MONEY AND BANKING

SECOND EDITION

MONEY AND BANKING

C. LOWELL HARRISS

Professor of Economics, Columbia University

ALLYN AND BACON

Boston

TO MY WIFE, AGNES

FIRST PRINTING . . . MAY 1965

THIRD PRINTING . . . JUNE 1967

PREFACE

REVISION of a textbook enables an author to draw upon a wider range of experience—his own and that of others, both students and teachers. This revision reflects, and I am confident benefits greatly from, extensive and varied experience. Within every chapter there has been substantial re-writing. Yet my own observations, and those of the majority of other users, confirmed my belief that the original structure serves well the pur-poses I seek. These are described in the following adaptation from the preface to the original edition.

This book is designed for the teacher who has only one semester or quarter for a basic course in money and banking. The goal will be to help the student gain an understanding of essentials. But as knowledge accumulates, as we learn more about the topics traditionally covered in money and banking, we also find that other phases of economics also bear closely upon the subject. Our potential responsibility grows. Class time, however, does not increase. In fact, colleges of business administration and liberal arts find that relatively new topics rightly press for attention. The competition for time becomes more intense each year.

Inevitably, therefore, the teacher of money and banking faces a diffi-cult task. How can the course be planned to assure that first things come first? The selection of materials in this volume represents one set of judgments as to which aspects deserve precedence—my own view, now reënforced by the reports of many who have used the first edition.

We are dealing here with monetary practice, theory, and policy. The basic course cannot ordinarily discuss monetary theory in depth. There-fore, our discussion is planned for the course which seeks to cover the major elements of contemporary theory without the penetrating and thor-ough analysis of refinements appropriate to the more advanced level. Where views differ—and this condition is by no means rare—I try to in-dicate the areas of controversy. The student is not expected to trace the development of ideas; his time will be devoted to modern tools of analysis and modern problems. He will study at a level of difficulty which is challenging but which does not involve the complications which are likely to be more frustrating than constructive at this stage.

This revision, as well as the original edition, places relatively heavy emphasis upon issues and problems of public policy. The discussion focuses on matters of broadest significance, whereas details of passing concern are ignored. Instead, the student will examine issues which are likely to be relevant indefinitely. What are the recurring problems? What are the underlying factors, the alternatives, the kinds of choices faced by the public? The discussion of these questions is directed at a level appropriate for the student, yet I believe that it is sufficiently developed to lay the foundation of persisting value which the modern individual needs to discharge civic and business responsibilities. Issues of current controversy are examined—but without any pretense that a professional consensus exists when such is not the case.

Banking is important not only for its influence on the levels of employment and prices, but also for its vital role in the processes of production and distribution. In covering some of the major elements of banking as a business, my goal has been to give the student of business and of economics a grasp—perhaps even a little of the "feel"—of banking in its more practical aspects. Of course, there is no pretense of dealing with the many interesting materials which are included in more specialized courses.

Those of us who work with college students just above the elementary level are constantly baffled by the problem of how much to assume has been retained in truly useful form from earlier study. The introductory economics course will have dealt with many elements of money and banking and fiscal policy. However, only the exceptional student will have so mastered the material that he can build upon it at once. The majority will have a set of impressions which are helpful but far from adequate. Reviewing is imperative and is aided by the groundwork provided by the elementary course. The new theoretical and empirical material, woven with what has been studied earlier, will add value and meaning to the student's progressive understanding.

New, up-to-date material has been included, but rarely as a net addition. Any substantial lengthening of chapters, I believe, would impair their usefulness. The historical section, however, has been expanded considerably to meet the requests of numerous teachers; although it remains at the end of the volume, it can be used, in whole or part by part, at any time in the course.

Extensive rewriting has sought to enhance clarity. Use of illustrative material has been increased, and there are more references to articles and books. A forthcoming manual for teachers will include suggestions for classroom presentation and testing material.

Many people have helped in one way or another—with the original edition and this revision. To all, I extend my thanks.

C. Lowell Harriss

New York City
February 1965

CONTENTS

PART ONE

MONEY

CHAPTER 1   *WHAT MONEY IS AND DOES*

MONEY, somewhat like an airplane, is marvelous when it works well, frustrating when immobilized, and tragic when it crashes. Money is indeed one of man's greatest inventions—or developments, for it has evolved over untold centuries. Men use money, as they do many things, with only vague notions of what it really is or how a monetary system functions. This day-to-day use may not require understanding of monetary theory. But management of an economy's money does require such understanding, for "Money will not manage itself." If our money is to serve us well, those responsible must have a great deal more knowledge than that which comes as part of the ordinary course of living.

Defining "money" and staking out the boundaries of the monetary system both require extensive discussion. Yet the gist of the conclusions can helpfully precede the study. *Money,* we shall find, *is anything generally accepted in exchange or in the payment of debt.* Currency—paper and coins—is, of course, money. Yet we pay most of our bills with checks. The bulk of our money, in fact, consists of deposits in checking accounts. Consequently, the monetary system includes far more than the arrangements for issuing and handling currency. It is largely the banking system—the banks with which individuals and businesses deal, the Federal Reserve banks with which these banks deal, and the agencies of government which regulate banks. For some purposes, however, other financial institutions and even banks outside this country must be considered part of the monetary system.

MONEY AND ECONOMIC LIFE

Just as money is interwoven with almost all of our personal life, it touches all aspects of the functioning economy. More than that money is the intermediary or means by which Americans transmit most decisions about production, consumption, and the vast majority of economic matters.

At one time economists may have thought of money as little more than a passive medium or means used to achieve economic ends. Today, however, experts agree that money itself can influence the real aspects of the economy. Or, speaking more accurately, production, income, and well-being are influenced by two somewhat different kinds of action in the sphere of money: (1) the way people use the monetary system to change the stock of money, and (2) the rate at which they spend (turn over) whatever money exists, *i.e.,* the speed or velocity with which money moves from one owner to another.

Money is part of the framework of the economy. We build around it. If the monetary system changes, other things are affected, even if we may not see the connection clearly. Because money performs different functions it affects the economic framework in a variety of ways which are related yet distinct. A development in one place will influence others, but not all equally.

"Cranks" and even devoted specialists may, it is true, exaggerate the importance of money. To focus on money risks the slighting of other fundamental requirements of economic welfare. Creating goods and services, for example, produces *real* income, *i.e.,* the things which satisfy human wants. Creating money, however, does not produce real things. The most sweeping monetary reform will not itself build houses or solve the problems of poverty.

On the other hand, seriously defective monetary policy, such as governmental actions greatly increasing or reducing the quantity of money, can lead to economic chaos that spreads through family, social, religious, and business life. The disruption can produce sweeping and terrible effects beyond the ability of most Americans to imagine. Disastrous monetary policies have involved mammoth inflations. Quite different, but also tragically disruptive, is monetary policy that leads to, or aggravates, depression, as in the 1930's.

Not all human illness is completely excruciating and disabling. Similarly, not all monetary sickness is critical. Yet poor monetary policy may bring trouble which, though far from disastrous, is serious. For example, for over 40 years preceding 1958, France suffered grievously from chronic monetary sickness which not only caused painful economic distress but also aggravated political, social, and military difficulties. Our country, too, has suffered from monetary policies which we now see were needlessly defective. Families have had less real income, less security, less satisfaction, less opportunity, and less success than if better monetary programs had been followed.

Human welfare depends more than many of us can appreciate upon the skill with which monetary affairs are handled. Two of mankind's major economic problems—moderating the ups and downs of prosperity and depression, and increasing the rate of healthy economic growth—are related closely to management of the monetary and financial system.

WHY SEEK TO UNDERSTAND MONETARY AFFAIRS?

Cannot the public leave to skilled "mechanics of money" the job of maintaining the monetary system in good working order? Most people do so, or think they do, just as they leave aircraft maintenance to technicians. Inevitably, however, the managing of money is influenced by government. And all voters have something to say, not only about who shall act as government officials in Congress and the Executive Branch; voters also influence the monetary policies which these officials adopt. We may say, then, that monetary policy which affects everyone is made to some extent by ordinary people. Few, unfortunately, are qualified for such responsibility.

Most voters are not even competent to decide who are the monetary experts, to say nothing of what is the wisest policy. We can deal with many other technical matters in a strikingly different way, relying for example upon experts selected by scientific tests to keep airplanes in good order. We can avoid risk of air crashes and maddening schedule disruptions by the alternative of using land transport. No one, however, can escape the disruption which results from folly, stupidity, or mere ineptitude in selecting and implementing monetary policies. All of us may suffer needless distress because of the monetary decisions of non-experts—voters seduced by glamorous visions of monetary ease, or elected officials insisting upon monetary stringency when business is sluggish.

Much as one might want to leave national money management to experts, complete delegation is impossible where the masses vote. (Dictators find control over money to be one of the more powerful weapons dominating the public.) Not only the broad duties of citizenship but also the personal concerns of self-interest require that as many modern men and women as possible understand the monetary system. Self-interest is twofold—to formulate wise policies for everyone, and to adjust personal and business affairs to whatever does develop, good or bad.

Some aspects of money's influence may seem clear. Courses in economic principles show something about the ways by which money affects economic life. We learn how specialization and the division of labor depend upon a medium of exchange which frees us from the unimaginably confining limits of barter; how monetary mismanagement may create unemployment or inflation; how avoidable frictions in financing business may hinder economic growth. Principles courses also show what sometimes seems a mystery—how banks create and destroy "checkbook money" and thereby affect employment and price levels.

Yet the citizen can do better for society and himself if he knows more about money and banking than he carries away from the principles course. Students with a special interest in business and economics, in government generally or in finance specifically—subjects which are deeply affected by monetary changes—have greater reason for pursuing this broad subject. Why is it sometimes hard to borrow? Why is the interest charge annoyingly high? Why do funds enter, or leave, the country? And so on.

A book such as this cannot provide all the answers. Facts change and principles are disputed, even by the experts. Conclusions once widely accepted now stand substantially modified. Of necessity, then, those principles, facts, and conclusions which we now accept must be applied to constantly changing conditions.

THE VARIED PURPOSES WHICH MONEY SERVES

For decades economists have distinguished four functions of money. This classification puts side by side concepts which are not truly comparable, and which cover more than does any usable definition of money. Nevertheless, the fourfold classification does help one to understand what money is and the varied ways in which it serves us.

All four are parts of a more fundamental function of money—to improve well-being by helping mankind obtain larger real incomes. Money is a means to other ends. It aids in getting the goods and services which satisfy wants. These services and goods must be produced and, for the most part, exchanged. Money facilitates exchange. In doing so, it helps make possible the division of labor, specialization, and, thereby, the whole apparatus of production and distribution. To comprehend the whole, we look at the four specific functions, leaving until later chapters what might be singled out as a fifth—the linking of an economy to the rest of the world.

Unit of Account (Standard of Value)

Life requires us to keep count of many things, including values. Counting requires units in which to count. The dollar is one such unit. In this sense it is abstract, as is the inch, pound, minute, or quart. No one ever saw or felt the dollar or the minute as a unit of account, but we employ them constantly in measuring. The use of the dollar in this sense is to help us quantify, to keep track of amounts.

The quantities which we measure are values or worth. Bread and circuses, houses and vacations, guns and butter, are widely different in physical characteristics. Yet they have in common something we call value. Values are bigger and smaller, more or less; they involve amounts.

To be able to measure these amounts is highly desirable indeed. If the unit or basis of measure is common to all, the values can be compared quickly. Hence money functioning in its role as the unit of account is sometimes termed "the standard of value."

The element counted, measured, or compared—worth—is expressed as price. The unit of account, in fact, is the thing (or concept) in which prices are quoted. Being able to express the worth, and the changes in worth, of myriads of goods and services in a common term—dollars— permits easy comparison. And comparisons are essential for exchange. Try to conceive the problems of carrying on business if each item had to be compared with others on the basis of the particular characteristics of each: a quart of milk equaling a pack of cigarettes, one-fifty-thousandth of the house we like, one-thirtieth of a textbook, and so on.

The values we wish to count and compare are not only those involved in exchanges. We also want to know how our affairs have prospered, how we stand economically, and the relative merits of available alternatives. A unit of account is indispensable. With it businesses and families can keep records that summarize their affairs and thereby help guide their decisions. Can one even imagine the frustrations of trying to judge how well a firm is doing by using accounts expressed only in physical amounts, the different types of man-hours used in producing goods on hand, the change in conditions of machines of various ages, the raw materials used up?

Comparison and measurement are possible even though the standard, the unit of account, does not exist as a tangible object which is, or might be, exchanged. Essential for comparison is a recognized, usable concept for measuring one kind of magnitude—worth. A ton of coal and a bushel of wheat are different in most ways. Yet because both have weight, they can be compared in this respect if there is an appropriate unit of measure, a system of weights. The two products have another thing in common— worth. This, too, can be measured if there is a standard of value. All economies have such a standard: dollar, pound, franc, ruble, peso, guilder, yen. The dollar as a unit of account is to our money, which we also call "the dollar," somewhat as the yard is to a yardstick.

Ordinarily, the national government, as an act of sovereignty, specifies the unit of account. People may, however, decide among themselves to count values in some unit other than the one specified by the government. They may settle upon a foreign unit of account (Germans after World War II conducted business among themselves in terms of Swiss francs) or even upon some tangible thing. Such action is ordinarily a sign of financial disease.[1] One's own money must be "sick"—rapidly changing in worth,

---

[1] People in different countries may deal with each other in terms of the money of some other land, such as the dollar or pound sterling (British). Such arrangements often prove convenient and do not necessarily indicate lack of confidence in the money of the other lands.

for example—if people prefer to use something else as their unit of account. But they may because, unlike the minute or mile or ton, which today differ not a bit from that a generation ago, one monetary unit does change in what it represents, compared with the past or with the money of other lands.

Medium of Exchange

Money serves as a medium of exchange; such a characteristic is the necessary requirement emphasized in the definition of money. In exchange for our services, the employer gives us dollars. We then exchange them for shoes and lunches and hundreds of other goods or services. The ability to use money frees us from the need to barter, *i.e.,* to make exchanges in the form of things for things. We can get bread or electricity without searching out each person in the long chain of production, finding what specific service he wants, and if we can provide it, then arranging the deal. Trying merely to envisage the complexities of barter may suggest, or begin to suggest, the incalculable usefulness of whatever might make barter unnecessary. With money, each complete exchange of goods or services can be separated into two independent parts: one item is exchanged for money, and then that money is used to buy something else. Each part can be handled as a transaction distinct from the other, but with a common element, money.

Money is generalized purchasing power, a broad nonspecific claim on the economy. (Or, the other way around, money is a general debt of the economy to the holder of money.) In exchange for something very specific, such as the services we render this week, we get money with which we can purchase any of a huge variety of things. The range of choice extend further in some places than in others. The larger the variety of goods and services obtainable with any given number of dollars, 10,000 items as against 1000, the greater our effective economic power and freedom.

Exchange, and with it specialization, the division of labor, and mass production are possible if people will accept what others offer. Money differs from all other things in the extent of its acceptability. It will almost always be taken in exchange, for anything. If one had to select a single feature to distinguish money from the other forces which facilitate the division of labor, this unqualified acceptability would stand out. What, then, creates such complete acceptability? Confidence—but in what? The confidence which counts lies in the belief that others in turn will accept money, and will do it without question. Yet because this answer can hardly satisfy (why do the others accept?) the inquiry must be pushed further. What factors make for general acceptability?

Throughout history there have been not a few cases in which money was accepted because it consisted of materials which were themselves useful. The civilized world presents no such cases today. Although the metal in coins has some nonmonetary worth, rarely is it more than a small fraction of the amount for which the coin is accepted as money. Certainly, our acceptance of paper currency or a check does not rest on any worth of the ingredients.

One reason why we accept money readily is this: the price of money is certain. In relation to the unit of account, money has a fixed price. (Though value in the sense of purchasing power changes, the price is constant. This is true of nothing else.) The price of a dollar is a dollar, but the price of anything else can change. In part, people accept money so willingly because it is definitely related to the units in which financial obligations are expressed. As a result, we arrange our affairs so that we can discharge our debts with money, whether this debt involve tomorrow's lunch or a long-term home mortgage. Is there, then, any wonder that we accept money readily? Acceptability declines when, as happened long ago with some state bank notes and Civil War greenbacks, the market price of currency is not the amount stated on its face.

One cannot understand the acceptability of money without reference to liquidity. *Liquidity* refers to the ease with which something can be converted into money at a price that is not subject to change. Liquidity is a matter of degree, with money as the perfectly liquid extreme. Having money, one can "jump economically" almost any way. Money can be used to acquire a limitless variety of things because it is so generally desired. Other kinds of property—tea, government bonds, books—are also desired, but not so widely and uniformly as money. Hence they are less liquid. The number of dollars they will bring is subject to some question; moreover, the process of converting to cash is something of a problem. Money, in contrast, is liquidity. As such, it serves a need and gains acceptability.

Law plays a part in accounting for the acceptability of some of the money stock. Government says, in effect, "If you have a financial obligation and offer to meet it with United States currency, the courts will accept the money if the creditor will not. As far as the law is concerned, you will then be clear. On this debt the creditor will have no more rights against you in court. Interest no longer accrues." Thus a tender of currency discharges the legal responsibility. This characteristic of currency makes it legal tender. Coins and paper money are now legal tender. Demand deposits are not. Bank deposits, however, are convertible into currency and thus close indeed to legal tender.

Law does not require that economic agreements be made in terms of legal tender. People may become reluctant to commit themselves to pay or accept the unit of money in the future, perhaps because of doubt about its purchasing power. They become less willing to arrange their affairs to require monetary settlements. Over the long run, legal tender status accounts, at the most, for only a small fraction of the acceptability of money. What, then, is the explanation? We accept some things as money because we believe that people will accept them from us, and so on.

The next two functions derive from the first two.

Store of Value (of Purchasing Power)

The transactions for which money serves so well as a medium of exchange do not as a rule take place instantaneously. Ordinarily, a family receives dollars one day and pays them out over days or weeks. For a time, it holds purchasing power, and in the form received: money. Its price is fixed in terms of the unit of account, and there is confidence that it will be accepted in the future. As a result, money can serve as a store of value.

In exchange for goods or services today, I can get money which gives me a claim on others. This is a claim which I can exercise at once or at some time in the future, distant or near. Money, therefore, gives those who hold it economic freedom through time. The use of money eases the problem of synchronizing through time our rendering of services and our purchasing the services of others. Unfortunately, one man's freedom to use money now or later can be a source of difficulty for others. It is the freedom to demand the services of others either today or in the future, perhaps years later. The way in which the public uses money as a store of value has something to do with the generation of business cycles.

The holding of money gives power which is more than merely the power to postpone purchases to a more convenient time. The holding of money is also the holding of an option on what to buy. Moreover, the possession of money helps assure one's capacity to pay any debt due in money. The inability to meet obligations can sometimes be the source of great loss. Illiquid assets may have to be sold under distress conditions; a business may be closed down or management control lost if a company does not have money to pay its dollar debts. If for some reason the flow of money into a firm or household falls below the rate at which dollars must be paid out, money in the bank can permit the necessary payments to continue. A wise person or business will hold money as a sort of insurance. It is a store of value to be used, not so much for expected purchases as for the unforeseen.

Money, of course, is not the only thing that functions as a store of value. Other kinds of property also serve, and in some respects they can serve more advantageously than money. Money, for example, brings no income while being held. A house or a bond or business will provide services, bring in rent or interest, or help earn profit.   Money, by its very nature, remains fixed in price.   While holding dollars, one sacrifices the opportunity of gaining more dollars but gains assurance of ending with no fewer dollars.   The purchasing power of these dollars, however, may rise or fall; the prices of things we wish to buy with money may change.   In holding dollars, one does assume some risk of gain or loss in their purchasing power; the basket or bundle of goods which cost X dollars at one time, may cost $2X$ or $X/2$ at another.

The amount of wealth that we try to hold in the form of money will depend partly upon our forecasts of changes in the amount the dollar will buy.   Holding money as a store of value involves costs, the sacrifice of alternatives; they must be compared with the costs and benefits of holding other things.   In estimating such costs, one must consider the income, if any, which each alternative asset would bring, the expense of safe-keeping facilities, physical deterioration, taxes, and so forth.   Money has some distinct advantages as a form in which to hold wealth.   Today, for example, storage of some forms of money in a safe place free from taxes and deterioration costs very little, and "selling" it costs nothing at all.   Yet memories of the way the dollar lost buying power after World War II lingers on and makes some people reluctant to hold money as a store of wealth except for payments in the near future.[2]

Standard of Deferred Payment

The fourth of the functions follows from the others.   We need something to serve as a standard of payments to be made in the future. Economic life above the most primitive levels requires productive facilities —houses, factories, railroads—which last for years, and all sorts of arrangements which extend through time.   Both capital equipment and the less tangible but always essential commitments which tie the past and present to the future can often be obtained more readily by contracts providing that one person turn over something now in return for a promise of something in the future.   In the typical case a person saves money and lends it, often through a financial institution, to a business or government which wants to construct or to buy productive facilities of some sort, not the least being housing.   Often both parties prefer to express the agreement in money.

What if the only basis for making long-term contracts were in terms of physical things?   Then arranging for the future would be stupendously difficult.   For example, houses, machines, and most other physical objects change as they are used.   Rarely can a person use something, especially

---

[2] Measuring the purchasing power of the dollar is discussed later.

over a period of years, and then return it in the exact original condition. Moreover, someone having specific things today, or the money to buy them, may not want the same items in the future. He will, of course, want something later, but frequently not the physical thing—a dynamo or office building—which will be useful to someone now. And in a progressive society, tangible things which are highly desirable at one time often become outmoded. Who would make a contract to exchange the price of a 1965 truck for such a truck in 1975 (plus interest) when all experience leads us to expect improvements in trucks?

True, a person who has saved for the future may buy physical assets such as real estate; he may buy equities such as corporation stock. But who knows their worth in 10 or 20 years? No one can be sure. And what if one wants certainty? To meet such a demand, we need an agreement in fixed terms. A debt contract is the answer.

When contracts for future settlement cannot conveniently be made in terms of physical things, what alternative will serve? The unit of account is the obvious answer. This unit may have the same name as the familiar and convenient medium of exchange. Money will thus be used naturally at both the initiation and the termination of the agreement. If both parties wish, the contract can in a sense serve as a store of value because the terms can be rigidly fixed, or can be set to vary with changes in the price level or some other factor. Being able to make agreements in money terms is valuable beyond calculation to a society which wants economic growth.

Money is used to help tie together the present and the future in a definite, understandable, and indispensable way. Without this service of money, modern economic life would be impossible. Contracts in money terms can be specific and binding. Consequently, the people who prefer such certainty can make agreements which involve the exchange of payments now for others in the future. The use of money as a standard for deferred payments facilitates the efficient division of labor. The gain is an increased use of capital equipment and in general the provision of a more secure and prosperous future. When the future worth of money is in doubt, *i.e.,* when money cannot serve well its function as a standard of deferred payment, the process of economic growth suffers.

QUALITIES OF GOOD MONEY

All four functions are important. Economic life depends upon how well money performs them. What, then, will help or hinder money from doing its jobs effectively? What is the difference between money which serves well and that which serves poorly? Is there something a nation can do to get better rather than worse money? Although answering these questions takes up much of this volume, we can indicate a few points now.

The mechanics of carrying on business are eased if the unit of account is convenient. For us this means, among other things, being divisible by ten and reasonably related to the size of ordinary transactions. The British system of pounds, each pound equal to 20 shillings, each shilling equal to 12 pence, is a little harder to use than a decimal system. The monetary units in some countries are so small that ordinary transactions require large numbers—a nuisance. The Italian lira, for example, is worth less than one-sixth of our cent. Experience shows that people can adjust to any unit of account. Change in the unit, however, disturbs calculations and is more than a minor inconvenience.

Coins and pieces of paper ought to be convenient in size and shape, durable, quickly recognized, hard to counterfeit, easily transferable, and available in adequate quantity.[3] The economy also needs safe, convenient, and inexpensive arrangements for handling money—currency and bank deposits. Theft, loss, and, in the case of paper currency, burning, are risks which can be reduced by use of the proper facilities for storage and handling.

Even more important, perhaps, is that money be integrated into an effective payment mechanism. Banking systems here and in several other countries provide such mechanisms.[4] Obviously, a modern exchange economy could not function without efficient arrangements for transferring money from one person to another.

Families might try to rely on currency kept at home, paying cash for everything. Businesses, however, need something safe and larger than the treasurer's pocket. They could conceivably provide their own vaults for the safekeeping of currency. But even if they did so, how would they make or receive payments in other regions? A few businesses would be able to afford their own facilities for receiving and disbursing money, but only a few. Special businesses, however, can and do serve the public by handling the payments process. As these businesses—banks—have developed, they have come to *create* as well as to *hold* and to *transfer* money. Consequently, our money is an integral part of the system for making payments.

Some such system is indispensable if an interdependent economy is to operate efficiently. Today's monetary problems include few serious deficiencies in the arrangements for making payments inside countries

---

[3] U.S. mints in 1964 were unable to produce coins rapidly enough to meet growing demand. As a result, the conduct of business became somewhat more difficult. The mistakes of official planning could not be corrected quickly because old mints had been abandoned long before replacements were ready.

[4] Post offices in some lands offer convenient and efficient facilities for making payments, somewhat like checking accounts. Deposits are received and are then transferred when the owner directs by what is essentially a check. Lending is not involved.

which have highly developed economies. Within less developed lands and among nations, however, the monetary payment mechanism leaves more to be desired.

Men may properly congratulate themselves on having developed money which meets the requirements mentioned so far. However, one characteristic which is even more important remains, not only to be mentioned but also, unfortunately, to be realized. If money is to perform well its function as a store of value and as a standard of deferred payment, the *purchasing power* of a unit of money must be essentially *stable* over the years. Nevertheless, in many lands conditions have been, and are, by no means satisfactory. Men have less than the firmest confidence in the future purchasing power of their money. The reasons for uncertainty, and the results, receive attention later. Suffice it here to note that we can record real progress as students when we see that money which performs some of its functions well may do poorly in other respects.

WHAT MONEY IS: DEFINITION

Efforts to define "money" can lead to a long sentence, too involved to be manageable, or to one more precise but incomplete. Somewhat different things perform one or more of the functions of money. Our unit of account is the dollar. Although expressed as the equivalent of one-thirty-fifth of a troy ounce of gold, this dollar is an abstract concept. Gold serves only slightly, or not at all, in performing the other functions of money. A definition in these terms is much too narrow.[5]

So we repeat the definition given earlier, adding one element: *Money is anything which has a fixed price in terms of the unit of account and which is generally accepted in exchange or in the discharge of debt.* Money is property which the owner can use to pay off a definite amount of debt with certainty and without delay.

Strange as it may seem, our money consists of debt, the debt of government or of certain types of privately owned businesses such as banks. Like other debt, this kind is an asset of the person to whom it is owed. Obviously not all debt is money. The debt which does serve as money gets its worth not from anything inherent in the money itself. The worth exists because the promise of the debtor makes, or helps make, the "piece of paper"—the debt instrument—generally desired and always accepted.

Whether a kind of property can be used to discharge obligations de-

[5] During the Civil War some businesses tried, with only limited success, to keep accounts in terms of gold dollars, while most people and businesses used circulating dollars (greenbacks) which had purchasing power very different from that of the gold dollar. Other countries have had experience with using more than one unit of account.

pends upon its acceptability. Something perfectly acceptable in one place (New York) may be less acceptable in another (Paris), and much less so in still another (Peiping). At any one place and time some kinds of property can be used to discharge debts, but less readily than some other kinds of property. Moreover, there are types—for example, time and savings account deposits in banks—which have a fixed price in terms of the unit of account and which serve as a store of value. Yet they are not themselves generally accepted in exchange. Though not money by our definition, for important purposes they are very close substitutes.

Just where, then, is the line between money and "not-money"? Economists do not agree but many would endorse some such statement as this: " 'Moneyness' is to some extent a matter of degree. When we study a specific problem, we must try to allow for the influence of anything which for that problem is a near money."

One thing about money is obvious—after being pointed out. Although money is used, it is not "used up" as it moves from hand to hand. The same money goes from person to person, year after year. Goods and services are produced and consumed. They *are* used up. But in getting money in payment for our services, and using the money to obtain goods and services from others, we receive and pass along money. It flows through the economy without, for the most part, being destroyed and then replaced as it is used. Yet the flows of money do rise and fall, increase and decline. It is these changes which make the study of money so important.

THE STOCK OF MONEY IN THE UNITED STATES

What makes up the stock of money in the United States today? There is "pocket money." Metallic coins and paper currency are money (although they cannot always be used with certainty to pay debts—mailing coins to pay a debt of $63.24 may be impractical and unsafe). Most payments however—about 90 percent of the dollar totals—are made by check. We generally accept checks, but not always and not always without question. Sometimes one must wait to learn whether a check is good. So it is not the checks themselves but the amounts (deposits) in solvent banks which can be drawn upon by check that are properly considered as money.

These *demand deposits* are money, sometimes called "bank money" or "checkbook money." Any given deposit has a "price" which in terms of the unit of account, the dollar, is fixed. We readily accept these deposits and know that others will accept them. A deposit in a New York bank is acceptable to a Californian because he knows that he can have it transferred to his own bank account without difficulty. He then has a deposit—money—which he can use.

Figures on the components of our money stock appear in Table 1.1. No one can doubt what bulks largest. Demand deposits total almost four times as much as coins and paper money combined. (Time and savings deposits are now greater than demand deposits and have been growing more rapidly.) Today's monetary problems are predominantly problems of bank deposits rather than of coins and paper currency. So we pass over the latter, though presenting a little background before proceeding directly to the process by which demand deposits are created.

TABLE 1.1

Money Stock of the United States, November 1964

	Billions	Percent of total
Coins[a]	$ 2	1
Paper currency[a]	32	20
Demand deposits[b]	124	78
Total	158	
(Time and savings deposits[c]	$173)	

[a] Outside banks.

[b] Excluding interbank deposits, United States government deposits, and cash items in the process of collection; these adjustments are made, in effect, to avoid double counting.

[c] Includes $48 billion at mutual savings banks.

Source: *Federal Reserve Bulletin*.

MONEY AND MONETARY STANDARDS

The fascinating history of the evolution of money is too long to summarize here. The obstacle is not only the mass of material which would claim attention. An additional problem would arise from the introduction of ideas which are partially or wholly wrong for the modern world. They would get in the way of an understanding of today's needs and opportunities. We must be content with a few highlights. Obviously, however, this section and later references to the past are in no sense a history of money and banking. Somewhat more of United States experience is sketched in Appendix A.

Two Types of Controls on Money Creation

Even the dullest dreamer can enthuse over the thought of having a simple way to create money. A person with such power would not need to find out what goods and services others desire—real things. Nor would he need to work to produce and exchange these things to get money with which to buy for his own needs. By creating money, he could get the products of others more easily. Yet if everyone were able to do so, we would quickly starve in a world overflowing with money.

Obviously, however, if we are to have money and thus escape from the confining restraints of a barter economy, someone must have the power to create money. Strong imperatives to use this power exist for anyone having it: to help pay an army, expand a business, or consume plentifully. What a temptation to abuse! The public needs protection against flooding of the economy with money, because "too great" a change in the quantity of money will have far-reaching and adverse effects. Men have devised two rather different kinds of controls.

1. One control limits money to whatever cannot be produced easily, such as gold. The public defines as money some commodity which is physically difficult to create, requiring work about as hard as that needed "to make an honest living." In such cases money is *asset money*—sometimes termed "full-bodied money." This term properly applies if the worth of the material as a commodity for other than monetary uses equals its value as money. The limits on the production of the material restrict the amount of money. Costs of producing the commodity influence the quantity supplied. For hand-to-hand circulation pieces of paper, called notes, and which represent the commodity stored somewhere, can serve. They are essentially warehouse receipts and may be called "representative full-bodied money."

2. The second type of control is legal. Men use the power of government to restrict the creation of money. Such control becomes especially important when money has become *debt,* like ours today. The money may be either entirely debt—"fiat money," such as Civil War greenbacks—or token money, such as coins whose metal content is worth only a fraction of the stated value. How much easier to go into debt than to create real assets. The law, however, can restrain the growth of those debts that serve as money, now chiefly the demand deposit obligations of banks.

Commodity Standards

Men have used dozens of commodities as money. One author found 170 materials and objects that have served as money—for example, *non-metallic* commodities include oxen, tea, beer, stones, slaves, skins, yarn, shark teeth, tiger claws, furs, wine, and tobacco.[6] Not every item served over a large area, for all the modern functions of money, or for long. Yet many things other than metals have been tested as commodity bases for money. All have been abandoned.

Tobacco, for example, proved unsatisfactory because of changes in the quantity from year to year. Harvests varied, and so did consumption. Such changes in the quantity of the monetary unit upset its value relative to the worth of other goods. The absence of fixity magnified the difficulties of measuring relationships among values. The quality of tobacco leaves also varied. It was necessary, therefore, to define quality standards as a base and then to determine how various batches of the crop compared with the base. Judgment was necessary, accurate measurement in fact rarely feasible. Disputes interfered with the confident and efficient conduct of affairs.

Acceptability as money in other areas was not assured. Non-uniformity of money among colonies hampered trade. Transportation was difficult; if large amounts were involved, movement might be impossible. Division into small and strictly comparable units proved difficult. Practical difficulties, including loss from handling the leaves and the physical bulk of amounts with much value, made use in ordinary transactions clumsy. Fire and water could do great damage. Storage was costly, deterioration or improvement with aging always a possibility. As a store of value, tobacco was not satisfactory. Moreover, monetary use tied up in largely idle form a resource which had some worth in alternative uses.

To varying degrees, other nonmetallic commodities, when serving as money, have somewhat the same defects as tobacco. Living things, in addition, may die from disease or age, as well as disappear in consumption.

The advantages of metals over other commodities appeared in ancient times. Quality and quantity could be determined accurately and often easily. Metals were durable, subject to little or no wastage in the form of deterioration. In use, metals wore out only slowly. Storage required slight effort. Divisibility or combination into larger masses was easy. Small, uniform, identifiable units—coins—could be made. Durability gave rise to what in the case of money was a decided advantage: The total quantity of a metal changed only slightly from year to year. Although output did rise and fall, no single year's addition made much difference in the total that had been accumulated from the production of past centuries. Short-run changes of value were limited. Yet the stock of money did not necessarily grow with an expanding economy—a growth which modern analysis shows to be extremely desirable. Moreover, the metal which served as money is not available for other purposes. Monetary use in-

[6] Paul Einzig, *Primitive Money* (London: Eyre and Spottiswoode, 1949). In camps for prisoners of war and in the disruption following World War II, cigarettes often served as a medium of exchange and as a standard of value.

volved costs—the sacrifice of alternative uses of the metal or the resources to produce it.[7]

Coinage provided a way to escape conspicuous difficulties of using metal in ordinary transactions—determining purity and weight. In minting coins, the sovereign put the metal into forms of standard weight and purity. The seal of the king's image was stamped to signify the contents. Coins became almost synonymous with money. Use of metal was simplified, but not to the extent we know today. The king might begin to cheat by putting in less of the precious metal than he certified. Others might "clip" some of the metal. Wearing out in use was common until methods of alloying to harden were developed. Alert members of the public would not accept the coin at face value, as we do today, but for their estimate of the market value of the metal contents. The worth of the commodity became the determining factor. Eventually, minting techniques improved to prevent various methods of withdrawing some of the metal contents. Then coins passed, as today, by count instead of by weight.

Two metals—silver and gold—became most widely used as money. In relation to other commodities they were not plentiful; they were desired enough to have high worth per pound. If the metals used as money were not somewhat "scarce"—copper or iron, for example—the amount to be lugged around for even modest purchases would have exceeded the capacity of purses and at times the strength of ordinary men.

For centuries, silver, not the more valuable gold, was the chief constituent of money. Gold was so very scarce relative to other things that most transactions would have required infinitesimal amounts of the yellow metal—bits too tiny to be usable. Silver, being less valuable, proved more convenient. Choice of metals to use as money rested upon relative degrees of scarcity. The usefulness of silver and gold as money, in turn, increased their value. This point deserves emphasis. *The addition of monetary demand to that for ornamental and industrial uses increased the total demand for the metals.* The use as money eventually came to account for a significant part of the price of gold and silver.

The influx of silver from the Americas into Spain in the sixteenth and seventeenth centuries was followed by loss of purchasing power of silver (rising prices of other goods and services). Profound and extensive economic changes followed. Then, in the nineteenth century, discoveries of new gold fields and improved methods of refining made gold relatively more plentiful. Greater monetary use became feasible. Gold gradually displaced silver—rather more by accident than by reasoned choice. As the use of silver for money dropped, an important part of the total demand for

---

[7] In this country today, for example, the stock of money should probably grow by more than one percent of net national product each year. If all or even most of such an amount had to be metal, the real cost of producing it would be a heavy burden on the economy.

silver disappeared. Its price fell. Gold had won as the monetary standard.

"The" Gold Standard

The gold standard developed gradually and without conscious, deliberate effort of informed men to analyze alternatives and to select the best. There have been so many variants, and they have functioned under such different conditions, that economists, bankers, and statesmen may not agree fully on the exact elements of "the" gold standard. But the general principles can be outlined. They combine the two types of restrictions on the creation of money—the *physical difficulties of production* and *legal controls.*

A government utilizing the "classic" or "pure" gold standard defined the monetary unit, dollar or pound, as so much gold of a specified fineness. The unit was made legal tender. Gold coins were minted and made available for circulation. They contained specie worth the face value of the coin plus some hardening metal. The government permitted the holder of other forms of money to buy gold at the fixed price. The owner of gold could exchange it for another form of money. In other words, government, or a central bank acting for it, agreed to buy and sell gold *at a fixed price* for either domestic or foreign use. Coinage of gold, or melting down coins to get bar gold, was unrestrained. (It was "free," except for a charge to cover the cost of fabrication.) Gold could move freely from industry and arts to the monetary system and back. It could also move freely into and out of the country.

Were the amount of paper currency in circulation, and the total bank deposits, tied to the quantity of monetary gold in the country? Some connection existed. Nevertheless, it varied widely in nature and in amount; in this respect conceptions of "the" gold standard differ. Long before 1900, the amount of gold in every monetary system was only a fraction of the currency and bank deposits *potentially* convertible into gold.

The *domestic* features of the gold standard were substantially modified decades ago, then largely abandoned. With minor exceptions the coinage of gold has disappeared. Governments[8] will generally *buy* gold in unlimited quantities at a fixed price, paying in paper money or bank deposits. Sales of gold for domestic use, however, are made only under tight restrictions. For example, it is not generally possible to exchange currency or bank deposits for gold bars to hold as an asset. Gold for dental, artistic, and industrial uses, however, will be made available to

---

[8] Or a central bank, such as the Bank of England, may act officially for the government.

those willing to pay the price. In settling international transactions, gold serves somewhat as it did in the past; but the variations from country to country are numerous. In due course we shall examine the merits and weaknesses of the gold standard—making only one more point here: There is no assurance, or even presumption, that the amount of gold—or the quantity of money based on it—is the amount which is most appropriate for the economy, at any one time or as conditions change.

Token Money; Bank Notes; Managed Paper Standards

Money today is debt, not asset, money.[9] In other words what we use for money is generally accepted because it represents promises to pay. These promises—by governments or banks—may be supported by assets, but it is not the assets which pass as money.

Coins became "token," or partially debt, money when the value of the metal content, as metal, fell below the face amount. Why did not the public, then, buy silver and manufacture coins which in money terms would have been worth more than the cost? Government assumed a monopoly over coinage and limited the quantity. This limitation prevented coins from falling in purchasing power to the worth of the metal. We use coins without thinking about the market value of their contents.[10]

Governments, however, may keep an eye out for the difference between face value and the market price of the ingredients. The difference is a profit, or *seigniorage*. Sometimes government may deliberately substitute cheaper materials to increase this profit.

Use of paper currency began centuries ago and developed gradually. First there were pieces of paper which were receipts for gold or silver on deposit with a goldsmith, usually for safekeeping. These pieces of paper came to be transferable from one person to another, in a sense passing the ownership of the gold or silver. Holders of the notes, it turned out, would not as a rule insist upon redeeming them for specie. The goldsmiths found that they could issue notes with a face value much above that of the specie which they kept in their safes.

The notes which were not matched by specie had originally been

---

[9] Some writers prefer the term "credit money." This term may emphasize more effectively the importance of the capacity and reputation of the institution or government supporting the money.

[10] If the market value of the metal rises above the face value of coins, as can easily happen during a substantial inflation, melting them down for sale as bullion becomes profitable. In fact, some nickels minted during World War II with an unusual metal content became worth about seven cents for their metal in 1964. And the silver dollar has become worth almost a dollar as metal so that minting of the "cartwheels" has ceased; in 1964 public demand for the coins, for numismatic rather than bullion purposes, rapidly exhausted the Treasury's stock on hand.

issued to borrowers from the smiths. These lenders, who had now become bankers, received interest on the amounts which they had loaned. When it was no longer necessary to match notes fully by gold or silver and when the lending of notes would bring an interest income, the temptation to over-issue often proved irresistible. Governments, too, issued paper money to pay for purchases. As issuers, banks and governments made promises to redeem in gold or silver which they would not always keep. The public confidence in the promises dropped. Some notes became completely worthless, and others lost purchasing power as larger and larger amounts were issued.

The history of money in the nineteenth century is in no small part a story of the search for methods of controlling the issue of paper money. This money pretended to be asset money. Men were inclined to think of each bank note as representing gold or silver in some bank vault, of the note as a sort of warehouse receipt. Yet the currency was predominantly debt. Specie backing was rarely more than a small fraction of the volume of notes outstanding. To control the issue of currency, it was necessary to limit the incurring of debt. Moreover, it was necessary to make the limits effective even when an increase in such debt seemed highly attractive. One type of control was to restrict the notes which a bank could issue to some multiple of its capital or of its holdings of specie.

Gradually, however, note issue became in effect the monopoly of government (even though banks might be used for issuance). A series of events broke the tie between bank notes and specie, at least for domestic use. The public became accustomed to the use of paper currency. While the acceptability of such money was growing, a new type—demand deposits—and the use of checks became increasingly important. Their use, in effect, pushed the modern world even farther from asset to debt money.

Governments today print currency with little or no regard for specie holdings. Paper money is not convertible into gold, at least not for domestic use. Of course, the currency is generally accepted as a medium of exchange. In one country after another experience shows that gaining acceptability of inconvertible paper money for *internal* payments is rarely a problem. As a practical matter the public has little choice. Some kind of hand-to-hand means of payment is essential. The purchasing power of this currency, of course, is another matter. It will depend not upon the existence of "backing." What counts is the total quantity of currency in relation to several other factors, such as the volume of other forms of money—bank deposits—and the quantity of real goods and services available for purchase.

Difficult problems arise in managing paper currency. The chief difficulty is to limit the issue of new money when governments are seriously pressed for funds. Time and again the issue of *fiat* currency, paper money which is not convertible into specie, has gone along with rampant inflation.

It seems that a close tie of currency to specie would have prevented such inflations. Not a few people believe, therefore, that the freeing of currency from tight relations to specie is an open temptation to inflation.

With some exceptions, however, the causes of big inflations are to be found in forces, such as war, which are too powerful to be controlled by the insistence upon convertibility of currency into precious metals. People have given up asset money and the metallic standard not because they thought paper better in principle. They have done so because under the circumstances they would not put up with the limitations which convertibility would impose. And there is a saving in real resources which is of no small advantage.

To varying degrees, all standards today are inconvertible. Some are so predominantly fiat that even the ties to gold for foreign trade have slight significance. Nevertheless, the standards of leading countries have a large element of convertibility for foreign transactions, even though little or none domestically. Such systems are not necessarily inflationary. They will not run themselves automatically and require management. But they offer hope of better monetary arrangements than those which grew up more or less haphazardly as different monetary standards were adopted, modified, and abandoned.

QUESTIONS

1. What would happen if the use of money were prohibited for a week?

2. What role does the citizen have in influencing monetary policy? Find examples of the discussion of monetary problems in the literature of the 1964 campaign for the Presidency.

3. What led to the use of gold and silver as bases for monetary systems? Could diamonds, cloth, or grain serve as well? Why?

4. Why is a check acceptable in payment of debts?

5. Discuss the four functions of money. What, if any, other things can serve each function?

6. What are the qualities of good money?

7. In what sense does money "tie together the present and the future"?

8. What is the difference between "money" and "near money"? Explain why "greenbacks" fit the first, time deposits the second, and common stock neither, category.

9. Distinguish between money and currency. How did the latter gradually become a subcategory of the former?

10. What is the difference between "asset" and "debt" money?

11. Describe two methods used to limit the creation of money? Why are limits established?

12. What are the meaning of, and the significance of, legal tender status?

13. Is it economical to dispense with the use of a commodity in the monetary system? Why?

CHAPTER 2   *DEPOSIT CREATION BY BANKS*

MOST of the money of the typical household, business, or government consists of the balance in the checking account at the bank. Such balances are debts of banks, payable on demand. They make up nearly 80 percent of the money stock of this country. What is the process by which commercial banks, along with their customers, create the deposits on which we can draw checks? [1]

DEPOSITS: ASSETS OR LIABILITIES?

The term "deposit" can be misleading. It is used as a verb, a noun, and an adjective. And as a noun it has significantly different meanings. We may, for example, think of a deposit as something that has been turned over to someone else for safekeeping. The person receiving whatever we hand over assumes a responsibility; he gives something, a promise. The transaction is two-sided. If we use the same term for both parts of the exchange, confusion is to be expected.

It is natural to think of a bank deposit as that which one gives to the bank. For the study of money, however, we must think of the deposit as that which one gets from the bank—the promise of the bank to do something. To a bank, deposits are liabilities. They are obligations due the bank's customers, the depositors. To these customers, however, a deposit is an asset. When it assumes these liabilities, a bank receives something (such as a borrower's note promising to pay later). Whatever the bank gets is an obligation or liability of someone else. To the bank, however,

[1] For present purposes we can think of a commercial bank as one which handles checking accounts. Virtually all banks except mutual savings banks are commercial banks. Institutions known as "investment banks" do not handle deposits in the ordinary sense; some did so before legal prohibitions were established in the 1930's.

it is an asset. The bank will not call this asset itself a deposit. Instead, the bank will record its new obligation, *i.e.,* the liability, calling it a deposit. It is due to, and owned by, the bank's customer.

Some bank deposits come into existence as the public hands currency to banks in exchange for increases in checking account balances. I may take currency to a bank and deposit it for credit to my checking account. This act reduces the amount of currency in circulation outside of banks and increases demand deposits. Deposit creation of this type is not large, however, nor is the corresponding deposit destruction when a person writes a check on his account and withdraws currency. The volume of demand deposits is more than thirty times the volume of vault cash held by commercial banks. Most deposits must have come into existence in some way other than by deposit of currency. This is what we are to examine now.

EXCHANGE OF DEBTS AS THE BASIS OF DEPOSIT CREATION

The process of creating demand deposits, in essence, is one in which commercial banks acquire debts of others—individuals, businesses, governments—in return for debts of the bank. These debts are deposits payable on demand. Private debts with low negotiability, *i.e.,* debts which cannot be easily transferred from one person to another, are exchanged for debts with very high negotiability, those of banks. My personal IOU would not be generally acceptable; its maximum area of circulation would be very small indeed, for not many people know me well enough to accept my debt from someone else. The liability of my bank, however, will be accepted by almost everyone the country over. Even if people far away do not know my bank, they have confidence in the banking system of which it is a part. If I can exchange my IOU for the bank's promise to pay, the acceptability of debt has increased to the point where the debt is money. Banks *monetize* debt. They charge for exchanging their debt for that of borrowers, *i.e.,* for the services they render in making debt more negotiable, more easily transferred.

A bank wants income. The amount it can earn will depend chiefly upon (1) the interest rate, *i.e.,* the price, that it charges for its lending services, and (2) the volume or quantity of lending it performs. If the bank insists upon charging an interest rate higher than the worth of its services to those seeking loans, there will be no borrowing and hence no deposit creation. Beyond some level, the higher the bank's charges, the less lending it will be asked to do, other things being equal. The competition of other lenders and the value of the bank's services to customers limit the height of its charges. What about the volume of debts (deposit liabilities) that a bank may incur? Here, too, there are limiting factors—

reserve requirements and the quantity of reserves available. Because the banking system's reserve situation has a controlling influence upon deposit creation, we look briefly at reserves.

WHY BANK RESERVES?

A person's debt will be worthless unless others have confidence in his ability and willingness (or those of someone supporting him) to meet the obligations involved. The same is true of a bank's debts, the deposits owing its customers. Bank assets which themselves have value help support the worth of the bank's debts. We accept checks more readily if we believe that banks possess enough wealth—assets—to honor the demands which depositors can legally make.

Bank assets can be of many kinds. Some get a formal, or informal, designation as "reserves." These are assets which can be exchanged for money at any time and without any appreciable doubt about the price they will bring. The reserve is something that is widely desired and has a good market—certainly not my IOU or that of the ordinary business. A reserve is always available to help the bank meet its obligations. Yet this is not the aspect of reserves which is of most interest.

A bank's obligation to keep reserves in some relation to its deposit liabilities will limit the possibilities of deposit creation. If the required reserve is something not easily obtained, such as a deposit at one of the twelve Federal Reserve banks, the amount of debt a bank incurs to depositors will be restricted. This limitation will help keep deposits from losing value as a result of "excessive" issue. Otherwise, a bank's search for income might lead it to grant more loans, and to create more deposits, than it "ought." Even minor economic strain might then reveal that the bank could no longer meet its obligations. Distress, even tragedy, would then ensue from bank failures, as happened all too often before 1934. Maintaining bank solvency, however, is still not the chief reason that society now requires banks to hold reserves.

Suppose that many banks in the ordinary search for income were to grant more and more loans. The total increase in buying as borrowers spent their new deposits could then lead to price inflation, a fall in the purchasing power of money. Reserve requirements, whether imposed by government or by bank management, help to keep banks—individually or as a whole system—from creating "too much" in new deposits.

Reserves can perform the functions ordinarily assigned them while making up only part of a bank's assets. Modern banks operate with *fractional reserves*. In this country minimum requirements are prescribed by law. For banks which are members of the Federal Reserve System, the legal reserve, other than vault cash, is the deposit at the Federal Reserve bank. In other words, member banks are required to maintain deposits at the Federal Reserve equal on the average to about one-sixth of the amounts which the banks owe in demand deposits. (For savings and time deposits only 4 percent—one twenty-fifth—is required.) Any amount above the minimum required is *excess reserve*. Its existence provides legal authority for the bank to incur larger liabilities to depositors and to acquire more income-earning assets. A bank's reserve position is of the utmost importance in its operations.

Cash in the vault now counts as part of the legal reserve. The bank must have enough currency on hand to meet any excess of currency withdrawals over deposits of currency. On the average, vault cash is about 1.5 percent of all assets. A banker, in addition, will hold certain highly liquid assets, such as short-term government debt, which he may term "secondary reserves"; these are not yet of concern to us.

BANK LENDING AND DEPOSIT CREATION

Banks, we can assume, must keep a legal reserve equal to one-sixth, or $16\frac{2}{3}$ percent, of the demand deposits subject to check.[2] Bank A receives an asset, a check, from a depositor, Z. To avoid complicating the illustration, we also assume that the check has not been drawn upon an account in another commercial bank. But is it possible for A to get such an asset without any other commercial bank experiencing a reduction in its reserves (assets) or its deposits (liabilities)? An example would appear if Z had sold a Treasury bill (3 to 6 month obligation of the Federal Treasury) to the Federal Reserve, receiving a check on the "Fed" in return; he deposits this check in A.

Bank A

Assets		*Liabilities*	
Deposit at (due from) Federal Reserve	increase $1000	Z's deposit	increase $1000

Bank A is a member of the Federal Reserve. It sends the check received to the FR for deposit in its account there.[3] This account is a

---

[2] Until World War II the average required reserve was nearer 10 percent. During and after the war the requirement was around 20 percent.

[3] Some agencies, such as the TVA, the ICC, and the SEC, are customarily referred to by their initials. This practice is economical. Custom has not yet developed comparable practice as regards the Federal Reserve. In this volume, however, we shall frequently use the letters FR to stand for Federal Reserve.

legal reserve for the bank. How, then, have its balance sheet entries changed?

A's deposit at the "Fed" earns the bank nothing. Yet this deposit is valuable because it provides a basis on which the bank can get something that will earn it income. This reserve, in fact, is large enough to support six times as much in deposits ($6000, which is $5000 more than at present). The realistic expansion potential for *A*, however, is very much smaller.

Suppose that a local grocer wants to add to his inventory and is willing to pay to borrow to do so. He applies to Bank *A* for a loan, offering his IOU. The bank now has "unused" reserves that will permit it to expand its deposits. Any expansion of accounts on which its customers can write checks, however, subjects it to the virtual certainty of a "cash drain." The cash demanded from it might be in currency, but we shall for the moment assume that the demand will be for some of the bank's deposit at the "Fed." In the typical case, for example, the owner of the demand deposit will write a check ordering the bank to make a payment to someone who uses another bank. To make such a payment, *A* will be forced to use its reserves—draw down its deposit at the FR.

Nevertheless, Bank *A* may feel that it can safely lend as much as $833; this amount is the excess of the original increase in its reserves ($1000) over the amount required as the reserve ($167) for *Z*'s deposit of $1000. So the bank agrees to lend the grocer $833 and credits his account with this amount. The bank's accounts as a result of these transactions then stand as follows:

Bank *A*

Assets			Liabilities		
Deposit at (due from) Federal Reserve	increase	$1000	*Z*'s deposit	increase	$1000
Grocer's IOU	increase	833	Grocer's deposit	increase	833
	Total increase	$1833		Total increase	$1833

The grocer has borrowed and agreed to pay interest so that he can make payments; why would he keep borrowed money in a checking account where it can bring no income? He soon writes a check to a wholesaler. The check itself is not of much use to the wholesaler. He benefits not by holding the check but by depositing it in his bank, *B*. This bank in turn demands payment, for the check itself is not what *B* wants. Bank *A* must pay. This payment is made by drawing down or debiting *A*'s account at the Federal Reserve, and crediting Bank *B*'s account there. The changes so far are the following *increases:*

Bank A

Assets		Liabilities	
Deposit at Federal Reserve	$ 167	Z's deposit	$1000
Grocer's IOU	833		

Bank B

Assets		Liabilities	
Deposit at Federal Reserve	833	Wholesaler's deposit	833
Total both banks	$1833	Total both banks	$1833

Bank *B* is now in a position somewhat like that of Bank *A* earlier. Its reserves have gone up more than is needed for the increase in its deposits. It can, then, meet the request of a customer—perhaps a manufacturer—for a loan. With a reserve increase of $833 might the bank incur added deposit liabilities totaling six times as much—$4998, *i.e.,* $4165 more than the $833? No banker would dream of trying to approach such a total. Bankers are too much aware of the cash drain. If the bank were to expand loans to this extent and if even a modest proportion of the added deposits were used to make payments to persons using other banks, the entire reserve of $833 (the deposit at the Federal Reserve) would move to the accounts of other banks, perhaps rapidly. Bank *B*, therefore, would more likely do essentially what *A* did—agree to lend only about the difference, $694, between (a) the required reserve, $139, or one-sixth of $833, and (b) the growth of its deposit at the Federal Reserve, $833. Let's say that it does so, with the following results:

Bank B

Assets		Liabilities	
Deposit at Federal Reserve	$ 833	Wholesaler's deposit	$ 833
Manufacturer's IOU	694	Manufacturer's deposit	694
Total	$1527	Total	$1527

The manufacturer, of course, has borrowed to be able to make a payment. He writes a check for $694. The recipient, a contractor who has repaired the factory, deposits it in Bank *C*. *B*'s deposit at the Federal Reserve goes down as *C*'s rises, producing the following:

Bank B

Assets		Liabilities	
Deposit at Federal Reserve	$ 139	Wholesaler's deposit	$ 833
Manufacturer's IOU	694		

Bank C

Deposit at Federal Reserve	694	Contractor's deposit	694
Total, Banks B and C	$1527	Total, Banks B and C	$1527

Bank C now holds reserves greater than it needs for the new deposit. It can, in effect, exchange the excess, five-sixths of $694, for an asset that will earn it income—a $578 note of a consumer buying a used car.

Bank C

Assets		*Liabilities*	
Deposit at Federal Reserve	$ 694	Contractor's deposit	$ 694
Auto buyer's IOU	578	Auto buyer's deposit	578
Total	$1272	Total	$1272

The seller of the car then deposits the buyer's check in Bank D, which receives payment from C's account at the Federal Reserve, drawing it down to $116 ($694 minus $578). The totals for the four banks as a result of these transactions now stand:

Bank A

Deposit at Federal Reserve	$ 167	Z's deposit	increase $1000
Grocer's IOU	833		

Bank B

Deposit at Federal Reserve	139	Wholesaler's deposit	833
Manufacturer's IOU	694		

Bank C

Deposit at Federal Reserve	116	Contractor's deposit	694
Auto buyer's IOU	578		

Bank D

Deposit at Federal Reserve	578	Auto seller's deposit	578
Total, Banks A–D	$3105	Total, Banks A–D	$3105

Deposits at the four commercial banks have grown $3105 as a result of these transactions—$1000 upon deposit of the original check of the Federal Reserve to the seller of the Treasury bill and $2105 as banks have created deposits for borrowers. The deposit at the Federal Reserve grew originally by $1000 and has remained the same; the ownership, however, has been shifting as one bank after another has been required to give up part. The grocer, manufacturer, and auto buyer have *borrowed and spent $2105 that had not existed before.* The banks have acquired interest-earning assets of $2105.

The original deposit of $1000 may be termed a *primary* deposit. The amounts resulting from bank lending may be called *derivative* deposits.

The process of deposit and loan growth need not end here. Bank *D* has unused lending potential. The process can continue as shown in Fig. 2.1. Each successive increment would, of course, be smaller.

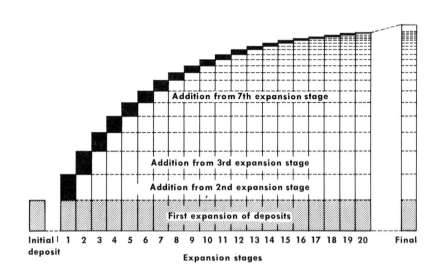

Addition from 7th expansion stage

Addition from 3rd expansion stage

Addition from 2nd expansion stage

First expansion of deposits

Initial | 1 2 3 4 5 6 7 8 9 10 11 12 13 14 15 16 17 18 19 20   Final
deposit

Expansion stages

FIGURE 2.1

Cumulative Expansion of Deposits

The largest possible increase of deposits at all banks would be $6000. The assets held then would be $1000 at the Federal Reserve and $5000 in IOU's of borrowers. The total would not, in fact, grow to this size because the cost of arranging and administering loans would be too high in relation to the interest income that they would yield the bank to justify the small transactions that would now appear. However, if we had assumed not $1000 but $1 billion coming into the banking system originally—and an increase of this size is possible—eventual growth to virtually six times the original injection is a realistic possibility.

The formula for the maximum deposit expansion is

$$\triangle D = \triangle A \times \frac{1}{R} \text{ or } \triangle D = \frac{\triangle A}{R}$$

where $\triangle D$ is the largest possible increase in demand deposits
$\triangle A$ is the addition to legal reserves
R is the legal reserve ratio.

Thus, if the legal reserve requirement is one-sixth, the largest possible expansion for $1000 of new reserves is $\frac{\$1000}{1/6}$ or $6000. When reserve requirements are set in percentage terms, as is the case in this country, R will be the figure of the percentage—say 16 (a bit under one-sixth, of course)—over 100, or 16/100. The practical limits are affected by the additional factors noted below.

Note—and this is vital—that the banks are not lending out what has been deposited with them. The banks are (a) *accepting* new assets (IOU's); (b) *creating* new liabilities; and (c) *shifting* ownership of the reserve. They are monetizing private debt. The IOU's of private individuals and businesses are exchanged for the debts of banks. These latter obligations are generally accepted throughout the economy. Such deposits payable on demand are money.

MODIFICATIONS OF THE SIMPLE PROCESS

The actual process is not quite so simple. Five possible variations will be noted here because they have bearing upon the substance of deposit creation.

1. A lending bank will not ordinarily lose the entire deposit it creates when it makes a loan. Some of the checks a borrower-depositor writes may go to other persons or firms using the same bank. Thus the grocer might have used some of what he borrowed to pay an employee who would deposit the check in his account at Bank A. Or the wholesaler might keep his account in A. The banker in deciding how much to lend will, perhaps somewhat unconsciously, consider the prospect that some of the deposit will shift from account to account in his bank, rather than going entirely to other banks. In fact, banks often have an understanding with a borrower that during the life of the loan he will keep on deposit in his account a fifth or so of what he has borrowed. When some of the deposit resulting from a loan remains in the bank, losses of reserves are obviously smaller than we assumed. The lending capacity of the bank is greater. But the lending power of other banks then grows less.

2. Any original depositor, such as Z, will often use some of his account to pay his bills. Except as the checks he writes are redeposited in Bank A, the permanent rise in its reserves is less than the original increase. Consequently, Bank A's "safe" lending capacity does not grow so much as in our illustration. But—and this is important—other banks will ordinarily get the reserves which A fails to retain.[4] A check on one bank cannot, as a rule, be of much use to the recipient until he deposits it in his bank. Ownership of the deposit at the Federal Reserve—the legal reserve—may shift rapidly. This shifting of ownership is from one bank to another. What one loses, others gain.

3. The people who get more money may not keep it all in demand deposit accounts. An increase in the use of currency for hand-to-hand transactions is probable. Currency withdrawn by depositor Z from Bank A will not necessarily return to other banks. In fact, this *currency drain* is by no means small. In the three years to mid-1964, currency in circulation rose $4.6 billion while demand deposits rose $7.5 billion. Moreover, the rate of drain is not stable. Bankers must allow for it more or less by trial and error.[5]

4. The public prefers to hold a substantial fraction of its total of bank deposits in time or savings, rather than in checking, accounts. Reserve requirements for time deposits average only about one-fourth of those for demand deposits. Therefore, the growth of deposits will depend upon the division between the two types, demand and time,[6] following an expansion of legal reserves.

5. Banks do not always lend as much as the legal reserves permit. It may seem desirable, for example, to build up some excess reserves. Or, the demand for loans may not be high enough to call forth all the borrowing needed for the full expansion.

For the banking system *as a whole,* lending capacity will rise about as indicated in the illustration, reduced somewhat by currency drain and

---

[4] Two exceptions will be noted but otherwise ignored for present purposes: (a) withdrawals of funds for foreign payments, and (b) shifts of deposits to government account at the Federal Reserve, which reduce commercial bank holdings there, and the total of member bank reserves.

[5] A growth of deposits increases the bank's needs for vault cash. When vault cash did not qualify as part of the legal reserve, the *vault cash "drain"* restricted deposit expansion slightly.

[6] The process of creation of time or savings deposits differs from that just described for demand deposits. To the bank the depositor hands over money, not his IOU.

modified by preference for time deposits.[7]   But how will the increase in lending capacity be distributed among banks after a few months?   The best answer to this question will be much less satisfactory than predictions of the total.

If *A* were the only bank in the economy, it would need fear no losses of deposits to other banks.   It could itself expand deposits to the full potential in our illustration ($6000 minus allowance for the increased use of currency).   What factors determine the "sharing" among banks of changes in legal reserves?   The size of the bank and its geographic and economic nearness to the point of injection of new reserves influence the result.   Otherwise, prediction is difficult.   Banks differ widely in size, and they number in the thousands.   The ownership of new deposits at the Federal Reserve, *i.e.,* the "resting place" of added reserves, after a few months is highly uncertain.   In Britain and other lands where a few banks with many branches cover the country and make up most of the banking system, it is not reckless to assume that changes in reserves will eventually be shared among banks in about the same proportion as existing reserves. Here, however, the individual bank faces disturbing uncertainties.   Its reserve position—and thus its lending power—is always a matter of some doubt.

Aspects of deposit creation remain for study later.   This chapter, however, has covered the essentials.   (The opposite process, which we have not discussed, is the chief means by which the country's money stock is reduced.)   The banker, concentrating on the phases of his business which we discuss in the next few chapters, may think that he merely "lends out what has been deposited" in his bank.   Yet whatever his conclusion, his actions lead to deposit creation (or destruction); the bank's loans (or their repayment) alter the total of amounts in checking accounts and thereby change the total of our principal medium of exchange.

QUESTIONS

1. In what cases is an asset of one person a liability of another? What is of special significance about the liabilities of banks?

2. What are bank reserves?   What functions do they serve?

3. "A single commercial bank can do little in creating deposits. The process requires many banks."   Discuss.

4. With the use of balance sheet entries show how commercial banks

---

[7] In the formula on page 33, *R* could be modified to allow for the relative importance of time deposits; *R* could be increased to allow for cash drain or a new factor added.

can "create" deposits after $1000 of currency is added to the assets of one bank. Assume the reserve required is (a) 20 percent; (b) 10 percent; (c) 5 percent.

5. Describe the effect of each of the following on the process described in Question 4: (a) currency drain; (b) the shift of deposits from checking to savings accounts; (c) the desire of banks to hold unused reserves; (d) a lack of demand for loans.

6. Are deposits in banks assets or liabilities? Discuss.

7. Do the profit potentialities of banks depend upon the size of the fraction prescribed for fractional reserves? Why? Illustrate from your answer in Question 4, assuming that banks receive six percent on loans.

8. What would cause a reduction in demand deposits throughout the banking system?

9. In what sense do commercial banks monetize debt?

PART TWO

COMMERCIAL BANKING

CHAPTER 3 *FORMATION AND OPERATION OF COMMERCIAL BANKS*

THE modern financial and monetary system has developed around commercial banks. These institutions are in no sense limited to commerce. They are the banks which most of us as individuals, and most businesses and governments, use in day-to-day transactions. Commercial banks accept funds for deposit in accounts from which the depositor may draw upon demand, by writing a check if he wishes.

Commercial banks also accept debts, promises to pay of businesses, individuals, or governments. In return the bank writes up the demand deposit owing to—and owned by—the borrower. The ability to *create* deposits in this way distinguishes commercial banks significantly from other financial institutions and helps account for extensive governmental control of commercial banking.

NATIONAL AND STATE BANKS: A PRELIMINARY VIEW

Approximately 4600 commercial banks are chartered by the national government. Nearly 9000 others have state charters. Including branches, this country has nearly 27,000 banking offices. All national banks and one-fifth of state-chartered commercial banks—most of the large ones—are members of the Federal Reserve System. While the United States does not have one central bank on the pattern of most countries[1]—Bank

---

[1] The Central Bank of the States of Equatorial Africa and of Cameroon and the Central Bank of the States of West Africa serve, respectively, five and seven of the newly created independent countries of Africa. This unusual arrangement grew out of conditions developed when these areas were under French rule. It is still too early to judge how satisfactorily these multination central banks will function.

of England, Bank of Morocco, Bank of Canada—the 12 Federal Reserve banks make up a system which is essentially a central bank for the economy. A national government agency, the Federal Deposit Insurance Corporation, insures deposits in all but about 300 relatively small banks.

Commercial banking is a business with many fascinating aspects. One suburban bank counted 125 different services it offered the public. Some operations, such as the handling of checks by the millions, may seem humdrum; without them, however, the rest of our economy could hardly function. The importance of commercial banks is not indicated adequately by such measures as the numbers they employ (less than one percent of the labor force) nor by the fact that they generate about 1.6 percent of National Income. They are an indispensable element of an interdependent economy. Commercial banks not only create the bulk of our money and help finance much of economic life. They also arrange or facilitate payments from one person or company to another, and among all regions.

Commercial banks are privately owned, incorporated businesses organized to earn income for their owners. In some respects, therefore, they resemble businesses generally. In other respects, however, they differ significantly, in formation, operation, and economic importance.

THE BALANCE SHEET AS AN INDICATOR OF THE NATURE OF COMMERCIAL BANKING

A bank's balance sheet, or "statement of condition," provides a useful place to begin our study. For many businesses the income statement reveals more about the vital activities than does the balance sheet; this does not hold for banks. Table 3.1 presents key balance sheet data for the entire commercial banking system (except a few small banks which in total account for less than one percent of all assets). Let us comment briefly upon the major elements.

Assets

"Cash" includes four major items.

1. *Vault cash* consists of the coins and paper currency on hand for meeting requests of depositors. Vault cash earns no income, but since 1960 it has counted as part of the legal reserve. Banks try to keep at least the minimum needed for orderly operation, *i.e.,* to meet differences between the inflow and outgo of currency. The requirements of each individual bank will depend upon (a) the deposit-withdrawal patterns of its

TABLE 3.1

Assets, Liabilities, and Capital of All Commercial Banks, December 1963

Assets	Amount (Billions)	Percent	Liabilities and capital	Amount (Billions)	Percent
Vault cash	$ 4.1	1	Demand deposits of individuals, partnerships, corporations, and states and localities[b]	$144.6	46
Deposits at the Federal Reserve	17.1	5	U.S. Treasury deposits	7.0	2
Deposits in other banks	12.3	4	Interbank deposits	14.5	5
Cash items in the process of collection	17.0	5	Time deposits[c]	100.3	33
U.S. government securities	63.4	20	Deposits of foreign governments and banks	5.3	1
Obligations of states and localities	29.8	10	Certified checks, etc.	4.5	1
Other securities	5.2	2	Miscellaneous liabilities	12.1	4
Loans and discounts, net[a]	156.8	50	Capital and surplus	25.8	8
Miscellaneous assets	8.4	3			
Total	$314.1	100	Total	$314.1	100

[a] After valuation reserves of $3 billion.

[b] Except banks and foreign governments.

[c] Excludes time deposits of domestic and foreign banks and governments.

Source: *Annual Report of the Federal Deposit Insurance Corporation for the Year Ended December 31, 1963* (Washington: The Corporation, 1964), pp. 133–4.

customers, and (b) the availability of currency from outside in case of need. If a bank, whenever pressed for currency, can go around the corner to the Federal Reserve or to other banks, its own holdings need not be so large as if it must rely upon sources in a city many miles away. For the commercial banking system as a whole, vault cash accounts for about 1.5 percent of assets.

2. For a bank, deposits at the Federal Reserve serve much as the balance in an ordinary person's checking account. They may be drawn upon at any time. Yet for a member bank deposits at the FR are legal reserves. Consequently, they have special importance. The amount that a bank can lend to earn income depends upon the size of its legal reserves.

3. Demand deposits in other commercial banks are also treated as "cash." Such deposits often bring no income directly, but they are highly useful in conducting business.

4. The fourth asset in this group is "cash items in the process of collection." Each bank will include here checks on other banks which it has received from its depositors and which it has sent for payment (collection) but for which it has not yet received funds. Despite excellent facilities for speeding the movement of checks, the total in collection at any one time is substantial. Each bank rightly treats the amounts due it as an asset. Yet they are not in fact a net asset for the system as a whole, even though they appear so when the accounts of all banks are added together. The claims represented by checks in the collection process are exactly offset by amounts which banks owe but which they have not yet recorded as obligations to other banks. How could a bank know how much it owes others for checks which its depositors have written but which have not yet reached it for payment?

"Investments," or "securities," make up a second major group of bank assets.[2] Most are debts of governments, chiefly the national government. Nevertheless, many banks also own bonds of state-local governments and of business corporations. The securities owned vary widely in important characteristics: for example, the time before they will be repaid; marketability; interest yield; and tax status.

The assets which make up the largest single group are acquired in the process of bank lending. They are the IOU's—notes and other promises to pay—which borrowers give the bank. By custom, these assets are called "loans." They provide the chief source of income. As shown later in Table 4.1, "loans" are of many types.

The final group consists chiefly of land, buildings, and equipment

---

[2] The term "investment" as used here has a meaning different frm the one we shall use beginning in Chapter 16.

used by banks in their own operations. The worth of such physical assets is much smaller, in terms of percentage, than for most business firms.

As is true of any balance sheet, the valuations placed on some assets will be open to doubt. For example, notes of borrowers often have no market in which their worth can be tested. Various rules have been devised for dealing with the different problems. Some uncertainty must always remain, however, and neither outsiders nor bank officers themselves will know exactly the range of reasonable doubt.

Liabilities

The bank's chief liabilities are what it owes its depositors. (Although the deposit is an asset of the depositor, it is a debt of the bank.) Demand deposits differ from time and savings deposits in several respects, and although time and savings deposits are not the same, we shall treat them as such when the differences are not important for the problem being discussed.[3]   (1) Demand deposits must be paid whenever the depositor directs.   On savings deposits, however, the bank has a legal right, which it will use only rarely, to wait 30 days or more before paying; time deposits are in general payable only after a fixed period.   (2) The owner of a demand deposit can withdraw it without contacting the bank.   (3) The percentage that the bank must keep as required reserves against time deposits is much less than for demand deposits.   (4) Somewhat different assets correspond to the two types of deposits—not legally but in the planning of bank managers.   (5) Finally, the bank pays interest on time, but not on demand, deposits.

The bank must distinguish (a) deposits due to individuals, businesses, churches, clubs, and other such entities from (b) those due governments or (c) other banks.   (Government deposits, especially those of the national government, must be secured by special pledged or earmarked assets,

[3] These deposits fall into three groupings: (a) Time certificates of deposit, "CD's," payable in not less than 30 days. Such certificates bring the "depositor" interest for periods when funds are not needed for business or other purposes. We shall discuss them later. (b) Open account time deposits which can be added to but not withdrawn until maturity (or upon special notice). Christmas clubs offer an example. (c) Savings deposits, evidenced by a passbook or other written receipt; only individuals and nonprofit organizations may own such deposits, and withdrawals must ordinarily be made in person. Banks must have the right to require at least 30 days' notice for withdrawal; they rarely use it. Until late 1964 the Federal Reserve limited the interest which might pay on time deposits to 4 percent for deposits payable in 90 days or more and 1 percent for those due in less than 90 days—with exceptions for deposits owned by foreigners. For savings deposits held for less than one year, the maximum was $3\frac{1}{2}$ percent. If state regulations set lower rates, they also apply to member banks. In November 1964 the ceilings were raised to 4 percent on all savings accounts and under-90-day time deposits and to $4\frac{1}{2}$ percent on time deposits of longer maturity.

almost always government securities.) Incidentally, published balance sheets rarely show details on types of deposits, not even the relation of demand to time deposits.

Remaining liabilities as a rule are relatively small in total. Banks always have some unpaid accounts outstanding, including wages accrued but not paid. Occasionally, there is a debt to the Federal Reserve when the bank has borrowed to get reserves; banks try hard, however, to avoid having such debt outstanding on the day to which a published balance sheet applies. Banks will also have outstanding pledges to meet certain obligations for customers under conditions that have been agreed upon. Miscellaneous liabilities are such things as income which may have been received but not yet earned, *e.g.,* interest paid in advance by borrowers and which must be refunded if the loan is repaid early; taxes due on profit, payrolls, and property; interest due on time deposits; and reserves for depreciation and possible losses on loans when these are not shown as deductions from the value of assets.

Capital Accounts

The last portion of the balance sheet shows the amount the owners have put into the business. The amounts received from sale of stock may be classed in part as capital and in part as capital surplus. Past earnings which have been left in the bank rather than paid out as dividends to stockholders will be designated as "earned surplus," "retained earnings," or some such term.

Preponderance of Debt

A thoughtful look at the balance sheet will reveal an interesting fact: The big amounts are debts. Most of the bank's assets are the debts of others. Even deposits at the Federal Reserve are debts of the Federal Reserve. Coins and paper money in a significant economic sense are a debt of government (or its agency, the FR). What a bank owns that is not a debt of others—its premises, for example—will make up a small part of its total assets. Liabilities, which are debts of the bank, also overshadow the ownership element which the stockholders have put into the capital accounts.

Now we can see the reason for calling banks "dealers in debt." The unusual nature of banks as profit-making businesses is suggested by a fact that we have noted earlier. Banks acquire the debt of others on which they receive interest. In return, they give their own debt, deposits. On about half of these deposits, however, commercial banks pay no interest.

BANK FORMATION

Historical Background

Modern commercial banking is the product of historical development. Over many generations, businesses such as goldsmiths, which had begun as providers of safe storage of gold and silver, or such as private banks, which made loans of the owners' own wealth, came to provide notes which were accepted in exchange. Gradually, more people learned to use these pieces of paper. Laws then granted some businesses the privilege of issuing their own debts in the form of bank notes. The notes could be given in return for interest-bearing IOU's of borrowers. The privilege of note issue became highly valuable; governments, therefore, restricted the opportunities to prevent overissue in response to profit opportunities. In this country until well into the nineteenth century, legislatures limited narrowly the creation of banks. Setting up a bank with power to issue bank notes required a special act of the legislature.

Then in one state after another, beginning in 1837, legislatures provided general rules governing the establishment of banks. Anyone meeting specified, often not very strict, conditions could set up a bank. To

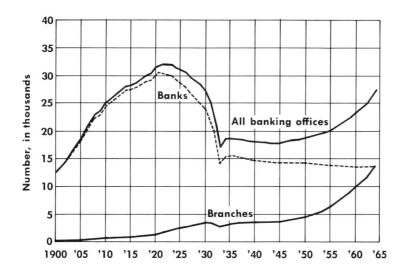

FIGURE 3.1

Commercial Banking Offices in the United States

create a bank under these "free banking" laws—and to a large extent under the National Banking Act, passed during the Civil War—became, it seemed, a "right" rather than a privilege. For several decades the establishment of banks was moderately easy.

Banking was profitable enough to invite great expansion in the number of institutions. This country held to a preference for "unit banking." Each banking office was ordinarily a separate institution rather than a branch of a large one. In 1850 the country had one bank per 27,000 persons; at the time of World War I over 27,500 banks averaged one for about each 3200 persons. Standards were so low, unfortunately, that many banks eventually collapsed. In fact, bank failures for a century to 1934 were a major source of economic difficulty.

Although the volume of money payments in our economy has grown substantially over the last quarter century, relatively few new banks have been permitted. In 1963, however, a relatively large number of new commercial banks—300—were established; half as many were absorbed by others or closed voluntarily. However, since 1100 new branches of national and state banks appeared, the total of banking offices grew. Early in 1964 the country had 5000 more banking offices than 6 years earlier.

Chartering

A bank must have a charter, state or Federal. The Comptroller of the Currency, an officer of the United States Treasury, is responsible for chartering new national banks. Charters will be issued only if the officials are persuaded that new banking facilities are needed, taking full account of the economic prospects of the community. Existing banks will generally try to show that new competition is not required to serve the public adequately. For many years defenders of the status quo would generally be successful if the community had more than one bank. Recently, however, the Comptroller has granted charters for new banks in localities where existing banks claimed that they were providing ample facilities and competing actively. He favors more banks and banking competition for a growing economy.

If applicants do establish that the economic situation justifies a new bank, they must meet other conditions. The personal records of those applying for a charter must meet exacting standards of probity and reputation. The proposed managers must also satisfy the government agency of their capacity to operate a bank efficiently. In all [4] but a few cases of rejection, the Comptroller has judged that the need was insufficient (or

---

[4] From 1960 through 1963 the number of state banks grew by three percent, compared with nine percent for national banks. State banks added 1200 branches, about 25 percent; national banks added 1900 branches, nearly 35 percent.

another application had priority), the income prospects unfavorable, or the management outlook unsatisfactory. A bank getting a Federal charter must arrange to join the Federal Reserve System and meet the requirements of the Federal Deposit Insurance Corporation.

Mergers eliminate about 150 banks a year. A small bank may recognize a shortage of qualified management for the future. It may be unable to meet the demands for loans, as in a growing community. The decision to merge may be determined by the receipt of an offer which is too good to turn down. A large bank may offer attractive terms because it wants more offices as a means of building business, especially in a growing community. The acquiring bank may seek larger lending power and the ability to make bigger individual loans. Or perhaps it may be seeking more prestige. Some states narrowly limit the possibility of merger. Congress in 1960 acted to ease mergers involving national banks. The Department of Justice, however, has strongly opposed some bank mergers which other Federal agencies had expressly approved. In two major cases the Supreme Court ordered dissolution. Federal policy on bank mergers strikes one as distinctly untidy.[5]

Branches, Groups, and Chains

The insistence on unit banking has been modified in much of the country. (In essence state laws govern because national banks are required to observe the limits set in each state for state banks.) Thirty-four states permit a bank to have branches, though in 17 states restrictions limit the scope for branching, *e.g.*, to a county. Some 2800 commercial banks had about 13,400 branches in early 1965; of these, 5400 were in the head-office city and only 4200 outside the county. A single board of directors and top management will control all the offices, but the local manager has a range of authority within which he is free to make decisions.

Several arguments favor branch banking. The large institution (a bank consisting of several branches) can develop a higher degree of specialization than can a small one. As a result customers may get better service. Some banking functions can be conducted more economically when the scale of operations is broad. The larger the bank, the larger the maximum loan it is permitted to make; and big companies sometimes need to borrow large amounts. Finally, it is argued that large banks are safer than small ones; loans and investments can be more diversified and management more competent.[6]

[5] E. S. Herman, T. G. Moore, and others discuss the issues in *The National Banking Review*, March 1964, pp. 391–423.

[6] The existence of many unit banks puts the economy to greater social cost in the form of examination and supervision than would be required if the number of separate institutions were materially smaller.

The chief argument against branch banking is that branching leads to concentration in banking and that this is dangerous, especially to the small business and small community. It is argued that a local manager of the branch of a bank with headquarters in another city cannot serve the town as well as can the banker whose business focuses on the locality. And may not big banks become monopolistic? One cannot answer with absolute assurance; but small banks in small communities can be monopolistic, and branch competition may sometimes lead to better and less expensive service. A recent study concludes: "Our analysis suggests that neither in terms of number of competitors, nor concentration (measures of actual competition), nor in terms of the condition of entry (potential competition) have the structures of local banking markets been adversely affected by branch banking in the United States. The weight of evidence suggests that, to the contrary, market structures are adversely affected by restrictions on branch banking." [7]

Multiple-unit banking has also developed in another form as 52 holding companies which operate about 1700 banks and branches in 32 states. A parent corporation buys voting control of individual banks. It can then operate them with whatever degree of central supervision it desires (within the limits set by government). Holding company banks have one-third or more of commercial bank deposits in 11 states, including Georgia, Minnesota, Oregon, and Wisconsin.

In some cases two or more banks are under much the same ownership. They may operate as a chain without the use of a holding company. A 1963 survey found the number of banks in such common ownership exceeding previous estimates considerably. Corporations engaged in other businesses occasionally own effective control of a commercial bank—with results not a matter of public record.

Capital

Laws set minimum capital provisions. For national banks these relate to size of community: $50,000 if the population is under 6000; $100,-000 if the population is from 6000 to 50,000; $200,000 if the population exceeds 50,000. The Comptroller may, however, require more capital. In addition, paid-in surplus must be at least 20 percent.[8] Minimum capital required for state banks is often as low as $25,000.

---

[7] B. Shull and P. M. Horvitz, "Branch Banking and the Structure of Competition," *National Banking Review*, March 1964, pp. 301–41. The authors give references to other materials on the subject.

[8] The price at which new stock is sold to the public might be $25, with $20 assigned to capital and $5 to paid-in surplus. National banks must accumulate surplus equal to the common stock. This requirement dates from 1935 and replaced one that imposed double liability on stockholders. Under the old rule a person owning stock in a national bank could be assessed (required to pay in again) as much as the par value of his stock to help meet the bank's obligations.

A bank's capital, including surplus paid in upon formation and retained earnings, provides protection for depositors—persons to whom the bank is obligated. The general acceptability of checks will depend upon public confidence in banks in general. Ample capital will give a solid basis for such confidence. As some loans turn out badly, the loss (above reserves for losses) can in effect be charged to the capital accounts of the stockholders.[9] Consequently, depositors cannot suffer until a bank's losses on loans and investments pile up to more than capital, including paid-in surplus and undistributed profits (plus the large protection provided by deposit insurance). How much capital is needed? There is no simple answer, and any rule will be crude. Practice and analysis have yielded no general agreement.

Capital might be related to the volume of liabilities. But in what proportion? Perhaps 1 to 10, a standard widely endorsed in the 1920's, would suffice. Yet needs for capital depend upon the quality of the bank's assets and the likelihood of losses. These in turn depend upon the caliber of bank management, general business conditions, the rigor of examination, and legal requirements. All vary from time to time and place to place.

One precaution limits the maximum size of the loans which a bank may make to any one borrower to a fraction of the bank's total capital. For example, the maximum which a national bank may lend to one borrower is ten percent of the bank's capital and surplus. Such a rule assures some diversification and spreading of risks. Yet the laws which require such diversification do not relate total loans to capital. The total may exceed the amount which capital can "protect."

For many years, there has been a downward drift in the ratio of capital to total assets, to *risk assets* (all assets minus cash and U.S. Government securities), and to deposits. Early in 1964 capital of FR member banks was about nine percent of total assets (compared with 15 percent in mid-1930's) and about 18 percent of "risk" assets. The averages seem satisfactory, but as with all average figures, these do not reveal how many banks fall how far below. Many nonmember banks have less secure capital ratios.

Profit Potentialities of Banks Operating on Fractional Reserves

Let us illustrate the profit possibilities of banking when capital (including paid-in surplus) is a small fraction of deposits. Assume that bankers believe, and the law agrees, that capital need only be one-tenth

---

[9] If capital, as stated in the bank charter, is impaired (reduced) by losses, new capital must be supplied—perhaps by assessments on stockholders—or the bank must be reorganized or closed. Reductions of surplus due to losses, however, call for no special action. Paid-in and earned surpluses are shown separately in the accounts, and all but the most unusual changes affect earned surplus.

of deposit liabilities. (For simplicity we may also assume that the bank owns its building and necessary facilities and that the assets purchased with capital funds are legal reserves.) Allowing for legal reserves which may earn nothing, the bank can then acquire earning assets of perhaps nine times the owners' investment, $900,000 of interest-yielding notes for $100,000 of capital. If the interest rate received is six percent, the annual gross income will be $54,000 on a commitment by the owners of $100,000—54 percent gross. Even if operating expenses are 50 percent of gross income—somewhat below the present expense level but above that often incurred in the past—net earnings would be 27 percent of capital.[10]

The dream of lucrative profit was wonderfully enticing when the ratio of capital (and required reserves) to deposits was small. In the 12 years through 1963 member bank profits after taxes averaged around 8.5 percent of capital and surplus. This rate falls below that for leading businesses throughout the country,[11] but above the rate earned by most regulated public utilities.

Bank owners have long faced this temptation—to build a large superstructure of earning assets and deposit liabilities on a given volume of net worth. Profits per dollar of owner's investment will then be larger than if the ratio of loans to the stockholders' investment were more conservative, that is, if there were more "cushion" for depositors. Bank costs include a substantial element which is fixed in the short run. Consequently, operating expense per unit of service performed, e.g., per dollar of loan, tends to fall as volume grows, adding to the temptation to grant loans of doubtful quality. If income-earning assets are $5 for each $1 of capital, the bank will have only half the income potential per dollar of owners' investment that exists with a ratio of 10 to 1. The risks, of course, also differ. At the 10 to 1 ratio, failure of only half as big a fraction of loans will produce any specific misfortune, such as wiping out half of the owner's capital.

The Problem of Adequacy of Bank Capital

Law and practice in this country have been lax regarding bank capital. They have also been too rigid for an economy of great diversity. The

[10] In the past to which this illustration applies, income taxes on banks were low or nonexistent; any such liability is included here in operating expenses.

[11] Reported earnings may, in the long run, turn out to be inaccurate. It is difficult to know in any one year whether the amounts set aside to cover future loan losses are correct, too high, or too low. The deductions made by some banks, one hears, have assumed future loss rates to be higher than a reasonable outlook for the economy will support; if so, true earnings will prove to have been greater than shown in published reports. For other banks, however, loss reserves may prove inadequate.

minimum absolute amounts required have been too small to assure that each bank will be large enough to operate efficiently. Capital requirements have not been related, as logically they might, to the bank's total liabilities. The rules of thumb used by regulatory agencies to allow for the quality of a bank's assets, and hence the likelihood of losses, are crude, to say the least.[12]

Why have lawmakers and regulatory officials failed to assure the public greater protection? Part of the explanation is found in the competition between the states and the Federal government. If one were to establish materially higher capital requirements, some banks in its system would attempt to shift their charters to the other. Their motive would be to preserve their income-earning potential and avoid added difficulty in meeting the competition of lenders operating with less capital. Such shifting of charters could go far to defeat the objective. Powerful in the past was the belief that bank formation ought to be encouraged to make it easier for the public to get banking facilities and, especially, loans. Antipathy to "money monopoly" leads to insistence upon a relatively large number of banks. And if there are many banks, some must be small.

Bankers have used political influence to retain favorable conditions resulting from past legislation. Yet banks have not ignored the problem. They have been using half or more of their after-tax earnings to add to net worth. Roughly 90 percent of growth of capital since 1945 has been retained profit. Moreover, bankers point out that increased effort to protect the quality of bank assets and the insurance of deposits do much to protect depositors against loss.

Much growth of capital seems essential for the years ahead.[13] Several hundred banks a year sell new stock to add to their capital. To do so, sales at prices below book value have sometimes been required. Small banks are narrowly limited in the potential market for their stock, as a rule selling largely to old stockholders. Broader public sale is difficult because the shares of stock of most banks have a very narrow market: the banks are small and local; moreover, the amount of information provided stockholders typically falls below reasonably adequate standards so that many careful investors are not attracted. Numerous banks have been paying some dividends in the form of stock to give stockholders something

[12] Some bank examiners will put pressure on a bank to increase its capital when the ratio of "risk" assets to capital plus surplus and undivided profit goes above some arbitrary level. But many types of virtually riskless assets—high quality mortgage loans due in the near future, state-local government bonds, loans amply secured by collateral of unquestioned value (life insurance cash values)—are treated on the same basis as loans already "sticky" but not in default. The standards used by the various regulatory authorities differ. The Federal Reserve Bank of New York applies a more refined guideline.

[13] See W. Lindow, "Bank Capital and Risk Assets," *National Banking Review,* Sept. 1963, pp. 29–46.

salable while the bank builds up net worth by holding on to cash.[14] The retention of earnings, of course, prevents cash dividends from reaching potential levels; stock prices tend to be lower as a result, hindering the sale of new shares on attractive terms.

Recently, sales of preferred stock and debenture debt (the bonds having claims subordinate to those of depositors) have received the approving smile of the Comptroller. Such security offerings, it is hoped, will enable banks to get funds at "reasonable" cost to protect depositors.

ASPECTS OF BANK OPERATION

A sketch of commercial bank operating problems serves several purposes. It will not prepare one to be a banker. Nor will it reveal all the services which banks provide. Yet a description of highlights will provide clearer comprehension, not only of the problems faced by bankers but also of the ways in which banks help us carry on the ordinary affairs of economic life.

Bank Directors

The owners of a commercial bank, its stockholders, elect *directors,* who in turn choose operating officials. For good reason, laws and government regulations impose upon these banks requirements and responsibilities which differ from those applying to corporations generally. (Requirements applying to state banks vary from state to state.) For example, directors must themselves be stockholders, and citizens. Most of the directors must reside in the community (defined broadly). They are subject to criminal prosecution for any of several actions, such as accepting a commission for making a loan, falsely certifying a check, or willfully making false entries in books or reports.

---

[14] The procedures for issuing stock dividends by national, and some state, banks are cumbersome. So are other rules about dealing with stockholders. See Advisory Committee on Banking to the Comptroller of the Currency, *National Banks and the Future* (Washington Government Printing Office, 1962), Part II. Shares of even the largest banks have not been listed on stock exchanges. One reason is that the banks do not make public as much information as required by the exchanges as a condition of listing. Study of annual reports and other information provided shareholders by a sample of 233 banks found the following percentages of *omission* of data: income statements, 19; major classes of loans, 65; valuation reserves, 38; relative amounts of demand and time deposits, 85; the number of stockholders, 69; etc. Yet such information would be expected by many potential purchasers of stock ("Why Banks Should Improve Their Stockholder Reports," *Banking,* April 1964, pp. 47ff, reporting on study by E. M. Lerner). Many types of data available for banks as a group are not revealed for individual banks.

Numerous rules limit the opportunities of a director to take unfair advantage of his position or of inside influence. Typically, the bank wants a director to do more than pass on loans and help in making policy decisions. He is also expected to help get both deposits and borrowers, and to do whatever else will make the bank more profitable. He receives prestige; an opportunity to guide an institution which is important in the community and in which he has a financial interest; personal contacts which may be helpful; and sometimes monetary compensation.

Bank Facilities

Banks have some needs for staff, equipment, and other facilities that differ, at least in emphasis, from those of other industries. One is the need for a vault system and other equipment for safekeeping large amounts of wealth—currency, notes (IOU's) of borrowers, and securities. These are highly negotiable and easily carried. They are as well inviting targets for thieves, and they are susceptible to damage by fire and water. Protective equipment of many types is essential—and expensive. So, too, are the special investigations of employees and necessary insurance against fraud.

Banks are service institutions. To provide the services most effectively, banking offices must be located conveniently for depositors, borrowers, and other customers.[15] Offering convenience tends to require the use of the more expensive locations in the community. It also requires dispersed operations. After the volume of business in one location grows beyond some size, part of any additional service can be rendered better by a new unit elsewhere than by expansion on the single location. A new banking office can be located to serve some customers more conveniently than would expansion of the old office.

The need for dispersal to give the best service does not require that each banking office be a separate corporation. To a considerable extent, however, the inescapable need for scattering banking offices has also encouraged the existence of thousands of separate banks.

One consequence of the dispersion of facilities to serve public convenience is some apparent duplication of overhead expense. This results in costs which a casual observer might consider waste. At each banking office, for example, an officer with responsibility for approving or rejecting loan applications must be on the spot even though little of his time may

---

[15] The mails and the telephone offer partial substitutes for convenience of location. Better roads and the general ownership of autos have made it possible for farmers and other residents of sparsely settled areas to travel farther than in the past to use bank facilities. As a result, the need for many rural banking offices has gradually disappeared.

be required for such work. Most of his time will be spent upon less exacting duties. Unfortunately, the small unit cannot provide all skills and facilities for which there is some need. As a result the public may not get service of as good quality as might reasonably be desired. Many banks are not only too small to provide efficient service, but, still worse, they have often been weak financially; as they failed, the whole economy suffered.[16] The public has "paid" more than inherently necessary to get convenient, dispersed banking offices, for, as noted earlier, branch banking offers an alternative.

Suburbanization, population shifts, and economic growth since World War II have created needs for new facilities to serve the public conveniently. The increasing use of autos has added to the appeal of bank premises which can offer parking space and even drive-in banking. Establishing new banking offices has become very expensive, but after two years or so the earnings of a new branch will ordinarily exceed costs.

Bank operations include the handling of great masses of paper. Every piece of paper is unique in some respect, though many are similar in most essentials. There are also vast numbers of transactions each of which may differ from any other. Every day tremendous numbers of valuable pieces of paper must be handled, but each is (or may be) different from the others. Every piece of currency is potentially counterfeit, every check signature possibly a forgery, every contact with a customer potentially an influence in getting more business, every loan application a possible source of income and perhaps of large loss. Some human judgment is required, ordinarily more than in the mass handling of parts and materials in factories.

Nevertheless, ingenious equipment and special methods and forms have been developed to help in processing checks, currency, coins, dividend disbursements, bond coupons, deposit slips, and payments on loans. Machines for accounting and for other requirements of banking improve every year. Complex computers and new methods save on labor and in many cases on floor space. Some banks find that their own operations do not require full-time use of their computers. To avoid the waste of keeping idle this extremely costly equipment, banks are using computers for a variety of customer services. Some banks are connected by wire, or use other means of communication (messenger or mail), so that one bank can use its computer to serve several others. Some new services are for other

---

[16] A bank provides a variety of services. For some the cost in relation to size of operations will differ significantly from the cost functions of other services. In general, apparently, long-run average costs decline rapidly as deposits rise to $1 million and somewhat more slowly to the $2–$5 billion deposit range. Average costs then remain approximately stable until deposits rise above $100 million, where unit costs again decline. Shull and Horvitz, *op. cit.*, p. 307. The authors emphasize that the data are incomplete and inconclusive.

types of business. Several, such as preparing payrolls, involve the processing of large masses of data. Others deal with more unusual matters, such as controlling inventories in a factory or warehouse. Frequently, confidential information is used, and banks have a tradition of dealing with such information with full respect for the customer's wishes. The companies served will usually not be large enough to own computers.

Bank Personnel

Bank employment is usually thought of as consisting of a few very good and responsible positions and a mass of routine and relatively low skilled jobs. Though something of a caricature, the picture until recently was not wholly inaccurate. But conditions now differ significantly from those of the mid-1950's.

Much uninteresting routine remains, even in banks which have kept in the forefront of mechanization. No one can say how extensively rising wage rates and scientific development will induce banks to adopt new methods. Automation of check handling in many banks has reduced the amount of labor needed per check. For a long time yet, however, human beings will have an essential, though declining, part in handling the mass work of bank operations. The skills required, for the most part, will be modest. The bulk of bank jobs will still present limited opportunity. These are the jobs that make the average earnings of bank employees— $76 a week in 1964 compared with $97 in insurance and $103 in manufacturing, wholesaling, and telephone service—somewhat unappealing to an ambitious young person. Today, one in six employees is an officer. Probably an increasing proportion of bank jobs will become highly responsible, interesting, and offer attractive compensation. Bankers feel, and each spring try to persuade students getting college degrees, that more good jobs will open up in banks than can be filled adequately by the younger men and women now in line. Some personnel gaps exist in small banks where no one is ready to replace managers who are nearing retirement. Most of the more promising jobs involve relations with customers, such as getting deposits and reviewing applications for loans, or management of security investments. These are the activities which provide the major source of bank income, the chief areas of competition, and the greatest possibilities of risk. For such work a bank will pay well. And new areas are opening while others, such as international finance and the use of computers, take on new importance.

The man, or woman, who succeeds in filling these positions competently will have started with good personal qualities and a reputation for the best character; special qualifications will be developed by experience based upon a good educational foundation. Banks have a long tradition of providing educational facilities for employees. After-hours programs, the use of which date from 1900, have been added to summer schools and classes at the college and graduate level.[17]

Banks organize their internal affairs in many different ways. A large bank may have 200 or more departments or divisions. They specialize to a high degree, for example, in specific industries or types of loans, or areas. They do so not only to improve the quality of their own operations but also to be able to offer their customers a wide variety of services. This is one basis on which banks compete. Medium-sized and small banks, of course, have less scope for specialization.

Wages, salaries, and fringes account for over 35 percent of bank operating expense. However, they are well over two-thirds of all expenses other than interest on time deposits and income taxes, a much higher fraction than for most industries. Fringe benefits tend to exceed the average for business as a whole.

The Struggle for Deposits

Banks compete for deposits. This phase of bank operations dominates the life of many bankers. The loans that a bank can make and the income that it can earn depend upon its legal reserves. One way for the individual bank to increase its reserves—chiefly the deposit at the Federal Reserve—is to get reserves belonging to other banks. How can this be done? Bank A can get some of Bank B's reserves by inducing a depositor in B to transfer his account, or part of it, to A.

When large corporations decentralize or expand their operations geographically, they tend to spread their use of banking facilities. One result has been added bank rivalry for deposits. In competing for deposits, banks cannot, as a rule, compete on the basis of price. That is, they cannot offer to pay more or less interest under the law—or any at all—on demand deposits. Great ingenuity and determined effort go into the non-price competition found among bankers. The growth of bank services to depositors, especially to businesses, is to some extent the outcome of the legal prohibition on competing for demand deposits on the basis of price, *i.e.,* interest. Moreover, large depositors are "permitted" to shift a portion of their total deposits from the demand to time category and thereby get interest on some of what in fact is virtually a working balance.

In competing for time deposits, commercial banks are restricted by

[17] The American Institute of Banking, established in 1900, offers a wide variety of courses in many cities. The American Bankers Association sponsors the Stonier Graduate School of Banking at Rutgers University.

FR and FDIC limits on the interest rate which may be paid. Other savings institutions generally pay more. They thus offer hard competition for savings. Some bankers grew critical of the arbitrary ceiling in the late 1950's; but in communities where there was little real rivalry for deposits, the banker often welcomed the rules which forbade his paying over 2½ or 3 percent on time deposits. In 1962 the maximum rate authorized by the Federal Reserve was raised to 4 percent. From 1954 to 1964 interest paid on time deposits rose from 6 to 35 percent of operating expense (other than income tax) of member banks.

Correspondent Relations

Each bank must be prepared to carry out transactions with any bank anywhere in the United States, and to some extent on all continents. It receives checks drawn on other banks. And checks written by its depositors may be presented to banks in any state and even in foreign lands. Consequently, a bank must have arrangements for doing business with banks elsewhere. Never, however, can it be certain with just which banks it may need to deal, when, in what capacity, or in what amounts. An extensive and flexible system is required.

This system exists. Gradual, voluntary development built a network of correspondent relations before the establishment of the Federal Reserve. Although the latter provides vital parts of the system which now links banks, the correspondent ties are still important. These enable banks in different localities to serve each other quickly, accurately, and at moderate cost. This set of arrangements performs many of the services which nationwide branch banks render in other countries. Every American bank will keep deposits in one or more large metropolitan banks, usually including a bank in New York City. These much-sought-after accounts, like other deposits, enable the city bank to acquire earning assets.

What are the services which city banks offer correspondents? One study found 48 distinct services. The city bank will help in handling checks and other credit instruments, in collecting and providing credit information for a "country" bank or its customers, and in making loans and investments. The city bank holds securities and takes care of the details involved in collecting interest and transferring ownership. It will give assistance on problems involving research, personnel development, transactions in foreign currency, matters of law and taxation, the handling of trust funds, etc. The city bank may also help a correspondent arrange to get reserves at the "Fed" if necessary or to lend a temporary excess to a bank with a deficiency. State banks not members of the Federal Reserve are generally allowed to treat deposits in large city banks as part of the legal reserve.

The correspondent system provides a means by which a bank in one locality (or its customers) can deal, regularly or only occasionally, with a bank (or its customers) in another community. Assume that Bank *A* in Albany has an item of business with Bank *B* in Butte. *A* will ask its New York correspondent, *M*, to help. If *B* also uses *M* as its New York correspondent, the matter may be handled at once. If *B* uses another New York bank, *N*, the process is only a little more complex. Bank *M* can settle with its neighbor, *N*.

Real economic advantage results from the concentration of such correspondent activities in a few centers, notably New York. Some types of operations, depending upon volume, can be performed at lower cost per unit, *i.e.,* there are economies of scale (within some limits). Centralization facilitates prompt, effective, and inexpensive dealings among banks which are widely separated. Yet each bank is free to choose its own correspondents. The city bank benefits not only from the deposits it gains; it will also use services of smaller banks when it needs to do business in their localities, for itself or its customers. At times loans to these banks are a source of income.

CLEARING

Businesses, governments, and households make payments by check. They receive payments in the form of checks. As a rule, the recipient of a check does not exchange it for currency but deposits it in a bank account. This deposit may be in the same bank as the account on which the check is drawn. If so, the bank merely reduces the amount remaining in the account of the person who wrote the check and increases the amount due the depositor receiving the check. The bank's totals do not change.

Very often, however, the recipient of a check will deposit in a different bank, *R*, from that on which it is drawn, *P*. How, then, can the recipient bank, *R*, whose obligations to its depositors have risen, get funds from Bank *P*? One possibility would be for *P* to move currency (or some other assets) worth just what the check calls for. This, however, would be more than a nuisance; it would also cost something. And before the physical transfer could be made, it might prove unnecessary; someone with an account in *R* might give a check to someone depositing in *P*, enough to offset the first transaction. Just as payments within a bank may balance, so may those from one bank to another. And so may the payments of one bank to and from all others.

How, then, can one bank settle or balance with others? It could do much of the job, but not all, by somehow getting together every day or so with each bank in the area. A simpler way, however, has grown up in most cities—*clearing* by an association housed at a central location. Each bank that is a member of the clearing association will sort the checks on other banks that it has received for deposit, one batch for each bank in the locality. The total amount of each batch, and the grand total, are computed. (Checks on banks in other communities are sorted separately.) Then at a time agreed upon each bank sends its bundles of checks to the clearing house.

Settling clerks at booths arranged by bank quickly add the totals of the bundles of checks—all that banks A through G have presented drawn on Bank H, all that A through F and H have presented for G to pay, etc. Each bank can then compare the total it has brought (in checks for collection from others) with what it learns the others have brought for it to pay.[18] The net difference is what it can receive from, or must pay to, the clearing house.

This settlement could be made in currency. In fact, something like currency, a clearing-house certificate representing gold or gold certificates on deposit, was once widely used for settlement. Another arrangement grew up in most communities, however—the use of accounts in correspondent banks in larger cities.

Today the settlement among banks in a city is usually made by debiting and crediting accounts at the Federal Reserve. Banks that are not members of the System may keep "clearing balances" at the FR to ease payments, although some also use correspondent banks in financial centers. For clearing with banks outside the locality, banks and the clearing house rely heavily upon Federal Reserve facilities.

The bulk of items will offset each other. The relatively small balances outstanding at the end of each day will also tend to cancel out over a week or so. Yet a bank may experience a predominance of clearings one way or the other. If it owes others—if it has an adverse clearing balance—it must arrange payment somehow. It may turn over assets acceptable to others, such as deposits at the Federal Reserve or at a correspondent bank. Or it may sell securities to get funds for payment. If it is in the happier position of having net claims on others, it can acquire from them assets to use in one way or another to earn income.

Payments of billions of dollars, and millions of checks, are handled every day quickly and efficiently, by *offsetting* them against each other. Without this magnificently effective mechanism, the use of checks would hardly have achieved the preponderant position it occupies in our payment system.

---

[18] The messenger returns with the checks which all other banks have presented for payment by his bank. Its clerks then proceed to debit them against the individual accounts of those who wrote them. To even out the work load over the day—and night—banks may exchange checks directly at times other than the clearing hours; the totals are included in the final settlement at the clearing house. The flow of check processing thus moves more regularly.

QUESTIONS

1. List and discuss briefly the items on the balance sheet of a commercial bank.

2. In what ways does banking as a business resemble and differ from other types of businesses?

3. Why do banks compete for deposits? What methods do they use?

4. What purpose does bank capital serve? Assume that a capital ratio (capital accounts to total assets) of 10 percent is considered satisfactory. What conclusions could we draw from a bank with a capital ratio of 5 percent? of 25 percent?

5. Discuss some of the advantages and disadvantages of "bigness" in banking. Comment on "branch banking" in the light of your conclusions. What is the situation in your state?

6. What is meant by a "correspondent bank"? What functions do correspondents serve?

7. Assume that X draws a check on Bank A for $100 which Y (the payee) deposits in Bank B. Describe the clearing process (a) when banks A and B are in New York, and (b) when Bank A is in New York and Bank B is in Chicago.

8. What is meant by favorable clearing balance? How are clearing house balances usually settled?

9. Discuss with a banker the kinds of problems he faces. What training and character traits are important or essential for a good banker?

CHAPTER 4 *COMMERCIAL BANK LENDING: MAJOR TYPES*[1]

MAKING loans lies at the heart of a bank's activities. Here is the major source of income. Yet loans also give rise to operating costs, and losses on poor loans may force a bank to discontinue operations.[2] To the borrower, too, these loans mean convenience, profit, growth, and even economic survival.

The significance of commercial bank lending is by no means limited to the bank and the borrower. Those with whom the borrower does business are affected only a little less directly than he. The whole economy, too, feels the influence. The deposits created, or wiped out when loans are paid off, are part of the stock of money; and changes in the amount of money in the economy can have substantial effects on the level of economic activity. There are, indeed, important reasons to study bank lending.

The loans have many aspects—the length of time they run, their purpose, the type of borrower, the kind of security given—each of which warrants attention. (Fortunately, however, we need not try to study all combinations of all aspects.) The understanding that we seek requires knowledge of both the loans and the process by which they are made and administered. This chapter deals primarily with types of loans. The next two deal with interest charges, collateral, credit instruments, and other related topics.

---

[1] The difference between lending and investment will be discussed later.

[2] For example, in one year, 1933, losses on loans and investments were 72 percent of gross income.

QUALITIES OF A GOOD LOAN

What kind of loan would a banker consider ideal? It would have a high interest rate, last indefinitely if the bank desired but be terminable promptly if the bank wished, and present no danger of any loss. The typical banker would prefer the loan to serve constructive purposes, such as aiding a developing business; he hopes that his work will serve others. The ideal loan would also help advance the bank's other activities, such as attracting deposits and stimulating demand for the varied services which the bank is equipped to provide. This model loan would be inexpensive to service, and, of course, meet requirements of law.

The ideal can never be realized fully. After all, the banker, as any businessman, can sell only the "package" which the customer wants badly enough to pay for. Competition will have an important effect on what any one bank can do. In essence, therefore, the bank must compromise, departing from the ideal on each particular loan, here on one feature, there on another. The bank's management will also, in a sense, compromise in the pattern or assortment of loans it has outstanding at any time. It seeks an assortment which represents the best attainable average, leaning one way at one time and another when conditions are different. A banker need not be very smart just to match competition, or to score well in achieving one or two qualities of the ideal loan. The real test of skill is in the total arrangements or combinations he negotiates. Is he good enough to outdo his competitors and also to make attractive profits? Differences in lending skill are not small.

The ultimate proofs of such skill yield their results only over decades. The wise bank management looks to the future. It tries to build the good will and reputation which, along with financial strength, will aid its growth.

THE SELF-LIQUIDATING COMMERCIAL LOAN [3]

Loans to businesses for financing short-term needs make up the biggest single type of bank lending. These loans, and the theory of their place in the economy, have several names: "the self-liquidating commercial loan" and "the real bills doctrine," for example. The features of such loans differ greatly. The term "commercial" is still used even though there is no longer any thought of restricting the loans to commerce. The word "liquidating" in this usage means that the activities which the loan helps finance generate or bring in cash to repay the debt. Those who have believed that the self-liquidating commercial loan ought to be the

[3] See B. H. Beckhart, ed., *Business Loans of American Commercial Banks* (New York: Ronald Press, 1959).

main element of bank lending—a group which included the framers of the Federal Reserve System—emphasize certain central points.

Nature of Commercial Loans: Traditional Theory

The thinking runs somewhat as follows: Banks shall loan to finance the planting, growth, purchase, processing, storage, transport, and sale of raw materials, inventory, and finished products. Each firm having a part in the successive stages of the whole process—various farms, mines, manufacturers, wholesalers, retailers—may borrow in turn. Sale of the goods at the end of each stage will provide the firm with money, received from buyers, to repay its loan. Thus, it appears, the loan liquidates itself. It makes possible, or at least facilitates, a transaction which ends by bringing in cash. Each stage will be concluded within a moderate period—nearer three than six months, as a rule, except for loans to farmers.

The loans directly aid the process of production. Do they not make possible the creation and distribution of goods and services which would not otherwise come to fruition?

Not all of a company's need for financing operations, it is held, can properly be met by bank loans. The minimum month-in month-out requirements for payroll and materials, representing basic needs, ought to be financed out of the firm's own permanent capital, equity or debt. It is the more exceptional needs, especially those of seasonal peaks, that banks should finance. In doing so, banks free business from the waste involved in holding funds idle in slow seasons. Thereby, the theory adds, the banks can raise over-all economic efficiency by shifting society's limited funds to the businesses in which they can serve the economy most effectively at a particular time.

Numerous modifications of the seasonal reasons also provide occasions for firms to borrow on short term for essentially self-liquidating purposes: to take advantage of ordinary or special discounts for prompt payment, to seize a special offer, to go ahead with minor types of improvements which will be paid for out of income but which are useful at once, and to finance customers. Perhaps even consumer financing fits logically into the scheme, but few original advocates would have gone so far.

Advantages to the Lending Bank

The basic arrangement, according to its proponents, has more than the worthy advantage of relating loans to production. Does it not also assure that bank loans will be highly liquid, convertible into a fixed amount of cash on short notice? (Banks with liabilities payable on demand have unusual need for liquidity.) The sequence—an increase in the borrowing firm's bank account, the payment for raw materials and labor, sale of goods, receipt of money from the buyer—is generally termed "self-liquidating." Obviously, however, the goods produced do not change into money. Yet if the loan facilitates production (defined broadly) which provides for the loan's own repayment in cash, it also provides for bank liquidity. In other words, each loan comes due not very long after it is made and when sale of the product ought to assure availability of funds for loan repayment.

Moreover, a bank may be able to stagger such loans, so that every week some will fall due. Then if it becomes pressed for funds—either to meet demands of depositors or to take advantage of better lending opportunities—it can for a time reduce the volume of new commitments or lend only where yields reflect better conditions. A bank, the argument proceeds, will never be more than a few weeks from the maturing of a large portion of its loans, *i.e.,* from the ability to arrange for an improvement in its liquidity position.[4] If the general business outlook is gloomy, the bank can lend more conservatively and thereby protect itself against both potential loss and growing demands of depositors.

The repeated testing of borrowers offers another advantage, it is claimed. If a business cannot pay its debt to the bank fully at the end of a cycle of its production, *i.e.,* if its operations are not successful enough to yield funds for repaying all it has borrowed, then something must be wrong. The bank is alerted. The firm must be watched closely. Perhaps it should get no loan next season, or a smaller one, or a loan under conditions giving greater assurance of prompt repayment. The bank's chances of loss should be reduced if the relation of the loan to the production process automatically requires frequent scrutiny. Consequently, there is another welcome result: The bank gets help in protecting its solvency, *i.e.,* maintaining assets worth more than deposits and other liabilities.

The testing of borrowers has still a further advantage. It permits the banker to find out which businesses are in a favorable position to use funds profitably and creatively. The bank can then serve both its own and the public interest by gradually shifting its loan accommodation from poorer to better uses. In doing so, it helps improve the allocation of productive resources and over-all economic efficiency.

The commercial loan, it is argued, serves the general public interest in a broader way: Credit expansion—the creation of money—will be appropriate to the "needs of trade," matched (it is hoped) in each case by an increase in the real worth of goods or services. How, then, can lending be inflationary? More goods match more spending power.[5]

---

[4] The higher liquidity may result not from an increase in assets but from a decline in the liabilities, deposits, that are payable on demand.

[5] Perhaps we should anticipate the answer. If the economy's resources are fully utilized, the business borrowing to produce more must bid the resources it needs away from other uses. This process tends to raise prices.

The bank may not always get a legal claim to specific and salable goods. The loan terms, however, often provide that something tangible, perhaps a staple commodity easily sold in a well-organized market, be pledged as security. The bank can itself seize and sell the property if the borrower refuses to pay. Assuming that original valuation is conservative, the real things safeguard the lending bank's solvency. (This tie to real things helps explain the British term "real bills"; the document received as collateral for the loan is a "bill of exchange" which is related to the transfer of ownership of commodities.)

Although economists, we should now note, may deplore the role of commercial loans as contributors to business cycles, the banker has good reason to think of these loans as highly desirable. Interest rates obtained, even after allowing for losses and operating expenses, tend to be higher than those on most alternative uses of lending capacity—at least if the banker is skillful. One reason why borrowers will pay somewhat "higher" rates is that over a few weeks interest is not large in relation to other business costs. A wholesaler is not likely to let the difference between five and six percent a year on a ninety-day loan deter him from operations which can gross ten percent in that time, or 40 percent on an annual basis.

The banker will recognize another desirable result from many of these loans. They can provide funds for small and local firms which would otherwise have difficulty in financing operations on the scale that they can conduct effectively. The bank gains more than the interest yield plus any satisfaction from helping a friend or neighbor. The financing, indirectly perhaps, aids the whole local economy, the community's business in general, as well as particular firms. Good loans will help build a broader base for more banking business over the years.

Disdvantages to the Lending Bank

Yet there are disadvantages. If this type of lending is to yield the full potential of success, the banker must know a good deal about the borrower —his (its) character, business, financial position, record, and outlook. Such information may at times be hard to get—and wrong. Vital factors call for judgment which requires knowledge that the banker may be in no position to gather. How, for example, can one evaluate the severity of the competition which the borrower may face?

The typical bank in making business loans of this type is limited largely to local firms. The promising opportunities in the community may be relatively scarce. The temptation to "reach out" may warp judgment and lead to mistakes. In making short-term business loans, the banker must consider the effects of any loan on his future relations with borrowers; he may be taking risks or making other current sacrifices which eventually prove costly. Friendship and personal ties can exert undue influence. At times, too, competition among lenders may cut prospects discouragingly.

Furthermore, a bank cannot count upon sustained volume of demand for business loans. Firms may repay unexpectedly or fail to renew. And every day a bank's "money" (lending capacity) is idle is a day irretrievably lost. Lending that is limited to financing seasonal peaks—perhaps in total not much over half of the year in the locality—may prove inadequate as an income producer. (Today, however, it is easier than in the past for even small banks to fill in such gaps by lending in the national market, described in Chapter 6.)

Some companies grow to expect "continuous borrowing." Banks find that they cannot eliminate or terminate, even temporarily, "short-term" loans to many businesses. The borrower comes to depend upon the loans for "regular" operations. Modern production is far more generally a continuous process than the commercial loan theory seems to recognize; a bank's insistence that a loan be cut to zero would frequently force a business to curtail its normal activity. Such contraction might serve no apparently useful purpose; more apparent, however, would be the damage to the community. The borrowing firm, having been deprived of loans against its will, might try to take its banking business elsewhere.

In effect, therefore, banks sometimes find themselves providing what is essentially permanent financing, plus varying amounts of additional accommodation as seasons and the general level of business change. Despite the principles that theorists may enunciate, businesses, especially successful, growing firms, come to rely upon "short-term" loans for permanent working capital needs. An annual "clean-up" of the debt may be required and yet in fact be little more than a formality, arranged by such expedients as borrowing elsewhere.

The liquidity envisaged in the theory, therefore, turns out to be an illusion. Time and again—though not extensively in the mild recessions of recent years—the illusory nature of the presumed liquidity has become most evident when liquidity has been most needed. Just as a bank has faced unusual cash requirements to meet its obligations to depositors during periods of business contraction and financial stringency, or just when a particular firm, area, or industry gets into difficulty and needs cash, "short-term" loans cannot be repaid. The bank cannot get the cash it wants. It finds itself compelled to "carry" a borrower when he is in trouble. It hopes to keep his business over the long run and sometimes to prevent distress from spreading in the community.

The bank, it is true, may have the legal right to seize real goods that have been pledged to support the loan. But taking possession will not in fact seem desirable except in the most unusual conditions. Very often these are just the conditions under which sale to protect the bank will be most difficult because demand for the products is weak.

Banks must expect another unwelcome result of commercial lending:

Loans that turn out to be poor will involve the bank in business operations, such as getting the company back on its feet or out of business. These activities distract from banking as such and often prove distasteful.

Trends

Commercial loans declined in absolute and relative importance after the early 1920's. Leading businesses came to finance their own operations by long-term borrowing, sale of stock, or reinvestment of earnings. Many had little or no need for short-term borrowing. Banks became more cautious, especially after the business decline which started in 1929. In all parts of the country the total volume of business dropped—in physical terms and even more so in dollar amounts. Improved transportation and communication reduced the amount of inventory needed to conduct a given volume of business. Idle capacity enabled suppliers to give prompt delivery. Many a business could count upon meeting sudden needs without itself borrowing to carry the inventories which would be appropriate for peaks only.

During and after World War II, however, commercial lending grew substantially. Many of the conditions noted in the last paragraph were reversed. The tremendous increase in both the physical volume of business activity and the price level expanded business need for funds to finance operations. Firms that once thought they would never need short-term bank loans began to seek such financing. Moreover, banks had lending capacity which enabled them to accommodate business, and borrowers had improved their financial strength by retaining earnings from past profits. The business outlook inspired optimism. These and other reasons account for a rise in loans to business, chiefly but not entirely commercial loans. Increasingly, these loans are related to the company's business in general rather than to particular transactions.

Month after month, however, the economic expansion that began in 1961 failed to generate the increase in loan demand which would have been expected. Changes in tax laws enabled businesses to hold on to more of their receipts and thus finance more of their own activity. Better control of inventory and faster delivery reduced borrowing needs. Large corporations financed more of their own operations from funds raised in the money market, as discussed later. Moreover, these big nonfinancial firms also provided more and more financing of small business through trade credit, *i.e.,* the time allowed for payment for goods and services. Firms offering such credit do so primarily to help sell their output; they can often raise funds from nonbank sources at lowest interest rates. Their customers then have less need for bank accommodation.[6]

[6] See P. S. Nadler, "Second Banking System," *Banking,* July 1963, pp. 39 ff; and M. H. Seiden, *The Quality of Trade Credit* (New York: National Bureau of Economic Research, 1964).

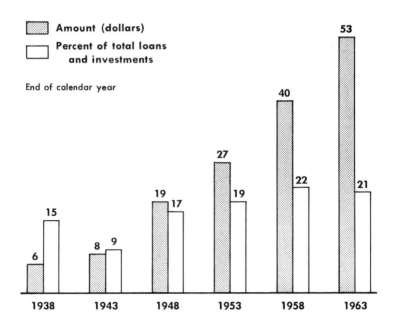

FIGURE 4.1

**Business Loan Growth, 1938–1963
(All Commercial Banks)**

Source: *Federal Reserve Bulletin*

Accounts Receivable Loans and Other Special Forms of Lending to Business

Special types of business lending which do not fit clearly into the pattern of the traditional commercial loan nevertheless have some of the basic economic characteristics.

1. One type is accounts receivable financing. (Lending agencies other than banks also make such loans.) The borrower is a business which gives to the bank as collateral, perhaps by assignment, the "receivables" which represent the business's claim on its customers. Assume, for example, that a manufacturer needing working capital has sold goods to a retailer with payment not due for thirty days. The seller has offered to wait for his money as a means of making the sale, but he wants dollars at once.   Therefore, he turns to his bank.   It agrees to a loan of perhaps 70 to 80 percent of the amount due.

The bank and the borrower usually agree in advance both on the maximum dollar amount that may be borrowed and the percentage of the receivables, as well as on the "mechanical" arrangements.   The business, for example, will probably agree to make special indication on its records of those accounts that it has pledged as collateral.   It may promise to send the bank all remittances that it gets in payment of those accounts.   The extra record keeping required imposes costs on both the business and the bank.   Borrowers, however, are willing to pay enough for such accommodation to make it profitable for the lender; banks, for their part, are willing to lend for less in such cases than if there were no collateral.

2. Some industries utilize loans backed by collateral which consists of *goods that are warehoused in the field* or on the premises of the borrower, and to which he has constant access.   A firm with relatively small resources of its own can get substantial seasonal financing by this means. Special cautions are needed to protect the bank, cautions about the quantity and quality of the goods, the reliability (on all scores) of the borrower and perhaps of the company operating the warehouse, the likelihood of price fluctuation and deterioration of the pledged collateral, and the extent of the market.[7]   Banks will advance from around 65 to perhaps 85 percent of the value of the collateral.

3. *Installment loans for the purchase of machinery and equipment* are of two general types: (a) to a business buying the equipment; (b) to the seller.   In either case the bank gets a claim on the specific machines, trucks, or other income-producing equipment.   Repayment on a monthly or other regular schedule is required.   Many special problems arise.   In some cases banks participate only indirectly; they finance an intermediary lender who specializes in loans of this type.

TERM LENDING

Term lending accounts for around 40 percent of the total of bank loans to business, relatively much more than before World War II.   A term loan is one to a business for over one year but ordinarily for not more than 10 years, with 3 to 4 years much the most common.   (Some equipment installment loans are included but not real estate loans.)   Sev-

---

[7] Some banks and other lenders suffered large losses on field warehouse loans in 1963.   A large dealer in vegetable oils pledged, and lenders accepted, forged receipts for oil which was not in storage and which in some cases had never existed.   This sad episode prompted an increase in vigilance over warehouse lending.

eral banks may join in making a large loan.[8]   Sometimes the loan is part of a financing program which runs even beyond 10 years, with an insurance company providing the part of the total that extends beyond 5 or 8 years.   Loans may be for $1000—some loans to veterans—or for tens of millions.   One Pennsylvania bank in ten years made 6000 "small" term loans averaging about $5500; gross yields were over 6 percent and losses only 1/20th of 1 percent.   A business getting a term loan may also receive short-term accommodation.

Although a term loan does not supply permanent capital, it does provide funds on which the borrowing firm can definitely count for a considerable period.   The money may be used for any of many purposes—maintaining inventory, financing customers, adding trucks or machinery or office equipment, air conditioning, refurnishing a hotel, buying out the interest of a partner, or possibly even constructing new plant facilities.

A definite *schedule of repayment* ordinarily provides for retiring the loan by the end of the term.   The amount at risk declines.   The normal expectation is that the debt can be repaid out of earnings and depreciation funds.   In a sense, the loan is about as self-liquidating as the more traditional commercial loan.   The company which repays such loans out of earnings in effect converts debt into equity capital over time.

The term loan commits the lending bank for a longer period than the ordinary self-liquidating loan.   In fact, however, some term loans are essentially the formal and frank recognition of what had become the dominant reality (but not an absolute certainty), namely, that banks would repeatedly renew short-term loans.   Certainty is an advantage which can offset disadvantages that arise out of the loss of flexibility.   The borrower knows that he will have funds, though in decreasing amount as his regular amortization payments reduce the debt.   The lender knows that he has an income-producing asset and a scheduled return of the loan principal.

In practice, term loans sometimes sacrifice certainty to get flexibility. The parties can agree to adjust the key features, such as repayment schedules and the interest rate.   The basic commitment remains, however. The lender cannot count upon selling the term loan contract as he can a bond with an equal period to run; the resulting lack of liquidity restricts the volume of term-loan contracts that any one bank will wisely hold.[9]

[8] A bank may find a local business with a well-founded need for a bigger loan than the bank itself can make.   A city correspondent may be willing to join in the loan and perhaps help arrange a syndicate to provide the full amount.

[9] Since there is no ready market for such loans, banks, curiously enough, rarely encounter any problem of valuation.   The face amount due is ordinarily the value used in the accounts; bank examiners consent.   The worries that can come with fluctuations in bond prices do not appear.

Several things help explain the growth of term loans. In the 1940's, rising price levels and the expanding physical volume of business multiplied business needs for working capital, needs that seemed likely to last indefinitely. Banks, on the other hand, could not use their full lending capacity for traditional short-term loans because the demand was too small. But there were potential borrowers who wanted money that they could count on for a substantial period, often to buy machinery and equipment with a life of several years. Yields on bonds eligible for bank ownership were low. Rules and attitudes of regulatory authorities became more favorable.

Moreover, until the early 1950's, businesses could at times save on interest by refinancing, *i.e.,* arranging new term loans to repay borrowings which had been incurred earlier and had some years to run. Another factor has more lasting significance. The business borrowing privately on a term loan avoids the disclosure and expense involved in public sale of new securities. Such costs may be prohibitive for smaller firms. Relatively small, growing businesses sometimes find that America's financial structure fails to provide adequate facilities for supplying capital in acceptable ways at reasonable cost. The term loan helps fill many gaps. It permits a bank, perhaps one in the locality, to provide substantial financing on more than a temporary basis. The firm's owners need not share control, as a sale of common stock would require. The loan can usually be negotiated without long delay and concluded at distinctly less cost than is needed to meet SEC and state "blue sky" laws for a public sale of new stock or bonds. Small businesses get capital that might otherwise be unobtainable. Commercial banks may thus perform part of what has been considered the investment banker's job, a part that the latter has found he cannot do at tolerable cost.

As a rule there is no mortgage or pledge of specific assets. The borrower, however, agrees to methods of general financing and operation which are specifically designed to protect the lender—limits on dividends and on additional debt, for example. The regular repayment requirements force a certain discipline on the borrower. The bank will, or should, scrutinize the firm's affairs, especially its longer-run prospects, more thoroughly than traditional commercial lending requires. Success with term lending requires that a bank develop the appropriate attitudes and staffs. Very possibly, the vast majority of banks will find an adequate staff prohibitively expensive; the potential volume of term loans is too small. These banks may, then, make only an occasional term loan where circumstances seem especially favorable—or participate in syndicates for which others provide the skilled engineering, research analysis, and follow-up.

SECURITY LOANS

Security loans, at times a major source of bank income, are of different types. Banks lend to those who wish funds to buy (and hold) stocks and bonds. The borrower may be an individual, a business, or a broker arranging to finance his customers. Federal Reserve margin requirements, however, limit the power of banks and brokers to lend for the purchase of listed stocks. In 1964, for example, a bank was permitted to lend only 30 percent of the purchase price of listed stock. Bank loans on bonds, however, are not subject to such limits.

Many loans backed by securities pledged as collateral are made for purposes other than the purchase of stocks and bonds. By pledging securities as collateral, any borrower, whether a large business or a humble individual, can expect better terms when he borrows, for whatever reason. In such cases, assuming no legal restrictions, the percentage of the market price of a security which a bank will lend varies through a wide range. Quality, price, marketability, and bargaining determine the result. A loan otherwise risky can be made safe by security backing.

The sale of newly issued securities sometimes requires short-term borrowing from commercial banks. For example, the investment banking firm, or its syndicate, may not sell an issue of bonds or stock as quickly as expected. And by a certain date it may be required to provide the business or government whose securities are involved with more cash than yet received. The necessary funds may then be obtained by borrowing from commercial banks, the unsold securities serving as collateral.

Dealers in outstanding securities also borrow to carry on their regular business, which is to buy stocks and bonds at one price and, they hope, sell at a higher price.[10] The "inventory" that is essential will probably require funds far greater than the dealer himself can supply. He will normally borrow from his bank, the amounts fluctuating widely, even in short periods. From the point of view of the bank, the uncertainty about the quantity of borrowing demanded from week to week detracts somewhat from the appeal of loans to brokers and dealers. Yet competition for this type of loan, especially in the largest cities, is sometimes so vigorous that the profit margin gets very thin. In effect, lending capacity for which there is no other demand may be used to finance security transactions, for a few days or indefinitely.

The borrower gives the bank physical possession of the securities purchased or pledged. When those originally pledged are sold, others

---

[10] The capacity in which they act is distinguished from that of a broker, who is a middleman between buyer and seller and charges a commission on the transaction. The dealer himself becomes an owner, buying even when he knows of no one specifically to whom he can sell. He may own a security only a few minutes—or many days, or even longer. Discussion of an unusual form of lending, the repurchase agreement, appears in Chapter 6.

may be substituted. Many such loans, especially those to brokers or for the purchase of securities, are terminable without prior notice by either the bank or the borrower. Loans subject to "call" may last only one day. Banks, of course, are reluctant to curtail a loan to a valued customer against his will. They are quicker to alter interest charges as conditions change. "Loans to brokers" are highly liquid (unless financial distress approaching panic develops), because of arrangements enabling a broker to borrow elsewhere if his bank wishes to cancel the loan. However, banks do not as in the past rely on these "street" loans to provide needs for liquidity because the total volume available is too small.

If the bank feels compelled to sell the pledged securities to get money and to protect itself against loss, the sale will tend to depress prices. If market prices are declining, the added pressure pushing prices even lower will aggravate the decline. A cumulative process may get under way. Security loans have influenced the whole economy, at times unfortunately. In the 1920's such loans financed a feverish boom on the stock market. (By no means all loans originated with banks.) Then in 1929 loan cancellation and the forced sale of stock added to the wave of selling on the stock exchanges and required more loan cancellation. The resulting financial troubles created real distress for business. Stricter limits on loans to buy securities are designed to prevent recurrence of excess. But banks have lost opportunities for what would be profitable lending as speculators turn to nonbank lenders and to foreign banks. Borrowing from banks may, of course, be directed toward financing purchases of bonds and unlisted stocks. The borrower may use other collateral and tell the bank that the loan is "nonpurpose," one for a purpose other than buying listed stock; he may then use the proceeds to pay for stock.

LOANS TO GOVERNMENTS

Banks sometimes lend to governments for short periods. (There is no sharp distinction between commercial bank lending to governments and bank investment in—purchase of—government securities, which we examine in Chapter 7.) Localities and states find that the inflow of tax revenue does not always match the outflow of expenditures. At some times of the year a loan from the bank proves a convenient device for filling gaps. The government which is able to borrow in this way can maintain the schedules of disbursements and tax receipts as determined for other reasons, without building up deposits which will be idle during parts of the year. Pressures for government economy, however, have forced many a state and locality to find ways to get along with smaller reliance on short-term borrowing.

In lending to state and local governments, banks face widely differing situations. Some such lending is highly competitive. Yet, especially where localities are involved, one or a few local banks may have a monopolistic position. Political preference is not unknown. On occasion, a bank may feel an obligation to grant loans to a local government when some other action might seem preferable.

The ability of the borrower to repay is usually beyond question. Sometimes, however, there is doubt about the ability of the locality to pay on schedule or at a time convenient for the bank.

The Federal government borrows on short term from banks to aid in refinancing outstanding debt or to meet temporary gaps between tax receipts and expenditures. This is true even when for the year as a whole it may have a net revenue surplus. And when it is running more than temporary deficits, it may resort to the banking system for loans which in fact are almost permanent—a topic about which more will be said later.

CONSUMER LOANS (OTHER THAN
FOR REAL ESTATE PURCHASE)

Commercial banks lend on a large scale to individuals to finance personal expenditure.[11] Such loans appear in several forms. In essence, however, these loans are generally for financing the purchase of durable consumer goods (autos being outstanding) or the payment of "lumpy" expenditures, such as medical bills, taxes, insurance premiums, home repair, tuition, or vacations. The contract usually calls for systematic repayment, most often in monthly installments, over a period of one to three years. Some loans, however, call for payment all at once—but with renewal not unknown. The bank may aggressively seek consumer loans by advertising and other solicitation. It may also rely heavily on businesses that sell to consumers, such as auto dealers, to supply loans; the bank will pay commissions to the merchant.

Lending to college students is one of the new fields. Social pressure to keep the interest rate down will limit the profit potential. In some

[11] Installment buying grew rapidly with the spread of auto ownership in the 1920's. Banks, however, were slow to engage directly in such lending. Other lending opportunities were ample. Loans for consumption seemed alien to the traditional belief that bank credit should be used to finance productive business. The administration of installment loans required different facilities from those that banks had developed. State anti-usury laws did not always permit charging interest rates high enough to cover costs. Some banks doubted that they could get enough loan volume to justify the overhead costs. A certain stigma attached to lending to consumers, a stigma growing out of centuries of loan-shark activities. Gradually during the 1930's, however, commercial banks developed the necessary facilities. They built up consumer lending, not only to finance purchases of durables but for other personal purposes as well.

cases, however, state or other guarantees help reduce risk. Evidence that banks desire to build personal loan business is found in new developments. Revolving credit, or "check credit," provides, for example, a family with a maximum debt which it may incur without new negotiation; borrowing is about the same as writing a check. Other plans automatically grant a loan when a person makes a purchase at a participating store. The seller, in effect, is freed from the need to give customers credit; the merchant pays a service charge for getting money from the bank at once.

Personal loans are not usually tied in with a productive, profit-making venture. Banks rely heavily upon the income prospects of the borrower and upon the moral risk, his apparent willingness to use his income and wealth for the repayment of the loan. The bank, however, may retain (but will go to great lengths to avoid using) power to seize the auto or other property of the borrower. Consumer loans are sometimes backed by securities, life insurance policies having cash surrender value, a savings account, or other collateral. A cosigner may give the bank more protection.

The bookkeeping and other services required for making and collecting installment loans impose costs which may be relatively much greater than those of the other types of loans discussed so far. Interest rate charges are also higher. Since the average size of consumer loans is modest, a substantial volume is ordinarily needed to cover minimum overhead and make this business profitable.

Installment loans of commercial banks rose from $1 billion in 1939 to $10 billion in 1954 and $23 billion in 1964. Banks then held over half of total installment loans. One-third was for the purchase of autos. Outstanding noninstallment consumer loans by banks were over $5 billion in 1964. Despite the growth from year to year, repayments generally exceed 90 percent of new credit granted. Net profits result.[12] Losses have been small, even during recession. Banks, in screening applicants, try to eliminate those who are bad risks, without undoing the effects of expensive promotion. Experience has also shown how to accommodate those who get into difficulty; reasonable treatment proves rewarding in keeping losses low and customer friendship high. Loans for home repair and modernization often carry Federal Housing Administration insurance.

Banks have overcome varied obstacles in building a good volume of business in consumer loans. One, for example, was the slightly forbidding manner of the old-time lending officer. Another was the apprehension of some "ordinary" people about seeking help from banks.

[12] A detailed study of the experience of 9 commercial banks found that net operating income in 1959 on all earning assets was 3.4 percent, while that on consumer credit was 5.3 percent. Losses were less than one-quarter of one percent. P. F. Smith, *Consumer Credit Costs, 1949–59* (Princeton: Princeton Univ. Press for National Bureau of Economic Research, 1964), p. 59 and p. 78.

One practical problem is how to build good relations with merchants, especially auto dealers, who are in a position to send borrowers to the bank. How will the bank's other relations to the merchant be affected? Will he expect more credit for himself than seems wise? And what if, to close a sale, he wants to grant the buyer more favorable terms, such as a lower down payment, than would the banker? Moreover, among the best customers of some banks are businesses which in turn lend to consumers; the cross-currents of competition are complex.

Banks usually, though not invariably, charge less than do other lenders to consumers.[13] One reason is that banks tend to be more selective about the risks they will assume. As more people come to realize that banks' charges on auto, personal, and consumer loans generally are lower than the charges of most competitors, the knowledge ought to help banks build volume.

REAL ESTATE LOANS

"Real property"—land and buildings—plays a greater role in bank lending than the figures on "real estate" loans suggest. Commercial banks lend to finance the purchase and construction of real estate. Moreover, real estate is often pledged as collateral for a business or security loan, but if the proceeds of the loan are not to be used to buy or build, the loan does not fall in the real estate category. Stand-by commitments to builders to assure them funds until new houses are sold are essentially business loans. So, too, is interim mortgage financing; a bank lends to a mortgage company or other real estate lender while the latter arranges the sale of mortgage loans to those institutions which will hold them permanently.

Disappointing, even disastrous, experience with real estate loans made in the 1920's[14] for a time led to substantial reduction of such loans among bank assets. Then new loan forms and arrangements were developed in the 1930's. Construction expanded. Banks sought out good interest yields. Since World War II real estate loans have grown substantially, from about $5 billion in 1945 to $41 billion in 1964.

Real estate loans ordinarily run for many years, 20 years or even more now being common. A bank whose liabilities are payable on de-

---

[13] The average charge of 9 consumer finance companies studied by Prof. Smith was 24.04 percent; for 10 sales finance companies, 9 commercial banks, and all Federal credit unions, the rates charged were 16.59, 10.04, and 9.13 percent, respectively. Smith, *op. cit.,* p. 78.

[14] The settlement of new areas plus urban growth in the nineteenth century created a strong demand for real estate loans of many types. Yet loans were often based on speculative, inflated prices which later fell. Then banks, and their communities, suffered. The National Bank Acts of 1863 and 1864 prohibited real estate loans by national banks. The establishment of the Federal Reserve relaxed the restrictions somewhat, and Congress has liberalized the rules since.

mand must be cautious in acquiring assets which become due only after many years. Yet banks do make long-term real estate loans. How do they justify such apparent risks? For one thing, commercial banks have savings or time deposits which to a large extent are in fact permanent. Although some such liabilities must be paid every day, and all may legally be withdrawn on short notice, the bank management may feel that there is no realistic probability that the mass will be much reduced on short notice. (Real estate loans by commercial banks equalled 30 percent of time deposits in 1941 and 33 percent in 1964.)

Some essentially permanent assets, therefore, seem appropriate, *if* they meet other requirements—(1) good yield and (2) only slight risk. Some real estate loans qualify. Yields have compared favorably with the interest obtainable from other possible uses of lending capacity. *Carefully made* real estate loans, it is argued, involve little long-run risk; the real estate pledging the loan will be worth substantially more than the debt, so that, if necessary, the bank can recover whatever is due it by sale of the property. Gaining secure protection from risk, of course, is not "self-achieving"; good real estate lending requires intelligent care.

Institutions which grant real estate loans today have safeguards that did not exist, or were much less generally available, in the past:

1. There is the now common requirement that the debt be repaid systematically, often month by month. As a result, the amount at risk declines, usually more rapidly than the property depreciates. Moreover, the lender can count upon a definite element of liquidity as principal returns regularly. As mortgage loans have become longer, however, the average repayment of principal each month has tended to drop.

2. A second safeguard is Federal Housing Administration insurance, or Veterans Administration guarantee, of mortgages. On such loans the lender will lose little or nothing even under adverse conditions.

3. The liquidity of mortgage loans is greater than in the past; today there exists a broad market in which a lender can sell many mortgages, though not necessarily at a price he likes.

The law now permits national banks to lend on real estate mortgages up to the larger of (1) the amount of capital stock and surplus or (2) 70 percent of time deposits. Individual loans may reach 50 percent of appraised value if the loan matures in five years and 60 percent if the loan matures in ten years (or if 40 percent is amortized in ten years). (Obviously, then, appraisal standards become important in determining the actual loan limits.) Insured and guaranteed loans, however, are exempt from these limits because other safeguards provide protection. On the other hand numerous detailed provisions restrict national banks in lending on real estate and in adapting to the changing conditions and opportunities of today's economy; prohibition of loans on unimproved land, for example, adds difficulties to the financing of new real estate projects. State banks often have more latitude.

Real estate loans should be made only after careful, and somewhat costly, investigation of the property (including the community) and of the borrower. Ultimate success depends at least as much upon the borrower's determination and financial ability as upon the security offered by the property itself. Servicing such loans involves costs which can eat up a significant part of the apparent yield. Even highly mechanized administration of monthly payments made regularly may come to a fifth or so of the gross interest yield. Costs rise greatly if the bank has difficulty collecting. They rise still more if it must foreclose the mortgage and take over the property. For many years, however, the interest obtainable has been enough higher than the gross yield on many other types of loans to warrant the extra handling costs. Another advantage is worth noting. The lending bank has its money "working" steadily, except for small sums that come in monthly as amortization payments. A banker has little problem of replacing real estate loans frequently because on the average they fall due at rare intervals only. Real estate loans are relatively more important for small banks than for large.

Most bank real estate loans are on residential property, but some are made on farms and business property. Many types of competition face any lender who seeks to make real estate loans. Life insurance companies, savings banks, savings and loan associations, trust funds, and others, in fact, have a bigger place in this market than do commercial banks. Commercial banks have no distinctive comparative advantage (except in lending for short periods to help finance construction and in some cases in small, local markets) over other financial institutions in making real estate loans. A bank's interest charges and other terms must be at least as good as those of other lenders.

LENDING TO FARMERS

Bank loans to farmers are relatively less prominent than a generation or more ago, when agriculture played so much larger a part in our economy.[15] Yet to many farmers, and to some banks, farm loans are highly important. Modern farming requires considerable financing per operator.

Although most farm loans are a form of either business or real estate

[15] We ignore here crop price support loans, which, even when technically made to the farmer, are not agricultural loans in the ordinary sense. They partake to a great extent of bank loans to government, with crops as collateral but with the farmer having an option to recover.

loan, they often require special knowledge of the particular farm and farmer. Natural misfortune—drought or pest infestation—can bring serious losses. Some bankers actively try to couple lending with advice and other aid for better farming practices. Facilities for short-term seasonal loans and for long-term land purchase appear to be more satisfactory than those for medium-term needs. (However, sellers of farm machinery have been helping to finance purchase, though not as a rule through local banks.) Banking laws contain various provisions designed to help banks accommodate farmers. Moreover, a variety of governmental lending agencies aid the farmer. In general, they are designed to supplement rather than to compete with commercial banks.

Table 4.1 summarizes the loans of commercial banks. Within each category, however, there are significant variations. Other types exist, notably open market loans, which are described in Chapter 6. We turn next, however, to a discussion of the various features or elements of lending. In a sense these "cut across" aspects already discussed.

TABLE 4.1

Commercial Bank Loans by Type, July 1964

	Amount (billions)	Percent of total loans
Commercial including open market paper	$ 55	34
Agricultural	8	5
Loans for purchasing and carrying securities	8	5
Loans to banks and other financial institutions	13	8
Real estate loans	41	25
Consumer and other loans to individuals	37	22
Other loans	4	2
Total	$166	100

Details do not add to the total because of rounding.
Source: *Federal Reserve Bulletin.*

QUESTIONS

1. What is meant by the "self-liquidating commercial loan" or the "real bills" theory of bank lending? What are the alleged advantages? What are the flaws in the theory?

2. What, from the bank's point of view, are the qualities of a good loan?

3. How can a bank reduce the risk of loss on loans?

4. In what sense is the "self-liquidating commercial loan" liquid?

5. What are term loans? How does the "self-liquidating" criterion fit them?

6. Account for the rise since World War II of bank loans to consumers; to business.

7. Define "call loans," "accounts receivable financing," and "field warehouse loans."

8. What factors make real estate loans more satisfactory for a commercial bank than before the 1930's?

9. What characteristics would seem to be necessary in a good lending officer?

10. Discuss the constructive uses and possible abuses of bank loans on securities.

CHAPTER 5   *THE LENDING PROCESS AND BANK CHARGES*

THIS chapter continues the discussion of bank lending.   It deals with points related to lending but having broader significance for the financial system. Finally, bank charges are discussed.

SPECIAL FEATURES OF LENDING
AND THE LENDING PROCESS

Line of Credit

Some borrowers, businesses especially, arrange a "line of credit" with a bank.   A more or less formal agreement designates explicitly a maximum which the borrower may owe at any one time. The agreement virtually assures the firm this much "accommodation" whenever it wishes during the period set, unless there is a material change in its financial position.

The bank may insist (1) that the borrower maintain a minimum balance of a certain size (probably a percentage of the loan), and (2) that at least once during the year the borrower owe nothing, i.e., "clean up" his debt.   The bank saves some operating expense by making its credit investigation before establishing the line of credit and not again each time the customer asks to borrow under the agreement.   The firms most attracted by this arrangement are those whose needs for funds are irregular and unpredictable—finance companies and importers, for example.   A treasurer likes to be able to pick up his telephone or walk over to the bank and get dollars at once, use them as he wishes, perhaps for only a few days, and repay at his convenience.

Sometimes the bank makes a binding commitment.   More often, however, it has no legal, but a very strong moral, obligation to lend if it possibly can. Does it make a special charge for such promises? Practice varies. Interest at the full rate is charged only for the funds that the borrower actually uses. If the bank makes a firm commitment, the borrower will often pay around 0.5 percent on amounts not "taken up." (The effective "charge" may consist, at least in part, of a promise to maintain a balance of a certain size, greater than the company would prefer.) The company believes that the assurance of being able to get funds when needed justifies the cost. Some firms may establish lines of credit at several banks.

Banks, too, may ask for lines of credit from their city correspondents. The bank can then meet seasonal needs which are expected, and unanticipated requests, promptly and without embarrassment to customers.

Legal Restrictions[1]

Laws not only prescribe general rules which govern reserve requirements but also impose more specific limits on bank lending—amounts, types, methods, etc. The limits have grown up to meet evident needs for protecting the general public, notably as depositors. The laws, however, have not necessarily kept abreast of changing conditions. Some laws, such as those against usury, apply to all lenders. Others, however, are for the banking system alone. The significance of many for the economy as a whole justifies no more than passing note here. But bank directors, who have complete responsibility for loans, must watch the laws carefully. Lending officers who in fact make the decisions must observe many legal rules designed for various purposes. State restrictions are often less confining than those of the national government.

National banks may not lend to any one borrower more than an amount equal to 10 percent of capital and surplus, except in the case of (1) endorsed commercial paper and banker's acceptances, *i.e.,* short-term loans that are highly liquid and well secured; for these there are no limits; and (2) loans backed by United States government debt , nonperishable staple goods in storage, and livestock; such a loan may reach 25 percent of capital and surplus. The rule seeks to assure diversification. The bank will not concentrate its loans in a few firms, assuming dangerously large risks in individual cases or slighting other businesses that need accommodation.[2]

---

[1] All banks are subject to general laws of the states in which they operate. In addition national banks are subject to laws passed by Congress. State banks must comply with state banking law, and, if members of the Federal Reserve or FDIC, must comply with provisions of laws governing those institutions.

[2] Details of rules can create anomalies. If a bank lends to a parent corporation and to its subsidiaries, the 10 percent limit applies to the whole group; but if there is no loan to the parent, the 10 percent limit applies separately to each subsidiary.

In recent years, the rule has prevented some banks from taking advantage of opportunities, such as building up their business with growing firms; the growth of bank capital has lagged behind the growth of the economy in general. Undistributed profits have not counted in computing the limits, except for amounts that the directors vote to transfer to the surplus account. In 1964, however, the Comptroller "held that undivided profits which are in fact earned surplus may be considered as unimpaired surplus funds" in computing loan limits, but the Federal Reserve refused to concur.[3] Who will prevail? Only time will tell.

National banks may not make loans on their own stock as security.[4] Nor may they lend more than $2500 to an executive officer, defined in 1964 to apply to policy-making officials only, excluding administrative officers. Although this dollar limit is now unduly low, experience confirms the wisdom of restraining officers from using bank lending capacity for their own affairs.

Collateral and Other Security

A bank's risk can be reduced or eliminated, and an applicant's chances of success in getting a loan can be enhanced or assured, by the pledge of bonds, stock, real estate, life insurance policies, a lease or rental contract, inventory, equipment, accounts receivable, or other property as collateral. (Whatever the borrower has on deposit in the bank is also a sort of collateral.) The additional or supporting guarantee of someone with good credit may also serve as collateral. Insistence upon collateral serves another purpose; it provides an effective and objective means of disciplining borrowers. Many loans are unsecured, however—in the past, at least, more often than conditions justified. In the days of expansion into new areas and the development of new businesses in a land short of capital, the practice of lending without collateral was widely, but not always wisely, favored.

If the bank cannot collect from the borrower, it can sell the collateral or proceed against the guarantor. If the borrower goes into bankruptcy, the collateral gives the bank a position distinctly superior to that of creditors generally. Other things being the same, a bank prefers collateral even though some cost is involved in handling and preserving the property. Yet

---

[3] *The National Banking Review,* June 1964, p. 599; *Federal Reserve Bulletin,* June 1964, p. 711.

[4] This limit prevents an old abuse. A person would (apparently) agree to supply capital to a bank by purchasing its newly issued stock. He would get the money for payment, however, by borrowing from the bank, giving the stock as collateral. In substance, the bank got no capital, depositors no protection.

often if the applicant for a loan had really good collateral, he would not be trying to borrow.

The major types of secured loans can be noted:

1. When a bank borrows from another bank, it provides collateral.

2. Investment dealers, too, even if their character and financial standing are the highest imaginable, invariably supply collateral when borrowing from a bank. Loans to brokers and others to buy or carry stocks and bonds are covered by marketable securities that are usually worth appreciably more than the loan.[5] The borrower would rather pay interest than sell the collateral; he expects the assets to rise in price, or to yield more than the interest he must pay on his borrowings, or to enable him to keep control of his business.

3. Businesses may pledge commodities as collateral. Various devices are available to make this arrangement possible. For example, if a manufacturer wishes to pledge raw materials but also needs to have them to process and sell, he can give a *trust receipt*. The bank gets first claim on the proceeds of sale, protected by the strict laws that govern trusts. *Warehouse receipts* and *bills of lading* may also be pledged. The actual seizure and sale of commodities by a bank will be a last resort, one rarely used. (If the proceeds of sale do not cover the debt, the bank has the right to try to get the remainder from the borrower.) A *mortgage* can give ample security; it may also give less than expected, depending upon the terms and the market price of the property when the loan falls due. Good appraisal of the property when the loan is made, and occasional checking to determine that maintenance and insurance are adequate and the taxes paid, are essential if mortgaged property is to provide sound security.

4. The bank may request, or the applicant may offer, guarantees by someone other than the borrower. Then if the borrower fails to pay, the lender can fall back upon the resources of the guarantor. For example, the principal stockholders of a closely owned corporation may be asked to assume personal responsibility for a corporation debt. Limited liability will not then shield the real borrowers from obligation while their control of the corporation offers an opportunity to manipulate assets and cheat the lender. Sometimes one corporation in a group, perhaps the parent, guarantees the debt of another to help it borrow on favorable terms. Relatives and friends may also cosign or endorse a personal debt, perhaps for

---

[5] Today, only a large and sudden drop in security prices would ordinarily threaten the lending bank with loss. The chief exceptions arise from loans which are not subject to the regulations applying to transactions in securities traded on organized stock exchanges. Considerable risk may exist when securities pledged do not have a wide market.

such good reason as helping a son start in business, or possibly without much that could be considered a reason.[6]

5. In the last 20 years the Federal government has become a major guarantor and insurer of loans—to veterans, to small businesses, to firms producing for national defense, to farmers pledging crops for price-support loans, to some firms doing business abroad, to builders of tankers, to farmers for buying and improving farms, to purchasers of residences, to builders of new apartments, to companies in "redevelopment areas," for subsidized housing, for college dormitories, and for an increasing list of purposes. Depression and war had much to do with the growth of government guarantee. In some cases, notably FHA loans, the borrower must pay something for the insurance. If this charge is adequate, as it has been to date, the government incurs no out-of-pocket cost. There is, however, a hidden cost. The insurance or guarantee adds to the supply of debt which in fact is backed by the Treasury. To sell its own debt then, the Federal government must offer at least slightly higher rates of interest than if it did not have its own competition. Even indirect Federal credit backing helps the borrower to get more favorable terms and frees the lender of much or all risk.[7]

A special study of loans outstanding found that in 1957 just half of all business loans were secured by collateral or other assets. The smaller the borrowing firm, the higher the proportion of loans secured; thus 78 percent of the dollar value of loans to firms with assets under $50,000 were secured, with only 18 percent where the firm's assets exceeded $100 million. Plant and other real estate was the most common type of security, especially for longer loans. Loans secured by United States government securities, other bonds, life insurance, savings accounts, and stocks accounted for about 11 percent of the total.[8]

ANALYSIS OF BORROWER'S CREDIT

In making a loan, a bank wants to be sure that it will be able to collect on schedule what is due, and without great cost to itself or hardship

[6] "Going on" a note for a friend can be the source of great trouble, in both personal and financial relations. The importance of cosignatures and endorsements is relatively smaller than in the past. Banks find difficulty (and arouse antagonism) in proceeding against friends of borrowers who do not pay.

[7] The extent to which the bank must pass on to the borrower the net advantages of government assistance will depend in part upon the extent of competition for the loans involved. The desirability to the bank of government insurance or guarantee, then, will depend upon complex evaluations of the effects on yields and of the risks eliminated.

[8] Caroline H. Cagle, "Security Pledged on Business Loans at Member Banks," *Federal Reserve Bulletin,* September 1959, pp. 1114–1129.

to the borrower. The bank seeking to maximize profit, however, will not limit itself to loans on which it can be positively certain of collecting every dollar due. Such standards would force it to pass up loan opportunities which would in fact turn out successfully. There is a big difference between (a) avoiding, as a bank should, loans which can involve very large loss, and (b) refusing to make loans which may possibly bring some loss. The wise policy is to make loans which, while appearing secure, have a little risk and occasionally may involve some loss. The banker should try to lend a borrower no less than he can use constructively to his own advantage, while paying an "appropriate" interest rate.

The lending officer's task calls for much skill. He must judge the repayment probabilities of those who want to borrow—their ability and determination; in doing so, he will evaluate the opportunities that the borrower will have for profitable use of the loan, and of many more over the years. Modern credit analysis is an integral part of the preparation for sound bank growth. This work, in essence, has much in common with that of the small town banker, who also must judge his neighbors and their prospects. In form and method, however, a city bank's procedure in analyzing credit today differs widely from that of the country banker.

The Three "C's"

Bankers, it is said, often judge on the basis of "C's"—character, capacity, and capital. This approach is reasonably adequate where personal or small business loans are involved. Almost by definition, a person applying for a loan has a financial problem. The "trouble" may be the result of either very good or very poor business. Yet in a not unrealistic sense the state of an applicant's affairs is not the best. His resources are in some sense inadequate. Will a loan improve things on balance? How?

For the majority of personal and smaller business loans, much does depend upon *character*—the moral factor, a borrower's respect for his obligations, his determination to live up to an agreement. If this persistence is low, the bank may have expensive trouble collecting even though the borrower's financial position is not really bad. If his affairs go poorly, the bank's difficulties can be substantial. When the borrower's character is high, however, the bank has a measure of assurance; even if he suffers economic adversity, he will make a determined effort to pay. Some people who might like to default will know that for purely pragmatic reasons they must try hard to pay. A bad credit standing is a serious, at times a fatal, business handicap.

Many degrees of character exist. Appraising a human being can be difficult, especially when little or no experience has been accumulated. If the banker is dubious, he is not likely to tell the applicant about the doubts. He may refuse on other grounds or insist upon terms which in effect constitute rejection. Or he may demand enough collateral to eliminate risk.

Capacity as used here involves the ability of a borrower to earn income—his education, energy, experience, job or business outlook, or, if a business, its facilities (in the broadest sense) for operating profitably. More specifically, capacity often means the competence to use successfully the money requested.

Decisions about both character and capacity rest upon judgments—about the borrower, the general business outlook, and the prospects of the particular industry and firm. Bankers may differ. Ascertainable facts can narrow the range of doubt, but they cannot always be sufficient.

The third "C," *capital,* is usually more definite. It is the wealth which the borrower has and may use to repay a loan if income is inadequate. Sometimes, of course, the capital may be used as specific collateral for the loan. In other cases, however, the proper evaluation as to whether capital can really support a loan is more difficult, requiring careful analysis.

When the applicant is a large, medium-sized, or even small business, the enlightened and effective study of capacity and capital involves analysis of all pertinent data obtainable—true analysis, not cursory review. The banker who neglects to base a decision on analysis and facts overlooks a valuable lesson of experience: Even apparently short-term loans may offer (1) the opportunity of developing a long history of profitable business, or (2) the risk of involving the bank in extended trouble. Although there will always be a judgment element in lending, progressive banks will try to develop and make greater use of quantifiable criteria. Where does a bank get data?

Sources of Credit Information

Banks get information on both character and finances from their own records, from the potential borrower, and from a variety of sources outside the bank. If a bank has loaned to an applicant before, or if there is a checking account or time deposit, its own records may reveal as much as the banker needs to know. The record certainly ought to yield facts that will be helpful. Too often, however, vital information about the bank's experience never gets from the officer's head to written records. Illness, death, retirement, and simple "forgetting" then cause the loss of valuable data. Often, especially in smaller cities and towns, one or more of the directors has had business dealings with a prospective borrower. The applicant himself, knowing more than anyone else about his affairs, can supply data on income, the intended use of loan funds, and other relevant factors. Yet the banker has a role here, for some skill may be needed to elicit all the facts that would be useful.

The regular financial statements of a business, especially if audited by public accountants, will often suffice. In this respect conditions have improved immensely with the development of accounting and auditing. Still, some extra reports may be needed. Part of the banker's job is to know which facts to seek in each case. Kinds of data which are highly relevant to one industry, or at one time, may be of slight importance in other circumstances.

Bankers look at the "current ratio," current assets (those which are or will become cash within one year) in relation to current liabilities (those which must be paid within one year). This ratio indicates something about the likely net inflow of money, or the potential inflow, during the period before the loan will become due. To judge the reliability of the reported current ratio for his purposes, the banker must judge the quality of accounts receivable, the marketability of the inventory, the general state of business, and what the ratio will be at several different times during the year. There are other significant "ratios" (sales to inventory or sales to receivables) and items to be studied, varying from case to case. The company's condition and record can be compared with standards for the industry. Especially important are the trend of the firm's affairs, the past record of profit in relation to sales, and the prospective use of the loan.

The banker should pay careful attention to the amount of the owner's investment (net worth) in relation to the size of the firm's business and especially to the amount of the loan. He may prepare a pro forma balance sheet of how the accounts would appear if the loan were granted and used as proposed. What counts is net wealth. Sometimes not even the borrower is aware of all his assets, such as his ability to borrow on life insurance. On the other hand, important liabilities, such as commitments on long-term leases, are not always thought of as debts. Yet they must not be overlooked in determining the net capital position. Are taxes overdue?

The bank may work out with the borrower a budget of the firm's affairs for at least the period of the loan. This picture will help reveal what the loan will mean to the business and the amount of cash likely to be available for repayment. To get and analyze such information, the bank may want to investigate on its own even though the financial statements have been certified by qualified accountants.

Other sources of information available include reports of credit-rating agencies. One of the outstanding is Dun and Bradstreet. It collects and supplies extensive financial data on businesses of all types, on particular industries, and on state and local governments and other banks, through a far-reaching confidential mutual service.[9] Businesses with whom the applicant has dealt (perhaps other customers of the bank), employers and friends, and public records of such things as lawsuits—all these provide facts and judgments. Sometimes, especially when longer-term loans are in question, careful study of the outlook in the industry or area will be made or obtained from some outside agency.[10]

The Scope of Credit Analysis

A thorough credit analysis often requires penetrating study of a variety of facts. Many little pieces of information may be needed to get the whole picture, or a single fact may give a vital clue. The amount that a bank can afford to spend in studying a single case is limited, but the limits are not clear. A loan may be a "one-time" matter or the beginning of a long and profitable series. Avoiding one serious loss justifies a lot of research. A few of the biggest banks have specialists on many subjects; some banks have extensive arrangements for gathering, interpreting, and filing information. A well-managed small bank will have peculiarly valuable data concerning a few firms or the economy of the locality, information which it will use and which it may make available to its correspondents.

The broadly oriented credit analysis of modern banking at its best can provide a basis for suggestions by the bank of ways in which the borrowing firm can raise its efficiency. Giant businesses may have no need for bank financial advice, or they may; but thousands of businesses can benefit from counsel which an alert, informed commercial bank can give. A bank which can make a good record on this score will thereby lay the basis for expanding its lending and its other services over the long run.

Often the practical problem is not whether a loan can safely be made but how much and on what terms. For several years before and after World War II, banks were "short" of good opportunities to lend, especially to businesses. The problem was not so much the screening of a multitude of loan applications to select the best, as it was the development of greater volume. Individual banks, and banks as a group, found that other lenders were competing for some of the largest and most attractive loans. As the demand for loans rose after the war, and as banks devised new methods of competing, there developed concern over the possibility that

[9] A national organization serving banks, Robert Morris Associates, supplies extensive and varied data.

[10] This broader study is also important for helping decide where to try to *promote* lending. A study of technical features of an industry may reveal unsuspected ways in which a bank might try to build loan volume.

competition would tempt banks to relax their credit standards. Might not loan quality deteriorate? Concern continues. Evidence remains inconclusive.[11]

LOAN SUPERVISION: DISTRESS LOANS

Having made a loan, a bank should not just "forget" it until the due date. Accumulating experience may reveal opportunities for profitable and wise increase, or some other mutually beneficial change, in the loan. Then, too, unfavorable developments may warrant the proverbial "ounce of prevention." Of course, most loans will present no troubles, but the banker cannot be certain which will work out with no difficulty. Therefore, he must check, not every loan in detail continually, but those which for one reason or another show signs of trouble—perhaps because the stock market has tumbled, business generally is sagging, a particular industry is suffering, or the borrower himself gives evidence of being in difficulty. The bank manager will also look for signs of unusual promise. Informal contacts with the borrower, formal financial statements, a visit to the place of business, a study of what is passing through the bank account, discreet inquiries—all these can prove useful. For installment loans the bank needs a reliable system for bringing any delinquency promptly to the attention of someone who will begin action.

When probings suggest trouble, perhaps more serious than the borrower recognizes, the banker in his own interest and that of the business may properly suggest action. Doing so will require tact; the proposal, of course, may be rebuffed. But if the borrower is receptive, the bank can try to help develop a constructive program. The banker may at times help in executing a "rescue" program.

A small fraction of cases will, as time passes, lead to real doubt about the ability of the business to survive. The banker's choice can then be difficult. If he insists upon being repaid under the rights provided in the contract, he may get all his money; but he may seem to be helping destroy a business. At the minimum, he is likely to lose a customer. Yet if he agrees to delay, he may sacrifice part of his loan, prolong the agony of a business death, and extend the period of the firm's operating losses. Ob-

---

[11] Loan "quality" defies simple definition or measurement. General business conditions make apparently good loans poor and poor loans good. Under any set of circumstances, however, some loans fail to meet reasonable standards of quality. If there are many such, the whole financial structure will suffer. A special study of a sample of reports of bank examiners found that for the years 1951 through 1957, loans criticized as excessively risky involved around one percent of the loan total. This percentage was lower than that found in somewhat comparable studies for earlier periods. A. J. Wojnilower, *The Quality of Bank Loans: A Study of Bank Examination Records* (New York: National Bureau of Economic Research, 1962).

viously, no general prescription can apply. Despite popular impressions, banks probably tend toward the side of leniency and tolerance. On the whole, apparently, such policies have proved to be wise; unquestionably, successes in "workouts" have been numerous.

For 25 years the economy has prospered. Bankers have had generally favorable conditions in which to handle difficult cases. No long recessions nor deep depressions have created and magnified problems on a large scale. If a depression were to occur, or if banks were to make an undue proportion of poor quality loans, the handling of distress cases would prove perplexing and disturbing beyond anything ever experienced by most of today's bank officers.

BANK CHARGES

Banks charge for their services. These charges, like prices in general, serve to induce economy in use and to provide the incentives for suppliers to make the service available. In some respects and at some times, however, the "prices" which banks charge will influence the economy in ways rather different from those of other prices. These influences, for the most part, are examined later, not here.

Interest and Discount

Two methods of charging interest are used. One is the familiar charge as an annual rate on a principal sum, payable at the end of a period. Six percent per year for six months on $100 is $3.00. The borrower must repay $103 at the end of six months.

The second type of charge is discounting—in effect, deducting the interest in advance. If a six-month loan for $100 is to be discounted at six percent, the borrower receives only $97 (the $3 charge being, in a sense, withheld in advance). He must pay $100 at the end of six months, $3 more than he received. Since he received $97 instead of $100, and thus had less of the bank's credit or funds to use during the period, the cost is over six percent—almost 6.2 percent. Discounting may permit a bank to charge slightly higher effective rates than if it were to quote straight interest. (At times the courts may tolerate effective rates which are above the legal limit if the rate of discount is at or below the figure set by law for interest as such.)

Experienced borrowers of other than small amounts will not be induced to pay more by such a technicality of form. Casual borrowers, however, especially those seeking small loans, may be misled, especially when agreeing to installment and personal loans. When a discount loan is repaid in equal installments, the true cost—expressed as a rate of interest—is roughly twice the rate of discount. With minor exceptions, the borrower has the use, on the average, of only half the money for the period. Thus, a discount loan of six percent repaid in installments costs the borrower approximately 12 percent on the funds available to him for use.[12] The advertising for auto and personal loans generally quotes rates as a discount rather than as straight interest—and as a percent of the original amount rather than the *average* balance. The result, and doubtless the intent, is an impression of cost much below the actual amount.

Occasionally, there may be a convenience advantage to borrower or lender in using one form rather than another, but the difference is rarely important.[13] For simplicity, we shall generally use the term "interest" to include discount.

Banks are well situated to collect interest frequently; they can charge the borrower's checking account with the amount due. If interest is collected monthly, the bank receives a somewhat higher effective rate than if it collects at the end of each six-month period.

The Level and Pattern of Charges

The rates that a bank can charge depend upon many factors of demand and supply. The vigor of competition varies widely. Big borrowers have many alternatives for seeking a lower rate, small borrowers few.

Cost as a factor influencing the supply of funds for bank lending differs somewhat from the costs of most businesses. One measure of cost to the bank always exists—an alternative use of lending capacity. For example, the interest rate obtainable from government securities measures

---

[12] The precise calculation is complicated. A formula used by the Federal Reserve in a study of consumer purchases is

$$I = \frac{2m\,D}{P\,(n+1)}$$

where I is the rate of charge
m is the number of payments in one year
D is the interest or discount charge in dollars
P is the principal or cash advance
n is the number of payments to discharge the debt.
See R. W. Johnson, *Methods of Stating Consumer Finance Charges* (New York: Graduate School of Business, Columbia University, 1961).

[13] Income tax considerations sometimes create a preference for discount over interest, or vice versa. A bank or other purchaser of a bond or note buying at a discount gets income in the form of appreciation in price. If the increment is treated for tax purposes as capital gain rather than as interest, there can be a tax saving which is not offset by a tax disadvantage of the borrower. Banks in their *ordinary* lending, however, cannot benefit from any difference in income tax treatment of discount and interest.

one alternative which must be sacrificed in lending to a business. The expenses of attracting deposits, especially time deposits, also serve to some extent as a measure of cost. Another factor is the difference in service rendered where such differences do put the bank to *variations* in expense. Banks differ in the extent to which they try to compute such cost variations and reflect them in interest charges.[14] Finally, the chance of loss, which does vary, is a cost which should somehow be considered. Unfortunately, computation in advance is impossible for any particular loan; but by using past experience, a bank can make an explicit allowance which may prove generally accurate on the average.[15]

A bank will have a prime rate for top-quality loans. All banks in the area will ordinarily charge the same prime rate, with that in New York setting the general level for the country. Other rates will then range upward. Fig. 5.1 shows the relation between the prime and average rates. The amount that a borrower pays will depend in part upon his ability to qualify for the prime rate—a matter that can be subject to negotiation. Most borrowers can never hope for the prime rate; whatever they pay in excess may be subject to bargaining if they wish, or it may be more or less set on a take-it-or-leave-it basis by the bank. Table 5.1 shows that businesses with large assets pay lower rates than do small companies. Surprisingly, secured loans tend to cost a little more than unsecured; not, of course, because of the collateral but because of other factors which the collateral did not offset fully.

Partly because interest rates are small figures, people sometimes fail to recognize that differences which may appear small are large in relation to the absolute amounts. For example, 6 percent is one-fifth (20 percent) above 5 percent. The factors which are peculiar to a specific case of a general type of loan will rarely influence the rate by 100 percent, but a range of one-third or so will often be subject to bargaining. Though 6 percent is 3 *percentage points* above 3 percent, it is 100 percent higher.

For some loans the demand is highly inelastic; only state laws may

[14] Indirectly, however, differences in servicing and related costs enter the terms of many loans in the form of compensating-balance requirements.

[15] Taxing authorities now allow as current expense deductions certain additions to reserves for losses. The limit is a total reserve which, after actual losses have been charged against it, equals three times the average annual loss rate of any consecutive twenty-year period beginning after 1927 multiplied by current loan volume. The complexity of the formula has apparently discouraged some small banks from trying to set up reserves. The amounts permitted are widely criticized as unduly low; they are below those allowed some types of financial institutions. For all banks, bad debt reserves average around 2.5 percent of loans outstanding. But variation among banks is large, and illogical. Banks with smallest losses in the past, whether because of good judgment or failure to make loans involving risk, qualify for lowest reserves now regardless of the present nature of their lending. A smaller, simpler, more clear-cut and uniform formula seems desirable.

effectively limit what a bank can charge. Considerable inelasticity exists in the demand for many other loans; the borrower is willing to pay any of several rates and to borrow about the same amount at each. Yet a banker who looks to the future may wisely refrain from demanding as high

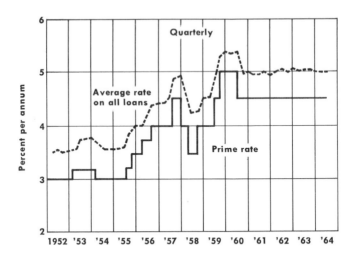

FIGURE 5.1

**Rates Charged by Banks on Short-Term Loans to Business
(19 Cities)**

Source: Board of Governors, Federal Reserve System

a rate as he might get. He may sense that the long-run demand for loans from *his* bank will be quite elastic even though short-run demand is inelastic. Moreover, because of the effects over the long run in attracting or repelling borrowers the charges on loans will influence the bank's ability to build up its deposits and other business. The good will of borrowers can be a significant aid in holding, and in getting, customers. The large personal or individual element in many loans, the fact that many borrowers have few if any alternative places to seek funds, or have any inclination to shop around, and the tendency of banks to establish patterns of rates—all these limit the possibility of adjusting charges in specific cases to meet each set of conditions.[16]

[16] Assume that a man wants to borrow $1000 for six months. The difference between $6\frac{1}{2}$ and $5\frac{1}{2}$ percent is $5 (minus any income tax saving). If the loan is $10,000 and the period a year, the difference, $100, may seem to warrant some effort to shop around.

Some room for adjustment does exist, however. One of the more common variations is the size of the "compensating balance," if any. The bank may want the borrower to maintain a minimum, or perhaps average, balance in his checking account over the life of the loan, with 20 percent

TABLE 5.1

Interest Rates on Business Loans, By Size of Borrower[a]

Total assets of borrower	Average rate of interest (percent)	
	Unsecured loans	Secured loans
Less than $50,000	6.5	6.5
$50,000 to $250,000	5.7	5.7
$250,000 to $1 million	5.2	5.4
$1 million to $5 million	4.8	5.2
$5 million to $25 million	4.5	4.8
$25 million to $100 million	4.2	4.5
$100 million and over	4.1	4.1

[a] Data cover all business loans by member banks in 1957; there were 1,185,000 loans for a total of $31 billion.
Source: *Federal Reserve Bulletin*, September 1959, p. 1121.

of the loan being a customary figure. The bank, thereby, in effect hopes to force the borrower to keep more in the account than he would otherwise. The results are (1) an increase in the net cost of the *useful* part of the loan to the borrower, and (2) for the bank, a reduction in the "cash drain" as new deposits are created (loans made). Any cut in the cash drain enables a bank to lend more to others, and thus earn more interest than would otherwise be possible.

Assume that a borrower pays six percent on a $10,000 loan and must maintain a balance of 20 percent of the loan when his balance would otherwise be $1000. In maintaining a balance of $2000, therefore, he keeps one-tenth of this loan immobilized; in effect, he pays an interest cost of almost 6.7 percent on the $9000 he uses. Clearly, variation in the size of the compensating-balance requirement is a way to adjust net terms.[17]

[17] See H. T. Shapiro and N. D. Baxter, "Compensating-Balance Requirements: The Theory and Its Implications," *Southern Economic Journal*, Jan. 1964, pp. 261–7.

Service and Other Charges

Banks now, more than before World War II, charge not only for loans but for other services.[18]   Such charges account for over eight percent of bank income, but substantially more in some cases.   Charges for handling checking accounts bring most noninterest income.

On large accounts the bank relates the activity in the account (the source of its costs)—number of checks written and deposits made—to the average or minimum deposit (the basis for estimated "earnings").   There is no charge if what the bank figures it "earns" on a balance (a rough equivalent of interest) covers the cost of handling the items.[19]   Otherwise, a service charge is imposed.   If the activity does not "cost" the full allowance, the depositor gets no direct refund.   Banks are not permitted to pay interest on demand deposits, but important customers can try for some benefit.   Those who borrow substantial amounts, for example, may get the cost of the loan reduced somewhat.   Large customers can try to arrange to keep larger amounts in the form of time deposits and receive interest.

The systems of charging for smaller accounts tend to be simpler: perhaps ten cents a check or $2 a month plus five cents for each check beyond a dozen or so.   (When the charge depends upon the number of checks, depositors have an inducement to write fewer checks, thus reducing the bank's work load.)   Extra charges if the balance falls below some minimum or average give strong inducement to the depositor to keep more on deposit than he might otherwise.   Consequently, the bank can expect more earning assets or a smaller "cash drain."

A variety of special services may occasion charges: handling securities and cutting bond coupons, collection of amounts due from others, issuance of cashier's checks and drafts, transfer of money by telegraph, frequent use of the safe deposit box, "insufficient funds" (N.S.F.) checks, mortgage or rent or utility payments, preparing payrolls, stopping payment on checks, overdrafts, closing savings accounts prematurely, night deposits, and credit information.   Banks are making increased efforts to

[18] Before World War I an important source of income, especially for smaller banks, consisted of charges levied on checks presented for collection; the Federal Reserve has largely eliminated this practice except for small, nonmember banks.

[19] One large Philadelphia bank, for example, allows a credit of 15 cents per month for each $100 balance over $300; its charge for accounts from $300 to $2499 was 75 cents plus five cents for each check and deposit, while for accounts of $2500 and over the charge was four cents for each check drawn and four cents for the first $500 of each item deposited and two cents for the excess.   Other banks in the same city had different schedules, some simpler, some more complex.   House Committee on Banking and Currency, *The Federal Reserve System after Fifty Years, Hearings* . . . Vol. 1 (Washington: Government Printing Office, 1964), facing p. 486.   This volume contains extensive information on bank service charges.

expand their income from such sources. Yet they encounter difficulty growing out of competition from other institutions and pressure from large customers, some of whom are well informed, *e.g.,* about the cost reduction resulting from the use of new electronic equipment.

QUESTIONS

1. What is a "line of credit"?   What are its advantages and disadvantages to the borrower?   to the lending bank?

2. Discuss the advantages and disadvantages to a bank of a loan for over, say, five years.

3. What purpose does collateral serve?   Give examples of types of collateral.

4. What are the "three C's"?   What role does each play in bank lending?

5. If you were a state legislator voting legal controls on state bank lending, what provisions would you favor?   Why?

6. What is the purpose of credit analysis?   What kinds of information may a bank use in making such analyses?

7. What problems does a banker face in deciding how to deal with possible bad loans?

8. What is "discount"?   How does it differ from straight interest?

9. What kinds of service charges do banks impose?   Why might a depositor in a bank be required to pay no service charges?

10. Why do interest rates on bank loans differ from one borrower to another?

11. Discuss with a businessman or a banker what is involved in deciding on the amount which a firm may borrow from a bank. Why may some borrowers not get as much as they believe they can use to advantage?

12. "Pro forma" is a term sometimes used in connection with banking.   Explain its meaning as used in this chapter.

13. Try to learn from a local bank how its correspondent relations influence its lending.

CHAPTER 6   *DEBT INSTRUMENTS, THE MONEY MARKET, AND BOND PRICES*

═══════════════════════════════

T<small>HIS</small> chapter opens with a description of the types of "instruments"—the pieces of paper—used in bank lending. We then discuss "the money market" where some of these debt instruments are bought and sold. Here the forces of demand and supply for borrowed funds produce the most sensitive interest rate changes. A brief discussion of the relation between interest rates and bond prices closes the chapter.

DEBT (CREDIT) INSTRUMENTS

Most borrowing is on open account. A person who buys from a store and says "charge it" hardly thinks that he is borrowing. Yet he goes into debt and gets credit. Ordinarily he pays no interest. Most transactions among business firms, including those which involve trade credit, utilize open accounts. No written acknowledgement of debt appears.

Sometimes, however, a formal proof of the debt is useful. It can remove doubts about the exact terms of the agreement—the amount, the date for payment, and other elements. Moreover, if the seller does not want to "carry" the buyer for the entire period, a piece of paper proving the existence of the obligation may permit the debt to be sold to someone else. Banks must insist upon receiving a written credit (or loan) instrument when making a loan.

By a loan, or credit, instrument we mean the piece of paper or other evidence of the conclusion of an agreement or contract. (Since credit and debt are opposite aspects of the same thing, a credit instrument is also a debt instrument, and vice versa.) There is no clear distinction between a loan instrument and an investment instrument. In general, however, loans involve the bank and the borrower *directly,* while investments are bought and sold in broader, more impersonal, markets.

In Britain and some other countries many bank loans are made in the form of *overdrafts* of checking accounts, negative balances on which the bank charges interest. The "borrower" signs nothing which indicates his promise to pay. This practice is not approved in the United States.[1] Our procedure calls for some written evidence of a borrowing transaction with a bank; the statement will contain the major facts but not necessarily all the details as agreed upon by the parties.

The instruments used are either *promises* to pay or *orders* to pay. In fact, however, orders often also include promises. The following discussion of these instruments omits many technical elements.

Negotiability

Before dealing with specific types of instruments, we examine a feature of credit instruments which has much to do with the smooth functioning of business and finance—negotiability.

A negotiable instrument is one whose ownership can be transferred by delivery (with endorsement in some cases) without complications of assignment: *B* can make *C* the owner by the simple process of handing the piece of paper to *C.* The instrument itself must be in writing, signed by the one who is eventually to pay, and payable on demand or at a determinable future date. It must be an unconditional promise (or order) to pay a certain sum of money; it may be payable either "to order"—*i.e.,* to a specific person, business, etc.—or to the "bearer."

The person receiving the instrument, the transferee, gets good title—the claim belongs to him beyond any question—if certain conditions are met. To satisfy these requirements is generally easy. The chief conditions are: (1) the instrument on its face must be regular and complete, *i.e.,* one can look at it and see all the essential facts; (2) the transferee takes it in good faith, giving value, (3) before it is overdue (or if it had previously been dishonored, without the recipient's knowing of the past failure to honor the instrument); (4) finally, the person accepting the instrument does so without knowledge of any defect in the title—*i.e.,* in the claim to ownership—of the person from whom he receives it.

Legally, negotiable instruments (such as promissory notes or checks) can be transferred from hand to hand like currency. The instruments

---

[1] Banks extend credit in this way only as an accommodation for a day or so to depositors whose records indicate that the deficit will be only temporary. If a depositor's account does not have enough to cover the checks drawn on it, the bank can refuse to honor the checks, returning them to the person who has tried to collect, marked "insufficient funds."

themselves, and the ease with which they can be transferred, differ widely. In contrast with currency, they are not ordinarily the obligations of government (or its agent) but of private individuals or businesses.

A problem inevitably arises. On the one hand, obstacles are certain to arise in the transfer of private debt; on the other hand, the easy exchange of such IOU's will often aid the transaction of business. To help solve the problem, merchants and other businessmen gradually developed rules to facilitate the easy transfer of debt and credit instruments. These rules have become the basis of the Uniform Negotiable Instruments Act, which all states have adopted. Our financial system has developed around conditions which would not have been possible without the wide acceptance of the provisions of this act. The fluidity, the liquidity, and the broad efficiency of the whole economy are enhanced by the extensive use of negotiable instruments. These evidences of debt gain in acceptability because their negotiability eases the possessor's ability to dispose of them later if he wishes.

The "holder in due course" of a negotiable instrument (the one who acquires it while meeting the first three of the conditions noted above) need not worry about defects in the title of the person from whom he gets it (the fourth of the conditions noted above). This fact is significant, for a "debtor" does have certain *absolute* defenses which will prevent anyone from collecting on an instrument, whether or not it is negotiable: forgery; legal incapacity of the maker, such as infancy or insanity; and lack of delivery of an instrument before it is completed. The last calls for brief explanation: Assume that a note is signed but not completely filled in and is then lost; someone finds it and fills it out. In such a situation the signer is not liable because he did not deliver a completed instrument.

The debtor also has *personal* defenses (such as fraud on the part of the person to whom the note was given, lack of consideration, failure to meet specified conditions, and several others). These affect the right of the person who is at fault to collect from others. Such defenses, however, do not go or pass along with the transfer of a negotiable instrument. A seller of goods, for example, misrepresents his product but concludes a sale and gets a negotiable promissory note from the buyer. The buyer can cite the fraud as a defense against his being compelled to pay. However, anyone acquiring the note in good faith and for value, unaware of the fraud, can collect from the debtor.[2]

A person receiving a *non-negotiable* credit instrument by assignment or by purchase gets only the rights of the previous owner. These may not be complete. The use of such instruments requires more care than the use of negotiable instruments.

For the most part, the technical requirements for negotiability are not

---

[2] In this case the buyer of the goods is the debtor.

difficult to satisfy. Consequently, business benefits from the widespread use of a highly convenient device for facilitating transactions.

Endorsement

Negotiable instruments made in favor of a named payee—to the order of someone—can be transferred by endorsement. (An instrument payable to "bearer" rather than to a specific person may also be endorsed on transfer.) The person to whom the instrument is payable signs, usually on the back. If he signs only his name, the endorsement is "in blank," *i.e.,* it imposes no restrictions upon further use. His endorsement may, however, have restrictions, qualifications, or conditions. If the endorser names a specific person or firm as payee, the latter must endorse before the instrument can be transferred again. Or an endorsement may specify that the instrument is for deposit, for collection,[3] or for payment upon the happening of some event, such as delivery of a product.

All of us have endorsed a check, but few of us may have known what we were doing. When a person endorses without qualification (though perhaps with conditions as illustrated above), he warrants that the instrument is genuine, that he has a valid title to it, that he knows of nothing that would impair its validity or make it valueless, and that he will make up any losses which a future holder may suffer because of the instrument. (Various requirements must be met if a person receiving an instrument is to recoup any losses from a prior endorser; among the most important is prompt presentation for payment.) Endorsements can add to the acceptability of an instrument because they indicate that one or more persons beyond the original debtor will be liable.

Promissory Notes

The most common instrument received by banks in their lending is the promissory note. This is (1) an unconditional promise in writing (2) made by one person (or a business or government)—the maker—(3) to another—the payee (or to bearer)—(4) to pay a specific amount of money (5) at a fixed or determinable future date or upon demand. The note must be signed by the one promising to pay. It may also be signed by others who agree to pay if the maker fails to do so.

Promissory notes are usually negotiable. They may pass from hand to hand, with endorsements. Some notes are as simple as an ordinary

---

[3] A bank or individual accepting a note "for collection" holds it as agent of the endorser. The proceeds collected are held in trust for the endorser.

personal check. Others, however, are complex, with a great deal of "fine print"; these details generally favor the lending institution whose legal staff composed the wording, with various special powers which are rarely used. The note may provide for repayment in installments or on a single date. Payment may be on demand, in which case the borrower as well as the lender is free to end the transaction; yet the loan may continue indefinitely.

Buyers of goods sometimes give the seller a promissory note instead of cash immediately. If he wants funds at once, the seller may endorse the note and turn it over (at a discount) to a bank in return for cash (rather than waiting until the note is due). The note is then a *double-name* instrument. The bank expects to be paid by the buyer of the goods, the maker of the note; but the bank can also call upon the endorser if the original signer fails to pay.

Orders to Pay: Drafts

The other major type of instrument is an *order* to pay. (Fundamentally, this is also backed by someone's promise; the instrument itself, however, is different from an IOU.) The familiar personal check is such an order; the depositor tells his bank to pay.

Other forms of orders are *drafts* or *bills of exchange*. The person who orders payment is the *drawer,* the one to receive payment is the *payee*. The one who is ordered to pay is the *drawee*. Any of these may be individuals, business firms, or banks. Drafts may be payable on sight, *i.e.,* on demand when they are presented.[4] They may be payable at a specific date, perhaps 90 days after they are made, or a given number of days after being presented for payment.

The drawee of a draft is not necessarily obligated to pay it. He may not have the required resources, or he may not recognize the claim of the one making the order. Hence this type of credit instrument in its simple form has defects, especially as a basis for bank lending. If X (the drawer, a retailer buying goods) gives A (payee, the selling manufacturer) a draft on B (drawee, X's bank) ordering B to pay A in sixty days, A may have trouble using the draft as a basis for borrowing at his bank. Who knows whether B will pay?

One modification, however, can make a big difference—*acceptance*. The drawee may write on the draft, "accepted," with the date and an

---

[4] When paying with a check, a person must have the funds in the bank account when the check is delivered. When a draft is used, however, the funds need not be in the account until the draft is presented. Businesses are making increasing use of drafts to take advantage of this day-or-two difference in the amounts which must be held in the bank.

official signature. By doing so, he agrees to honor the obligation. The drawee thus gives or substitutes his own financial standing and his explicit acknowledgment of the debt for what had been only an implication that he would pay. What had existed before was the drawer's implicit promise that the drawee—bank *B* in the case above—would turn over the funds to the payee on the date specified. If the drawee who has accepted is better known than the drawer, or has greater financial strength, the addition of his promise makes the "paper" more desirable. For example, banks which would not lend on the basis of the drawer's order (an implied promise) may do so when the draft has been converted into an acceptance.

An illustration of the use of a draft and the role of acceptance will be helpful. A buyer of cotton for processing may not wish to pay for it immediately. The seller, willing to make the sale but also anxious to be certain of payment, ships the cotton by railroad on an order bill of lading. He also draws a draft on the buyer for payment in sixty days. The seller has the draft sent to a bank in the buyer's locality along with the bill of lading. The buyer cannot get the cotton from the railroad until he has *accepted* the draft (thus promising to pay); he must accept to get the bill of lading. The seller now has the buyer's signature acknowledging his obligation to pay. The draft has become a *trade acceptance*. When the acceptor is a bank, the instrument becomes a *bank acceptance*.

The seller may hold the draft until it is due. Often, however, he uses it to get money from a bank at once. A common practice is to endorse the draft and sell it to a bank (or some investor seeking short-term assets) at a discount which allows the bank the equivalent of interest. The details vary. The seller of the cotton may himself endorse the draft when he originally draws it, attach it to the bill of lading, sell both to a bank, and rely upon the bank (and its correspondents) to take care of the rest of the arrangements. Or the buyer of the cotton (drawee) may in advance get a promise from his bank that it will accept a draft. This promise will be evidenced by a *letter of credit* which can be sent to the seller and will aid him in selling the draft to his own bank.

A bank accepting drafts makes no loans in the process. It will charge, however, for making its credit available—for the risk it assumes in promising to pay if its customer fails to do so, for tying up possible lending power, and for the clerical effort involved.[5] A businessman seeking funds will wisely pay the charge if the additional backing of a bank enables him (or someone with whom he is arranging a deal) to borrow on sufficiently more favorable terms. Various restrictions limit the acceptances a bank may make and have outstanding.

Drafts, and their more refined version, acceptances, are useful in

---

[5] The bank's balance sheet will show as a liability "acceptances outstanding" and as an asset "customers' liability."

financing trade. They aid in matching the flow of credit with the flow of goods. They prove especially helpful when businesses which may not have close and long-standing financial ties wish to deal on other than a cash basis. Drafts provide a tangible evidence of an amount due, a piece of paper which can be exchanged by purchase (sale) or endorsement in financial markets. Consequently, they offer a better basis for financing than open-book account debt. The association of acceptances with tangible products, often staple commodities with well-organized markets, gives such instruments the character of self-liquidating debt that fits well into the commercial loan theory of banking. Acceptances are used relatively more in financing foreign trade than for domestic business.

DEBT INSTRUMENTS USED BY GOVERNMENTS

Governments borrow on a large scale. For the country as a whole, Federal, state, and local governments combined almost always spend more each year than they collect in taxes. The gap is made up by borrowing. Moreover, governments often issue new debt to get money to repay debt which is falling due. What kinds of debt instruments do they sell?

The variety may seem endless. It includes many more features than need be discussed here. "Municipals"—debt instruments of states and localities—are more varied than Federal issues, but the basic features are essentially the same with one important exception. The interest on municipal debt (but not on Federal debt) is exempt from Federal personal and corporation income tax.

United States debt has a special attraction for banks, for they must pledge such debt as security for Treasury deposits. Federal debt may also be used as collateral if a bank borrows from the Federal Reserve.

Treasury Bills and Certificates

In borrowing for a year or less the Treasury offers two types of securities. Bills are sold each week on a discount basis, *i.e.,* they do not bear interest but are sold for less than the face amount which will be paid upon maturity. In mid-1964, bills yielded about 3.5 percent. Sale is by auction on the basis of competitive bidding. An exception is made, however, for a bidder seeking up to, perhaps, $200,000; the full subscription will be allotted at the average price resulting from competitive bidding. Bills ordinarily run for 13 weeks, but the Treasury also offers 26-week, and on occasion essentially one-year, issues.

Bill denominations range from $1000 to $1,000,000. Bills are payable to bearer, are interchangeable, and are bought and sold in an active and highly competitive market. The amounts offered each week vary according to the Treasury's need for cash, but most of the proceeds go to repay the owners of bills which mature during the week.

Treasury certificates of indebtedness usually mature in one year. They are sold at less regular intervals than bills and are apparently being supplanted by other debt forms. Certificates pay a designated rate of interest, which the Treasury sets according to market conditions at the time of issue. Certificates are bearer obligations with denominations from $1000 to $1,000,000. They are bought and sold in the open market.

Notes and Bonds

Notes are an intermediate-term issue. They run from 13 months to 5 years, bonds longer than 5 years. Savings bonds are widely publicized and available at all times for sale to the general public on a discount basis and usually in rather small amounts. Other bonds and notes are issued on a few occasions a year. The interest rates are set according to market conditions prevailing at the time of original sale. The law, however, prohibits a rate of interest above 4¼ percent on bonds. If the free market rate is higher, the Treasury cannot sell new bonds—except at a discount from par, which it refuses to do other than for minor amounts and, of course, savings bonds. If market rates are higher, the Treasury must rely upon shorter-term securities, on which the law permits whatever rate of interest is needed to sell the issue. The original buyer of a bond or note may hold until maturity or (except for some issues) sell anytime after purchase.

The features of Federal bonds and notes vary greatly in details. A few issues will be accepted in payment of certain Federal taxes. Bonds appear in both bearer and registered form and for denominations ranging upward from $500. Some issues are callable before maturity, *i.e.,* the Treasury may repay them at par before the final due date. Issues of notes and bonds differ in details. The variations add a little to the difficulty of comparing the attractiveness of issues and make for somewhat thinner markets in particular securities.

Municipal debt is often in serial form, with maturities staggered over many years.

COMMERCIAL PAPER, REPURCHASE AGREEMENTS, AND TIME CERTIFICATES OF DEPOSIT

Most loans are the outcome of direct contact between banker and borrower. In New York and a few other cities, however, there is an impersonal or open market in "commercial paper." In this market anyone with funds to lend for a short period may buy short-term debt of well-known, financially sound businesses.[6] Much of the borrowing is done to meet more or less temporary needs for additional working capital.

The buyers of such debt, *i.e.,* those who lend, include commercial banks, corporations, state and local governments, and foreign banks or businesses. The buyer may deal with commercial paper "houses." These are brokers who specialize in handling debt of this particular type. They make the credit investigation and arrange the initial terms of each loan. (The large finance companies, such as those financing installment purchase of autos, issue their own paper directly.) The loans may run from a weekend to a year or more as the two parties prefer. The debt is ordinarily sold in denominations of from $5000 to $100,000 and on a discount basis. The volume outstanding varies, but in 1964 averaged about $8 billion, almost twice the 1960 amount.

The borrowing firm can get funds from widely dispersed lenders impersonally, without the need to establish continuing relations. It can count upon the broker to sell the notes on the most favorable terms possible at the time. The cost tends to be less than the prime rate charged by banks. Relatively few, around 420, top-credit firms have ready access to this market. This opportunity strengthens their bargaining position when dealing with commercial banks. Large corporations at times find the issue of commercial paper more convenient than arrangements to borrow from many banks, each of which is limited in the maximum loan that it is permitted to grant any one borrower.

Although interest rates obtainable tend to be lower than on business loans, a bank can lend in this "open market" when other opportunities do not use up all its lending capacity. In this way, too, a bank can get diversification in its business loans. This consideration is important for some banks, *e.g.,* those in one-industry areas. The notes are not ordinarily salable, but the issuing dealer or corporation will usually agree to buy back obligations if the lender encounters unexpected need for cash.

Repurchase agreements now play a large role in short-term financing. Assume that *B* owns a Treasury bill or some other security with several days, weeks, or even months to run to maturity. *B* wishes funds at once. Instead of selling the asset outright, *B* may "sell" it temporarily, promising to buy back (repurchase) on a specific date, usually within 16 days but sometimes much longer, and at a specified price. The temporary purchaser may be a non-financial corporation, a securities dealer, the Federal Reserve, a commercial bank, a state treasurer, a pension fund, etc. The buyer can get some benefit from dollars not needed immediately but which

---

[6] N. D. Baxter, *The Commercial-Paper Market* (Princeton: Princeton University Econometric Research Program, 1964).

it will want shortly to pay taxes, dividends, or some other obligation. Repurchase agreements can be tailored precisely in amount and timing to the needs of one or both parties. Interest yields tend to be low; they take the form of difference between the original price and a slightly higher repurchase price. This type of transaction, once familiar to a sophisticated few only, now attracts many participants.

The volume of negotiable time certificates of deposits—CD's—grew from nothing in early 1961 to over $10 billion in mid-1964. Before 1961 commercial banks encountered more and more difficulty in competing for corporation funds seeking short-term investment. FR regulations set the maximum interest rate payable on time deposits at only one percent on deposits up to 90 days and 2.5 percent for 90-day to 6-month deposits.

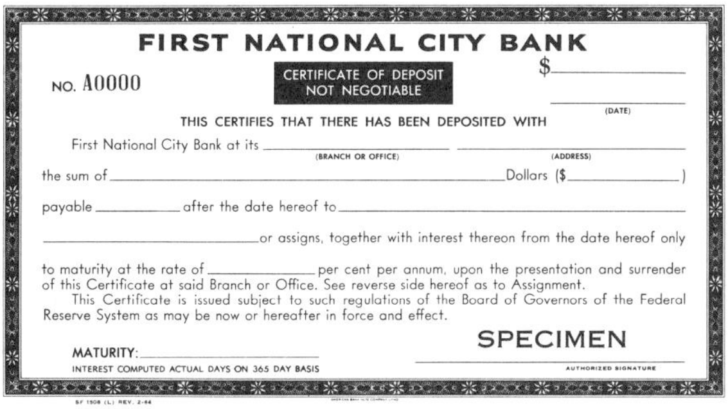

FIRST NATIONAL CITY BANK

NO. A0000 | CERTIFICATE OF DEPOSIT NOT NEGOTIABLE | $ _____

THIS CERTIFIES THAT THERE HAS BEEN DEPOSITED WITH

First National City Bank at its _____ _____
(BRANCH OR OFFICE) (ADDRESS)

the sum of _____ Dollars ($ _____)

payable _____ after the date hereof to _____

_____ or assigns, together with interest thereon from the date hereof only

to maturity at the rate of _____ per cent per annum, upon the presentation and surrender of this Certificate at said Branch or Office. See reverse side hereof as to Assignment.
This Certificate is issued subject to such regulations of the Board of Governors of the Federal Reserve System as may be now or hereafter in force and effect.

SPECIMEN

MATURITY: _____
INTEREST COMPUTED ACTUAL DAYS ON 365 DAY BASIS   AUTHORIZED SIGNATURE

NOTICE TO ASSIGNEES

No assignment hereof shall be binding on this Bank until this Certificate, assigned by the payee below, shall have been received by the Branch or Office specified on the reverse side hereof. This Bank has, by law, the right to set off any indebtedness of the payee to it due, or which it may mature, at the time of such receipt.

I assign this certificate

To _____
(Name and Address of Assignee)

_____
(Signature of Payee)

FIGURE 6.1

Outstanding Time Certificate of Deposit

Much of the time these rates were "below the market." Moreover, if the depositor withdrew before the end of the period originally agreed upon, he forfeited all interest. The combination of (a) maximum rate often lower than that on high-quality short-term assets, and (b) extreme inflexibility, in effect excluded banks from a large and growing market. Corporations were economizing on demand deposits and buying short-term securities. Banks answered with the negotiable CD.

Leading banks issue CD's in denominations of $500,000 or more, while some banks go as low as $2500. The interest rate offered must be no higher than the ceiling set by the FR's Regulation Q: until late 1964, 4 percent for over 90-day certificates, then 4½ percent. Yields of CD's have been slightly higher than on Treasury bills. Maturity dates are adjusted somewhat to meet market preferences, e.g., just before a date for tax payment. A CD can be sold in the open market by the original depositor or by any later owner, but no one can get the funds from the issuing bank before the CD matures. Issuing Banks (required to hold a non-yielding legal reserve of 4 percent) may have difficulty in using the depositor's funds to get yields which make CD's a source of much profit. But "something is better than nothing."

THE MONEY MARKET

The financial district of New York City is small in area. Yet it is the center or focal point of a market which serves the whole country and even the whole free world. More accurately, there are different markets which are related, both closely and remotely.

One is called "the money market." The things bought and sold are short-term debts: Treasury bills and other short-term government securities, commercial paper, time certificates of deposit, repurchase agreements, bankers' acceptances, call loans, and "Federal funds." (The last are deposits at a Federal Reserve bank which banks that are short of reserves acquire from banks with excess reserves.) Daily money market transactions in U.S. debt due in less than one year often exceed $1.5 billion; other transactions make the total very much larger.

Physically, the market in New York and the markets in other cities will be found to consist of bank trading rooms, brokers, dealers, and perhaps others, all linked by telephone. There is no single meeting place, but there is the most highly developed of communication facilities. These communications connect the traders within New York, and also the markets in various cities over the country—and the world—with New York. Thus a huge number of traders are actually or potentially in touch with each other. Any tendency for price to change in one part of the market becomes evident in other parts. The market is extremely well organized, and yet the organization is not rigid. Significant elements of flexibility, informality, and adaptability exist.

The *borrowers, i.e.,* those who issue the securities which are sold, consist of the United States Treasury, some states and localities, corporations which sell commercial paper, security brokers and dealers, commercial banks, and businesses engaged in foreign trade. They will seek financing in this market if conditions are more favorable than elsewhere, chiefly interest cost in relation to the period for which funds are desired. At any one time, of course, the securities available for sale or purchase are not only those just being issued. Securities which have been outstanding for days, weeks, months, or perhaps even years are constantly offered by previous purchasers who want money at once rather than later when the loan matures (become due for repayment).

The *lenders, i.e.,* those who provide the funds, are commercial banks (from the largest in the country to some of the smaller), foreign banks, insurance companies and other financial institutions, business corporations, state and local governments, some individuals, and on occasion the Federal Reserve. They have funds which they do not need at the moment. By lending for a few days or weeks, they get some interest. (In mid-1964 each day's interest on $1,000,000 was about $100.) Today's lender may have been last month's borrower. A city, or corporation, treasurer can sometimes cover a month's salary, or much more, by shifting resources briefly into short-term paper. Here is a market in which many participants deal on a day-to-day basis, and in large totals. In August 1964, for example, dealers in U.S. government securities had average daily financing of $4.2 billion. New York City banks provided 27 percent, other banks 22, non-financial corporations 41, and a large variety of other lenders 10 percent, respectively.[7] The large role of corporations is impressive.

The money market is highly competitive. For one thing, "the product" is largely homogeneous. Of course, the short-term debts bought and sold are by no means identical. Some are further from maturity than others; not all debtors are equally reliable and well-known; other elements differ. Yet most issues are close substitutes for most others. If the price of one starts to get even a trifle out of line with the prices of others, the high degree of interchangeability makes itself felt. These debts are almost money. The range of price fluctuations is so small that risk of loss is minimal.

The large volume of transactions also helps to make the market highly competitive. The quantity of debt instruments available for dealing is substantial. The tens of billions of dollars of Treasury bills and

[7] L. Freeman, "The Financing of Government Securities Dealers," Federal Reserve Bank of New York, *Monthly Review,* June 1964, p. 108.

certificates in themselves make up a huge base. The number of buyers and sellers—actual and potential—runs into the thousands or tens of thousands. No one really knows at any time how many buyers and sellers might enter on one or the other side of the market. But the number, already large, appears to be growing. The overwhelming majority are so small in relation to the total that individually or even in manageable groups they can have no perceptible influence on the whole. Some, however, are large enough for their transactions occasionally have more than negligible effect on price (at the margin) in the very short run. And, of course, the Federal Reserve Bank of New York, acting for the System and for foreign central banks, buys and sells on a scale large enough to affect the whole market. Sometimes the "Fed" stabilizes; sometimes it acts to change the level of prices and interest rates.

A third characteristic contributing to the effectiveness of the market is the existence of many middlemen. They work on very small commissions or mark-ups, with the spreads between "bid" and "asked" being a small fraction of one percent. Dealers try to build volume, competing on the basis of price and service. While personal friendship and business connections may on occasion have some influence, the dealer system typifies the impersonal market. Buyers and sellers stand an excellent chance of getting the best price possible.

Bids for, and offers of, short-term debt in the money market indicate the relative strength of the forces of demand and supply. The sales made are at prices, and these are readily translated into yields. (Most dealings are in discount rather than interest-bearing debts.) In other words, the yields on short-term debts traded in the open market are determined by demand and supply. These yields or prices are available to anyone who can deal in this market—a very open market indeed.

A part of the market which is important for monetary developments consists of shifting of Federal funds. Deposits at the Federal Reserve bring the depositing bank no income. A bank with more than it needs to meet its reserve requirements will naturally seek to put the excess to use. On the other hand, a bank whose reserves are below the legal requirement will want to build up its reserve position. In the money market it can often do so. Through firms specializing in this service, one bank can in effect borrow some of another's deposits at the "Fed." It borrows for one day at a time, ordinarily in units of $1,000,000. The interest rate depends upon the balance between demand and supply; the rate, however, will not ordinarily go above the cost that a bank would encounter in borrowing from the Federal Reserve. The bank owning the excess can, of course, use it to buy other assets and will not lend its excess reserves for a rate below that obtainable on high quality short-term paper.

Borrowers or lenders who do not have access directly to the money market—the owner of a small business and perhaps his local bank—will

Table 2: Matrix of alternative portfolios

Including short-term tax-exempt securities

Program	Percentage Composition of Portfolio						Yields			Weighted Yield Factors (1)						Weighted Yield Factors (2)						Weighted Returns on Portfolio	
	TB	OT	CD	CP	TE			(1)	(2)	TB	OT	CD	CP	TE		TB	OT	CD	CP	TE		(1)	(2)
A	40%	30%	10%	10%	10%		TB	3.31%	2.85%	1.324	1.047	.375	.370	.380		1.140	.930	.327	.315	.320		3.50%	3.03%
B	30	30	10	10	20		OT	3.49	3.10	.993	1.047	.375	.370	.760		.855	.930	.327	.315	.640		3.54	3.07
C	30	20	20	10	20	×	CD	3.75	3.27	.993	.698	.750	.370	.760	=	.855	.620	.654	.315	.640	=	3.57	3.08
D	30	20	10	10	30		CP	3.70	3.15	.993	.698	.375	.370	1.140		.855	.620	.327	.315	.960		3.58	3.08
E	20	20	20	10	30		TE	3.80	3.20	.662	.698	.750	.370	1.140		.570	.620	.654	.315	.960		3.62	3.12
F	20	20	10	10	40					.662	.698	.375	.370	1.520		.570	.620	.327	.315	1.280		3.63	3.11

Notes to Table

TB: 91-day U.S. Treasury bills.
OT: Other U.S. Treasury securities (one-year maturity).
CD: Certificates of deposit.
CP: Commercial paper.
TE: Tax-exempt securities.

In Yields matrix, column *(1)* shows rates prevailing on May 1, 1963 (CD rate is for one-year maturity of money-market banks, TE rate is for obligations rated "A" or better, of approximately one-year maturity); column *(2)* shows 1962 averages (TB rate is for new issues. CD rate is average of 6-month and one-year maturities of money-market banks, TE rate is for obligations rated "A" or better, average of 6-month and one-year maturities). CP rates in both columns are for 90-day paper of prime finance companies.

Weighted Yield Factor for each investment medium in a given program is derived by multiplying the percentage of portfolio represented by that specific medium times the applicable yield.

Weighted Return on Portfolio for a given program is derived by summing Weighted Yield Factors in applicable matrix.

It is arbitrarily assumed no single class of investments other than Treasury securities is to exceed 40% of portfolio in any program.

Each basis point (0.01%) of yield has a value of $1,000 per $10,000,000 invested per annum.

Alternative Portfolios for Use of Short-Term Funds Reproduced, with permission, from "Money-Market Investments —the Risk and the Return," copyright © 1964 by Morgan Guaranty Trust Company of New York

be affected at least a little by changes in the level of interest rates in the great financial centers.[8] The connection is sometimes close and obvious; much more often it is indirect. Yet to some extent the charges made by the individual bank in its lending result from forces operating throughout the economy which determine interest rates in the money market.

Another tie must be noted: that between the money market (for short-term debt) and the capital market (for long-term debt). In fact, there are not two clearly distinguishable markets but two with wide overlap. For some actual or potential borrowers and lenders, long-term securities can be substituted for short-term, and vice versa. The balance of forces of demand and supply in one sector of the market will spill over into others. Levels and changes of interest rates in the money market influence long-term rates and in turn are influenced by them.

INTEREST RATES, YIELDS, AND SECURITY PRICES

The description of discounting in Chapter 5 pointed out that a bank may choose to take its income in the form of an excess of the face amount of a loan over the amount actually turned over to the borrower. The borrower pays no interest as such but does pay back more dollars than he receives. The securities bought and sold in financial markets often combine interest and discount. When they do, the computation of yield must obviously include both. Only a little less obvious is another fact whose full significance will appear only as we proceed. The market price of a security will fluctuate with changes in market rates of interest. We look first at the computation of yield.

In mid-1964, 3.5 percent Treasury bonds due in 1980 were selling for 91. For $910 one could buy a $1000 bond which would pay $35 a year in interest and mature in 16 years, paying $90 more than the purchase price. The $35 a year is 3.72 percent of the $910 cost of the bond. This is the "running yield." Clearly, however, it does not adequately measure the bond's full yield to the owner. Some allowance must be made for the gradual but certain rise in price as maturity approaches.

The computation requires two kinds of adjustments. The first is the amount that the "investment" will change as maturity approaches. For example, if a person bought at a discount, his commitment will increase month after month (assuming stable market rates of interest) as the bond rises in price. In essence, he will reinvest some of the yield each month or year. If he retains the bond for which he paid $910 when the passage

---

[8] Small businesses, we noted in Chapter 4, may receive more generous trade credit when bigger corporations get funds on more favorable terms in the money market. Each month's activities in the money market are summarized in the *Monthly Review* of the Federal Reserve Bank of New York.

of time has raised its price to $950 he sacrifices the alternative of committing $950 elsewhere. His average investment is his purchase price plus the face (maturity) value divided by two. Thus if he paid $910 for a bond maturing for $1000, his average investment is $\frac{\$910 + \$1000}{2}$, or $955.

How does one take account of the appreciation element in computing yield? If the bond has 16 years to run, its appreciation each year may be $6. However, one gets only an approximation of the right yield by adding the annual coupon, $35, and the $6 and then dividing $41 by his average investment, $955. The exact computation must take account of compounding. And compounding calculations are not easy for most of us.

Fortunately, detailed tables are available. They show all the possibilities in which one is likely to be interested. In the case of the Treasury bond mentioned above, the full yield is 4.24 percent. A 1½ percent note due in October 1968, and selling for $910 in the summer of 1964 would yield 3.69 percent to maturity, more than twice the rate specified in the contract.

Bonds also sell at premiums, *i.e.,* for more than the number of dollars which will be paid at maturity. In the summer of 1955, for example, 3¼ percent Treasury bonds due in 1983 but callable in 1978 were selling for about 106. A buyer paying $1060 for a bond would get $32.50 a year interest, but he would know that when the bond was paid off, he would receive $60 less than he paid for it. Making allowance for this factor, he would find the yield to call date on his $1060 would be 2.89 percent. (The 1964 price was $870, the yield to the 1978 call date 4.24 percent.)

The general principle is easily illustrated by the case of a perpetual bond (or a piece of real estate) which has no maturity date. Assume that we know how many dollars a year the bond will bring in—perhaps $50. We can also find the rate of interest prevailing in the market on assets of the same type. Perhaps this is 5 percent. Then how much would one pay for the bond, or, if the owner, how much would one insist upon receiving? The answer is given by the simple formula

$$\text{capital value} = \frac{\text{annual yield}}{\text{market rate of interest}}$$

In this case we find that the bond is worth $1000 $= \frac{\$50}{0.05}$.

Now suppose that the market rate of interest for such debts drops to 4 percent. The yield generally obtainable is less than before. The old bond, however, will continue to bring in $50 a year. How much, then, is it worth now? Applying the formula, we find that its price should be

$1250. In other words, this is the capital sum which if invested at the current four percent rate of interest will bring $50 a year. What if the market rate of interest rises to six percent? Anyone with money to lend can get more per year per dollar of capital. This bond, however, will continue to bring the same amount—$50. How much will it now be worth? Dividing the $50 by six percent, we get the answer: $833.33. When the bond has a maturity, of course, the prospect of getting the face amount—perhaps next week, perhaps not for 30 years—will enter into the calculations of worth today.

Tax considerations complicate price and yield computations. Yields which take the form of capital gains or losses are often (but not always) taxed differently from interest. For example, a bank buying a $1000 Treasury bond with a 2½ percent coupon rate for $880 will pay, we assume, Federal-state tax at the rate of 50 percent on the $25 a year interest. The rest of what the bank gets, however—the $120 rise in price to maturity —is taxed at 25 percent and only when finally realized by sale or redemption. Assume that the bond matures in 1972. The yield before taxes is 4.13 percent. If the owner is a corporation, such as a bank subject to a combined Federal-state income tax rate of 50 percent, the yield *after* tax would be 2.06 percent if all the income were taxed as interest, but roughly 2.4 percent if the appreciation element, the $120 rise in value to maturity, were taxed as capital gain. (Yields on bank loans will not qualify for capital gains treatment.) A bank realizing capital losses finds them treated differently for tax purposes. Losses may be deducted in full from other income, *i.e.,* from income that may be subject to tax at around 50 percent. In figuring yields, the complexities involved in taking accurate account of tax elements are formidable. Experts, however, make the major factors readily available to buyers and sellers.

QUESTIONS

1. Describe three types of "debt instruments." How do promises to pay differ from orders to pay?

2. What is meant by "negotiability"? Give an example of a negotiable and of a non-negotiable instrument. What is the significance of endorsement?

3. Describe "commercial paper" and the market in which it is bought and sold.

4. What is meant by "double-name" paper? Is it "safer" than "one-name" paper? Why?

5. How does a "trade acceptance" differ from a "banker's acceptance"? How are they used?

6. What types of debt instruments are issued by the United States government? How do they differ?

7. What is a time certificate of deposit?

8. What is the difference between the money market and the capital market? How are they related to each other?

9. What is bought and sold in the money market? What factors help to make this market competitive?

10. What effect will a general rise in interest rates have on the market prices of outstanding debt? Why?

11. A bond with ten years to maturity sells at $900. Its annual coupon yield is $40. Determine the running yield and the approximate yield to maturity (ignoring taxes).

CHAPTER 7   *COMMERCIAL BANK PORTFOLIO POLICY*

LOANS of the types discussed in Chapter 4, along with currency, deposits at the Federal Reserve and in correspondent banks, and miscellaneous assets, would rarely meet all of a commercial bank's asset needs. Most banks also own bonds.[1] Such holdings in fact account for about 30 percent of commercial bank assets. This percentage is higher than before the 1930's, but below the 60 percent reached in 1945.

PURCHASE OF SECURITIES

The U.S. Treasury and many states and localities require that any bank wishing to receive deposits must pledge government debt as security. Holdings of public debt for this purpose account for about 5 percent of bank assets.

The object of a bank in adding more securities to its assets may be to help meet any one of three needs which we discuss later: liquidity, solvency, and income. The results of purchase or sale, however, will include influences which extend beyond the bank to other parts of the economy. Most important is the fact that a commercial bank's purchase of a bond can have the same effect on the stock of money as does a bank loan. The bank may seem to be using the funds deposited with it, exchanging one asset for another. When a bank acquires additional assets, however, it creates additional liabilities (deposits).

---

[1] Although the "pieces of paper" held are not always bonds, it is convenient to refer to all these assets as "bonds" except when there is specific reason to distinguish various types. Banking literature usually refers to assets of this group as "investments." However, because we use the term "investment" differently in much economic analysis, its use here will be sparing.

Difference Between Loans and
Security Holdings (Investments)

No clear line separates (1) loans from (2) purchase of bonds or other securities. The bonds which a bank acquires are debts—usually of a business or a government—just as are the notes of borrowers. A few distinctions, however, apply generally: an investment security is usually purchased in the open market and may be sold there at any time; any one bank ordinarily holds only a part of the total issue; bonds have maturities that generally extend beyond those of the typical bank loan; the bank acquiring a security rarely deals directly, as it does in lending, with the borrower.

Securities That a Bank May Buy

The laws governing commercial bank ownership of securities are both precise and vague.[2] Except for (1) issues of the United States government, or issues guaranteed by it, and (2) debts of state and local governments, a national bank's total holdings of the obligations of any one debtor must not exceed 10 percent of the bank's capital and surplus.[3] Otherwise, laws and their official interpretations allow banks wide discretion in (1) the selection of particular issues to buy and (2) the amounts to hold.

Congress in 1927 authorized national banks to buy "bonds, notes, or debentures commonly known as investment securities" under regulations issued by the Comptroller of the Currency.[4] His rules reflect a desire to prevent bank purchase of speculative assets; the regulations emphasize that marketability is highly desirable. Yet they do not mark clear limits, except for prohibitions against (1) the purchase of debt that is in default as to either principal or interest and (2) bonds that are convertible into stock at the option of the issuer.

[2] Member banks may own stock in their FR bank and in safety deposit and trust company affiliates. A bank receiving stock in discharge of a debt may hold it temporarily. Federal law explicitly forbids a national bank to own stock of another national bank.

[3] The 10 percent limit, and others of a technical nature, originated many years ago to meet needs of the time. Today, these rules lead to some anomalous results and occasionally put national banks at some competitive disadvantage compared with state banks and other lenders.

[4] States issue "legal lists" of bonds eligible for purchase by savings banks, life insurance companies, trustees, etc. Rulings of bank examiners constitute somewhat comparable guides, or limits, for commercial banks.

What Is Available in the Market

Today's banker seeking to buy securities finds a wide variety from which he may select. Government and corporate debts eligible for commercial bank purchase are outstanding in amounts many times as large as banks would conceivably wish to own. The increase in marketable United States government debt during World War II vastly enlarged the opportunities of commercial banks to buy securities. The detailed features of the issues—rates and forms in which interest is paid, time to maturity, security, tax features, denomination, etc.—vary widely.

Some securities are better than others—better, that is, in terms of what they will give per dollar put into them. Some are better than others for a particular bank's needs at any one time. The selection problem of a bank is now complex just because the variety of opportunities is great. A banker may, and many do, decide (perhaps unconsciously) to seek something satisfactory without necessarily "reaching" for the very best. Such a decision simplifies the problem of choice. Ignoring the variety now available may not lead to serious error. Yet the variety does exist for banks wishing to try to maximize earnings.

Risks in Holding Debt Securities

Two kinds of risk exist in the ownership of bonds: (1) The debtor may not meet the terms of the contract; (2) Interest rates in the market as a whole may rise. Both risks are undeniable, and both call for analysis, but of different kinds.

1. The first, which for simplicity we shall call the *risk of default* (sometimes termed the "credit risk"), depends upon the ability and willingness of the debtor to (a) pay interest as specified in the contract and (b) repay principal on the maturity date fixed in the agreement. Much debt outstanding today presents no appreciable default risk. Some governmental and private debt is so well secured that meeting the contract terms is about as certain as anything in life. Other debt is almost, but not quite, so free from risk of default. Still other bonds are preponderantly safe but with risk that is more than negligible. And so on down a scale of many gradations. The banker's problem is to judge the gradations.

Default may result from poor management in business, from the failure of a regulatory commission to grant adequate railroad or utility rates, from the decline of an industry for any of several reasons, from the economic difficulties of a locality which reduce taxpaying capacity, and, accentuating everything else, from general economic depression. Default on debts of foreign businesses or governments may result from restrictions on convertibility of currency (see Chapter 19), revolution, war, and political change, as well as from more familiar types of economic distress. Evaluating accurately the chances of default calls for more skill than banks sometimes recognize. History contains myriads of mistakes in judgment: buying bonds for more than they eventually "paid out," or failing to buy bonds when prices were below their eventual worth. As conditions change, so may the quality—and market price—of a bond.

Risk is less desirable than certainty. Other things the same, people will pay more for riskless than for risky bonds. Yet how much more? Risk exists because doubt exists. Views about the significance of risk in specific cases will vary. Some bonds, therefore, may sell at prices which overvalue the risk of default, others at prices which undervalue it. The relative prices of securities reflect differences ("errors") in the appraisal of chances of default.

For many years, however, the dominant tendency of bankers has been to buy only debt with such slight chance of default that the price differentials due to this risk must be small. Such conservatism may melt away as bank management moves into the hands of men who have never experienced a wave of substantial defaults. If so, some bankers, as at times in the past, will accept more than a negligible possibility of default if other terms, including the prices of bonds, seem to justify the chance of loss. Inherently, of course, it is impossible to know in advance whether the price adequately compensates for risk, or what reserves should be accumulated to offset losses.

The default risk can take two slightly different forms. (a) The more obvious appears when a business (or a government) shows some signs of being unable or unwilling to live up to the contract.[5] The *existing* economic outlook may not give positive assurance of smooth sailing for the debtor. Five years after a company has sold bonds which have 20 years to run, a banker may see that the firm's affairs have turned for the worse, an existing fact. (b) The prospects of some debtors 25 years from now will be more secure than the prospects of others. Obviously, such differences are difficult to appraise long in advance. Utilities or local governments which clearly have economic capacity to carry their existing debt for the next 5 years may have distinctly uncertain futures beyond, say, 30 years.[6]

2. The *interest-rate* risk exists because changes in conditions in financial markets will alter the balance between the supply of, and the demand for,

[5] The more that banks buy debt with long maturity, the more of this second form of risk they assume.

[6] A borrower's outstanding debt may be well within its economic capacity. However, the corporation or government may incur additional obligations at a rate above that of the growth of its ability to pay interest and principal. Fear of default may then affect all its debt.

loanable funds. The market will reflect such changes and alter the prices of outstanding bonds. A rise in interest rates will reduce the price of outstanding debt. The lack of certainty about the level of future interest rates means that there is a risk, an inescapable risk, in dealing in debt. Interest rates *will* change.

A debt contract is fixed. (Although recontracting is possible—the parties may agree in advance that some provisions are subject to change —the limits of such change will ordinarily be fixed.) Each party does the best it can under the circumstances, when making a contract or when buying or selling bonds or other debts issued earlier. Under different circumstances one or the other party might have done better; when once committed, however, neither can alter the terms of that contract. New contracts and new dealings in old contracts are quite another matter. They will reflect any changes in market conditions.

Present alternatives, not those of the past, are what count. Assume that lenders are now able to get more for the use of their funds (higher interest rates) than was possible earlier. As a result, outstanding debt which was negotiated at lower interest rate levels will be less attractive, per dollar of face value, than before. The price of old debt will sink as interest rates rise.

Three actual experiences will illustrate. An issue of 3⅞ percent Treasury bonds which sold at over 110 in 1958 sold as low as 92 in 1960. From March to September 1959 the average price of high-grade corporate bonds fell more than 5 percent. In 8 months from October 1957 one issue of Treasury notes rose from 88 to 97. Prices of bonds which are completely free from any risk of default—and which offer no chance of paying off more at maturity than face value—may rise and fall through a wide range. Capital gains and losses on top-quality bonds can be more than minor.

Significance of Time to Maturity

If a bond is near maturity (the date when it will be paid fully) even substantial changes in interest rate levels will bring only slight movements in its price. The reason is clear. Any "abnormality" in the rate of interest specified in the contract, compared with prevailing market rates, will bring loss or benefit for only a short time. If the debt has many years to run, however, its market price can get much above or below the face amount. For a long period the interest to be paid—the fixed number of dollars—in relation to face or maturity value will be above or below the rate prevailing in the market currently.

Early in 1964, for example, 3 percent Treasury bonds due 2 years later were selling for 98, while 3 percent bonds due in 1995 were selling at 98, while 3 percent bonds due in 1995 were selling at 84. But note the closeness of the yields, taking account of the rises in price that will appear as maturity approaches: 3.88 percent and 3.89 percent, respectively.

Although short-term debt can carry little interest rate risk, long-run debt can involve a substantial amount. *This risk exists even if the debtor is the United States government or the richest, most prosperous business in the country*—debtors who will pay every cent they owe on time. Their debt contracts, once fixed, become more or less attractive, *relative to others that become available,* as the economic world changes.

There is no way in which a bank can truly protect itself against such risk. Of course, if it buys only short-term issues, it can avoid all but insignificant capital losses on securities it holds. Yet it also loses any opportunity for capital gain from changes in market conditions. And if interest rates do fall, it must accept the full brunt of the decline. For example, suppose that it can buy short-term debt yielding 4 percent and long-term debt yielding 5 percent; it selects the short term. Then long-term interest rates fall while short-term rates are unchanged; it can continue to get 4 percent, but it no longer has the opportunity which it once gave up to get 5 percent. If short-term rates also fall, the bank's loss from its earlier decision not to take the 5 percent rate is even clearer.

A bank or any other lender assumes an inevitable risk. The income obtainable from a capital sum will change. Therefore, contracts which fix the income from a certain capital cannot protect against changes in the market price of the debt agreement (bond) representing that capital if new interest rates come to prevail in the market. The longer the period of a commitment, the greater the chance for unforeseen developments. An unsophisticated investor might conclude that if he is buying to hold to maturity, he need not worry. If the price falls for a time, he may feel no loss because he will not sell. But at the same time he has sacrificed the opportunity of taking advantage of more favorable conditions.

Selection of Securities

A bank trying to decide on the purchase or holding of securities should first formulate its objectives. What does it want to achieve thereby? Since there are likely to be different objectives which may conflict somewhat, the answer is less simple than may appear. Some explicit ordering of priorities is essential if the decisions are to be the best possible. It is not enough to say that the securities account should "fill in the gaps" remaining after the loan account has been arranged as well as possible—the gaps of regional or industrial diversification, liquidity, stability of price, ease of administration, etc. The banker needs some notion of the size and relative significance of any such gaps if he is to fill the right ones.

With a knowledge of objectives, a bank may itself begin to sort out specific securities to buy or sell. Because of the wide choice now available, however, few banks can be adequately staffed to do an expert job. Here the bank competes in the big leagues without, ordinarily, being a big leaguer. It must compete for investment values with the giant insurance companies, the great trust funds, the real financial experts. Major metropolitan commercial banks do maintain research groups to study the interest rate outlook in general and individual securities, issue by issue. A big bank's own investment needs as well as those of trust accounts give a large enough volume to justify the expense of adequate analysis.

Many other banks, though large, can do only part of their own job. If they attempt study of the whole market, they can hardly do well; but if they concentrate on screening for their own needs the more general recommendations made by outside sources, they can reasonably hope for good results. The sources of information may be larger correspondent banks or any of various specialized services. The great mass of small banks must rely predominantly upon outside advice. Few managers and directors of the country's thousands of banks are qualified by training, or have the time, to do a first-rate job of research on bond selection.

PRIORITIES IN ASSET POLICY

A bank, like any individual or business, must choose. One of the basic choices is how to apportion its assets among possible uses. This choice may be made with great care, but accident often plays a bigger role than is recognized and desirable. Four uses of a bank's funds can be distinguished: primary reserves, secondary reserves, customer demands, and open market purchases for income.[7] Their significance will be discussed as we proceed.

Thinking of them in terms of priorities is helpful. Nevertheless, *at the margin* all are of equal importance. The banker, in other words, will maximize only if each use is satisfied up to the point where a dollar devoted to it brings as much benefit as a dollar devoted to any of the others, but no more.

Primary Reserves

Attention first goes to what the banker may call "primary reserves"— (1) currency as needed for ordinary operations with a margin for emergen-

[7] Roland I. Robinson, *The Management of Bank Funds,* 2nd ed. (New York: McGraw-Hill Book Co., Inc., 1962).

cies, plus (2) other reserves required by law, plus (3) whatever deposits at correspondent banks are clearly necessary for smooth operations. Although the amount of primary reserves needed by a particular bank is not determinable precisely, the area of doubt is relatively small. (Although the amount of required reserves will vary with deposits, actual requirements are computed as an average for a period.)

Protective Investments (Secondary Reserves)

Second priority goes to assets which assure funds "(1) for likely and indeed almost forecastable cash needs, (2) for remote, unlikely, but possible cash needs." [8] The need for some such assets is much clearer than is the guide to the amount.

What kind of property will meet such needs? It must be something that on almost a moment's notice can be converted into cash with no more than insignificant reduction of the principal. The obvious solution is the ownership of high-quality short-term debt actively traded in the money market.

The widely used term "secondary reserves" covers this second-priority group, but it often applies rather more broadly. The term has no legal significance and does not have a clear definition in banking or economic literature. We can use it, but with caution.

Customer Credit Demands

Having assured its own safety, *i.e.,* its ability to continue to exist, a bank's third priority goes to its borrowing customers. One job of commercial banks is to make funds available to the local community, predominantly its businesses. This is a function for which the bank is (or ought to be) especially equipped, more so than any other financial agency. The function is important to the locality. And of those lending services which the bank can perform, this generally offers the recipient benefits not obtainable elsewhere—and offers the bank the greatest profit potential.

Open Market Purchase of Securities for Income

If the first three uses have not absorbed all of a bank's funds (or lending capacity), the remainder should be used as well as possible in producing additional income. Such income will serve the immediate in-

[8] *Ibid.,* p. 15.

terest of the stockholders. It can also further the long-run interest of everyone having direct or indirect dealings with the bank, assuming that some of the income will be retained to make for a stronger institution. Of course, long before a bank will buy securities to satisfy this fourth purpose, it acquires some to make up its secondary reserve—quite another matter in principle, though hard to distinguish in practice.

Note that none of these four includes one which interests the economist: namely, the bank's role in adding to, or reducing, the nation's stock of money. The omission is no oversight. The individual bank is *not* properly concerned with regulating the nation's supply of money. That is the responsibility of the central monetary authorities.

The bank's most demanding problems arise over decisions that involve the second, third, and fourth priorities. The problems are discussed now in a somewhat different framework.

PORTFOLIO MANAGEMENT

The term "portfolio," as used in modern finance, refers to the total of an institution's loans and investments. Within the freedom permitted by law, and consciously or unconsciously recognizing the four priorities, how should a bank decide the composition of this total? How may the decisions influence the economy?

Portfolio management involves the search for three broad objectives: (1) liquidity; (2) solvency; and (3) income. Challenging difficulties arise when the three conflict. A mistake in overemphasizing one may result in costly sacrifice of other objectives. Elements of both art and science are involved. The skills demanded of bank management differ markedly from those required in most other businesses. And from one bank to another the needs vary. Officers must always be alert to the peculiar, and perhaps changing, requirements and opportunities of their institution. The self-liquidating commercial loan may seem to fill all the needs. In fact, however, it fails in various ways; or, more accurately, it proves incomplete.

Liquidity

The liquidity problem of commercial banks calls for repeated emphasis. (1) Most of a bank's liabilities are payable upon demand. If the bank cannot meet them, it cannot stay in business. The demand of depositors may be for currency; more commonly, it is for a deposit at another bank, as happens when a depositor sends a check to someone in another city.　(2) Quite another need for liquidity grows out of the third priority above: A bank will be wise to retain capacity to lend on short notice to good customers or prospective customers.

A bank can satisfy liquidity demands by holding "cash"—currency in its vault and deposits at the Federal Reserve (especially those above the legal requirement) or at correspondent banks.　Yet neither form of cash —currency or demand deposits in other banks—brings any income.　(Interest-bearing time deposits in correspondent banks may be usable and, in fact, almost perfectly liquid.)　Both appear "dead weight" as far as earnings are concerned.[9]　Thus the bank has persuasive reason to "economize" such holdings.　But what is economical?

Each bank must answer this question for itself.　To do so wisely, it will study the normal day-to-day balance between inflow and outflow of funds and keep enough extra cash to meet the exceptions it observes.　It will also analyze seasonal variations and arrange for them.　The ease or difficulty of compensating for an error will influence the decision.　If the bank were to find itself with more cash than needed, would it find no obstacle, or perhaps a bit of trouble, in buying some short-term security? Would it face any practical difficulties in selling such an asset quickly to obtain cash?　These, however, are not the really serious questions.

More difficult are the problems that can arise because of uneven, unpredictable, and sudden demands for cash.　In a system made up of many individual banks rather than a few giants with branches, unusual demands may occasionally be large in relation to the single bank's resources for meeting them.　One thing that will create just such demands is a loss of depositor confidence in the bank.　In the past such demands occasionally appeared on a scale large enough to cause distress extending far beyond any one bank or region.　Fortunately, as Chapter 8 will describe, although individual banks are not completely immune, the banking system has been adapted to ward off, and to help banks meet, these depositor "runs."

Less dramatic pressures may appear in the course of ordinary affairs. A decline in local business may lead to an outward flow of deposits.　A few large depositors may draw unexpectedly on their accounts to make payments elsewhere—for inventory or capital equipment, debt repayment, or purchase of financial assets.　Some may decide to use other banks. The U.S. Treasury, too, will at times make large withdrawals from its deposits at commercial banks, though not without notice.　The inflow of funds may drop, for one or more of several reasons.

Larger outflow, smaller inflow, or both can generate enough pressures on primary reserves to embarrass the bank.　If it has kept legal reserves

---

[9] The services provided by a correspondent bank, though not a form of money income, are aids to the earning of income.

at what seemed a reasonable minimum, a small decline in deposits may be large in relation to the assets that are freely available to meet demands. The deposit slide, of course, reduces the legal reserves which the bank must hold, but by only a fraction of the decline in deposits. The legal reserve, though in one sense perfectly liquid, can give only narrowly limited help in meeting liquidity needs; the assets that constitute legal reserves can be used to satisfy customer demands for funds only at a cost, such as a penalty charge paid to the Federal Reserve.

To meet exceptional needs for liquidity, banks look to their *secondary reserves* (protective investments).[10] These are assets which can be sold on very short notice—in a matter of minutes in the major financial centers —without risk of appreciable loss of value. The appeal of these assets for this purpose results from a combination of two kinds of confidence—confidence in finding a buyer (marketability), and great assurance that sudden sale will not cause significant loss by depressing the price.

But who buys? The purchaser may be another bank, perhaps one receiving more cash than ordinarily (conceivably from the depositor who is withdrawing from the bank that is selling). Or the buyer may be a dealer who specializes in such assets and now purchases to help "make a market" or to build his inventory. Sometimes the buyer is a business with funds for temporary investment. The individual bank can always find buyers. Such assets do make *it* liquid.[11]

From the mid-1930's until after World War II, short-term, highly liquid assets brought yields much below those obtainable from the less liquid securities. For example, Treasury bills in the late 1930's yielded less than one-half of 1 percent and bankers' acceptances about 1 percent. Longer-term Federal and state-local bonds brought well over 2 percent, mortgages and business loans substantially more. Consequently, ownership of the most liquid short-term debt at the sacrifice of business loans, mortgage loans, or long-term government bonds involved significant loss

[10] Liquidity differs from saleability. Long-term government bonds can be sold immediately; over a few weeks, however, the price obtainable may vary, perhaps by as much as a full year's interest, or more. The bond is saleable but not liquid as we use the term.

[11] Can the liquidity of the financial system as a whole be assured? Domestically, *i.e.,* ignoring international aspects, it can. The essential requirement is an agency "outside" the system which can inject new money in paying for securities. If necessary, it can buy to absorb an increase in offerings of securities by banks and other sellers. In this respect the Federal Reserve can be a buyer from "outside" the commercial banking system. Ordinarily, the money that one bank and its customers give up goes to others. Liquidity (cash) shifts around but does not grow. The liquidity of the commercial loan, for example, depends upon the existence of buyers able and willing to pay for what the borrower has to sell; his commodities are not money, not liquid. Arrangements which meet the needs of individual banks to liquidate assets do not necessarily solve what may be the bigger liquidity problem; but our concern now is for the bank, not the system.

of earnings. More recently, however, the differential has been much less. The cost of getting liquidity by owning short-term assets has generally been moderate but not negligible—around one percentage point.

Another method of meeting liquidity needs is the spacing of loan and security maturities to bring a continuous inflow of funds, or an inflow adjusted to probable variations in the need for cash. Loans repayable in installments often qualify well on this score. The bank can also adjust the rate at which it makes new loans or investments to help meet any changes in liquidity needs. If a large portion of total loan volume is short-term, the bank may seem amply protected. In fact, however, loans, even good ones, are not always collectible when due. Borrowers expect renewals, especially when economic pressure is heavy; the bank's good customers must be accommodated; the interests of the locality cannot be ignored. The fraction of short-term loans that is truly liquid may be hard for the banker to estimate accurately. And even if his portfolio puts heavy emphasis on longer-term bonds, it may in fact be effectively liquid if maturities are spaced so that at all times some securities are within a year or so of the date on which the borrower will pay every dollar specified.

Finally, a bank can arrange to borrow from other banks, and in the case of member banks from the Federal Reserve. As a means of meeting liquidity needs, however, borrowing can rarely serve more than temporarily.

Solvency

A bank is solvent when its assets are worth enough to meet all its deposit liabilities (financial obligations).[12] These obligations are in dollar terms. Insolvency means not only that the owners have lost what they put in but also that claims of depositors cannot be met fully. A bank may operate while insolvent—year after year if the insolvency is not discovered. It may be able to meet the demands made on it every day because these demands never equal the total that might be made at any one time. Yet if examining officers discover the insolvency, as they are likely to do, or if depositors make exceedingly heavy demands, the bank will perhaps be forced to close. Insolvency has caused many bank failures and enormous harm to the public.

What will cause insolvency? Losses on bad loans and a drop in the market value of securities in the bank's portfolio may suffice to wipe out a bank's capital. Occasionally, a commercial loan which seems fine will turn sour for any of several reasons. In a recession many such loans can

---

[12] Capital, surplus, and undistributed profits are not treated as obligations for this purpose. If assets are worth more than the liabilities to depositors but not by so much as owners have provided, capital is impaired, but the bank is solvent.

get into difficulty. The dangers depend upon the size of the bank's capital (including surplus and undistributed earnings) in relation to assets whose worth is not certain. Actual declines in asset prices may come from default (or fear of default) by the borrower or from interest rate changes.

Trouble tends to arise from this fact: Loans with the greatest risk frequently offer the largest opportunity for earnings. Such loans are often of the type which seems to serve the most pressing needs of business. These are the needs of the small, local, growing firm at almost any time, and the needs of still more businesses when conditions are depressed. A bank may risk its solvency in pursuing normal and proper objectives—the profit obtainable for itself from an extra third or so in gross yield from accommodating businesses which seem really to need funds and which willingly pay interest rates above those on more secure loans. Many such risks are taken with good results. Yet some disappointments are inevitable. To protect its solvency, the bank must keep losses few in number and small in size. Laws and regulations, imposed in part to preserve solvency, prevent some errors.[13]

Income

The earnings aspect of portfolio management must be related to needs for both liquidity and solvency.[14] In the short run, in fact, income considerations must be subordinated to the others, or seem to be. What may appear to be a conflict in the short run disappears as one takes a longer view; the best earnings in the long run require careful respect for liquidity and solvency needs.

Obviously, a bank needs income to pay wages and other operating expenses. Hopes of profit have led owners to provide the capital that makes the bank possible. Profit in fact, as well as in expectation, is necessary if the banking system is to prosper and to serve the public well.

One starts by looking at the gross interest yield of different loan and investment opportunities. Ordinarily, this is easy to determine; the net yield, however, is not. For example, the market price may fluctuate. If an asset must be sold either to meet liquidity needs or to take advantage

---

[13] Another factor lies somewhat beyond the banker's own control. Whether under the law a bank is deemed to be solvent will depend not only upon the assets it owns but also upon their valuation for legal purposes. Value is not always crystal clear. Sometimes the doubt ranges widely. The standards of asset valuation, then, may be important in determining solvency. These standards can influence the composition of the portfolio. Chapter 9 discusses the rules applied by bank examiners.

[14] Banks distinguish between "earnings" and "profit." Speaking generally, the former corresponds to the difference between operating income and operating expense. Profit consists of earnings plus or minus net realized gain or loss on loans and investments.

of new and better opportunities; if market prices of one type of asset change relative to the prices of others; if a borrower does not repay the full amount due; or if a loan is repaid unexpectedly—if these or other comparable developments occur, the bank may get, or be able to get, more or less than foreseen when it acquired an asset. Consequently, when a loan is made or an asset purchased, prediction of the *net* yield is subject to more than a minor margin of error. Occasional losses are inevitable and must be treated as normal operating expense. But what is the proper allowance to make on the average? Views may differ considerably.

The cost of servicing assets will affect the difference between gross and net earnings. Some loans and investments can be handled with slight expense; others cost a good deal to service (relative to gross yield), even with the best of equipment and methods. A few loans will cause so much trouble, chiefly the time of responsible officials, that servicing expense eats up all the income and even more. Within wide limits the costs of administering a loan of a particular type are about the same whether the loan is small or large; therefore, the larger the loan, the greater the percentage of gross income that becomes net.

Important expenses of a bank are largely fixed, at least for short periods—vaults, office equipment, most of the staff. The short-run marginal cost of administering any one loan can be very slight. Long-run average costs, of course, are likely to be much higher. The decision about making any one loan, or buying any one investment, can rest on the fact that it *alone* may add only a tiny amount to operating cost. A single loan's contribution to net profit can be much greater per dollar than the average. A bank's net income can vary significantly, depending upon the volume of operations.

Sensitive concern for income will lead a bank to adapt its lending to help build opportunities for future earnings. The purchase of a short-term government security—instead of lending to a local firm—may offer a comfortable and definite return with no chance of loss over the next year or so. Yet such "playing safe" offers no opportunity to expand profitable lending or to attract deposits. If a business will grow more with the bank's loan accommodation than without it, the bank itself stands to earn more over the years.

A bank's long-run earning and growth prospects are likely to be bound up with the locality. Loans favoring local businesses and residents can bring a bank benefits that are not to be expected when it uses its resources to buy securities in the national money markets. As we emphasized in Chapter 3, a bank's prosperity depends upon its success in building up its deposits. Most deposits of most banks come from local persons or firms. Some sacrifice of other conditions desirable in lending and investment policy is justified to help build deposits and also to advance such other income-producing activities as trust administration. When lending capacity is strained, out-of-town borrowers may reasonably, if reluctantly, be turned down to favor those at home.

Seasonal demands of customers require careful study. A bank's earnings will depend upon how fully it keeps "loaned up." Banks do have an advantage over most businesses. Loans and investments earn income every day, Sundays and holidays included, whether or not the bank is open and its personnel are at work. On the other hand, every day that lending capacity is not used—that "funds" are idle—is a day lost forever as a source of income to a bank. Consequently, there tends to be an earning advantage in assets which have a long life or which do not mature on a rigid schedule. Bonds, call loans, and commercial paper bought and sold in the open market are attractive in this respect. Unexpected repayment is not common, and any time a bank does get repaid it can at once "put the money to work" again. A loan, however, is more obviously a two-sided affair. It comes into existence only if there is a "demander," someone wanting to borrow. The bank's directors cannot just decide to lend more and proceed to carry out the policy. Conditions of demand for loans will affect the outcome.

Net profit also depends upon the tax treatment of different types of income. (1) Interest on state and local government debt is exempt from Federal income tax. Interest from Federal debt is exempt from state tax. Corporation income tax rates around 50 percent (on income over $25,000), and a rise in gross yields from state-local debt, have combined to induce commercial banks to raise their holdings of tax exempts from $5 billion in 1947 to over $30 billion in 1964. (2) Any portfolio "yields" which are taxable as long-term capital gain rather than as interest will bear only half the regular tax, because only half is included in taxable income. Losses, however, are generally deductible in full. Sometimes *tax switching* as interest rates and bond prices change can aid net profit materially; losses will be deducted in full, while half of capital gains are free from tax.

As noted earlier, the selection of securities may be made with great care and concern for maximum profit. Or the bank may settle for some "second best." Many banks follow more or less general rules, with prominent weight given to such factors as spacing maturities evenly.

PORTFOLIO CHANGES SINCE 1930

The relative importance of different kinds of assets in bank portfolios has changed markedly in the last 35 years. For highlights, see Fig. 7.1.

A large drop in loans to business after 1929 was a result of both demand and supply conditions. Demand fell because declines in both the level of prices and the volume of business reduced the need of some firms for borrowed money. They could finance depression operations with fewer dollars and perhaps without any borrowing. This condition was especially true of some large firms with best credit ratings. On the supply side, banks became more cautious. Having had bad experience with loans, they were distrustful of the ability of many applicants, under depres-

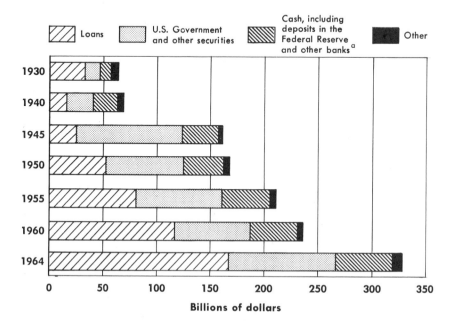

ª Coverage varies slightly for different dates.

FIGURE 7.1

**Assets of All Commercial Banks, by Type
(Selected Dates 1930–64)**

Source: *Statistical Abstract* and *Federal Reserve Bulletin*

sion conditions, to use funds successfully and to repay on schedule. Consequently, banks tended to set higher standards. This caution persisted even after banks had come to hold excess reserves and when they still needed income.

World War II changed demand and supply conditions fundamentally. Lending began to rise. The volume of industrial production expanded.

Costs rose. Businesses needed more money to finance operations. Profits multiplied. Risks dropped; some loans were guaranteed by the government. Banks had ample reserves. Lending mounted, with rising interest rates.

The rise in borrowing was not merely a wartime phenomenon. Many of the same conditions remained even after fighting stopped, though excess reserves disappeared. The profitability to business of using additional funds continued to outstrip the resources available to many firms. Bank loans to business grew.

Government securities made up only a small fraction of assets during the 1920's. In the 1930's, however, the decline in business loans and the growth of Federal debt brought bank holdings of government securities to equality with loans. With large excess reserves, banks could lend to the Treasury without sacrificing other lending opportunities. Competition for Treasury debt under such conditions drove interest rates to exceptionally low levels.[15] The money and capital market mechanisms developed so that "country" banks, as well as those in big cities, found that they could deal in short-term government debt and other money market assets. Banks became accustomed to holding government debt, to buying and selling it, and to relying upon it for a considerable part of their income.

Commercial banks bought government debt heavily when Federal budget deficits during the war multiplied Treasury demand for borrowed funds. In an important sense this lending was largely costless—to accommodate the Treasury, banks did not have to sacrifice other loan possibilities. (Servicing larger deposits, however, did add to operating expense.) The interest rate on short-term loans remained almost minuscule, as low as 0.375 percent a year, but still profitable. Shortly after the ending of hostilities, the Treasury used excess cash balances to retire some bank-held debt.

Thereafter, banks, especially those in large cities, gradually reduced their holdings of Federal debt because they saw better lending opportunities elsewhere. Among the more attractive alternatives were mortgage and other loans having United States government insurance or guarantee. Yet Federal debt still accounts for about 15 percent of gross income of member banks. The relative importance varies widely among banks. A continuous rise in time deposits has added some reason, or justification, for commercial banks to hold more long-term bonds, including those of state and local governments. Leading banks have become accustomed to altering their holdings of bonds to gain flexibility for other lending.

---

[15] Short-term rates dropped below 1 percent on top-quality obligations. Long-term Treasury issues yielded more, over 2.5 percent, but did not generally appeal to banks, which feared a decline in market price if interest rates were to rise to, perhaps, the 3.5 percent of a few years earlier.

1. Most customer loans can offer a higher rate of return than government debt. Yet almost all commercial banks hold government debt. Why? Why may municipals be preferred to Treasury obligations? Do the latter have any advantages?

2. "There are basically two types of risks in holding debt securities. When the debtor is the U.S. Treasury one of these risks is virtually eliminated; the other remains, however, and is very real indeed." Discuss.

3. Construct an arithmetic example to show that bond prices fluctuate more sharply on long-term issues than on short-term issues for a given change in the interest rate.

4. What are "primary reserves"? What function do they serve? Are they synonymous with legal reserves? With required reserves?

5. What are "secondary reserves"?

6. Why are some types of assets better for assuring bank liquidity than others? Discuss.

7. "In addition to liquidity and solvency another rather prosaic factor—income—must be taken into consideration as portfolio policy decisions are made." Discuss. How, if at all, may the various considerations conflict?

8. Under what, if any, circumstances might a bank make a commercial loan at a net interest yield below the after-tax yield from state-local government bonds?

9. Why have commercial bank holdings of Federal debt dropped in recent years even though bank assets have grown substantially?

10. Explain why bank lending to the Treasury during World War II was almost costless, whereas in doing so today a bank encounters significant cost.

11. How can a bank operating in only one city get adequate diversification in its portfolio?

12. How may objectives of portfolio policy conflict?

CHAPTER 8   *BANK FAILURES*
AND BANK SAFETY

BANK failures have characterized every financial crisis, every one of our great depressions. No one can ever know how much all of mankind have suffered because of bank failures. Is such suffering now a thing of the past? We have good reason to believe that bank failures in the future will be the exception. Beyond question, our bank deposits are very much safer than before 1935.

BANK FAILURES

The difficulties of one large English bank are charged with aggravating America's economic troubles in the early 1890's. The failure of an Austrian bank, the Credit Anstalt, precipitated the financial calamity that shook the economy of the whole world after 1931. The United States, however, has the unenviable distinction of the worst record of bank failures.

They extended over a long period; on the average, dozens of banks failed every year from the Civil War to World War I. Throughout the generally prosperous 1920's, about 600 banks failed each year. Then conditions grew even worse.[1] The three years 1930–1932 brought over 5000 failures. And by March 1933 strains were so bad that President Roosevelt ordered every bank closed temporarily. Even though most re-opened soon, the country had 4000 fewer banks at the end of 1933 than a year earlier. But a mighty reform had begun. Since 1940 only around 80 banks—most of them very small—have failed. Today's college student, having grown up in an era almost without bank failures, needs a brief description to understand their significance.

---

[1] The banking situation deteriorated very much more than underlying economic conditions in any sense required.

Nature and Cause of Bank Failures[2]

A bank, like any business, will be considered a failure if it cannot pay its debts when they fall due. The position of a commercial bank, however, differs significantly from that of other businesses. Most bank obligations are payable upon demand, and others (time deposits) are payable on short notice.

A bank's inability to honor its obligations may, as we have seen, develop from two rather different sources: (1) insolvency, where the assets may not be worth enough; or (2) lack of liquidity, where assets may not be salable quickly enough to get the cash demanded. American insistence upon unit banking, and the small size of most of our banks, have made them susceptible to both types of economic illness.

As long as an ordinary business, such as a retail store or a manufacturer, can pay its debts to the reasonable satisfaction of persons demanding payment, it will continue to operate. It may do so even though at any one time it is unable to pay all it owes. Banks, however, must report the major outlines of their financial position to government authorities. Official examiners look carefully, not only at the bank's records, but also at what it actually has on hand. Therefore, if a bank's assets are not worth enough to meet its obligations, the insolvency is likely to become known. Unless the deficiency is corrected promptly, the authorities will demand that the bank cease operating. It cannot then incur additional obligations, and its assets can be preserved for equitable distribution to all depositors.

Bankers and regulatory authorities, although there may be doubt about valuation of many items, usually know whether a bank is on the right side of the solvency line. To determine the adequacy of liquidity is more difficult. Whatever suffices one day may be excessive, or inadequate, the next. So much depends upon what depositors do! If many suddenly decide to exercise their legal right to demand cash payment at once, they create a serious danger for the bank—and for themselves and other depositors.

Insolvency arises from trouble over assets.[3] One sort of trouble comes from the hankering of bank employees, or owners, for money. Occasionally, but rarely, they yield to temptation and take enough from the vault to make a bank insolvent. Banks try to protect themselves by purchasing insurance ("bonding" employees), but the temptation to keep costs down sometimes leads to inadequacy of coverage. More important

---

[2] Banks before the establishment of the Federal Reserve sometimes suspended payments in currency while continuing to honor checks.

[3] For individuals, in contrast, insolvency may arise from an increase in liabilities, such as a damage claim resulting from an auto accident.

as a source of difficulty are assets that do not prove to be worth as much as the banker expects when he accepts them. Many banks have had too little capital for the risks they have assumed. Hindsight shows that wiser management would have kept risks more in line with capital and earning power. The local nature of each unit bank deprived many of opportunity for reasonably adequate diversification.

Businesses are not always able to repay loans in full. The supposedly self-liquidating loan "freezes." The borrower's note turns out to be worth less than its face amount; if the borrowing firm itself goes bankrupt, as hundreds over the country do each month, the note may be worth much less than the amount loaned by the bank. What in good times is mediocre banking appears to be incompetent in bad times—and this country has had a distressing number of bad years. Even when business in general is good, crop failures, depression for a key local business, or poor management make some loans uncollectible.

A person who has borrowed to buy stock and pledged it as collateral may not have cash to pay, and the collateral may fall in price. Or the bank may have made mortgage loans which will not be paid on schedule; the market value of the underlying real estate may be less than the amount due. Bonds purchased as investments have sometimes fallen enough in price to embarrass a bank. Unfortunately, misfortunes of these varied types tend to pile up more or less at the same time, *i.e.,* during economic recession. Bank capital has melted away in declining asset prices, and insolvency has then closed banks' doors.

The typical *liquidity* problem is associated with a sharp increase in depositor demands for cash. Why should many depositors, or a few large ones, suddenly raise their demands for cash? The chief explanation is that depositors lose confidence in their ability to get cash from the bank if they wait. Fearing that the bank may close, they sense that protection against annoying inconvenience, perhaps serious loss, requires immediate withdrawal of their money. When many get in this mood, they start a "run" on the bank, an almost sure-fire way to force the bank closing they fear.[4] The merely psychological, purely emotional, element can be decisive. Such a run, started perhaps by failure of another bank or by a rumor, with or without foundation—possibly even malicious in origin—may bring ruin within a few days (or hours). It may do so even to a

---

[4] Runs may consist of depositors in long lines waiting for their turn at the withdrawal window. The strain may degenerate into true panic; it may, however, disappear if the bank displays evidence of ability to meet demands. A less obvious type of run develops when large depositors draw down their accounts substantially and suddenly. Perhaps they merely stop making new deposits, while continuing to withdraw from existing deposits. In such a situation the bank's managers may have a chance to forestall disaster by satisfying the uneasy depositors.

bank which had been comfortably solvent and with ample cash for usual demands. On occasion the total currency resources of the locality have proved inadequate, and transport from other areas has been too slow to meet the emergency before banks have been forced to close.

Trouble may develop on a broader scale if people seek to get gold to send abroad. Such a gold run may force the whole monetary system to contract, and perhaps by a multiple of the gold loss. Few persons now alive have experienced such a condition in this country. But troubles which arise in the domestic economy of one country, and seriously affect major conditions there, will have repercussions in other lands as well.

Effects of Bank Failures Before 1935

A bank failure (or to lesser extent suspension of payments) brings a variety of distresses. Let us sketch the results as they used to develop before the reforms of the 1930's. The freezing of deposits is miserable for depositors; dislocation and distress spread rapidly and broadly. Individuals and businesses cannot pay their debts, except with funds that they happened to have outside the bank. The man who was prosperous yesterday may be unable to pay his milk bill today. Those, including consumers and producers, who must repay their loans to the closed bank—loans which would have been renewed—are forced to reduce buying below what it normally would have been.

People within the community understand and try to be tolerant. Barter can meet some needs. Yet transactions outside the immediate locality cannot be settled by barter, even with the best of good will. An inevitable contraction of the volume of business plagues not only the town where the bank failed but others far away where money is not being received for past shipments and where incoming orders drop. Trouble breeds more trouble at many points.

The brood of difficulties includes forced liquidation of the failed bank's assets. A supervisory authority appoints someone to wind up the affairs and gradually pay off depositors as fully as possible. The bank's assets must be disposed of for cash. Some bonds can be sold on national markets without depressing prices, but selling on any large scale—as is probable when many banks fail—can force bond prices down enough to embarrass other financial institutions.

The notes of local businesses, and local real estate loans, present stubborn difficulties. The businesses which have borrowed from the bank will have suffered from the tying up of their deposits and from general economic disruption in the community. Yet they must try to find cash to meet the demands of the bank receiver. With such an overhanging obligation, a firm will find it hard, perhaps nearly impossible, to locate another supplier or bank to grant new credit. Since the company's borrowing from the bank may have played an important part in financing its operations, it now finds the going extremely difficult. In effect, the business is expected to increase its savings (reduce debt) just when its ability to earn income has been substantially impaired. Many a business has been forced by bank failure to discharge workers, reduce inventory, and delay purchase of plant and equipment.

The bank's receiver will try to sell, not only the bonds owned by the bank but also property, including the real estate, held as collateral for loans which are not paid off in cash; the sales depress prices that are already weak. Even the knowledge that such properties must eventually be sold will tend to send prices down. New investors and lenders will hold off, hoping for the lower price. Moreover, other lenders, including banks, find the value of their assets, and hence their solvency, threatened.

Bank failure deprives the community of banking facilities. The difficulties thus created are more than mechanical. If the closed bank has been the only one in town, its loss will hinder the efficient conduct of business. Using currency to make payments is cumbersome and risky. Dealing with out-of-town banks for depositing and clearing of checks is a nuisance. Businesses will find difficulty in developing new banking relations which permit borrowing, even at a bank surviving in the community. One reason, for example, is that losses in the closed bank will have weakened the financial position of its depositors and thus made them less promising as borrowers who will be able to repay.

The slowing of business will have dulled the prospects of profitable use of borrowed funds. Other banks become more cautious, possibly even reducing loans to their regular customers, just to avoid the chances of getting into trouble; their reserves are limited. The personal ties which influence the extension of bank loans cannot always be developed quickly. Consequently, business suffers from partial paralysis because firms can borrow less than before—and less, even, than their prospects may justify. Rebuilding financial institutions to serve the locality as well as before may require years.

Even after waiting a year or more, depositors ordinarily recovered less, perhaps much less, than the amount they had had in their accounts.

Bank failure is a kind of trouble that typically spreads. Confidence is undermined. If one bank closes, people get afraid that others will fail. The psychology of alarm grows; the forces of business contraction feed on their own degree of intensification—perhaps gradually, perhaps fearfully. And here is an indispensable element of the explanation of the severity of business depressions in this country before World War II.

City banks were subject to difficulties of a special type. Their "country" correspondent banks, to meet customer demands, would draw on deposits in the city bank.[5]   If a city bank closed, the deposits of correspondent banks became immobilized, multiplying trouble.   Banks tried to help each other.   Yet they generally found their combined power narrowly limited, unless they could turn to a central bank which had both the power and the willingness to create money.[6]

Today our banks seem safe.   What accounts for our present sense of confidence in bank safety?   For one thing, there is governmental supervision of banks; for another, deposit insurance.   In addition, the Federal Reserve has ample ability to supply funds and would undoubtedly do so; in the early 1930's, unfortunately, the "Fed" failed to utilize its powers in time and on the scale which conditions required.

BANK EXAMINATION

Federal and state examination of bank operations is a continuing element of government effort to protect the public.

Although a bank's directors are responsible for seeing that it is run as the law requires, and as prudently as needed to protect stockholders, sad experience has shown that neither owners nor depositors can rely fully upon the competence and judgment of the directorate.   Nor can they trust free competition to produce good banking.   The competitive process would tend to eliminate weak banks, but in doing so it would work considerable hardship.   Much money entrusted to banks by depositors, much capital, many jobs, and valued sources of borrowing have vanished because of poor banking.   The public, therefore, seeks to protect the general interest (including that of the stockholders) not only by laws and regulations but also by occasional investigation to see that they are being obeyed.

Several different agencies examine banks: the Comptroller of the Currency (national banks); the Federal Deposit Insurance Corporation (insured banks not in the FR); the Federal Reserve (state member banks); and the various state banking authorities.   Overlapping, duplication, and inconsistency in examination standards, though not yet eliminated, are less annoying to banks now than in the past.[7]   (Neither the FR nor the FDIC will rely upon the reports of state bank examination, but FDIC and FR examinations are often conducted jointly with those by the state.)   A

[5] This greater susceptibility provided the original reason for higher reserve requirements for New York, Chicago, and certain other city banks which were likely to hold relatively large deposits for correspondent banks.

[6] Before the Federal Reserve was established, with the power to create money as needed in emergency, groups of banks operating through clearing house associations sometimes issued certificates which were used to settle transactions.

[7] FR officials object to proposals to shift the System's examining duties to the FDIC to reduce inconsistency.   They argue that the knowledge gained from examination assists in the general regulation of banks and also in making and executing monetary policy.

special training system for examiners of national banks has operated for many years. Facilities for training examiners of state banks have differed greatly in quality; what many states could not afford individually is now being done cooperatively at the University of Illinois by a newly established school for training state bank examiners. Examination rules have been modified to emphasize long-run factors. Banks bear the costs, which, however, continue to rise. Room for economy certainly exists—cutting the time of bank officers in answering the same question for different purposes, reducing the effort spent on inquiry which the bank's own internal checking system will control, adaptation of examination reporting forms to new forms of mechanical accounting, etc.

The *examiner seeks to find facts.* In addition, he may recommend to the bank and to his supervisors how operations might be improved. Examiners come to a bank without prior warning. They begin work when the bank is closed for regular business, immediately sealing vaults and records and making a quick check on currency holdings and certain other key matters. Then over a period of days or weeks they examine various aspects of operations, permitting the bank staff to have access to vaults and records.

Examiners pay most attention to assets. To compare liabilities as shown on bank records with what depositors believe the bank owes them is exceedingly difficult. The inability to check accurately and systematically on recorded deposit totals is unfortunate because falsification of records of liabilities (deposits) is the most common method used in defrauding a bank. Spot checking of a sample of deposit accounts, however, can help.

The major purpose of examination is not to detect fraud or embezzlement. If there has been such, the examiner may find it. Moreover, the inevitability of outside examination must help offset the temptation to falsify and steal. Yet the dominating objective of examination is to learn whether the bank is operating within the limits that protect the public interest from unwise, though perhaps perfectly honest, banking. Are loans well made? Are borrowers being required to meet the terms of their agreements? Does the bank actually possess the securities that it claims to hold as collateral? Are loans and investments valued accurately, and losses charged adequately? Is there diversification and lack of favoritism to officers or directors? Is capital being enlarged with liabilities? Are general operating practices safe and sound? Is management competent?

The examiner will "comment" upon specific items, such as loans that seem poor. He may make recommendations about general practices. Such suggestions can help a bank appreciably, for examiners get a wide variety of experience and can draw upon knowledge which is not generally available to the officers of a single bank, especially a small one. However, examiners' recommendations do not ordinarily have the force of directives and will not usually be enforceable if the bank fails to act. National banks do not see the confidential section prepared by the examiner for the Comptroller.

The 1920's revealed a weakness of the examination system, one which unfortunately accentuated business fluctuations. When business generally was flourishing, examiners tended to accept bank valuations of assets and bank judgments about borrowers. This practice eased loan expansion in the upward phase of a business cycle. During a recession, however, examiners insisted that loans were not always worth as much as the banker reported. Some had to be "written down," producing a book loss that was charged against capital accounts, threatening solvency. If the examiner saw evidence that the borrower's business was deteriorating, the bank might be pressed to reduce the loan, adding to the borrower's troubles. Moreover, if the market price of bonds, even government bonds, fell, examination rules required that the bank value them at the reduced market price. This, too, brought book losses, weakening the reported capital position and reducing the ability, and certainly the willingness, of banks to lend. Business suffered.

In essence, liquidity and solvency objectives were being mixed or confused. For determining solvency, immediate, short-run liquidity standards were being applied to the valuation of assets. This was done even when no immediate liquidation was required and when the dollars obtainable in the longer run would be substantially greater. If banks were told to sell assets (perhaps because the quality seemed to have deteriorated) the selling depressed market prices, added to losses generally, and put additional pressure on other banks.

Today, bonds of the quality generally held by banks are valued at what the bank paid for them even if the current market price is less. (If the bank paid above par, the excess must be charged off gradually.) Thus transitory market conditions are subordinated to what seems to be the potential of ultimate realization. Lower-grade bonds (not in default) are valued at the average price of the last 18 months; half of any net loss of worth must be deducted in computing capital. Bonds in default and common stock must be carried at the market price. Consumer loans more than 90 days delinquent must be charged off in full—probably not unreasonable; but to class all delinquent mortgage loans as substandard takes no account of the worth of underlying real estate.

It has been suggested that bank examination policies might vary to exert a countercyclical effect—becoming more exacting in periods of rising business and laxer during recession. However, the practical possibilities of constructive results are narrowly limited. The present system seems tolerably satisfactory, at least as long as banks have a considerable portion of high-quality, short-term assets and do not face liquidity crises just when bond prices are depressed.

Two or three times a year the government "calls" upon banks, presumably without prior warning, for extensive detail on their financial position. This information permits the authorities to make a general check upon each bank.[8] In some cities clearinghouse associations also examine member operations. Large banks generally have their own internal auditing staffs which constantly check upon the work of the rest of the bank; many banks hire outside auditors.

These arrangements provide substantial assurance that banks comply with the law. The process also assures the review, often the critical and constructive review, of some of the intangible factors that are so important in banking. Examination, however, does not prevent poor, nor assure good, judgment by bankers. It does not make good laws nor necessarily lead to the best of regulations. And, of course, examination cannot change features of a banking structure which might be inherently weak.

DEPOSIT INSURANCE

Fortunately, however, one basic change made in the 1930's profoundly improved the banking structure. Most of us can sleep with assurance that in the unlikely event that our bank were to fail we would not lose a penny. The improved position, an improvement somewhat like that which was gradually achieved in the nineteenth century in bettering the quality of bank notes, owes much to the insurance of deposits.

Hoping to avoid the evils of bank failures, 8 states, led by Oklahoma in 1908, set up systems by guaranteeing the deposits in state banks. For some years these systems seemed moderately successful, but they proved inadequate when the strain became heavy, especially because of agricultural distress in the states involved. By the late 1920's all had failed, as had the guarantee systems which were tried before the Civil War. Although the record did not necessarily prove that insuring deposits was impossible, it reinforced a widespread doubt that any system, even one with risks distributed over the whole nation, could be successful. There was even a question, especially among bankers, as to whether a try was desirable.

Leading Congressmen, however, insisted. They were responding to what was undoubtedly a real, if not a clearly formulated, public demand. The Federal Deposit Insurance Corporation was established in 1934. Each bank pays a premium which is determined by fixed rules. This is all

---

[8] In fact, however, call dates have coincided with end-of-quarter reporting dates. Who could be surprised? For those dates when statements are published, banks engaged in "window dressing" to show a more favorable impression than the facts justified. In 1963, however, the Comptroller of the Currency surprised the banking world by announcing an unexpected call date. While having the disadvantage of reducing the comparability of statistics from year to year, this action helped bring into the open, and then possibly reduce, "window dressing."

of the bank's responsibility for costs. Foolish lending by some banks, or just bad luck, will not raise the costs to other banks.[9]

The coverage is wide. Every bank belonging to the Federal Reserve must have deposit insurance; most others, including mutual savings banks, have met the requirements, so that banks with about 99 percent of deposits belong.[10] Risks are spread over the entire country. Moreover, the amount of risk is limited to the first $10,000 of each person's (or firm's) account in each insured bank. Any depositor can multiply his protection by establishing accounts in several banks, but large companies can generally have only a small fraction of their total deposits covered. Each member of a family may maintain an insured account in a single bank.

The system also includes provisions for helping prevent the development of trouble and hence the need to pay claims. Bank examination gives the FDIC an opportunity to detect weakness and to start remedial action before trouble snowballs.[11] The FDIC has developed ways of working unobtrusively. Where trouble does occur, FDIC aid comes smoothly and in ways that create a minimum of disturbance to the local economy.

Insured banks pay a gross premium of 1/12 of 1 percent of their total deposits including interbank deposits but excluding those of the U.S. Treasury (for which banks pledge special security). Premiums have been more than ample to cover losses. The reserve grew to be so large that Congress in 1950 provided for annual premium refunds; as long as the reserve is above $1 billion, 60 percent of the excess of premiums over operating expenses will be returned to insured banks.

When a bank needs help, the FDIC may do one of four things: (1) It may let the bank close and pay each depositor up to $10,000 in cash or a deposit at another insured bank; (2) While permitting the bank to close, the FDIC may set up a new national bank and establish accounts for depositors of the old bank, dollar for dollar, up to $10,000; (3) It may lend to the bank, purchase assets, or make deposits so that the bank can continue to operate; this method is especially appropriate if the difficulty centers around liquidity; (4) The FDIC may arrange to merge the bank with another insured bank, guaranteeing the latter against loss.

[9] This statement is not strictly true because very heavy losses by the FDIC would endanger the refunds which all members now receive from excess premiums.

[10] To get insurance, state banks that are not in the FR system must agree not to pay interest on demand deposits and to subject themselves to various other rules, including examination by the FDIC. Original plans envisioned use of deposit insurance to bring more banks into the Federal Reserve by eventually limiting insurance to member banks.

[11] This provision does much to meet certain early objections to deposit insurance. One was that good banks would suffer from the incompetence or rascality of other bankers. Another was that insurance would remove the incentives of depositors to insist upon high standards of bank management; bank examiners can probably do as well as any but a few depositors, and far better than most, to discourage bad banking.

The FDIC relies primarily upon the fourth method. This and the third provide protection for *all* deposits, not merely the first $10,000. These methods also minimize adverse publicity and threats to confidence. Continuation of banking facilities for the community, especially borrowing relations, is assured more readily than if a new bank must be established.[12]

After arranging an adjustment, the FDIC proceeds to help manage affairs to get as much as is possible out of the assets of the troubled bank. It shares in the total amount recovered on the basis of the proportion of insured to total deposits. Originally, the FDIC had $150 million capital subscribed by the Treasury and nearly as much from the Federal Reserve banks. All has been repaid. Losses have been $30 million since 1934, while operating costs have been small. No expense has fallen on the Treasury. To meet extreme needs, the FDIC may borrow up to $3 billion from the Treasury.

The FDIC provides a vast reservoir of liquidity for specific banks and the entire financial system. Insured banks can count upon effective help in a liquidity crisis. In essence, the money-creating mechanism of the national government can be used in an emergency to make the banking system liquid. Each year the FDIC discovers a few banks which, though not on the brink of closing, show evidence of being in danger. If there is apparent delay in correcting defects, the FDIC will threaten to withdraw deposit insurance. In most cases the threat brings reform.

Might the present system be improved? Would it not be wise to require all banks to join? There *is* a national interest in the banks of every community. Trouble that starts with one bank failure can spread. Business suffers, even in communities removed from the one where the bank closed. Nevertheless, the danger of widespread distress growing out of failure of uninsured banks appears slight.

Increasing the amount insured above the first $10,000, is desirable. (The insurance charge applies to all deposits, not just to the amount insured.) Removal of the inducement to spread deposits over several banks would save depositors trouble; banks having fewer but larger accounts could render a bit better service. Owners of large deposits would have no reason to draw down their accounts on suspicion of trouble, action which itself can *cause* distress for a bank.

---

[12] A dozen or so bank failures in 1963–65 revealed a risk largely overlooked before. In some cases persons from outside the community bought enough of the stock of a bank to gain control, apparently at very enticing prices. The new owners then made loans outside the community, loans which bank examiners later declared sub-marginal or worthless. The recipients of the loans allegedly had close ties to the new owners of the banks, used up the loan proceeds, and then were unable to pay back the loan. Regulatory authorities have inadequate power to prevent such "looting" because shifts in bank ownership and control can occur, the loans made, and the funds transferred from the bank before officials have notice of any change. The publicity growing out of recent failures may have weakened somewhat public confidence in banks generally. Any such result is indeed regrettable.

Moreover, if insured banks were to close, the immobilization of deposits above $10,000 would hurt the general economy. Most such accounts are owned by businesses, and frozen deposits will not meet payrolls, buy raw materials, or pay taxes. The welfare of the masses, therefore, is involved in the insurance of large deposits; extension of coverage would not be chiefly a rich man's gain. The added cost would probably be insignificant, but it might not—and the chief obstacle to greater coverage is the fact that the dollar losses would be higher.

An excellent record of bank safety over 30 years does not assure equal success in the future. Though prospects look good, one cannot be positive that arrangements now in existence will meet all the needs that may arise. Somewhat comparable confidence proved ill-founded a generation ago when the Federal Reserve failed to prevent financial disaster. Bank capital, surplus, and undivided profit remain lower in relation to deposits than some observers believe to be desirable for the public. Perhaps more loans of poor quality are being made than bankers allow for in setting up loss reserves.

OTHER PROVISIONS

The insurance and guarantee of many loans contribute to bank safety by reducing the chances of large loss. The development of a broader secondary market for mortgage loans (see Chapter 12) has made them more liquid. The monthly or quarterly amortization of many loans reduces the amount at risk and brings in funds which can help meet liquidity needs.

The prohibition of interest payment on demand deposits, and the ceiling imposed on time deposits, were adopted to discourage banks from "overcompeting" and incurring unduly high expenses. The extent to which the regulations do in fact contribute toward the intended result arouses debate. Additional protection for depositors comes from bank accumulation of reserves for losses and income tax provisions allowing tax refunds when a bank (or any business) suffers net loss.

QUESTIONS

1. "It is very possible that perfectly solvent banks may fail, whereas banks of questionable solvency may go on for years." Comment on this statement made in the early 1930's.

2. Discuss the factors which may lead to the failure of a bank.

3. What were the results of a bank failure in, say, the 1920's?

4. "Bank failures cause great hardships. Fortunately, since the 1930's, major steps have been taken which make widespread failures very unlikely if not impossible." Discuss.

CHAPTER 9 *STRUCTURE OF THE FEDERAL RESERVE SYSTEM*

THE Federal Reserve System is not a "central bank" in the European sense. Nevertheless, it has a central role in our financial system. The businessman will never deal with it directly, and yet he can never be free from its influence.

The System is partially government, partially private. It is more private than the U.S. Treasury but less so than a national bank. It is an instrument of government. Yet its decision-making methods and personnel are in important respects separated from both the political process and the ordinary authority of Congress and the Executive. It can exert tremendous influence; at the same time, however, many forces limit its power to bring about the economic results it favors. Congress has given it great powers but no specific objectives, means but no clear ends.

STRUCTURE AND GENERAL OPERATIONS

The establishment of the FR in 1914 offers one of the few examples of major banking and monetary action that was the outgrowth of legislation which in turn was the result of careful study. So much financial legislation has been a response to emergency, not the fruit of deliberate and rational analysis of how best to provide for long-run needs. True, the chief impetus for the study that led to the FR was the Panic of 1907. But Congress did allow time for study and did take advantage of the findings.

Economic conditions, of course, have changed profoundly in half a century, and we know a great deal more about how the economy operates. Has the System changed appropriately? It has certainly changed. Congress, largely under the pressure of emergency in the 1930's, has modified the applicable laws. The System on its own has evolved methods of operation that differ significantly from those envisioned when the framework was built. Nevertheless, one can find intelligent questioning about the adequacy of what has evolved, adequacy for present needs. More common appears to be the rather complacent view that the present structure needs no revision, except perhaps for minor details. Our study must not assume, uncritically, that the System is about as good as it could be.

Federal Reserve operations fall into two significantly different categories: (1) The System performs essential, but largely routine or mechanical, services; (2) It influences the supply of money and thereby the general level of the national economy. Although what it does on one score will affect accomplishment on the other, the two types of operation are largely different. Conceivably, one might be done well, the other poorly. To understand either, however, one needs some grasp of the framework.

Board of Governors

At the top is the Board of Governors. This body is the chief agency for giving unified direction to a system which otherwise lacks essential elements of a central bank. The Board has seven members (governors) appointed for 14-year terms by the President of the United States, subject to Senate confirmation; he designates one as chairman, one as vice-chairman, for 4-year terms. Congress in 1935, in a move to reduce Treasury influence over the FR, removed from ex officio membership the Secretary of the Treasury and the Comptroller of the Currency. Compensation is low in comparison with that of top officials throughout the banking system who have only a small fraction of the responsibility. (The Governors receive less salary than several of their employees.) Every second year the term of one member expires. No president can "pack" the Board or assure that a majority will be generally sympathetic to Administration policies. Reappointment is not permitted after a person has served one full term.

The law specifies no qualifications for members but requires the President to "have due regard to a fair representation of the financial, agricultural, industrial and commercial interests and geographical divisions of the country." A member while serving (or within two years of resigning before the expiration of his term) may have no connection as officer, director, or stockholder with any bank or trust company. Members may be removed for cause by the President of the United States. Proposals to reduce the size of the Board and to make the term of Chairman coincide with that of the President receive considerable, but not unqualified, support inside and outside the System.

The Board levies on the 12 FR banks for its operating funds—about $8 million a year. Thus it is free from both Congressional and presidential control of its spending and need not fear budgetary influences on its operations.[1]

The Board, sitting in Washington, makes policy.[2] Much authority has come to it from Congress. And by virtue of its central position, the character and quality of its members, and the knowledge provided by its extensive research organization, the Board has acquired significant, though not clearly outlined, power beyond that which is specified in the law. Formally and informally, it shares power with officials of the 12 banks, the Treasury, and others.

Not the least important outside and indirect influence is that of Congress, even when no legislation is involved. Congressional pressures may exert more influence than outsiders can appreciate; any important policy, for example, will have critics in Congress. Demands for justification of whatever the System does, or fails to do, will require careful preparation of arguments and the marshaling of evidence. Board members, especially the chairman, must devote much time and energy in testifying before Congress and in other "educational" work. Tiring hours on the witness stand and dozens of public speeches are part of the job of informing and persuading the public.

The Board's monthly *Federal Reserve Bulletin* presents a wealth of statistical information and carries articles about a variety of topics. Other regular and special studies present data and analysis—rarely if ever critical of any of the System's prior actions.

The Twelve Federal Reserve Banks

The existence of 12 separate FR banks is the result of Congressional fear of centralized control of the monetary system, a desire to prevent any "Wall Street" money monopoly.[3] Might not such control, by inflexibility

---

[1] Congressional scrutiny of expenditures by the Board and the 12 banks may call public attention to outlays which a critic believes inappropriate. Such publicity doubtless leads to tighter internal control than would otherwise prevail.

[2] For two of numerous discussions of Federal Reserve activities see D. C. Hastings and R. M. Robertson, "The Mysterious World of the Fed," and G. L. Bach, "Federal Reserve Organization and Policymaking," in Committee on Banking and Currency . . . House . . . , *The Federal Reserve System after Fifty Years,* Vol. 2 (Washington: Government Printing Office, 1964), pp. 1519–25 and 1393–8, respectively.

[3] The 12 banks, however, do not compete with each other, nor with commercial banks. The First and Second Banks of the United States had aroused antagonism because they competed with privately owned commercial banks. The founders of the FR eliminated this potential source of rivalry by creating institutions to cooperate, not compete, with existing banks.

if not callous disregard, sacrifice some regions or industries to the interests of others? Congress wanted to avoid any such risk; it sought to assure diversity and regional variety. Boundaries were set to mark productive areas having more or less economic unity. Each bank is separately incorporated, with headquarters in a city important to its region's economy; twenty-four branches provide facilities in that many more cities. Thus, 36 cities where most of the country's business is done—the major metropolitan areas—have essentially equal "central bank" facilities.

The banks' capital has come from the sale of common stock to commercial banks who have become members; each member bank buys stock in an amount equal to 3 percent of its capital and surplus. The capital of the FR thus grows as member banks increase their own capital and surplus. Dividends of 6 percent, the maximum allowed, are paid annually. All additional earnings now go to the U.S. Treasury; because of large holdings of United States debt and rising interest rates, these extra profits are impressive—an estimated $910 million in the 1965 fiscal year.[4]

Each bank has nine directors grouped in classes A, B, and C, to assure representation of various interests: banks, borrowers, and the public generally. Member banks, each with one vote,[5] elect class A directors from the ranks of bankers and class B directors from industry, trade, and agriculture (generally, that is, bank customers). Class C directors, thought of as representatives of the general public, are appointed by the Board of Governors, which designates one as chairman and one as deputy. The chairman, who is also designated as Federal Reserve Agent, must have "tested banking experience," a requirement that may be interpreted broadly. Some Class C directors are economists and university officials. Terms are for three years; one term in each class expires each year.

The directors choose a president, subject to the approval of the Board of Governors. He is chief executive officer. As such, he not only supervises operations but is also responsible for carrying out policies set by Washington.

Each of the 24 branches has a separate board of directors of from three to seven members; the majority are chosen by the directors of the

---

[4] Why do not the member banks, owners of the stock of the FR banks, get the profits? These profits, unlike ordinary corporation earnings, are not the result of successful risk taking by the stockholders, nor of skillful management by their agents, the operating officers. FR profits result from special powers granted by Congress, powers which involve monetary authority and are essentially governmental. One also hears the argument that when those who operate the FR Bank have no prospect of appreciable gain or loss from changes in its charges and in interest rates generally, they may be freer to decide in the public interest alone.

[5] Voting is somewhat more complex because banks are divided into three size groups and elect by group, in which each member has one vote. Neither a few large, nor many small, banks can dominate.

parent bank, the rest by the Board of Governors. The branch manager is an official of the parent bank.

The 12 banks report weekly to the Governors and are examined periodically under the Board's direction. The presidents meet in special conferences at least three times a year to discuss matters of mutual interest —from detailed problems of operation to the broadest trends of the economy. The presidents get together on other occasions and have direct telephone connections for conversations at any time. As a result, the widely dispersed system, while allowing each legally separate unit the freedom to adapt to regional conditions, can operate on a unified and consistent basis when action involves the whole country. Today's extensive coordination is the outcome of consultation and highly developed communication arrangements rather than of dictation from Washington.

The New York Bank is the largest and most influential. The judgment and actions of its officers in day-by-day purchase and sale of government securities for the whole System in implementing open-market policy, and in major Treasury financings, have much influence on the smoothness and efficiency with which the whole monetary system operates. The New York Bank acts for the other eleven banks in most matters involving international finance. Its influence also reflects the fact that its members include the banks in the country's leading financial center, banks whose services reach to every part of the nation and to much of the world beyond.

Member Banks

In requiring all national banks to join the system, Congress assured a broad base that would include most of the country's commercial banking. Its "invitation" to other banks to become members has led state-chartered banks (including some mutual savings banks and trust companies), with about 30 percent of all the country's demand deposits, to join. Yet in refusing to try to compel state-chartered banks to join, Congress has chosen to keep the system less than fully comprehensive. In fact, most banks (55 percent of all commercial banks) are not members; though generally small, they are nonetheless important to their communities; they account for $23 billion of demand deposits, one-sixth of the national total. Nonmember banks are especially numerous in the South and West.

To join, banks with state charters must generally meet the same minimum capital requirements as national banks and convince the Board that their management is competent. They must also come under the same regulations and observe the operating conditions prescribed for other members, such as restrictions on lending practices (maximum size of loan, and loans to officers, for example), reserve levels (and reserves in a form which brings no income),[6] reporting, and par clearance of checks.[7] These requirements can impose some loss of opportunity for profit.

What are the advantages of membership? Members have the privilege of borrowing from the FR if they are short of reserves. In view of the difficulties banks have had in times of financial distress, one would expect bankers to be willing to make appreciable sacrifices to be confident of FR help. Members also have continual use of the System's highly effective mechanism for clearing checks and transferring funds. A member bank gets access to other operating aids, including many kinds of information and advice. Finally, the 6 percent received on the capital stock is a good yield for a perfectly secure asset.

For small banks, however, the potential value of these advantages has been largely eliminated. Nonmembers can obtain most of the operating services, such as check clearing and transfer of funds, at little or no cost. They do so by dealing with a correspondent bank which is a member, or by qualifying as a "clearing bank." (A nonmember clearing bank gets the privilege of using FR facilities by maintaining an account of adequate size and by meeting certain other conditions.) Moreover, nonmember banks can get funds for regular seasonal needs or emergencies from their city correspondents which are members. Banks that have not joined thus obtain, indirectly but effectively, the elasticity which is a fundamental "selling point" for membership.

[6] All states permit (nonmember) banks to include deposits at correspondent banks as part of the legal reserve; most of the deposits would be needed in any case. Some states permit state banks to include certain income-producing assets in their legal reserves. Member banks must submit to various other restrictions, such as bans on interlocking directorates and use of affiliates, both of which some states permit. See H. P. Gray, "Bank Regulation, Bank Profitability, and Federal Reserve Membership, *National Banking Review,* Dec. 1963, pp. 207–20.

[7] Despite persistent effforts of the FR, some 1600 nonmember banks still refuse to remit to out-of-town banks at par. Member banks must clear at par, but these others prefer the income produced by the charges. These charges are not those which a bank may impose on a customer for the expense of handling a check on an out-of-town bank, especially the sacrifice of the use of funds for a day or two. The charges against which the FR has been fighting are those, say 1/10 of 1 percent, that the bank on which the check has been drawn deducts from the amount it is ordered to pay, while charging its depositor's account the full amount. Eight states have laws specifically permitting non-par payment of checks. Banks point out, among other things, that making payments outside the community involves costs; deposits with correspondent banks, for example, earn no income. Non-par payment is more than a nuisance and sometimes more than a slight cost to outsiders cashing checks. It has also led to complicated check routing. For example, bank *A* getting a check on bank *Z,* which deducts a charge of 0.1 percent, may send the check to bank *B,* which gives credit at par; *B,* in turn, may send to *C,* etc., until the check reaches a bank to which *Z* will remit at par, perhaps another bank in its own locality. This inefficient process can tie up funds for days and deprive a business of prompt credit to its account of amounts due it and needed for operations.

Problems of Broadening Membership

Many economists believe that our system would be better if all commercial banks were members of the FR.[8] The entire public has an interest in money and in what commercial banks do. Even apparently local actions by a bank can have effects beyond the particular community. High standards of banking must be assured. Banking is "affected with a public interest" even when the bank is a privately owned, profit-seeking business. Moreover, private and public interest in banking are not always identical.

The most effective monetary policy, one that can protect the wide public interest adequately, must cover the entire economy. If some banks are outside the FR, their operations are excluded from the full force of control. Being freer, they may follow policies which conflict with the national interest. (The public interest requires monetary regulation which on some occasions will seem onerous, even highhanded, to some bankers and their customers.) The exemption of some banks from FR control may bring them a competitive advantage over member banks. This possibility may at times limit a little the freedom of FR officials, especially in imposing policies of restraint. The System must face the possibility of losing banks which fear the competition of nonmembers, or which want to take advantage of greater profit opportunities where requirements are less stringent. (State member banks might withdraw while national banks might seek state charters and then withdraw.) And should not all banks share in the costs of central banking arrangements which serve the entire financial system?

What are the arguments against compulsory membership? For one thing, avoidable compulsion is undesirable. The availability of "nonmembership," it is claimed, gives even members an alternative of escape from distasteful or dictatorial regulation and respects "states' rights." Banks with small staffs object to the burden of FR reporting requirements. The most influential consideration, however, is the desire of banks outside to keep the greater earning opportunities they now enjoy. Membership would raise their effective reserve requirements; even if the percentage required were no higher than at present, it would be an addition to amounts which must be kept at correspondent banks for operating purposes (and which now count as legal reserves for nonmember banks). Some city banks, incidentally, would lose interbank deposits, a fact which helps explain part of the opposition to compulsory membership.

The effectiveness of monetary policy, it is argued, suffers little when

[8] Some of the largest nonmembers are mutual savings banks which would have little to gain from membership. Nor would there be much public advantage in their membership. Their activities have relatively little effect on the supply of money, and other regulations assure the public of essential protection.

only 16 percent of demand deposits are outside the System. Moreover, deposits of most nonmembers are insured. Depositors and the general public can count upon important protection against loss when a nonmember bank is operated poorly.

The Federal Open Market Committee

Early in the 1920's the Federal Reserve banks began to buy short-term debt, including Treasury obligations, in the open market for the income that the securities would earn. Such earnings were needed to help pay operating expenses when member bank borrowings were low. The purchase and sale of such debt, however, affected the money market. The conditions in which the FR was exercising credit control were altered by actions designed to yield it income.

The desirability of coordinating the actions of the 12 banks became evident. Since the buying and selling of all 12 banks was done in New York, the actions of one might conflict with the interests of others. Moreover, only by accident would the net changes be those that a coordinated study would prescribe for the whole economy. A special committee was formed to facilitate joint action, but it was only partially successful. The Board in Washington felt that its own influence was inadequate. In 1935, therefore, Congress voted legal status and power for the Federal Open Market Committee. The Group now consists of the 7 members of the Board of Governors, the president of the New York Bank, and presidents or vice-presidents of 4 other banks selected on a rotating basis.

The Committee meets every three weeks. It controls the System's open market purchases and sales of securities (and also of foreign currencies). In making policy, it draws upon the facts and judgments supplied by the Board and its Washington staff and also by all 12 banks. Special staff reports are distributed in advance and supplemented by oral briefings. Members also seek information from banking and business leaders. The fact that Committee members have other key positions assures that views from a wide range of sources will bear upon decisions. The Board of Governors, constituting a majority, can exert ultimate control if the members will act as a unit.

After a review of actions taken since the last meeting, each member presents his views. The Chairman then formulates the "consensus." If any change in policy seems called for, a new directive will be drafted and voted on. Along with continuing directives adopted each year, the new statement constitutes the guide for the Account Manager. He sits with the Committee, hears all the discussion, and later conducts actual operations. The record of the directives appears many months later in the

Board's *Annual Report,* but in language so vague that even an expert cannot be certain about what was intended, either means or ends.[9]

The New York Bank executes the policies for all 12 banks. It also carries out purchases and sales of foreign currencies for the government under the jurisdiction of the FOMC.[10]

Federal Advisory Council

Each of the twelve banks appoints a member of the Federal Advisory Council. These men, usually prominent bankers, meet with the Board of Governors at least four times a year to study and to make recommendations on matters which relate to Federal Reserve operations. The Council's direct influence seems to have been small. The indirect influences may be greater. The recommendations it makes do get publicity in banking and government circles, and serve at least an educational function. Moreover, the discussions give these leading bankers perspective which helps them interpret general policies to the banking community over the nation.

Other Elements

This description of the System's formal structure has not included all elements. The FR banks have various arrangements for learning, regularly and systematically, what is going on in business and finance through-

[9] The following example was adopted July 9, 1963:

It is the Committee's current policy to accommodate moderate growth in bank credit, while putting increased emphasis on money market conditions that would contribute to an improvement in the capital account of the U.S. balance of payments. This policy takes into consideration the continuing adverse balance of payments position and its cumulative effects and the high level of domestic business activity, as well as the increases in bank credit, money supply, and the reserve base in recent months. At the same time, however, it recognizes the continuing underutilization of resources.

To implement this policy, System open market operations shall be conducted with a view to continuing the present degree of firmness in the money market.

Votes for this action: Messrs. Martin, Hayes, Balderston, Bopp, Clay, Irons, King, Mills, Scanlon, and Shepardson. Votes against this action: Messrs. Mitchell and Robertson. Board of Governors, *Fiftieth Annual Report . . . 1963* (Washington: The Board, 1964), pp. 92-3.

[10] The procedures of the FOMC have come under considerable criticism. Representative Patman argues that the influence of bankers has undue weight. When 12 members and three times that many staff members are together in one room, it is argued, neither deliberation nor confidentiality can be expected. The vagueness of the decisions leaves very extensive discretion to the operating staff and a few Washington and New York officials. Attention, it is said, focuses on the next three weeks rather than on the longer run.

out their districts—and in the minds of representative bankers and businessmen. This information is analyzed by professional staffs and presented to the president and directors. Similarly, the Board of Governors has an extensive organization for gathering and interpreting information.

In Washington and throughout the System some of the country's best-trained economists study both current trends and the basic, long-run problems of the economy. Nevertheless, there is substance in criticisms of the research and analysis emanating from the professional staff as failing to take account of new thinking and evidence from economists in academic circles. One reason for such a lag is the reluctance of, or restriction on, staff to publish materials which do not conform more or less closely with Board thinking and policy. Each of the banks publishes a monthly bulletin which presents statistics about national and regional conditions and articles on special topics.

Officials are in constant touch (but not always in agreement) with the Treasury, the Council of Economic Advisers, the FDIC, and other governmental agencies. The FR has connections with state banking officials and with monetary authorities abroad. The 12 banks have examining staffs and provide various facilities for members, such as training programs. The Interdistrict Settlement Fund, maintained in Washington, clears payments among the twelve banks.

FEDERAL RESERVE SERVICE OPERATIONS

We deal with the System's service functions only briefly, not because they are of slight importance. In fact, by facilitating the smooth and effective functioning of the financial system, the service operations make an indispensable contribution. Fortunately, however, they present few problems of current general significance.

Check Clearing and Other Payment Services

Each FR bank acts as a clearinghouse and as a paying center for its member banks (and for nonmember banks which have clearing privileges). One-fourth of the FR employees are engaged in check clearing. They process about 5 billion checks a year—$1500 billion worth in 1963. Except as member banks choose to clear through correspondents or even directly with out-of-town banks, checks which cannot be cleared locally go to the FR bank or branch.[11] The checks, in effect, are credited to the

---

[11] Checks on banks which do not remit at par must go through separate channels because the Federal Reserve will not process them.

account of the bank that sends them. Checks which are drawn upon a bank in the same FR district are charged to the account of that bank at once and sent to it.[12]

Checks that are drawn on banks in other districts are sent, usually by air express, to the appropriate FR bank for collection. Each FR bank notifies the Interdistrict Settlement Fund in Washington of the total which each of the other eleven FR banks owes it. These amounts will be credited to its account, and it will be charged with checks sent to it by each of the other eleven banks. The Fund balances the various amounts and notifies each FR bank of the net change in its position.

A member bank gets credit for the checks that it deposits at the FR according to a time schedule which has been drawn up to reflect roughly the time required for collection. Most checks on banks in the same city as the FR bank are credited immediately. Checks on somewhat less accessible banks are credited the next day, and those on the banks farther away are credited on the second business day. In fact, however, collection sometimes takes longer even when mails are not disrupted. The arbitrary schedule, therefore, is somewhat inaccurate; it sometimes grants immediate credit when not justified and never holds up credit more than two days. Consequently, banks as a group get something of an "extra."

A bank will receive credit for some checks before they are debited against the account of the banks on which they are drawn. Here is the origin of "float." The total of "cash items in process of collection," checks that are on their way to the banks on which they are drawn, tends to be larger than that of "deferred availability cash items." The latter are checks for which credit has not yet been granted because the arbitrary time period has not expired. The difference is the float. It is the amount which banks have received in credit at the FR but which has not yet been charged to the account of banks on which the checks are drawn—a sort of interest-free loan from the FR to member banks. Weather that is bad enough to ground air mail, or a general rise in the volume of payments, will increase float for a day or more.

Routing symbols speed the clearing process. These appear as a fraction in the upper right-hand corner of the check. The figures on top indicate the city or state and the specific bank. The denominator shows how the check is to be routed: to which FR district, whether to the head office or a branch, and whether the funds become available on the same day or after one or two days.

The FR also collects for member banks what are known as *non-cash items*—a variety of drafts, notes, bills of exchange, and acceptances. A

---

[12] What happens when a member bank faces a net claim against it at the FR and a demand which its balance cannot meet without falling below its legal requirement? It may borrow or sell an asset and deposit the proceeds, checks on other banks. Or it may conceivably have extra currency which it may deposit.

bank having such a claim payable in another city can use the System's services, probably after paying a small charge.

The FR also offers member banks and their customers facilities for transferring funds by telegraph over its network of leased wires. Any member bank, by mail, telegram, or other means, may instruct its FR bank to charge its account and wire any other member bank any amount in a multiple of $1000. If the receiving bank is in the same district, its account will be credited immediately. If the receiving bank is in another district, its FR bank will receive the telegram and make the credit. Settlement between the two Reserve banks is made on the same basis as check clearing—through the Interdistrict Settlement Fund. This wire service is provided free. A business firm or any bank customer can ask its bank to arrange telegraphic transfers. Within an hour, for example, a bank in Los Angeles can buy a Treasury bill in New York, arrange the payment, and receive its security; the security sold in New York is canceled and a new one issued in Los Angeles on the basis of telegraphic instructions. Consequently, funds which would otherwise be idle in transit are kept "working" all the time.[13]

Agent for the United States Government: Other Services

The FR is the Treasury's chief banker and its agent in public debt transactions. Without any charge the twelve banks accept deposits and process the checks for the vast mass of Treasury financial operations. The FR performs an enormous volume of paper work involved in issuing and redeeming government debt—204 million items worth $683 billion in 1963. It handles more than 15 million bond coupons per year in paying about $5 billion in interest for the Treasury. Although most of the activity is routine, good performance facilitates the smooth operation of the economy.

The FR has other functions, including the analysis of economic conditions, storing gold, the arrangement of international payments, and the issue of currency.

CURRENCY

The System has two somewhat different responsibilities for the nation's currency: It takes charge of the essentially mechanical but always

---

[13] Another arrangement for avoiding idleness of funds is the system of Federal Reserve Exchange Drafts. These are acceptable at any FR bank or branch for immediate rather than deferred credit. A bank receiving permission to use such drafts can make prompt transfers; its account is reduced each day for the drafts issued that day. This system is not widely used, however, because most banks find the use of facilities of their city correspondents as satisfactory as the FR draft system.

important details of getting currency into the economy, and it holds the legal reserves for outstanding paper money.

Routine Issue and Reissue

The FR performs a great volume of paper work in handling the nation's currency. It is an intermediary between the Treasury—the Bureau of the Mint and the Bureau of Engraving and Printing—and the commercial banks. If the public wants more coins and paper money to carry on transactions, the FR arranges for minting and printing, and then disbursement. It also provides for seasonal changes, holding extra amounts in periods of low demand to be able to meet public wishes in peak periods. The 1963 record shows the handling of 4.8 billion pieces of currency, worth $32 billion, and 8.7 billion coins. When it receives paper money that is too worn for further circulation or coins that are mutilated or short-weight, it arranges for their destruction and replacement. Its staff keeps on the alert for counterfeits. The costs of these essentially governmental functions are charged to FR operating expenses.

Each FR bank issues its own paper money, subject to regulations fixed by Congress. All such currency is legal tender and an obligation of the United States, as well as of the issuing bank. The Bureau of Engraving and Printing prints a stock of each variety of Federal Reserve note—denominations ranging from $1 to $10,000. These notes are held in Treasury vaults until requested by the Board of Governors, which in turn hands them over, upon request, to the agent of the FR bank for whom they were printed. He must, however, provide proper collateral, as described later. The notes are shipped to the FR bank for issue to member banks for their customers. The Federal Reserve Agents' Settlement Fund in Washington is used to pay the Treasury for new notes and to clear notes of different banks. Worn-out currency or any being returned for redemption is exchanged for collateral.

Demand for Currency

The quantity of notes outstanding depends upon what the public wants. The FR's position is in a sense passive, accommodating the general public. Seasonal fluctuations are evident, as is longer-term growth.

Changes within a year are dominated by the approach and then the passing of holidays and other seasonal movements. However, the possibility of a shift in public psychology, such as occurred during panics in the past, does exist; exceptional demands for currency might develop suddenly. Over the longer run the public's demand for currency is affected by the forces which determine the demand for money as a whole. (See Chapter 13.) In addition, changes in the relative importance of the use of checks and any other substitutes for currency influence the long-run demand for paper money and coins.

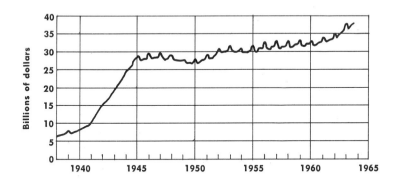

FIGURE 9.1

Currency in Circulation, Outside Treasury and Federal Reserve Banks, 1938–64

Reserves

For each dollar of paper currency it issues, the FR must provide a dollar of collateral. At least 25 percent must normally be gold certificates; these are issued by the Treasury, which is the legal owner of the monetary gold itself. A FR bank gets gold certificates by the process described later. Some certificates will be held by the FR agent in his redemption fund in Washington; they count in meeting the requirement. Gold certificates used as reserves for deposits until the requirement was removed in 1965 did not count as reserves against currency.[14]

The rest of the collateral can be (1) debt of the United States government; (2) commercial paper—notes, bills, drafts, or acceptances acquired by a FR bank in rediscounting or lending to a member bank, subject to various technical requirements; (3) bills of exchange endorsed by a member bank; and (4) bankers' acceptances purchased in the open

[14] Gold certificates held in the Interdistrict Settlement Fund may be counted as reserve for notes.

market. The assets pledged, *including those which yield income,* remain the property of the FR bank. But they are held in special custody by the FR agent. The currency issued is the offsetting liability of the bank. When new currency goes into circulation, the FR bank exchanges one liability for another. It gives currency, its own debt (bank note) but reduces the amount it owes the member bank by debiting that bank's account.

The Board of Governors has legal authority to modify the requirements for currency reserve; it may require additional collateral, limit the amount of issue, or suspend the reserve requirement. If the gold certificate collateral is less than 25 percent, the bank must pay a penalty rate. This is only 1 percent a year if the deficiency is not over one-fifth. If the gold certificate backing falls below 20 percent, however, the penalty rises steeply. In short, there is significant flexibility which is nevertheless subject to restraints.

The present rules governing FR notes differ considerably from those which have applied in the past. One change was the 1945 reduction in the minimum gold certificate requirement from 40 percent; each ounce of gold will now "back" more currency. A change in 1932 permitted the use of collateral other than commercial paper. Specifically, Congress authorized the use of government debt to make up some or all of the difference between the gold holding and the full value of the notes. This modification was highly important. The amount of commercial paper held by the FR banks, *i.e.,* rediscounted for member banks, will not necessarily be related in any logical way to the country's need for currency. In the early 1930's, for example, the FR faced unusual difficulties in providing currency. A truly serious, and quite unnecessary, emergency might have developed because of inability to provide enough currency. The System had little eligible commercial paper. Therefore, it had to provide abnormally high gold coverage for currency, and at a time when gold was not plentiful.

The original rules rested on the theory that an elastic currency is desirable. When business expands, the argument ran, more currency ought to be issued; when business contracts, so should the volume of outstanding currency. The expansion and contraction of business, it was assumed, will be related closely to business borrowing from commercial banks and their rediscounting at the FR. Therefore, linking the supply of currency to the volume of commercial paper held by the FR ought to insure some of the elasticity appropriate to a healthy currency. Yet, even if such elasticity were desirable (we shall see later that this is hardly true), a close connection between currency and rediscounted commercial loans would not necessarily give the *best* amount of elasticity in the economic world that has in fact developed. Federal Reserve holdings of commercial paper do not fluctuate as originally expected. More important, the total amount of such paper held by the FR has not been large enough to back a volume of currency appropriate to modern needs.

What is now the purpose of having reserves or "backing" for paper money? The economic reason is not to make currency convertible into some tangible thing which in itself has value. Our currency today is not convertible in this sense. The purpose of reserves is to limit the issue of paper money. At best the method now used is crude, unnecessary, and largely ineffective.[15] Most economists would probably favor repeal of the requirement. Two arguments are made against such change. For one thing, the Fed's emergency powers should enable it to prevent serious disturbance if strains appear. The more persuasive argument, however, rests upon fear that the public, here and abroad, might misunderstand and to some extent lose confidence in the dollar; foreigners might then step up their demands for gold in exchange for the deposits held in this country. We return to this subject in Chapter 20.

QUESTIONS

1. "The present-day structure of the FR is a compromise between the two camps of 1913—those who wanted a central bank like the Bank of England and those who distrusted 'Centralism' and 'Monopoly.'" In discussing this statement, describe the structure. Why do you suppose that centralization has developed?

2. What are some of the advantages and disadvantages of being a *member* bank? Discuss with a banker.

3. What would you judge to be qualities required for effective service on the Board of Governors? What kinds of information do Board members need?

4. What are the functions of the FR other than controlling bank reserves? Who pays the costs?

5. What is the Federal Open Market Committee? What does it do?

6. What is the meaning and significance of the "float"? Other things being- equal, what effect would you expect widespread fog, sleet, and rain to have on member bank reserve balances? Why?

[15] For many years one could say that the requirement was harmless. By 1960, however, a defect had become apparent. The requirement of partial gold coverage for currency tied up specie which could not then be used to meet foreign demands for gold. Since gold still has a useful role to play in settling international balances, are we not foolish to keep some $8 billion immobilized to restrict currency issue when other methods exist?

7. What are the reasons for the requirement of gold certificate backing for currency issued by the FR?

8. What influence can the President of the United States have on week-to-week actions and policies of the FR? How can Congress influence the System?

9. What are the FR "service" functions?

10. Examine the monthly publications of a few of the twelve Federal Reserve banks.

11. Give arguments for and against requiring all commercial banks to join the FR.

CHAPTER 10 *MEMBER BANK RESERVES*

THE lending capacity of a member bank depends upon its reserves. The reserves of the banking system as a whole depend to a large extent upon action by Federal Reserve officials. Their control of reserves involves control over the ability of the banking system to create (and pressure to destroy) the demand deposits which make up most of our stock of money. And changes in the stock of money, as we shall see in Part Three, influence the economy profoundly.

This chapter describes the role of reserves and the way that they come into existence. The following chapter analyzes the FR's control instruments and their use.

MEMBER BANK RESERVES

The Federal Reserve has rather little influence on changes in the volume of currency in circulation. It does, however, have substantial influence on the volume of demand deposits. The System exercises its power by (1) holding and (2) regulating (a) the quantity and (b) the use of most member bank legal reserves, *i.e.,* the expansion potential. Bank reserves (sometimes called "high-powered money") are important, and their control is important, because the country's stock of money depends heavily upon the reserve position of banks.

The discussion which follows applies, with a few exceptions, to FR member banks only.

Legal Reserves

The law requires each bank to maintain a reserve of no less than a specified fraction or percentage of the amount it owes its depositors. The legal reserve of a member bank is vault cash plus the bank's deposit at the FR. For simplicity, we shall generally omit reference to vault cash and focus on member bank deposits at the FR. To the bank legal reserves are of paramount importance because they determine the amount of other —and income-producing—assets the bank can hold. The relation to bank earning assets is once removed in that the legal reserve is related to the bank's liabilities, the amount it owes depositors; in creating these deposits, of course, the bank acquires earning assets.

Congress itself has made two distinctions regarding legal reserves. It has distinguished (1) between time (and saving) and demand deposits and (2) among banks according to the size of the city in which they are located.

Table 10.1 shows the rates required in 1964 and at selected dates in the past.

Reserve on Time Deposits

The reserve requirement for time deposits—now 4 percent—is uniform throughout the country. The Board has power to vary this requirement from 3 to 6 percent. The level may seem rather low, substantially less than one-third of the average rate required for demand deposits. One justification for an apparently low level is that time and saving deposits present less of a potential liquidity problem than do demand deposits. The typical owner of such a deposit does not build it up and then draw it down every month or so. Time deposits overall are relatively stable except for a growth trend. In fact, however, any general loss of confidence in a bank would probably lead to withdrawals of time deposits on a scale great enough to create serious difficulty.

A second reason for the low requirement stems from the fact that time deposits, by most definitions, are not part of the money supply. They do not expand and contract in the same way that demand deposits change. Nor do they shift from one owner to another. Consequently, it is argued, the control needed to protect the general public interest can be less rigorous than that applied to demand deposits. Finally, there is a practical consideration. Member banks pay interest on time deposits but receive none from the FR. They would suffer in competition with nonmember banks if the reserve requirement were high, tying up more assets in nonproducing form.

Classification of Member Banks

Until 1962 banks were classified in three groups. New York and Chicago were central reserve cities; other large cities were designated as

TABLE 10.1

Member Bank Reserve Requirements, Selected Dates
(Percent of deposits)

| Effective date of change[a] | Net demand deposits[b] | | | Time deposits |
	Central reserve city banks	Reserve city banks	Country banks	
1917—June 21	13	10	7	3
no change until				
1936—Aug. 16	19½	15	10½	4½
1937—May 1	26	20	14	6
1938—April 16	22¾	17½	12	5
1941—Nov. 1	26	20	14	6
1942—Aug. 20	24			
Oct. 3	20			
1948—Sept. 16	26	22	16	7½
1949—May 1	24	21	15	7
Aug. 1	23½	19½	13	6[c]
Aug. 25	22½	18½	12	5
1951—Jan. 25	24	20	14	6
1953—July 1	22	19	13	
1954—July 29	20	18	12	5
1958—Feb. 27	19½	17½	11½	
April 17	18½	17	11	
April 24	18	16½	11	
1960—Sept. 1	17½			
Dec. 1	16½	16½	12	5
1962—Oct. 25				
and in effect				
Aug. 1964	c	16½	12	4
Limit of range permitted by law[c]				
Minimum		10	7	3
Maximum		22	14	6

[a] Minor details of timing omitted.

[b] Demand deposits subject to reserve requirements which, beginning in 1935, have been total demand deposits minus cash items in process of collection and demand balances due from domestic banks.

[c] The Central Reserve City classification ended in July, 1962. Prior to 1959, the minimum and maximum legal requirements against net demand deposits of central reserve city banks were 13 and 26 percent, respectively, and the maximum for reserve city banks was 20 percent.

Source: *Federal Reserve Bulletin*, July 1964, and *Annual Report of the Board . . .* for 1959.

reserve cities, and all others as "nonreserve," commonly called "country." Reserve requirements varied. The threefold grouping was a legacy from a distant past. When the National Banking Act was passed, banks were required to redeem their own bank notes. It seemed desirable that extra funds for this purpose be held in New York and some other cities. Though the redemption system was dropped in 1874, the old basis for classifying national banks remained.

By that date reserves were thought of as serving chiefly to assure bank liquidity. Banks in New York and Chicago faced a special liquidity problem because they owed large deposits to correspondent banks. These deposits might be drawn down upon short notice and for suddenly developing reasons. Therefore, the banks in these two cities had an exceptional responsibility to protect their liquidity position—to serve their own interests, those of their correspondents, and of the public in general.[1]

Many banks in other larger cities also held some deposits of banks (including state banks) in neighboring localities. These were deposits on which owners might begin to draw heavily upon short notice. The liquidity needs of a bank owing such deposit liabilities were greater than those of banks which owned the deposits and could claim them, banks in smaller cities and towns. Thinking based on such conditions was carried over into the FR System. Reserve requirements were set to meet liquidity needs which seemed to differ among types of banks.

Whatever justification might have once existed for the threefold classification disappeared long ago. The creation of the FR, in fact, abolished the system of redeposited reserves for member banks. With it went the logic, if any, of the classification. Most of the business of New York and Chicago banks is "regular" banking. The handling of interbank deposits is only a small part of their activity. Moreover, banks in other localities, including some in nonreserve cities, hold interbank deposits—relatively more on occasion than do some New York banks. In short, bank location no longer indicates the type of business done, nor the need for reserves. Congress, accordingly, eliminated the "central reserve city" classification. In 1964 there were 48 reserve cities.[2]

The remaining twofold classification rests upon an obsolete theory of the role of required reserves, namely that they exist to provide liquidity. A more rational system would treat all banks equally.

---

[1] Note, however, that if the law requires that a reserve be maintained, the assets which make up that reserve cannot be used in discharging obligations.

[2] Around 150 banks in reserve cities had been classed by the FR as country banks because of the nature of their activity.

The Purpose of Legal Reserves and the Present
Differences in Requirements

The need for reserves depends on the purpose they serve. What is it? Today, the function of required reserves is not the assurance of liquidity. Under a fractional reserve system, a reserve which is required is not, in fact, available for meeting depositor demands. How could it be used to meet demands on a bank for cash? Only an "excess" can serve to meet depositor requests for cash.

The principal purpose of the reserve requirement is to help in controlling the volume of money.

The present differences in rates, however, complicate rather than aid in achieving smooth control. Shifts of deposits among banks—from a country to a reserve city bank—change total reserve requirements. The change, however, will not necessarily serve any useful purpose. For example, little if any economic significance attaches to a shift of deposits from Urbana to Chicago or from Saratoga to New York City; the reserves required, however, increase by more than one-third in such cases. A movement of deposits the other way—from New York or Chicago to a "country" bank—reduces required reserves substantially.

More strikingly, shifts from time to demand deposits increases the total reserve needed per dollar of deposit by two- or threefold. A shift the other way has the opposite effect. Efficient monetary management is made more difficult by the differences in reserves now required by law and regulation.

The Level of Required Rates

If required reserves are to be only a fraction of deposits, we ask, "What fraction?" What will serve the public best, one-twentieth or nineteen-twentieths or some figure in between? The issues involved in such questions require the kind of analysis discussed in later chapters, except for two points: The smaller the fraction or percentage, (1) the larger the profit potential for banks, but (2) the greater the problem of monetary control. In regulating reserves, for example, the monetary authorities cannot predict the effects of changes so accurately when each dollar of reserve will permit up to $10 of deposits as when the dollar will permit no more than $5 of deposits.

To some extent the present *level* of rates is the outgrowth of conditions of the 1930's. At that time owners of gold seeking protection from political and economic trouble in Europe sent the yellow metal to this country. This influx added substantially to our monetary reserves.[3]

---

[3] See Chapter 19.

Commercial banks found their reserves building up to far more than was required. But no one could be sure how long this "hot money" would remain. A potential danger existed. The stock of money—demand deposits—might expand on the basis of gold which could suddenly leave the country if conditions abroad improved. Both the expansion and the contraction on a large scale of the stock of money could hurt the economy.

To reduce the potential danger from such excess reserves, Congress gave the FR power to raise reserve requirements up to twice the previous maxima. The Board made use of this authority. At the time of Pearl Harbor the requirements were at the maximum permitted by law and twice the level prevailing from 1917 to 1936.

The System might then have reduced the requirements to provide reserves for deposit expansion to help finance World War II. It did so to a small extent only. As the major method of enlarging the lending power of banks, the FR bought government debt. Various changes, both increases and reductions, have been made since 1945; but the net movement has been down, as shown in Table 10.1.

Vault Cash

From 1917 to 1960 vault cash was not allowed as part of the legal reserve. This refusal resulted from developments during and after World War I. At that time it seemed wise to concentrate gold holdings in the FR. One method of doing so was to discourage banks from holding gold coins. The authorities also wished to discourage banks from holding more FR notes than was essential, since the gold coverage requirement for notes was higher than for FR deposits. "Excess" note issue would mean "inefficient" use of gold.

Banks with easy access to currency suffered only a little from the exclusion of vault cash from legal reserves. New York and Chicago banks in 1959 held currency equal to only about 0.6 percent of net demand deposits. Banks farther removed from offices of the Federal Reserve, however, had to keep more of their assets in this relatively unprofitable form. The 1959 average for country banks was 3.5 percent of demand deposits, for reserve city banks 1.7 percent. Nonmember state banks were generally allowed to treat vault cash as part of legal reserves.

The problem was not only one of discrimination among banks. Monetary control was also involved. If the public converted one form of money (currency) to another (demand deposits) there was a change in the total of gold reserves required.[4] The shifts complicated the job of the monetary authorities.

[4] The amount of gold coverage per dollar of money changed tremendously. For currency the gold reserve was about 25 percent. For demand deposits, however, it was 25 percent of 12 or 16½ percent in 1959.

Computation of Reserve Requirement

In computing the demand deposits against which reserves must be held, the bank adds all deposits which it can be required to pay in less than 30 days. More exactly, it adds together all those that do not fall into one of the three categories of time deposits. The bank must also include such items as certified checks outstanding and amounts due to the FR on account of collections the System has outstanding against the bank. It may then deduct (1) amounts subject to withdrawal on demand which it has on deposit at other banks, (2) cash items in the process of collection from other banks, and (3) checks (and other items) on hand which it will present for payment or collection within one day.

Banks in reserve cities report weekly, country banks twice a month. Each bank must compute reserve requirements for each day and must take an average over the period. Its holdings of reserves during the same period are also averaged. Consequently, deficiencies of some days may be offset by excesses of other days.

What if reserves fall below the requirement? The law specifies a penalty: a tax or fine of 2 percentage points above the rediscount rate. Moreover, while it is deficient, a bank must not make new loans or pay dividends. It may lose its national bank charter and FDIC membership if a deficiency persists for long. As we shall see, member banks have more than one way to avoid the penalty by acting to meet the requirement.

TWO ISSUES

Reserves as Idle Assets

The reserve brings the member bank no income. Of course, the income which the FR gets from the assets it owns does pay the System's operating costs. Member banks get nonmonetary benefit in the form of services, such as check clearing. In general, however, the banker is likely to feel that a large part of the reserve is a sterile waste. He sees a cost in the holding of more assets in this form than his bank requires for clearing and for meeting customer demands for cash.

In fact, however, member bank reserves have come into existence with little or no sacrifice on the part of the commercial banking system. The individual banker observing his own operations may conclude that he turns over to the FR an asset which then brings his bank no income. Yet for the banking system as a whole, the opposite is more nearly true. The individual bank got the asset as a result of an earlier use by the FR of its power to acquire (income-producing) assets and to create deposits. The reserves for each particular bank (and for all member banks combined) result primarily from actions by the Federal Reserve, based on the power granted to it by Congress to issue currency and to create credit, *i.e.,* deposits for member banks. International gold flows and currency drains for domestic circulation complicate the analysis; nevertheless, commercial banks did not create the deposits at the Federal Reserve and did not sacrifice significantly as the FR acquired assets.

However, even if the requirement did impose a real economic cost on the commercial banking system, would this be unreasonable? Would this not be a cost which the community could appropriately impose upon banks if they are left with an opportunity to recoup somehow? Reserves serve an important public purpose; they provide a device for monetary control. And the commercial banking system continues to end each year with at least a comfortable net profit.

Assume that reserve requirements were lower, other things remaining unchanged. Member banks would then increase their loans and security holdings, *i.e.,* earning assets. In doing so, they would create deposits, thus adding to the country's stock of money. The desirability of such an increase would depend upon the general state of the economy.

Reform

The system of reserves has been modified in recent years. Still, it is not ideally adapted to conditions today. The geographical discrimination, for example, is obsolete. Reform plans, however, must recognize that country banks insist upon a favorable rate, if not necessarily below the level of big cities at least on a level which will offer good scope for attractive earnings. If the reserve requirement for country banks were raised substantially, many would shift to state charters and leave the FR. Reduction of relative discrimination against reserve cities could take the form of reducing their requirements. This could be done without going much below the rates which existed in the past. Yet rates around 10 percent may not be best for monetary control; when potential leverage is nearly tenfold, the prediction of bank response is more difficult than when the requirement is higher.

More sweeping changes deserve serious consideration. One would be to base required reserves on deposit turnover. For example, if two banks had the same deposit total, say $50 million, but one's debits to accounts during a week were $20 million and the other's $25 million, the required reserves for the latter would be higher. A second possibility would be to relate reserves to loans and investments rather than to deposit liabilities. Reserve requirements could be made to vary with the kind of asset held—less, perhaps, for government securities than for business loans. Neither of these two proposals, despite their merits, has gained much of a following in official circles.

The committee of high Federal officials appointed by President Kennedy to report on financial institutions favored, with one dissent, a graduated system. A relatively low rate would be required on the first $5 million or so of deposits, a higher rate on the next $95 million, and a still higher rate on deposits over $100 million. Such a schedule would eliminate differences among banks due to city classification. Small banks would obviously be favored. The committee justified such treatment in part on the grounds that it is the smaller banks which are most likely to use state charters and stay out of the FR if its requirements are higher; in part because smaller banks keep larger proportions of assets on deposit at correspondent banks where they receive no interest; and in part because small banks are unable to manage their reserve positions with precision so that they tend to hold excess reserves.

The committee of bankers appointed by the Comptroller favored lower and uniform requirements on demand deposits and elimination, eventually, of all reserve requirements on time and savings deposits. The latter recommendation rests upon several arguments: that time and savings deposits are not money and that reserves do not therefore serve to influence changes in the country's stock of money; that the competitive position of banks would be improved vis-à-vis other thrift institutions for which there are no reserve requirements; and that shifts between time and demand deposits are not in fact large enough to interfere with monetary policy controls.

The Commission on Money and Credit, which included many non-bankers, also recommended, with one dissent, the elimination of reserve requirements on time and savings deposits and uniform requirements for demand deposits. Other suggestions include payment of interest by the Federal Reserve and limited allowance of high quality, income-earning assets as part of the reserve.

In brief, there is widespread agreement that the system of reserve requirements is in need of change, but as yet there has been no crystallization of views about the precise nature of the revisions which would serve the country best.

BUILDING RESERVES: THE INDIVIDUAL BANK

How can a single bank build up its deposits at the FR? Four methods are possible. The first three are available only if some other bank has the funds. In such cases what one bank gets, another gives up. Since these three methods involve the whole system, we merely mention them here, to deal with them in the next section.

(1) One method is to buy excess reserves in the market for "Federal funds." (See Chapter 6.) Conditions of demand and supply determine

a price for the use of another bank's reserves, usually somewhat below the cost of borrowing from the FR. Accommodation of this sort may, or may not, be temporary; a bank which is a borrower one day may be a lender the next. Other methods available to a member bank include (2) sale of securities (secondary reserves), receiving payment in funds which can be drawn from the accounts of other banks at the FR; (3) drawing down deposit balances at a correspondent bank; (4) borrowing from the FR (rediscounting). We begin with the fourth.[5]

Member Bank Borrowing—Advances and Rediscounting

Membership in the System enables a bank to borrow from the Federal Reserve, paying interest at the rate set by the FR. The member bank turns over its own IOU to the FR and gets a deposit. The borrowing resembles closely that of a business arranging a loan from a commercial bank. Although the deposit which the member bank obtains brings it no income, the increase in reserves will enable it to acquire more earning assets (and incur more liabilities) or to hold on to those it has. We consider this method at greater length in Chapter 11, but the essential changes can be illustrated simply.

Federal Reserve Bank		Member Bank	
Member Bank's IOU [a]			
Assets	Liabilities	Assets	Liabilities
IOU of member bank +$100	Member bank deposit +$100	Deposit at FR +$100 (reserve) (increase in required reserve: none; in legal reserve: $100)	IOU to FR +$100

[a] This example ignores the amount (the interest or discount) which the borrowing bank pays the "Fed" for the accommodation.

Each institution has increased both its assets and its liabilities by the same amount. No other bank has lost or gained reserves or other assets. The member bank borrowing has increased its legal reserves by $100.

[5] When vault cash did not qualify as legal reserve, a fifth possibility existed. The bank could send currency from its vaults to the Federal Reserve.

CREATION OF RESERVES FOR THE SYSTEM
AS A WHOLE

How do *banks as a group* get reserves? With some exceptions they can get reserves only if the Federal Reserve increases its liabilities, *i.e.,* the deposits of member banks. To do so, it must acquire assets. Member bank borrowing, just noted, is one of three major ways by which the "Fed" gets assets. Each, of course, may operate in reverse. One of the two remaining methods involves gold flows, the other open market operations. The illustrations below assume an average reserve requirement of 16 percent.

Gold Inflow

If gold flows into the monetary system (from imports, new mining, industrial use, or dishoarding), the Treasury buys it. Payment is made with a Treasury check. The seller deposits this check in his bank. The

Federal Reserve Bank		Member Bank	
Sends Treasury Check			
Assets	Liabilities	Assets	Liabilities
Gold certifi- cate + $100	Member bank deposit + $100	Deposit at FR + $100	Deposit of seller of gold + $100
	Treasury deposit − $100	(Required reserve + $ 16	
	+ $100	Excess reserve + $ 84)	

commercial bank will then turn over the Treasury's check to the Federal Reserve. The member bank's deposit at the FR rises; the Treasury's deposit, however, drops by the same amount.

To replenish its account, the Treasury issues a gold certificate to the FR, which thus has more assets—gold certificates. It also has more liabilities—the increase in the deposit of the commercial bank in which the seller of gold put his funds. The Treasury's deposit balance is the same as before it bought the gold. The member bank has $84 more of reserves than required for the $100 deposit of the seller of gold. If the Treasury purchases silver, member bank reserves also increase.[6] Changes in reserves resulting from movements of gold and silver are largely beyond the control of System officials.[7] Foreign trade and investment are now the main determinants of gold flows.

Open-Market Purchase of Securities

Banks will also get reserves if the FR buys government debt or some other security. The FR has complete, or nearly complete, control over this type of change in its assets. Here is much the most important instrument for altering member bank reserves.

The Federal Open Market Committee, we assume, tells the New York Bank to buy securities for the System's account. (Its own reserves are adequate.) The "Fed" will pay the seller with a check drawn on itself. The seller, perhaps an insurance company or an individual, deposits the check in a commercial bank which redeposits it in the FR. The FR has gained an asset which earns it income. In return it has assumed a liability, the increase in the member bank's deposit account. This deposit is a legal reserve. The process is simple and effective.

Federal Reserve Bank		Member Bank	
	Federal Reserve Check		
Assets	Liabilities	Assets	Liabilities
Security + $100	Member bank deposit + $100	Deposit at FR + $100	Deposit of seller of security + $100
		(Required reserve + $ 16	
		Excess reserve + $ 84)	

Purchases of assets by the FR have provided much of the largest part of the increase in reserves since the 1930's. Note that the FR creates what it uses for payment—its own debt, the deposit that it owes the mem-

[6] The Treasury is now a seller, not a buyer, of silver. When it did buy, sellers of silver deposited Treasury checks in commercial banks, which in turn deposited the funds in the Federal Reserve. The Treasury rebuilt its account by issuing silver certificates. These, unlike gold certificates, are not legal reserves of the FR.

[7] During the 1930's the Treasury kept changes in gold holdings from having their full potential effect on the monetary system. It "sterilized" gold. In effect, it chose not to issue to the FR gold certificates for all the gold it received.

ber bank. This debt, unlike a bond, yields the owner no interest. Will it, then, always be accepted? It certainly will, for it is valuable. In effect, a member bank can use most of this amount—$84 in our illustration —to acquire earning assets. And member banks *as a group* can build up their loans and deposit liabilities to a multiple of the $100 original purchase by the Federal Reserve.

Treasury Balances and Bank Reserves

By far the biggest single owner and user of money, and the biggest borrower, is the United States Treasury. Congress has given it special powers; its officials have at times acquired others. As a result, its financial transactions influence the monetary system.

The Treasury is permitted to keep deposits not only in the FR banks and branches but also in insured commercial banks. An obvious reason for using banks in communities large and small is the convenience to taxpayers of depositing locally. More important, however, is the fact that exclusive reliance by the Treasury upon FR facilities would complicate banking tremendously.

Tax payments are not closely synchronized either in time or location with government spending. (Government debt operations, largely refundings, also produce big and uneven movements of funds.) Suppose that all checks received in payment of taxes (or for sales of bonds) were deposited at once in the Treasury's account at the "Fed." The typical commercial bank would find that its deposit at the FR (its legal reserve) had dropped as depositors' checks for taxes were credited to the Treasury. For banks as a group, the resulting decline in reserves in months of peak income tax payment could easily be one-quarter of *all* reserves. Lending capacity would obviously fall. Later, then, when the Treasury spent from its account at the FR, commercial banks would get back deposits at the FR—legal reserves—as government employees and suppliers deposited Treasury checks.

The total volume of reserves and of bank lending capacity—and the distribution among banks—would change erratically, with no economic rationale. The money market would churn around in a confusing, disturbing way, adding to the uncertainties and costs of banking. If the differences between flows into and out of the Treasury were small, the disturbances would be minor. But fluctuations today are large in relation to legal reserves.

To minimize disturbances, the Treasury maintains Tax and Loan Accounts at about 11,000 commercial banks. When the Treasury receives a check drawn on one of these banks for taxes or from the sale of a bond, it deposits the check in the bank. The bank's total of deposit liabilities, its reserves, and its required reserves remain the same. When the Treasury expects to use the funds to make payments, it (through the FR) issues a "call" upon banks. They are notified that on a designated date the FR will transfer a certain percentage of the amount in the Tax and Loan Account from the bank's account at the FR to the Treasury's. Small banks get two weeks' notice; the biggest banks, however, get less advance warning, perhaps only a few hours. The Treasury then makes disbursements from the balance at the FR.

Most of the time around 90 percent of the Treasury's deposits are in commercial banks. And the Federal Reserve in its day-to-day open market operations attempts to offset temporary fluctuations which might result from Treasury receipts and disbursements. Consequently, the monetary effects of unevenness in the flows of funds to and from the government are rarely disturbing. The Treasury receives no interest on its deposits at commercial banks. It believes, on the basis of special studies, that the services which the banks render the government without charge do provide reasonable compensation for any possible loss of interest.

Other Factors

Total member bank reserves change in other ways. From day to day, such changes can have appreciable effects on individual banks and, if they are not offset, on the whole system. Shifts in and out of accounts of foreign banks at the FR can alter member bank deposits there; for example, if a foreign bank acting for its government or for a business firm uses funds on deposit at the FR to pay for goods bought in this country, member bank reserves rise. A rise or fall in "float," and shifts of deposits between member and nonmember banks, will change reserves. Finally, shifts of deposits among banks with different reserve requirements, and from time to demand deposits or vice versa, alter the total of *required* reserves but not the total of reserves in existence.

THE RESERVE EQUATION

The elements which go into determining the total of member bank reserves can be gathered together and expressed in a sort of equation. The form in Table 10.2 is that used in the *Federal Reserve Bulletin*. The first three items (combining to the total shown in item 4) make up the FR assets (or in the case of Treasury currency, potential assets) which might be matched by deposits owed to member banks—except that in fact there are other claims offsetting part of this total, the amounts in items 5 through 8. The difference, item 10, plus currency and coin held by commercial banks, is the total of member bank reserves, item 12.

TABLE 10.2

Member Bank Reserves, Reserve Bank Credit, and Related Items, 1964 [a]
(Billions)

Factors Supplying Reserve Funds			
1. Federal Reserve credit		$36.8	
a. United States government securities	$34.6		
b. Discounts and advances (member bank			
borrowings)	.3		
c. Float	1.8		
2. Gold stock (certificates)		15.5	
3. Treasury currency outstanding		5.6	
4. Total			$57.9
Factors Absorbing Reserve Funds			
5. Currency in circulation [b]		37.5	
6. Treasury cash holdings		.4	
7. Deposits other than member			
bank reserves		1.2	
a. Treasury	.9		
b. Foreign	.1		
c. Other	.2		
8. Other Federal Reserve accounts		1.3	
9. Total deductions			40.4
10. Member bank reserves at Federal Reserve			17.4
plus			
11. Vault cash (currency and coin)			3.2
12. Total member bank reserves			20.5

[a] June 30, 1964.
[b] Currency in circulation represents not only FR notes but also most of the Treasury currency of item 3.

Because of rounding details do not add to total.

Source: *Federal Reserve Bulletin,* July 1964.

Other things being the same, increases in items 1, 2, 3, and 11 raise member bank reserves; of these, of course, 1a is generally the most important. Increases in items 5, 6, 7, and 8 reduce reserves.

BALANCE SHEET OF THE SYSTEM

The assets, liabilities, and capital accounts of the twelve FR banks combined are shown in Table 10.3. Clearly, there are two major assets and two major liabilities. Note that items which correspond to items in Table 10.2 differ slightly; the tables apply to different dates.

TABLE 10.3

Balance Sheet of the Federal Reserve Banks, 1964 [a]
(Billions)

Assets		Liabilities and capital accounts	
Gold certificates	$15.2	Federal Reserve notes	$32.3
Cash	.1	Deposits of member banks	17.0
Discounts and advances (borrowings of member banks)	.1	United States Treasury deposits	1.0
United States government securities	34.5	Foreign owned deposits	.1
		Other deposits	.2
Cash items in the process of collection	6.2	Deferred availability cash items [b]	4.4
		Other	0.1
Bank premises and other assets	0.5	Capital and surplus	1.6
Total	$56.7	Total	$56.7

[a] June 24, 1964.

[b] Amounts which will be due member banks within one or two days for checks which are being cleared. The "float" on this particular date was $1.8 billion, the difference between (1) deferred availability cash items and (2) cash items in the process of collection.

Because of rounding details do not add to totals.

Source: *Federal Reserve Bulletin*, July 1964.

QUESTIONS

1. What, if any, is the logic of imposing reserve requirements which are lower on time than on demand deposits?

2. What is the major purpose today of requiring banks to hold reserves? Would not banks in their own self-interest hold adequate assets for customer needs?

3. "There is no longer any good reason for requiring banks in a few cities to hold percentages of deposits as reserves which are larger than those held by banks in other cities, towns, and villages." Discuss.

4. What would be the probable effects of permitting the Federal Reserve to pay interest on the legal reserves of member banks?

5. "The methods by which an individual bank can get reserves are essentially different from the methods available to the banking system as a whole." Discuss.

6. How can a member bank increase its legal reserves?

7. If the reserve requirements of all banks were the same, would there still be any economic significance to the way the Treasury handled its deposits? Explain.

8. In what sense are reserves "idle assets"?

9. What is the "reserve equation"? What items are of greatest importance?

10. How might reserve requirements be modified?

11. Compare an increase in gold holdings with open market purchases as methods of altering bank reserves.

12. Explain how shifting of deposits can alter reserve requirements.

13. In recent years the United States has been losing gold. Can the effects of such losses on bank reserves be offset by open-market operations?

CHAPTER 11   *ANALYSIS OF FEDERAL RESERVE CONTROLS OVER BANK RESERVES*

THE Federal Reserve has three major instruments for influencing the lending capacity of member banks. Two—open market operations and the discount rate—influence the amount of reserves. The third is the power to modify reserve requirements, *i.e.,* the amount that a member bank must hold for each dollar it owes its depositors. We now examine these instruments or tools of control. The objectives and some of the problems of control remain for discussion in Part Five.

Of necessity, each must be discussed apart from the others. Yet the effects of any one depend upon how officials are using others. Coordination is a prerequisite for success.

REVISION OF RESERVE REQUIREMENTS

The FR's power to change reserve requirements dates from Congressional action in 1935. Table 10.1 shows the range within which the FR may now fix requirements and a few of the rates in effect since 1917.

Immediate Effects of Change

A change in the percentage required as legal reserve may apply to all banks, to all those in reserve cities only, or to all country banks only. A change may apply to demand deposits or to time deposits or to both. The revision does not alter the amount of legal reserve but initially has two effects: (1) A rise in the percentage required will reduce any existing excess reserves and perhaps create a deficiency; a reduction in the requirement will cut down or eliminate a deficiency or create or enlarge an excess. (2) The change will alter the possibilities of multiple creation of deposits. For example, assume that banks have $20 billion of reserves, that no significant amount is excess, and that the average reserve requirement is 20 percent. The FR then cuts the average to 16⅔ percent. The deposit multiplier rises from 5 to 6. Excess reserves now appear—about $3.3 billion, enough (ignoring currency drain) to permit a $20 billion expansion in deposits.

Use of Power to Vary Requirements

The power to change reserve requirements is used infrequently and with caution. This tool will rarely be appropriate for meeting a temporary condition. For one thing, the smallest change readily made—half a percentage point—is 3 percent of total required reserves. Such a change would be larger than is desirable for most temporary situations. Variation in the requirement applies so broadly that its use is most appropriate when a more or less permanent change is desired. The banker learning of a change in reserve requirements will probably interpret the action as laying the basis for rather general revision of his lending policy.

A change in reserve requirements applies to all banks in the classes affected. It operates more broadly than do the other two instruments of control, changes in the discount rate and open market operations. The direct influence of changes in reserve requirements is not limited to those banks which are borrowing from the FR nor to those whose reserve position will be affected appreciably by open market operations. Alterations can be announced to become effective after a period of time which will allow banks to adjust gradually.

If the banks have great excess reserves, as was the case early in 1936 (reserves held then were about double requirements) an increase in the requirement may have little effect.[1] If banks are about fully loaned up, however, an increase in requirements can exert compelling pressure. In response, bankers may increase their borrowings from the FR so that total reserves rise and offset some of the effect of the higher percentage require-

---

[1] What is *legally* an excess reserve may not exceed the amount the banker *wants*. Although the 1936 increase in the legal requirement brought little bank response, a rise in 1937 had an effect. The banks had excess reserves in 1937. But the amounts remaining above the legal requirement may well have been desired by banks, *e.g.,* for liquidity reasons. At least some contractive effect on the stock of money did follow when excess reserves were reduced from $2.2 billion to $700 million in half a year, as legal requirements were raised.

ment. Individual banks may also seek relief by selling secondary reserves. Such sales, however, cannot help banks as a group unless the buyer is the Federal Reserve. (Sales from one bank to customers of another will shift, not increase, reserves.) Open market action can do much to accentuate or offset the effects of changes in reserve requirements, to ease the transition from one level to another. Unfortunately, the response of bankers cannot be determined in advance with certainty.

Large and discontinuous change is generally undesirable in monetary affairs. The mere announcement of a change in reserve requirements makes news. Presumably the public will conclude that the FR is changing policy. Who can know what the psychological reaction may produce? If a change proves to be too big, partial reversal is difficult, if only as a matter of prestige; much harm may be done before the error is recognized and admitted.

A cut in the requirement increases the earning possibilities of banks. A given volume of reserves will support larger deposits. Bankers welcome such reductions. The downward movement since 1951 reflects to some extent FR desire to enable member banks to meet rising costs and to compete with non-member banks whose requirements were lower and also with financial institutions (see Chapter 12) whose holdings of "sterile" (non-income-producing) assets are relatively smaller. Critics of reducing reserve requirements point out that open market purchases would have much the same effect while benefitting the U.S. Treasury; FR earnings and refunds to the government would be greater.

Opposition to increases in requirements would be strong unless the FR were to pay interest to member banks. However, an emergency requiring sudden, large increases in Federal spending might appropriately be financed by direct sale of Treasury debt to the FR with a rise in reserve requirements to offset the addition to reserves as the Treasury pays out.

CONTROL OF MEMBER BANK BORROWING:
DISCOUNT RATE

The second of the major powers involves the access of member banks to Federal Reserve credit, *i.e.,* the ability of banks to borrow at the "Fed" to get reserves.[2] The chief, or at least the most obvious, device for exercising this control is the discount rate, *i.e.,* the charge to the borrowing bank.

---

[2] This power has developed into something markedly different from what the founders of the Federal Reserve had in mind. They wanted (a) to insure that money would be available if panic conditions led the public to demand increasing amounts of cash and (b) to provide for an "elastic currency," amounts rising and falling with the seasonal and other "needs of trade."

Each of the 12 banks sets its own rate, subject to Board approval; in fact, the separate banks rarely act except all at once. Rates are almost always uniform over the whole country. Action must be taken every 14 days, if only to reaffirm explicitly an existing rate. Ordinarily, rate changes follow interest rate moves which have appeared in the money market.

Let us look briefly at the process of borrowing. Federal Reserve loans to member banks take two main forms. One is the discounting (or rediscounting) of notes that the bank has received from its customers. The second is lending on a bank's own note supported by collateral. In both cases the individual bank takes the initiative.

Discounting

In discounting, a member bank endorses and sends to the FR "paper" (IOU's received from its borrowers) which meets standards of eligibility. The "Fed" then deducts interest (discount) and credits the member bank's account with the remainder.

What is eligible? Present criteria still reflect pre-1914 thinking—that bank lending should consist of self-liquidating commercial loans. Congress, therefore, restricted eligibility to notes, drafts, or bills of exchange running for not more than 90 days (9 months in the case of agricultural loans) given to the bank for loans to finance the production and distribution of goods.[3] These legal limitations remain, although by general agreement they are obsolete.

In addition, the FR possesses, and on occasion apparently utilizes, discretionary authority to judge acceptability. The criteria include the credit worthiness of the borrower and of the transactions involved. Here is emphasis on loan quality, a characteristic which is difficult to define precisely.

The funds obtained by the bank do not as a rule support a loan to the business whose note is pledged. The lending capacity may not go even to a somewhat similar business. Loan expansion resulting from discounting may be used for purposes of which the FR would disapprove. Nevertheless, wide departures from FR standards are not likely to persist long. System officials have, and will use, the discretion to refuse future accommodation for a bank if they believe that its lending is really inappropriate.

Experience gradually revealed disadvantages with the discounting process. Essentially mechanical problems were annoying. To illustrate,

---

[3] Notes for buying or carrying U.S. government securities are also eligible, but not notes to finance other security transactions.

the amounts and maturities of customers' notes are not always convenient. A bank's dealings with a borrower may get a bit clumsy if his note is at the FR rather than in the bank's vaults when he wants to repay. Borrowers may not like to have the bank disclose their affairs to the FR to the extent which may be required to establish the eligibility of borrower notes. And not least important, banks at times have needed help without having had the "paper" which met eligibility standards; thus, discounting has occasionally proved impossible in the emergencies when strains were great.

Advances: Member Bank Borrowing

The more common method today is for a bank to request an advance or loan from the FR, usually for 15 days. The borrowing bank in return gives its own note supported by collateral equal to at least the amount borrowed. The collateral may be commercial paper that meets the standards of eligibility for discount. Usually, however, for practical reasons of convenience, government debt is pledged. The actual securities used are often those which the member bank has sent to the "Fed" for safekeeping.

Congress has given the FR authority to accept a member bank note secured by other types of collateral which satisfy the FR, *e.g.*, notes pledging term loans. Such collateral may be more readily available than traditionally eligible paper or government debt. However, a *penalty* interest charge is made when the FR consents to the use of such assets—$\frac{1}{2}$ percentage point above the rate on other borrowing. This power to use its discretion gives the FR freedom which can help in emergency. The penalty rate, however, is a vestige of older thinking about the superiority of self-liquidating short-term commercial loans. Justification for the penalty is hard to find.

Use of Federal Reserve Borrowing Facilities

A bank's desire to borrow will depend upon conditions in the market as a whole as well as upon those peculiar to the bank itself.[4] Many banks as a general rule try other means of getting reserves before going to the FR. The bank may turn to the market for "Federal funds." It may sell securities. Or it may try to borrow from a correspondent. The ability

---

[4] Banks (with FR cooperation, at least until recently) have resorted to "window dressing." On their public statements they do not like to show indebtedness to the FR, a reluctance that reflects a deepseated belief that a well-run bank will not itself borrow. Member banks, therefore, arrange to pay back all or some of their debt for a day or two at the end of the month on which they are to issue a public statement. They meet the legal reserve requirement by borrowing enough more on other days to maintain the necessary average for the period.

to do so, of course, depends upon the reserve position of other banks. The greater the volume of excess reserves held by other banks, the greater the opportunity of banks short of reserves to satisfy needs without borrowing from the "Fed." On the other hand, a tightening open-market policy (described later) creates pressure which induces banks to seek FR loans.

Access to the "discount window" at the FR may be denied, *i.e.,* a member bank does not have an unqualified right to borrow. Congress has made it clear that the System may refuse bank requests for loans. Officials apparently never make a blunt refusal.[5] They act to forestall applications which they will not wish to grant. Each of the 12 banks tries to maintain consistent standards which distinguish "appropriate" requests from those which will probably be denied. (Standards differ somewhat from area to area.) Consequently, a banker can have a good idea about the types of applications which will be unwelcome and which will subject him to criticism.

Occasional errors in a bank's forecasts of its reserve position are to be expected. When the errors lead to a shortage of reserves, bank borrowing at the "Fed" is appropriate—but not often and not for prolonged periods. Similarly, seasonal shifts of deposits or loan requests will sometimes be greater than could reasonably have been expected. Such surprises provide approved reasons for turning to the discount window. A bank's *normal* seasonal needs, however, should be handled, the System believes, without recourse to FR credit.

Officials do not consider "continuous" borrowing proper, borrowing either at the FR or in the market for Federal funds. If there is need to "make good loans to good customers" beyond the bank's capacity, the bank evidently is short of capital or is failing to liquidate securities. The FR does not believe that it should go into "partnership" with a bank in such cases. The System conceives of its lending as a means helping to meet temporary and exceptional need. Federal Reserve credit is not intended for such purposes as helping to finance a growing community or the construction of a school or other desirable project (except for brief, and rare, emergencies). While the standards of appropriateness are admittedly subject to interpretation, the System's management asserts that the standards are "consistent from year to year."

Influence of the Discount Rate

The discount rate is a price, one which, for substantial periods, is fixed rather than free to move with changes in demand and supply. Yet

---

[5] C. R. Whittlesey, "Credit Policy at the Discount Window," *Quarterly Journal of Economics,* May 1959, pp. 207–16.

the supply is not elastic in the ordinary sense. The System will not make unlimited quantities of loan accommodation available at the price. What, then, is the significance of the rate itself? and of changes in it? The answers vary considerably. Men who have studied these questions confess to uncertainty. For banks with excess reserves, or a banking system with large excess reserves, the discount rate has minimal influence.

The rate itself is not so important as its *relation to other rates*. The same applies to *changes*. The degree to which banks use the discount window at the "Fed" will depend, among other things, upon the cost in relation to other costs of getting reserves and upon the prospects of using the lending capacity obtained.

The discount rate, ordinarily well below bank lending rates, is designed not as a penalty, but more as a deterrent.[6] Consequently, a bank may often be able to lend at least as much to its customers as it borrows from the FR and charge a higher rate than it must pay.[7] A rational banker seeking maximum profit, it would seem, would borrow, or not, as indicated by his reserve position in relation to loan demand. The rate, and changes in it, should not have much effect, for there will usually be a gross profit on loans which are made possible by borrowing from the "Fed." Why would a banker act differently as a result of changes in the rate? There is a related question which stems from the fact that FR officials have long had a policy of discouraging member bank discounting as a source of profit. If such attitudes are influential, will a rate change have much effect? Despite the implied negative answers to both questions, changes in the discount rate do have effects.

For one thing, rate changes do alter somewhat the attractiveness of discounting. The rate does influence profit margins on bank lending. A rate increase will deter some borrowing and induce the bank to make other adjustments. For it, the difference may be slight, but for the banking system as a whole, the effect on the aggregate reserve position can be significant. Discount rate increases usually follow upward moves in the market. Increases in the FR's rate will be made at a time when banks are raising their own charges. As a result, some borrowing by bank customers may be discouraged, reducing the need for greater reserves, but the responses of this sort are not likely to be large.

Another result of a rise in the rate is clearer. As low-yield short-term securities mature, banks seeking to repay the "Fed" will more often

---

[6] In Britain, for example, the cost of borrowing from the Bank of England generally exceeds the yield on the assets held by the institutions ("discount houses") which use the Bank's lending facilities.

[7] An increase in reserves permits banks as a group to expand loans—create deposits—up to a multiple of the increase. An individual bank, however, would safely lend only the approximate amount of the increase. Incentives to use the discount window would be much greater if the borrowing bank could count upon making all the additional loans which the banking system as a whole will be able to make.

press their borrowers to pay more in cash. Or banks will sell securities outright, using their secondary reserves. (No new reserves are created by such sales, of course, even though individual banks gain reserves at the expense of others.) Such sales tend to reduce security prices or yields on outstanding debt increase. Consequently, the issue and sale of new securities will require the offer of higher interest rates and become somewhat less attractive—except that the magnitudes are probably too small to have any perceptible effect.

The power over the discount rate is power to influence bank access to the FR. Other things being the same, the higher the rate in relation to others, the smaller the use banks will try to make of borrowing from the FR in relation to other methods of getting reserves. Undoubtedly, under any given set of circumstances there is a rate which will largely choke off member bank borrowing. No one can be sure how high this rate will be, nor to what extent, in moving up, the FR will discourage such borrowing significantly before it eliminates all but emergency member bank borrowing. Such uncertainty is a basic defect of this element of our system of monetary controls.

Will a reduction in the rate induce any increase in borrowing? The direct effect may be small. Because of the tradition against borrowing, the results may be much less than from an increase of equal size. If banks do not want to borrow—if they have ample reserves or if those banks that are short can get reserves more cheaply in the Federal funds market or by selling assets—lowering the rate may have little effect.[8] Yet, ordinarily, at least some banks will tend to make greater use of discounting in preference to other methods of getting reserves, the lower the discount rate is in relation to other rates in the market. Thus if discounting costs 3 percent and Treasury bills yield 3½ percent, a bank will tend to borrow at the "Fed" rather than to sell bills. The tendency would be even greater if the spread were, say, from 3 to 4 percent. But if the bill yield is 2½ percent, a sale of bills is preferable to discounting at 3 percent.

Changes in rate have some "announcement effect," some psychological impact. They suggest something about the system's view of the economic outlook and the general kind of monetary policy that the FR can be expected to pursue. At least some indirect effects develop. But we have no way to measure them. Moreover, misinterpretation is easy, and some reactions may be perverse. A reduction in the rate, for example, may lead many people to conclude that the FR expects poorer business; private buying may then decline. The FR may "follow the market" or try to

---

[8] In 1964 all member banks incurred costs for discounts and advances of $8.7 million. Their gross income from loans was over $4.9 billion. In 1959, the last year of relatively large member bank borrowing from the FR, one out of three member banks borrowed at some time during the year. They paid a total of $28 million to the FR.

lead it. Rarely can we know which the officials are attempting. What is economically significant is the relation of the discount rate to market rates, not the relation of the present rate to that of the past. But the announcement applies to the latter. The public is more likely to look at discount rate changes alone rather than at their relation to what has been going on in the market.

One disadvantage of the discount rate is the jerkiness of changes as they are actually made. These discontinuities are an obstacle to smooth monetary adjustment. A system once used in Canada has merit. There, the discount rate was tied automatically to the market rate, being set each week at ¼ of 1 percent above the most recent average rate on Treasury bills.

A final point requires emphasis. The FR's discount rate does not make the market rate of interest. The latter depends upon a total which includes many other conditions. (See Chapter 15.) The "Fed's" lending is only one of the many factors which affect market supply and demand for loanable funds. Unfortunately, there is a popular tendency to attribute far too much interest-rate influence to the actions of System officials in setting the discount rate. Another point also deserves mention. Use of whatever power the FR does have to change interest rates is not necessarily in the public interest. Some groups may want easier borrowing, or easier credit, and call for the Federal Reserve to do what it can to reduce interest rates. Such action might, or might not, aid the economy.

Lender of Last Resort

The FR's power to lend to member banks constitutes a safety valve, an escape hatch, an "emergency resource." When unforeseen trouble arises, the individual bank can get accommodation rather than put pressure on its borrowers.

Note a vital difference between an individual bank and the Federal Reserve. When a commercial bank increases its liabilities, it faces the limits which will arise from adverse clearing. Its ability to expand is thereby restricted. The power of the FR is strikingly different. The System can *create* what is needed to meet unusual demands to the extent that they arise domestically. It can create deposits. It can issue currency. Therefore, except as the demands for additional funds come from abroad, the FR can meet the needs of member banks.

OPEN MARKET OPERATIONS

As the "Trading Desk" at the Federal Reserve Bank of New York buys and sells in the money market, it conducts open market operations.

It does so for the whole System. It does so every business day. Sometimes it acts to counteract temporary disturbances, action it calls *defensive*.
In contrast, it also pursues a *dynamic* policy as it buys or sells to raise or
lower the level of lending power of banks.

Authorities are in general agreement that this is the instrument to
which we should look for major control of the monetary system.

Effects on Bank Reserves

When the FR buys government debt, or commercial paper, in the
open market,[9] it pays with its own debt or liability—a check on itself.
The seller deposits the check in his bank, which then sends it to the FR;
the commercial bank's deposits (reserves) thus rise. The member bank
can then (1) increase its loans to customers, or (2) enlarge its own purchases of government debt or commercial paper, or (3) repay debt to the
"Fed," or (4) lend any excess in the Federal funds market, or (5) enjoy
greater liquidity.

The FR can also sell government debt. When it does so, the purchaser writes a check on his bank account. The FR then deducts this
amount from the bank's deposit (reserve). Since this process of contraction was not described earlier, we illustrate it here:

Federal Reserve   Member Bank

    ←————————Check of Buyer of Treasury Bill

Assets	Liabilities	Assets	Liabilities
Treasury bill − $100	Deposit of member bank − $100	Deposit at Federal Reserve − $100	Deposit of buyer of Treasury bill from FR − $100
		(Required reserve − $ 16	
		Other reserves − $ 84)	

[9] Until 1955, the FR set rates at which it would buy bankers' acceptances in any
quantity offered. The purpose was to help build a market for this type of credit instrument. Purchases were sometimes named "involuntary" open market operations.
Rarely were they important, however. The newer system of buying such assets as a
part of discretionary open market action represents no substantial change. Repurchase agreements have much the same effect as outright purchases, but for a short
time only.

The FR may choose to let Treasury bills mature and not replace them. In such a case the Treasury's deposits drop by the amount it uses to pay the "Fed." Any effect on the banking system appears as the Treasury makes larger calls than it otherwise would on its deposits at commercial banks.

Ordinarily in buying or selling, the FR does not know which banks will be affected directly. It does know that in a market as active as the money market any significant change in one place will soon be felt widely —but not evenly.

Effects on Bank Lending

The power that can be exerted by open market operations is greater at some times than at others. The response of banks, and of their customers, is not automatic. Many variations of conditions are conceivable. Banks, for example, may be changing their demands for (excess) reserves.

If banks have more excess reserves than they want, modest FR open market sales to reduce reserves may have slight effect on bank lending. However, if the banks are loaned up fully, open market sales will force bankers to adjust somehow to the reduction in reserves. For a time, of course, the banks that are pressed can seek help at the discount window— at a cost; but continuous borrowing is not permitted. Some other action is eventually required. Individual banks can seek relief by selling short-term securities, but a second bank loses the reserve gained by the first. Bank customers will find borrowing more difficult. Interest rates will rise. The FR *can* sell enough assets to force any amount of monetary contraction (with a resulting rise in interest rates) which it believes desirable. Yet in forcing down bank lending and the stock of money, the FR may overshoot its goal.

The power to increase bank reserves by open market operations is also clear and strong. What is not so clear is the amount and the speed of bank and customer response to an increase in bank lending capacity which results from FR open market operations in creating reserves. The public reactions are not always the same, especially in amount. If the current demand for loans is active, it can be satisfied more fully when reserves increase. The money stock will rise, and the newly borrowed funds will be spent. If there is little demand for more loans, however, expansion of demand deposits may be slow.

Banks, however, will not ordinarily hold large excess reserves. If customers do not want to increase their borrowings, banks will try to increase their earnings by the purchase of securities, paying with newly created deposits. The stock of money grows. Money becomes "easier."

Use of Open Market Operations

Open market operations are under the control of the System. It can speed up or slow down actions. Gradual, unspectacular action is possible. Policy can be reversed without headlines that may bring unexpected public response. Authorities can "feel out" the market. Or they can act with quick and impressive vigor. In carrying out daily operations, technical competence of a high order has been gained. Major policy matters, however, present far more difficult problems, as we shall see in Part Five.

FREE RESERVES[10]

Open market operations and discount policy are closely related. Some banks will be discounting while others hold excess reserves. Most member banks, in fact, cannot pay close attention to their reserve position in the sense of making daily adjustments. Only the large banks can afford a skilled officer to maintain hawk-eyed watch of reserves. Moreover, when a bank, especially one outside the main financial centers, has only a small excess, the gain from any feasible use may not seem worth the trouble.

Numerous factors are always changing bank reserves in relation to requirements. One figure "nets" the results of all the factors, bringing everything into focus at one point. This is the figure of "free reserves." The figure is positive when excess reserves for all member banks are above borrowings by all member banks. It is negative when borrowings are greater than holdings of excess reserves. Fig. 11.1 shows monthly relationships. Note what happened from the boom of 1957 to the recession trough of 1958 and then as recovery gained force into 1959. From one week to the next, changes in the figure may not indicate FR policy. But over a few weeks the totals are more likely to suggest policy. They do *not,* however, show either total reserves or changes in the total.

Negative free reserves are ordinarily assumed to indicate, in a loose way, "tight" money—a positive figure, "easy" money. It goes without saying that the size of the figure and the trend both make a difference. Unfortunately, we have no comparable measure of the demand of banks for (excess) reserves. If, for example, bankers for some reason increase their desires for reserves more rapidly than reserves grow, even though the free reserve figure is positive, money may actually become tighter. In short, what is happening to free reserves may not always tell the "net" of

---

[10] See A. J. Meigs, *Free Reserves and the Money Supply* (Chicago: University of Chicago Press, 1962).

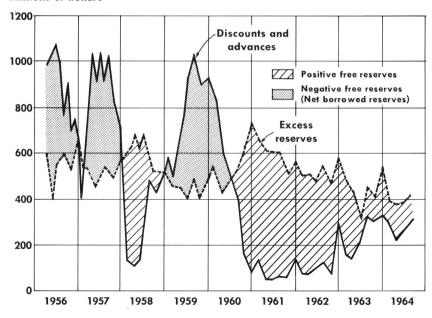

Millions of dollars

FIGURE 11.1

**Excess Reserves, Member Bank Borrowings, and Positive and Negative
Free Reserves, 1956–63**

Source: *Federal Reserve Bulletin*

all the relevant changes. The significance of any given total, positive or
negative, or any change, will depend upon other conditions, and changes
in them. Yet this "weekly barometer" of monetary change is one of the
most widely used.

MISCELLANEOUS POWERS

The FR has other powers, the effectiveness of which is difficult to
weigh.

Tradition

Tradition is important. Over a period of years the FR has helped
build attitudes of its officials and of commercial bankers. Well-entrenched
traditions have developed. They are not necessarily tools in the sense of

variables which can be modified in the short run. They are part of the framework in which other instruments of control are used. They influence results in ways which would not otherwise be expected. Perhaps the most important—the tradition against continuous borrowing—has already been discussed.

Moral Suasion

Moral suasion, or "psychological pressure," by the FR has influence which defies measurement. The large number of banks and other financial institutions in this country makes the problem substantially different from that in most lands. Abroad it is often true that a few men at the head of key institutions make policy for most of the financing which is done by banks and insurance companies. Where this concentration prevails, the heads of the central bank can exert, directly and often in face-to-face discussion, great influence on the whole financial system. In the United States the corresponding power is of another, lower, order of magnitude.

By testimony before Congressional committees and in written reports, by speeches and pronouncements, public and private, FR officials indicate how they think bankers should be acting in the light of current conditions. In frequent contacts with individual bankers and groups of bankers, FR officials can express disapproval of certain kinds of action—lending to finance "speculation"—or approval of others. System leaders will at times try to persuade, to exhort, to convince a bank to act in ways that are not those most obviously in its immediate interest. Some appeals may be to sacrifice the interest of the bank to that of the country as a whole. Others may emphasize longer-run aspects, or perhaps the less obvious features, of current actions. Conceivably, pressures may be re-enforced by threats of penalties, more likely vague than specific.

What are the results? At the least some decisions will be made differently because of FR persuasion. A little bit of effect here, a little there, may add to a total that is significant at the margin. More than small effects may appear at times, but at other times—chiefly in periods of great exuberance or serious depression—the total result of moral suasion can easily be insignificant. The Program for Voluntary Credit Restraint during Korean hostilities yielded some of the results its sponsors sought—but far from all.

The uncertainty of the outcome, therefore, makes moral suasion an unreliable instrument. It is defective in another respect. To the extent that bankers are led to modify their actions, they may sacrifice their own interests to those which the FR believes serve the public. Banks which refuse to cooperate do not share the burdens, and they may gain a competitive advantage over those more responsive to official persuasion.

Margin Requirement and Other Selective Controls

One outgrowth of the 1929 stock market crash was the establishment of controls on bank and broker lending to buy securities (see Chapter 5). The Federal Reserve now determines the margin requirements for dealings on securities exchanges and some bank lending to buy stock. If the margin requirement is 70 percent, a buyer can borrow only 30 percent of the purchase price; the balance must be paid in cash. The significance and the logic of control by the monetary authorities of the use of credit for stock market activity are both debated.

The general public does have an interest in reducing the extremes of fluctuations in stock prices. Use of borrowed funds feeds the boom; repayment of loans under stress as the market drops deepens the plunge. In the late 1920's general business conditions did not call for tightening of money generally. Yet excesses on the stock market, financed largely by borrowed money, seemed to call for action. The burst of the bubble hurt the whole economy and contributed to the forces which brought about the Great Depression. We want nothing of the sort again. Yet does not the use of *monetary* powers for a type of selective *credit* control, by confusing two problems, run the risk of clumsiness in dealing with both? In general, an economy seeking to use the market system to allocate resources acts inconsistently when it imposes on the use of funds for one purpose limits which are vastly stricter than those elsewhere.[11]

The requirements since 1937 have unquestionably reduced the pyramiding of borrowing to buy on a rising market; no one can say by how much. Defenders of this selective control believe that reliance upon *general* monetary restraint to produce a comparable effect in the particular sector would have hurt business generally. The free demand for loans to buy on the stock market can be disturbingly volatile.

During World War II and the fighting in Korea, the System had varying control over lending to finance installment purchases and purchases of houses; Congress also gave it power to guarantee loans to private business to finance facilities needed for military output. From the 1930's to 1959 it had the power, which it almost never used, to make direct loans to busi-

---

[11] One criticism is that not all types of securities and not all lenders are in effect controlled. Exempt lenders can charge higher interest rates than if the market were free. Banks can lend more on unlisted stock or on bonds than on stock traded on exchanges. Another line of criticism focuses on the low level of lending which has been allowed at some times—only 10 percent from October 1958 to the summer of 1960. (Contrast this with the very much higher rates for other purposes.) A third defect is that any FR action in changing the requirements will be interpreted as an official judgment of the appropriateness of the prevailing level of market prices. For this reason—as well as for normal doubts and inertia, plus the human reluctance to imply that earlier decisions may have been wrong—action will almost inevitably be timed poorly.

ness for working capital.   It is authorized to lend up to $5 billion directly to the Treasury; this power, last used in 1958 (and on a small scale), permits the Treasury to operate with smaller cash balances than it would otherwise consider prudent.

Today's problems and their setting, the whole economy, have changed as the FR has used its power for half a century.   New conditions have presented new opportunities, problems, and challenges.   Changes continue to do so.   Some developments, in addition to the strains of two world wars, are the decline of the relative importance of the self-liquidating commercial loan, the growth of government debt, the insurance of bank deposits, new types of business and personal finance, great expansion in Treasury financing, the flourishing of competitive types of institutions, and the change in the position of our economy in that of the world.

QUESTIONS

1. What would be the result of an increase in reserve requirements?

2. "It is not so much a change in reserve requirements, or in the discount rate, or in open market operations as the net effect of all together, which will determine the course of bank lending capacity."   Discuss.

3. Why is discounting now used relatively less than borrowing by member banks?

4. Show how sale by the FR of securities in the open market affects member bank reserves; a purchase.

5. What is "continuous borrowing"?   How does the Federal Reserve regard it?

6. "There is no logic to discouraging member banks from using the 'discount window.'   Any 'excess' use can always be offset by open market sales."   Discuss.   Distinguish between the effect on individual banks and on the banking system as a whole.

7. What is the significance of changes in the FR discount rate?

8. "The ability of member banks to borrow at the Federal Reserve in effect provides insurance against a serious liquidity crisis." Discuss.   Can the Federal Reserve always meet the demands? Why?

9. In what sense is use of the discount rate "discontinuous" while open market operations are "continuous"?   What, if any, is the economic significance of the difference?

10. Explain the meaning of "free reserves." Assuming no other major changes, what will be the economic significance of a decline in free reserves?

11. What would you judge to be indicated by a reduction by the Federal Reserve in the margin required for the purchase of stock?

12. " 'Moral suasion' may serve usefully during war or a great national emergency. In general, however, it is not a method on which this country can, or ought to try to, rely." Discuss.

CHAPTER 12 *INTERMEDIARIES AND OTHER FINANCIAL INSTITUTIONS*[1]

COMMERCIAL banks, because of their role in creating money, play a unique part in the economy. They serve us in many more ways. So do other financial institutions, as they perform functions which are essential for prosperity and progress. Some of these functions are also performed by commercial banks. Each passing year, however, seems to narrow the differences between commercial banking and other financial institutions in terms of providing many economic services, including:

1. receipt of savings and their use to purchase income-producing assets; the institutions supply credit and help make funds available for capital formation;
2. provision of assets which have a high degree of liquidity;
3. management and administration of wealth;
4. insurance (combined sometimes with savings);
5. investment guidance;
6. marketing of securities, especially those newly issued;
7. lending to consumers and to special kinds of businesses;
8. safekeeping of securities and related services of many kinds.

This chapter presents, not a reasonably complete analysis, but a brief description of an apparently miscellaneous group of institutions, agencies, activities, and practices—and something of their economic significance.

---

[1] A highly useful source of information about fifteen types of institutions covers much more than the title suggests. . . . Committee on Banking and Currency, House . . . *Comparative Regulations of Financial Institutions* (Washington: Government Printing Office, 1963).

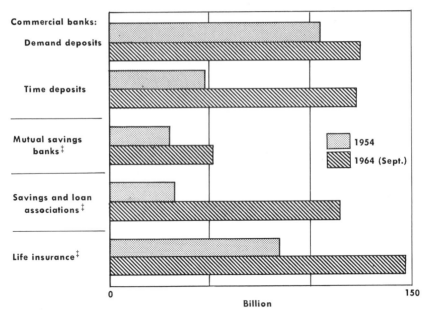

FIGURE 12.1

Growth of Selected Financial Magnitudes, 1954–64

FINANCIAL INTERMEDIARIES

Many of the institutions to be discussed fall into a group called "financial intermediaries." Their growth is part of the development of a more productive, and a more complex, economy, one in which the public receives more kinds of services to meet more needs and desires.

Some people receive more income than they want to spend on consumption. Therefore they save. The dollars saved in themselves are of limited usefulness. They create nothing which constitutes income. Yet many businesses, individuals, governments do want to spend more than their own income. To do so they must get dollars from someone else[2]— the saver or his agent.

Both the saver and the user of his savings can be served constructively

---

[2] In some cases, the need is met by credit which takes the form of permission to delay payment.

by efforts which bring the two together. Many agencies do just that—but indirectly. The person who does the saving and the one who uses the dollars rarely come face to face. Rather, officials of financial intermediaries exercise judgment and make the decisions about where the funds are used in financing new investment.

The institutions receive money without, as a rule, giving the saver any promise as to how dollars will be used, or by whom (a certain business or locality). The saver, of course, often does get a promise. Usually it is definite, such as the institution's promise to pay (or lend) in cash on short notice. The intermediary, having made such a promise, then acquires assets, such as the debt of someone who wants to use the money to build a new house, factory, or utility extension. Or the intermediary may buy an asset which has been outstanding for years, *e.g.,* a municipal bond or a share of stock. Ordinarily, the use that the seller of the asset makes of the cash, though perhaps important for the economy, is of little or no concern to the financial intermediary.

Several aspects of the role of intermediaries are important:

1. These agencies play a part in *resource allocation.* As they try to offer savers the most attractive terms possible within the limits set by their standards, and as they compete for the securities, new and old, which are being offered for sale, these intermediaries help establish the prices and yields of debt and equity securities. These prices reflect the wishes and judgments of the public. The more effectively these attitudes are tested, the more sharply that buyers and sellers are forced to compete with each other, the better are the chances that the best judgments will prevail. As a result, resources will flow to uses in which their creativity promises to be highest.

2. The existence of intermediaries enlarges the opportunities available to both the saver and the user of funds. As more financial institutions (numbers and types) become available, the range of choice for the public grows. What were once local markets become national and even international. Markets which once dealt in debt only become markets for equities as well. What were once markets for only large sums handle small amounts. And so on.

3. Financial intermediaries play an active part in the process of balancing the totals of (a) what the public saves out of income with (b) what others want to spend on new investment goods. Any failure of an economy to use savings to pay for the creation of new capital goods, or any failure to induce enough saving to pay for all the construction and real investment which is being made—either lack of balance will create undesirable conditions.

4. Intermediaries influence the feeling of liquidity in the economy. These institutions do not create means of payment, money. They do not give out more money than they receive. Yet their functioning does make people feel more liquid. Most types of intermediaries get money from the saver and promise to pay him money. As far as access to dollars is concerned, the saver's position seems hardly changed. What he has received can be almost "interest-bearing money" in his thinking. The intermediary, of course, does not hold on to the money but uses it to buy a security or make a mortgage loan. The seller of the security, or the borrower, now has money and spending power he did not have before. There is no change in the quantity of money in the economy. Nevertheless, the feeling of command over money has grown. The seller of the asset unquestionably has more money. Meanwhile, the depositor in the financial intermediary has good reason to feel that if he wishes he can get about the same number of dollars on short notice.

"Financial mediation" also plays a large role in consumer buying, especially house purchase. Chapter 4 dealt with commercial bank lending to consumers. Yet much comes from other sources. And consumers in placing their savings can choose among many alternatives other than savings accounts in commercial banks.

MUTUAL SAVINGS BANKS

Millions of depositors had about $48 billion in accounts at 506 mutual savings banks in 1964. These banks, operating in one-third of the states but heavily concentrated in New York, Massachusetts, and Connecticut, are chartered by states, not as stock corporations to operate for profit but as mutual associations all of whose income belongs to members. A few mutual savings banks today are giants with assets of around a billion dollars.

Early in the 1800's a few humanitarians recognized two facts: that large numbers of people with modest incomes would benefit from thrift, and that the economy would gain if the money thus saved were made available for lending (where risk was minimal). What, then, would encourage both saving and the constructive use of funds? The answer seemed to be the provision of safe, secure institutions to receive savings and then to invest them constructively but conservatively. At that time entrepreneurs seeking profit were establishing banks, but not the kind which the family with small savings would be wise to trust.

To meet a real need, therefore, public-spirited leaders got permission from state legislatures to set up special banks. These would be organized not for profit but for safety, combined with the use, not the hoarding, of wealth. Humble people could, in a sense, pool their small savings. Useful investment would become practical when the funds were combined into far more than the few dollars any one family could accumulate. Furthermore, the cooperation of many families would permit diversification in asset holdings and also greater liquidity than the individual could obtain by buying any of the assets then available.

In Philadelphia and Boston in 1816 mutual savings banks (following British precedents) began operating. Key founders became directors, serving without pay. The depositor, though a co-owner, had—and in 1965 still has—no part in selecting directors, for they appoint their successors.

A savings bank can acquire earning assets only by purchase with funds which have been deposited. Unlike a commercial bank, it cannot create money, means of payment. A borrower from a mutual savings bank will not want to receive in return for his IOU an account at the savings bank because he cannot use it to make a payment, as he could use a demand deposit at a commercial bank. Thus, when a savings bank lends, the borrower must get what depositors have put in (currency or a demand deposit). The savings bank loses cash equal to 100 percent of the loan.[3]

Safety is a paramount consideration in selecting the assets of savings banks. State laws require the holding of cash or other liquid, but income-producing, reserves of from 3 to 10 percent of deposits. States long required mutual savings banks to confine their buying of assets to a list of conservative issues—the "legal list"—chiefly top-grade corporate and government bonds and well-secured mortgages. After World War II, however, inflation and low yields on high-quality bonds led some states to permit mutual savings banks to put a portion of their funds into common and preferred stock, multifamily housing projects, and a variety of other assets. Mortgage loans account for about two thirds of all assets.

A few savings banks are large enough to maintain skilled investment staffs. Many, however, must rely on outside advice, such as is provided by leading city banks. Savings banks are under pressure to keep their assets earning income so that depositors can be offered rates of return which are reasonably close to those paid by other thrift institutions.

The banks rarely exercise their legal right to demand 30 to 90 days for payment of deposits. In the short run total deposits are stable, while growing from year to year. Consequently, a predominance of long-term assets presents little liquidity risk. A portfolio of prime bonds and mortgages costs less to manage than the typical commercial bank portfolio of the same size, with its loans which mature frequently and require re-examination. Savings banks have another operating-cost advantage over commercial banks. The activity per account is far less; relatively few entries are made from month to month.

Directors decide what portion of net earnings will be credited to the

---

[3] The same *may* be true of *a* commercial bank but *not* of the commercial banking system.

accounts of depositors as interest (commonly designated "dividend," because whatever is paid is a division of income). The remainder builds surplus. Since owners have provided no equity capital, there is strong reason for building a cushion to protect depositors—and the solvency of the institution. Reinvested earnings average about 9 percent of deposits.

Total 1965 assets of $55 billion were 3 times the amount at the end of World War II. Competition for deposits takes forms other than the stated rate of interest; for example, starting to credit interest as of several days before deposit, compounding at shorter intervals, or offering premiums for new accounts.

Mutual savings banks serve chiefly the more or less regular saver of modest income. They provide a convenient place for putting savings where dollar amounts will be safe and easily converted to cash, managed economically, and where the net earnings are the exclusive property of depositors. The depositor thinks of these funds as highly liquid, and for each individual they are. For any large group, however, cash could be provided on short notice only by the liquidation of assets which might have to be sold at some sacrifice.

Therefore, to reduce the danger of disturbance that might result if a few large depositors were suddenly to try to withdraw, laws fix the maximum individual deposit. This factor helps the bank to get along safely with smaller amounts of cash than might otherwise seem necessary. (A person or family can easily exceed the apparent limit by depositing in several institutions or under several names.) Most deposits are insured by the FDIC, but all banks do not belong; those in Massachusetts and Connecticut have state deposit insurance systems. Although only three savings banks belong to the Federal Reserve, those in New York, which account for most deposits, have a sort of central bank of their own—the Savings Bank Trust Company, a commercial bank which has membership in the FR.

The original benevolent aspect now seems of minor importance, but the spirit of careful trusteeship is very much alive. Meanwhile, other types of institutions have developed to offer competitive services. As commercial banks have raised the rate of interest paid on savings accounts, the competition for deposits has intensified. Savings banks also face competition as they seek to invest in high-quality bonds and mortgages. Competition, of course, works more than one way. Savings banks have broadened the range of assets that they will acquire and the services that they provide—safe deposit facilities, trust services, collection departments, sale of cashiers' checks, and life insurance—competing with commercial banks in more and more activities. Some tension has grown out of the efforts of commercial banks to acquire savings banks (with their deposits and surpluses).

To the depositor his savings account is a highly liquid asset, almost as liquid as money. These deposits cannot serve the "medium of exchange" function of money, but they represent a store of value with qualities of liquidity virtually as high as demand deposits.

SAVINGS AND LOAN ASSOCIATIONS

Few if any financial developments of our times can match the growth of savings and loan associations.[4] Assets rose from $9 billion in 1946 to nearly $115 billion by 1964. Most associations are mutual organizations which have grown on a pattern established more than a century ago. Originally, a group would pool savings, each member contributing regularly on a fixed schedule, to provide enough money for a few to build houses. The first borrowers would repay regularly, putting funds back into the pool. It could then finance others wishing to build houses. When all had been satisfied, the particular plan terminated.

The neighborhood aspect has largely disappeared. And the original arrangements to compel regular savings have also lost favor. What remains is the idea of pooling savings to accumulate funds to finance home purchase or construction and borrower repayment on a regular (monthly) basis. A person entrusting funds to a savings and loan association does not, technically, make a deposit. He buys shares and gets an ownership interest. He need have no intention of ever using these savings to buy a house.

If the shareholder (depositor) wishes to make a withdrawal, he asks the association to repurchase his shares. It is obligated to do so, but not immediately; for many years, however, associations have been able to repay on demand, except in a few cases in which mismanagement appears to have accounted for insolvency or the inadequacy of liquidity. The public has come to think of these "deposits" as about as liquid as those of savings banks. Managements tend to plan accordingly. They hold vault cash, deposits in commercial banks, and other highly liquid assets in an amount which, with the anticipated inflow of funds, will meet demands for cash. The "deposits," then, are another form of wealth which in the owner's calculations are very close to being as liquid as money.

Except for currency for daily transactions, modest amounts of deposits in commercial banks and government bonds, the premises, and a few miscellaneous items, savings and loan association assets consist of loans backed

---

[4] The organizations described in this section have a variety of names, such as building and loan societies, cooperative banks, homestead associations. The details of state laws and of operating procedures vary, of course. Some associations are not mutuals of the type described here but profit-making corporations whose stock is widely, or closely, owned. For data see the annual *Savings and Loan Fact Book* published by the U.S. Savings and Loan League, Chicago.

by mortgages on urban real estate, chiefly residential, in the same community. Loans are repayable on a systematic schedule, usually monthly, over 20 years or so. Mortgage loans guaranteed by the Veterans Administration or insured by the FHA are made for longer periods—and for larger percentages of the appraised value of the property—than rules will generally permit for conventional mortgages. It is difficult to generalize about the quality of mortgages held. But a serious recession, locally or for the whole country, might create for some institutions both a solvency and a liquidity problem. Such was the case, on a disastrous scale, in the early 1930's. At that time shareholders asked for cash just when many borrowers had to cut their repayments.

Congress has provided for national chartering of associations, hoping to assure higher standards than some states had tolerated. Less than 30 percent of the 6300 associations operate under Federal charters, but two out of three belong to the Federal Home Loan Bank System, patterned somewhat on the Federal Reserve. The eleven Home Loan Banks, organized geographically, supervise member associations. In addition, the FHLB banks can, and do, borrow publicly to provide associations with funds somewhat as a central bank lends to commercial banks which face liquidity problems.

Accounts may be insured up to $10,000 by the Federal Savings and Loan Insurance Corporation, roughly as bank deposits are insured.[5] Although 30 percent of associations remain outside the insurance system, they account for only about 5 percent of all assets. Liquidity needs, except in an unusual crisis, can be met by monthly receipts from borrowers as they repay mortgages. Reserves average about 8 percent of "deposits."

Shareholders receive dividends (interest) from net earnings after the directors have set aside what they believe desirable to build reserves (surplus). The payments to account holders average around 4¼ percent but with at least one out of five associations paying more. Until around 1963, payments were at markedly higher rates than those paid by commercial or savings banks on savings accounts. This differential has given savings and loan associations a competitive advantage in seeking "deposits."

The advertisements of California associations in New York newspapers provide only one of several examples of active search by some associations for "deposits" from other areas. The appeal is higher yield in California. As investors, the associations compete significantly in only one market, that for mortgages. Here, however, they are in a league of

---

[5] FSLIC and FDIC insurance may appear to be about the same. The differences, however, might prove important in a period of financial strain. Early in 1965, for example, the FSLIC reserve was around 0.9 percent of insured accounts. The FDIC figure was nearly 1.4 percent.

their own. Their nearly $100 billion of mortgage loans was 40 percent of all nonfarm mortgage loans outstanding. The local element remains strong, but reduces geographical diversification.

LIFE INSURANCE COMPANIES

Insurance companies are more than businesses that spread risk. They are also major financial institutions. The purchase of life insurance often involves an agreement to save.[6] The premiums which companies receive, therefore, average more than is needed to pay for the pure insurance provided currently. The excess builds up savings—to help pay for insurance at older ages when the chance of death is greater or to furnish funds to be paid back to the insured as an endowment or annuity. Life insurance companies also sell annuity contracts and pension plans which require the accumulation of savings. The companies invite beneficiaries of policies to leave the proceeds "on deposit" for distribution in monthly payments. Consequently, life insurance companies by 1965 held assets worth about $150 billion, growing around $7 billion a year.

State laws govern the property which life insurance companies may acquire. With minor exceptions, they are restricted to assets which will eventually return a fixed and certain number of dollars: nearly half in government and high-quality industrial, railroad, and utility bonds; one-third in mortgage loans; real estate leased to others on long term; preferred and common stock; policy loans, cash, and miscellaneous assets.

As investors, insurance companies are important in markets for a somewhat larger variety of securities than are dealt with by savings banks and savings and loan institutions. Sometimes life insurance companies, individually or in groups, buy newly issued bonds directly from a corporation. In doing so, they provide a significant part of total demand; their $45 billion increase in corporate bond-holdings since World War II is nearly 40 percent of the net growth of such debt. Their mortgage loans account for 20 percent of the total postwar growth. Such loans are often made by staffs which the companies maintain in different parts of the country. Some life insurance companies, however, rely heavily upon

---

[6] Life insurance companies differ greatly; what is said here applies to the companies which account for the great bulk of the business. Most life insurance business is done by mutual companies directed by men with a sense of responsibility to act conservatively. Scores of new and relatively small companies, however, though meeting the law, do not provide high standards of protection for the insured. Companies providing fire, auto, and other insurance have not become major institutions for financing other than purely insurance activities. The premiums they receive just about cover costs, so that funds for investment do not grow rapidly. For data see the annual *Life Insurance Fact Book,* Institute of Life Insurance, New York.

independent correspondents to make the arrangements which must be done locally.

Policies which build up accumulations for the insured ordinarily promise him a rate of interest—2½ or 3 percent as a minimum; the company must earn at least this much. Moreover, in competing for new business, companies seek higher yields to enlarge policyholder dividends —reductions in the annual net cost. Managements will not change much of an entire portfolio from one year to another. They do make shifts, however; and they direct their new funds—$500 million a month, net— into the assets which appear most attractive. Here, then, are well-informed investors of large amounts who operate on a national scale and who constantly try to take advantage of developments in the capital market, competing at some points with commercial banks as well as with others who put funds into low-risk assets.

An aspect of life insurance that has monetary significance is the sense of liquidity provided to tens of millions of policyholders. They can borrow approximately the savings in a policy, or surrender it for cash.[7] Raising cash in this way is much cheaper than most consumer borrowing. The potential runs into tens of billions.

Can we conceive of enough policyholders seeking cash at the same time—during a business decline or when market rates of interest have risen above those specified in the insurance contract, or when inflation causes doubt about the wisdom of holding claims to dollars—to create a liquidity problem? Something of the sort seems most unlikely but cannot be ruled out as impossible. If it were to develop, companies would be forced to draw down their bank balances, reduce greatly their mortgage and other lending out of receipts from premiums and repayment of older debt. They might sell assets under conditions that are not favorable.

Again, we note a fact whose importance is difficult to judge: People know that cash can be obtained quickly and with certainty. This sense of assurance must reduce the desire to hold bank balances and other assets to the extent that they serve to provide liquidity.

SAVINGS BONDS AND POSTAL SAVINGS

The Treasury began in the 1930's to offer bonds of small denomination for general public sale. Here was a secure investment designed for

---

[7] Reluctance to borrow on life insurance seems strong. Companies do not encourage such borrowing, even though the return to the company after allowing for costs of administration will exceed that from other assets. This attitude contrasts sharply with that of finance companies and banks, which urge the public to borrow. Outstanding policy loans in 1964 were around $7 billion.

the ordinary person. World War II brought aggressive efforts to increase the sale of these bonds as a method of absorbing purchasing power. Dollars used to buy such bonds would not then support inflationary pressures in markets for consumer goods and services. Sale has continued, but the net amounts outstanding have changed little. The 1964 total of $49 billion was $3 billion above the 1945 end-of-year amount.

The features of the bonds have varied in somewhat lagging response to market conditions. Three general characteristics must be noted. (1) The bonds are redeemable at the option of the owner and at prices fixed by the contract. These assets, in other words, are highly liquid. The bondholder can get a definitely determined amount of cash upon his own demand, cash which the Treasury must raise somehow. (2) The interest yield in the early period is substantially less than later. Consequently, the owner has an incentive to hold on to the bond. (3) The interest (appearing as discount in most cases) and the other features compete with the terms offered by others. The Treasury both provides and must meet competition.

The Postal Savings System was created in 1910 to offer an absolutely safe place for the common man to deposit savings—something that thousands of communities have not always offered. For various reasons use of the facilities has declined, so that total deposits are only about $400 million.

FEDERAL AIDS TO FINANCE HOUSING AND AGRICULTURE

Housing is important in everyone's life. Moreover, the construction of new housing has much to do with the state of the economy. The Federal government became active in residential finance with the hope of improving the quality of living facilities while also raising the level of economic activity.[8] The net results are debatable if only because no one knows what would have developed otherwise. Unquestionably, however, the financial system is affected by Federal policy.

Federal Housing Administration insurance of mortgage loans and Federal guarantee of housing loans to veterans have reduced the risk of lenders and have broadened the market for such loans. Of course, not everyone, not even every veteran, wishing to buy a house can get such help. Conditions are imposed to protect the lender, the government, and the borrower.

[8] G. H. Break, "Federal Loan Insurance for Housing," Commission on Money and Credit, *Federal Credit Agencies* (Englewood Cliffs: Prentice-Hall, 1963), pp. 1–65; see also E. Bloch, "The Federal Home Loan Bank System," and J. Gillies, "Federal Credit Programs in the Housing Sector of the Economy: An Aggregative Analysis," Commission on Money and Credit, *Federal Credit Programs* (Englewood Cliffs: Prentice-Hall, 1963), pp. 160–257 and 425–506, respectively.

One condition is a ceiling on the interest rate, imposed with the commendable objective of enabling the borrower to get the lowest rate possible. At times, however, the rate has been below the market level. Funds for such loans have then become scarce. A bank which can get 6 percent on a good-quality conventional mortgage loan will not lend at 5 percent on an FHA loan. Many would-be borrowers cannot then get an insured loan. Or they pay more by subterfuge, such as by signing a note for $16,000 but in fact getting only $15,000. Nevertheless, FHA and VA loans have financed one-fourth of the new housing "starts," and over one-fifth of the post-1950 increase in mortgage debt on nonfarm one-to-four-family dwellings.

The eleven Federal Home Loan Banks were set up in the 1930's to aid housing finance. Most savings and loan institutions are associated with the FHLB of their area. Membership subjects the association to supervision, but gives it access to borrowing or rediscounting privileges somewhat as does FR membership to banks. The FHLB System, therefore, increases the liquidity of savings and loan associations. Where does the FHLB get cash to meet the requests of member associations? It does not have the power of money creation, as does the Federal Reserve. It sells its own obligations in the open market, around $4 billion being outstanding in 1964. It accepts deposits and capital from its members—over $2 billion by 1964. Moreover, in an emergency, the FHLB can borrow from the Treasury. In 1963 its advances to member institutions were $5.6 billion; repayments were $4.3 billion. In mid-1964 advances outstanding were $4.8 billion.

The Federal National Mortgage Association ("Fanny May") provides a secondary market for FHA and VA mortgages. It buys mortgage loans from lending institutions and sells them to other institutions when conditions seem favorable. In 1960 it bought $1.2 billion and sold $0.4 billion; in 1963, however, purchases were $0.3 billion, sales $1.1 billion. FNMA will also buy to hold mortgage loans for itself; its 1964 holdings were $4.6 billion. The FNMA gets funds (1) from the sale of its stock to those institutions from which it buys mortgages, (2) from the sale of its own obligations in the market, and (3) from the Treasury. The market for funds for mortgage lending has become more nearly national than local or regional.

Other Federal aids to housing finance include a variety of direct and indirect subsidies for "public housing," urban renewal, college dormitory facilities, and military housing. Popular support for "easy" housing credit does not prove that the benefits to the public as a whole are actually those expected. The fact that land prices and construction costs have risen much more than prices in general may be due in part to financial aids which have stimulated housing demand more than demand for other uses of savings. If so, the aids have been no unmixed blessing.

TABLE 12.1

Participation of Federal Government in Housing Finance[a]
(Billions)

	1952 [b]	1964 [c]
Federal Housing Administration mortgage loans insured	$10.8	$45.0
Veterans Administration	14.6	31.0
Federal National Mortgage Association mortgages owned	2.2	4.5
Federal Home Loan Banks, advances	.6	4.8

[a] Selected programs only.
[b] End of year.
[c] September.
Source: *Federal Reserve Bulletin.*

Congress has also set up special lending agencies for farmers.[9] The production cycle on the farm is often longer than that of most businesses; the $40,000 to $80,000 or more of capital needed for many commercial farms ordinarily exceeds what the farmer himself can have accumulated by the time he wants to begin operating. The lending resources of local banks are not always adequate, and competition is often slight. A system of Federal Land Banks, now fully owned by local farm loan associations, dates from 1916. The associations (essentially cooperatives) administer farmer borrowing on long term from these banks. The funds come from the sale of FLB bonds in the open market and from repayment of earlier loans.

Indirect help for farmers is provided by Federal Intermediate Credit Banks. They lend, by discounting, to institutions which have made loans to farmers for periods up to five years. A commercial bank, for example, may lend to a farmer to buy equipment; the loan may then be converted into cash, at a discount, by use of these Federal facilities. Special Federal agencies and programs help in financing farmers' cooperatives, the construction and repair of farm housing, rural electrification, the rehabilitation of small, poor farms, and disaster relief. The interest and other costs charged are often below rates prevailing in free markets (markets to which the farmer may not in fact have access) and frequently below what the Treasury pays for loans of comparable duration.

[9] D. G. Johnson, "Agricultural Credit, Capital and Credit Policy in the United States," Commission on Money and Credit, *Federal Credit Programs* (Englewood Cliffs: Prentice-Hall, 1963), pp. 355–423. D. E. Hathaway, "The Federal Credit Programs for Individual Farm Development," Commission on Money and Credit, *Federal Credit Agencies* (Englewood Cliffs: Prentice-Hall, 1963), pp. 319–84.

TRUST FUNCTIONS AND PENSION FUNDS

Increasingly, modern banking includes trusteeship. This activity, a specialized business in itself, lies largely outside the scope of our study.

In general, a trust is created when someone (the trustor) gives the legal title to property to another (the trustee) for the benefit of a party other than the new legal owner. The beneficiary may be the trustor, his close relatives, or a person or group entirely unrelated. The trustor may be a private individual, a business or government setting up a pension plan, a corporation arranging to issue bonds, or some other group. Obviously, in giving up title to wealth, one wants to be sure that the trustee is not only honest but also competent to manage prudently. Banks, as a rule, qualify.

In competing for trust business, banks have several advantages over an individual: They are accessible every business day—never traveling, preoccupied with personal affairs, or incapacitated by sickness or senility; banks do not die and can assure continuity; they offer skill, experience, group judgment, and mechanical facilities which far transcend anything the usual individual can provide; they are financially responsible and subject to regular government supervision; they are impartial where family and other interests may conflict.

As trustees, banks have become responsible for vast amounts of property—no one knows exactly how much, but in 1963 the trust departments of national banks held almost $100 billion. In many cases the bank shares control or has no control of investment decisions. Growing wealth, tax advantages of using trusts, the expansion of pension plans, and increasing recognition of the advantages of banks over individuals as trustees help explain the growth of activity by banks.

Laws require that trust activities be distinctly separated from other banking functions. The same building and vaults may serve; the same investment personnel will often advise. Yet the securities are kept clearly segregated from the bank's own. If the bank fails, the trust assets remain for the beneficiaries, not the depositors. Some trust responsibilities, such as those of settling an estate, may end after a year or two. Many extend for generations. The ordinary personal trust, however, will rarely last for a century because of state laws against perpetuities.

Much of this business is costly to administer. The specific provisions of each trust must be observed scrupulously, with careful accounting for each item of income and each payment to a beneficiary and full compliance with tax laws.

To manage a trust department well requires skills that are expensive to develop. If performance is to be good, overhead costs are inevitably high. They must be spread over a large volume of business if profit is to be substantial.[10] The compensation received, usually a percentage of principal and of income, is often specified by law—and often not enough to provide much profit except where a trust's assets run into hundreds of thousands of dollars or where the requirements are simple. Several hundred banks manage "common trust funds." Each of these serves many beneficiaries; the pooling of assets is designed to make trust services available for small funds, the average participation being around $25,000.

Pension plans have grown so rapidly in the last quarter of a century that they now account for vast holdings of wealth and substantial additions each year. Excluding the Social Security programs of the Federal government, assets of pension funds were probably around $115 billion in 1964. One-third or more of the total of assets was held by life insurance companies and the trust departments of national banks, and have thus been included in the earlier figures. Plans other than those administered by insurance companies receive nearly $7 billion a year, chiefly from employer contributions and income from investments. Annual benefit payments exceed $2 billion. State banks including large trust companies in Chicago, New York, Philadelphia, and San Francisco administer many plans. But many are administered by representatives of the company, by the union, or by a group representing both.[11] Asset selection of trusts, and to lesser degree of pension funds, emphasizes conservatism, but less so than in the past. Some trust agreements specify the assets to be held —a piece of real estate, an interest in a business, the proceeds of a life insurance policy. State laws were once narrowly restrictive, limiting trust assets for the most part to highly conservative bonds. Today, however, most states prescribe the "prudent man" rule, which permits trustees to use their judgment within a wide range. For example, purchase of common stock is permitted if the interests of beneficiaries are likely to be served thereby. Increasingly, trust provisions give the trustee great discretion. In 1962 almost one-third of trust assets held by national banks were common stock. Pension funds (other than those for government employees and those handled by insurance companies) were nearly 40 percent in common stock.

Property in trust will generally be invested with care and often with

[10] One uncertainty in estimating net earnings is the possibility of being "surcharged" for mistakes. At any time before discharge by the court which has jurisdiction, a trustee faces the possibility of being required to compensate for errors.

[11] Special tax provisions enacted in 1962 permit unincorporated business and professional persons, such as lawyers and doctors, to set up retirement plans for themselves and their employees with current deduction of contributions in computing taxable income. National banks seeking to provide the necessary services received approval of the Comptroller of the Currency. The Securities Exchange Commission, however, objected on the grounds that the proposed plans would circumvent registration requirements.

skill. Preservation of capital rates high as an objective, but saving on taxes and long-run growth often rate equally as high. The continually expanding responsibility for handling the accumulated wealth adds to bankers' importance in the economy, partly because the totals grow rapidly and partly because trustees receive more and more discretion.

Some banks exercise trustee functions for owners of corporate debt. The basic responsibilities are to see that the corporation meets the terms of contracts, and to take action to protect bondholders if the debtor in some way fails. Banks also act as trustees in receivership, with responsibilities of varying importance. As registrars and transfer agents, some banks perform indispensable, but largely routine, functions for corporations and the stockholding public.

INVESTMENT BANKING

A group of institutions which few of us would think of as banks—businesses which do not accept deposits and rarely lend money—perform functions termed "investment banking." [12] Until the 1930's some commercial banks engaged in such activity. Congress then forced the separation of commercial banking from the "merchandising" of newly issued securities, the heart of investment banking. Consequently, investment houses today are perhaps best thought of not as banks so much as "securities merchants" and financial advisers.

A large corporation wanting to raise additional capital is likely to consult an investment house.[13] The latter will investigate the firm from all relevant points of view—physical and technical, legal, economic—and advise on the specific problems. If the outlook seems mutually promising, efforts will be made to negotiate an agreement about the type of securities to be issued, the detailed terms, and the ways of meeting requirements of the Securities Exchange Commission, state authorities, and other official agencies.

The resulting agreement is an underwriting. It may commit the investment firm to buy the securities itself, for resale, or to buy any of the issue which it does not sell in a public offering. In either case the corporation gets assurances about the dollars it will receive and the obligations it assumes. The investment firm assumes risks in the form of

[12] Stock exchanges and the over-the-counter market provide facilities which the public can use for the purchase and sale of stocks and bonds issued in the past. Investment banking firms, some of which have partners with stock exchange membership, act as brokers and dealers in handling outstanding securities as well as selling new issues.

[13] States and localities planning to borrow usually proceed somewhat differently. They decide on the bonds they want to issue and then ask for competitive bids from groups of investment banking firms.

promises to supply funds. It must either have ample funds of its own or access to money—ability to borrow at commercial banks. To spread the risks, several underwriters often form a syndicate, perhaps with representatives in all important regions of the country, to share the responsibility. This group then attempts the public sale. Underwriters hope to sell for enough more than they promise to pay the issuer to cover marketing costs and earn a profit. Success or failure may hinge upon a general turn in financial markets as well as upon the judgment and effort of the firms involved.

Buyers may be individuals, financial institutions, or any of a variety of organizations with funds from new or old savings. The skill with which investment firms investigate and judge the opportunities for creative use of money, and the vigor with which they try to sell, will help determine the efficiency with which new savings go to those uses in which they can be most creative—and perhaps even whether some will be used at all.

The elaborate, highly developed investment banking system, unfortunately, remains largely inaccessible to relatively small and growing firms. The expense is too high. When a firm of small or modest size wants to raise money by the sale of a new issue of securities, the investment banker must incur costs which would be minor in relation to a large transaction but which are great indeed as a percentage of the amount that the small firm seeks. Whereas the small business may sometimes use the biggest bank for short-term lending, it cannot expect the large investment houses to sponsor its securities in sale to the public without an investigation which must be costly—often prohibitive—in relation to the size of the issue.

MUTUAL FUNDS

The demand for and supply of stocks and bonds are influenced by buying and selling of a type of financial intermediary, commonly termed "mutual fund" or "investment trust." These funds or trusts issue and sell their own securities, which are usually shares of stock. The money received, over $1 billion a year in net increase, is used to buy a diversified group of securities. The teacher, laborer, doctor, or pensioner who is willing to pay the "loading" commission plus other expense charges of around 7 percent can thus acquire an interest in a large number of stocks without need to study each.

Some funds specialize in one type (chemical industry stocks, for example); others emphasize diversification. The managers can invest more carefully and more wisely than can the ordinary saver. Their selection efforts presumably raise the average of rationality in financial decisions. Selling efforts have undoubtedly broadened stock ownership as people who would not venture to buy a share in this and a share in that corporation, buy into mutual funds.

Many funds agree to repurchase their own shares whenever the owner so demands, and at a price determined by the current market price of the assets in the portfolio. Consequently, the shares are as liquid as stocks listed on the stock exchange. Public demand for cash might conceivably develop on the broad scale. Mutual funds would then be forced to sell stock, depressing prices, perhaps in cumulative fashion. The danger, however, does not seem to be inherently greater than if the public owned the securities outright.

GOVERNMENT LENDING TO BUSINESS
AND FOR VARIED SPECIAL PURPOSES

The country's overall facilities for private financing have gaps.[14] Their size and seriousness are open to debate. But they have aroused enough concern to lead governments, chiefly the Federal but also many states and even more localities, to set up special arrangements for financing. The proliferation within the last decade has created such variety that mere description of major types would require scores of pages. Their newness precludes reliable valuation. Some provide direct loans. Others extend aid indirectly through some form of insurance, assumption of residual risk, or tax favoritism.

The Small Business Administration advances loans to firms of modest size and insures other lenders against most loss. Commercial banks participate in SBA financing. Borrowers pay ½ percent as insurance to cover loss by lenders. Small Business Investment Companies provide equity capital and long-term loans to "small" businesses (gross sales not over $5 million, annual profit after tax not over $250,000). SBIC's are privately owned but can receive Federal loans up to $400,000 through the SBA; income tax treatment is favorable. The Area Redevelopment Administration provides technical assistance, makes grants to local governments for public facilities which will increase employment, and provides loans for urban industrial and public facilities; over 1000 localities classed as "disadvantaged" qualify. Urban renewal projects, railroads, ship operators, college students, exporters and others receive varying types of Federal assistance in borrowing.

Increasingly, state and local governments seek to attract business by borrowing, using government credit to borrow (on a tax exempt basis)

---

[14] See J. W. McKie, "Credit Gaps and Federal Credit Programs," and also J. F. Weston, "Analysis of the Technical Components of the Federal Credit Programs," Commission on Money and Credit, *Federal Credit Programs* (Englewood Cliffs: Prentice-Hall, 1963), pp. 311–53 and 587–614 respectively.

to build and lease facilities for private use. The total dollar amounts have yet to reach large figures. Nevertheless, a relatively new competitive element has been introduced into the country's financial structure.

NONBANK LENDING

To Business

Earlier chapters have referred to nonbank lending to businesses. The variety of services, some very highly specialized, and the competition among suppliers both become more intense and more numerous as lenders become more skilled and more vigorous in trying to appeal to borrowers.

Some nonbank lenders specialize in accounts-receivable financing of about the type done by commercial banks as described earlier. Some commercial finance companies, known as "factors," and especially prominent in the textile industry, purchase accounts receivable outright with no recourse against the seller. Several manufacturers, perhaps through subsidiaries, and some finance companies finance the installment purchase of equipment; the machinery or equipment serves as collateral, and the loan is repaid on a regular schedule. These activities have their close counterpart in commercial bank services; often the competition is direct.

The businesses served tend to be small manufacturers and wholesalers. The position of the nonbank lender frequently rests upon his specialized knowledge of the industry or his personal contact with the borrowers. Willingness to assume risk also accounts for the success of the finance company in getting business in competition with banks. Data on the extent of such financing are sketchy. Figures for leading commercial finance companies and factors for 1950 to 1962 show a fourfold growth to $18 billion of financing. Charges frequently exceed 12 percent.

To Consumers

About $72 billion of "consumer debt" was outstanding in 1964.[15] Only $23 billion had been made directly by commercial banks. Why had not these lending institutions done more to meet an important need? Part of the reason was a lack of aggressiveness and imagination by bankers. Restrictive laws also played a part. In addition, some services which consumers want may be of a kind not provided as efficiently by banks (especially small banks) as by other lenders.

---

[15] The figure includes $3 billion for home repair and modernization loans but not loans to buy housing.

The demand for personal loans exists because people want to spend more money than they have on hand or than they can or wish to get by liquidating assets. The spending may be for a dire necessity or a frivolous luxury. It may be of the most productive sort to help raise income— another year of education. It may be to buy something which requires a large but infrequent outlay, such as an operation, a vacation, or an auto.

A variety of nonbank agencies now lend to individuals. The services which each provides differ. They also change. Before examining these agencies, let us look at one aspect of personal borrowing.

Regulation to Protect the Borrower. Individuals often desire consumer loans intensely; frequently the demand rests upon weakness. Through necessity or ignorance, a person seeking money will at times agree to exorbitant terms if they are the best obtainable. And throughout history, the supply of funds for consumer borrowing has been far from plentiful. Moreover, in each local market the supply has tended to be concentrated in a few hands. The risks of loss have often been great, and the expenses of servicing large in relation to the size of the loan.

Borrower and lender tend to be in highly unequal bargaining positions. The borrower, perhaps having no other place to turn, is much more anxious to get money than the potential lender is to make any particular loan. The two can reach voluntary agreement but on terms that cost the borrower heavily. If such cost is small in relation to the borrower's wealth or income, and if the duration of the loan is short, no serious harm may result. One danger, however, at times tragic, exists in the market for consumer loans. The borrower may get trapped. So much of what he pays the lender, week after week, turns out to be interest, that he is unable to reduce the debt itself. Perhaps the last thing the lender wants is repayment of principal; he may even prefer an occasional default which will bring penalty interest rates. Year after year the borrower may pay and pay, with only death bringing escape. Even in this country today, not a few borrowers seem more concerned with the size of the monthly payment than with the interest cost or even number of months.

To prevent results which can be truly vicious, governments have enacted usury laws, setting maximum limits on interest rate charges. Over many centuries and in many countries the results of these laws have been disappointing. Laws seek to keep interest charges down to what seem reasonable levels. Inevitably, however, the rules, if enforced, will cut to a fraction the funds available for lending where risks and other costs are high. Consequently, the artificial limitation on supply forces rates above the level which would otherwise prevail—and above the legal limit. Men will evade laws. Some people want loans badly, and others are willing to accommodate, at a price. Disobeying the law to meet the demands adds risk for which the lender will demand compensation. The borrowers who suffer most are likely to be the weakest and the poorest. A law intended to help the neediest may in fact hurt them.

Lending costs do vary. The expense of handling a small loan, ignoring entirely the risk of loss, may amount to a considerable percentage of the principal. If the loan is for only a few weeks, the cost expressed as an annual rate may seem utterly unreasonable. Assume, for example, that the labor, material, and office costs of handling a loan are $5. Then, a person who borrows $50 for a week and pays only the $5 as a charge may seem to be paying interest of 10 percent a week or 520 percent a year. Yet the lender has no yield on his money. If the loan were $2000 for a year, cost of $5 would be negligible. Actually, the cost of making almost any loan will probably be at least $5. In seeking to protect borrowers, therefore, why not limit the rate of interest but give the lender freedom to impose charges to cover expenses of administering the loan? Well, nothing can be foolproof. Unscrupulous lenders would use any freedom, any scope for discretion, to evade the law and to exploit weak borrowers.

Unlicensed Lenders. Most of us lend to friends and borrow from friends with no thought of an interest charge. Sometimes we borrow more formally, signing a note and agreeing to pay interest. The mutual benefit from such lending may be clear. Sometimes, however, the two parties are in unequal bargaining positions. The borrower, perhaps having no other place to turn, is likely to be much more anxious to get money than the unlicensed lender is to make any one loan. The interest charged in such situations may be usurious.

Pawnbrokers. Prosperity and competition have been hard on pawnbroking. A useful, but disparaged, activity is the granting of loans with personal property—jewelry, furs, cameras, etc.—as security. Most such loans are for only a few dollars, made in a few minutes, and eventually repaid; if the loan is not repaid, the pawnbroker can sell the property pledged. His gross charge is likely to be at an annual rate of 36 percent or so. Chief users have been the poor, but many a person "down on his luck," *e.g.,* actors and authors, has sought funds from a pawnbroker. The cost for a few days can be unimportant; and if one has property to pledge, such borrowing may seem wise. Criticism, however, especially the alleged refusal of the pawnbroker to lend a high enough fraction of the worth of property, plus the danger that stolen property will be pledged, and the apparent height of rates that could be charged in a free market, have led to considerable regulation. Other types of personal loans and rising incomes have not eliminated the usefulness of the pawnbroker. They have, however, reduced his relative importance—and, along with rising costs of operation, his net income.

Industrial (Morris Plan) Banks. Special institutions to lend to industrial workers (chiefly manufacturing and clerical) began to operate shortly before World War I. The best known are the Morris Plan banks. Originally, they did not accept deposits. The money for their loans came from sale of stock. Lending was essentially like that of personal finance companies today: the amounts were small, systematic repayment was required, the interest charged was around 15 percent. The institutions emphasized "character rather than collateral." They pioneered in co-maker loans, with the borrower getting the signature of two others who could be called upon to make up any losses. More and more, however, these institutions have broadened their activities until today they are generally banks, accepting deposits, qualifying for FDIC insurance, and operating profitably.

Installment Sales Loans. Autos and many other durable consumer goods, and some not so durable, are now purchased "on time." The buyer usually gives the seller a down payment and agrees to pay the balance over weeks, months, or years. Details vary greatly. Usually the lender can repossess and then sell the thing purchased if the debt is not paid. In some cases he retains ownership until the loan is retired; in others he takes a mortgage. The seller of the product may himself make the loan, probably with borrowed money. More commonly, he arranges with a sales finance company that specializes in loans of this type. These firms borrow publicly in the money and capital markets and from commercial banks. A few corporations have sales finance subsidiaries. In fact, General Motors Acceptance Corporation in 1963 had almost twice the assets ($5 billion) of the next largest sales finance firm. Charges on the great bulk of loans, especially those for purchase of autos, generally range from 10 to 15 percent. Frequently, however, charges are higher. Extra cost can be hidden in the price of the article or quoted as a service charge. Furniture, jewelry, and clothing purchased on time where the terms that seem to be offered are "easy" are likely to cost heavily in financing charges. One proposal before Congress for several years—"truth-in-lending"—would require sellers to tell buyers the charge being made for non-cash payment, expressed as simple interest per year, whether 8 or 128 percent.

Personal Loans. Loans for personal use not specifically tied to the purchase of any particular item are usually but not always on an installment basis. "Small loan," "personal finance," companies lend modest amounts (up to $300 or, in some states, more) on the personal note of the borrower. A chattel mortgage on furniture or autos, or possibly an assignment of salary, may be demanded. Lending companies, however, are reluctant to use extreme measures for collection except as a last resort.

The interest charge seems high, with 3 or 3½ percent a month being legal in some states. Competition, however, tends to reduce the charge for safer loans. Yet the costs of record keeping and collection plus some losses are large in relation to the small amounts borrowed. State regulations have developed to protect borrowers, some of whom would be too weak or ignorant, and would buy to protect themselves. Millions of consumers have used such borrowing facilities with satisfaction, have established their credit, and probably feel confident of their ability to borrow again.

Where do the lenders get money? In addition to their own capital, they borrow in the open market and from banks.

Credit Unions. One remarkable development of the years since World War II was the growth of credit unions. True, the 20,000 units of 1964 were only about double the number at the time of Pearl Harbor; but assets of $8 billion and loans of $6 billion were about 8 times the 1950 figures.

A credit union is a "cooperative" operating under special Federal or state law. It is formed by a group of people with some common interest —they work for the same employer, belong to the same fraternal organization, club or labor union, live in the same neighborhood, etc. Each member buys shares. The money he pays in, perhaps in small amounts on each payday, is used for loans to members for any of a wide variety of purposes. The interest charge averages slightly less than 1 percent a month on the unpaid balance. Operating expenses are ordinarily low, the employer or other organization gives free office space, and credit union personnel almost always donate their services. Tax exemption offers an advantage over commercial lenders. Loss rates have been under $\frac{1}{5}$ of 1 percent; the close association of members helps in screening loan applications and in assuring collection.

Borrowers are covered by insurance provided by a mutual insurance company. Owners of credit union shares receive dividends of around 4 percent. Redemption of shares ordinarily presents no difficulty, but the unions are by no means so liquid as an individual member believes *his* share, or his capacity to borrow, to be.

Charge Accounts. The most widely used type of consumer credit is that obtained from the seller on open account. We buy and say "charge it," giving no formal evidence of our obligation, but with mutual understanding that we will pay soon. Retailing and the provision of many kinds of services—telephone and other utilities, medical, and dry cleaning for example—flow more smoothly if payment does not have to accompany each transaction. Our economy operates more efficiently because consumer borrowing of this sort is possible. Someone must bear the cost, however. Retailers are trying to charge openly for such lending or to grant discounts for cash payment. The 1964 total of charge accounts—around $6 billion—was nearly twice the 1950 figure. For a time, in the 1950's, one form of consumer charging grew: the use of credit cards.

Businesses which give the customer time to pay may themselves get the money from bank loans or by borrowing in the money market. But some firms provide the funds out of permanent capital.

ECONOMIC SIGNIFICANCE

One important aspect of the economic significance of the institutions and activities discussed in this chapter has been mentioned several times—the effect on liquidity. Savers turn over currency or demand deposits to financial intermediaries. In return they receive a claim which in some cases almost entitles the holder to cash on little or no notice. The institution then uses what it has received to acquire an income-producing asset of far less assured liquidity. We shall return to this subject in later chapters.

A second issue arouses concern within the financial world. The various types of institutions find themselves in different competitive positions. When such differences result from the traditions and practices of the companies or groups themselves, public policy will not ordinarily be involved. Many differences in competitive position, however, result from governmental policies, both Federal and state.

Laws and regulations, for example, impose strict limitations upon the establishment of new banks and banking offices, while some competitors face little or comparable restriction. Bankers chafe at the requirement that they hold reserves which produce no income while other financial institutions in more or less direct competition are free from any such requirement.

From state to state capital requirements vary widely for institutions of the same kind as well as for different types of institutions.

Tax treatment of commercial banks, savings and loan associations, life insurance companies, credit unions, etc., to say nothing of governmental institutions, remains significantly unequal but less so than before recent changes in the law, especially in 1962. Restrictions on the type of loan or investment which may be made, and upon the potential sources of capital and other funds, are subject to restriction in some cases, not in others. Governmental participation subsidizes here, creates distressing competitive inequality elsewhere. Some borrowers and savers have access to better financial facilities than do others. And so on.

In an economy which changes as constantly and as rapidly as ours, laws and regulations get out of date. Keeping them reasonably modern proves exceptionally difficult. Sometimes no problem becomes evident until conditions have gotten so encrusted that change would upset vested interests which have no small power. Typically, there is no general consensus on what modification would best serve the public. Clearly, however, much unfinished business of modernizing the financial structure remains.

QUESTIONS

1. Where do the functions of commercial banks and of other financial intermediaries overlap, and where do they differ? What is unique about commercial banking?

2. In the light of the history of their development, discuss the role of the mutual savings bank in the financial market today.

3. How do savings and loan associations differ from mutual savings banks? What do these types of institutions have in common with each other that they do not have with commercial banks? In your community, how do rates of interest offered savers compare?

4. How do financial intermediaries affect liquidity?

5. What is "Fanny May"? What is its role?

6. Discuss the possible economic effects of a doubling of the amount of wealth held in trust over the next fifteen years.

7. "An investment bank is not really a bank at all. Yet it plays a vital role in our monetary system." Comment. From a prospectus on a recent offering of new securities compute the cost to the firm raising new capital.

8. Discuss the possible economic effects of "easy" consumer loans. What are the costs of such loans in your area?

9. Why do you suppose that commercial banks lend to personal finance companies which compete with banks for consumer loans?

10. In what sense are life insurance companies savings institutions?

11. Discuss with the manager of a credit union the methods and problems of operation.

PART THREE

MONETARY THEORY

CHAPTER 13 *QUANTITY APPROACHES TO THE STUDY OF MONETARY THEORY*

EVERY economy which uses money must have some sort of monetary policy. It must put theory into practice. The policy may be pernicious, poor, good, or excellent. It must rest on theory, whether or not the policy maker is aware of the theories which underlie action. The lives of everyone, including persons yet unborn, will be affected by existing and developing monetary policies—and the theories on which they rest. But how? and to what degree?

Economists differ in their answers to such questions. We also differ somewhat in our interpretations of the way by which monetary influence operates—the path or chain of reactions which relate monetary change to price levels, to employment, and to the growth of the economy. Therefore, it is necessary, and fortunately it is helpful, to examine different ways of "looking at" the role of money. Before examining them, however, let us look briefly at the concerns of monetary theory.

SCOPE AND IMPORTANCE OF MONETARY THEORY

Monetary theory in one sense is concerned with the influence of money on the economy—on production, distribution, economic growth, and the major subdivisions or aspects of these broad groupings. In a more concrete sense, however, monetary theory deals with a few very important elements of economic life, chiefly the levels of prices and of employment.

Money touches virtually all economic transactions, and also many decisions that do not seem to be realized in transactions. Consequently, money has a pervasive economic influence, an influence decidedly greater than one might expect from a "medium" (of exchange), an "intermediary tool." An understanding of this influence gives not only insight into economic processes but also guidance for decisions of the utmost practical importance. Monetary theory helps us judge what can be expected from different kinds of actions by both government and private agencies—actions over which man has control. They involve matters about which we *must* choose, even if by default. Human beings must "manage" money, consciously or unconsciously. The difference between good and poor management can make the difference between a healthy, prosperous economy and one with needless misery, waste, and poverty. Comprehension of "correct" monetary theory can be of inestimable value.

Yet gaining such comprehension is not easy. Just as money touches virtually all economic transactions, monetary theory today seems to be almost a part of most other phases of theoretical economics while merging into several of the more applied fields of economics. No clear boundaries set off monetary theory from other aspects of economics, or of business or politics. Thus, a thorough analysis of modern monetary theory requires crossing into several areas which are themselves important parts of the domain of economics. Nevertheless, it is wise—but difficult—to limit such excursions.

The scope of monetary theory has broadened in recent decades. The dominant, though not the exclusive, concern in the past was over the forces determining the purchasing power of money. Theorists, in other words, tried to answer the question, "What brings changes in the worth of money in relation to goods and services?" [1]

Clearly, price-level change has profound significance for human welfare. Yet price-level movements are not the only important result of monetary change. For more than a generation now, monetary theory has been concerned explicitly with the effects of money on economic fluctuations, on the level of employment, and on the rate of economic growth, as well as with the effects on the purchasing power of money. In fact, all are interrelated.

A warning, however: Monetary theory is a developing body of knowledge, not yet "set." Different emphases have adherents. Consequently, some overlapping and even repetition will appear.

---

[1] When the unit of money was tied closely to a commodity, such as gold or silver, there was occasion for monetary theorists to try to relate the value of the monetary unit to that of the commodity or, more significantly, to the resources needed to produce more of the particular commodity which served as the monetary base.

TRANSACTIONS VERSION OF QUANTITY
THEORY: EQUATION OF EXCHANGE

Sometimes the old takes on new interest, not because of the fickleness of fashion but because the old seems to have merits not found in younger rivals. Such a revival of prestige appears to be developing for "quantity" approaches.

The quantity of any good or service available affects its worth or importance relative to the worth of other things. Money is no exception. One fruitful approach to the study of money is to examine its quantity— and the changes in its quantity—in relation to the other things in which we may be interested, including the economy as a whole. A good starting point is the equation of exchange, starting with essentially the form developed by Irving Fisher, a distinguished Yale economist who worked extensively on monetary theory before World War II.

The Basic Equation

We begin with a truism, identity, or tautology: The total amount of money paid out in an economy in a given period of time is the total amount of money received. Think of two aggregates for the whole economy, (1) payments and (2) receipts. They are two sides of the same thing, two aspects of the same process.

Each can then be separated into two parts for more revealing study of significant elements. The *payments* total consists of (a) units of money and (b) the frequency with which they are used. The *receipts* total can be divided into (a) the goods and services sold for money and (b) their prices. A simple equation will now express the relation, with the four elements distinguished:

$$MV = PT$$

This is the *equation of exchange.*[2] To learn what it can teach, we must understand the meaning of the four elements.

Money. The M is the total quantity of money: coins and paper currency but mostly deposits in checking accounts.[3] This concept is essentially similar to that used throughout this book.

---

[2] Any use of the equation with statistics would require that each of the four elements be expressed as an index number. Appendix B deals with index numbers.

[3] Questions arise in defining M for use here. Is it wise to include currency in bank vaults? Would results be better if time deposits were included? If so, to what extent? Is a Treasury note which can be used to pay taxes in fact money? For purposes of the discussion at this point, such questions are not highly significant.

Velocity. The *V* is velocity of circulation of money, the exchange or *transactions* velocity. It is a measure of the speed with which money moves through the economy. We usually express it as the number of uses a year, the number of transactions in which an "average" unit of money is used. (One distinctive characteristic of money, we recall, is that as money is used it is not "used up." Grain, electricity, time, paper, machinery, and most other things are exhausted as they are used. Money, however, flows without being consumed.) Some parts of the stock of money move very often or rapidly, some slowly; some may be idle for the entire period. Small coins serve in hundreds of transactions a year. Ten thousand dollar bills, on the other hand, may lie in bank vaults for months on end.

The figure needed for our equation is an average, as a rule an annual rate. It must be a weighted average, *i.e.,* one which takes account of the varying size of different units of the money stock. Assume that a dime is used 400 times and a $100 bill twice during a year. What is the average *V* of these 402 uses of 2 units of money? To get a figure, we relate each unit to one dollar. The dime, then, moves the equivalent of 40 times one dollar. The $100 bill moves the equivalent of 200 times one dollar. Thus we get a total of 240 times one dollar for the 2 units of money. The average of 120 is the figure we seek. The *V* of demand deposits is the number of times a dollar is used in transactions, passing from one account to another as checks are written and deposited and accounts debited and credited.[4]

More will be said about velocity later. Our concern here is over the notion or concept—a measure of something. In a superficial but still useful sense, the concept of transactions velocity is simple. Money moves from hand to hand, and from bank account to bank account, at some rate of speed. Speed varies. It can be measured; we search for a measure of this speed. If on the average each dollar of the money stock is used in a transaction every week, the *V* figure for a year would be 52; if each dollar is used once every two weeks (approximately the fact), *V* is 26 per year.

In a realistic sense, however, the concept *is* complex. Measurement presents formidable problems. This *V* applies to every use of money in a transaction. To learn the size of *V,* one needs facts that are not directly available. No independent measure of velocity by some sort of counting of uses, even on a sample basis, seems possible. A speedometer or counter on $5 bills, for example, is hardly feasible. An indirect method offers the best approximation: dividing (estimates of) total money payments by the quantity of money. Fortunately, we have data on the use of the major

[4] The concept of transaction needed here, as we shall see later, suffers from lack of precision. Shifts of funds between one bank and another, or from one branch to another while owned by the same business firm, may not involve transactions in a sense significant for purposes here. And yet they may.

element of our stock of money—turnover of demand deposits. The total debits to demand deposits can be divided by the average amount of such deposits during the period. For use in guiding public policy, the data on demand deposit turnover are tolerably good measures of transactions velocity.

Level of Prices. P is an average of prices; or, more accurately, it is an index number which measures the general price level. And a *general* level it is, for it must include everything on which money is spent. The concept is moderately clear. Most of us, at least, readily see meaning in the notion of a measure of the range or height of prices of a large variety of things, such as consumer goods. Yet when *everything* must be included—military equipment, real estate, freight rates, common stocks, professional services, raw materials and goods in process of manufacture —as well as consumer goods and services, the concept loses any semblance of clarity. The reality becomes very much harder to measure than the average of consumer prices.

Many prices, for example, are not easily determined—such as the prices at which 20-year-old houses sell. Some prices rise while others fall, and many fluctuate from day to day. Weighting of the relative importance of the thousands of items necessarily included in a comprehensive index would be a herculean task, even if there were agreement on the principles to be applied. Yet if the price level measure we use is to be complete, everything on which money is spent must have a place, and a place which reflects the item's relative importance.

Although great progress has been made in constructing price indexes, there is no prospect of getting an index tailored for measuring this P. The Consumer Price Index of the Bureau of Labor Statistics has broad but far from complete coverage. The implicit price deflator developed by the Department of Commerce for use in computing real national product applies to all final output of goods and services. But it, too, has serious shortcomings.

Transactions. T stands for the physical or real items, the goods and services, which are exchanged—traded or transacted—for money. This mass far exceeds final output, or gross national product. Each element sold must be weighted to give it the relative importance it deserves. This T includes real estate and securities. It includes labor services and business inventory. The total is as conglomerate as P. In fact, the two are tied together intimately, for each transaction has both a P and a T element.

The variety of transactions for which we use money, though not infinite, is too great for most of us to conceive. Often the same thing exchanges for money many times during a year. If so, it must be counted each time that it is part of a transaction which uses money—whether starting as a raw material and being processed in stages by several firms, or as a share of common stock being bought and sold many times. But what is a feasible unit of measurement? Weight, time, acreage, number, and other physical measures might each have its place; obviously, however, no one of them can meet all needs. Many elements of T will change in about the same direction—the quantity of shoes, milk, boots, and medical services rising or falling at about the same time. The magnitude of particular changes, however, will differ. Even if there were agreement on method of computation, and none is to be expected, the data needed are seriously inadequate. We can measure neither the absolute size of T, nor changes, except very crudely. Yet the *concept* does prove useful. We do think of larger and smaller aggregates of goods and services.

Understanding to Be Gained from the Equation of Exchange

What can this equation teach us about the influence of money? Several generalizations giving valuable insights appear. Most important as a starter is this lesson: In studying the broad aggregates of the economy, we shall find the influence of money related closely to three other major elements. Any change in the quantity of money may work out its effects on one, two, or three other elements of economic life. Equally true, however, is another lesson: A result which we may be inclined to attribute to money may be partly the outcome of other forces that either reinforce, or partially offset, the influence of money.

These lessons may seem too general to be useful. Yet to see important interrelationships, no matter how simple, is to be equipped to protect ourselves from errors often made in the past and still not unknown. Merely to be able to avoid mistakes is in itself a valuable "possession." Fortunately, more positive gains also come easily.

An increase in the quantity of money will possibly—even probably—lead to a rise in the general level of prices, but not necessarily. Conceivably, V might fall, or T rise, enough to offset the increase in M. In other words, there is no inevitable and fixed tie between the quantity of money and the level of prices, or between changes in the quantity of money and changes in the purchasing power of the dollar. Nevertheless, we can expect a close and important connection.

Suppose, for example, that the economy is producing essentially as much as its capacity will permit; output cannot increase appreciably. An increase in M will then lead to an increase in P—unless (1) V falls or (2) there is an increase in T in ways that do not require much use of productive facilities (perhaps stock market transactions or sales of real estate involving no additional construction). Most probably, the price level will rise. (Under these conditions V is unlikely to fall.) If velocity actually rises, the increase in P may be greater, proportionately, than the growth of M. If T drops for some reason, the price-level rise will tend to be greater than otherwise. In short, when productive capacity is fully employed, increases in the quantity of money almost certainly will lead to increased spending and higher prices.

Let us now assume a strikingly different starting condition, one of substantial unemployment and large potentialities for increases in T from greater production. An increase in M can help boost output and employment. For if there is an increase in the quantity of money, someone owns it; if the owners use it to buy goods and services, the new buying adds to demand for output. If V is generally stable, MV (total spending) will rise following an increase in M. Prices may go up, of course; but if there is substantial idle productive capacity, competition will limit the ability of businesses to get higher prices. Output will increase as demand grows. The expansion of employment and of T will ordinarily be highly desirable.

Another question. Is an increase in M essential for an increase in price levels? Not inevitably, for velocity increases may conceivably "finance" a rise in the price level without a change in the quantity of money.[5] Yet the historical record shows no large price-level increases which have not been associated with increases in M. Changes in the quantity of money have unquestionably been associated with changes in the purchasing power of each unit—dollar, franc, pound, or peso.

Such "uses" of the equation enlarge one's general understanding of the economy. More specifically, they can help prevent errors, such as the conclusion that an increase in the stock of money will inevitably lead to a rise in the general level of prices. Either a drop in V or an increase in T may "prevent" a rise in the price level. Nor should one assume that productive capacity is always being used fully when M starts to rise. Yet the simple "quantity theory of money" relied on this assumption.

Another avoidable error is the belief that prices on the average will vary in some close, or even fixed, proportion with the quantity of money. Price levels may go up or down in the same relative amounts as the quantity of money; but such conformity is not necessary. In an economy whose output grows from year to year, such a result is highly improbable.

Another erroneous conclusion will no longer mislead us—a belief that during a depression an increase in M will certainly work itself out, fully or predominantly, in greater production. It may not. A drop in velocity can reduce, or nullify, the potentially stimulating effect of an expansion of M, though complete offset is highly improbable. A partial, but not complete, offset in the form of wage and price increases seems far more prob-

---

[5] The price level would rise if output were to decline without changes in M and V, a relationship which seems improbable.

able. For example, people already employed may be able to get higher wages per hour and thus absorb some of the effect of the increased M. Such a development, however, will reduce the potential expansion of employment.

One conclusion stands as both valid and valuable: The nearer the economy is to capacity output, the greater the likelihood that a rising MV will be felt in higher prices rather than in a larger output of goods and services.

Inadequacies of the Equation

"Uses" such as those just illustrated are far from adequate for guiding policy. The equation does not show causal relationships. The monetary authorities, for example, need greater certainty about the specific reactions to be expected from a change in M under real-life conditions—directions of responses and their magnitudes.

Knowledge of the equation does not permit us to say for certain how a change in the total on one side will be divided between the two elements. Nor can we eliminate the difficulty by putting three elements on one side, e.g., $P = MV/T$, for two of the three may react to M rather than remain stable. We should like to be able to examine carefully all of the magnitudes involved, to measure, and to predict the amounts by which three would each change (or not) if the fourth rose or fell by some known amount. The conditions for such assured success, unfortunately, are not yet of this world. Today's margins of error are wide, but not hopelessly so.

Whatever economists may have written to the effect that price levels will vary directly and proportionally—a 2 percent increase in the quantity of money leading to a 2 percent increase in the level of prices—the analysis here shows that the relations are more complex. Of course, if V were stable, as some economists once assumed, or if it changed in some definite and predictable way, the effects of changes in M would be more accurately foreseen.

Another problem arises from doubt about changes in T. Declines are always possible, even from depression lows. Increases, too, are (almost) always possible, even when war has strained the economy to what seems to be its limits. As output rises, however, further growth becomes more and more difficult. Although this conclusion is undeniable, it can be of only limited help in the prediction of what will actually happen. How much can—and will—output increase from any existing level? Working overtime, for example, permits much, but not unlimited, flexibility. Moreover, stock market, other financial, and real estate transactions can expand to "absorb" much increase in the use of money, diverting effects from goods and services.

Another annoying limitation is the impossibility of measuring P and T with any statistics now available, or likely to become available. Important parts of both the price structure and the volume of trade, it is true, are measured in index numbers: wholesale and consumer prices, industrial production, common stock prices and share turnover, retail sales, and many others. Yet we have no reliable composite or aggregate measures. A comprehensive index of consumer prices may serve fairly well as P for long-run measurement. Analysis of short-run changes, however, requires knowledge of what happens to prices that are not in an index of consumer prices. This defect, however, is small compared with the weakness of the best measures of T.

M and V, too, present measurement problems, although figures of bank clearings with adjustments that are feasible give a moderately satisfactory measure of the bulk of MV. In normal circumstances payments made with coins and currency probably change in about the same proportion as check payments; even if they do not, they are such a small part of the total that any variation will have only a minor effect on national flows of money.

Finally, the equation does not compel, nor even does much to assist, one to try to understand human motivations and the forces which make for economic change.

In short, the transactions form of the equation of exchange helps in understanding broad relationships and long-run tendencies.[6] But as a guide for economic policies as decisions are made from month to month, the equation at best can give little help.

INCOME VERSION OF THE EQUATION OF EXCHANGE

Another way to look at the relation of the quantity of money to economic life is better adapted to the statistical material available. Moreover, it focuses attention on income-creating uses of money.

The Elements of the Income Version

The income version can be expressed as $MV_y = P_yR$. (The subscript y is used because the letter Y has come to be widely employed by economists to signify "income.")

---

[6] An example on a somewhat limited basis appears in H. Barger, *Money, Banking, and Public Policy* (Chicago: Rand McNally & Co., 1962), p. 92. For T, Professor Barger uses the Federal Reserve Index of Industrial Production and for P the Bureau of Labor Statistics Index of Wholesale Prices. For the period 1940–1960 MV/T as predicted from computation rose from 100 to 230; the Wholesale Price Index actually rose from 100 to 234. The closeness of the two figures is impressive.

One element, M, is the same as before. The price measure, P_y, however, differs. It applies to the prices of goods and services that make up *final output*. Excluded are (1) prices in intermediate stages of production and (2) prices of things which are transferred for money but which are not final output, such as buildings constructed in the past and securities. For this measure, an index of consumer prices is more nearly adequate than it is for the transactions form of the equation. Most final output does consist of consumer goods and services.

The velocity figure, V_y, is "income velocity." Definitions differ somewhat, but the central notions are similar: Income velocity is the speed with which money on the average completes a full circuit in creating income. It is frequently expressed as the year's gross national product (or income) divided by the stock of money, *i.e.*, GNP/M.[7]

One may think of income velocity as the frequency with which an average unit of money passes a given point in the income circuit. (Sometimes, in fact, the term "circular velocity" is used for this concept.) We express this rate of flow as the number of times a year that the average dollar appears as a dollar of income—around three times. The speed of this flow is much below transactions velocity, for there will generally be many transactions involving the use of money during the production of a unit of final output or income. Almost every time a dollar is used, some income is created, but often only a few cents' worth. The income part of a dollar of transaction in the typical case is usually only a small part of the payment. (Excluding most purely financial transactions, payments of about $1550 billion were made in 1956, when the gross national product was about $420 billion and the money stock approximately $140 billion.) On the average, therefore, the creation of a dollar of income requires several dollars of transactions.

The R stands for the real goods and services that make up national income; in other words, R is *final output*. Since P_y is an index of prices of the goods and services which are real output, and R comprises these real things, P_yR is the gross national income or output. Whichever measure—gross national income or gross national product—is chosen, it can be related to the stock of money to compute V_y. The fact that income velocity can be computed with statistics available makes the income approach more promising than the transactions version.

Using the Income Version

Most of the points made in discussing the transactions type of the equation apply generally here. Other things being the same, the larger

---

[7] Gross national product is discussed in Chapter 16.

the quantity of money, the higher the level of prices. Yet other things can and do change. The effects of a rise or fall in M will depend, for example, upon what happens to velocity and upon the capacity of the economy for greater output. However, because all the uses of money are not reflected in the constituents of this equation, a possible source of "disruption" exists. A change in the use of M for purposes not reflected in R may "upset" preestablished relationships. For example, the volume of purely financial transactions can change enough to influence the total use of money.

Income and Financial Flows of Money

Financing the processes of production, consumption, and investment involves the flow of money in what may be called the "main money circuit." Other uses of money are also large, uses in what may be termed the "financial circuit." The largest consist of borrowing and then debt repayment and the purchase and sale of stock, bonds, and real estate. How do the two circuits compare in size?

The Federal Reserve's detailed study of money flows permits us to separate the two circuits for 1956. The total payments in the entire process of creating income (the main money circuit) were about $1550 billion. Other studies found that debits to demand deposit accounts in all commercial banks (not counting interbank transactions) were about $3015 billion. These, in fact, do not cover all payments because uses of currency are not included. Yet the second total will include most of the payments in both circuits.

The difference between the second and the first—$1465 billion—is essentially the total use of money in financial transactions. It appears to be about as large as the use in the income circuit. Obviously, it is much too great to be without influence on the various uses of money which make up the total of monetary flows.

CASH BALANCE APPROACH

The cash balance approach to monetary theory[8] focuses attention on the *holding* of money, rather than on its movement (velocity). The most developed version uses the demand-supply method of analysis which serves so well in price theory.

---

[8] This formulation is sometimes called the "Cambridge" version because it has been developed and widely used by economists at Cambridge University, England—such men as Alfred Marshall, A. C. Pigou, and Sir Dennis Robertson.

Transactions Version

Families, businesses, and governments want to hold money, *i.e.,* cash balances. What these three groups (plus other economic units, such as nonprofit organizations) hold at any time *is* the stock of money at that time. Every bit of money is owned by someone, and no one can hold money that does not exist. The demand for money to hold *must* equal the supply; for the moment we ignore the aspect of "price," *i.e.,* whatever serves to balance quantities demanded and quantities supplied. Why is there such a demand? And why does it change? How much money does anyone willingly hold, instead of using it at once to buy goods and services, to pay his debts, or to purchase income-earning wealth?

The person with money wants the amount which will give him a certain purchasing power in terms of goods and services, including the power to invest in durable goods, inventory, or securities. For this purpose "he" is a family head, the treasurer of a great business or a small private organization, or the manager of a government's finances. The equation expressing the essential condition for the whole economy can be formulated as $M = KTP$.[9]

M is the total quantity of money, by now a familiar concept—except that for this purpose the arguments for including time and savings deposits as money are more persuasive than before. P is the general price level, essentially the P of the transactions version; it includes prices of all those things on which holders of money may want to spend. T is the volume of goods and services, again meaning somewhat the same as in the transactions version of the equation of exchange.

What is new is K. This is the fraction of a year's total transactions for which the public—families, businesses, and governments—wishes to hold purchasing power in the form of money. Perhaps, on the average, we want always to have enough cash to buy a month's purchases, including the payment of a month's wages if we are an employer.

Obviously, K relates closely to V. In fact, it is V turned upside down, or $1/V$. If V is 24, then money is used for transactions on the average 24 times a year. The amount held at any time on the average, K, is $\frac{1}{24}$ of the amount spent in a year.

One must eat, wear clothes, and have shelter. But there is no comparable necessity for holding money as money. What determines our demand for money is not any need for money as such but the need for it as a means to other ends. Chapter 14 will discuss the many considerations which affect the holding of money.

There are difficulties in the concept of K. Probably few of us could give an enlightening answer if we were asked about our "demand for cash

---

[9] All four items are index numbers.

(or money)." The concept is not well suited to statistical measurement. Yet this approach requires one to think about important things which one might otherwise overlook. It leads us to look at motives, at the reasons why people do what they do with money. Why, for example, does any buying unit want to hold buying power rather than what money will buy? How much does he want to hold? Why may his actions change?

Income Version

The holding of money can also be related to income rather than to transactions:

$$M = K_y pR.$$

In this case K_y is the fraction of the year's income (or output) which the public wants to hold in cash; R is some measure of national income or product, probably the GNP; and p is the price level of the goods and services making up what is included in R. Thus if K_y is one-third, the public wants to hold in money an amount equal to four months' income. In other words, the average of prices multiplied by the final output of goods and services produced in a year is a dollar total three times the quantity of money.

Using the Cash Balance Approach

The cash balance formulation in either the transactions or the income version, like the equation of exchange, is a truism. Yet it, too, is useful and in a somewhat different way from the equation of exchange. To repeat, it requires us to look at human desires. The activating force in any economic change—or in any lack of change—is something people do. The cash balance equation tells us to examine the demand for money; to learn, if we can, why people hold money rather than spend it; to find out why from one time to another people having power to dispose of cash choose to hold more or less; to study velocity (or its opposite).

What the public really wants to hold, the argument runs, is not so much a specific number of monetary units as a certain amount of *real purchasing power, i.e.,* of goods and services obtainable by using money.[10] Other things being the same, the higher the level of prices, the greater the amount of money the public will want to hold. Similarly, the lower the

---

[10] Statements of the Cambridge equation sometimes imply that the quantity of real purchasing power which the public wants to hold is fixed in relation to real income or to some other variable. There is no convincing reason to expect such fixity, however.

price level, the smaller the number of dollars we wish to hold in cash. Yet, of course, "other things" do change. If the public wishes to alter the amount of real purchasing power that it will hold in the form of money, there will be a change in the demand for money. This change will bring other effects. Let us look at the working out of results.

Effects of Change in the Demand for Money

If for some reason the demand for money drops—if the stock of money in existence has come to represent more in purchasing power than businesses, households, and other parts of the public wish to hold—people will seek to reduce their money holdings. They will try to exchange money for real things, or to buy services, by spending more. As the public thus enlarges its buying, output will increase (unless the economy is at peak capacity). The price level will also rise. The closer the economy is to full employment, the greater the difficulties of expanding output to meet the increased desire for things, *i.e.,* to reflect a decline in the demand for money. The amount of money is what it is; the public as a whole cannot hold less than exists.

The attempt to hold less money brings a "corrective" as the public responds to higher prices.[11] The rise in the price level is a drop in the purchasing power of a unit of money. The worth of a dollar declines when demand for money falls, just as does the worth of anything for which demand falls. The public then finds that in order to keep the same total of purchasing power in real terms, it must hold more money than it had expected to want to hold. If people then try to build up their holdings of money, assuming no change in supply, their attempt will affect business—depress it a little.

Assume a money stock of $150 billion, full employment, and a desire to hold money equal to one-fourth of a year's income. The income is $600 billion. The public then changes its demand for money, deciding to hold only one-fifth of a year's income in the form of money. People begin to try to reduce their holdings of cash by spending more. The greater demand for goods raises prices. At higher prices, however, more money must be held to equal the amount of purchasing power desired. When the price level has risen to the point where the money value of na-

---

[11] This process or its outcome is termed the "Pigou effect," after the British economist. It plays a prominent, but debated, role in more advanced theory. See Don Patinkin, *Money, Interest, and Prices* (Evanston, Ill.: Row, Peterson and Co., 1956). For analysis with attempts to measure, see Thomas Mayer, "The Empirical Significance of the Real Balance Effect," *Quarterly Journal of Economics,* vol. 73, no. 2 (May 1959), pp. 275–291. For other criticism, see John H. Power, "Price Expectations, Money Illusion, and the Real-Balance Effect," *The Journal of Political Economy,* vol. 67, no. 2 (April 1959), pp. 131–143.

tional income is $750 billion, the quantity of money desired, one-fifth of a year's income, equals the amount in existence.

Let us now look at the other possibility. Suppose that people for some reason want to hold more money. If there is no increase in the stock of money, they must in some sense be frustrated because there is only the same amount to hold. It seems inadequate. Households and other economic units, however, will try to build up their holdings by reducing outpayments. (Velocity declines.) The reduction in spending will in turn reduce the demand for goods and services. As one person succeeds in holding more purchasing power in the form of money, someone else must be disappointed. He may try even harder to cut his spending. When businesses seek to build up cash balances, they may not only buy less but also try to sell more, converting inventory and other goods into cash. Such sales will depress prices.

Eventually, assuming no change in underlying conditions, the level of prices will be such that the amount of money in existence represents the real purchasing power which the public wishes to hold, under the circumstances, in the form of money. Each dollar now gives a greater command over goods and services than it did when the process started, because prices have fallen. (The lower dollar volume of business requires less money for financing.) Heads of economic units no longer need to try to change their holdings of money. In fact, as the fall in prices reduces the number of dollars which people need to hold in order to have any given amount of real purchasing power, buying will rise a little. Business will get a bit of a lift.

This line of analysis seems reasonable—but it is not complete. The quantity of money will probably rise or fall as the other conditions change. In our economy movement to new price levels will in itself almost certainly alter M. Such changes may counterbalance, or accentuate, the changes taking place in K or K_y. If the demand for money rises, people in trying to satisfy the higher demand are not limited to holding on longer to the cash they receive. They may also borrow more from banks. To the extent that the increased demand for money is matched by an increase in the quantity available, total buying need not drop; neither prices nor real output will fall. A decline in the demand for money, on the other hand, may lead to retirement of bank loans, a process which reduces the quantity of money. And a problem that we encountered earlier remains—the uncertainty about how changes in total buying will be divided between price changes and alterations in the physical volume of output.

The cash balance approach, as we try to pursue it, becomes more like those discussed earlier. It cannot give the precise results we should like. Both M and T, as well as K, K_y, P, and p, are variables which are most certainly free to change. Moreover, K and K_y cannot be determined by independent investigation; one finds them by determining velocity. Yet this approach does alert us to think about the motives which influence the demand for money, to hold or to use. Such inquiry is essential if we are to understand the influence of money on our lives.

QUESTIONS

1. With what problems is monetary theory concerned?

2. What is the "general price level"? What is required to measure it?

3. Assuming that V is constant, in what circumstances would an increase in M be most likely to change P? to change T? Why? In which situation would an increase in M be more desirable?

4. What is the difference between "income velocity" and "transactions velocity"?

5. How does the transactions version of the cash balance approach differ from the income version?

6. "The equation of exchange is both inadequate and immensely useful." Discuss.

7. How may changes in the use of money for financial purposes influence the price level?

8. Under what conditions would an increase in V be most likely to stimulate employment? raise prices? Why?

9. Estimate the fraction of a year's spending which you try to hold in the form of money. Why do you not try to hold more?

CHAPTER 14   *VELOCITY AND THE DEMAND FOR MONEY*

"MONEY is a busy traveler," but busier at some times than at others. Each approach sketched in the last chapter uses some measure of (1) the speed with which money flows through the economy or the frequency with which a unit is used, or, conversely, (2) the demand for money to hold, either briefly or indefinitely. Both "money sitting and money on the wing" require study.

Why do people hold the amount of money they do, rather than more or less? What is the relation of their money holdings to their income, their wealth, the volume of business they conduct, and a host of other factors? What will bring about a rise or fall in the amount of money that any economic unit holds? Why do some economic changes work out in the form of attempts to build up or draw down cash balances—alter velocity—rather than in efforts to increase or reduce the stock of money? In a sense, most of the forces of life bear upon the answers to these important questions. The motivations of governments, businesses, and households vary; and the discussion here cannot pretend to cover all aspects.

WHO HOLDS MONEY

A useful way to begin understanding why money is held is to look at who owns the money in existence. Although data are neither complete nor up-to-date, relationships are probably much the same as in 1960 (see Table 14.1). Businesses, not including farms, owned more than half of all demand deposits and governments about half as much as individuals. Clearly, most of the demand for money is by governments and businesses, not households. The same conclusion would be reached even if we assumed that virtually all coins and currency outside banks were owned by individuals.

TABLE 14.1

Ownership of Demand Deposits, Insured Commercial Banks[a]

	Percentage of—	
	Total dollar amount	Number of accounts
Domestic business		
Corporate	39	4
Noncorporate	12	7
Individuals—personal	26	79
Nonprofit organizations	4	5
Farm operations	4	5
Trust departments of banks	2	[b]
Foreigners	1	[b]
Government		
Federal	3	[b]
State and local	10	[b]

[a] January 1960.
[b] Less than half of one percent.

Source: *Federal Reserve Bulletin*, April 1960, p. 367; governmental holdings estimated by author from other data in the same issue.

In terms of dollars, over 90 percent of demand deposits were in accounts of over $1000. Nearly 65 percent of all demand deposits were in accounts of over $10,000.

A discussion of the demand for money which centers on family motivations would give a distorted picture. We shall start with Keynes's threefold classification of motives. These motives, and the money holdings to serve them, are not sharply distinct; to some extent the same dollar may be used for all three purposes. Yet the differences are sufficiently marked to warrant separate treatment in discussion, even though empirical study cannot distinguish them clearly.

THE TRANSACTIONS MOTIVE

Every economic unit needs money to handle its ordinary transactions. We conduct our economic affairs with money and can be seriously inconvenienced if cash is not available. The family or business gets money for what it supplies to others and pays money for what it receives from others. At any time, then, the amount that it holds in the ordinary course of events will depend to an important extent upon the money volume of its receipts and payments. General Motors must always have more money to handle its massive business than the local service station, the city of Los Angeles more than the typical town. And, of course, the larger a family's expenditures, the more money it must have on hand on the average.

What is true for individual economic units also applies to the whole economy. The greater the national income—whether as a result of rising prices or rising output or both—the larger the need for money to finance transactions. The changes, however, are not necessarily in the same proportion.

Of course, the amount of money which any economic unit will hold to finance its transactions will depend upon more than the dollar volume of its business. The *frequency* of payments and receipts makes a difference —whether weekly, monthly, or quarterly. The higher the frequency, the smaller the average cash balance that must be on hand to finance transactions smoothly. (This is another way of saying that the greater the velocity of circulation, the smaller the funds needed to finance a given volume of payments over time.) *Regularity,* too, is important. The more assuredly one can count upon what will come in and what must be paid out, the less, on the average, one needs to hold in cash.

Moreover, the relationship between the time when funds are received and the time when payment must be made affects the need for money in the bank. The closer the timing of the two, the more rapid the velocity of circulation or the smaller the average holding of cash. For example, if I get my salary on the last day of the month and must pay my major bills on the first, my average bank balance over the month will be lower than if the big bills are not due until the middle of the month. Some businesses have major seasonal fluctuations which give rise to widely varying needs for money to carry on their normal affairs.

The amount to be held for financing transactions varies somewhat with the speed at which payments can be made. A business which sends checks by air mail or which can telegraph payments may find that it can get along satisfactorily with a smaller average bank balance than if payments were made by slower means; the firm holds money a shorter time while its check is getting to-the recipient. Moreover, if the latter uses the fastest means of collection now available, the funds remain in the payer's account a day or two less. Every day saved in clearing checks reduces the total stock of money required in making payments of any given total amount.[1]

Various transaction needs for money result from special considerations. For example, loans are often for more than borrowers will spend at once. Tax receipts of governments, though coinciding with expenditures

---

[1] A complete statement of the points in this paragraph would be more complicated. See R. T. Selden, "Monetary Velocity in the United States," in *Studies in the Quantity Theory of Money,* ed. Milton Friedman (Chicago: University of Chicago Press, 1956), pp. 179ff.

better than in the past, are synchronized less closely with payments than is the income of the typical business or family. (Property taxes, the major source of local revenue, are often collected in only one or two installments a year.) The amounts which governmental treasuries hold, and the amounts which taxpayers accumulate to meet their liabilities, depend upon factors differing somewhat from those that affect most transaction financing. Another special condition exists when a business accumulates cash to cover depreciation or to retire debt due later; the expected use of the money may be months, or an indefinite time, in the future. The ability to use ordinary charging or a credit plan reduces at least a little the need for money because there is less reason to hold funds for unusual transactions. The corporation which pays its dividends once a year will be likely to hold more cash for this purpose (on the average over the year) than if the same total were paid out on a quarterly basis.

The extent of business integration influences the need for money. Transactions carried on in the same firm can be financed by debits and credits to internal accounts; less money is required than if the business involves different firms.[2] A shift of economic activity from sectors that are more or less self-sufficient to those more fully in the exchange economy raises the need for money for transactions. Thus, the general extension of the market economy, and the related growth of urbanization, have increased the proportion of our economic life requiring the use of money. The relative importance of foreign trade may also influence the need for money for financing transactions because the payment conditions differ somewhat from those for domestic business.

Humble families, giant businesses, and governments at all levels hold some deposits in the bank because the bank adjusts its service charges to the size of the balance. Whether the "extra" holding serves a transaction motive may be disputed; but it does help pay for, and thus provide, the convenience of a checking account. It probably accounts for much of what may appear as idle bank balances. On the other hand, attempts to keep funds "working" affect transactions velocity; a corporation or government treasurer who buys and sells short-term debt, perhaps from day to day or week to week, with funds not needed at the moment may produce an astonishingly high turnover figure for the average balance in his account.

Finally, the availability of substitutes for money to use in transactions will influence the need for cash; a few U.S. Treasury obligations, for example, can be used for the payment of some taxes. Not many such direct substitutes for money exist, but many close substitutes can be held as partial alternatives for the funds needed for transactions. Moreover, pay-

---

[2] The effects of integration on the transactions need for cash are easily exaggerated. Payments for labor, the major cost item for most firms, must be about the same whether production is carried on by several firms selling to each other or by one only.

roll, dividend, or other checks received can be used to make payments by endorsing them over rather than by depositing and writing a check; the greater this practice, the lower the recorded turnover of deposits in relation to income.

THE PRECAUTIONARY MOTIVE

Holding money is desirable not only to pay for the transactions which we know about but also because money on hand gives a type of protection, a sort of insurance against some risks. Holding money rather than other assets for this purpose eliminates delay and any danger of loss in "sale."

The future always has uncertainties. Some contingencies may develop that can be met best with money readily available. They may be misfortunes: in a family—illness, accident, fire, or loss of job; in a business —a failure of someone who owes money to pay as expected, a machine breakdown, a rise in the price of essential inventory; for a government— taxpayer default, a natural disaster, or a rise in the relief rolls. Suddenly, needs for money increase. For some risks, of course, one may insure; someone else will then provide the unexpected requirements for cash.

The need for money can also increase because of unexpected difficulties in renewing loans. And if trouble arises because one does not have funds, it may then breed more trouble, piling up in cumulative fashion and hindering efficient operations. A business, a government, or a family which gets a reputation for being "slow pay," or which shows signs of being in financial trouble, may suffer as others refuse normal accommodation. The wise manager will take some precautions against adverse developments.

The contingencies of an uncertain future, of course, also involve opportunities for good bargains, for getting unexpected business, for acting quickly to gain an unusual short- or long-run benefit. Having ready cash may make possible the seizure of opportunity that would otherwise be lost.

The amount of money that anyone will hold as a precaution will depend in part upon his estimate, perhaps unconscious, of the likelihood of contingencies developing and of their probable significance. Expectations are crucial, and they are the outcome of varied and varying factors, rational and irrational. The more unstable an economy is expected to be, the greater the probable precautionary demand for money. Rising real income will also, one suspects, increase the money holdings which serve to provide peace of mind. In this sense cash balances are probably a "superior good," *i.e.,* one for which the quantity demanded rises in greater proportion than increases in income.

Precautionary holdings of money will depend upon the economic unit's judgment of its ability to get money in other ways if necessary or desirable—notably by borrowing or by sale of assets on satisfactory terms. A firm with an established line of credit at the bank can treat this as a substitute for precautionary holdings.   Usually, this ability to borrow in itself depends to some extent upon the possession of cash or near moneys which are good collateral.[3]   Suppliers are more willing to extend credit to firms in a strong cash position.   Banks, too, recognize that lending is less risky to a borrower who customarily has more cash than is required for his regular transactions.   The maintenance of a consistently strong cash position enhances a firm's ability to borrow if it wishes.

The possession of highly liquid assets and close substitutes for money reduces the need for holding money itself to satisfy precautionary needs. Time and savings accounts can serve almost perfectly for individuals and small businesses.   State and local governments and large businesses will prefer Treasury bills and commercial paper.   The tremendous growth since World War II of financial intermediaries which provide highly liquid assets to the public must have reduced markedly the precautionary demand for money.

The importance of the precautionary motive will vary from time to time.   Unfortunately, there is no way to measure its significance at any one time or its changes.   Nor can this motive be distinguished clearly from the others.

THE SPECULATIVE MOTIVE

Men's holdings of money are also influenced by speculations on its value.   Perhaps it is a bit surprising to speak of money as a speculation. Dollars are always dollars.   From time to time, however, they purchase different amounts—of raw materials, common stocks, real estate, ordinary household articles.   In even short periods of a few weeks, some prices change by large percentages.   Not a few of us sometimes try to outguess the market, *i.e.,* to guess better than the others who buy and sell.   Anyone expecting a fall in the prices of what he intends to purchase will be inclined to build up his holdings of money.   But if he expects prices to rise, he will speed up expenditure, reducing his cash holdings.

The actual amount rationally held to satisfy speculative needs will depend, among other things, upon access to money not presently owned —notably the ability to borrow from banks and to dispose of near moneys. Such access, like other things, is not without its uncertainties.   Least secure, probably, are judgments about ability to borrow in the future if conditions have changed materially.

---

[3] Most economic units can meet emergencies in part by using some of the money normally held for transactions. In effect, then, those with whom one ordinarily deals extend loans by waiting somewhat longer than is customary for payment.

Expectation is decidedly important in connection with this speculative reason for holding money. And expectation is the result of a variety of tangible and intangible factors. Attitudes toward future price changes differ from person to person. Sometimes opposing views will about balance; they may shift in individual cases, of course, but continue to offset each other. And then, for one reason or another, the expectations of price changes may move markedly in one direction—a large net shift. If so, the rise or fall in spending which results may have considerable effect on the economy.

The most dramatic examples of changing expectations about money's future worth have occurred as inflations have progressed—in Germany in 1923, in the Confederate States, and in China in the 1940's. The public has seen prices rise and has come to expect further rises. People then try to spend cash more quickly, to substitute goods for money. Velocity goes up, sometimes to great heights indeed. New expectations grow out of the new conditions and in turn create still newer conditions.

Fortunately, most changes in expectations are not so unsettling. But changes do occur. In a sense modern society is always liable to at least some monetary disturbances which arise out of changing expectations about prices. The monetary changes in turn, will affect national income.

The speculative motive relates to beliefs about the future value of money—but not to such beliefs alone. To some extent, speculations about business developments and the volume of activity will also lead to changes in the desire to hold money. For example, a firm which foresees opportunities for an expansion in volume may build up its cash to be able to take advantage of developments at the appropriate time. If it expects volume to drop, it may let its cash run down to be replenished as inventory is sold or accounts receivable are collected.

Speculative holdings of money also depend upon expected changes in interest rates. The holding of cash rather than a bond or other debt fixed in dollar terms is a speculation on the interest rate. Such debts are to some extent substitutes for money. Their prices are tied closely to interest rates. Someone who expects bond prices to rise (interest rates to fall) will shift from money to bonds. Conversely, one who believes that interest rates will rise (bond prices to drop) will prefer to hold money. This topic will receive separate coverage later.

INSTITUTIONAL CHANGE AND THE DEMAND FOR MONEY

The amount of money held for any or all reasons will depend in part upon the institutions of the economy. Perhaps the most important for this purpose are credit institutions. The ability to borrow easily, whether at the department store or the bank, affects the amount of money required to conduct a business and to serve other needs. However, except as the amount of money can change, what is true for economic units as separate entities is hardly possible for the economy as a whole; if one group can count on getting more credit, some other must stand ready to grant it.

A good market for the sale of new securities enables businesses and governments to finance new capital projects without long prior accumulation of cash. And the more plentiful, the closer, and the more varied the substitutes for money, the less the need for money itself.

Other factors, too, have changing influence over time—the extent of the barter part of the economy, urbanization, the speed of mails, the way taxes are collected, changes in income distribution, the pattern of foreign trade, expectations about price level change, and doubtless many more. Not all work in the same direction. Measurement of the significance of any one is hardly possible. From year to year the net effect of all may be hardly perceptible. Over a period, however, some of these forces have made—and will make—a difference in velocity and in its counterpart, the demand for money.

COSTS OF HOLDING MONEY

Holding money serves useful purposes. It also involves costs. Money held in a checking account serves each of the three functions described above, but it cannot be used for other purposes. It brings no income (except as it helps cover the costs of the services rendered by the bank). In keeping money, therefore, one sacrifices the opportunity to get the benefits that could come from the possession of the best thing(s) that might be obtained in exchange for cash. The alternatives might be assets offering protection against inflation, consumer goods capable of bringing a great variety of satisfactions, or new equipment useful in the business. As a rule, however, the benefits obtainable from such alternatives are not readily measured. It is hard to compare them because they differ among themselves. They also differ from the benefits gained from the possession of cash. Is there, then, any simpler way to measure the cost of holding money?

The simplest measure of the relevant sacrifice might seem to be the interest that could be obtained from an asset with high liquidity. This is an asset with enough "moneyness" to be a close substitute for money, something highly similar to cash. The asset which qualifies will be one which can be "sold" on short notice at a price subject to little or no change.

Such income-producing assets do exist. The most common types are high-quality debt due to mature in the near future, time and savings accounts, and (government) debt redeemable at the owner's option. These assets, however, are so like money that they may not accurately reflect all the significant alternatives to holding money. Can short-term interest yields, for example, show adequately the effects of expectations about changes in the general price level over time? Hardly. No clearly "best" measure of the cost of holding money is evident. Sometimes the correlation of velocity with short-term interest rates has differed from its correlation with one or more series of long-term rates.

The general relationship, however, is clear. To illustrate, let us assume that potential substitutes for money bring low yields—perhaps around 1 percent a year. This substitute, then, is only a little more attractive than cash. The inducement to shift from money to the substitute will be small. The potential gain can be outweighed by the expense, trouble, and inconvenience of acquisition and later disposition of such an asset, plus a slight chance of at least a little loss. The higher the yield obtainable, however, the greater the inducement to shift from money to other assets. When interest rates rise, innumerable corporate and government treasurers and even households will find ways to get along with less cash so that they can acquire income-producing assets. When short-term assets yield 3.65 percent, $1,000,000 brings in $100 a day. The costs of actual purchase and sale of securities for substantial amounts can be covered quickly. Thereafter, the interest adds to net income—and, per dollar of income, one of the least difficult to garner. An additional factor is that as interest rates rise, borrowers will try to get along with smaller loans than otherwise and operate with less money; they also have greater incentive to reduce cash balances to pay off debt.

Moreover, the higher the level of interest rates, the smaller will be one disadvantage of sacrificing liquidity. This disadvantage is the risk of loss from a drop in the price of a fixed interest security. As we saw in Chapter 6, if interest rates rise, the prices of outstanding fixed interest obligations fall, especially those whose maturity is not near. The owner suffers a loss. When the level of interest rates is "low," the risk of such loss cannot be ignored because a rise in the level is possible. When interest rates are already "high," however, there is less chance that they will go up and perhaps a reasonable chance that they will go down. If a drop does occur, the owner of bonds benefits from a capital gain that he would not have received had he held money.

In short, other things being the same, the higher the rate of interest, the greater the incentives to economize on the holding of money, and the higher the velocity of circulation of the money which does exist. Yet other things do change.

FACTS ABOUT VELOCITY

The forces underlying the motives for holding money unquestionably change. Do the combined effects of various changes just about offset each other so that, on balance, velocity (or the desire to hold money) remains essentially stable? Or is there a long-run trend up or down? Or do changes pile up predominantly in one direction at one time and in another at other times? If so, do they produce a total effect with a significant result?

A look at the record of history will give helpful answers. Any such look, of course, requires measurement which is difficult; in significant respects it yields uncertain results. Neither the data nor the concepts are fully satisfactory, and different computations yield different results.[4] Causal relations are uncertain. Conclusions must be somewhat tentative. Fig. 14.1 shows three measures of velocity from 1919 to 1963. The following points derive from analysis of the historical record:

1. *Income* velocity dropped over the long sweep of history from 1839 to the end of World War II. The 1899 figure by one computation (with time deposits treated as money) was 1.87 and that of 1950 around 1.24. The secular decline has not been regular, and its size depends on the measures used. Yet the long-run correlation with per capita real income seems significant; as real income rose, the demand for money cash balances in real terms also rose, *i.e.,* income velocity fell. Will the same trend operate in the future? Only time will tell. Since World War II both income and transactions velocity have risen. This departure from trend may be only an offset to highly exceptional developments during World War II. Yet we have testimony that higher velocity has reflected deliberate efforts to economize on holding of money and to cope with problems arising from "tight" money during periods of high prosperity.

2. Whatever the long-run trend, the short run is at times marked by instability. The 1932 figures of transactions velocity as measured by demand deposit turnover, and of income velocity, were less than two-thirds those of 1929; income velocity in 1942 was about 40 percent above that in 1940; in the last quarter of 1950 the rate was a fifth higher than that in the first quarter of 1950. In the twelve months to June 1964, the turnover of demand deposits rose by nearly one-tenth from a level which was one-tenth higher than that two years earlier.

3. In general, income velocity rises during business expansions and falls during contractions. In twelve cycles with mild depressions from 1876 to 1954, income velocity rose 0.08 per month during expansions and dropped by 0.32 per month in contractions. In six cycles with deep depressions the rise during expansions averaged 0.02, the fall during contrac-

---

[4] One source of doubt relates to the treatment of time and savings deposits in commercial banks.

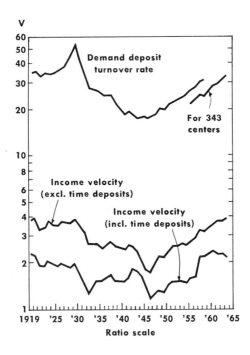

FIGURE 14.1

Three Measures of Aggregate Monetary Velocity

Source: Joint Economic Committee, *Employment, Growth, and Price Levels . . .
Hearings,* Part 4. Prepared by R. T. Selden

tions averaged 0.69 per month. War cycles are excluded.[5] A unit of
money is put to harder work when business is generally rising, and is allowed to take things more easily when the level of economic activity sags.
There is a seasonal low during the first quarter of the year and a high in
the last. Table 14.2 shows something of velocity changes during business
expansions and contractions from 1947 to 1959. The changes have clearly
been of major significance.

4. Another fact is evident. Income and transactions velocities do not
always move together. The probable explanation of divergencies is that

[5] Joint Economic Committee, *Employment, Growth, and Price Levels . . .
Hearings . . . Part 4* (Washington: Government Printing Office, 1959), p. 693.
The data come from testimony by R. T. Selden.

TABLE 14.2

Comparison of Changes in Money Supply and in Income Velocity During Upward and Downward Movements of Gross National Product, 1947–1959

	Year and quarter							
	1947 I	1948 IV	1949 IV	1953 II	1954 II	1957 III	1958 II	1959 II
Income velocity[a]	2.09	2.43	2.37	2.93	2.84	3.33	3.22	3.45
Percent change in GNP	+17.7	− 3.4	+43.5	− 2.7	+24.8	− 3.0	+11.5	
Percent change in money supply[b]	+ 1.0	− 0.7	+15.9	+ 0.6	+ 6.3	+ 0.1	+ 4.3	
Percent change in velocity	+16.3	− 2.5	+23.6	− 3.1	+17.3	− 3.3	+ 7.1	
Absolute change in money supply (billions of dollars)	+ 1.1	− 0.7	+17.3	+ 0.7	+ 8.0	+ 0.2	+ 5.8	
Approximate monetary equivalent of change in velocity (billions)[c]	+17.6	− 2.7	+25.6	− 3.9	+21.9	− 4.4	+ 9.6	

[a] Gross national product divided by money supply.

[b] Money supply consists of demand deposits adjusted plus currency outside banks; in billions of dollars, seasonally adjusted, average for beginning and end of the quarter. Board of Governors of the Federal Reserve System.

[c] Estimated by multiplying the money supply for the previous period by the percentage change in velocity since that period (e.g., the $17,600,000,000 estimate for the period from the first quarter of 1947 to the fourth quarter of 1948 equals $108.2 billion × 0.163).

Source: Joint Economic Committee, *Staff Report on Employment, Growth, and Price Levels* (Washington, D.C.: Government Printing Office, 1960), p. 345. Minor alterations made by author.

the use of money for financial payments does not move closely with income. A rise in stock market activity, for example, may raise transactions velocity. People seek to use money less as a "store of value," spending it to buy securities. Money circulates outside the flows which create income. Transactions velocity rises and income velocity falls (or rises less). Conceivably, changes in real national income may arise out of a change in the desire to engage in financial transactions.

5. What about the correlation between interest rates and velocity? Over the long run the facts do not show a relationship which economists agree is significant.[6] Clearly, however, the rise in velocity since World War II has accompanied a rise in interest rates. Although many other things also happened in this period, there is no doubt that rising interest rates have provided incentives for economizing on the holding of money.

6. Transactions velocities in different sectors of the economy vary markedly.
a. The turnover of demand deposits in New York City greatly exceeds the average for the rest of the country. The chief explanation is the centering in New York of financial activity which brings rapid turnover of money. The rate in 6 other large cities is also markedly higher than in most of the country. In June 1964, for example, the seasonally adjusted turnover rate in New York was 94.5 per year; in 6 large cities, 47.1; and in 337 other reporting centers, 30.5.
b. Even more striking are figures on the velocity of deposits held by certain financial firms. In the month of February 1959, a group of firms dealing in United States government debt turned over their demand deposits at an annual rate of 11,264. The velocity of deposits of member firms of the New York Stock Exchange was 299 per year.[7]
c. The transactions velocity of demand deposits of nonfinancial corporations in 1962 was more than 4 times that of consumers. Farm and noncorporate firms and the Federal government used deposits more than twice as rapidly as consumers in 1956 and about two-thirds as fast as corporations. State-local governments used deposits, on the average, very slowly in 1956; but evidence leaves no doubt that since then many have become sophisticated and energetic in using funds efficiently.
d. Another computation reveals large differences among groups of businesses. Though the actual amounts have certainly changed since 1956, as have perhaps the relationships, it is interesting to note that retail food corporations and wholesalers achieved turnovers of about 35 a year in 1956, compared with an average of just over 20 for all nonfinancial

[6] Joint Economic Committee, *Employment, Growth, and Price Levels . . . Hearings . . . Part 10*, pp. 3435–43.
[7] George Garvy, "Structural Aspects of Money Velocity," *Quarterly Journal of Economics,* vol. 73, no. 3 (August 1959), p. 443.

corporations, about 13 for public utilities, and 8 for mining corporations.

e. Finally, the size of business is significant. Nonfinancial corporations with assets under $50,000 in 1955 recorded average turnover of about 24 compared with 20 for all nonfinancial corporations. One major development in the 10 years to 1955 was the almost doubling in velocity achieved by corporations with assets over $100 million; here we find evidence of the success of corporate treasurers in economizing on the size of cash balances. By 1962 the average for all nonfinancial corporations was half again as high as in 1955.

7. The demand for money, and hence velocity, according to a leading student of the subject, can best be understood by distinguishing between "permanent" income and "measured" income.[8] The latter, measured income, is the amount actually received. Permanent income is a longer-term concept. It is the income that one expects, not forever of course, but for the foreseeable future. It is this to which families and businesses look in their planning. Transitory changes in income—differences between measured and permanent income—have very different effects on the quantity of money demanded than do income changes which are expected to be more or less permanent.

The velocity of circulation of money is certainly not so stable as the velocity of light. Movements of money are not so predictable as those of the tides. Changes, however, are not widely or wildly erratic. They are unquestionably great enough to help account for movements in national income. Their own causes, however, are not always clearly indicated by the best evidence available. Consequently, monetary authorities cannot know in advance how velocity reactions will affect the outcome of a change in monetary policy—or a failure to change.

WILL VELOCITY RISE MORE?

Can velocity continue to rise as it has since World War II? If so, will it? These questions are important for monetary policy. Answers are not clear. Some increase, of course, will always be possible if people want it badly enough. More and more people have learned that their affairs can be conducted with relatively fewer dollars than they had once felt necessary. One company learns about the economizing methods used by others. Computers reveal quickly and frequently the prospective inflow and outflow of cash for the days ahead; cash can then be kept more nearly at the minimum in relation to short-term, income-producing assets. State

[8] Milton Friedman, *The Demand for Money: Some Theoretical and Empirical Results,* Occasional Paper 68 (New York: National Bureau of Economic Research, Inc., 1959).

and local governments adopt better methods.   After some point, however, the obstacles are certain to grow and eventually to outweigh the benefits of additional action.

Many holders of money have probably reached the practical limits of economizing in its use with the techniques now available; others must be near that position.   An unknown number, however, could gain from using methods now available.   Some rise in average velocity is possible.   The potential range cannot be measured.   Nor can we know the odds on such a rise occurring, or of a drop back to lower levels.

CONCLUDING COMMENT: MONEY IS FOR USING

Holding money brings advantages.   But they are limited.   Having devoted most of a chapter to the reasons for holding money, we do well to add a closing word.   "Money is for spending."   The spending may be for consumption.   It may be for investment.   Or, more probably, for some combination.   Whatever the object of expenditures, the important fact remains.   In any given time period under conditions otherwise the same, the larger the public's *holdings* of money, the greater its *spending*.

The two elements—the stock of money and the volume of spending—will not necessarily vary in the same proportion.   The discussion in this chapter has shown why we need not expect proportional changes.   Except in the most unusual of circumstances, however, the *direction* of change will be the same.   When we have more money, we tend to spend more.

QUESTIONS

1. The amount of money held to satisfy the transactions motive is sometimes designated as M_1.   What is this transactions motive? When would you expect M_1 to be greater—in a time of brisk or of slow business?   Why?

2. What other factors (beside the briskness of trade) influence the demand for M_1?   Which of these can be classified as "institutional"?

3. The remainder of the money stock (M_2) is held to satisfy *two* additional motives.   Discuss each.   Under what circumstances will the desire to hold M_2 be greatest?

4. What is the connection between the stock of money and the rate of interest?   Explain how they are mutually governing.   (Hint: Consider holding bonds as an alternative to holding money.)

5. Why might the desire for liquidity change?

6. "Velocity is difficult to predict. Although we have learned something in the past decade, predicting velocity with the accuracy needed for wise monetary policy may prove to be a stumbling block for a long time to come." Discuss.

7. Try to discuss with a businessman his firm's policy about its holdings of money.

8. Discuss the significance of the figures in the last line of Table 14.2.

9. What is the difference between "permanent" and "measured" income? How may it be related to holdings of money?

CHAPTER 15   *INTEREST*[1]

INTEREST occupies a prominent, though disputed and shifting, position in monetary theory. Some aspects of interest theory have little direct connection with the concerns of monetary theory and policy. Others play a central role.

The controversies of the Middle Ages over usury were by no means the first attempts to examine interest, nor did they lead to conclusions which satisfied a changing world. As "classical" and "neoclassical" economics developed, the analysis broadened. The main stream of economic study as it concerned interest dealt with (1) the forces influencing the supply of, and the demand for, savings and (2) the share of total income going to owners of capital. What, economists asked, is the relation of this share to the formation of capital? What are the underlying "real" forces? More specifically, what determines the ability and willingness of people to forego current consumption so that resources can be used to form capital equipment? And what influences the productivity of new capital facilities? Marx emphasized another aspect; he argued that receiving interest is theft.

By the end of the nineteenth century, a new concern demanded attention. Banks were playing an increasing part in the lending process. In the short run, certainly, their actions could influence the interest rate, whatever the deeper forces of the real economy. Moreover, there appeared to be possibilities of more or less conscious, deliberate direction of the economy by one or a few central bankers. These men had some power to alter the rate of interest. But how much? And with what results? Questions such as these touch monetary theory closely.

THE GENERAL NATURE OF INTEREST

Interest is the price paid, and received, for a service—the use of funds on loan. The service can command a price because it is both *useful* and

[1] S. Homer, *A History of Interest Rates* (New Brunswick: Rutgers University Press, 1963).

scarce. The price, like any price, serves a dual function: (1) It both (a) restricts the use, and (b) directs or allocates the use, of something whose supply is not unlimited. (2) It also induces "production," or the creation of a supply of loanable funds.

The forces inducing the supply, and restricting the use, of loanable funds operate at two related but different levels. There are the deep, basic, underlying forces; they change, but as a rule slowly. There are also the surface forces, which account for assertions that "interest is a monetary phenomenon." Temporarily, the surface forces may exert a powerful influence. At any moment they may properly dominate the thinking of responsible officials. These conditions can change rapidly. The influence of one may be superseded quickly by others and forgotten before another year rolls around.

Some parts of interest theory are complex. For example, the ties between the underlying "real" level and the short-run "monetary" level are anything but simple. Furthermore, the study of interest is one aspect of economics in which "other things being the same" is an unusually risky assumption. Fortunately, however, major points can be understood without intricate analysis.

Of course, there is not just "a" rate of interest but several rates prevailing at the same time. Differences in rates arise from several sources, some of which have been discussed in earlier chapters—servicing costs, risk of default (including collateral, insurance, and guarantee), variations in tax treatment, marketability, repayment terms, and the period for which the loan is to run. Table 15-1 gives examples.

TABLE 15.1

Varieties of Interest Rates, Late 1964

Treasury bills, 10 days from maturity	3.65
Bonds	
U.S. government, 2 years from maturity	3.89
U.S. government, 34 years from maturity	4.09
New York City, 5 years from maturity	2.85
Pennsylvania Railroad, 17 years from maturity	4.75
American Telephone and Telegraph, 21 years from maturity	4.38
Prime rate, New York City banks	4.50
Short-term business loans of less than $10,000 by banks in 11 Southern and Western cities	5.31
Uninsured mortgages on new homes, national average	5.77
Auto and other consumer loans,	generally 12.00 or higher

THE DEMAND FOR BORROWED FUNDS

The demand for loans has different aspects. There is, for example, the *type* of demander—demands of business, of governments, and of householders—each of which may then be classified in more detail. Or we can think of the *time period*—short, medium, long. Or the *purpose* for which the money will be used—purchase of productive equipment, personal consumption, paying for war, refunding an earlier debt. Or the *places* involved—urban or rural, East or West, domestic or foreign. And so it goes.

On what does the demand rest? Although the reasons are varied, all have at least one common element—a preference for something *now* rather than in the future.

Table 15.2 summarizes the debt structure of this country just before World War II and on three dates since.

TABLE 15.2

Public and Private Debt, 1939, 1949, 1959, and 1963: Gross Amounts at End of Calendar Year
(Billions)

	1939	1949	1959	1963
Federal government[a]	$ 50	$266	$322	$ 348
State and local governments	20	21	62	87
Corporate				
Long-term	52	68	157	212
Short-term	35	72	179	236
Farm	9	12	24	33
Nonfarm mortgage[b]				
1–4 family residential	16	36	124	172
Multifamily residential and				
commercial	10	15	36	63
Commercial [b]	4	8	16	20
Financial [b]	6	6	13	21
Consumer[b]	7	17	52	70
Total [c]	$208	$520	$986	$1260

[a] Includes agency and other debt not subject to statutory Federal debt limit.

[b] Individual and noncorporate.

[c] Details may not add to totals because of rounding.

Source: *Survey of Current Business.*

Business Demands

Businesses want resources—assets—to use in earning income. The usefulness of assets varies widely, of course. Both physical and economic productivity of plant, equipment, and inventory differ from time to time and place to place. Yet from time immemorial, equipment—a fishing net, boat, machine—has been productive. The use of the facilities has enabled mankind to get more of what it has wanted than was involved in the total labor, materials, and other resources required to make the equipment available.

A business ordinarily acquires such productive capacity by purchase. (Renting and leasing are also possibilities. Generally, however, they are available because other businesses assume the responsibilities and obligations of ownership.) A business can pay with funds provided by the owners or with money that it borrows. Getting money from non-owners—by borrowing—involves costs. Anyone giving up the use of his funds sacrifices the opportunities of using them himself. He will not do so unless he expects the rewards to be as great as those of the best alternative use.

A business can benefit from borrowing if the expected advantages from new assets—whether to expand capacity or to reduce costs—are greater than the costs. The costs, of course, will include the interest to be paid on borrowed funds. When the productivity of the added facilities does seem likely to exceed costs, a business without adequate funds is wise to seek a loan. For example, a businessman learns of a new machine which he can buy for $1000. He feels confident that its output will add about $70 a year to his income after allowing for depreciation and expenses of operation. Such a return is a 7 percent yield. If he can borrow $1000 at 6 percent—$60 a year—he should do so and buy the machine. If the cost of a loan is 5 percent, the project is even more attractive. But if he must pay 8 percent, he would be foolish to borrow and buy.

It is the productivity of capital equipment and plant which accounts for the basic, underlying—the *real*—origin of the great bulk of business demand for loans. This demand rests upon estimates of advantages and disadvantages. Some are not related in any real sense to the productivity of the assets to be required.

Disadvantages, for instance, lie in the *nature of debt* itself. Borrowing may lead to trouble. Debts, with minor exceptions, must be repaid according to the terms of a contract. The borrower must somehow get money to turn back to the lender. Such an obligation can be onerous. If a firm cannot repay, it faces difficulties which may be extremely serious. Some managements attach more importance than do others to the possibilities of getting into trouble through borrowing. Opinions will vary with expectations about business in general, the firm's own financial strength, and the flexibility offered in the debt contract.

There are, however, advantages that affect the demand for debt, at least as contrasted with equity financing. If the cost of debt is less than the prospective reward that must be offered to get new equity—6 percent as against 8 percent—debt has relative appeal. Some of us seek high leverage; the greater the proportion of debt, the higher is the potential for the owners of common stock if the firm prospers. Moreover, when a business obtains funds by borrowing, the power to manage need not be shared with lenders; in contrast, the sale of new equity ordinarily creates new voting interests and can weaken management's position. Tax considerations also give rise to special reasons for preferring debt to equity. Interest is a deduction in computing taxable income. Dividends are not. With tax rates at present levels, debt has significant tax advantages over equity finance.

Some business demand for new loans is to refund earlier borrowings that are falling due. The strength of this demand depends upon the desire of the firm to avoid reducing the volume of its operations, the availability of funds from depreciation, profits, the sale of inventory or financial assets, and the possibilities of getting equity capital.

Finally, expectations about changes in the price level or in the level of interest rates—and either vague or clearly formulated reasons for holding some fraction of assets in cash—will influence the desire to borrow, at least in the short run. Business demand thus rests not only upon the basic forces of capital productivity but also upon what may be only a temporary monetary condition.

One unsettled question of monetary theory, the influence of the rate of interest on the amount of borrowing by business, will be examined as we proceed, especially in Chapter 23.

Government Demand

The total demand for loans now includes a big element of governmental borrowing. The largest part today represents no net demand because it is for refundings of old Federal debt. Some growth of Federal debt occurs in most years, however, as spending exceeds taxes.

Most of the postwar growth of government debt has resulted from state and local government borrowing—chiefly for schools, highways, water and sewer systems, and other more or less long-lived facilities. As communities we borrow to pay for such wealth because of the creativeness of what is obtained. The facilities produce services that we value but which we could not get if they had to be paid for—*e.g.,* the services of school buildings—in taxes at the time of construction.

Population growth, the building of new communities, a reluctance to pay higher taxes, and rising standards of public service, all these help to explain the heavy demand for state and local borrowing. Of course, no careful estimate of gains in relation to costs is possible. Here is a demand for borrowed funds that is the product of forces many of which are not subject to careful economic calculation, but which rest basically on expectations of the productivity of capital and on the inadequacy of financial resources otherwise obtainable.

Family (Consumer) Borrowing

American families and individuals borrow enough to make their part of the total demand for loans a significant fraction of the whole. Some of this borrowing is for business purposes, such as a family seeking to expand an unincorporated business; and some, such as borrowing for the purchase of securities, presumably rests on calculations which are a bit like those of business.

Part of consumer borrowing is to meet emergencies. A great deal more, however, is to get the use now, rather than later, of durable consumption goods. These include not only autos and furniture. Houses are even more important. Total consumer demand is subject to fluctuations which result from a variety of forces. The basic elements of the demand, however, arise from the belief that property which can be acquired by the spending of borrowed money will bring benefits and that getting those benefits sooner rather than later is worth some extra payment (of interest).

Religious organizations, hospitals, clubs, and other nonprofit associations also borrow. They do so for somewhat the same reasons as families. Borrowers expect to spend the money to get something—usually a building or equipment—which will provide desired services. Presumably the services are worth more now than in the future, enough more to justify payment (of interest) to speed up their acquisition.

THE SUPPLY OF FUNDS FOR LENDING

Major Sources of Saving

Income not used for consumption provides an important source of funds for lending. People save for many reasons. While in general we prefer the present to the future, we will make some sacrifice of satisfactions today in the hope of satisfactions in the future—for ourselves or our heirs. Of course, the public's ability and willingness to forego consumption now for the sake of years ahead are limited. Table 15.3 shows estimates of savings made in 1963; the margins of error are not small.

Saving often takes the form of a temporary accumulation of money,

TABLE 15.3

Gross Savings and Capital Consumption, 1964
(Billions)

	Gross saving	Capital consumption	Net saving
Consumers and nonprofit organizations	$102	$53 [a]	$49
Business sector	57	45 [b]	12
Financial sectors	2	0	2
Federal government	−11 [c]	—	−11 [c]
State and local governments	− 3 [c]	—	− 3 [c]
Total	$148 [d]	$99 [d]	$49 [d]

[a] Includes new debt incurred and depreciation of durable consumer goods and housing.

[b] Primarily depreciation.

[c] Borrowings in excess of debt repayment.

[d] Columns may not add to totals because of rounding.

Source: *Federal Reserve Bulletin.* Data from flow-of-funds computations are seasonally adjusted annual rates in second quarter.

chiefly bank balances. Some such savings are destined for uses that have no close connection with the market for loanable funds; other savings are definitely earmarked for lending. There is a remainder which may or may not be loaned. A variety of conditions will influence the decision—such as the desire to purchase equities or real estate or to hold money. Therefore, the total amount of new savings that may be in the effective supply of funds for lending depends upon both the volume of saving and the strength of attractions that compete with those which potential borrowers will offer.

Another element in the overall supply of potential funds for lending is a part of what businesses accumulate as they charge over $45 billion a year (1964) to cover depreciation. Ordinarily, such receipts are used to replace equipment or to repay debt which was incurred to buy the original asset. Yet on occasion, there is leeway to lend some of the funds.

Two other sources of supply exist. They can account for much of the *temporary* change which is tied so closely with monetary theory and policy. (1) Banks if they have the necessary reserves can create deposits and lend them. (2) Cash balances built up in the past and not essential for carrying on today's affairs can be offered in the market for loans. Businesses, governments, and households will sometimes be in the unusual position of standing ready to lend or borrow; at high interest rates they will lend, and at low rates borrow. Fig. 15.1 illustrates a possible case.

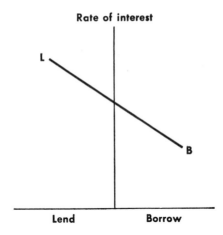

FIGURE 15.1

**Demand-Supply Schedule of Loanable Funds: Hypothetical Case
of an Individual Economic Unit**

New Saving: Influence of the Interest Rate and Other Factors

The amount of saving depends upon many things, but our knowledge
of their relative significance is seriously inadequate. The *size* and *trend*
of *income* are certainly important. The higher the income—family, business, or national—the greater, as a rule, the volume of saving. The relationship between income and saving, however, is a complex of many things,
including somewhat obscure psychological forces, all of which influence
behavior.

Individuals. Does the interest rate appreciably affect the amount of
saving by individuals? Much saving is certainly remote from the influence
of the rate of interest as either (1) an inducement to save or (2) a source
of income out of which saving is possible. The practical problem is
whether *at the margin* there is any significant responsiveness in the short
run and the long. Let us think in terms of an *increase* in the interest rate
as we look at the varied forces.

Higher interest rates have an inducement effect—higher "pay" for the
service of saving will influence some people to provide more of the service.
But we do not know how much more. Higher interest rates give savings
banks and other institutions a more impressive "selling point" and may
lead them to advertise more aggressively; higher interest income may enable

these institutions to provide services which ease and encourage saving. One response is beyond dispute. When some borrower or financial intermediary offers to pay higher rates of interest than do close competitors, dollars flow to get the better yield. If owners of funds for lending (or deposit) show such positive response to differentials in rates obtainable, they may well react similarly in dividing income between consumption and saving.

Nevertheless, forces also run in the other direction. The higher the rate of reward (interest), the smaller the capital sum needed to provide any given level of consumption desired for the future. Perhaps equally important, however, higher interest rates make it less necessary for some people to dip into capital for living expenses. Retired persons, for example, will find that a rise in interest income permits fuller preservation of capital and thus operates to reduce negative saving (capital consumption).

Some saving is done by debtors as they repay. The higher the interest rate, the greater their inducement to get out of debt soon. Yet as more of the monthly payment goes to interest, less is available for retiring principal. When interest rates on home mortgage loans rose in the 1950's, for example, the average duration of FHA home loans rose from 20 to nearly 30 years; the monthly payment, then, included less for debt reduction, *i.e.,* saving. The reactions of lenders as they receive more or less return of principal each month are doubtless mixed.

A short-run rise in interest rates will be part of a tightening monetary situation, one aspect of which is likely to be greater pressure on some borrowers to repay loans. Banks will shorten somewhat the periods for which they will make loans; in doing so, they require borrowers to save to repay more rapidly. (But in the short run tightening money may put national income lower than it would otherwise be and thereby, in a sense, depress the saving actually done, regardless of the intentions of those economic units affected.)

Moreover, an interest rate increase will mean that the prices of outstanding bonds will fall; such capital losses will probably discourage consumption slightly and thus indirectly increase saving. A rise in interest is a rise in the income of the recipient; it will make possible an increase in the amount saved—notably as accruals in savings accounts, life insurance reserves, and pension funds. The ultimate effects of any change in the interest rate level are certain to differ from the effects in the first year.

Perhaps $12 billion of saving each year results from employee and employer contribution to pension funds, a sort of forced saving. The yearly contribution is not much influenced by interest rates. Much saving also results from commitments which are made freely but which when once made cannot be changed except at considerable inconvenience or cost; mortgage and installment debt repayments and the savings in life insurance are examples.

Businesses.   In the short run, certainly, the amount of business saving depends more upon income than upon the interest rate.   The higher the level of profit, the more that is available for keeping in the business, above customary or expected dividends.   In recent years dividend payments have been much more stable than has profit.   The difference, saving, is a residual.   For example, after-tax profits fell $2.5 billion from 1959 to 1960; dividends actually rose by $800 million, while retained earnings, corporate savings out of profit, declined $3.3 billion.

Longer-run management decisions about retaining income will depend largely upon estimates of the probable advantages from the use of funds, chiefly in the business itself.   But other factors, such as complex tax considerations, also exert influence.   Some business saving in any one year, like personal saving, results from past commitments, especially those to repay debt.   The extent to which business savings affect the supply of funds for lending (or reduce the demand for loans) will depend upon still more and varied considerations about which meaningful generalization is difficult.

Governments.   Two rather different factors influence the amount of government saving.   In neither case does the rate of interest play a direct role of appreciable importance.   One factor is the prior commitment to repay outstanding debt; states and localities ordinarily set tax rates to bring in enough revenue to retire the debt as they have promised.[2]   The second factor is the level of national income.   If national income is higher than was expected when tax and spending decisions were made, governments may have budgetary surpluses, or larger ones than planned—a form of saving.   A deficit resulting from low or declining national income is a form of negative saving.

Conclusion.   In the short run, the amount that the whole economy saves will fluctuate considerably because income rises and falls.   Except as interest rates may affect national income, we cannot be confident about the net influence of interest rates, and changes in interest rates, on total saving.   From month to month and from one year to the next, changes in interest rates have scarcely any influence on the public's saving practices.   For the longer run, however, it is much harder to speak with confidence.

Source of Funds for Lending

The availability of funds for *lending* depends not only upon the amount being saved and the other potential sources noted above.   The

---

[2] The national government has also established a sort of compulsory saving to accumulate funds for social insurance benefits.   Additions to social insurance funds, the net new savings, are now insignificant.

willingness and the ability of the persons in control of funds to enter into *loan* contracts are also important. For a time, savers may build up their holdings of money. Or they may wish to put more of their funds into shares of stock or other equities, real estate, or business property. Other things being the same, if there is a change in the desire to hold either money or equities, there will be a change in the supply of funds for lending.

The desire to hold money as completely liquid wealth became a central element of interest theory in the 1930's. John Maynard Keynes, the distinguished British economist whose work we shall examine in Chapter 16, was responsible for the new emphasis. The supply of funds for lending, he said, depends crucially upon "liquidity preference." Liquidity in itself brings some benefits, notably the freedom to take advantage of improving opportunities. People will not give up these benefits, either in lending or in buying equities, except for a reward which promises to be at least slightly greater than the value which they attach to liquidity. The reward on a loan contract is chiefly interest. If the rate of interest is not so high as the value a saver puts on liquidity, he will not lend his money. Keynes suggested that for the whole economy there is a level below which the "pure" interest rate will not fall because of the value of liquidity—a long-term rate of around perhaps 2 percent.

The lending actually done reflects the existence of both a preference for, and an aversion to, loans (or equities). This consideration will appear especially significant when there is a belief that the price level will change. A loan contract ordinarily provides for the return of a specific number of dollars. If a person believes that dollars will become worth less, he will as a result become less willing to enter into debt contracts.

Assume that a saver can use his funds to buy common stock or real estate or some other property whose value is not fixed in terms of dollars. If he expects the dollar to lose purchasing power (inflation), he will become more anxious to get such real assets rather than bonds, mortgages, or money, which seem likely to become worth less in real terms. He will lend his money only if the interest and other advantages are great enough to match the best that he can obtain from something else, allowing for the change in prices. But if he expects the purchasing power of money to rise (the price level to fall), he will become more willing to lend, less anxious to buy property.

The supply of funds for lending is also influenced by a legal factor. Life insurance companies, savings banks, trusts, savings and loan institutions, pension funds, and sinking funds for debt retirement must use the money entrusted to them as contracts and laws prescribe. Laws often require that the bulk of assets be fixed dollar obligations—bonds and mortgage loans. Even if the officers believe that the dollar may drop in purchasing power, or that some other asset will yield more, they must buy fixed dollar obligations. The requirements today, as we saw in Chapter

12, are not absolutely rigid. Nevertheless, as the public entrusts wealth to fiduciaries, it is also directing funds into the market for loans. Therefore, the total supply of funds for lending, as contrasted with the purchase of equities, may be greater than if everyone were freer.

DETERMINATION OF INTEREST RATES

Interest rates obviously exist. Why are they what they are? The "loanable funds" approach examines the process through *flows* of funds. The "liquidity preference" approach focuses on *stocks* of money (and close substitutes) in relation to desire for liquidity.

Demand and Supply of Loanable Funds

New savings flow into the market for loanable funds, constituting a supply. There is also a demand. As bids and offers appear, the persons making them try to reach mutually satisfactory terms to arrange a deal. A

Inelastic demand and supply

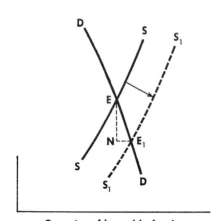

Elastic demand and inelastic supply

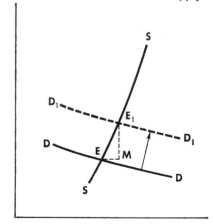

Quantity of loanable funds

When supply increases from SS to S_1S_1, the quantity of loanable funds demanded rises only slightly, NE. The equilibrium rate of interest drops relatively more, EN, than the quantity increases.

Quantity of loanable funds

When demand increases from DD to D_1D_1, the quantity demanded rises by EM. The equilibrium rate of interest rises relatively more, ME_1, than the quantity increases.

FIGURE 15.2

Demand and Supply of Loanable Funds and the Determination of Interest Rates: Hypothetical Cases

key element of these terms is price, the rate of interest. The forces of demand and supply will determine a price, the rate of interest. Fig. 15.2 illustrates two cases.

If demand and supply of loanable funds change—and they do, rising and falling, becoming more or less elastic—the interest rate and the amount loaned both change. These various changes, especially those involving the amounts saved out of income and the amounts invested in new capital goods, will affect the level of economic activity, as we shall see in Chapter 16. New conditions of demand and supply then appear.

Liquidity Preference Theory of Interest

Keynes singled out two elements as being of decisive importance in the determination of interest rates—liquidity preference and the stock of money. The liquidity preference theory is illustrated in Fig. 15.3. (1) There is a demand for liquidity. The quantity of perfectly liquid wealth desired for precautionary and speculative purposes depends (among other things) upon its cost as measured by the interest rate. (The amount of

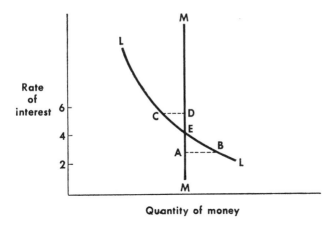

It is assumed that for the time being the stock of money in existence is fixed; MM, therefore, is vertical. LL is the demand for money, the reflection of liquidity preference. E is the equilibrium rate of interest, about 4 per cent. If the interest rate were higher, the public would want to hold less money than exists; the attempt to dispose of CD of money holdings—perhaps by the purchase of bonds—would reduce the interest rate. If the interest were below E, however, the public would try to get more money—AB; but if, as we assume, the money stock is fixed, their efforts to sell bonds to get money will increase the rate of interest, not the stock of money.

FIGURE 15.3

Liquidity Preference Theory of Interest Rate Determination: Hypothetical

money demanded for transaction purposes will depend primarily upon the size of national income.) The higher the rate of interest, the smaller the holding of money for liquidity purposes and the greater the holding of bonds. In short, the demand curve for money to serve liquidity preference must slope downward, though its shape and location (on any given scale) can hardly be known. (2) Perfectly liquid wealth is money. The amount in existence is fixed at any moment, though over even short periods the amount of demand deposits which banks create will depend somewhat upon the rate of interest obtainable from loans and securities. (3) The quantity of bonds outstanding affects price and yield.

When the quantity of money demanded equals the amount supplied, the interest rate is determined. Equilibrium exists. If for some reason the interest rate goes higher (prices of bonds go lower), some holders of money will try to exchange money for other forms of wealth, such as bonds. The purchase of bonds raises their prices and thus reduces yields —interest rates. If the interest rate goes below equilibrium, however, owners of bonds will try to shift to money; such selling of bonds raises the return available.

An increase in the stock of money will lower the rate of interest, other things unchanged, while a reduction in the money stock will raise the interest rate. The amount of response will depend upon the elasticity of the demand for liquidity.

The complete process involves more than is covered by the preceding discussion. As the more advanced analysis takes account of the effects of changes in interest rates on the economy, of the factors which underlie the demand for liquidity, of the results of attempts to increase or reduce the holding of money for all purposes, etc., the elements of the loanable funds theory enter.

Short- and Long-Term Rates

Loans extending for different periods of time but essentially the same in other respects have different interest rates. Fig. 15.4 shows some past relationships for debts of high quality. There has obviously been no simple relation between long- and short-term rates. The long rates fluctuate less, because week-to-week economic changes which are significant temporarily are of no consequence over a decade. Weekly and monthly figures show more clearly than the annual data of Fig. 15-4 that short-term rates go up and down more frequently than long-term rates. Fig. 15-5 (page 272) illustrates.

The difference between long- and short-term rates in free markets will rest largely on uncertainties. They are greater at some times than at

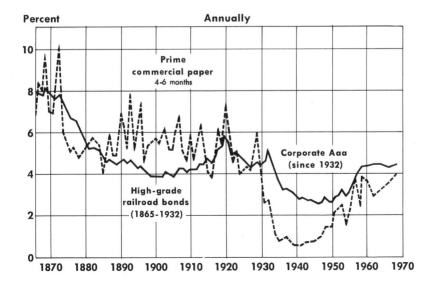

FIGURE 15.4

Long- and Short-Term Interest Rates: 1866–1964

Source: Board of Governors, Federal Reserve System

others. If both borrowers and lenders were confident about the future, yields on different maturities would tend to come together.

When the rates for different maturities are not identical, lenders (the buyers of bonds or other debt instruments) who are accepting the *lower* rate do so because they believe that the other rate is likely to change unfavorably (for the owner of bonds) causing the price of the bond to fall. Other lenders—and borrowers—disagree. Fig. 15.6 (page 273) shows yield curves for taxable Treasury securities on two dates. On both occasions long- and short-term rates were different. The *patterns* and the *levels* of rates also differed.

If the long-term rate is "low," there is reason to expect the short-term rate to be lower. Lenders channel funds into the short-term portion of the market. They recognize that long-term bonds bought now will go down in price if, or when, the long rate rises. Any increase in the funds offered for short-term lending, of course, will tend to depress the short-term rate; any reduction of supply of funds for long-term lending will tend to raise the long-term rate. Under such conditions, the difference between the rates will narrow. The prices of bonds will rise, and the flows of funds will change in response.

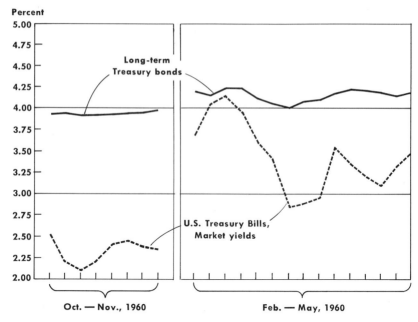

FIGURE 15.5

Comparative Fluctuations of Short-Term and Long-Term Interest Rates, Selected Periods[a]

Source: *Federal Reserve Bulletin*

[a] The periods have been selected to illustrate the greater stability of long-term rates. In many periods, of course, short-term rates are nearly as stable as long-term.

The higher the long rate, to repeat for emphasis, the less the chance of a further rise and the greater the chance of a decline. Lenders who have choice will try to channel funds from short- to long-term contracts to get more permanent advantage of the "high" rate which may not continue. Borrowers, however, try to make greater use than otherwise of short-term loans and less of long. The forces of demand and supply will tend to bring a new relation between short and long rates.

Relations between rates will be discussed again in Chapter 23.

Interest Rates and Bond Prices

Changes in interest rates, as shown in Chapter 6, have an effect, or take a form, rather different from what one observes with other prices. If demand and supply move to alter the price of shoes, there will probably be no observable effect on other prices. Changing interest rates, however, do have evident effects on one other group of prices—those of bonds.

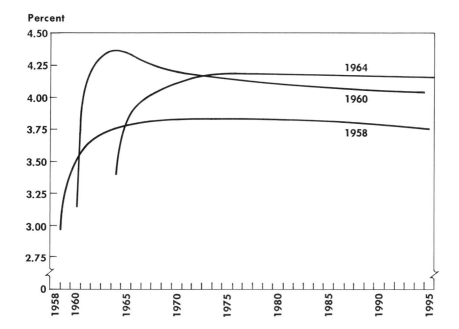

FIGURE 15.6

Yields on Taxable Treasury Securities, Three Dates
(Fixed Maturity Issues Only)

Source: *Treasury Bulletin*

The market for loanable funds is not limited to new savings and to new loan contracts. Existing bonds and other debts are bought and sold. Anyone supplying funds for lending may buy debts already outstanding. He is not limited to a market which reflects merely the demand for new borrowing. Available to him are debt contracts which were issued earlier. And he is in competition, in a sense, with persons who have saved earlier —many of whom continue to seek more attractive terms and will take advantage of better offers by lenders.

Similarly, potential borrowers in trying to get funds are not limited to sources of new savings. The borrower can also try to get loans from those who have provided money to someone else earlier and have an asset (for example, a savings account or a bond) which they can liquidate. Who will not welcome an opportunity to make a better deal? Both borrowers and lenders in trying for the best terms possible must meet the competition of those who made agreements earlier but who seek better conditions.

At any one time, of course, only a small fraction of those who have borrowed or loaned in the past are seriously "in the market" to rearrange, or to buy or sell, existing loans. The great mass of debt is stable and securely held. Some, however, is shiftable; the ower or owner is willing and able to try for something better. As opportunities change, some old debt will change hands—and price. There is enough such movement to influence the whole market. Marginal shifts of a small fraction of the total debt in existence can be large in relation to the net flow of new funds into and out of the market. Those who try to buy or sell bonds or mortgage loans which have been outstanding for years may not realize that their actions influence interest rates which apply to new loans. Yet such ties exist.

The market for United States government debt and other high-quality obligations, we know, is extremely sensitive. Actual and potential buyers and sellers are legion. The volume of debt that may be traded is huge. There is also a considerable variety, but with neighboring types that are not sharply differentiated. Knowledge about what is going on is widespread. Large, well-informed institutions are prominent. The elements of a good market exist.

In the short run, it is true, deliberate official and private activity can "disturb" or stabilize prices for particular securities or interest rates. Over the months, however, such intrusions are likely to have little net effect (except as the interventions constitute open market activity which changes legal reserves). In the longer run the changes that count are the outcome of forces of many types from many sources. Wherever they seem to originate, their ultimate influence will be felt to a varying degree in all parts of the financial market.

As these forces change the prices of outstanding debt, they are also changing interest rates—in the opposite direction. If the demand for borrowed funds rises with no change in supply conditions, or if demand remains the same but supply drops, the interest rate will rise. As part of this process, existing government (and other) bonds fall in price to the point where funds placed in them bring yields at the new and higher market rate. Holders of 3 percent bonds due in, say, 10 years can get the face value if they wait till maturity; however, if the rate on new loans is 4 percent, the price of the old bond will be enough less than par to yield 4 percent to maturity. Any buyer would be foolish to pay a higher price.

If demand and supply conditions lead to a drop in the level of interest rates, the prices of outstanding government and other debt rise. Owners will not sell except for a price which is high enough to bring a capital sum that will maintain the same stream of income at the lower interest rate. Prices of short-term debt, of course, change little because maturity is not far off. Prices of long-term bonds, however, may fluctuate over a wide range. The wealth of bondholders changes. Such changes can influence buying and investing quite independently of any identifiable alteration in the flows of income and saving.

To summarize, when interest rates are "high" there are two reasons for holding bonds—the current yield is attractive and the chances of a rise in bond prices are good, or at least much better than when interest rates are "low." And when interest rates are low, the holding of money gains in attractiveness. The loss of interest is "small," and there is no risk of a fall in price of the asset (money) as there is if one holds a bond.

Interest Rates and the Prices of Non-Debt Wealth

The demand-supply conditions that influence interest rates and bond prices bring changes beyond the market for debts. Many owners of funds to "put to work"—those who have saved out of income or who owned a security which has been repaid—are not limited to bonds, other loans, and cash.

Common stock offers an obvious alternative. If interest rates rise, bonds become relatively more, and stocks less, appealing. Stock prices tend to fall, though not in the clear pattern of bond price change. Any corporation seeking to sell stock, and any owner of outstanding stock, must meet the competition of higher bond yields. The converse is true if interest rates fall.

Or we can look at the same basic relation in another way. If stock prices rise or fall, other things being the same, the relative attractiveness of bonds changes. The flow of savings will shift to reflect the new conditions. Interest rates will show the effects.[3]

Another alternative is to buy real things. Assume that the long-term rate of interest drops (bond prices rise). What does a person with funds to invest now find? Bonds are less attractive than before, but the purchase of other forms of wealth has become relatively more inviting. If the expected productivity of buildings, inventory, or equipment remains unchanged (or if it declines less than the interest rate) expanded purchases are to be expected. For example, an apartment house that had not seemed quite worth owning when good bonds yielded 5 percent might be

---

[3] No simple comparison of bond and stock yields can be adequate. The rational investor will consider not only stock yields but also earnings. Some people, for tax purposes, may prefer stock with little or no current dividend yield but with earnings plowed into the corporation to build capital gains. Moreover, equity earnings may rise—*e.g.,* a leading corporation in a growing industry in a growing economy. Bonds and other fixed contracts offer few if any such growth prospects.

purchased when bond yields fall to 4 percent.[4] Higher demand for such real assets as buildings or equipment, of course, will raise the price and reduce the yields. If the building could be constructed, or if new machines could still be produced, at the costs that had prevailed before, more new (or old) savings would be used to buy real things rather than bonds. Money spent in this way will no longer "press down" on the price of loanable funds. Meanwhile, the increase in the quantity of productive capacity will tend to reduce marginal yields. Thus, the difference between the interest rate and the yields on real wealth will narrow. (An initial rise in interest rates tends to produce the opposite results.)

Shifts between lending and the purchase of real assets are impeded by a host of imperfections. Many persons find that in practice the number of close alternatives may seldom be large. Nevertheless, small changes at the margin can produce results whose significance transcends the size of the particular change involved.

The expected net productivity of real capital facilities influences the rate of interest, not only through the demand for loanable funds but also through the demand for equity investment. Net productivity depends upon both gross yield and costs; costs include those resulting from the outlay for original purchase, *e.g.,* depreciation. Thus, the cost of producing equipment will affect the rate of interest in a basic, but indirect, way.

BANKS AND THE RATE OF INTEREST

What, if any, effect does the banking system have on interest rates?

Confusion between Credit and Money

Borrowers want money. They have no reason to care whether the money is newly created or whether it is the result of saving out of income. The significance for the economy, however, is tremendous.

The demand for loans—often expressed as a demand for credit—can be met out of the supply of savings. There is a price, an interest rate, which will balance the quantities of credit demanded and supplied. The "thing" which changes hands is money. In Chapter 14 we saw that there is demand for money as such; there is also supply. The supply-demand of credit and the supply-demand of money are essentially different. But

---

[4] Our concern here is *not* with the possibility that lower interest rates will lead to more *borrowing,* and expansion in demand deposits, to stimulate the buying of such property.

confusion between them is common. Much misunderstanding results from the fact that commercial banks both grant credit (make loans) and create money (demand deposits).

Commercial Banks as a Source of Loanable Funds

Some of the supply of loanable funds, and especially some of the *change* in the amount supplied in the short run, results from commercial bank lending in the form of money creation. This lending need involve little real cost in the sense of labor and materials. Under some circumstances the creation of demand deposits for one borrower or many may not require any sacrifice of desirable alternatives. The public, through government, can influence the amount of such lending by the rules that it makes to regulate banks in their creation of money.

Is it not possible, then, to use the banking system to control the rate of interest? More tempting, perhaps, is the possibility that by enabling banks to "manufacture" money more easily, man can lower the cost of borrowing. At any given time, society, using government, can permit banks to expand their loans—extend more credit—even though there has not been a penny more of voluntary saving. This fact is undeniable. Another fact is also undeniable. Such loan expansion increases the stock of money.

An increase in the volume of funds available for lending will tend to reduce interest rates. But this is not the only result. As the new money is spent—assuming full employment and no change in velocity—the price level will rise. Will this rise affect interest rates? It ought to induce some lenders to try to get a higher yield as compensation for the loss in value of money. Some owners of bonds will sell, perhaps to buy stock or real assets. Some holders of money will shift to goods. Borrowers will tend to seek larger loans to benefit from rising prices. Both demand and supply thus move to raise interest rates.

Furthermore, interest rates will go back up unless banks add another injection of money. Banking policy cannot lower interest rates, except temporarily, unless injections of new money into the economy are continued. Such a practice will be self-defeating in a world of essentially full employment. For as the growing stock of money circulates, the upward pressure on prices will continue until borrowers and lenders cannot ignore what is happening.

When there is substantial unemployment, however, the effects of the increase in bank-created funds for lending—money—may appear primarily as greater output, with little rise in prices. Higher incomes may then do as much to stimulate saving or to raise the demand for borrowed funds. The relative magnitudes will depend upon a host of conditions whose net effect will not be clear, certainly not before the process has gotten under way.

What about the power of the monetary authorities and the banking system to raise interest rates? Again, the basic forces of demand and supply dominate. Banks have influence in the short run. By reducing reserves or raising reserve requirements, the monetary authorities could force banks to reduce loans outstanding. Interest rates would tend to rise. But for the longer pull they would not rise a great deal unless the process were repeated and repeated, something which is most improbable.

Briefly, and explicitly excluding inflationary possibilities, bank actions over any extended period will not have much effect on the level of interest rates. The influence in the short run is quite another matter. Monetary policy which leads banks to raise or lower the level of interest rates from month to month can certainly be effective. Changes in short-term rates that are large in percentage terms can result from alterations in bank lending. Such changes in lending may result from forces apparently outside the banks—a decline or a rise in business demand for loans—or from official actions which alter the capacity of banks to make loans.

A Note on Magnitudes

Demand deposits grew $2.5 billion a year in the 1950's. From January 1960 through June 1964 the annual growth was $2 billion.[5] Net debt in this country grows by nearly $50 billion a year. Demand-deposit growth has been a small percentage of the growth of debt (credit).

An addition of 10 percent to the annual supply of funds for lending would reduce interest rates for a time. Suppose that banks were given enough reserves to enable them to create $5 billion *more* of demand deposits each year. Interest rates on bank loans would tend to fall. By how much no one can say for certain. But we are able to say that the more than doubling of the annual increase in the money stock would not be insignificant. Each act of deposit creation adds to the supply of loanable funds only once. The money, however, will continue to circulate. A five-year program of adding to the money stock (above the existing rate) by 10 percent of the expansion of debt would cumulate into a total mone-

[5] In the 4 years 1960 through 1963 demand deposits grew by less than $1.4 billion a year. The Federal Reserve was then, and still is, criticized for failing to permit growth in the stock of money which would be more in line with the potential growth of the economy. During this period, however, time deposits at commercial banks rose by $10 billion a year, 3 times the average of the 1950's; velocity increased by one-tenth. The FR probably concluded that such rapid growth in both a close substitute for money and in deposit turnover called for slowing the growth rate of demand deposits.

MORGAN GUARANTY TRUST COMPANY of NEW YORK

DOMESTIC MONEY MARKET RUN-DOWN

OPENING RATES: 11/17/64

	90 DAYS		180 DAYS	
U. S. TREASURY BILLS	3.58	%	3.76	%
FEDERAL AGENCY ISSUES	3.86	%	3.96	%
PRIME FINANCE AND INDUSTRIAL PAPER				
FINANCE COMPANIES (ADDITIONAL RATES BELOW)	3.875	%	4.00	%
INDUSTRIAL COMPANIES	4.00	%	4.00	%
INTEREST ARBITRAGE (FULLY HEDGED)				
UNITED KINGDOM TREASURY BILLS	3.66	%	----	
UNITED KINGDOM HIRE PURCHASE DEPOSITS (PRIME)	4.30	%	4.45	%
GOVERNMENT OF CANADA TREASURY BILLS	3.48	%	3.61	%
CANADIAN FINANCE COMPANY PAPER (PRIME)	4.20	%	4.40	%
BANKERS ACCEPTANCES (WITHOUT OUR ENDORSEMENT)	3.75	%	4.00	%

PUBLIC HOUSING AUTHORITY NOTES (PHA's) 2.00 %(3.95 %)* 2.05 %(4.00 %)*
(OTHER TAX EXEMPT RATES BELOW)

TIME CERTIFICATES OF DEPOSIT (NEGOTIABLE) ISSUED BY M. G. T. CO.

90 - 119 days 3.90   5/3/65 and longer 4.00
120 - 4/30/65 3.95

BANKERS RATES

			EFFECTIVE DATE
N. Y. FEDERAL RESERVE BANK DISCOUNT RATE	3.50	%	July 17, 1963
M. G. T. CO. RATES FOR:			
SHORT TERM PRIME COMMERCIAL UNSECURED CREDITS	4.50	%	August 24, 1960
BROKERS LOANS (UNDER REGULATION "U")	4.50	%	August 23, 1960
DEALER LOANS SECURED BY U. S. GOV'TS.	4.00	%	FLEXIBLE
FEDERAL FUNDS	3.50	%	FLEXIBLE

PRIME FINANCE COMPANY RATES

5 - 14 days	3 1/4% - 3 5/8%
15 - 29 days	3 1/4% - 3 3/4%
30 - 59 days	3 1/2% - 3 3/4%
60 - 119 days	3 3/4% - 3 7/8%
120 - 270 days	3 7/8% - 4%

TAX EXEMPT MUNICIPAL NOTES AND BONDS

3 MOS. 2.00-2.05 % (3.95-4.05%)*
6 MOS. 2.05-2.10 % (4.00-4.09%)*
9 MOS. 2.10-2.15 % (4.07-4.17%)*
12 MOS. 2 1/8-2.20% (4.08-4.26%)*

FIGURE 15.7

Domestic Money Market Run-Down

Reproduced with permission of Morgan Guaranty Trust Company of New York.

tary growth large enough to affect the economy significantly, in all probability putting upward pressure on the price level.

"Market" and "Natural" Rate

The distinction between the "market" and the "natural" rate of interest can help one understand underlying economic issues. The *natural* rate, a concept associated with the Swedish economist K. Wicksell, is that rate which basic demand and supply conditions would produce. It reflects the *real* forces of capital productivity and of the public's willingness to save. The natural rate would be essentially the yield expected from newly created capital (net after allowing for risk and other costs) at the margin where the last dollar of new savings is invested.

"The" *market* rate is that which prevails in fact. It can differ from the natural rate because banks influence the supply of funds for lending.

If the market and the natural rates differ, the level of prices or the volume of production, or some combination, will tend to change as follows:

1. If the market rate is *below* the natural rate, then the marginal productivity of new equipment is above the market rate of interest. Consequently, borrowing (financed partly by bank loans) and real investment will both exceed the savings which the public wishes to make. (The creation of new demand deposits is not a form of real saving.) The quantity of producer and consumer goods demanded will be greater than the quantity supplied at prevailing prices. The price level will move upward.[6]

2. On the other hand, if the market rate is *above* the natural rate, the costs of adding new equipment, including interest, will exceed the benefits. Business investment will drop. Prices and national income will also fall. A decline in the demand for borrowed funds will then help reduce the interest rate.

Deep and powerful forces determine the natural rate. Deliberate and conscious official control, the argument continues, can do virtually nothing in the short run to alter the natural rate. The market rate, however, can be influenced by the monetary authorities. If they knew the natural rate, they could help the banking system bring the short-run market rate more quickly into line. In this way adjustment toward equilibrium

---

[6] Several related forces contribute to the price level change. Much depends, of course, upon the extent to which resources are utilized. Keynes, as we shall see in the next chapter, called attention to another element affecting the outcome. Changes in national income affect both saving and the demand for investment goods. Thus the underlying conditions of supply and demand of loanable funds depend in part upon price level trends.

could be speeded, cyclical fluctuations reduced. Practical use of this line of analysis requires knowledge of the actual natural rate. Unfortunately, man has no way to obtain this required figure. Once again, we find a concept or theory which gives insight but has no operational usefulness.

INTEREST AS A TOPIC OF CONTROVERSY

Interest has been, and remains, a controversial subject. We note a few points which have some current concern.

Is there an element of exploitation in interest? Does the lender provide a useful service? Does not the payment of interest transfer money from the "have nots" to the "haves"? When the commercial banking system creates deposits for lending, what justification can be found for charging interest? Such questions raise several issues.

An old argument is that the person who provides loan funds, unlike the person who labors with his hands, performs no useful service. Critics also say that he undergoes no hardship, makes no real sacrifice. What does he do? He abstains from consumption. He waits. He lets others have the use of what he might consume. In doing so, he enables them to produce more or, in some cases, to enjoy life more today.

The saver-lender may consume later. (In fact, of course, capital has accumulated over centuries only where savers have failed to consume all their wealth before dying.) Humans are mortal. Waiting to consume will often, but of course not always, involve sacrifice. Even more clearly, abstaining from consumption—even waiting to consume—must be recognized as rendering services of value to others. The failure to consume, by freeing resources for other uses, is worth something to others. It is a service for which, like many others, free men willingly pay.

Yet is there, really, subjective cost for the saver-lender? Quite possibly much saving involves no sense of "going without." Many a worker, for example, will have no awareness of any personal sacrifice due to the employer's contribution to a pension fund, even though the payment is a substitute for higher wages. At the margin, however, conditions are decidedly different. Some saving does involve real cost. Perhaps no one can convince others of the appropriateness in a deep human sense of any specific reward for whatever sacrifice is involved. Fortunately, such doubt is not a matter of serious import, any more than are corresponding doubts about the rewards for labor.

Whether or not saving involves much real cost, there is an economic cost in making a loan. The lender sacrifices liquidity. Far more important in the long run, he gives up the opportunity to obtain and enjoy the yield of productive assets. He foregoes alternative uses of his wealth. This sacrifice is a cost. It must be paid by anyone who wants another person to incur it.

In the past, certainly, payment of interest did often transfer income from lower to higher income groups. Perhaps there is enough to be condemned in such a result to create a meritorious argument against public policies which make for higher interest rates than would otherwise prevail; *i.e.,* perhaps there would have been better alternative means of achieving the objectives sought from interest rate policy. However, broadening the ownership of debt has gradually and substantially changed conditions. The vast majority of the public, directly and through such intermediaries as life insurance companies, Social Security, and savings institutions, receive much of the total interest paid. (Top wealth groups generally own more common stock and other equities than debt.)

For commercial banks a rise in interest rates will create portfolio losses—and also increase earning capacity. Judgments of the eventual result may well depend upon the degree of banking competition. A generally competitive banking system will tend to pass on to customers increases in interest earnings above costs. The process, however, may take quite some time. And there may be more than a few places where banking competition is not vigorous. On balance, the effects of interest rate changes on income distribution do not appear clear enough to justify a place of influence in the determination of monetary policy.

QUESTIONS

1. "Conditions of demand and supply for loanable funds in the aggregate determine the rate of interest." Comment.

2. What is the liquidity preference theory of the rate of interest?

3. What factors influence the amount of saving? the supply of funds for lending?

4. What is the relation between the productivity of capital and the rate of interest?

5. How does the productivity of new capital equipment influence the rate of interest?

6. Find examples of several different rates of interest in the market at the same time.

7. Explain the concepts of the "market" rate and the "natural" rate of interest.

8. What functions does interest serve?

9. Why are people willing to pay interest? What constitutes the demand for, and supply of, loanable funds?

CHAPTER 16   *NATIONAL INCOME APPROACH TO THE ROLE OF MONEY* [1]

Massive and prolonged unemployment in the 1930's created new challenges for economists. One response overshadowed all others—that of J. M. Keynes. He made a bold effort to attack the great problem of the era, the tragedy of widespread and apparently endless unemployment. His primary concern was neither business cycles nor short-run but temporary failures to reach full employment. Keynes sought to learn what determined the *general level* of employment, year in and year out.

Since the publication in 1936 of his famous book *The General Theory of Employment, Interest and Money,* his analysis has aroused strong emotions and stimulated extensive study. Moreover, it has influenced the most abstract of economic theories and the most practical of governmental (and private) policies.

Keynes's approach emphasizes *national income* rather than price levels, as had so much of monetary theory.[2] The new analysis concluded that the quantity of money and monetary policy are likely to be of secondary importance, at least under depression conditions. (Velocity was left rather outside the major Keynesian analysis.) Both the analysis and the policies which it suggested aroused vigorous debate. The dust stirred up by the controversy has not all settled, and still clouds some views. Yet

---

[1] See H. G. Johnson, " 'The General Theory' After Twenty-Five Years," *American Economic Review,* May 1961, pp. 1–17; a modern analysis which emphasizes monetary aspects is F. Modigliani, "The Monetary Mechanism and Its Interaction with Real Phenomena," *Review of Economics and Statistics,* Feb. 1963, pp. 79–107.

[2] Thus, Keynesian analysis is sometimes designated "income theory," "receipts and expenditures" or "income-expenditure" approach. Expenditure in the sense of total demand, buying, plays a crucial role.

we must certainly benefit from looking at the problems of a modern economy through the windows opened by Keynes.

MEASURES OF NATIONAL INCOME AND PRODUCT

The 1930's witnessed the extensive development of national income accounting, providing indispensable tools for the Keynesian type of analy-

TABLE 16.1

National Product and Income Measures and Amounts, 1964 [a]
(Billions)

Gross national product		National income	
Consumption		Compensation of employees	$365
Durable goods	$ 59	Income of unincorporated en-	
Nondurable goods	180	terprises (nonfarm) and	
Services	166	professions	40
		Farm income	13
Gross private domestic		Rental income of persons	12
investment		Corporation profits before tax	58
Construction		Net interest	27
Residential	26	Total national income	$515
Other	23		
Producers' durable equip-			
ment	36		
Change in business inven-			
tories	3		
Net exports of goods and			
services	7		
Government purchases of			
goods and services			
Federal	66		
State and local	64		
Total GNP	$628		
Less—			
Capital consumption allow-			
ances	54		
Net national product	$575		
Less—			
Indirect business taxes	60		
Miscellaneous adjustments, net	1		
National income	$515		

Personal income		Disposable personal income	
Disbursements to employees and other labor income[b]	$348	Personal income	$495
		Less—	
Income of unincorporated enterprises (nonfarm) and professions	40	Personal taxes	59
		Total disposable personal income	$436
Farm income	13		
Rental income of persons	12		
Personal interest income[c]	36		
Dividends	20		
Transfer payments received	38		
Less—			
Personal contributions for social insurance	13		
Total personal income	$495		

[a] Seasonally adjusted annual rates during third quarter. Because of rounding details do not add to totals.

[b] Differs from "Compensation of employees" by the amount of employer payments for social insurance and private pension plans.

[c] Includes interest received on government debt; such interest is not considered as part of national income.

Source: *Survey of Current Business.*

sis. Two general sets of measures have come into common use. One covers output or *product*—the goods and services produced. This is the money value of final output for the whole economy. The other set of measures applies to the *income* received for the services rendered in production.

Measurement of the components and of the totals in itself proves to be an interesting area of study. Measurement problems, however, are of only slight concern for monetary theory. Table 16.1 summarizes the relations between the chief measures of national aggregates.

CIRCULAR FLOW OF INCOME

The national income approach looks at the flow of money in both (1) the creation or generation and (2) the use, of income. Fig. 16.1 illustrates the circular flow.

Money is more than an essential lubricant of the economic machine. Money is also a means by which people produce change. Although the real, the fundamental or activating, forces may be largely nonmonetary, they exert their influence through the use—or nonuse—of money.

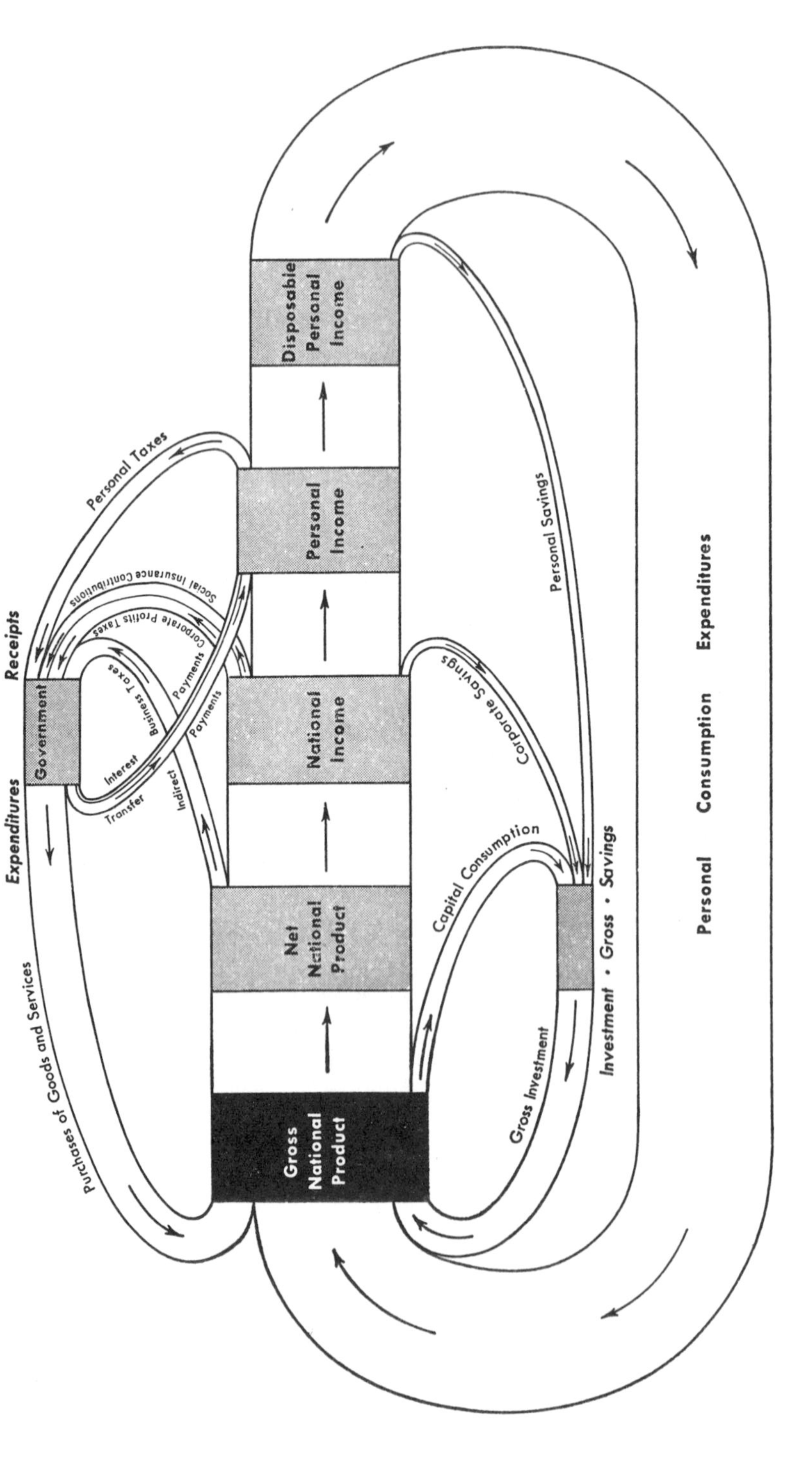

FIGURE 16.1

Flow of Income and Expenditures   Courtesy of the Twentieth Century Fund

Effective Demand

Goods and services are produced, and jobs exist, because there is effective demand, people able and willing to buy. Total demand or buying can be subdivided for analysis into 4 classes: consumption, gross, private domestic investment, net export of goods and services, and government purchasing of goods and services. We shall discuss them later. The relative importance of each for late 1964 is shown in Table 16.1. The buying for consumption, $405 billion; plus the buying of new investment or capital goods, $87 billion, plus Federal-state-local government buying, $130 billion, plus $7 billion difference between exports and imports, make up total demand. This demand consists of dollars being spent.[3]

How does money come into the hands of spenders? For the most part, we get money as payment for what we do as producers. In general, what is paid out as the costs of providing goods and services is the income of producers (wages and salaries, proprietors' earnings, corporation profits, rent, interest, and miscellaneous items). For the economy as a whole, the two totals—expense (costs, out-payments) and income—are equal. The production process generates enough income to buy all the output at prevailing prices. In other words, the potential money demand is adequate to buy everything created at the prices in effect.[4] If the money income generated (and no more) is all spent, the levels of total income will not change. Particular prices and types of output, of course, may move up and down, but not the aggregates for the whole system.

Change in National Income: Preliminary Statement

However, the total of money spending does change. Why, or rather, how? Keynes answers, not in the form of reasons for change in M or V as such, but with reasons why the public alters its buying.

For one thing, a family (or a business or government) may *save;* it spends less (on consumption in the case of a family) than its income. Assume that it does so—getting $8000 as income after taxes but spending only $7000. Will total buying in the economy drop as a result? The answer depends upon what happens to the $1000 which has been saved. If these new savings are turned over to someone else, perhaps through a savings bank, and are all used in paying for newly produced capital goods

---

[3] A few relatively small items, though valued in dollars, do not result from the use of money in the period in question. A person living in a house is counted as receiving income equal to the rental value of the space.

[4] The conclusion that all the income will in fact be spent for consumption plus new capital goods is known as "Say's Law" after the French economist J. B. Say.

—houses, dams, factory equipment—the flow of spending in money amount will not change.

The dollars saved, however, may be held idle—for example, as a larger deposit in a checking account. They are not spent, not used to buy the products or services of others. (Remember that this deposit of the saver is his property, and only he can use it.) The flow of income contracts (that is, V declines). What happens if the money saved is used to repay a loan at a commercial bank which is not matched by new borrowing? The two acts—saving and debt reduction—have led to a drop in the stock of money, not to buying which is demand for goods and services. The crucial question, then, is, "Why is money that is saved not used somehow to pay for newly produced goods and services?" The suggested answer will appear later.

On the other hand, total spending during one month sometimes exceeds the income that has been received for output during the previous month. The total of goods and services which we are able and willing to pay for with money may be greater than the income we have received for what has just been produced. Demand becomes greater than it was a month ago. Where, then, does the money to finance the added buying come from? What can pay for a rise in buying? We can get the extra money by (1) drawing down cash balances (higher V) or (2) inducing banks to create more money for us. But why will a whole economy try to buy more (in money value) than it did during the preceding period?

Keynes concluded that in facing such questions we ought to seek most of the answers—the aspects of strategic importance—in the reasons which lead businesses to change their spending on such capital goods as plant and equipment. Buying of this type will rise if there is improvement in the prospects of net income, business earnings in excess of costs.

Symbolic Statement

The major elements of the Keynesian formulation can be presented in the following symbolic form:

$$Y = C + I + G$$

where Y is gross national income
                C is consumption
                I is gross investment
                G is government purchase of goods and services.

For the sake of simplicity we shall not generally distinguish between measures of product and income. We shall also ignore (net) foreign transactions.

CONSUMPTION BUYING

What accounts for most spending?   Why do economic groups change their buying?   About two-thirds of all spending is for consumer goods and services, and we look at this aggregate first.

The Consumption Function

The major force influencing the total amount of consumer buying is the income being received—disposable income.   Keynes argued that at any income level the portion of disposable income used to buy consumption goods and services will be essentially constant from period to period. He believed, in other words, that the function relating consumption spending to income is basically stable.   By "function" we mean that one variable, in this case consumption, depends upon, or is determined in part by, the other—income, in this case.

From one income level to another ($10,000 compared with $7000), the percentage of disposable income used for consumer buying varies. For large groups, though not for individual families, Keynes believed that the pattern of variation will be broadly predictable.   The relation between the amount of disposable income and consumption buying at different income levels is the *propensity to consume.*   The larger the household's income after tax (other things the same), the smaller the proportion used for consumption and the greater the percentage saved.   This general relationship applies for the whole country at any one time.[5]

Study of the past will disclose the basic relation between consumption buying and disposable income.   By using disposable, rather than personal, income, we eliminate complications presented by income taxes. The study provides a tool for prediction.   Fig. 16.2 shows historical relationships.   In recent years consumption has averaged about 93 percent of personal disposable income.   What worth has this tool?

At any one time, the disposable personal income being received is known within a small range of doubt.   With this knowledge, if the consumption function were stable, we could determine how much consumption buying or demand to expect in the month (or months) ahead.   And this is the demand which will give rise to the major element of national

---

[5] Our discussion skirts some problems.   One arises in shifting the conclusions drawn from the analysis of *family* buying at different income levels to total consumer buying at different levels of national income.   The original Keynesian analysis concluded that as national income rises, the percentage saved will rise.   The crucial conclusions, however, require no more than that the absolute amount saved increases as income moves from one level to one higher.

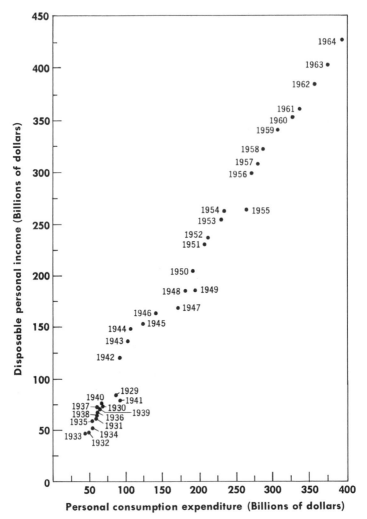

FIGURE 16.2

Relation of Personal Consumption Expenditure and Disposable Personal Income

Source: Department of Commerce

income in the period. Such predictive power would indeed be valuable. Do we have it? Some, but less than we should like.

Consumption Depends Upon Factors Other Than Current Income

The original Keynesian analysis of consumption now seems unduly simple. Intensive studies of the factors influencing consumption have shown why today's level of consumption spending results not only from the income just received. Other things also exert influence.

The income we expect in the periods ahead will affect buying now. The portion of current income that we spend on consumption will be different, depending upon whether we expect income in the future to rise or to drop. Data on expectations are being improved, but uncertainty will always remain. If differences exist, as the family sees it, between "permanent" income and actual income, the former may have more bearing on consumption buying in the short run than the latter. But the notion of "permanent" income, a post-Keynesian element, rests to some unknown degree on experience, and experts are not agreed on the usefulness of the concept. Clearly, however, spending on consumption at any one time is related to what has been spent in the past, and thus to past income. Basic patterns of consumption change, but rather slowly, it seems. Even though income rises or falls appreciably, basic consumption spending may change only gradually. The family whose income after several years at $10,000 has fallen to $8000 will probably spend differently from the family whose income has been stable at $8000 or the one which has just moved up from $7000.

If a family has supplied itself rather completely with *durable consumer goods,* it is likely to spend less out of any given income than if it feels pressing needs for a refrigerator, an auto, a record player, a fur coat, and other more or less durable items. And if past purchases of durables have not been fully paid for, present buying will reflect not only the lack of insistent need for new items but also the compulsion to use some of current income to repay debt incurred for past purchases. In contrast, an increase in a family's income may lead to a much larger temporary rise in spending as the family borrows to buy some major item. The condition of durable consumer goods also makes a difference. If for some reason the furnace, washing machine, tires, and rugs have become generally dilapidated, spending for replacement will likely raise consumption buying to an above-average percentage of income. Moreover, expectations of price changes, or of the appearance of new models, influence buying in the short run.

Wealth from past saving, inheritance, gifts, rise in the price of assets (capital gains), or other sources, affects consumption buying—somewhat independently of income. A person or family with substantial wealth will probably consume differently from any given amount of income than will a family with little or no wealth, or large debts.

The ease with which one can borrow affects the timing, the objects, and perhaps the total amount of spending. The easier it is to borrow, the more many families will spend at any one time. Marked relaxation of the terms allowed on installment sales will stimulate buying. But since borrowers must repay, the net difference between tough and easy credit terms may be only temporary. Suppose that borrowing to buy is made easier and that spending on consumer goods rises for a time. Thereafter, although some families may buy more than "normal," others will be repaying "excess" debts incurred earlier. Debts incurred to buy a house, of course, can earmark a part of one's income for a big fraction of life.

Liquidity, the amount of money and near moneys held, will influence consumption spending. A family with less money than it feels desirable —for transactions, precautionary, and speculative purposes—will tend to use some of its income to build up its cash. To do so, it will spend less than is normal for its income level. Under any given conditions, the larger the holdings of money and other highly liquid assets, the greater will be the tendency to use income for consumption. Holdings of near moneys reduce the need to use income to build up one's liquid position. With only a little effort, an owner of non-cash liquid assets can use them to get money to pay for new consumption goods, perhaps on impulse and often without any close relation to the rate at which income is being received.

Past decisions influence today's consumption buying not only because of debts incurred but also because of other actions which restrict, or later enhance, freedom. When once made, commitments to save in the form of life insurance, pension and annuity contracts, or savings clubs, limit freedom to use income for consumption—not so rigidly as debt repayment contracts but often substantially. Later, however, they often provide funds which, though not income (but return of savings), are available for use to buy consumption goods. Every year more older persons finance much of their consumption out of such receipts.[6]

Intangible factors influence consumption spending. For example, choices of the present as against the future—time preference—are the result in part of personality factors and of other forces that are hard to identify and harder to appraise. Social pressures to keep up with the Joneses, or to avoid ostentation, the intensiveness of selling effort, habits once formed—all these affect us. Rising prices of securities and other assets make some people more willing to spend even if the capital gains are not converted into cash income. Falling prices of assets may do the opposite. War and fear of war, natural disasters or exceptionally fine vacation weather, changes in the political climate, a period of national mourning or an epidemic—these and other unpredictable or unusual developments exert varying significance.

What we do through government influences personal consumption.

---

[6] The bulk of what is received consists of return of past savings and interest accrued in the past. A portion, however, may be interest, dividends, or rentals during the year on the capital accumulation.

The availability of streets and highways, for example, affects auto spending; the level and pattern of taxation affect all spending. And for the economy as a whole, the size of the population, family composition, age distribution, the degree of urbanization, the pattern of occupations, seasonal change, the distribution of income, the availability of vacations, and other factors exert forces of varying weight. Some lead to lasting change, but only gradually. Others may have important short-run influences. In short, so many things enter into the decisions which underlie our consumption spending that the tie between income and consumption seems less stable than Keynes expected.

Marginal Propensity to Consume (and to Save)

The consumption function and the propensity to consume, just examined, are averages. To study the role of consumption most effectively, however, we must examine not average, but *marginal* relationships. Here, as in price theory, study of the margin, the sensitive area of change, reveals more than will the study of a total which lumps many things together. How much of a dollar *increase* in (disposable) income will go into an *increase* in buying of consumer goods and services? [7] How much of a dollar drop in income will be reflected in reduction of consumer buying?

Table 16.2 illustrates possible relationships. In Fig. 16.3 the marginal propensity to consume is measured by the *slope* of *CC*. If income is $6000 and consumption buying is $5400, the average propensity to consume (*APC*) is 90 percent or, in a customary type of expression, 0.9. If income rises $500 to $6500 and consumption rises $300 to $5700, the average propensity to consume is 0.88, but the marginal propensity to consume, *MPC*, is 0.6. Only six-tenths of the *change* in income has gone to buy new output of consumer goods. If consumption had risen to $5900, the average propensity to consume would then have been 0.91; the marginal propensity to consume, however, would have been 1.0, as all of the $500 would have been used for consumption. In this case, then, *MPC* would be nearly twice as high as in the first case, and would even be above *APC*.

The marginal propensity to *save* is the difference between the whole change in disposable income, *i.e.*, 1, and the marginal propensity to consume.

---

[7] For present purposes we do better to think in terms of disposable income rather than personal income. Complications presented by income taxes are thus eliminated.

TABLE 16.2

Marginal Propensity to Consume (and to Save): Hypothetical Case

Disposable income	Consumption buying	Average propensity to consume	Increase in income	Increase in consumption buying	Marginal propensity to consume	Marginal propensity to save
$Y_d{}^a$	C	APC	$\triangle Y_d$	$\triangle C$	$MPC = \dfrac{\triangle C}{\triangle Y_d}$	MPS $(1-MPC)$
$5500	$5000	0.91		—	—	—
			$500			
6000	5400	0.90		$400	0.8	0.2
			500			
6500	5700	0.88		300	0.6	0.4
			500			
7000	5950	0.85		250	0.5	0.5

ᵃ The symbol Y is often used for income concepts other than disposable income; the subscript d is used here to make clear that disposable income is the concept we are using.

INVESTMENT EXPENDITURE

The decisions which determine expenditure on new investment goods result from considerations which differ in kind from those that determine consumption.

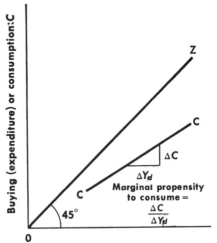

If all income were spent on consumption, CC would be identical with OZ.

FIGURE 16.3

Definition

The term "investment" is used popularly—and sometimes in this book —to apply to purchase of financial assets as well as to the buying of productive equipment. In studying national income, however, we think of investment as the purchase of newly created capital goods, new productive capacity, including business inventory and housing (but not government facilities). Gross investment includes replacements for existing facilities; net investment is gross minus the loss of value of existing capital facilities during the period.

Investment goods are purchased in the hope that they will create money income and not, as a rule, to serve the buyer's needs directly. New housing, however, often results from a combination of both motivations. The builder who makes the decision to go ahead with a housing project, of course, expects to make a money profit. Many buyers, however, hope for services of value which will eliminate the need to make money payments later in the form of rent. Buyers of apartment buildings, however, do so for an income return.

In studying employment and national income, we must distinguish outlays for newly produced capital equipment from expenditures on capital goods produced in the past (such as a secondhand truck or a five-year-old motel). Today's buying of a factory built two years ago creates no jobs now (except for the agent negotiating the sale); the payment for the factory is a transfer. Such buying of old capital equipment can rise and fall with no perceptible effect on national income. In contrast, expenditure for facilities as they are built pays for current output, for productive services—chiefly labor—devoted to creating new things. If expenditure of this type fluctuates, employment and national income are involved.

Although investment goods make up a much smaller part of GNP than consumption goods and services, investment has a decisive role in determining the level of national income. One reason for its prominence in the analysis is that investment is unstable; in the 1950's, for example, consumption rose every year, but investment (gross) rose during five of the years and fell during the others. Another reason is that the volume of investment may be affected by interest rate changes over which the monetary authorities can exert some influence.

Business Investment Planning

Business firms do most of the buying of capital equipment and inventory. The major objective is to improve their ability to produce goods and services which can be sold to advantage. A business will be wise to buy investment goods if it expects the gross benefits obtainable to be greater than the gross costs. The costs include those of getting funds, or of the best alternative sacrificed, all future amounts being discounted by an appropriate rate of interest. More accurately, a business ought to try to maximize the present worth of the assets it has available.

Note the key importance of expectations! What is happening now affects investment decisions chiefly because of the influence of events now upon the predictions of businessmen about the future. Keynes argued that investment will not be made unless the marginal efficiency of capital exceeds the interest rate. What is the *marginal efficiency of capital* (MEC)? It is not an engineering or scientific concept. Nor is it the economist's concept of marginal productivity as that which is now being produced at the margin. Yet MEC is essentially *expected* marginal productivity. One can think of it as the benefit expected above all costs except interest. The marginal efficiency of capital, as sometimes defined, is the rate of discount which would make the present value of net returns expected from a new item of capital equipment equal to the amount that would have to be paid to acquire the capital good.

Most investment, other than inventory, can prove itself only over the years. Today's decision to invest, or not, must rest on expectations. These usually involve considerable uncertainty—about both costs and benefits. Some cost items—though few—may be known definitely. Although the businessman may know the purchase price, the corresponding operating expenses, depreciation and obsolescence, appear over an indefinite future; they are always subject to doubt. If funds are borrowed, the interest due (and probably the repayment requirements) may be known definitely. If the firm uses its own funds and finances internally from retained earnings or depreciation funds, it incurs a cost which may be a bit obscure. This cost is the sacrifice of whatever it could get by using the money in some other way, such as lending or repaying debt. Even if today's alternatives are clear, those of the future are not. Finally, who can be sure about other types of cost five years from now—wage rates in relation to productivity, for example?

Other uncertainties of new investment projects add to the problems of business planning. The benefits from a project can rarely be predicted with assurance; they will come in a future which will have many surprises. What will added output sell for, five years from now? How much will a reduction in man-hours per unit of output save in dollars, in three or in thirteen years? Some firms make the most careful investigation of investment opportunities, using every relevant type of analysis and source of information. Many businesses, however, act at least partially on superficial hunch, dominated, perhaps, by current market conditions. Changes in inventory will rest on decisions made in ways that differ considerably from those used in passing upon the advisability of spending on equipment and a new plant.

A business, in judging the costs and the benefits of an investment, must allow for the fact that both will appear over a period of time. At the time when an investment project is being considered, the worth *now* of dollars in the future is not the number of dollars to be paid or received 3 or 10 years later. These dollars must be "discounted." Today, the value of a dollar due in a month is not the same as the value of a dollar receivable in 10 years. Nine years and 11 months make considerable difference. But how much? The amount depends upon the rate of interest used in discounting.[8]

If different firms use different rates of discount, or if they expect different time schedules or receipts or payments, their estimates of the *present* worth of various alternatives will differ. So will their investment decisions. The market rate of interest will set certain minima. In the real world, however, there are always some people who believe that conditions will turn out better than others predict.

Fig. 16.4 illustrates two hypothetical curves of the marginal efficiency of capital. If the prevailing rate of interest is 5 percent, investment in one case will be about $60 billion, in the other $80 billion. An investment project will seem desirable if the expected receipts as discounted exceed the expected costs as discounted including interest (actual or imputed). What, then, influences these expectations?

Some increases in investment result from current increases in consumption and other investment. This type, called "induced," though thought of as responding to current consumption, is nevertheless forward-looking.

The businessman's judgment of future consumer demand plays a dominating role. Investment goods find their *ultimate* market in the de-

---

[8] A dollar receivable in ten years is worth 68 cents now if it is discounted at 4 percent but about one-quarter less, 51 cents, if the discount rate is 7 percent.

To illustrate the Keynesian type of calculation, assume that a machine is expected to bring $1000 a year above maintenance and operating costs and that its life is expected to be five years with no salvage value. Let us also assume that the going rate of interest is 6 percent and that there is no expectation of change in the purchasing power of the dollar. The $1000 expected a year from now is worth today $1000/1.06.

The $1000 coming in 2 years is worth, now, $1000/(1.06)^2.
The $1000 coming in 3 years is worth, now, $1000/(1.06)^3.
The $1000 coming in 4 years is worth, now, $1000/(1.06)^4.
The $1000 coming in 5 years is worth, now, $1000/(1.06)^5.

The present value of the series is approximately $4215. This is the amount one could wisely pay for the machine under the circumstances. If it can be purchased for less than this, then the marginal efficiency of this capital is higher than 6 percent.

For analysis of many of the practical problems of business investment, see Ezra Solomon, ed., *The Management of Corporate Capital* (Glencoe, Ill.: The Free Press, 1959).

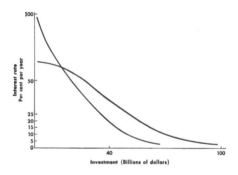

FIGURE 16.4

Marginal Efficiency of Capital (Investment Demand) Curves; Two Hypothetical Cases

mand for consumer goods and services, plus those of government.[9]   The outlook for consumer demand—as a whole and for specific products— becomes a major element in the forecast on which investment decisions must rest.   The better the demand outlook, the higher the probability that an expenditure on capital equipment will prove wise.   (Of course, managers of a dozen firms may differ greatly in their forecasts.   More-over, two or more companies may invest to supply the same consumers.) *Additional* capacity is not likely to raise visions of producing profit if a considerable amount of similar plant and equipment is idle.   Under the same conditions, however, *cost reducing* facilities may be attractive.

Belief that national income is going to rise will create expectations of greater consumer demand.   Similarly, the incentive to invest will rise if there is a shift of expectations about the consumption function which indicates greater consumer buying and less saving out of a total income of any given size.   Age distribution and the rate of family formation affect this country's consumption function, and certainly business expectations about demand for housing.   A general belief that demand will be essen-tially stable (or will grow regularly) will lead to more stable investment than (a) if demand is expected to fluctuate or (b) if expectations fluc-tuate.   Investment for style change (*e.g.*, the annual auto models) or for the production of an entirely new item may in itself stimulate consumer demand.

---

[9] For example, decisions to invest privately in new machinery to make military equipment, or in buildings to lease as post offices, rest on judgments of demand which the public will express through government.

Factors not directly related to consumption buying affect investment. The term "autonomous" is commonly applied to much of the investment described in this paragraph. Scientific progress which changes the techniques of production generally requires new investment; jet planes replacing those with pistons offer an example. Improvements in the ways of doing things—*e.g.,* electronic methods of processing checks in banks— often call for different kinds of equipment. New locations to reduce costs will necessitate added expenditure on plant. In industry after industry, the search for lower production costs is a big reason for investment. Technical development leads to types of machinery which use fewer dollars of input per dollar of output. The speed of technological progress has much to do with the opportunity for profitable investment. In some cases, however, changes in the cost of inputs, or in the value of certain outputs, make the purchase of new equipment desirable even though no engineering advance is involved.[10] A technique may first become worth using when the price of one or another input changes.

The *prices* of capital goods have affected investment tremendously. In the short run, the expectation of a *change* in the price of machinery, housing, or other capital equipment, may lead to either speeding up, or delay, of investment which is going to be made in any case. Over the longer run, the level of prices of investment goods will influence the total quantity bought. The higher the prices of such goods, the lower the chances of profiting from their use. The elasticities of demand for different capital goods, of course, vary widely. For some machines and structures, demand is highly inelastic—but not for all capital goods. An increase in the prices of houses, factories, machinery, etc., will reduce the quantity demanded under any given conditions of income, expectations, and interest rates. When construction costs rise, for example, fewer new houses and schools will be constructed; and some that are built will be a bit smaller than before, and of poorer quality than if building prices had not risen.

The influence of interest as a determinant will be considered later.

Many other things influence private investment. Taxes, government spending, international affairs, the functioning of financial markets, the availability of funds from past activities and current earnings, the extent of monopolistic restraints, the opening of new suburbs with their needs for utilities, zoning and other governmental regulation, the pressure

[10] The author once studied a sample of (internal) investment projects considered by a large corporation. The firm at that very time was re-examining expansion, modernization, and replacement proposals that it had rejected earlier to see which had recently been made desirable by a new wage rate increase. Some rejected projects with a relatively large labor-saving element had become attractive enough to undertake, because man-hours had become more expensive while capital costs had risen relatively little.

to improve plant safety, suspicions about what competitors will do, profit prospects in other lands and the outlook for foreign competition—all these are among the varied considerations which are known to influence investment.

And replacement! As the stock of capital goods grows, the total spending required each year to offset depreciation also grows. Such spending is part of gross, but not of net, investment.[11] It requires resources. It creates demand for labor. It does not, however, bring the benefits of new productive capacity unless, as is sometimes the case, a dollar spent on "replacement" also includes some improvement.[12]

Stability in investment spending is hardly to be expected. If only because of changes in psychology, or in the feelings of businessmen, expectations may vary from time to time regardless of basic conditions. But the conditions themselves do change. Variations in expectations may in fact be much wider than the real elements of the economy would seem to justify or require. Businessmen can get unduly optimistic or pessimistic. As a result, real investment totals may swing through a broader range than the underlying conditions will eventually prove has been justified. Increasingly, however, investment is being planned carefully with long-run considerations dominating. The big utilities, manufacturing companies, and many developers of commercial and residential real estate projects are guided by detailed studies of long-run prospects. Investment by no means always rests on careful, rational calculation. Yet much business expansion and modernization grow out of well-considered plans, influenced, of course, by expectations which involve uncertainty. Fickle guesses do not dominate. Disappointments, however, are not rare.

BALANCE BETWEEN SAVING AND INVESTMENT

The difference between (a) personal income received after taxes, *i.e.,* consumer disposable income (*CDI*), and (b) spending on consumption (*C*) is personal saving. In addition, businesses and governments may—and on balance do—save. We designate total saving by the symbol *S*. This saving is a part of the income stream which does not constitute demand for new output—which does not regenerate itself—unless it is used

---

[11] Owner-occupied dwellings present special problems. Which outlays are merely for maintenance, which for improvement? How much of aggregate household budgets are subject to change for net investment, plus or minus, in the house?

[12] If the costs of producing capital goods were stable, so that technical progress could be incorporated in new equipment without involving higher cost, then replacement might be at lower cost (per unit of potential final output). Because of inflation, however, today's cost of replacing the productive capacity built years ago is very often greater than the original cost, even after allowing for technical progress.

to buy new investment goods (*I*).[13]   Here is a point which Keynes emphasized.   If some of today's saving is not spent on new investment, the level of national income will drop.   Fig. 16.5 illustrates.

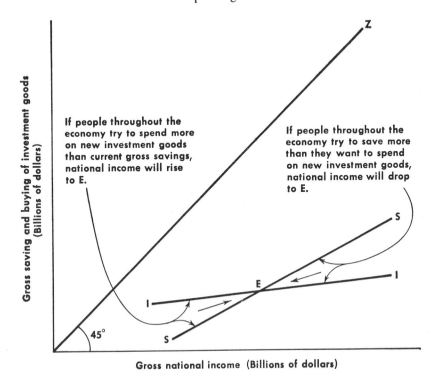

FIGURE 16.5

Relation of Balance Between Saving and Investment and Equilibrium

Actual (realized) saving *must* equal actual (realized) investment, *i.e.,* when the books for any day or longer period are closed, the saving actually accomplished will be found to have equaled investment by Keynesian definitions.   Both are the difference between income and consumption. Keynes showed how this balance will be achieved by a change in national income.   As national income moves toward *E,* the point of equilibrium under existing conditions, the amount of saving and of investment will change.

Let us look at the case in which people throughout the economy want

[13] Some government spending included in *G* is investment—the new school building or water supply system.   For our purposes, however, little advantage would be gained from trying to distinguish between the part of government buying which is to provide goods and services currently and the part which constitutes capital facilities to provide services over several years.   Any statistical study would need to take care to use consistent concepts of government saving and investment.

to spend more on investment than they want to save out of income. Thus *I* exceeds what the public plans to save, *S*. Such a condition can exist, for example, when businesses get new money, deposits newly created by banks, or when investment is financed by money which was saved in an earlier period but which has been held idle. When investment outlays are greater than the savings that are being attempted, national income will rise and generate more savings. Throughout the economy, families find income above that of the prior period, with the increase not spent immediately.

What people plan or intend is frequently termed *ex ante*. The actual results are *ex post*.

To a considerable extent decisions to save and decisions to invest— to expand plant and equipment, add inventory, and build housing—are made by different people for different reasons. There is no obvious reason why they should harmonize. Yet the national accounts must balance. What happens must produce results which are what they are. The output that is not consumed (ignoring government) is the net investment for the period. But the totals of *C* and *I* do not necessarily add to the national output which full employment would create.

CHANGE IN LEVELS OF NATIONAL INCOME

The flows of income and of product move constantly (though not necessarily evenly), day after day. For study, however, it is helpful at times to think in terms of lags, the income of one period (month) being available for use in the next. If all income is used to buy goods and services, and if there is no other source of spending power, total demand will equal the price of the output that generated the income. No change in aggregate demand will then appear.

Yet not everything received *must* be spent. Individuals, businesses, and governments do save. Moreover, some of gross income, *i.e.,* some of the money which businesses receive, goes to offset depreciation. Businesses may, or may not, use these funds at once to pay for the replacement of equipment. Any saving (whether gross or net) which is not used to pay for new investment goods reduces the flow of income. And, of course, some of what we receive as payment for services goes to pay taxes; being beyond the recipient's effective control, it is not part of his disposable income. It is, however, available for government to use a bit later.

The flow of income is largely self-financing. Nevertheless, the relation between the receipt and the use of income is not necessarily close. Certainly, both underspending and overspending of income are possible. Economists and laymen have sometimes disputed whether there is enough purchasing power to buy all that the country is producing. We can give an answer. Assuming no change in the price level, there is always enough income to buy all output. The income (including profit and loss) which is the cost of output is potential purchasing power. It is available. Yet it may not all be used.[14]

Families, businesses, and governments have varying amounts of freedom to refrain from spending all of their income. (Foreigners with income from sources in this country are usually under no compulsion to spend all of it here.) Moreover, even if all income received is used promptly for buying, it may not be enough to create a demand in the next period for all the output which the economy is then able to produce. Suppose that the income just received had been generated by an economy operating at less than full employment. Then, even if all income were spent, it would not create enough demand to induce capacity output at existing prices.[15]

On the other hand, the public may try to spend more than it has just received as income. Where can it get the money? It can use deposits newly created by banks (or currency from the printing press) or funds that had been idle, received in earlier periods but not yet spent. Total demand will now exceed that in the previous period. The larger demand may work out in higher prices or in greater production of goods and services or in some combination. Demand is not necessarily limited to income. Buyers may draw on unused savings of the past or borrow in ways that lead commercial banks to create new deposits.

In short, although the income flow is potentially always self-sustaining, there is no inherent reason why spending in one period should equal the income generated in the period just preceding. And, of course, the income level of the recent past is not necessarily the level which the public should seek for today or next month.

MULTIPLIER AND ACCELERATOR

Two magnifying forces require explanation. When one part of the national income stream changes, other parts of the interconnected whole will feel some effect. Keynesian analysis makes heavy use of the concept of the investment multiplier. Another—the accelerator—fits conveniently into the same general discussion. The multiplier involves the magnification of national income resulting from a change in investment. The ac-

[14] The error in Say's law as commonly expressed is the portion which concludes that because mankind is poor income received will be used, not held idle.

[15] If the level of prices were to fall, the money demand could buy a larger output, perhaps all that the economy could produce. The fall in prices, however, would itself bring changes in income.

celerator involves magnification of investment buying stemming from a change in consumer buying.

Multiplier

An increase in investment spending can bring a significantly larger ultimate increase in total spending because it leads to a rise in consumption. (A decline in investment can be expected to bring a magnified reduction in consumption.) For example, $1 added to investment outlay may well bring an increase of $2 or more in consumption buying as time passes. The symbol K is customarily used for the multiplier. It is the reciprocal of the marginal propensity to save.

Analysis of the multiplying process, the way an increase in I leads to a growth in C, has absorbed much professional attention. Early enthusiasm about the possibility of using this concept as a predictive device has been largely disappointed. The real world is in fact so complex and so changing that future responses are always uncertain. The hope of finding a numerical measure of the multiplier—say 3—which can serve as a reliable guide for policy actions seems destined to be frustrated. The concept, however, does help illumine significant relationships and probable responses. It alerts us to look at elements which are of practical significance even though their size cannot be predicted accurately.

The multiplying process works essentially as follows: A net increase in investment spending increases the incomes of those who build the machines and apartments and provide the other goods and services that make up the investment. With larger incomes the recipients will increase their spending on consumption. Such a rise in buying adds to total demand and thereby to national income (in money and perhaps in real terms). Yet the first round increase in consumption buying will be somewhat smaller than the original rise in investment spending because some of what the public originally received as added income will be saved. (For present purposes we shall treat increases in tax payments which are not matched by added government spending as increases in saving.) Let us assume that one-third of the increase in income is saved and that investment outlays do not change. Then only two-thirds will constitute added demand for consumer goods and services. Now suppose that the suppliers of these newly demanded consumption goods and services also use two-thirds of the increase in their incomes to buy consumer goods—and so on in successive stages.

The added income in each round provides the basis for an addition—though by a smaller absolute amount—to consumption buying in the next stage. (If investment drops, declines in income proceed in the opposite direction.) These rounds or stages, of course, are not instantaneous; they

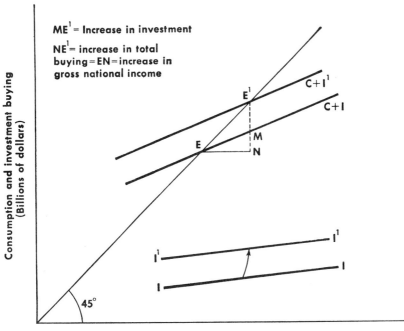

An increase in investment leads to a multiplied increase in national income.

FIGURE 16.6

The Multiplier

follow each other. The fifth stage is many months after the initial investment spending. How many? The interval depends in essence upon the income (circular) velocity of money.[16] If income velocity is three per year, the fifth round will occupy the 4 months at the middle of the second year after the original impact. This fifth round, of course, is small compared with the total of what has gone before. Most of the multiplication occurs in the first 18 months or so. If we calculate in terms of periods of 3 months and if in *each* period investment is $1 billion higher than before the process started, *e.g.,* $20 billion each quarter instead of $19 billion, the level of income in, let us say, the sixth period will be higher by perhaps twice or three times the period's $1 billion increase in investment itself. Fig. 16.6 shows the beginning and "ending" conditions with a multiplier of around 2.

---

[16] Lags present both conceptual and measurement problems. If my income rises this month, I may at once spend all of the increase which I have any intention of using for consumption. The gross receipts of retailers rise at once. Yet only a part of these receipts are net income. The rest must be used to cover costs; the suppliers to the retailers, however, earn more income as larger orders are filled, and so it goes—taking time.

The multiplier as a figure, we noted, is the reciprocal of the *marginal propensity to save,* or $K = 1/MPS$.[17] If one-third of each dollar of added income is saved and two-thirds used for added consumption buying, then the eventual increases in consumption will add to $2 for each $1 of original investment. The investment plus the total added consumption will come to $3. The increase may be in real income, in money income as prices rise, or in some combination. Of course, what actually happens will depend, among other things, upon the stability of patterns of consumption and saving, whether any additions to either consumption or saving themselves lead to a change in investment, what happens to interest rates and to the stock of money, and other elements of economic life. A modern society is not a machine. The responses do not proceed as if "other things" remain as they had been, for businesses and consumers adapt to changing reality.

Accelerator

The acceleration principle deals with short-run change of a type which Keynes was not considering in his theory of the determinants of the general level of employment. The accelerator involves the magnified increase (or decrease) in investment buying which results from an increase (or drop) in consumer buying. No single figure applying to the whole economy is suggested, but in particular industries there will at times be a relatively large response in the buying of new capital goods and inventory.

A certain *stock* of capital, including inventory, is needed to provide for a certain *rate* of final output. If the final output increases or declines, the stock of capital equipment which makes it possible may change. Such changes are at times imperative. These alterations in the stock of capital

---

[17] The algebraic derivation is as follows:

$$K = \frac{\Delta Y}{\Delta I}$$

$Y - C = I$ and $\Delta Y - \Delta C = \Delta I$. Then substituting for ΔI, $K = \dfrac{\Delta Y}{\Delta Y - \Delta C}$. Dividing both denominator and numerator by ΔY, we get

$$K = \frac{\dfrac{\Delta Y}{\Delta Y}}{\dfrac{\Delta Y}{\Delta Y} - \dfrac{\Delta C}{\Delta Y}} = \frac{1}{1 - \dfrac{\Delta C}{\Delta Y}}.$$

Since $\dfrac{\Delta C}{\Delta Y}$ is the marginal propensity to consume, subtracting it from 1 leaves the marginal propensity to save. Thus $K = \dfrac{1}{MPS}$.

goods and inventory will create a relatively big, albeit temporary, move in some parts of the economy.

Table 16.3 illustrates a possibility involving inventory.

TABLE 16.3

Accelerator Principle Involving Inventory: Desired Inventory to Be Twice Sales: Hypothetical Case

Period	Sales (no. of units)	Percent change in sales	Desired inventory (no. of units)	Purchases[a] (no. of units)	Percent change in purchases
1	200	—	400	200	—
2	200	0	400	200	0
3	250	+25	500	350	+75
4	300	+20	600	400	+14
5	200	−33	400	200	−50

[a] Amount to replenish sales and to provide for the change in inventory.

An increase in consumer demand (25 percent from the second to the third periods) leads to a much greater percentage increase in business demand for inventory—75 percent in this case.

Similarly, the demand for investment in plant and equipment may change much more in percentage terms than the consumer demand which occasions it. Table 16.4 shows what might happen.

TABLE 16.4

Acceleration Principle Involving Plant and Equipment: Hypothetical Case[a]

Period	Consumption (no. of units)	Percent change	Plant and equipment (no. of units)	Purchase of plant and equipment (Number of units) Additions	Replacements	Total	Percent change
1	10,000	—	1,000	0	100	100	—
2	11,000	+10	1,100	100	100	200	+100
3	11,000	0	1,100	0	110	110	− 45

[a] It is assumed that one unit of plant and equipment is needed for each 10 units of consumption and that one-tenth of the equipment on hand in the prior year will be replaced each year.

Relations as rigidly fixed as in the two illustrations are uncommon. Many factors affect actual results. But the tendency toward magnification and instability undoubtedly exists.

Consumer purchases of "productive capacity" also provide examples. If a family's demand for a particular type of service goes up, perhaps for auto transport, the rise may lead to the purchase of a second car. This car, or any of many other kinds of durable consumer goods, may be thought of as "consumer investment." Spending for such goods may fluctuate through a wider range than do changes in demand for the services they provide.

GOVERNMENT SPENDING [18]

Today governments in this country spend amounts equal to more than 30 percent of GNP.

Transfer payments, such as social security benefits, aid to farmers, and welfare aid, plus interest on public debt, add up to roughly one-fourth of total governmental spending. These amounts (except interest, to some disputed extent) do not purchase goods and services for general public benefit. This spending, then, is not directly part of the demand for output. Yet the recipients of social security benefits and of other transfers will generally spend the money; these payments, therefore, finance consumer demand not long after they leave government treasuries. The remainder of government spending pays for services (*e.g.,* of mail carriers, soldiers, and teachers) and goods (*e.g.,* bridges, missiles, fire engines). Some is consumption, some investment, and much not easily classified.

The forces determining the total, and the pattern, of Federal, state, and local spending result from preferences and conditions which both resemble and differ from those in the private economy. Although most of the total is fixed, at least in the short run, parts do change with every new local, state, and Federal budget. Some of these parts can be altered deliberately to raise or lower the aggregate demand for output. Discussion of this potential controllability occupies much of Chapter 24.

INTERNATIONAL BALANCE

The fourth element of GNP we designate as F—the difference between exports and imports. Rarely does it approach 1 percent of the total.

---

[18] Taxation is not considered explicitly here. To a large extent it has been taken into account implicitly in computing the amount spent privately. (a) The income available for both consumption and investment spending is largely what remains after taxes. (b) The prices of both consumer and producer goods and services include tax elements, often hidden.

People in other countries buy goods and services here; in doing so, they add to the effective demands on our economy. On the other hand, some of our purchasing power goes to buy goods and services produced abroad. Such demands financed out of our incomes draw upon other economies. The two contrasting demands may balance. Or one may be appreciably greater than the other. As far as total employment and the price level in any one country are concerned, what counts is the *net difference* between these demands. In national income accounts, therefore, we find the item "net foreign investment." This measures the amount by which international transactions add to, or subtract from, the aggregate demand for domestic output.

The volume of purchases across international boundaries, and changes in these amounts, depend upon such things as the levels (and changes) of prices and incomes in different countries, the freedom with which trade and investment can cross international boundaries, relative investment prospects within a country and outside, and political stability. One difference between these and the factors which affect domestic consumption plus investment plus government buying, has special significance for our purposes: To a large degree foreign factors lie beyond the power of any group within a country to control, or perhaps even to influence. Predicting them, too, may be exceptionally difficult. Chapter 18 returns to these problems.

RESTATEMENT

The level of gross national income can be thought of as being equal to spending on consumption plus saving plus personal taxes ($Y = C + S + T$), on the assumptions that the net foreign balance is zero and that government spending is equal to taxes. This formulation is an alternative to the one given earlier. The latter showed the level of national income as being equal to spending on consumption and investment plus government spending for goods and services. (Again we ignore net foreign investment and assume that G equals T.) In general, therefore, $Y - G$ (or T) $= C + S = C + I$. After the event (*ex post*) $S = I$. Planned (*ex ante*) savings, however, may differ from planned investment. Two different groups make the saving and the investment decisions and may have rather different intentions.

What, then, is the equilibrating factor which in fact brings S and I into equality *ex post*? Changes in the level of income, Y, bring S and I into balance. Assume that originally planned $I = 60$. Planned S is also 60 and income is 500; then C is clearly 440. The average propensity to consume is almost 0.90. Now let us assume that investors decide to increase their outlays to 70 and that the marginal propensity to consume is stable at ⅔. What happens to equate S and I?

The additional 10 of *I* enters the income stream. New jobs are created (or old ones bring more pay). As consumers receive more income, they spend more, but not the full amount. For each dollar of added income, consumption rises by $2 and saving by $1.

The level of *Y* increases not only by the original (autonomous) increase of 10 in *I* but also by increases in *C*. For the economy to reach equilibrium these increases must be large enough to induce an increase of 10 in *S*. In order for *S* to expand by 10, *C* must rise by 20. Adding the increase in *C* to the 10 increase in *I*, we find that the new level of *Y* is 500 + 20 + 10, or 530. The multiplier is 3, as an increase in investment of 10 led to an increase in *Y* of 30. The following example will illustrate:

	Original period *A*	Investment	First period *B*	Second period *C*	Ultimate period *N*
C	440	increases	446⅔	451⅑	460
S	60	by 10	63⅓	64⅘	70
Y	500		510	515⅚	530

WILL THERE BE THE RIGHT AMOUNT OF BUYING?

The four types of buying—$C + I + G + F$—create demand for labor and output. Income results. What relation does this new income have to the income that has just been received—more, less, or the same? Is it about the "right amount"? What forces may operate to change it? And for better or worse? For answers we must look at the relation between saving and investment.

If the amount which people throughout the economy want to save out of any given income (*ex ante*) is greater than what the public as a whole want to spend on investment (*ex ante*), national income will drop. Yet if *ex ante* saving is less than *ex ante* investment, national income will rise. Since the groups making the saving and the investing decisions are not the same, is there any assurance that a good balance will be reached?

Keynes concluded, and the conditions when he wrote left no doubt, that market processes could not be counted upon to move the economy to the best level, full employment.[19] At some times people may want to invest more than they are freely willing to save. If so, *i.e.,* if the exuberance and optimism of business stimulates buying of investment goods beyond the public's desire to save, income will rise—and with it saving.

---

[19] In 1936 Keynes wrote with little explicit concern for price-level changes, and for good reason. Expanding the use of idle labor and capital was overwhelmingly the dominant problem.

The resulting higher income level may be one of full employment at the same price level as in the past.

If the economy, however, had been at full employment, the price level must rise. In such circumstances there is no assurance that under the new conditions (1) the desires to invest will *drop,* or (2) the desires to save will *rise,* by enough to prevent another upward move of the price level. What will be the outcome? Prices will rise more, but eventually costs will catch up with earnings prospects.

Keynes feared, however, that the opposite imbalance might tend to be self-perpetuating. Imagine an economy that has reached a high level of income. Prosperity raises savings above what businessmen want to invest. Total buying then drops. Employment will fall unless, as is highly improbable, prices and wage rates go down enough to "absorb" the full effect of the decline in total demand. The downward inflexibility of prices and wage rates makes impossible an adjustment without growing unemployment.

In short, a full employment level of income is not necessarily self-sustaining. Nor is that level necessarily one of stable prices. The explanation, we repeat, is that the portion of their income which people try to save may fall short of, or exceed, what the public wants to spend on new investment goods. Realized (*ex post*) saving and realized investment do balance. Changes in national income produce the balance. Keynes believed that the balance or equilibrium could be reached at any of several possible levels of employment. An economy might settle into equilibrium before reaching full employment. But is there not some corrective force?

Interest Rate as an Equilibrating Device

Assuming that at high levels of national income people want to save more than will be used to buy new investment goods, perhaps the interest rate can change to produce a better balance. Keynes was pessimistic on this score. The analysis gets complicated. A complete "system" must take account of complex interrelations among many elements. Yet we can summarize the dominant features.

The quantity of saving, Keynes believed, responds only slightly to changes in interest rates; in other words, the supply schedule of saving is highly inelastic with respect to interest rate change. Consequently, wide fluctuations in interest rates can be expected to bring relatively little alteration in the quantity of saving attempted.[20]

[20] The effects of the interest rate on the amount of saving may be the result primarily of the effects of a change in the interest rate on national income. If a drop in the interest rate stimulates the economy, it may thereby lead to an *increase* in saving.

Planned investment, according to Keynes, will depend upon the relation between the marginal efficiency of capital and the rate of interest. With an adequately high marginal efficiency of capital throughout the economy, the interest rate might naturally bring a reasonably good balance between planned saving and planned investment. And if the rate of interest resulting from market forces failed to produce a desirable balance—perhaps because of price and resource rigidities—the monetary authorities might intervene constructively.

Keynes believed that the rate of interest depends upon the relation between liquidity preference and the stock of money. The monetary authorities can change the stock of money. If investment tends to be too high, the money stock can be reduced to raise the interest rate. This action will reduce the level of new investment, as is shown in Fig. 16.7. On the other hand, if investment is too low, an increase in the stock of money which lowers the rate of interest will stimulate investment.

At some low level of interest rates, however, increases in the money

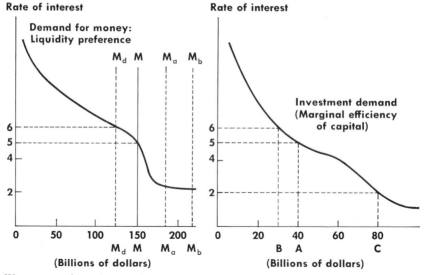

We assume given demand for money, liquidity preference, and investment demand curves. A decrease in the stock of money from MM to M_dM_d will raise the rate of interest from 5 to 6 percent. The volume of investment will drop from OA to OB. An increase in the stock of money from MM to M_aM_a will lower the rate of interest to 2 percent and raise investment of OC. However, an increase in the money stock to M_bM_b will not reduce the rate of interest significantly because of the desire for liquidity. The quantity of investment will not rise beyond OC because at this point the value of liquidity is above the marginal efficiency of capital; the economy is caught in the "liquidity trap."

FIGURE 16.7

Monetary Change and the Volume of Investment: Simplified Keynesian System

stock will not reduce the interest rate because the public will prefer to hold money rather than bonds. Here is the "liquidity trap." The marginal efficiency of capital may get so low—say 1¾ percent—that businesses cannot afford to pay the 2 percent which would be required to induce savers to exchange money for fixed interest obligations or other investment properties. At levels of national income below those of full employment, Keynes believed, savings may exceed what the public wants to invest. If so, hoarding in the form of money cannot be offset by monetary policy which reduces interest rates.[21] Keynesians believed that this unhappy situation is more than a possibility for advanced economies. Whether or not such conditions existed in the depths of the depression of the 1930's, the Western world has been very far indeed from any such hazard since World War II.[22]

One inadequacy of the simplified version illustrated in Fig. 16.7 stems from the fact that the demand for money cannot be assumed to be "given"—stable—as national income changes. When national income goes up, the need for money for transaction purposes will certainly rise. The demand for speculative balances may also change, though the direction of such response is not absolutely certain. The total M must be divided into at least two components, frequently designated as M_1 for transactions balances and M_2 for speculative balances. M_1 will vary more or less directly with Y (gross national income). If national income rises, then, the M_1 part of the demand for money will also rise. Unless M_2 falls by an equal amount, which seems most unlikely, the total demand for cash balances rises; so will the rate of interest if M remains stable.

---

[21] The argument, much simplified, runs as follows: Giving up control of funds by lending them to someone else prevents one for the time of the agreement from making a better contract if opportunities improve. Suppose that the interest rate is around 2 percent. This is not very attractive for a lender. But it may seem better than what will be obtainable later, say 1½ percent. On the other hand, however, rates may rise. If they do, today's 2 percent loan agreement will have been a mistake. From a level of 2 percent, which kind of move is more probable? All history indicates that the chances of a rise from 2 percent are much greater than those of a fall. Loan contracts made at the 2 percent level, especially those for other than very short periods, are more likely to prevent the lender from using the wealth to better advantage than they are to prove higher than the best under new conditions. In a sense, therefore, the supply of funds for lending (except for short periods) will disappear when interest rates are below the value placed on liquidity. The public prefers money to bonds at the best bond yields available. Presumably cash also seems better than equities and tangible productive property.

[22] Would liquidity-trap conditions continue indefinitely? Writers stimulated by Keynes but disagreeing pointed out that in theory adjustments would eventually release the trap without a change in the underlying conditions. The response, named for a prominent exponent, is called the *Pigou effect*. As wages and prices fall during continuing employment, real wages (the purchasing power of money wages) tend to remain unchanged. But the real value of each unit of money goes up; the real value of money balances increases. Consequently, fewer dollars need to be held to equal the desired purchasing power. Some of the money balances will then be used to buy consumption goods. Business will pick up.

A rise in the rate of interest will tend to discourage investment. Consequently, to maintain the rate of interest associated with the investment which raised national income, the stock of money must grow. Fig. 16.8 shows one stage of the adjustment process.

More problems arise. Investment is not so sensitive to interest rate changes (not so "interest-elastic") as Keynes believed. Much investment

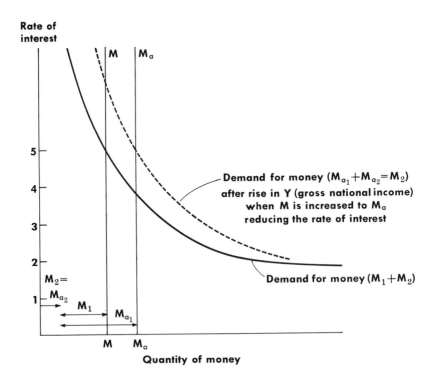

When the quantity of money increases to M to M_a the rate of interest drops from 5 to 4 percent. Investment increases, raising national income. The transactions demand for money, M_1, goes up to M_{a_1}. The rate of interest will rise, discouraging investment.

FIGURE 16.8

appears to be largely independent of at least moderate changes in the rate of interest. Even though the marginal efficiency of capital is higher than the rate of interest, imperfections in capital markets may be great enough to prevent potential borrowers and lenders from making all the agreements which would be mutually profitable. Monetary policy, as we shall see in Chapter 23, may not be able to overcome this obstacle, quite independently of any liquidity-trap explanation of failure of investment to settle at a level consistent with full employment.

Quantity of Money

Keynes concluded that monetary policy operates through the rate of interest.   But there are other avenues.

Chapter 13 ended on the note that "money is to be used," to meet needs for liquidity and for transactions, in goods or investment.   The "store of wealth" use of money is not the only use.   The monetary authorities, it would seem, must be able to add to the stock of money until businesses and households find that their demands for cash balances have been fully met.   Then the owners of additional money as it becomes available will increase their use of money for purposes other than liquidity, perhaps for adding to consumption, perhaps for equity investment.   Even though we do not know the strength of the forces which would follow the saturation of demand for liquidity, they must exist.   They will act to supplement the interest rate as an equilibrating device.

Prices or Jobs

Will changes in total buying appear as changes in prices or in real goods and services?   Nothing in the income approach throws much light on the answer to this question.   Of course, if an economy is at full employment, any rise in total demand will bring higher prices.   But will a drop in total demand lead to a large enough drop in prices so that real income and employment remain the same?   Although one can imagine an economy with prices and wage rates so flexible that they would adjust downward to prevent unemployment, such is not the type of economy in which we live.   Keynes, in fact, reasoned that falling price and wage levels would themselves create new difficulties.

Prices are by no means completely inflexible.   Resources are not entirely immobile.   As demand drops, some prices will fall.   But to what extent?   And with what effect on jobs?   No one can be sure.

Nor do we know how much of rising demand will be offset by rising prices before full employment is reached.   Fig. 16.8 shows one possibility.   For nearly 20 years this issue has tantalized both economic theorists and statesmen facing the practical problems of economies operating somewhat below reasonable aspirations.   Experience leaves no doubt that growth of total demand will affect the price level before resources are utilized fully.   Bottlenecks appear.   Here and there demand presses so firmly against capacity that prices rise.   Rising demand flows into fully employed sectors while others have unused resources.

Moreover, at any given level of total demand, the volume of employment realized depends in part upon average wage rates per hour. Wages, of course, are not only income and buying power. They are also costs. Such interrelations add to the difficulties of using income theory to deal with the problems of an economy having unemployment which by general agreement is too high but far from massive and in which price and wage levels go up far more easily than they go down.

CONCLUDING COMMENT

Economists do not all agree about either the validity or the importance of many elements of the national income approach to understanding of money and monetary theory. Yet there is no doubt that this approach forces us to look at economic forces which are of unquestioned importance and which do not come explicitly to our attention when we rely upon quantity approaches. There is also no doubt about the existence of "gaps" in income theory of the type outlined above. One of the most important is the absence of systematic analysis of the role of money in the ups and downs of business. Keynes concentrated on the forces determining the general level of national income. He thus devoted his major effort to the dominant economic problem of the 1930's. This problem, however, is not the only one of importance on which money has great bearing. Another is the problem of cycles, the subject of the next chapter.

QUESTIONS

1. GNP = consumption + investment + government expenditure on goods and services + net foreign investment. Using the above, explain how what is paid out in factor costs is the same as what is received as income. Show that gross national product and gross national income are two aspects of the same thing.

2. What is meant by saving? by investment in the Keynesian sense? Why may plans for saving and investment be unequal?

3. Why must *ex post* savings equal *ex post* investment? How does changing income act as an equilibrator?

4. What is the consumption function? What is the "multiplier"? How are they related? What may cause them to change?

5. What is the "accelerator"?

6. In what sense are decisions to save and decisions to invest made by different people for different reasons?

7. What factors influence consumption spending? investment spending? government spending?

8. What is the marginal efficiency of capital? What would cause it to rise? to fall?

9. According to Keynes, how does monetary policy influence the interest rate?

10. In the Keynesian system, what is the relation between the rate of interest and the volume of investment? What, if anything, can the monetary authorities do to influence the level of national income?

11. What effect will a change in expectations have on the level of national income?

12. How can the relation between investment and saving influence (determine) the level of national income if actual (realized) savings and investment are identical?

CHAPTER 17 *MONEY AND BUSINESS FLUCTUATIONS*

FLUCTUATIONS in business have long absorbed much of the interest of students of money and banking. The men who framed our laws on banking and finance did so with cyclical problems very much in mind. The sequence of prosperity and depression—not "boom and bust"—was a serious concern for decades before the 1930's. Then for a time this interest in cycles was overshadowed, first by worry about the persistence of mass unemployment, unrelieved by a period of prosperity, and second by war-induced inflation.

The memory of ups and downs grew dimmer. Post-war fluctuations were so small, and so dominated by a high general level of activity, that many persons—especially young people—had little reason to be aware of the problems of cycles. Yet the sharp, though short, recession of 1957–58, the mild drop of 1960, and the inadequacy of the recovery to 1964 may be sufficiently fresh to keep us alert to the fact that fluctuations did not disappear with either World War II or Congressional passage of the Employment Act of 1946.

The study of business fluctuations is in itself a major division of economics, one whose analysis requires many times the space allotted here. We will, then, concentrate on monetary factors. Economists disagree about many an aspect of cycle theory. Beyond question, however, money and banking have a powerful influence on what actually does take place. In the past some economists concluded that cycles were monetary phenomena in the sense that money caused the trouble. Other economists argued that money was more truly passive, transmitting pressures originating elsewhere but not in itself acting to create cyclical change.

Such extreme views are now passé. Today there is no doubt that cycles are influenced significantly by (1) the way in which people use money (velocity) and (2) the amount of money that they have to use.

Yet there is difference of informed opinion about the scope of the role of money and of banks in modern cycles.

The "model" used below has been oversimplified, partly to help us concentrate on the relation of monetary policy to cyclical change. This problem is of deep significance. It ties in with man's hope for acting to improve his accomplishment in a portion of economic life where failure has been common.

DEFINITION

Two leading experts define a business cycle as follows:

Business cycles are a type of fluctuation found in the aggregate economic activity of nations that organize their work mainly in business enterprises: a cycle consists of expansions occurring at about the same time in many economic activities, followed by similarly general recessions, contractions, and revivals which merge into the expansion phase of the next cycle; this sequence of change is recurrent but not periodic; in duration, business cycles vary from more than one year to ten or twelve years; they are not divisible into shorter cycles of similar character with amplitudes approximately their own.[1]

Cycles have varied greatly. No two are alike. Despite some regularity, fluctuations are by no means rigidly periodic. Some follow the seasons, and do so for such clear reasons and with such certainty that we do not treat these ups and downs as part of "the" business cycle.[2] Not a few fluctuations here and abroad have been "distorted" by exceptional developments such as wars, political upheaval, and natural disaster.

Duration varies considerably. On the average, "short" cycles work out between 3 and 5 years; other movements—intermediate of about nine years and long-term ups and downs of fifty years or so—may have a cyclical pattern. However, there is too little evidence applicable to conditions of the twentieth century to support a solid conclusion about the significance of cycles which do not average around 50 months.

There is, however, abundant evidence that every cycle contains divergent trends, with some parts of the economy affected differently from others. From 1957 to mid-1958, for example, buying of autos and parts *dropped* about 20 percent; buying of food and clothing *rose*. Outlays on producer's durable equipment fell by almost one quarter. In the expansion from

---

[1] A. F. Burns and W. C. Mitchell, *Measuring Business Cycles* (New York: National Bureau of Economic Research, 1946), p. 3. Cycles of different lengths are sometimes identified by the names of economists who studied them—Kitchin for the shortest, Juglar for the intermediate group, and Kondratieff for those of longest duration.

[2] That is, in measuring cyclical change, we adjust for normal *seasonal* variation.

1961 to 1963 consumption buying rose at an annual rate of 4 percent, residential construction 11 percent. Fig. 17-1 shows for recovery periods in 3 recessions how 2 important types of economic activity—business fixed investment and consumer buying of autos—differed from each other and also from cycle to cycle.

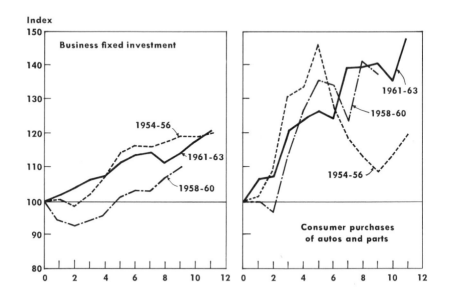

FIGURE 17.1

Business Fixed Investment and Consumer Purchases of Autos in Three Cyclical Expansions, by Quarters

Source: *Survey of Current Business,* January 1964

Some change can be thought of as originating outside the economic process (as narrowly defined)—weather, wars, inventions, political change. Such initiating forces are called *exogenous.* In contrast are changes, called *endogenous,* which develop within the system as it operates. Although by no means sharp, the distinction helps in understanding cyclical change. Much of what we shall be discussing is endogenous. But it is not to be thought of as inevitable. The changes which the system itself produces will depend upon the nature of that system and the way men respond. Both the system and the reactions change—and can be changed.

At any moment the condition of the economy, and the direction of change, are the result of many and varied forces which in combination have produced the prevailing situation. Changes in the structure of our economy since 1930 and since World War II—taxes, role of unions, availability of knowledge about cyclical trends, the banking system—have altered the strength of forces which (1) may initiate a new move in business and those which (2) account for (a) *responses* (for "contagion" and cumulation) and (b) eventually the reversal. We shall see in Chapter 24, for example, that "automatic stabilizers" now exert considerably greater effect than before World War II in reducing the amplitude of cycles.

MONEY IN THE PHASES OF THE CYCLE

So much happens in so many different ways that study requires a simplifying device. One helpful method is to divide fluctuations into phases—four are common, (1) revival and expansion; (2) peak; (3) contraction and recession; and (4) trough. We shall look at money's role in the broad processes of expansion and contraction, without trying to deal specifically with each of the four phases.

One distinctive feature of business fluctuations is that some elements make for *cumulation* or the self-generation of change. Once a movement up or down gets started, it creates forces which push it farther along in the same direction. The way in which we use money and the way in which banks expand and contract deposits, both contribute to the process of cumulation. Yet cyclical movements never go on forever. Cumulation *is* eventually offset by other forces. These, too, are influenced by the monetary system.

Revival—The Upswing of Expansion

Assume that economic conditions begin to improve after a period of considerable unemployment. Businesses, sensing a better outlook and in some cases already enjoying a pick-up in orders, will tend to enlarge their operations. More raw material and other inventory are needed to handle the bigger volume of orders on the books or in sight. Some machines that have grown obsolete must be replaced; others need extensive repairs. Rising consumption brings the *acceleration principle* (Chapter 16) into operation here and there, especially in the purchase of inventory.[3]

Cost-saving equipment appears desirable. The new product whose

---

[3] Large increases in consumer buying may lead to no large outlays for plant and equipment where there is ample idle capacity, where price increases seem more attractive, or where the surge of demand is not promising enough to warrant commitment of capital for the long term. Conversely, relatively small growth of consumption can sometimes bring a big capital investment—*e.g.,* the few dollars a month which people in a new suburb spend on telephone service can require big outlays for new lines, central office equipment, and instruments.

development had been shelved now seems worth risking. The existing stock of housing and of other structures appears to be unsatisfactory for a variety of reasons, especially if population has grown (or shifted to new areas) during a period of low construction. Investment spending thus rises. Effectively, but not deliberately, businesses start the *multiplier* process as they increase their buying of investment goods and pay out more in wages and for materials, equipment, and construction. These payments are income to the recipients. When used for consumption, they stimulate demand for still more investment.

At once we ask, "Where do consumers and businesses get the dollars to finance added spending?" Some of the payments are made with money that had been held idle in checking accounts, the M_2 balances discussed in Chapter 16. They had not been needed for transactions and were used only as a store of liquid wealth, as speculative holdings. V rises. Total M also grows. Greater borrowing from banks accounts for some, or much, of what happens in the world of money. Demand deposits, the major form of money, grow. Fig. 17.2 shows what happened in two expansions and

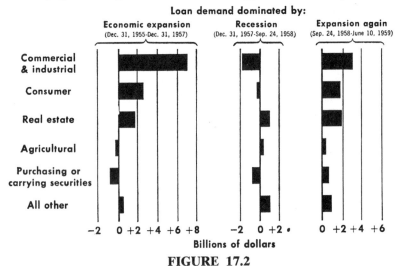

FIGURE 17.2

Changes in Member Bank Loans

Adapted from W. Lindow, "Forecasting of Loan Demands," *Banking,* May 1960, pp. 52 ff. Data from Federal Reserve Call Reports.

one contraction. During the 1958–59 expansion demand deposits grew almost 4 percent in a twelve-month period. What accounts for such an increase?

When expansion starts, banks will have excess reserves; they totaled about $500 million in the spring of 1958, and also in early 1961, the troughs of 2 cycles. Banks, of course, want to raise their net income. As the economic outlook improves, they become more willing to expand business loans. At first here and there, and then more generally, businesses seek to borrow to take advantage of new and more promising opportunities. Consequently, the actions which businesses and banks take in their own interest leads to an increase in the stock of money. For example, in the year of economic expansion to the summer of 1959, commercial bank loans to business increased by nearly 10 percent. Borrowings are made to get dollars to spend.

Many employees (and some businessmen, stockholders, and recipients of interest) now have more to spend on consumption as a result of the rise in investment. For many families the marginal propensity to consume will be above its customary level—a period of depressed income will have seen the wearing out and the using up of clothing and other semidurables and durables. The multiplier, then, will probably be higher than ordinary. Moreover, the expansion of consumer spending will not be limited to the increase in family incomes. Households, like businesses, are generally in a better position to borrow. Many do, and buy autos, furniture, and other such items. Fig. 17.3 shows changes in consumer borrowing by quarters

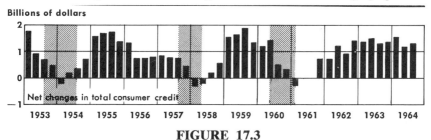

Billions of dollars

Net changes in total consumer credit

1953 1954 1955 1956 1957 1958 1959 1960 1961 1962 1963 1964

FIGURE 17.3

Changes in Consumer Credit
(Seasonally Adjusted, Quarterly Data)

Source: Board of Governors, Federal Reserve System.

ᵃ Second and third quarters of 1961 less than $100 million.

since 1952; the shaded areas are periods of recession. During the 1958–59 expansion, short- and intermediate-term consumer credit outstanding rose by 20 percent—$9 billion, about $500 million a month—no minor amount.

As effective consumer demand grows, business improves even more. The cumulative process is in swing. Profits rise, far less than wages in dollar amount but substantially in percentage terms.[4] The expansion of

[4] From the first quarter of 1961 to the fourth quarter of 1963 (a long expansion which had not ended), the annual rate of compensation of employees rose $48 billion, almost 18 percent. Corporation profits after taxes rose 40 percent, $8 billion, one-sixth of the rise in wages.

output takes place under favorable conditions. Costs, for a time, go up less rapidly than business volume, while prices can be raised somewhat without undue difficulty.

As consumer demand rises, the need for some kinds of producer goods grows. The accelerator takes hold in new spots. The investment demand of some businesses increases by more in percentage terms than the rise in consumer buying—to change the stock of capital to accommodate the new rate of consumption. To some degree, the multiplier then converts the investment increase into further expansion of consumer demand, spread over months. Moreover, rising profits provide equity capital (especially undistributed profit) which not only pays for investment but which also supports borrowing, including some from banks. Public sale of new securities grows easier as business improves and profits rise.

Many firms find that as prosperity develops they need still more money to finance expanded activities. An increase in physical volume and a higher price level combine to enlarge the transactions demand for money. Better profits realized—and a more optimistic outlook for future profit—make businesses safer risks as far as banks are concerned. And for many months banks will be able to expand loans without any serious restraint resulting from "tightness" of legal reserves.[5] For a time business growth can be financed without a corresponding increase in voluntary saving.

As new money continues to enter the economy, it finances more expansion. In doing so, it helps spur the rise in profit, the growth of optimism, and the increase in price levels. In combination these make more borrowing and money creation likely. Rising prices induce some borrowing based on hope of speculative gain—such as a business acquiring inventory before it is needed or an individual buying common stock "for a rise." Customers "buy ahead" to fill their needs before prices go up further or, in the case of businesses, to protect against interruptions in production due to delays in delivery. Cumulation gets impetus.

Interest rates rise. Consequently, economizing in the holding of money becomes increasingly desirable—*i.e.,* using money to pay off debt, to buy interest-yielding securities, or to keep borrowing at a minimum. There is more reason to try to make each dollar, or each million, finance a greater volume of transactions.

More money flowing around the income circuit, and moving on the average more rapidly, represents greater spending. Enlarged buying stimulates growth in production. The expansion of GNP will not be exclusively in physical volume. Some of the rise will be in prices, sporadically at first and then more and more generally.

---

[5] Individual banks will sell securities (secondary reserves) to get dollars to lend on terms more attractive than the yields of the securities.

The Peak and the Ending of Expansion

When does expansion become full-fledged prosperity and reach its peak? Substantially full employment, good earnings, and inspiring profit prospects certainly characterize prosperity. They appear, perhaps gradually, even as expansion tapers off.

Why does expansion end? For one reason, bottlenecks appear as types of capacity here and there become fully utilized. Physical limits become evident at some points, not all foreseen. Economic restraints become even more numerous. Pushing further ahead becomes expensive. Costs increase for various reasons, not the least of which is a deterioration in the quality of labor available for adding to output. Meanwhile, expansion in the volume of things for sale creates some difficulty in getting the higher prices needed to maintain profit margins. Where profit margins drop, expansion becomes less attractive.

Some business, consumer, and government borrowers are deterred by higher costs of construction or of machinery or consumer goods. Major building plans are completed. Because needs are less urgent and costs higher, new projects are not so extensive. A slowing of the rate of growth of consumer spending (even when the total is still moving up) cuts the need for additions to inventory and to plant and equipment. The earlier growth of debt now requires larger totals for repayment, forcing an increase in savings. Rising income leads to progressively larger increases in personal and corporation tax liabilities. Therefore, the private sector is not free to spend as large a fraction of increases in income.

Monetary factors also help account for the ending of expansion. Banks find their reserve position tighter. To add to loans, a bank must sell higher-yielding secondary reserves or borrow from the FR. In either case and after allowing for risk, the net advantage of a loan may be small. Moreover, a bank is not supposed to be in debt to the "Fed" for long. Whatever improvement in its reserve position one bank makes by selling secondary reserves other banks lose (unless the "Fed" increases total reserves). Some banks "ration" new loans. Businesses have trouble getting the funds for as much expansion as they want. Interest rates rise. Bond prices fall; some owners suffering capital losses become more cautious in their spending.

Injections of new money are less frequent. Velocity can grow, of course, to finance a rising dollar volume of business, but finding ways to make money "do more work" becomes increasingly difficult. Some holders of money prefer to reduce their spending when costs are so high and, failing to use the dollars to buy securities, hold money idle. The monetary stimulants to the economy grow less potent.

The mere reduction in the upward pressure on the economy may lead to a downturn rather than merely to a leveling off and sustained prosperity. If general expansion stops, will not growth industries suffer an actual decline? Conceivably, growth in one sector will appear at about the same time as another sector stops expanding. To date, however, full offsetting has never appeared; prosperity has never lasted indefinitely.

On some occasions—1837, 1873, 1893, 1907, and 1933—a true money crisis has developed, precipitating serious economic distress. More often, money becomes "tight." Monetary stringency of a sort appears. Few people may directly experience any unusual difficulty in getting funds to finance their activities. But those who do have trouble must curtail their buying plans. In doing so, they may affect the affairs of others.

Contraction and Recession

Monetary forces may or may not have a great deal to do with the turning of expansion and prosperity into a recession. There is no doubt, however, that once contraction begins, our system of money and banking helps send the economy downward. Of course, neither bankers nor borrowers deliberately want to cause business to get worse. Moreover, in recessions since World War II monetary aggravation has been milder than often in the past. Nevertheless, cumulative economic contraction feeds on monetary forces, as well as on others.

Businesses have less need for funds as sales drop. Some firms reduce their debts to banks. Others, such as those which let inventory run down, build up cash balances or try to do so, reducing V. As business buying falls, consumers have less income. Their buying drops, giving business further reason to curtail activity. New consumer borrowing stops growing and may decline, while loans incurred in the earlier expansion require repayments which absorb potential purchasing power.

Declining business activity will mean lower profit and hence less safety in loans. Banks become more cautious, as conditions require them to make larger allowance for risk in lending. On some loan applications no feasible interest rate may adequately cover the higher risks. The loans which during expansion were justified on the assumption of rising profit seem subnormal when falling profits appear to be general. New loans and renewals drop below repayments. The resulting reduction in the stock of money—or failure to grow with economic potential—in itself helps make business less good.

The number of business failures rises, embarrassing the banks to which the firms have been in debt. Before 1934 recessions also brought numerous bank failures, spreading distress. Falling commodity and security prices remove some of the support or collateral for loans. Consequently, banks call for payment of marginal loans, perhaps compelling businesses to sell inventory when they would not wish to do so; some such sales may have to be made under distress conditions. The added pressure to sell in itself tends to reduce prices on a weak market. Moreover, the wiping out of some of the stock of money, as loans (and deposits) are reduced, accentuates deflationary forces. Falling prices encourage a reduction in V, as some families and businesses decide to try to hold more money (whose value is rising) and fewer goods.

The marginal efficiency of capital falls, drastically in some cases, not because technical factors become less favorable but because economic prospects grow discouraging. For many firms the expectations of near-term gain from added investment may in effect collapse. Even a substantial drop in interest rates cannot compensate for dismal short-run prospects. For example, if part of a firm's present plant is not utilized, going ahead with expansion can seem foolish (though cost-cutting projects may still seem wise). Businesses use some of their depreciation funds to repay debt, acquire interest-yielding securities, or build up bank balances rather than to buy productive equipment for replacement.

The operation of the money system makes the disease of economic contraction more contagious.[6] Without consciously desiring to do so, banks help spread the infection. And so do myriads of other economic units. Falling consumer and business expenditures reduce not only the demand for labor but also the stock of money, as loans are repaid. The extent depends upon factors peculiar to each situation. For example, the larger the number of bad loans made during the boom, the greater the job of adjusting—of working them off—later. Moreover, the decline itself breeds difficulty. Expectations dim. The financial community becomes more cautious.

The Trough: Preparation for Expansion

Contraction does not go on forever. There is a trough. Then recovery starts. Why? Part, but only part, of the answer can be found in the way in which the monetary and banking systems function and the way in which they tie in with other economic processes.

---

[6] "The Commercial Banking sector . . . doubles its net acquisition of assets in upswings as compared to downswings and also doubles its holdings of State and Local Government issues. . . . Also in the upswing, the [banking] sector greatly increases its net acquisition of mortgages and extends bank loans (primarily industrial and agricultural) rather than liquidating them as it does in downswings." The study covered 11 years through 1962. P. H. Hendershott and J. L. Murphy, "The Monetary Cycle and the Business Cycle: The Flow of Funds Re-Examined," *National Banking Review,* June 1964, pp. 531–50 at p. 538.

After a time the contraction of demand deposits slows down. The poorer loans are weeded out; borrowers get their debts to the bank reduced to a more conservative level. The sale of inventory and securities needed to get funds to repay loans becomes substantially completed; thus one exceptional force depressing prices almost melts away. The reserve position of banks eases; those banks which may have found themselves under pressure to discourage loans while building up reserves get into a satisfactory position. Banks purchase securities; the sellers now have larger demand deposits. With fewer dollars needed to finance transactions, more are available for purchase of securities. Bond prices rise. The wealth and liquidity of the owners improve, leading some to become more willing to spend. Banks, large and small, actively seek "good" loans. Bankers offer lower interest rates. As a result some borrowers become more willing to borrow or less anxious to repay loans to banks.

Here and there firms with innovations to develop get funds, push ahead, and, on the basis of success, borrow more. If prices have gone down, less money is needed as a store of value; more can be spent. Some consumers step up their buying of durable goods. The process described early in the chapter is under way.

Conclusion

Although even the experts' knowledge of fluctuations—especially of causal forces and relative importance of interrelated factors—has gaps, the uneven expansion (and at times actual contraction) of the stock of money will certainly account for some lack of stability in the economy as a whole. This conclusion holds even though for over one third of a century we have been free from widespread bank failure and old-style financial crises. Changes in our willingness to hold money, V, also play a part. Both are largely endogenous. Impulses from "outside," exogenous change, can produce magnified effects because the initial force leads to, among other things, changes in the stock of money—or in velocity.

The commercial loan principle of banking, while presumed to accommodate business, has contributed to cyclical instability. The argument for the principle, we recall, was that bank loans will rise and fall "appropriately" with changes in real production. Serious weaknesses, however, undermine the main argument.

1. Even under "normal" application, changes in loans, and hence in the stock of money, may vary with *prices* as well as with physical quantities. Consequently, price fluctuations will be accentuated by loans that change the total quantity of money. Such fluctuations are themselves a source of disturbance to the efficient and desirable production of goods and services.

2. Once money is created and injected into the economic system, it continues to flow. The total rise in spending associated with an increase in money is not the initial amount—which may all go to enlarge real output —but some much larger quantity. (The same applies to a decrease.) The full effects on national income are a multiple of the original expansion, perhaps desirable, perhaps not, but only by accident what could be termed "appropriate."

3. Finally, it is not only changes in the quantity of money which influence the stability of the whole economy. The use we make of a given stock of money also influences the level of national income.

Cycles are not exclusively monetary. Yet they are influenced greatly by what happens in the realm of money. Monetary action has at times certainly done more to increase than to dampen cyclical fluctuations. The past has left us with a banking system having elements which are, to say the least, congenial to cycles. Yet it is an *administered* system. The managers of money can seek to use their powers of control to reduce fluctuations.

EVIDENCE FROM MANY CYCLES

Figs. 17.4 and 17.5 present some of the results of a massive study of the evidence on cycles.[7] A reasonably complete summary of the method used would require more space than is available, and besides is not necessary. The figures show two sets of averages, one of the stock of money, the other of income velocity, for non-war cycles for nearly a century. Measurement is from the peak of the cycle shown by the vertical line at "0." The negative (left) side shows the months before the peak, expansion; the positive (right) side covers the months after the peak, *i.e.,* contraction. For cycles with major swings (deep depressions) the stock of money grew during expansions, then stopped growing and actually declined somewhat during contractions. During milder cycles, the stock of money grew much more rapidly during the expansion phase than during contraction.

[7] M. Friedman and A. J. Schwartz, "Money and Business Cycles," *Review of Economics and Statistics,* Feb. 1963, with comments by H. P. Minsky, A. M. Okun, and C. Warburton, pp. 32–78.

Velocity rose during expansions of both the large and the milder cycles, but more during the ones with the bigger swings. During contraction periods, velocity fell off, but more so in large than in more moderate cycles. The authors point out that such findings by no means prove that money operates as a dominating causal force. One may even argue that the causal process goes from non-monetary forces to the monetary. Yet there can be no question that the findings are consistent with the theory that, whether as initiating or permissive (making possible) elements, monetary forces play a major role in business fluctuations. In Chapter 23 we look again at parts of the process as we discuss policies to reduce fluctuations. A set of findings rather too complicated and controversial to present here show very close relation between fluctuations in the rate of change in the stock of money and net national product. In both cases monetary changes have a relatively larger cycle, increasing more since 1908 than before; this result suggests that Federal Reserve in this respect has not improved on prior arrangements.

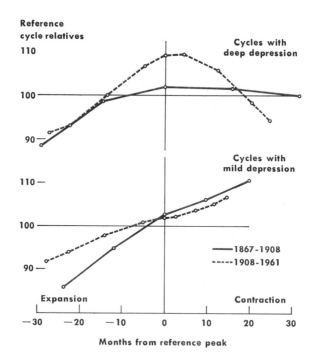

FIGURE 17.4

Money Stock: Average Patterns for Mild and Deep Depression Cycles (1867–1961)

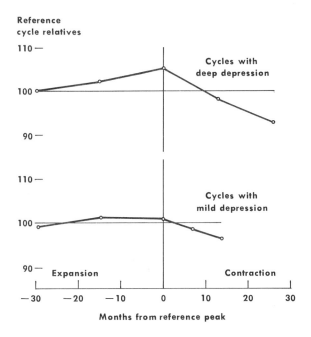

Reference
cycle relatives

FIGURE 17.5

Income Velocity: Average Patterns for Mild and Deep Depression Cycles, 1870–1958

ARE CYCLES UNDESIRABLE?

Business cycles are mixtures of good and bad.[8]   Every cycle has phases which involve hardship.   Individuals and businesses suffer because of what happens in the overall economy.   They find themselves overwhelmed, or at least profoundly influenced, by a general decline in national income.   Yet during other phases of the cycle, individual economic units get support from a pleasing buoyancy around them.   Almost everyone then seems more successful, economically happier, because others are enjoying greater prosperity.   The movement upward in itself gives a positive stimulus to most businesses and to the families dependent on them.

Can we strike a balance between the benefits and the losses from the ups and downs of business?   Or, more fundamentally, can we judge the net results of cycles?

---

[8] The depression of the 1930's was unquestionably one of the great catastrophes of modern history.   Fortunately, other business fluctuations have brought no such extreme disaster.

Need for Change

A first point is of central importance. Change is both inevitable and highly desirable. Changes in tastes, techniques, population, and so much in life create new needs and opportunities. Some highly desirable forms will inevitably involve the rise and, at some time, the decline of one or another segment of the economy. The persons directly affected may welcome or oppose some of this change. They may not, of course, always appraise their own interests wisely. Some people are over-optimistic, others too apprehensive, about the probable effects of some change upon them. The interests of the people most affected are not necessarily identical with those of the whole economy. Unfortunately, there may be no way to get those who benefit to compensate adequately for the losses of others.

The conditions which bring about many desirable changes will sometimes come together—this is often true in seasonal fluctuation. When war or natural disaster strikes, the need for making many changes at the same time rises sharply. Ordinarily, however, the flux of life in a huge and diverse economy is so great that a moderately even distribution over time of the real "need" for change would seem more normal, more to be expected, than a serious bunching.[9]

In other words, no apparent technical or economic factor gives reason to expect marked cycles (except seasonal) in the changes that are normal in a growing economy. An expansion here, a decline there, essential stability in most places, would characterize the economy adapting to the new opportunities which are desirable. The more stable the level of employment and of prices in general, and the greater the mobility of resources and the flexibility of individual prices, the larger the probability that change will distribute itself rather evenly over time—or at least more evenly than has been the case in the past.

Constructive changes both require and produce some unemployment of men and equipment. If a new industry is to develop without undue difficulty, it must be able to draw on resources, including labor, not otherwise fully employed. If the public is no longer to buy items for which its demand has fallen, if consumers are to buy the new instead of the old, they must be free to alter their buying. Such freedom, however, is freedom not only to demand more man-hours from some workers but also to create unemployment for others.

---

[9] This conclusion conflicts with that made famous by Prof. J. Schumpeter. On the basis of learned study, he concluded that innovation proceeds in wavelike movements. His conclusions, however, rested on study of an era in which research, by present standards, was sparse and technological and managerial development less rapid. The technical opportunities for the whole economy are not likely to be dominated today by more or less haphazard successes in a few types of research.

Disadvantages of Cycles

The amount of unemployment which appears in business recessions, however, exceeds any amount which can be considered useful in the process of constructive change. Consequently, the cycle involves waste in the form of undesired and unconstructive idleness of men and capital equipment. Society loses real income which might be produced by people who would like to make use of their time and property. Other things associated with this loss—the personal insecurity and human distress that comes from worry and doubt about the future—add to the indictment against cycles.

Fluctuations bring not merely resource idleness but also inefficient allocation. Conditions during each stage are not those which will prevail over the long run. Yet decisions about investment, choice of occupation, and other matters with more than temporary significance must always be made.

Commitments are inevitably influenced by what is taking place. Even if the persons involved (the young man taking his first job or the directorate of a giant corporation voting next year's investment plan) try to make some allowance for what they believe is an abnormality, they cannot have a completely adequate basis for adjusting. Decision making must suffer. One inescapable result is that some plans are made less well than if they had been formulated when the economy in general was free from cyclical disturbance.

Prosperity as a Source of Economic Loss

The prosperity phase of the cycle, so universally welcomed, is not an unmixed blessing. It spawns careless, over-optimistic decisions that create needless distress later. After a period of generally rising business and expanding prosperity, some people will act without the rational examination of alternatives which is needed to make a commitment that will prove wise over the long run. Boom encourages activity which is not sustainable.

The mistake in such a commitment is itself wasteful, an example of the poor allocation of resources referred to earlier. It produces an additional evil, however. Its "correction" will almost certainly bring trouble to others. For example, the closing of one business may hurt each of many others. The suffering spreads. If many such mistakes are made at about the same time—and a boom is likely to lead to a clustering of decisions that prove to be mistakes—many errors may have to be corrected at about the same time later. As a result, the economy must shoulder a period of concentrated distress which is not only serious in itself; the added difficulty is that the concentration also breeds greater trouble than would arise from the sum of each element as a unit. For example, even a relatively small overexpansion of capacity may doom a whole industry to a considerable period of distress and low profits. An upswing, in short, tends to plant seeds of trouble which will sprout when the rise stops.

Benefits and Evils of Recession

Thus expansion and prosperity, good as they are, bring some undesirable results. Does depression, on the other hand, have any desirable features? Surprisingly, perhaps, good things are sometimes credited to depression, if only implicitly.

Depressions do eliminate inefficient firms, those which use resources poorly; productive capacity is forced to shift to uses of greater efficiency. Poor business also impels firms which have only discouraging prospects to seek aggressively for some better use of their resources. The pressure of depression, moreover, forces all business to try for cost-saving methods, to do a better job. Workers may also try harder to do the best they can. In such cases productivity rises. These related points have merit, but they do not tell the whole story.

Depression weakens firms and in itself *creates* trouble. In other words, depression does not merely eliminate the results of earlier error. It actually produces distress and waste. Those firms and activities which fail in bad times are not only the ones destined to die because of mistakes made earlier. The casualties include firms which, had it not been for the difficulties added by the depression, would have lived to serve the public constructively. If these firms had survived, their use of resources might well have been better than whatever use develops later. No one, of course, can measure such loss and compare it with benefits from the depression-speeded weeding out of activities which ought not to survive. Still, the net result must be social loss.

The argument that depression compels greater efficiency has an unattractive counterpart. For one thing, firms with losses, suffering the distress of depression, cannot finance modernization. Consequently, they cannot take advantage of developing opportunities to raise efficiency.

Moreover, bad times induce some unions to press for make-work rules or to protect workers by use of methods which are retrogressive. Fear of depression is one reason that unions sometimes oppose technical progress that may eliminate some jobs. After all, finding new jobs is harder when business generally is in recession. Moreover, businesses, fearing slack times, may succeed in restricting competition and thereby deprive the public of the benefits of greatest potential efficiency. Depression also creates an additional kind of waste. Businessmen must devote effort to revising plans and to solving problems that grow out of the depression, a diversion that would not be necessary if the cycle did not occur.

Let there be no doubt—pressure to do one's best helps powerfully to raise productivity. Fortunately, we do not need depression to create effective pressure; vigorous competition during prosperity can suffice. Yet prosperity itself does not assure as much competition as is needed to keep everyone at his best. In fact, boom, especially if it seems likely to continue, may lead to slackening of effort and to a costly weakening of willingness of workers to do their best.

The recession-depression phases of cycles are sometimes condoned, perhaps even welcomed, as helping check the long-run tendency toward inflation. And the boom is condemned because it spurs inflation. Some observers suggest that in the decades ahead the hope of avoiding chronic inflation may fail unless there are occasional price "shake outs" of the kind that in the past have come only during recessions. The recessions since World War II, however, have done little to reduce the level of prices. Recession is not a solution to the problem of inflation. We must look for ways to prevent creeping inflation without incurring the wastes of business contractions and depressions.

Concluding Comment

General economic expansion *does* add a buoyancy which is itself stimulating, in obvious and also subtle ways. And recession does just the opposite. We have no scales for balancing the results. However, the average accomplishment of the economy must be below what would prevail if we enjoyed a high level of prosperity without the extra stimulus of cyclical expansion and the drag of recessions.

On the whole, cycles have been undesirable—at least when compared with greater stability at high employment levels. The case for trying to reduce fluctuations is overwhelming. (But it is not a case for putting the economy in a strait jacket—if we could.) We would be foolish not to try to use monetary and other powers to prevent extremes of boom and depression, to keep contractions and expansions from snowballing, from cumulating and building on themselves. Nevertheless, before discussing the use of monetary theory in monetary policy, we need to examine the relation of one land's monetary system to the economies of other countries.

QUESTIONS

1. What is the "business cycle"? How may it be separated from the seasonal and irregular fluctuations which appear frequently and in many parts of the economy?

2. What causes an expansion to continue? a contraction?

3. How does the expansion gather momentum? What causes it to end? Do the same factors account for the ending of contraction? What is the role of money in the two processes?

4. Explain how an elastic money stock tends to behave during the business cycle. Would an inelastic money supply bring significantly different results? Why?

5. Could the multiplier and accelerator appear if the stock of money were stable? Discuss.

6. What industries would you expect to be most influenced by cyclical change? Why?

7. "No one will tolerate deep depression or hyperinflation. Yet mild business cycles are a not entirely undesirable part of a free society." Comment.

8. "The business cycle will never disappear as long as people are free to use, or to hold on to, their money." Discuss.

9. "In the past, people have been much too concerned about the ups and downs and have not paid enough attention to the general level of economic activity. Cycles matter little if recessions are balanced by booms. What counts is how big the economic pie is." Discuss.

PART FOUR

INTERNATIONAL FINANCIAL
RELATIONS

CHAPTER 18 *INTERNATIONAL PAYMENTS*

INTERNATIONAL trade and finance are subjects for extensive and specialized study. Such study, of course, is not appropriate here. Economists differ somewhat in drawing lines between those aspects of international finance which must be included in a study of money and banking and those which can be omitted without serious loss. This volume will deal chiefly with the means used in making (1) payments, including those involving capital, across national boundaries and (2) the way in which financial connections, again including capital transactions, tie different economies together—their price level movements, employment, growth— or keep them apart.

It is hard to live a day without consuming something which requires someone in this country to make a payment in another land. On the other hand, millions of Americans could not enjoy their present incomes if it were not for payments they receive from foreigners. Both types of transactions, payments made and payments received, involve at least two currencies, the dollar and some other. This chapter deals with the process of payment when two currencies are used.

DOMESTIC AND FOREIGN TRADE:
CERTAIN SIMILARITIES AND DIFFERENCES [1]

In some respects international economic affairs do not differ from domestic: people benefit from specializing in production and from exchang-

---

[1] Changes in the net excess of exports over imports act on domestic national income as does an increase in domestic investment, as described in Chapter 16, with potential multiplier effects. A decline in exports or a rise in imports acts somewhat as a decline in investment. Changes in income levels may thus be transmitted from one economy to others. These responses will receive only incidental attention in this volume.

ing the fruits of their efforts. The broader the market, the more advanced the division of labor. We can produce more efficiently and consume more abundantly when we specialize and trade on a wide basis than when we limit ourselves to the opportunities of a single area. The trade must almost always utilize money, for the possibilities of barter are narrow. The easier it is to exchange moneys of different lands, the greater are the opportunities for profitable exchange of goods and services.

Another similarity between domestic and foreign business is that most of both types of economic activity—outside the Communist sphere—are carried on by private firms and individuals. Though we often speak in terms of a whole country and its foreign economic affairs, governments as such do rather little of the actual negotiating, trading, and paying. Governments do participate, often extensively, in fixing the framework within which economic affairs with foreigners must be conducted. Nevertheless, most buying, selling, and investing are done by private businesses seeking to advance their own interests.

National frontiers have an important economic influence, not so much because the boundaries have inherent economic significance as because they distinguish areas within which different political powers operate. The number of independent nations has increased substantially since World War I, and continues to grow. As people in an area get political independence and establish a new nation, they acquire legal power to set up their own monetary and financial system.[2] The existence of separate currency systems gives rise to problems which do not exist for domestic transactions. Most of the problems with which we shall now deal result from the use of political sovereignty to establish monetary systems which are both separate from, and yet tied to, those of other countries.

PAYMENTS ACROSS NATIONAL BOUNDARIES

Most payments from one country to another, whether for businesses or individuals, are made through banks. What facilities are available?

Banking Organization

In all of the major, and most of the minor, population centers of the non-Communist world, banks stand ready to serve those who wish to make or receive payments across national boundaries. The origins of such

---

[2] The group also gains the power to erect tariff and other barriers or encouragements to trade, to restrict emigration and immigration, and to establish its own laws affecting commerce, investment, taxation, and the whole of economic life.

banking arrangements go back centuries. The nineteenth century witnessed substantial development, with the British banks far in the lead but not without rivals. The disruption of international banking due to World War I, though extensive, was far from complete. Renewed growth in the 1920's was interrupted by the depression and World War II. Since 1945, however, the development has been more rapid and on a broader base than ever before.

A relatively few banks have emphasized the establishment of branches in foreign centers. Many more built up correspondent relationships, often through the banks which had branches. Central banks had special ties with each other. U.S. banks were virtually prohibited from having branches abroad until passage of the Federal Reserve Act. Even then the restrictions were so narrow and onerous, the focus of banker attention so predominantly domestic, the competition so keen, and other arrangements for transacting foreign business so satisfactory, that only a small handful of American banks built up even small systems of foreign branches before World War II. After the war, too, with the restrictive laws still in effect, the development of branches was slow. Correspondent ties grew, however. Meanwhile, leading foreign banks were reestablishing old branches and associations and building new ones just when American businesses were vastly expanding their foreign activities. Some U.S. bankers sought more freedom to meet the competition abroad of foreign banks, for serving both U.S. and foreign companies.

Congress and regulatory authorities eventually (in the 1960's) relaxed the restrictions. U.S. banks operating abroad under special laws may now carry on some activities and services permitted to native banks but not allowed in this country. New York State permitted branches and agencies of foreign banks in New York to perform essentially the operations U.S. banks sought permission to perform abroad, so that foreign governments would grant U.S. banks more opportunities. The results have been encouraging. By 1964 about 165 branches were operating, but building up competent staffs in foreign lands proves exceedingly difficult. Most U.S. banks rely primarily upon correspondents to perform the services abroad.

Over a dozen foreign banks have branches in New York City; around 20 have agencies in New York and some in other cities. Many more have representatives here. The branches and agencies are largely free from Federal Reserve and other regulation by U.S. authorities. In foreign business they offer tough competition. Branches of foreign banks may carry on deposit business as well as other banking activities; agencies may, and do, perform a very wide range of banking services but do not handle deposits.

In addition to lending for foreign transactions and arranging payments ". . . banks also extend services that are equally essential—the provision of information and know-how.   Banks offer customers doing international business credit information and data on foreign markets, help locate potential partners, selling agents and customers, and assist in overcoming language and currency obstacles.   In brief, banks bring buyer and seller together and create conditions under which the varying risks for credit and transfer of funds can be accepted by all concerned.   Their services are offered to both American and foreign exporters and importers." [3]

Basic Procedures

How does a person in one land pay someone in another?   In essence much of the mechanism is the same as that for payment by a Bostonian to someone in Los Angeles—commercial banks arrange for clearing, for the balancing or offsetting of claims and obligations of people in different areas.   Yet payments abroad involve different monetary units or currencies.   Although each transaction is ordinarily negotiated in one of the two currencies—in francs or in dollars, for example—the payment process is not complete until there has been a settlement in the other currency.   A look at the mechanics and the economics of simple cases will reveal the underlying elements.

To start, we assume that N, a librarian in New York, buys books from a London seller.   Let us look at two possible methods of payment.   (1) The price is quoted in British pounds which N must pay the British bookseller.[4]   The New Yorker has dollars, and he has obligated himself to pay pounds.   The natural place for N to turn is to his bank, which he finds ready to serve him.   The New York bank accepts N's order to pay the bookseller the pounds specified; the bank itself maintains an account in a London bank, an account in pounds, to provide just this kind of service. The bank pays out of its London account and charges N's account in dollars in New York.[5]   (2) Alternatively, the London bookseller may direct N to deposit dollars in a New York bank, in an account which is held by a London bank.   When the London bank hears from New York that the dollars have been deposited, it credits the bookseller's account in pounds in London.   In either case N ends with fewer dollars and the bookseller with more pounds.

[3] G. S. Moore, "International Growth: Challenge to U.S. Banks." *The National Banking Review,* Sept. 1963, p. 9.

[4] The mechanisms discussed in this section have features not covered here.   Details and modifications are omitted because the major objective, an understanding of the basic elements, can be achieved better by the simpler treatment.   The British bookseller, for example, might prefer dollars in a bank account in New York to use in buying American books.

[5] At this point we ignore the problem of determining the number of dollars to equal a pound and assume that the rate is known.

What if N (or the bookseller) deals with a bank which does not itself maintain an account in the other country—and only a few banks do? The payment process becomes only slightly more complicated. N's bank can arrange for the transaction to be made by a bank that does have the necessary account in the other country. The widely developed system of correspondent bank relations in this country, and branch banking abroad, makes convenient payment facilities available over most of the non-Communist world.[6] An Alabama bank, for example, can direct its New York correspondent to arrange payment in pounds, even far from London in a small English town (where the London correspondent of the New York bank has a branch).

Banks Obtain and Dispose of Foreign Moneys

Obviously, however, the New York bank cannot provide the facilities unless it has pounds on deposit in London. How does it get pounds?

1. It may borrow in London, paying interest. This method is used chiefly to meet temporary needs.

2. A more common method illustrates the economic process. Someone in New York has made a sale in England, agreeing to accept pounds. But he wants dollars. He turns to his New York bank. The latter tells him to have the pounds deposited in the account it keeps in a London bank. When the American has done so, his bank credits his account in New York with dollars. (This process is the reverse of that in which the London bookseller accepted dollar payment in New York.) The New York bank then has pounds to serve a customer like N who wants to make payments in England.

3. The New York bank can get pounds from Englishmen who want dollars. An English importer, for example, may have agreed to pay dollars to the sellers of American cotton; his needs can be met by giving up pounds in London for dollars in New York. If the New York bank and its London correspondent arrange such a transaction, the importer can be served.

The payment process is essentially one of clearing. Exports pay for imports, as the following diagram illustrates. Capital exports and imports, as well as those of goods and services for current use, make up part of the totals.

---

[6] The system of international postal money orders also provides a convenient mechanism for making payments in the currency of another country.

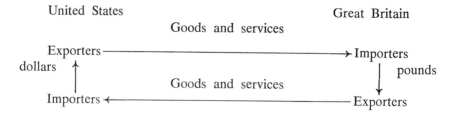

United States   Great Britain

We can describe the process a little differently. Importers in one country, England, must make payments to sellers in other countries. On the other hand, exporters from England have claims on persons in other lands who bought British goods. The two groups in England (importers and exporters) can get together and offset their claims and obligations. English exporters can get the dollars which are due them by making appropriate arrangements with importers in England. Assume that both groups have arranged the deals in pounds, not in dollars.[7] Then English exporters sell their claims to receive pounds to English importers, who use them to pay their pound obligations. The English importers replenish their holdings of pounds as the imported items are sold. In America a comparable exchange takes place. We repeat: The exports have paid for the imports, in both countries.

The clearing arrangements differ in many details from check clearing within a country. A relatively small group of banks and specialized dealers serve importers and exporters and their banks. However, before discussing this organization and the problems which arise out of differences in currency units, we shall say a little about the kinds of paper showing evidence of debts and claims in foreign trade. These documents differ, at least in relative importance, from those common in domestic transactions. It is these documents—more accurately, the claims which they represent—that are termed "foreign exchange."

Bills of Exchange: Cable Transfers

Foreign dealings frequently involve an extension of credit, *i.e.,* some delay in payment. The time required for shipment, perhaps weeks, creates a problem of financing goods in transit. Yet buyers and sellers may not know each other well, and facilities for credit investigation are not always adequate. Moreover, the buyer is likely to be beyond the convenient reach of the legal system of the seller's country so that enforcing agreements may be difficult.

For these and other reasons it is more common in foreign than in

---

[7] If the deals had been arranged in dollars, British importers and exporters would try to offset their dollar claims and obligations.

domestic dealings to attach evidence of title of the goods sold to the draft, acceptance, or other instrument associated with payment. Consequently, to get possession of the goods, the buyer must perform specific acts in connection with payment. (Of course, if payment must be made for a service rather than goods, no "things" are available.) The seller or his agent retains legal title to the products until he is assured of payment. It is customary for the exporter to "draw a bill" (draft) against the buyer or his bank. The exporter attaches the shipping documents to the bill and then sells it to his bank for his own currency at a discount which permits the bank to make a profit.[8]

The bank arranges with its branch or correspondent bank in the importing country for collection. The various documents are commonly called "bills of exchange" or "foreign exchange"[9] (though, as indicated above, the latter term has a broader meaning because it includes claims not represented by bills of exchange). Handling these documents requires specialized knowledge and facilities, partly but not entirely because of the variety of currencies involved. Such specialization has been developed in key centers—New York, London, and a few other cities.

The specialized dealers in foreign exchange are chiefly commercial banks. They make a market in foreign exchange. In doing so, they do more than provide the services of an intermediary having unusual knowledge and skills. In addition, they often extend credit. The coupling of credit extension with the handling of bills of exchange or other documents aids the process of international trade, the exchange of real goods and services, not merely the financing of transactions.

Among the more common of the bills of exchange is the "sight bill," which calls for payment when the bill is presented. A sight bill in French francs, for example, can be an order on a French bank to pay a given number of francs on sight. An importer in New York, who bought such a bill from his bank as he took possession of the goods from France, mails the bill to the French exporter, who gets francs immediately upon presentation of the bill. The sight bill effects payment, but with one important disadvantage—there is uncertainty about the time which will elapse between (1) the payment for the bill in New York and (2) the outpayment in France. Such uncertainty forces banks to sacrifice some opportunity to earn interest, because they cannot know exactly when payment must be

---

[8] Buyer and seller in arranging the transaction will agree on how the bills are to be drawn and handled. Sometimes the cost of financing, such as the interest lost by delay in payment, is in effect included in the price of the products and not stated as interest.

[9] The relative importance of bills of exchange is declining, even in London, where their use developed most fully. A draft (commercial) bill with documents attached is a "documentary bill." Drafts drawn by banks on other banks are "bankers' bills." A draft with no documents attached to it is a "clean bill."

made; to play safe, therefore, they hold some funds which are usually idle.

Modern communications offer a way to avoid such uncertainty and loss—the use of cable transfers. They have become increasingly common. "A cable transfer is . . . an order sent by cable to a foreign bank holding an account for the seller of a particular currency, directing that bank to debit his account and credit the account of the buyer [of the currency], or the account of the person designated by the buyer, with a specified amount." [10]   Cable transfers permit payment to be made in another country in a day or so.

Assume, for example, that a New York importer must make a payment in Paris not later than a specified date. He waits until the day or two before and then instructs his bank to charge his account dollars and cable Paris to pay francs as due. His bank makes arrangements with its Paris correspondent by cable. There is no time uncertainty, no needless loss of interest or tying up of funds. To illustrate another use of cable transfers, assume that an American business has received marks in Germany. It can convert them into dollars at once by selling the marks to a bank which can arrange by cable to get dollars paid in New York within a day or so. The German bank's payment may be from accounts it maintains in American banks.

Cables are fast, but air mail also permits rapid, and cheaper, communication. Consequently, air mail has helped maintain the use of bills. A Chicagoan, for example, uses dollars to buy a draft from his bank; he mails it by air to an Italian exporter. Two or three days later the exporter collects lira from the Italian bank on which the Chicago bank drew the draft. Rarely will there be more than one day of doubt about the time required.

Some bills are payable 30, 60, or 90 days after a specified date (or the sight date). For example, an exporter, A, sends a draft payable in 60 days in the currency agreed upon; the importer or his bank "accepts" and gets the goods, payment to be made in 60 days. If A wants money at once, he can sell the accepted bill to a bank, a specialist, or perhaps some business or investor with funds to lend. Such bills are sold at a discount which allows for interest. The price also varies according to the credit standing of the firm or bank obligated to pay. A draft that has been accepted by a leading bank will be worth more than one which is the obligation of only an obscure business.[11]   Hence such a business will be

<hr>

[10] Alan R. Holmes, *The New York Foreign Exchange Market* (New York: Federal Reserve Bank of New York, 1959), p. 18.

[11] The prospective discount will be considered in the original negotiation of the sale. If the amount involved is large, special effort can be made to arrange that the financing be done in the country with the lower interest rate. See "Bankers' Acceptances," Federal Reserve Bank of New York, *Monthly Review*, June 1961, pp. 94–100.

wise to get its bank to accept; the superior credit standing of the bank enhances the market value of the bill and thus reduces the cost of financing the transaction. When a bank "accepts," it does not make a loan or advance cash; it only promises to do so *if* the buyer fails to pay.

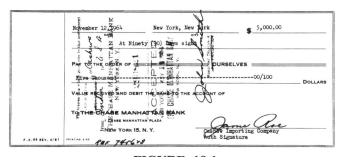

FIGURE 18.1

Banker's Acceptance Used in International Trade

Letters of Credit

Letters of credit permit the substitution of bank credit for that of the importer.[12] A firm wishing to import and not having the funds for immediate payment can go to a bank and arrange financing. A variety of conditions may be established, from the cost of credit accommodation to the specific details of the transaction. The bank then issues a letter (this may, in fact, take the form of a cable, perhaps to a correspondent bank abroad), promising to provide funds either for specific transactions or at the general direction of its customer.

The buyer of the letter of credit (the importer) turns it over in concluding an agreement to buy. The seller of the goods, upon proving that he has met the terms prescribed (proof that he may establish by attaching a bill of lading and other shipping documents to a draft), presents the letter of credit, probably through his bank, for payment. Usually, he will receive his own currency. The bank which has granted the letter may pay the foreign bank at once; or, if delayed payment has been agreed upon, it "accepts" a time draft promising the funds later. In the latter case there is a loan for a month or even considerably longer.

The letter-of-credit arrangement permits a buyer to eliminate uncertainties of financing a purchase abroad by substituting bank credit for his own. He will repay his bank in his own currency, perhaps after selling

[12] A letter of credit is not a negotiable instrument. Travelers at times use a somewhat different type of letter of credit. A tourist or businessman going abroad gets from his bank—either paying cash or borrowing—a letter entitling him to get funds from correspondent banks in other countries. Each time he presents the letter for cash, the amount obtained is endorsed.

the goods imported. The letter of credit may provide that the currency in which the agreement is conducted be that of a third country, such as the British pound or the United States dollar, in which active currency markets exist.

The technical features of bills and other devices for indicating what is owed and for extending credit in foreign trade have developed to meet various needs. The development continues as conditions change.

Travelers' Checks

The growth of tourism has stimulated the use of travelers' checks for payment away from home, especially in foreign countries. The American Express Company, Cook's, and a few banks sell the familiar type of check in various denominations. The checks are obligations of the seller, whose financial standing is beyond question. Anyone cashing them can be sure of receiving payment if the person presenting the check is the owner. He proves his ownership by countersigning, *i.e.,* by duplicating a signature he affixed when buying the check.

A tourist abroad cashing a travelers' check in dollars ordinarily gets the local currency. Either the person who accepts the check or his bank may return it to New York and get a dollar balance or present it to the local agent of the issuer (for example, a branch of American Express) in return for local currency. Those who sell travelers' checks must maintain funds over most of the world to meet claims. The costs are covered in two ways: There is a charge when the check is purchased—now ordinarily 1 percent; and the seller of the check has the use of funds, some of which can be invested at interest between the date of purchase and the date of cashing.

ORGANIZATION OF THE NEW YORK
FOREIGN EXCHANGE MARKET

The two great markets in foreign exchange, those in London and New York—and the dozen or so others of varying importance—are organized somewhat differently. The operation of the New York market, however, illustrates the basic features which have economic significance. This market is in a sense three-tiered.

The Three Tiers

1. The broadest tier consists of banks and their customers. The latter constitute the ultimate users and suppliers of foreign exchange. The banks serve them. Around 30 United States banks keep deposit accounts abroad in foreign banks, but 5 or 6 do most of the business. In addition, some of the branches and agencies of foreign banks in New York participate in the United States market by (a) their connection with finance and business in their own countries, and (b) their activity in the use of dollar balances owned by foreigners. A few dealers specializing in the purchase and sale of foreign bank notes—chiefly for tourists and businessmen who travel abroad—also make up part of this broad, first tier of the market.

2. The second tier is made up of 8 foreign exchange brokers. They serve the New York commercial banks in a highly specialized way. The banks do not deal with each other directly in buying and selling foreign exchange, but buy and sell through the brokers. Why? The brokers, as middlemen serving all, are able to provide each bank with a better market than any 2 or 3 banks could develop themselves.

3. The third tier consists of New York bank dealings with banks in other countries. These operations are conducted by the banks directly, not through middlemen.

All parts of the market, all tiers, are interrelated closely into a highly developed whole.

The foreign exchange market, unlike the stock or commodity exchanges, has no centralized meeting place, no fixed opening or closing time, and no formal requirements for participation except the informal acceptance of a code of financial and moral conduct that has evolved out of the working of the market itself. It thus may best be regarded, not as a place, but rather as a mechanism whereby buyers and sellers of foreign exchange are brought together. Buyers and sellers do not ordinarily meet face to face but carry on their trading primarily by telephone, and also by telegraph, cable, or mail.[13]

The New York market is part of the world market. The banks have connections in the far corners of the world, connections which are at the service of the man around the corner.

Methods of Operation

Commercial banks deal in foreign exchange to earn income. Not unlike the grocer, they seek to gain by selling for more than they pay. Moreover, they hope to build up other aspects of their business by providing good service. The balances that they maintain abroad in their accounts in foreign banks constitute basic working tools.

Banks *add* to these accounts by (1) purchasing balances abroad from

[13] Holmes, *op. cit.,* p. 10.

businesses, such as United States exporters who have been paid in foreign funds, individuals, and banks; (2) selling dollars in New York to foreign banks who will pay in foreign currency, *i.e.,* a New York bank will credit the account which a foreign bank keeps in New York in return for a credit in the account at the foreign bank in Rome, Rio, or Tokyo; (3) purchasing bills of exchange and a variety of items, such as travelers' checks and bond coupons; and (4) borrowing. (The amount held in any *one* country can be increased by shifting funds from another foreign land.) The banks draw down or *sell* their foreign balances as their customers request. The customers, of course, include correspondent banks throughout this country who act for their customers.

Foreign banks also buy and sell foreign exchange in New York, seeking to earn income. Sometimes they exert a heavy influence on one or the other side of the market in this country as they seek better terms from banks in New York than they can get abroad.

It is rare for any one bank to find its normal buying and selling just equal. On some days purchases will exceed sales, on some days the opposite. When a bank is buying more foreign exchange than its customers are demanding, it acquires foreign funds which serve no useful purpose. The excess represents the tying up of resources not immediately a source of income. But when the demands are greater than the supplies coming from its clients, it runs the risk of losing business by being unable to satisfy its customers. In either situation it may be able to improve its position by selling foreign exchange to, or buying it from, other banks. The financial community, therefore, has developed a highly organized wholesale, inter-bank market.

At the center of this market are the eight specialized and highly competitive *brokers*. The traders in the foreign exchange rooms of the leading commercial banks have direct telephone connection with the brokers and deal through them. The banks' traders, of course, seek the best terms available. Consequently, the brokers are able to match bids and offers from all the banks. Each broker's chance for profit depends upon his skill in competing with the others to offer attractive terms to the commercial banks. The result is a prompt and economical balancing of supply and demand, with, of course, price fluctuations. The commercial banks have strong reason to encourage competition and prevent collusion among the dealers.

Although several different currencies are actively traded in New York, the pound sterling accounts for about half the total of all transactions; the Canadian dollar is next in importance. In London the U.S. dollar is the most actively traded. Excellent systems of communications tie together the markets of cities in all continents, but especially those of New York and London. For example, a demand for dollars in London quickly appears as a supply of pounds in New York.

The prices of currencies vary. Moreover, the relationships among prices—pound to dollar or franc to mark—also change. The price relations may shift differently in different markets.

Arbitrage and Competition in Markets for Foreign Exchange

When relative prices of currencies change, opportunities for gain from *arbitrage* result. Arbitrage in foreign exchange is the attempt to gain from a temporary discrepancy in the prices of different currencies in different markets. To illustrate:

Suppose that the pound sterling is bid at $2.81 in the New York market and the Deutsche mark offered at $0.2390 in Frankfurt. At the same time, sterling is offered in London against the Deutsche mark at 11.75 Deutsche marks per pound sterling. An alert New York trader would immediately buy Deutsche marks against dollars in Frankfurt, sell the Deutsche marks in London for sterling, and get back into dollars by selling sterling in New York. Suppose that he purchased 1,000,000 Deutsche marks in Frankfurt at a cost of $239,000. With these Deutsche marks he could purchase £85,106 in London, and resell the pounds sterling in New York for $239,148. In effect he would, by arbitraging through the mark, be able to acquire sterling at a rate of $2.80825 as compared with $2.81 being bid in New York. The profit on the transaction would be only $148, but the entire operation would be completed in a few minutes. As a result of this arbitrage transaction there would be a tendency for the Deutsche mark to appreciate in terms of the dollar in Frankfurt, and to depreciate against sterling in London, while sterling would tend to fall in New York. Consequently, the cross rates among all three currencies would tend toward uniformity in all three markets.

The competition for arbitrage business is keen, not only among the traders in New York but also from traders abroad who have been actively engaged in such transactions involving the various European currencies ever since these operations were resumed in the European markets in 1954.[14]

As governmental controls on leading currencies have been relaxed since around 1950 and as the volume of world trade and investment has increased, the market for foreign currencies has grown. The ties between the leading world centers, the competition among banks in New York and those in more and more additional centers, and the active search of business firms with large international operations for the best terms possible—all these combine to add to the forces making the market for foreign exchange competitive. Competition exists not only at any one time but also, to some

[14] Holmes, *op. cit.*, p. 29.

extent, between the present and the future. This "time dimension" requires comment before we discuss the forces of supply and demand as they determine price.

"FORWARD" MARKETS

A dollar is a dollar, a franc is a franc. Each, and scores of other national moneys, will be bought, sold, and used next month and next year. But as they are used month after month, their relationships to each other constantly shift. Such changes create a type of risk for international business which does not exist in the conduct of a domestic business requiring the use of only one monetary unit. A United States firm with a contract to receive, or to pay, dollars in six months does not have to think about the price of those dollars (though their domestic purchasing power may change). If the contract is in pounds, however, the United States businessman faces an additional risk. He must think of the number of dollars that he will have to pay, or will get, for the pounds involved. Ordinarily, he cannot be certain what the exact relation of the pound and the dollar will be in the future. Here, then, is a risk which a manufacturing or commercial firm may not want to bear. The business will prefer to eliminate the risk if it can do so at a cost which seems reasonable.

The future or forward prices of currencies will interest anyone, speculator as well as businessman, involved in foreign trade and finance. A person who knows about the fluctuations in, say, the price of the pound in terms of dollars and who believes that today's relationship between the two currencies will change, may wish to put his belief to the test. He hopes to make money by doing so. What can he do? He can try to make a contract at today's prices; later when, he hopes, prices will have moved as he expects, he will "cover"—in essence, make just the reverse transaction.

To do so, however, he must find someone willing to do the opposite of what he wishes. How can such a person be found? The best prospect will be through an organized market, if there is one. And centering in New York and London there is such a market—one for currencies to be bought and sold in the future. It is made up partly of people seeking to speculate and partly of businessmen who want to avoid speculation. The latter wish to determine exactly what they must pay for or will receive from a contract involving a foreign currency transaction in the future. Banks act as the middlemen.

The dealings involve forward exchange. (These contrast with a "spot" contract, which is the ordinary type of transaction, one concluded when made.) A forward exchange contract is ordinarily between a bank and a customer or between two banks. On a specified date in the future, a certain amount of one foreign currency, say pounds, is to be delivered for a fixed payment in another, say dollars.

In one month—or 6 or 12—when the contract terminates, the spot rate of exchange may differ from the contract rate. If so, one party would have been better off not to have made the agreement, while the other will have gained. Both, however, have eliminated uncertainty. Ordinarily, at any one time, there will be businesses (and speculators) wanting to buy forward and others wishing to sell. A bank will serve both. It will try to maintain a fairly even balance of contracts, rather than having a net "position" one way or the other; if it does balance in this way, its losses and gains offset each other. How, then, does the bank benefit? It counts upon commissions to yield it a net income from the transactions.

Sometimes spot prices (*e.g.,* pound to dollar, franc to pound) are above futures, sometimes below. The relationship of the prices of spot and forward exchange will depend largely upon expectations of the future.[15] Some seasonal movements, of course, have high regularity. Yet supply and demand growing out of even normal commercial transactions will be influenced by expectations, as businesses decide to cover more or less of their future needs by forward exchange contracts. Purely speculative elements, however, are important and can account for swings of significant amplitude. Speculators, of course, may be about evenly divided so that their net influence is small. They may bunch together in offsetting an imbalance in the ordinary commercial market. Nevertheless, speculation can also be clearly destabilizing if expectations of change lead to a predominance in one direction and then a reversal.

The market for forward exchange, as for spot, is international. If the relative price of dollars to pounds for, say, contracts due in ninety days is more favorable in New York than in London, funds will flow from one center to another. They will, that is, unless there is some offsetting factor, such as a difference in interest rates which counterbalances the tendency for funds to shift. Or if interest rates in London and New York differ, short-term investment (*not* speculative) funds will move if the forward exchange rate is favorable. For example, assume that the interest rate on British Treasury bills is appreciably higher than the interest rate on United States Treasury bills. Then a New Yorker with funds for short-run, riskless investment may try to convert dollars to pounds to invest in London. He will do so, however, only if he can make a forward contract which will enable him, when he sells the British bills, to convert the pounds into dollars at a fixed price. And this price must be satisfactory.

If forward exchange is selling at a discount which is large enough to offset the interest rate differential, the transaction will not take place. Small differences in the prices of forward exchange can have significant influence on the amount of short-term money seeking to take advantage of higher interest rates abroad. And funds may actually flow from a high-

---

[15] Prices also reflect differences in interest rates in the two markets.

to a low-interest rate country—if the difference between spot and forward exchange justifies.

THE BALANCE OF PAYMENTS

How great will be the demand and supply of foreign exchange? They will be as great as buying and selling, lending and borrowing, giving and receiving, provide and require. The demand in the United States for pounds, francs, and other currencies will depend upon what importers, investors abroad, and others want. The supply of foreign exchange will depend upon what exporters, foreigners who wish to invest in the country, and others offer. Somehow the quantities demanded and supplied must balance.

Concept[16]

Though it is convenient to speak of "foreign exchange" as if it were a unit, what actually exists consists of a big variety of distinct currencies; transactions are carried on with all the world.[17] Does the smooth functioning of foreign trade require that the supply in one country of the currency of some other equal the demand? Must the supply of Brazilian cruzeiros in Italy equal the demand there? Fortunately, although some bilateral exchange does exist, there is no such exacting need. An economy's deficiency in one foreign currency can be covered by a surplus of some other if appropriate offsets are possible—and they are. Multilateral clearing goes on all the time, especially in London and New York.

Our concern, therefore, centers on the total for an economy. Do the claims on foreigners equal the claims against foreigners? In one sense they must, for accounts, broadly conceived, must balance. But the accounting balance may be achieved in ways that are not welcome, such as capital losses from failure to collect debts due.

One obvious way to study what is involved is to look at the two sets of accounts: (1) those which create a foreign demand for our dollars, and (2) those which supply dollars to foreigners. The two accounts present the balance of international payments.

---

[16] The balance-of-payments statement is not like a customary business balance sheet; it does not consist of a summary of the foreign assets and liabilities belonging to the people of a country.

[17] In fact, some of the potential complexity is avoided by the common practice of invoicing transactions in pounds or dollars rather than in less widely used currencies. Indians dealing with the Dutch may carry out the transaction in terms of British pounds. A Brazilian-French contract may be expressed in dollars.

Data

Various groupings of items are used. For mid-1964 Table 18.1 shows the annual rates of dollar totals of the major groups of items for which people in the United States could demand payments from foreigners (exports) and for which we became obligated to pay foreigners (imports). These are the international accounts.

The items of merchandise that we receive—coffee, bananas, Japanese cameras, German autos—obviously require payment. People from this country also get a great variety of services abroad, notably tourist services, such as a sightseeing tour in Rome; we also receive services provided by foreign businesses, such as insurance by a London company or a flight on Air France. Foreigners have provided some of the capital we employ in this country; we pay for its use. Moreover, our government makes military expenditures abroad which must be paid for in foreign currency. Privately and through our government we make gifts to foreigners, pay pensions to people outside the country, and make other transfers (transactions for which no goods or services are received currently). Many Americans have been lending to foreigners, buying stock of foreign corporations, and acquiring real estate abroad. Finally, United States firms have been acquiring capital facilities abroad, direct investment. All of these items create demand for currencies to make payments abroad.

Their opposites give us claims on foreigners. We export merchandise on a huge scale, provide tourist and other services to foreigners, get some repayment of loans made earlier, receive some capital for long-term investment, and obtain a variety of other claims on foreign funds. Moreover, the accounts have gaps which cannot be explained in detail.

The methods used by the United States in computing international accounts differ from those used in most other lands. Our presentations make conditions seem "worse" than would appear if we used the accounting procedures of most countries. The biggest single difference arises from the treatment of short-term capital. When foreigners acquire bank deposits or other short-term assets in this country, the amounts are shown in our accounts as an increase in our obligations—correctly. But when U.S. businesses or private individuals acquire bank deposits or other short-term assets abroad, these amounts are *not included* in our accounts. The asymmetry in our figures needs to be corrected in some way.[18]

Gold, though in fact a "good" or item of merchandise not unlike cotton, has a very special place in international finance and is therefore singled

---

[18] See P. B. Kenen, "Measuring the Balance of Payments," *The Review of Economics and Statistics,* May 1964, pp. 139–44. There are other large difficulties in both classifying and measuring balance-of-payments items.

TABLE 18.1

Balance of International Payments for the United States, 1964 [a]
Billions

Imports of goods and services— $		Exports of goods and services— $	
Merchandise	18.2	Merchandise	24.1
Military expenditures	2.9	Military sales	.5
Investment income payments	1.2	Investment income receipts, private	4.7
Other services	5.6	Investment income receipts, Govt.	.5
Remittances and pensions	.8	Other services	5.2

Balance on goods, services, remittances and pensions   6.3

U.S. Govt. grants and capital flow, net, excluding advance debt repayments

Grants	−2.2
Long-term loans and subscriptions	−2.8
Scheduled loan repayments and other	2.4

Private capital flows, net, excluding foreign liquid assets in U.S.

U.S. direct investments abroad	−2.1
U.S. long-term capital, other	−1.0
Foreign long-term investments in U.S.	.3
U.S. short-term capital	−2.5
Foreign short-term capital	.1

Errors, unrecorded transactions and seasonal adjustment   −.6

Balance   −2.7

Met by[b]

Gold export	.3
Foreign acquisition of bank deposits and other short-term assets	.8
Sales of special U.S. Treasury securities to foreign central banks and borrowing from International Monetary Fund	1.6

[a] Seasonally adjusted annual rate in second quarter. Excludes military exports under grants.

[b] Not seasonally adjusted. For the entire year the total of "balancing items" may differ substantially from the annual rates shown here.

Source: *Federal Reserve Bulletin.*

out for special note in presenting the balance-of-payments accounts.[19]

The purely mechanical facilities for handling the payments of these large totals, though undoubtedly capable of improvement, now serve well. More interesting balance-of-payments problems involve such questions as how different currencies become available and what mechanism brings adjustment. For although the accounts must balance, the forces bringing adjustment can differ in ways that have much meaning for humanity.

Balance is not necessarily equilibrium. When the conditions which have produced balance are not those which people prefer to alternatives, of prices, quantities, or changes in debt, something different will develop. The flows of goods and services give rise to most of the supply and demand. They depend upon relative prices, income, tariffs and other governmentally created obstacles or encouragements, and other factors which need not be discussed at this point. The role of capital movements, however, calls for attention.

Capital Transactions

Capital items appear on each side of the balance of payments. In some respects, of course, the economic problems that they present are essentially the same as those of goods and services for current use. Yet capital movements at times give rise to special balance-of-payment problems.

Short-run capital movements respond to essentially temporary conditions, though at any moment it is not always clear whether a condition is temporary or more likely to persist indefinitely. As the flows of trade create pressures for financing, debts from one economy to another rise and fall as buyers and sellers receive and then repay credit. Small, and even passing, differences in interest rates and in the relative prices of currencies —and expectations about price relations in the future—can lead to the shifting of funds. Sometimes, too, political hopes and fears influence short-run capital movements.

From day to day, then, the balance-of-payments position can change because of shifts of capital which are presumably temporary. These short-run moves may result from actions which are highly constructive in aiding the useful exchange of goods and services. The shifts may also come from disruptive actions arising from political disturbance or speculation which turns out to be destabilizing. The amounts may be small in relation to national income but very large in relation to the resources available for

---

[19] The terms "favorable balance" and "unfavorable balance" are sometimes still used. A "favorable balance" presumably exists when a country receives, or ends with the right to receive, gold or its equivalent. Whether or not such a situation is desirable depends upon the particular facts of time and place.

settling affairs without costly strain. The freedom which most of the time will aid the adjustment of underlying forces can at other times permit the aggravation of trouble.

Debt or equity capital for longer-run investment also appears in the total balance of payments. Two contrasting possibilities illustrate differences.

1. Assume that a firm in India borrows in Britain. A British investment banking organization sells bonds and receives pounds. The Indians then use the money to buy goods in Britain and ship them to India. In such a case the adjustment of the international balances takes place without direct effect on the payments mechanism. Similarly, when a U.S. corporation buys equipment here and sends it to a subsidiary abroad, the capital investment is made directly in the form of a real asset, not money. No international movement of funds is involved, except perhaps indirectly in the sense that something else that would have happened has not come about.

2. Now let us assume that the Indian borrower wants funds to spend in India. The transfer is then more complicated. How are pounds converted to rupees? The process is the same as that by which British importers make payment to Indian exporters. Borrowers in India get rupees from Indian importers in exchange for pounds provided by lenders in England. The pounds are made available to British exporters. India can import without exporting goods, though one may think of the IOU as an export. The British export without importing, except the IOU.

If the amounts involved in capital transactions, whether debt or equity, are large relative to the net balance on current account—the difference between the value of the period's exports and imports of goods and services —the adjustment difficulties may be substantial. The strains, among other things, will influence interest rates in the two countries and the relative attractiveness of borrowing in one economy or the other.

When the debt is repaid, or equity capital repatriated, the opposite conditions will tend to prevail. The borrowing country finds itself compelled to export to get foreign currency which it must use to pay its obligations rather than to buy goods and services for import.

International capital movements have contributed immeasurably to world economic progress. Unfortunately, they have also provided a mechanism by which trouble has been spread, or even created. Even capital transactions which are eminently justified for their long-run economic effects may give rise to serious disturbances in the international accounts. Trouble also arises at times from movements of "hot money." Capital shifts from one center to another, perhaps for political reasons or passing interest rate differentials, when little, if any, constructive economic purpose can be served. Many an economy faces the risk of temporary changes that are large in relation to the resources available for coping with them.

QUESTIONS

1. An American wants to buy a British auto. How can he (or his bank) make the payment in pounds?

2. What is a banker's acceptance?   a letter of credit?

3. How do travelers' checks figure in international transactions?

4. Show how arbitrage works to restore equilibrium in exchange rates.

5. Why do you suppose that some Americans buy stock in foreign corporations while foreigners buy stock in U.S. firms?

6. "The forward exchange market is made up of speculators and 'antispeculators.' "   Comment.

7. List the major debit and credit items on the balance of payments of a country.

8. In what sense must the balance of payments balance?   Since exporters and importers are not the same people and make free decisions, how can their transactions fail to create discrepancies in the balance of payments?

9. How do banks get paid for the services they render in arranging the settlement of payments across international boundaries?

10. What is the difference between short-run and long-run capital movements?

11. Why do banks which buy and sell foreign exchange deal with each other through brokers?

12. Discuss with a banker the methods that he uses in buying and selling foreign currencies for his customers.

13. What is arbitrage?   Does it serve a useful purpose?   Discuss.

CHAPTER 19   *THE RELATIVE PRICES OF CURRENCIES: EXCHANGE RATE CONTROL*

IN DAY-TO-DAY dealings we do not think of the dollar as having a price. It is the things which we buy with dollars that have prices. The American who buys abroad, however, must think of the price of money—the price of the foreign currency he must purchase with dollars before he can pay for goods and services in other lands. Foreign exchange, like coffee or oil, is bought and sold. Different currencies have different prices in relation to each other, *i.e.,* the dollar price of the pound differs considerably from the dollar price of the yen or the franc. How, then, do the prices of currencies in relation to each other get established? What brings changes? With what results?

THE CONCEPT OF THE PRICE OF A CURRENCY

The pricing of foreign exchange, and the role played by changes in currency prices in adjusting quantities supplied and quantities demanded, call for special attention. Although international financial accounts must balance somehow, there is no assurance that the amount of a currency demanded from abroad will equal the amount supplied at any specific price. Does not the price of a currency, like any other price, depend fundamentally upon demand and supply? And what does one mean when speaking of the price of this or that currency in the foreign exchange market?[1]

---

[1] The price of a currency as the concept is used here is not the same as its domestic purchasing power, but the foreign exchange price and domestic purchasing power are related.

The price of the dollar, franc, or other type of money is the amount of other currencies—or of some one key currency—which a unit of the money will buy. The dollar price of the British pound in 1964 was about $2.80 in the foreign exchange market, while the price of the Canadian dollar was about 92 U.S. cents. Prices of goods and services generally change to balance quantities supplied and quantities demanded. As a rule, however, the price of a currency in terms of most others is not free to change more than about 1 percent because governments act to control it.

Rarely will a government leave the price of its currency to the mercy of supply and demand when these two forces result from commercial and other private transactions. The ways in which public officials influence the price of currency are not always the same. The results, however, are always important, and important for domestic as well as for external reasons.

THE GOLD STANDARD

Let us start with the system used by this country now. It is essentially "the" gold standard as applied to international transaction. In major respects (but not all) it is the system which was effective over much of the world before World War I, to a considerable extent in the 1920's, to a much smaller degree in the 1930's.

Major Features

The dollar, in essence, is defined by law as being equal to a physical quantity of gold—one thirty-fifth of an ounce. Of greater practical significance, the United States government agrees to buy and sell gold at this dollar price for international dealings (specifically, to foreign central banks).[2] In other words, our government creates special elements of supply and demand for dollars used in foreign exchange. It does so by its willingness to accept or provide dollars on terms which are fixed in relation to something else, gold.

Many other governments, in effect, specify that each unit of their currency will equal a certain physical quantity of gold. For "approved" international transactions they will sell gold (or the equivalent, say dollar foreign exchange) at that price in their own currency. And they stand

---

[2] Sales of gold will also be made at this price for domestic use in industry and the arts. The exchange of paper money for gold coins or bars ceased in 1933; in this respect present practice here and in the rest of the world differs from that which was once considered to be an essential element of the gold standard.

willing to buy at that price, paying in their money. Consequently, many currencies are fixed in terms of the same thing—gold. They are, then, fixed in relation to each other. Therefore, in the foreign exchange market the price of one such currency in terms of another cannot vary much. Let us look at the mechanism by which demand and supply affect price under such conditions.

If I have dollars and want British pounds, I can get them, or my bank can get them for me, in either of two ways. (1) I can buy pounds in the foreign exchange market as described in the last chapter. (2) The Treasury will sell gold to my bank (in fact, the sale is to a foreign central bank which has received the claim from my bank) at a fixed price for conversion into pounds at a rate fixed by the British government. One of these two methods will ordinarily be cheaper than the other. The dollar cost of pounds in the foreign exchange market is quoted regularly and can be compared with the price of gold. The conversion of gold into pounds, however, involves costs which must be taken into account.[3]

To get a pound in London by the gold route may cost not $2.80, the official rate, but $2.82, the 2 cents reflecting costs. Therefore, the price I will pay for pound exchange in New York may be a trifle higher than the official gold equivalents of pound and dollar. But the price will not go above by more than the cost of sending gold from New York to London. Nor will the price go below the gold equivalents by more than the cost of bringing gold to New York from London. The person with pounds in London who wants dollars need not accept less than about $2.78 per pound. For he could (we oversimplify, it is true) use pounds to buy gold for transfer to New York to purchase dollars.

The price of British pounds in dollars may range between the equivalent of the "gold points," the upper and lower limits set by costs of shipping gold. The United States gold export point is reached when one pound equals $2.82; the United States gold import point is $2.78.[4] This range is not large enough to influence most importers and exporters significantly. But there are some marginal dealings which will be affected. Conceivably, some exports which would not offer good profits if sold in Britain for pounds when the pound is worth $2.78 are worth risking if the pound brings $2.82. And some imports that can be sold profitably if a pound costs $2.78 will not pay if the pound costs $2.82. Moreover, owners of capital for short-

---

[3] The costs are transport, insurance, and loss of income (interest) from use of the funds while they are being moved. For some years now, however, effective substitutes have replaced actual shipment across the ocean in the usual case. Gold transferred from United States to foreign ownership remains in FR vaults in New York. This earmarked gold is considered as having been exported.

[4] Today the Bank of England for the British Equalization Account buys and sells pounds to keep the price between $2.78 and $2.82. The range is essentially the same as that which would exist if gold actually moved across the ocean.

term investment may consider a move toward one limit enough to shift a decision.[5]

Changes in the relative prices of currencies can affect the volume of short-term investment and trade, and hence the demand and supply of foreign exchange. The changes tend to be equilibrating under the conditions we are assuming. Suppose that United States importers have increased their purchases in Britain above what has been the equilibrium level. The demand for pounds raises the price, say to $2.82. This increase in the cost of foreign exchange then tends to discourage imports and encourage exports, correcting the imbalance. Yet the total effect may be slight, for currencies on the gold standard can fluctuate only within a range too narrow to influence most trade.

Assume now that the dollar demand for pounds does not equal the quantity being offered and that there are no other currencies, *i.e.,* "pounds" stand for all foreign exchange. British importers offer more pounds for dollars than United States importers will supply. The dollar price of pounds rises to the gold point as British importers compete for dollars. A residue of unsatisfied British seekers of dollar exchange remains. They satisfy their needs by using their pounds to buy British gold at the official rate and transferring it to United States ownership for purchase of dollars.

Gold Movements and Price and Income Change

A movement of gold from British to United States ownership does more than settle payments. It has, or at least may have, importance which exceeds the significance of a movement of wheat or oil of the same total value. The shift of gold also changes the monetary base. In the example in which Britain exported gold, the British economy finds itself with a smaller monetary base, the United States with a larger one. Other things being the same, the United States monetary supply will tend to expand while the British supply will contract.

These contrasting monetary developments will in turn tend to change the flows of trade to bring about a reversal of the conditions which started the gold movement. Thus, what a great mass of people do in buying and selling across national boundaries can start a chain of monetary developments which will lead them eventually to alter their buying and selling. Let us look at the underlying tendencies.

---

[5] A drop in the price of pounds toward $2.78 offers a chance of profit. The price cannot go lower if Britain maintains its policies relating the pound to gold. The price can, however, go higher. If there is reason to believe that the price of the pound has fallen because of seasonal or some unusual developments which are temporary, a speculator can expect the price to rise later. As he buys pounds to hold for a time, he creates demand which tends to raise the price.

$$M_? \rightarrow P\uparrow \rightarrow Y_m\uparrow$$
$$\quad \hookrightarrow M\uparrow, X\downarrow$$

What happens in the United States, assuming that it "follows the rules" of the gold standard? Imports of gold expand the monetary base. The gold, in effect, adds to the deposits of member banks at the FR, *i.e.*, to their legal reserves and hence their lending capacity. Under the system of fractional reserves the potential expansion rises by a multiple. Money becomes "easier"; bank lending and purchase of securities both grow. Business improves. National income rises, at least in money terms; so do prices. The closer the United States had been to operating at capacity, the greater the tendency of prices to go up. Two important types of adjustment will follow.

1. The rise in prices makes this country a more inviting place for sellers in other countries; the higher our price level, the greater the prospects of selling to advantage here. On the other hand, exporting from America gets harder because higher United States costs and prices increase the difficulties of meeting foreign competition. Here and there some American goods and services are priced out of a part of the foreign market.

2. The *rise in income* in the United States leads to more domestic consumption of raw materials and finished goods from abroad. Americans also buy more services from foreigners, *e.g.*, tourist services. Moreover, higher United States incomes lead to domestic consumption of some goods that might otherwise be exported.

What is the net result of these responses? The import of gold has started developments which lead to a rise in imports and a decline in exports. The effects on the balance of payments are obvious—in direction but not in amount. Consequently, the rate of gold inflow will drop, perhaps even go into reverse.

Just the opposite forces will operate in the country that originally lost gold. Both income and price declines there will work to reduce imports and to raise exports. Perhaps gold will now begin to enter.

The combined results in the *two* economies of the *price* and the *income* effects act to offset the conditions which originally caused the movement of gold. The total equilibrating effect will hardly be ideal. Yet if the responses envisioned in the theory appear, they will keep economies from getting far from any position of original balance. Gold flows will not continue for long in one direction.

Though some of the price and income effects may begin soon after gold first moves, the full adjustment will take—well, no one knows just how long. Major effects will rarely appear in a matter of weeks. Much depends upon the responsiveness (1) of the monetary system to gold movements and (2) of the industrial system to changes in monetary conditions. These vary from one economy to another and from time to time. And in the modern world governments are unwilling to observe the "rules of the game" as presumably played in the past. Governments are reluctant to let gold movements influence domestic income and price levels. The automatic responses which were once assumed to exist—and which did operate, though less smoothly than we have indicated—have been curbed.

As a part of their domestic policies for full employment and price stability, governments to a varying degree insulate their monetary systems from the full effect of gold flows. Such cushions absorb much of the impact of movements of gold. In this country, for example, the FR by open market operations offsets the effects of gold movements whose influence on the domestic economy it believes would be undesirable if not counterbalanced. (In the 1930's the Treasury "sterilized" gold by failing to issue gold certificates on which the "Fed" would expand.)

Interest Rates and Short-Term Capital Movements

Another element of the adjustment works through interest rates. Shifts of capital, as already indicated, can produce effects which are prompt and sometimes troublesome. Suppose that a country receives gold as capital moves to it. Bank reserves and lending capacity will increase. One result may be a decline in interest rates. In the country losing gold, however, interest rates will tend to rise as money becomes tighter. These effects may appear long before other price changes exert any significant influence.

Because of divergent movements in interest rates, some owners of liquid assets (as distinguished from capital funds for longer-run investment) may find it profitable to shift funds to take advantage of *new* interest-rate differentials. This will happen if the relation of spot to forward prices of currencies will not require that all the interest-rate differential be used to buy protection from the exchange-rate risk. Such a shift or return of short-term capital tends to counteract the conditions that induced the gold movement.

If Britain loses gold and interest rates rise in London, while the inflow of gold in the United States produces the opposite developments in New York, what is to be expected? Some financiers in New York will sell short-term dollar securities, use the dollars to buy pounds, and then use the pounds to buy securities in London, such as short-term British government debt. In doing so, of course, the supply of dollars and the demand for pounds are increased. These results are just the opposite of those produced by the commercial and investment transactions which would have brought about the export of gold from Britain. The new capital flow tends to be equilibrating.

In practice, the easy shifting of short-term capital funds among countries on the gold standard is limited to a few major centers but is nevertheless very active among them. Interest-rate changes thus affect, and are affected by, relations among the prices of major currencies.

Pricing a Currency under the Gold Standard

With currencies defined in terms of the same thing—gold—and freely convertible into that commodity, their relative prices could change little. The maximum range of variation between any two would be the cost of a round trip of gold. Among major world financial centers this cost would generally be not more than about 1 percent. This amount, then, would be the limit of exchange rate fluctuations. A system of this sort can operate, however, only if gold is available for shipment, *i.e.,* if the economies have the gold and permit it to move. Moreover, the equilibrating results will not appear unless monetary systems and internal economies respond. Otherwise one-way movements may continue until no longer possible. Then some change *must* come.

One requirement for successful operation of the gold standard is a little harder to understand. It involves the relative amounts of gold in the monetary units. The economies must be so related to each other that underlying economic conditions, such as productivities and internal prices, are in line with the exchange rates set in pricing the currencies in terms of gold. Otherwise gold flows will persist, despite tendencies to "correction," until either the basic economic conditions change or until gold holdings are too large or too small to be tolerable. Then the exchange rates will be modified or restrictions placed on the movement of gold.

After a time of serious economic disturbances, such as war, who can know what relation between the gold prices of currencies is consistent with the deeper forces of the economies? A relation of £1 = $4 is obviously different from one of £1 = $3. The problem will be clarified as we examine the next topic.

CURRENCY PRICES WHEN EXCHANGE RATES ARE FREE TO FLUCTUATE

Let us now assume (1) that there is no official price of a particular currency in relation to gold or to other currencies and (2) that the price of this currency is permitted to fluctuate (or to "float") freely. Those who want to buy and sell foreign exchange will make the best deals that they can with each other, just as do those who buy and sell fruit or common stock. They cannot turn to a fixed price of gold as an alternative to the market price for foreign exchange.

At some price of the currency, quantities of foreign exchange demanded and supplied will balance; in an active, well-functioning, free market, the price of the currency will never get far from this level. But this equilibrium level will itself change through a range which is probably much wider than that between the gold points. Why the bigger range? For one thing, no purchase and sale of gold helps bring balance at a fixed level—adding to, or subtracting from, supply (or demand). For another, no gold movement helps induce the monetary changes which produce the more or less automatic adjustments under the gold standard. Nevertheless, an adjusting mechanism does exist.

To understand it, let us look at the Canadian currency—its dollar— when it was not tied to gold in the traditional sense and for which no rate of exchange was fixed. Without at the moment any increase in exports, Canadians begin to buy more from another country, which we call N, which we shall assume is not on the gold standard, and whose currency is called "pound." Canadian importers must now bid more vigorously for pounds. To get a given number of pounds, a Canadian finds that he must pay more dollars, perhaps $3.00 instead of $2.80, a prior equilibrium. Therefore, to sell imports at the same profit, Canadian businesses must charge more dollars. The adjustment process operates. The higher dollar price will tend to cut the purchases of imported products in Canada; a reduction in the demand for pounds follows.

Across the ocean in N, another part of the adjustment mechanism is working. N's residents find that each pound will buy more dollars and hence more goods in Canada. The price of Canadian goods in N falls as each pound now buys $3.00 instead of $2.80 in imports; there is an increase in the quantity of products from Canada bought in N. Imports into N rise, creating a larger demand for Canadian dollars.

Thus, in N, as well as in Canada, the change in the relative prices of currencies initiates trade adjustments. These in turn tend to offset the conditions that originally led to a movement in the price of foreign exchange.[6] If basic conditions are stable, the exchange rate will settle at an equilibrium level which will persist.

Purchasing Power Parity

What, then, will determine the price of a currency which is free to fluctuate without fixed ties to gold or to other currencies? In our illustration, what will be the equilibrium price of the Canadian dollar in terms of pounds? We look at the purchasing power of the currency, at home and abroad. What a currency will buy abroad and the amount it will buy at

[6] Other aspects of the adjustment process may include monetary and income effects in both countries.

home are related.   This relation is reflected in the price of the currency in the foreign exchange market.   Anyone's desire for a currency depends upon what it will buy him in real goods and services in his own land and in others.

The worth of Canadian dollars to an Englishman rests upon the things they will bring him.   So does the worth of his own pounds.   Therefore, the number of pounds that he will sacrifice to obtain 100 Canadian dollars must depend upon the quantity of goods and services that he can get for the pounds and for the 100 dollars.   At the margin he must expect equivalence.   If the ratio of the prices of the currencies does not reflect accurately their purchasing power in the two countries, alert traders will take advantage of the discrepancy.   They will buy things in one place and sell in the other until the ratio accurately measures the values of the currencies in goods and services.   A dollar will then buy no more when converted into pounds and spent in Britain than when spent in Canada.

In short, one or more currencies free from all restrictions on use abroad and with no ties to gold will be related to others so that their purchasing powers will be equal—as far as comparison is possible.   Things freely traded between the countries involved—especially staple commodities such as copper, petroleum, and wheat—will have the same price everywhere, allowing for transport costs and tariffs.   This conclusion will be true whichever currency is used in the figuring.   The prices of currencies, in other words, will be such that a buyer of, say, petroleum will get the same amount with a dollar as if he used the dollar to buy the other currency and then used that currency to purchase petroleum.

Practical Limitations

So much seems clear.   But it is not the whole story.   Most of the things that we consume—especially services and the service element in so many goods as they are finally bought by the consumer—are not traded internationally on a wide scale.   They differ in both obvious and obscure ways, so that accurate comparison is impossible.   Moreover, tastes and consumption patterns differ; a "market basket" appropriate to one economy will be ill-suited to another.   Consequently, no one can measure exactly what a unit of one currency purchases at home, taking an average of *all* the goods and services for which it can be used.   Nor can anyone measure what a unit of another currency will buy in its home country.   Obviously, therefore, it is impossible to use domestic purchasing powers to get a reliable indication of what the free rate of exchange of currencies "ought" to be.

Yet careful, though necessarily imprecise, comparisons may give a helpful indication.   If the rate of the pound, for example, has somehow reached a level where in Britain it will buy rather less of what the British want than it will buy abroad, trade will move to change the relation. The approach to this condition can probably be foreseen by comparisons of prices in Britain and elsewhere. As the British try to use more pounds to buy abroad, seeking better value by importing more, they offer more pounds for other currency. The exchange rate for pounds will fall. More pounds are then needed to get the same things abroad. The purchasing power of the pound in foreign lands has fallen. There has thus been a change in the relation between the domestic and foreign purchasing power—a reduction of the differential.

In a politically and economically stable world, domestic purchasing power of freely fluctuating currencies would change only slowly. So would their values in relation to each other. Nevertheless, short-run demand-supply changes would give rise to somewhat wider fluctuations than are possible under the gold standard, though by how much is hard to say because such a world does not exist. The one in which we live has presented, and still presents, a host of instabilities with which men must deal. The next chapter examines the chief methods of coping with the problems today.

Purchasing Power Parity: Relation to Gold Points

When currencies are related by fixed gold parities, the relations of gold contents must represent purchasing powers (within a range which is not easily predicted) if the parities are to last. Otherwise, gold will flow until conditions do change—in any of several ways or some combination. The change may consist of new internal price levels, higher in the countries receiving gold, lower in those losing it; the volume of employment and consumption in various lands will tend to differ from what would have prevailed if gold had not moved; productivity may rise more under competitive pressure where gold is leaving and business is contracting than where gold is being received and giving a stimulant to the economy; finally, the gold parities may be altered.

However, if the country losing gold—the one where prices are relatively high and the purchasing power of gold relatively low—has enough to meet an adverse balance for several years, the eventual reckoning may be long postponed. There is another possible obstacle to realignment of gold parities. As mentioned before, an economy receiving gold may not let the additions influence the domestic economy, *i.e.,* the monetary authorities may offset the potential effects of the gold inflow. If so, the gold price of its currency may stay out of line with purchasing powers for a long time. Other possible methods of adjustment are devaluation (described below), abandoning the gold standard, and domestic deflation. The first two are inconsistent with the traditional "rules of the game." The third may conflict with domestic policies for full employment.

MODIFICATIONS OF THE GOLD STANDARD:
EXCHANGE RATE CONTROL

Many men of influence have felt that neither the gold standard as it developed before 1914 nor a system of freely fluctuating exchanges would be most satisfactory. The older gold standard lost favor because some of the conditions needed for its smooth functioning seemed unattainable.

The Setting

The disruptions stemming from World War I presented greater obstacles than could apparently be overcome even in the prosperous 1920's. For one thing, after wartime and postwar inflation and a host of other changes which differed from one economy to another, there was no agreement on the appropriate parities to get currencies into stable relations with each other. For another, gold seemed poorly distributed over the world; officials of some countries felt that they had too little gold to operate the system as traditionally conceived.[7] Moreover, the additions to gold holdings from the output of the world's mines bore no rational relation to the growth of trade.

Then in the 1930's serious depression over the world, plus political crises in Europe, led to disturbing capital flows. Governments were not willing to let their internal economies respond "fully" to gold movements; the monetary adjustments called for by the "rules of the game" would have produced domestic changes which seemed undesirable. Should a loss of gold, due perhaps to fear of political disruption or a capital flight resulting from better prospects elsewhere, be permitted to bring deflation and unemployment if they could be avoided? Moreover, the gold standard seemed to be acting as an agency for transmitting trouble caused by the mismanagement of some economies. Would other countries not be wise to set up buffers?

---

[7] The "gold exchange standard," used by India and the Philippines before World War I, was extended in the 1920's as a partial solution for the apparent scarcity of gold. Country A ties its own currency not to gold but to another currency, that of B, which is on the gold standard. The central bank of A will buy and sell its own currency in settling foreign transactions at a price fixed in terms of the currency of B. The reserves of A consist of bank deposits and short-term securities in country B. Such arrangements enable A to obtain income from its monetary reserves rather than to hold wealth idle in the form of gold. B's affairs, however, become more subject to changes in A's balance of payments. And A stands to lose if B devalues its currency.

The gold standard got the reputation of being unduly rigid, except for an economy with a substantial "excess" of gold. A country tied to the world by the gold standard does not have full freedom to manage its internal affairs. And after World War II, the typical nation acquiring independence wanted more freedom than appeared possible under the gold standard. This argument was especially persuasive in cases where an economy had too little gold to finance even moderate strains in its balance of payments while following the traditional rules.

One alternative would be to leave the exchange rate free. The price of the currency would then rise and fall with demand and supply. But exchange rate fluctuations within the range that is possible in free markets can disturb business. At times such fluctuations may create chaotic conditions. Uncertainty about the future price of the currency must inevitably add to the risks of those engaged in foreign trade and finance.

In free markets, however, are not such exchange-rate fluctuations the result of forces of demand and supply to which business must adjust somehow? Some fluctuations certainly are the outcome of real economic developments.[8] Not all fluctuations, however, will result from the ebb and flow of normal business. Capital movements, which may or may not be speculative, can bring large short-run changes in the demand or supply of a currency and hence in its price. If so, business and investment may be upset for no good purpose.

No one can be certain about the seriousness of the difficulties which, under modern conditions, would arise out of freely fluctuating exchange rates. The consensus, however, has been that free markets in foreign exchange are not the best alternative to the gold standard.

Control of Exchange Rates

A widely used compromise involves a fixed rate or price of the currency, with controls on the *amount* of foreign exchange which may be bought and sold at the price. The price is ordinarily expressed in terms of gold (or some currency having a gold price). An official agency, perhaps the central bank, participates in foreign transactions more extensively than under the gold standard.[9]

---

[8] Even exchange rate fluctuations that result from basic economic conditions can present problems which differ significantly from those with which the ordinary businessman is familiar. There is advantage in eliminating them—or in converting them into something which businessmen can learn to use, *e.g.*, futures contracts.

[9] The types of control systems are numerous and vary from time to time. Russia and other lands with totalitarian governments conduct foreign trade through governmental agencies. The resulting monopoly permits central control of all the financial aspects of foreign economic affairs.

The agency may, as did the United States Stabilization Fund in the 1930's, buy or sell gold for the nation's currency to keep the price from fluctuating beyond a narrow range but without much restriction on private transactions. Imbalances of demand or supply can be offset within at least some limits. What became more common was for the agency to have a legal monopoly on the purchase and sale of gold and foreign currencies. Although such monopolies still exist, they affect a much smaller portion of world trade and investment than they did as late as 1954.

Nevertheless, the United States business firm which deals in Asia, Africa, Latin America, and parts of Europe will experience interventions of such agencies. For example, any exporter in one of these lands may be required to sell to the official agency all or most of the foreign exchange he receives, and sell at a price fixed by the agency. Other businesses in the country needing foreign currency to pay for imports can buy it from the control agency only. They pay an official price. The great difference from the gold standard is that not everyone can buy at the price set, and those who are permitted to buy will not necessarily get as much as they would like. Anyone who wants to contract to import must first assure himself that he will be able to get permission to buy foreign exchange. In some countries several different rates may prevail.[10] The control of foreign exchange gives the controllers vast power over the economy, power which penetrates far more extensively and deeply than is often recognized.

If the exchange rate (price) set is approximately that which would prevail in free markets, the system may run without much difficulty except for the nuisances of untying red tape. The purpose of control, however, is apt to be the maintenance of conditions markedly different from those of free market equilibrium. If the authorities can control quantities tightly, they may set a rate (or group of rates) which will differ appreciably from what would prevail in a free market, and they may conceivably make the rate prevail without creating apparent and large dislocations in the domestic economy. People *can* learn to live under such a system. Yet underlying stresses are inevitable.

Suppose that the rate for the pound is set at $4, when the relative dollar-pound purchasing power justifies a rate in a range around $3. If businesses were free to buy and sell goods, British exports would tend to be "low." British goods and services in foreign markets would be expensive relative to those of other countries. Imports into Britain, on the other hand, would be "high," as many foreign goods appeared to be less

---

[10] Brazil once charged importers of some items more than twice as much in cruzeiros as allowed to coffee exporters for the foreign currency they received. High and discriminating rates on foreign money serve as a tariff. Discriminating rates on exports act as subsidies of differing amounts. The dozen or so countries with complex multiple rate systems are moving toward simplification and eventual abandonment because of the difficulties revealed by experience. International Monetary Fund, *Annual Report, 1963* (Washington: The Fund, 1963), p. 70.

expensive than home products. If exchange rates were controlled, exports would still tend to be depressed; after all, the British have no way to compel foreigners to buy more than they wish at the $4 rate. The control system, however, would enable the British to restrict the use of pounds for imports to the quantity made available by exports. Much as British businessmen might wish to try to meet the domestic demand for foreign products, the foreign currency would not be available.

The authorities can also try to control capital movements. Suppose that official policy is to keep capital at home. The control agency can refuse to sell foreign exchange for the purchase of plant and equipment to be used abroad, to buy foreign securities or real estate, or to lend to foreigners—except as officials approve. British investors might relish the thought of buying bonds, stocks, real estate, or factories and utilities abroad if each pound would buy $4 worth; at home pounds buy less investment value.[11] But the inability of British capitalists to exchange pounds for foreign currency effectively prohibits them from making the investment abroad which they would welcome.

Such arrangements can continue indefinitely if controls are really tight. Yet subterfuges and illegal means of evasion are likely to develop, especially when the incentives are great and the administrative effectiveness of government less than the best. Few if any countries have the quality of civil service personnel needed to make exchange control operate thoroughly, if the incentives to evasion are large. Black markets develop. Bribery and corruption grow. Methods of doing business adapt to permit evasion; the cooperation of businesses and bankers in other countries with those who wish to disobey the law can add immeasurably to enforcement difficulties.[12] Men and women show unending ingenuity in devising ways to take advantage of economic opportunity in spite of legal obstacles.

To the extent that exchange controls are effective, the results are by no means fully obvious. Some of the worst consequences are hidden—the direction of economic activity into less than the best possible lines, the fostering of monopoly and the sheltering of domestic business from the stimulus of outside competition, the encouragement of corruption which tends to spread to other sectors, the needless delays in getting action from the control authorities, the loss of capital and skill which might come from

[11] Controls may also check a capital inflow if the exchange rate is fixed to undervalue the domestic currency relative to foreign currencies.

[12] Assume that S is an exporter of Spanish oranges, forced to sell the foreign exchange he receives at a price below what it is worth in free markets. Perhaps he can arrange to have a dummy corporation set up in Switzerland. He then sells through it so that it makes a large profit, which S will own—and keep—in Switzerland. The Spanish operations may show a loss, and S may bring in only the funds needed for current operations. The Swiss system of numbered bank accounts has for decades provided secure protection for those who wish to conceal their assets and activities.

abroad. Other results are less obscure but difficult to evaluate—the costs of compliance, the playing of one country or industry against another for benefits which at most are trivial, stupidity or inefficiency that bring losses entirely out of line with any conceivable benefits (such as the refusal to permit the purchase of spare parts needed to keep a big machine operating).

The exchange rate may be set below, rather than above, the level which would prevail in a free market. If so, imports will be discouraged, exports encouraged. Exporters will then have more foreign exchange to sell than importers want to buy at the rate. The economy will accumulate foreign funds, perhaps in the form of earning assets abroad, perhaps gold. If the domestic monetary system adjusts to gold imports as it would under the traditional gold standard, the underlying conditions, chiefly prices, will change. Incomes and prices at home will tend to rise and thereby alter conditions. The changes will in turn bring about a new balance of payments. Gradually, the free market rate will approach the control rate. Yet if the gold or equivalent is somehow sterilized—kept from supporting domestic monetary expansion—the original "disequilibrium" rate may continue for a long time. How long, no one can be sure.

Finally, we note modifications. Restrictions may apply to certain currencies only. After World War II, for example, many countries found themselves short of dollars and other "hard" currencies but able to balance supply and demand for many others. Dealings in "hard" money were then controlled, while others were permitted great freedom. A second modification applies to capital transactions. While foreign exchange may be sold for purchases of goods and services with virtually no restriction, any requests for funds to buy capital assets abroad are narrowly limited. This latter arrangement prevailed in Britain and other lands after the removal, in the mid-1950's, of the tight regulations of World War II. The knowledge that controls exist will in itself reduce the demands for funds so that no one has a clear notion of the magnitude of potential demand in a free market.

CURRENCY DEVALUATION

Assume that the conditions which create the pressures that lead to control of the exchange rate—domestic prices and incomes out of line with those abroad—are not temporary. Then a change in the price of the currency is probable. A continued loss of gold and foreign exchange in meeting deficits in the balance of payments invites currency devaluation as a solution. There have been many examples.

For instance, in 1949 Britain changed the dollar price of the pound from $4.03 to $2.80. A change of this sort—devaluation—makes exporting easier and importing more difficult. For a time it can provide an apparently easy way out of a difficult situation.

An American, for example, finds in 1949 that he needs only $2.80 to buy a pound's worth of goods and services in England, whereas before he needed $4. Clearly, his dollars will go farther, will now benefit him more, in England. Unless demand is completely inelastic, Americans who have been buying in Britain will increase their purchases. Some new buyers will enter the market for British goods and services. Presumably, the British are able to provide the larger quantities of goods. The additions may come from expanded output. They may also come from the diversion, somehow, of goods from British consumers, including, for this purpose, businesses investing in new plant and equipment. Presumably, too, the added output can be supplied at prices which do not go up by as much as the devaluation.

Meanwhile, Englishmen find that they must pay more pounds for the cotton or food or machinery that they had been importing. A pound which before would have bought $4 worth of goods from America now buys only $2.80 worth. British consumers whose incomes in pounds do not go up in the same proportion as the devaluation—and this condition will be the general one—will tend to reduce their consumption of imports. Yet if the demand for imports is highly inelastic, the spending in pounds for imports may rise by nearly as large a percentage as the devaluation. Supply prices from abroad, of course, may fall as a result of any drop in British demand.

In general, even though neither physical quantities nor money amounts of trading after devaluation are predictable with accuracy, two sets of forces affecting the British balance of payments can be expected. A stimulus to exports increases the supply of foreign exchange. A curbing of imports reduces the demand for foreign exchange. The result may be just what had been desired.

Obviously, however, when a country makes its goods cheaper to others—worsening its terms of trade—it is offering the fruits of its labor and capital and its natural resources for less than before. Consumers at home find their living costs rising as imports become more expensive. Business using imported raw materials can hardly welcome the higher prices.

Why not try to meet the problem of imbalance in international payments by reducing the prices of exports rather than by devaluation? In other words, why the price of the currency? The simple answer is that forcing down wage rates and other prices enough will be politically impossible. The resistances to wage and price reductions are powerful. Even if governments, by monetary or such other measures as direct controls or government finances, could force enough deflation—something which is by no means certain—popular resistance would be tremendous, perhaps irresistible. And frictions in the economy will probably be so obstructive that considerable waste in the form of unemployment will accompany efforts to force prices down. Moreover, the source of the disturbance may be distresses in other countries which reduce trade. Country *A,* for example, may be in trouble not because it had had inflation but because countries to which it sells have suffered serious economic distress. Why should countries like *A* "import" some of the trouble if exchange rate alteration will keep it out?

Devaluation in the short run can ordinarily be counted upon to help eliminate an adverse balance of payments. Actually, even in the short run, the results are less certain than surface indications might lead one to expect. For both exports and imports, supply and demand elasticities which influence the results are likely to be uncertain. Who can know how capital movements will be affected, whether free or controlled? The complexities involved go beyond what can be covered here. Suffice it to say that surprises are inevitable.

The longer-run effects of devaluation are even more difficult to predict. Other countries may devalue in turn, so that the relations of currencies revert to about their original status. The relations, however, may change as a result of new devaluations to patterns quite different from those just before or just after the original devaluation. In the longer run the conditions of demand and supply of goods and services change. Among the circumstances to which the conditions will gradually adjust will be the new relations of prices in different lands. These new prices will take account of the changes in the relative prices of currencies. Moreover, we must remember that demand and supply elasticities change more in the long run than the short.

Finally, a country devaluing will almost certainly find that upward pressures on domestic prices and costs cannot be resisted—if only because imports become more expensive. Gradually, then, its domestic prices go up to offset at least some of the effects of devaluation.

QUESTIONS

1. "For an American living in the United States to talk of the price of dollars sounds silly, but to talk of the price of pounds makes good sense." Explain.

2. "Under the gold standard the price of a foreign currency can vary over a range of only about 2 percent in the short run." Explain.

3. What was the automatic equilibrating mechanism claimed for the gold standard before the 1930's? Explain how it presumably operated. Show how the modern mechanism differs. What factors other than deliberate government policies may contribute to the failure?

4. Explain how the foreign exchange rate is established when the

rates are free to fluctuate. What are the advantages and disadvantages of this arrangement?

5. What is the "purchasing power parity" doctrine?

6. For what reasons might a country decide that control of foreign exchange rates is preferable to either the gold standard or freely fluctuating exchange rates?

7. Explain how exchange controls operate to keep the foreign exchange rate at the desired level. What disadvantages do such controls have?

8. What advantages might an economy expect from devaluation of its currency? Explain how these advantages may not result if several countries devalue.

9. "An upward revaluation (of our currency) will help prevent foreign inflations from disturbing us." Discuss.

10. What is the relation between interest rates and short-term demand and supply of foreign currency?

11. What would be the effect of an upward valuation of the German mark?

12. "Control of the exchange rate can accomplish most of the objectives of the gold standard." Discuss.

13. "A country which avoids inflation will not have balance-of-payments difficulties." Discuss.

14. "Free convertibility of currency is an aid to economic efficiency." Discuss.

CHAPTER 20 *PROBLEMS OF INTERNATIONAL FINANCE IN THE 1960's*

A VARIETY of important topics must now be covered, all too briefly. The first is essentially a continuation of the subject discussed at the end of the last chapter.

THE INTERNATIONAL MONETARY FUND

Reasons for Establishing the Fund

The terms on which the people of one country conduct trade with the people of other lands include not only costs and selling charges in some real sense (man-hours and machine-hours). Financial and monetary aspects of payment for each transaction are also significant, and to more than one country.

International payments are tied to domestic financial transactions, to money and banking, by connections that differ from such real factors as consumer taste and the techniques of production. Flows of foreign exchange, changes in liquidity, and varied aspects of finances affect more than one, or even the two, economies involved directly in a transaction. Trade and investment are affected by, and also transmit, forces of many types originating in many lands. What one country does will inevitably affect others. Yet some insulation of domestic from foreign finances is possible. Controls made effective by limits on buying or selling of foreign currencies have been described. Another method of seeking some insulation from outside forces is to let the price of the currency fluctuate freely under conditions in which more than minor swings occur and wide fluctuations are possible.

Monetary distress can spread like a contagious disease from one land to another, leading to more and more trouble within each. Attempts to insulate by controlling, or by failing to control, the rate of exchange at an inappropriate level have brought trade discrimination, economic warfare by manipulation of foreign exchange, and distortions of domestic economic life. The 1930's produced so much evidence of the disruption and the bad effects of both rigid controls and wide fluctuations—and so much despair over the possibilities, and doubt about the necessity, of restoration of the automatic gold standard—that a new approach seemed desirable for the post-war world.

Nations trying to "go it alone" would hurt each other. Cooperation was called for to serve the mutual interest. After extensive study, debate, and compromise, representatives of many nations meeting in 1944 at Bretton Woods agreed to set up the International Monetary Fund. By 1965 it had about 110 members. Table 20.1 shows major items in its balance sheet in 1964.

TABLE 20.1

International Monetary Fund: Major Balance Sheet Items, 1964
(Millions)

Assets		Liabilities	
Gold	$2,334	Member subscriptions	$15,665
Investments	800	Reserves and other	237
Currencies:		Total	$15,902
United States dollars	2,670		
Other	9,087		
Unpaid member subscriptions	993		
Other	18		
Total	$15,902		

Source: International Monetary Fund, *1964 Annual Report.*

Objectives

In a fundamental sense the objective is to facilitate the efficient development of world trade and investment and thus to help raise levels of income throughout the world. More immediately, the Fund's methods of helping the world economy involve closely related activities. It aims to promote stability in exchange rates and to develop a multilateral payments system which will encourage broad international financial cooperation.

Members must adhere to prescribed standards of conduct in their international monetary dealings. If "fundamental disequilibrium" requires a substantial revision of one or more exchange rates, the Fund can help make the adjustment orderly and thus reduce needless dislocation of business and the danger of competitive exchange depreciation. The Fund's most prominent activity consists of aiding members in meeting temporary balance-of-payments difficulties.

Obligations and Benefits of Membership

In joining, each member agreed to contribute gold and some of its own currency, on a quota basis, to a common pool of resources. Much the largest quota was that of the United States. Each member then has the right to draw upon this pool for gold or another currency if it faces a shortage of foreign exchange. The amount that it may draw depends upon (1) its own contribution plus (2) additional accommodation if in the judgment of the Fund's officials the facts of the situation justify such aid. Until a country returns the funds, it must pay a charge (interest).

Suppose that an adverse balance of payments develops out of an apparently temporary (not a fundamental) disequilibrium; the country must pay more abroad than it is receiving. If it does not have gold or foreign exchange, what can it do? Devaluation of the currency might be unwise for the long pull. To restrict imports by direct controls would bring costly disruption. Another alternative would be to force domestic deflation, creating unemployment, upsetting business at home.[1] Each possibility would initiate a chain of troubles which would extend to other countries. Fund membership, however, allows the country to borrow foreign exchange. The need for drastic action and the threat to other economies is greatly reduced.

Each country sets a par rate of exchange for its currency. This rate is the value defined in terms of gold or its equivalent. A member may devalue or alter the rate upward by 10 percent on its own initiative. Any larger change requires the permission of the Fund. What if the Fund objects? It cannot really prevent the action, but it can deny help which may be highly valuable at the time and later. Fund authorities are not inclined to veto a request. But they will attach conditions designed to help make devaluations yield the overall and long-run results which will serve the interests of the country and the rest of the world.

---

[1] The degree of distress in relation to the amount of corrective action would depend in part upon the number and strength of rigidities in the domestic economy.

Members are supposed to abandon exchange controls on current (noncapital) transactions unless the Fund explicitly grants exceptions. It has often given permission to impose controls to a country facing a scarcity of a specific currency. For example, when France had a shortage of dollars, the Fund approved French restrictions on dollar imports. Such regularization of the imposition of currency restrictions is designed to prevent the spawning of discriminatory controls, such as those which brought extensive trade disruption in the 1930's.

Problems of Operation

Use of the giant pool of currencies can keep temporary trouble in the balance of payments from causing costly internal distress and curtailing trade with other countries. Sometimes, however, there will be doubt whether a country's foreign exchange troubles are the result of temporary or more fundamental difficulty. If the source of trouble lies in the structure of the economy—productivities, prices, consumption patterns—temporary aid can do little to solve the problem. Help may only make things worse. It may delay adjustment and thus permit the sources of trouble to get more deeply entrenched.

Nevertheless, a breathing spell may enable the forces of correction— some of which may not be foreseen—to operate and reduce the problem. A poor crop or a major politico-economic development, such as the Suez crisis, can create exchange difficulties that are most likely to be temporary only. If an economy is short of foreign exchange because an exceptionally cold winter requires a big increase in fuel imports, aid from the Fund can make a helpful contribution to smooth economic adjustment. The situation is significantly different, however, if a shortage of foreign funds arises to a large degree from domestic inefficiency in production which makes the costs of export goods high—or if domestic inflation stimulates imports and discourages exports. Foreign exchange shortages may then result, in essence, from a basic maladjustment. It is the latter which really needs attention even though surface or temporary forces are also creating trouble (and may seem to be the cause). Fund aid is for *temporary* difficulties only.

Some exchange crises are clearly the product of fundamental difficulties just as some are clearly temporary. In other cases, even experts may not agree. If a currency is overvalued (as the German mark has seemed to be for several years), the Fund can do nothing in way of correction, other than persuade and help some of the countries which are adversely affected.

Those who planned the Fund wanted an agency which would not interfere with domestic economic policy. Beyond the familiar desire to avoid the infringement of national sovereignty, there was another concern. Leaders in many lands wanted to be free to pursue full employment policies. Economists, of course, realized that domestic fiscal and monetary policies which would stimulate employment might also cause balance-of-payments difficulties. An expansionist program in one country would tend to create just such difficulties if many other countries were in recession; the latter, because of poor business, would reduce their imports and their need to make payments to others. Meanwhile, the imports of the land with expansionist policies would tend to increase. It could expect balance-of-payments trouble.

Would it not be better to meet such difficulties by providing foreign exchange to the lands with full employment policies, rather than by forcing them to slow down and create unemployment? The founders of the Fund thought that the answer was clear. The Fund's discretionary authority, therefore, was limited. Consequently, Fund help may at times be superficial when something basic is needed—new cost-price relationships, higher productivity, or slower domestic monetary expansion.

Accomplishments

At first the Fund did rather little. Abnormal financial situations which developed during World War II, conditions of postwar disruption, large-scale dollar aid under the Marshall and other plans, Korean hostilities, the establishment of many new countries, and other developments largely unforeseen, all these overshadowed the Fund's power. Clearly, the climate was not favorable for building an exchange rate structure, or a general economic organization, which would reflect the underlying, long-run need—and the economic reality. As the 1940's passed, restrictions on the convertibility of currency remained more widespread, and more of an obstacle to efficient world trade, than had been hoped. As some economies worked out of their foreign exchange troubles, others got into an increasingly difficult situation. Calls on the Fund grew, chiefly for dollars.

Dramatic evidence of how the Fund can help meet a crisis appeared in 1956. As the Suez crisis deepened, it became clear that Britain and probably other countries would have to use their limited supply of dollars to buy oil in America. Doubts grew about the ability of Britain to maintain the exchange rate of the pound.

Foreigners with funds in Britain had reason to withdraw them at the existing rate of the pound merely as protection against loss in case the pound were devalued. There was no need for serious concern about the long-run balance between exports and imports on current account. But any substantial flight of capital would have strained Britain's foreign exchange reserve position, perhaps beyond the breaking point. The fear of just this eventuality could in fact create much of its cause—the precautionary and speculative selling of pounds to buy other currencies.

The Fund, however, met Britain's request for $561 million of aid and promised $739 million more if the need developed. With such assurance, the drain of foreign funds from London disappeared. What might have turned into a cumulating financial crisis was nipped in the bud. In 1961 the Fund helped arrange large standby credits from continental countries to prevent a possible "run" on the pound.

The Fund has been getting more calls for help. It will now make its assistance available to countries with economic development programs that require imports beyond immediate capacity to pay; but the Fund is not a source of permanent financing. If the Fund is to do its job, it must "revolve."

Several countries—France, Brazil, and Argentina, for example—have at times sought more foreign exchange than the amounts to which they were automatically entitled. They got more, but they had to agree to conditions set by the Fund. In a few cases Fund aid has been coupled with substantial amounts from bank and governmental sources. In prescribing conditions, the Fund has said, in effect, that a country getting extraordinary aid must act to remove the causes of the need for such aid. In doing so, the country would also prepare to participate more freely in world trade. Such "outside" advice was not always welcome—nor always followed— but it had influence.

The United States in 1963 arranged a standby credit of $500 million and drew on it in 1964, while getting assurance of larger drawing rights if such were to seem desirable. In 1964 the British pound again came under great pressure. The Fund gave substantial aid, but it was not adequate; additional buttressing came from central banks, including the Federal Reserve.[2]

DOMESTIC ECONOMIC DEVELOPMENTS AND PROBLEMS OF FOREIGN EXCHANGE

In most of the world, the relation between domestic economic policy and the foreign exchange position is more evident, and tied more closely to immediate problems, than in the United States. Our economy is so large relative to others, gold accumulated here in such huge quantities in the 1930's, and our ability to compete has been so effective, that we were for a long time free from the troubles of most countries. Consequently, in making national economic policy, we were able largely to ignore factors

---

[2] For analysis of actions of the Fund and the World Bank, as well as economic problems of world finance, we now have a quarterly publication, *The Fund and Bank Review: Finance and Development,* published jointly by the two organizations.

which are of crucial concern elsewhere. By 1960, however, our position had clearly changed.

How Difficulty May Develop

Let us review the process by which difficulties arise in a country's foreign exchange position. Assume that an economy's balance of payments presents no strain and requires no gold movement or change in short-term obligations to foreigners. Then the country begins, whether or not as a matter of deliberate monetary or fiscal policy, to experience a rise in domestic income. For a time there is no increase in prices. Rising domestic income in itself will increase the demand for imports for two reasons—businesses need more raw materials, and consumers spend more on goods and services from abroad. Exports, however, will drop as more of domestic output is used to meet home demand stimulated by higher income. The balance of payments will be strained, perhaps only gradually; reserves will be drawn down month after month.

Now suppose that prices, including those that are costs, move up as rising money income presses on the limits of productive capacity. Other countries, however, are not experiencing comparable developments. Price levels move apart; this divergence adds to the strain on the balance of payments. There will be a rise in imports whose prices have not risen as much as the prices of their domestic counterparts; in other words, residents of the country where prices are rising will substitute some foreign goods for the now higher-priced domestic items. Exporting becomes more difficult because higher prices (costs) at home make domestic goods harder to sell abroad. Thus, the "price effect" adds to the "income effect" in raising imports and reducing exports.

The foreign exchange position will deteriorate further as the demands for foreign currency exceed by more and more the quantity supplied from current transactions. Fear of currency devaluation may lead to speculative export of capital. Trouble may develop, or be accentuated, by the relation between interest rates and profit prospects both within and without a country.

Gold Standard Adjustment

The gold standard operating in the traditional manner would prevent trouble from developing to serious proportions. In the country losing gold, monetary changes would operate to pull down activity and prices, while lands receiving gold would feel a stimulus. These two forces would gradually "correct" the imbalance.

Nowadays, however, a country losing gold may find this sort of control, "dictation," unwelcome. It is almost certain to create some unemployment. Sacrifice of highly desired consumption or important parts of an investment program might then result. Certainly, the internal adjustments would be unpleasant to someone. If the economy receiving gold is operating at about full capacity, monetary expansion would tend to be inflationary. The country may have good reason to obstruct the traditional response. Automatic adjustment under the gold standard is by no means painless adjustment.

The Need for Aligning Economies

It is sad but true that keeping economies in line with each other will bring some distress and annoyance. But failure to do so will lead to greater distress as trade and investment eventually become more difficult. A country which has freed itself from the discipline of the gold standard cannot escape certain realities. Any disparity between internal and external economic developments is such a reality. True, an economy can maintain a domestic inflation (greater than that elsewhere) if it will let its currency decline in relation to others. Such a decline, however, will itself create problems—speculation against the country's currency, capital flight, almost irresistible pressure for more restrictions and controls.

Inflation at home, deflation abroad, or more rapid inflation at home than abroad, will put pressure on a country's balance of payments. So, too, can *relative* price changes. These may arise out of different movements of productivity or of alterations in demand and supply, which can develop from any of several conditions. The appearance of pressure on the currency may clearly demonstrate that a problem exists. But the balance-of-payments figures will not show the cause, or the relative importance, of different forces when more than one is operating. Of course, one cause may clearly overshadow others. Usually, however, time is required for the removal of doubts about the strength of forces. As time passes, conditions may worsen—or correct themselves. One forceful illustration of how conditions change is the topic of the next section.

FROM DOLLAR SHORTAGE TO DOLLAR SURPLUS

Perhaps it is wrong to speak of a "dollar surplus," but there is no doubt that (1) after World War II a "dollar shortage" plagued much of the world, and (2) by 1960 the situation had changed profoundly. Terms such as "shortage" and "surplus" are, of course, relative to something; in this case the basis of comparison is not always clear. Yet the change in 15 years is striking.

Postwar Problems and Aid

World War II destroyed or distorted productive capacity in much of Europe and part of the Orient. Tremendous need to meet desperate consumer requirements was evident. And the need for industrial recovery was also huge—to re-equip and develop European economies at the speed which seemed desirable, or absolutely necessary, in order to forestall social and economic chaos.

The United States and Canada made gifts of goods; they also made loans and gifts of money to buy other products and services. Yet as the immediate emergency passed by 1948, economists saw that a more persisting problem remained. The rebuilding of economies required more time and far more resources than were in sight. Resources would have to come from North America on a large scale.

How could Europe, Japan, and a few other areas get enough dollars? The problem was large, threatening, and in the opinion of some economists likely to persist indefinitely. To help, the United States, through a loan to Britain, the Marshall Plan, and other aids, provided gifts and loans of dollars and special help for raising productivity.[3] Foreign buying of merchandise in this country in the period 1946 to 1955 was more than $50 billion greater than our buying of goods abroad. Food and raw materials for emergency needs and modern machinery for equipping industry went to allies and former enemies.

Within only a few years the productive capacity of Western Europe and Japan was rehabilitated and then expanded. Most of these economies became able to export enough to pay for their imports, including those from the dollar area. Tight restrictions on purchases from the United States were relaxed, though not completely abandoned, by 1960. The European dollar shortage was largely eliminated, and one country after another accumulated gold and dollars.

True, the world continued to hear of a dollar shortage. Two factors accounted for much of the problem as it appeared in the late 1950's. (1) Lands seeking capital for investment (*e.g.,* India and the Philippines), or lands carrying burdensome defense loads (*e.g.,* Israel and Turkey), did not have the dollars or other foreign exchange needed to pay for the imports they wanted. (2) Some countries (*e.g.,* Brazil and Indonesia) had domestic inflation and faced the old, familiar difficulty. Their demands

---

[3] Among the important "other aids" was United States assumption of the lion's portion of the cost of mutual defense. The arrangements for sharing the costs of NATO were designed in part to help meet the "dollar shortage."

for foreign exchange exceeded the amounts available at current exchange rates. The United States continued gifts and loans to help meet both types of problems.

Balance-of-Payments Deficit for the United States

Suddenly, however, Americans became aware of a new problem. The rest of the world as a whole was getting more dollars than it wanted to spend here. Foreigners built up their bank accounts in New York and their holdings of short-term dollar obligations. Foreign central banks bought gold. In only a few months in 1958 they exchanged dollars for more than $2 billion, over 10 percent, of our gold. In less than 3 years (to late 1960) foreign holdings of gold and liquid dollar assets grew by over $8 billion. In the 4 years to mid-1964 short-term liabilities to foreigners as reported by U.S. banks grew by over $4 billion. Why?

One point should be made clear. For most foreigners, just as for most Americans, there was no surplus of dollars. Who will not always think of himself as "short" of dollars? What had happened was that demand and supply conditions had changed. When such a change occurs in, say, the egg market, the price of eggs will rise or fall to restore equilibrium. When a currency is involved, however, the problems of adjustment are rather more complex. The range within which relative prices of currencies were free to move remains much narrower than the range within which other elements of world economies were moving.

It is impossible, of course, in looking at the balance of payments, to pick out one or more items as accounting for the net result.[4] U.S. Government gifts and loans, private capital exports, the spending by tourists and soldiers abroad, restrictions of other countries on purchases here— each of these, and more, played a part. It is wrong to think of any one factor as either decisive or unimportant.

Interrelations are complex. If tourists were to spend less in Europe, how much would Europeans alter their buying in this country? To what degree do our large exports of merchandise to Canada depend upon our export of capital funds to Canadians?

Reasons for the United States Deficit

A glance at Fig. 20.1 will make clear the fact that United States exports are not only high but rising. Imports, however, are also high and

[4] Year-to-year changes, of course, may result from identifiable developments of particular items.

Billions of dollars

□ Exports[a]
▨ Imports

[a] Excludes military exports under grants.
[b] Annual rate in second quarter.

FIGURE 20.1

United States Imports and Exports of Goods and Services, 1952–60

Source: *Statistical Abstract* and *Survey of Current Business*

rising. If our economy had operated nearer full capacity after 1957, our imports would have been still greater.

If we exclude exports financed by U.S. gifts (*e.g.,* military and foreign aid) and military spending abroad, plus those dependent upon some form of government subsidy (farm products), the export record gives no bases for complacency. Moreover, foreign producers can increasingly use methods of production every bit as good as ours while paying lower wage rates. Our policy of raising the prices of certain farm products by governmental action has added to the difficulty of continuing our traditionally large export of farm products, except with subsidy. Our tariff reductions, on the other hand, have been large relative to those of many countries, encouraging imports here.

Substantial military establishments abroad require our government to spend dollars for maintenance. Furthermore, each year the military and civilian personnel who staff them spend about $1 billion of their pay abroad, which comes from the dollars of American taxpayers. We continue to make military grants in dollars to some of our allies and friends; but most military aid funds are now spent in this country. Our government presses our allies to pay more of the cost while also using more of the dollars here even if our prices are higher.

Capital export in excess of capital import makes up a third factor. (The dollars shown as capital export are to considerable degree used to buy machinery and other items in this country, thus financing some exports which would not otherwise take place.) Capital export is not new, and it will continue. Businesses, and not a few individuals, have been attracted by investment opportunities abroad. Some activities abroad, such as marketing and mining, can be done only on the spot. In addition many U.S. firms trying to develop foreign markets find that plants abroad are essential to meet competition or comply with local law. In numerous countries after-tax profit prospects have seemed more promising than here. Because interest rates are lower and facilities for borrowing generally much better in this country foreign businesses and some governments have borrowed on a large scale. Gradually, expanding earnings from foreign investments will provide growing amounts on the receipts side of the balance of payments.[5]

A fourth factor is our policy of aiding poor nations. Most of such aid is now "tied"; the funds must generally be spent here rather than used to buy goods and services abroad. Over the longer run, the development of regional associations, such as the European Economic Community, *i.e.,* the Common Market, may create difficulties for nonmembers, including the United States. The groupings have in fact already erected discriminations against goods from outside.

Outlook for the Dollar

The balance-of-payments deficit seems certain to continue for at least a few years. If it is on the scale that now seems probable, this country must be prepared for difficult monetary and economic problems.

The surface problem may seem to be loss of gold. Yet the actual loss of even billions of dollars worth of gold need not create trouble for this country. It might, however. We have tied our internal monetary system to gold by requiring minimum reserves. It is sometimes said that as a result most of our gold is not free to move to foreign ownership except by forcing monetary contraction in this country.[6] Fortunately, the Federal Reserve has emergency powers. Using them might be clumsy and the results possibly disturbing domestically—but again, adjustment might proceed smoothly.

What would be the effect of a large loss of gold on the attitudes of

---

[5] A considerable part of corporation earnings abroad are reinvested on the spot and not immediately brought to this country. Thus the profits returned to this country will not rise as much as the earnings abroad.

[6] Assume that M declines because of gold loss and that V is essentially stable. If P were to decline easily, then no drop in T would be necessary. But prices and wage rates are so "sticky" that much of a drop in MV would be felt in T, not in P.

foreign holders of dollars and on Americans as well? A large outflow of gold might cause many foreigners, and some of our own citizens as well, to expect restrictions on further withdrawal of gold or even a devaluation of the dollar. Such expectations would lead some to try to remove dollars at once. No one can be quite sure what the psychological reactions would eventually produce. Foreign central banks would probably continue their cooperation and resist demands for large drawings on gold here. Leading central bankers hardly want the dollar to get into bad trouble, for the repercussions would inevitably be unsettling, or worse. Still, the uncertainties are discomforting.

From month to month, interest rate changes influence the movement of funds for short-run investment. Domestic monetary policy, therefore, can accomplish something, temporarily. But the benefit will hardly be large enough for long enough to justify any appreciable restraint on the economy which is not justified on other grounds.

Ingenious arrangements, described from time to time in *Treasury Bulletin* and *Federal Reserve Bulletin,* provide opportunities for obtaining foreign currencies by borrowing and "swaps." These help in the short run. Such aid offers little promise for the longer run because the debt can scarcely grow indefinitely; when repayment is required, the original help on the balance of payments will be reversed.

What about the deeper problem? Is there a more than temporary maladjustment in underlying conditions? If so, are there forces working toward correction? The identification of maladjustment is not always easy.

Who can say, for example, whether net capital exports from this country represent some sort of maladjustment which will persist or will pass? Some, such as direct business investment, often bring not only high profit but also a substantial return flow of foreign exchange. In response to White House urging, Congress passed a 3-year "Interest Equalization Tax" on foreign borrowing in this country and on the sale of new stock—with many exceptions. Since the tax was to be retroactive to July 1963, the date it was first recommended, the proposal (even though not enacted until the summer of 1964) reduced capital export substantially in late 1963 and early 1964. In advocating the reduction of Federal taxes, the Administration argued in 1963 and 1964 that profit prospects in this country would improve. As a result, it was hoped, businesses would be less anxious to export capital.

The balance between exports and imports will depend upon the relative costs of production here and abroad. Will technical superiority (of U.S. producers) be more fleeting in the future than in the past? More and more economies now have the skilled labor and the capital to match or exceed us in many lines. In addition, American firms are increasingly able to use their best methods in foreign plants where wage rates are decidedly lower than in this country.

Can we develop enough new products to appeal on a large scale abroad? Will increased sales effort stimulate exports substantially? What will happen to domestic wage and other costs relative to those abroad? Businesses and unions concerned primarily with domestic markets may let costs and prices rise. They may have little or no export market to lose and yet may help set wage-price patterns which are bad for the import-export balance. A country can price itself out of enough foreign markets to have difficulty paying for as much as its people want to import.

Much will hinge upon our record in preventing price-level increases, compared with what happens abroad. In the mid-1960's Europe was experiencing strong upward pressure on prices and wage rates. Growing prosperity abroad will raise the demand for United States goods and services—but perhaps no more than rising income here may increase our own demand for imports.

The Federal government is trying to help businesses find markets, encourage foreigners to come here as tourists, and initiate a variety of other means of improving the balance of payments. Devaluation of the dollar receives little public discussion and seems unlikely. Such action would repudiate our promises. Moreover, there is considerable opinion that devaluing (reducing the gold equivalent) of the dollar offers little hope of accomplishing the objectives. Enough other economies would probably follow our example so that magnified disruption, rather than correction, might well result. A "floating" exchange rate, or one free to fluctuate through a wider range than is now permitted by the IMF, would tend to weaken this country's position as "banker" for much of world trade; one appeal of the dollar for use by foreigners is its stability. A "reserve" currency must not be one whose "price" is subject to question.

Higher tariffs, import quotas, limits on American tourist spending abroad, a "capital issues committee" to regulate the outflow of capital, and other direct controls all appear unattractive for various reasons. They, too, would invite retaliation. No solution is yet in sight. The magnitude of the problems ahead, of course, will depend upon the amount which foreigners decide to hold here for the financing of international trade and investment.

Euro Dollars

An integral part of today's international monetary machinery developed in the 1950's, not as a result of planning by governments or central banks but out of more or less spontaneous market forces. "Euro dollars" now finance a considerable volume of transactions over the world.[7]

A Euro Dollar, in oversimplified terms, is a dollar liability of a European bank. A bank in Europe receives dollars which Europeans—central banks, commercial banks, or business firms—have accumulated in New York or which Americans will lend (deposit with) it. Some of the dollars are kept as deposits in U.S. banks, but some are used to buy short-term, interest-bearing dollar securities in the New York money market. The European bank agrees to pay a certain rate of interest for these dollars. The supplier of dollars no longer has a claim on a U.S. bank; his claim is on the European bank, and is in dollars.

The European bank then makes a loan in dollars, not in its local currency, probably to a business. The dollar loan may be to a U.S. firm, such as a securities broker who can thus escape controls applying to U.S. lenders. The interest rate is higher than the bank pays to the supplier of dollars but lower than the interest rate on borrowing in local funds. The European borrower may himself want the dollars to pay for something in the United States; or he may sell them for some other currency. When his loan falls due, he must have dollars for repayment. He will generally hedge in the forward exchange market to eliminate risk of adverse movement in foreign exchange rates. The total cost of the transaction to him, therefore, is the interest plus the cost of hedging.

European banks must keep amounts equal to some of their Euro Dollar obligations on deposit in New York; but not to all, since a considerable portion of the dollar obligations of European banks will be used by the European borrowers to settle accounts from one business to another in Europe. The market for Euro Dollars is highly organized. Prices are quoted daily in the European financial press in terms of annual interest rates.

On December 24, 1964, for example, Euro Dollar deposits on call were quoted in London to yield 3⅞ percent, and for 3 months to yield 4¾ percent.

According to one commentator,

"What the Eurocurrency market has done is to give the Continent a money market of its own, using internationally minded London as its cen-

---

[7] Antecedents predate World War I. The development in the 1950's was speeded by the relaxation of controls on foreign exchange, the expansion of world trade and finance, the improvement of political relations among nations, various imperfections and differences in money and capital markets, and other factors. One of the latter apparently was Russia's desire to avoid possible U.S. restrictions on its use of dollars; as a result, the Russian-owned bank in London made large use of new mechanisms. The "Euro" in the term is something of a misnomer because other parts of the world, notably Japan and Canada, are involved. Moreover, currencies other than the U.S. dollar are used in essentially the same way.

tral depot and the internationally minded dollar as its currency. Because more funds, as well as goods and people, are moving across frontiers, it has given foreign exchange traders a bigger job of placing funds received on deposit and raising money to cover loans. Operating with top-speed telephone and telex communications, they move funds from areas where credit is cheaper and more plentiful to areas where credit is dearer and relatively scarce. Arbitrage—in spot and forward foreign exchange and in interest rates—is grease on the wheels." [8]

In 1964 from $5 to $7 billion of Euro-dollars were in use. One reason for the growth was, and remains, differentials in interest rates among many markets. Another has been the universal acceptability of the dollar. A French firm borrowing dollars rather than francs from a Paris bank can often make payments more easily over the world; many transactions can be settled as the dollars pass from company to company —and with some saving on exchange conversion expenses.

WORLD LIQUIDITY

As the physical volume of world trade continues to rise, even without any change in average prices, financing it will require more payments and presumably more internationally acceptable "money"—gold, dollars, and other "hard currencies." If there is also a general rise in the prices of things traded in world markets, the need for money financing will rise even more. Both forces have operated in the postwar period.

One result has been to create concern about the liquidity of the world economy. Some observers have feared that trade and the division of labor over the world may be hampered by lack of liquidity. People may not be able to take the fullest advantage of opportunities for trading and investing abroad because cash and credit are not available on an adequate scale. "Adequacy," however, is not easily defined. "Liquidity," too, is a concept subject to different interpretations when used in international finance.

The flow of goods and services—and of capital—is still restricted here and there, and perhaps at many points, because of what seem to be purely payment difficulties. What about the future? Will the amount of money or financing available in the international sector lag behind needs? What will serve? Gold certainly; dollars if they remain fully convertible; the pound sterling and perhaps other widely accepted currencies.

[8] N. O. Johnson, *Euro Dollars in the New International Money Market* (New York: First National City Bank, 1964), p. 12.

[9] On the date for which Euro Dollar yields are shown above in the text, 90-day CD's yielded 4.15 percent in New York; 90-day pound loans in London yielded 6¾ percent. For discussion of problems of measuring the magnitudes, as well as of the development and use of Euro-dollars, see Bank for International Settlements, . . . *Annual Report . . . 1964,* (Basle: 1964), Ch. V.

The output of gold will meet part of the problem, as it has for generations. For many years the deficits in the United States balance of payments have added dollar balances on a large scale to the stock of the world's liquid resources. Foreigners acquiring dollars have used billions to build up dollar balances to finance more and more trade. Will the process continue? If it does, how can the dollar be protected against sudden, large demands for convertibility into gold.

Economists are by no means in agreement on whether, in fact, a problem of insufficient liquidity lies ahead. Specific cases do not establish a general condition. Moreover, what is sometimes given as an example of illiquidity is more a problem of the absence of facilities for granting short-term loans.

Continued development of international banking is certainly a partial solution. Some leading students of the problem believe that before many years some sort of world central bank will be needed. Perhaps the International Monetary Fund could be transformed. Such a bank would create "deposits" which central banks would accept in settlement of international obligations. These deposits, it is hoped, would serve as monetary reserves for central banks. A shortage could be replenished by borrowing. How else, it is asked, can the world finance the growth in the volume of trade which is so desirable? The answer is not clear, but the practical difficulties of establishing a world central bank would be formidable even if leading nations were willing to cooperate.[10] The inflation potential frightens many bankers and economists.

SPECIAL AGENCIES FOR INTERNATIONAL LENDING

The need and the opportunities for profitable flow of capital across international boundaries are tremendous. The business world has invested huge amounts abroad directly out of profits, borrowing, and sale of stock in the home country. Banks in many lands have expanded their facilities and activities abroad. U.S. banks, for example, have tripled their annual volume of term (more than one-year) loans in less than a decade. And governmental and quasi-governmental sources have come to play a role. The latter justify comment.

[10] Perhaps we might build on the Bank for International Settlements rather than the Fund. The BIS was established to help handle German payments of World War I reparations after conditions became extremely difficult around 1929. Its present operations are small compared with those of the IMF. Yet they might be expanded. A second example of cooperation is the European Payments Union, which in the early 1950's proved highly effective in arranging the settlement of accounts among lands in Western Europe. One of several recent discussions appears in the *1964 Annual Report* of the International Monetary Fund. See also *International Monetary Arrangements: The Problem of Choice, Report . . . of 32 Economists* (Princeton: International Finance Section Department of Economics, 1964).

World Bank

The International Bank for Reconstruction and Development is designed to help finance investment.

The subscribed capital, all provided by governments, was $21 billion in 1965; only 2.2 billion has been paid in. The Bank has gotten most of its funds for lending by selling its own debt in the United States, Germany, and other lands. (In the early years this country was the largest supplier of funds, but more recently Europe, especially Germany, has taken the lead.) The Bank's debts are contingent liabilities of member governments, up to 80 percent of their quotas. In effect, therefore, the lender can count upon the United States, Canadian, and other treasuries to pay the debt if the Bank were to fail, a contingency which now seems most unlikely.

A government which is a member, a political subdivision, or even a private firm if it can get its government's guarantee, can apply to borrow from the Bank. The specific project will be examined carefully by the Bank's staff. The purpose of the investigation is to learn whether the proposal suits the economy and whether the financial arrangements are adequate. If the project is approved, the Bank will lend on terms designed to cover its costs and to provide a margin for safety. Loans now go almost exclusively to underdeveloped lands, generally for power, transportation, and communications facilities but on occasion also for agricultural and industrial projects. By 1965 almost $8 billion of loans had been authorized; repayments plus sale of loans to private investors were about $3 billion.

Two newer associated agencies help finance investment projects with greater risk than the Bank will undertake. The International Finance Corporation provides funds to risky but promising projects which can get some other financing. The IFC, for example, attempts to encourage private individuals having some funds but little experience, and foreign firms having little familiarity with operations in underdeveloped areas. The International Development Association will make long-term loans to underdeveloped countries at low interest rates. A portion of the servicing payments will be accepted in the local currency. The loans have generally been for relatively small amounts. Various governments help provide the subsidy, largely indirect, which is involved. The World Bank's excellent technical facilities will be available to help the IDA.

Export-Import Bank

In 30 years of life the Export-Import Bank has engaged in varied activities. Its major function is to make loans to foreign governments and businesses to finance purchases of materials and capital equipment in the United States when private lending is not available.   These are "tied loans"—the money must be spent in this country.   ExImBank also loans to foreign agencies to help them pay overdue debts to United States businesses and banks; it guarantees loans made to foreigners so that the United States bank or business will not suffer loss, and it shares loans with banks when they are not in a position to carry the full amount for the full period.

Loans vary greatly in amount.   Most have been to help encourage the export of particular commodities from this country—machinery, cotton, airplanes.   Yet important aid has also been given to help meet balance-of-payments difficulties and to finance longer-term development.   It will insure exporters against loss from war and expropriation.   The Bank gets its funds from the United States Treasury.   Over the years it has earned a net profit.   Loans outstanding in early 1965 were about $3 billion.

Other U.S. Government Agencies for Lending Abroad

The Agency for International Development is the successor to earlier agencies used to make loans and gifts for rebuilding Europe and Asia and loans for defense-related projects abroad and to insure U.S. firms against both expropriation and inconvertibility losses on new investments abroad. The major activity now is to administer economic aid for development, as distinguished from military assistance.   AID funds are primarily loans repayable in local currency rather than in dollars.   The United States government attempts to limit loans to projects with promise of aiding long-term economic growth.   There is some subsidy—how much depends in large part upon the worth of the "soft currencies" received in repayment.

Several other lending programs have been established by the United States government.   Some are already history. One large program consists of loans of foreign currencies received from the sale of agricultural surpluses.   Most of these loans are for local development programs, but up to 25 percent of the proceeds may be loaned to United States business firms for investment within the country.   Various arrangements for loans and guarantee of private loans, including programs for Africa and Latin America, are designed to serve in part as instruments of foreign policy.

QUESTIONS

1. What is the purpose of the IMF?   How does it correct short-run disequilibria? signal long-range maladjustment?   Why is it not useful to correct fundamental disequilibria?

2. What factors have caused the United States to lose gold in recent years?   If this situation were to continue, what steps might we take?

3. How was the postwar dollar shortage met? In what way, if at all, did this lead to the present dollar surplus?

4. "In 1958 most of the United States deficit was made up by gold export and in 1959 by short-term capital export." Explain.

5. What is the World Bank? Why is it that this "bank" can issue securities to finance investment projects that could never have been financed by themselves? What is the effect of this phenomenon on world economic development?

6. What is the Export-Import Bank? How does it aid American foreign trade and foreign policy?

7. What, if any, advantage would result from removing the requirement that the Federal Reserve hold gold certificates for currency outstanding?

8. How is domestic monetary policy related to the balance of payments?

9. Why does the United States have compelling reason to try to maintain foreign confidence in the dollar?

10. What is the problem of international liquidity?

11. "The Fund must not attempt to perform the job of the Bank." Discuss.

12. "If domestic business grows, we know that the stock of money must grow. The same is true of international trade. But the world's common money, gold, expands only slowly." Discuss. Do not ignore velocity.

PART FIVE

MONETARY POLICY

CHAPTER 21   *THE OBJECTIVES OF MONETARY POLICY* [1]

AMBITIONS are more easily raised than satisfied—an ancient truth which applies to modern economic policy. Some of us have come to expect a great deal from monetary action, or at least to seek both big and varied objectives. They, in themselves, call for explicit consideration. Yet before one can choose wisely among objectives, answers to other questions are needed. What can we expect to accomplish by monetary action? What is possible? For if policy is to be guided most constructively, it must be directed toward attainable objectives.

THE ART OF THE POSSIBLE

Several factors affect the attainments which are "possible" from monetary policy action.

1. The monetary authorities cannot directly change the income stream. What they do will not in itself constitute an increase or decrease in the flow of expenditures through the economy.

Nevertheless, the monetary authorities do have a good deal of power, even though the major actions work on the income stream only indirectly.

[1] Prevention of inflation is discussed in Chapter 22 and economic growth in Chapter 26. See Commission on Money and Credit, *Money and Credit* (Englewood Cliffs: Prentice-Hall, 1961), Ch. 2; H. G. Johnson, "Objectives, Monetary Standards, and Potentialities," with comment by A. P. Lerner; also G. E. Noyes, "Short-Run Objectives of Monetary Policy," with comments by H. Stein, J. Conard, and C. F. Christ, in *Review of Economics and Statistics,* Feb. 1963, pp. 137–55; L. S. Ritter, "Official Central Banking Theory in the United States 1939–61," *Journal of Political Economy,* February 1962, pp. 14–29.

The Federal Reserve changes the availability of money, or of close money substitutes. It can raise or lower liquidity. It can make borrowing more or less expensive and influence the prices of securities and thereby the wealth of their owners. The public, in turn, is free to respond. Such responses are not always foreseeable—in amount, in timing, or in location. Even the nature of the responses is sometimes doubtful. Although confident about the direction in which aggregate spending will change, there will be doubt about the division of the total of the change between prices and real goods and services.

2. Monetary policy operates broadly. The effects of change cannot be pinpointed. Even if an initial impact were to be focused by some sort of selective action, such as special treatment of mortgage or consumer lending, the results will gradually spread over the economy; other sectors feel the results, some promptly, others only after considerable delay. Monetary change works in a fluid environment. A change in level in one area will produce flows to other parts of the system—but not without delay and not with equal effect on the levels in various places.

3. Monetary action will not build houses or raise the productivity of manufacturing or make people friendlier. It will not in itself modify the underlying real elements of the economy. Monetary conditions, however, are an essential element of the framework within which we produce and consume. Within this framework men have a significant amount of freedom. Monetary policy works by modifying the general conditions within which men act. Many things other than the financial system also help make up the general framework of an economy—the tax structure, the policies of labor unions, the size of foreign trade, the age distribution, the extent of monopoly. Monetary action cannot overcome or offset them, at least not fully.

4. The public has no choice as to whether or not to have monetary policy. We are going to use money. We are also going to use banks, and banks are related closely to the amount and the flows of money. The public might decide to leave banks "free" (as free, perhaps, as shoe retailers) or to regulate them more narrowly than today. Either action would be a decision on monetary policy. Even apparent inaction is a form of policy. The practical question is not whether we shall have a policy but what kind it will be. Nor is there any doubt that we shall use the institutions of government. However we may interpret the constitutional provision giving Congress the power to regulate the value of money, Americans will unquestionably use government—Federal and state—in managing the monetary system. Even economists who outspokenly oppose broad governmental intervention in economic life will assign to government heavy responsibilities in regulating money.

5. The tools or implements of monetary policy, of course, help determine the "possible." The chief tools influence the stock of money and its close substitutes. If all money were created by government, public officials could control exactly the amount of money available to the public. When most money is created by banks, government can influence—but not completely control—the total.

(a) The monetary authorities cannot control the willingness of banks to lend or of customers to borrow. (b) Even if the quantity of money were controlled rigidly, no central authority would be able to control velocity or the changing desires for liquidity. All of us have some freedom to decide (i) how much of our total wealth we shall hold in money and in close substitutes for money and (ii) how many days shall elapse on the average between the receipt of income and the payment of our bills. The flow of money payments through the economy will not necessarily be steady even if the quantity of money is fixed. Nor will variations necessarily move in accurately predictable ways. The Treasury-FR kit contains no tool for controlling velocity directly. (c) The authorities do not know by how much either changes in interest rates or in the prices of securities will influence the volume of investment. Apparently, however, demand schedules for many types of investment goods are highly inelastic with respect to interest. Some students, but not all, believe that to affect the quantity of investment enough to influence employment substantially, wide, but financially disturbing, moves in the level of interest rates may be needed. We certainly do not know how big the marginal responses will be.

6. What can be accomplished also depends upon the ability of those with power and responsibility to predict accurately. The choice of what we ought to try to do will depend upon the extent of confidence in our ability to predict the effect of different kinds of action. Unfortunately, prediction remains an uncertain art.

7. Another factor affecting the possible is the quality both of the personnel who will make and administer policy and of their advisers. Will the people who must make the decisions be well qualified? The wise action that may be counted upon from one group of men cannot necessarily be expected from others. What assurance can the public have that those responsible for policy are competent to act as well as is required for success? The actions will require sensitive, delicate judgment and execution. A person or group not qualified to do the job well (no matter how competent to act on other problems) may in fact have decisive influence.[2] Serious errors may produce costly mistakes. The existence of this risk underlies

---

[2] For example, a banker who is well qualified to judge the quality of business loans may have little competence for deciding how much change in the quantity of bank lending will serve the public best.

the argument, discussed later, for trying to rely upon carefully devised rules in preference to frequent exercise of judgment.

8. Any realistic appraisal of what can be done will recognize that the general environment—political and social as well as economic—must influence the results. What might seem possible "in theory" may in fact be impossible because of practical realities. For example, two such different things as the temporary strength of a few leaders in Congress or delays in getting a half-dozen pieces of key information may modify significantly the hopes of success in dealing with a particular situation. Today we recognize another environmental factor—economic conditions in other countries. The freedom to use monetary policy depends in part upon what monetary authorities in other lands are doing. The "possible" in one country rests somewhat upon the "actual" in others.

9. The intermixture of *monetary* and *credit* policy seems certain to continue and to create unfortunate confusion. Society's need for money —as a medium of exchange, a store of value, a unit of account, a standard of deferred payment—is different from its need for credit. The attempt to meet desires for loans by creating money—or the destruction of money when the demand for credit slackens—is not likely to produce the best monetary policy. Yet the two are destined to be grouped together, with officials in and out of Congress more concerned about credit than about the stock of money. The desire to help one sector of the economy (farming) or restrict another (the stock market) can be satisfied, perhaps, by credit policy. Monetary policy, however, is not an efficient instrument for such purposes.

10. A final item in this list of elements affecting the possible is the singleness or consistency of objectives. Monetary policy may be directed toward one or more goals. Perhaps any one of them could be reached. Perhaps all are desirable. Yet they will inevitably conflict somewhat in the sense that the kind of action best suited to one will not be well designed for achieving others. We hope that policies for attaining important objectives will more often harmonize than conflict. But this happy state is by no means certain. In recent years we have often been confronted with rising consumer prices when unemployment was more than frictional; the monetary policy appropriate for one was unsuited for the other. The choice of which goals to subordinate may be more than merely troublesome.

The policy maker will frequently face conflict between short- and long-run considerations. Today's problems can take on importance which proves entirely out of proper relation to the longer-run needs. Adequate weighing of the concerns of different periods can never be done with confidence of success. The Federal Reserve has come in for no small amount of criticism for attaching undue weight to immediate needs. Perhaps it has erred in both directions. In any case the difficulties are inescapable and must be recognized, not ignored.

KINDS OF OBJECTIVES

Some goals are simple, some complex. Some are clearly the means toward other ends, while others are more nearly ends in themselves. Shall we, for example, settle upon a rather specific goal for the monetary authorities, such as a stable or slowly rising quantity of money? Or should we seek a goal embracing much more of economic life, such as maximum employment or the rapid growth of real income? We might select a monetary goal because it in turn promises to help us achieve a "goods and services" goal. Or, in slightly different words, we may pursue a monetary objective because if we do not realize it, the attaining of other goals will become more difficult. Monetary goals, like money, are means to other ends. It is hopeless to expect monetary action in itself to bring us to our real objectives—the goods and services we would get from the full employment operation of a free economy. Yet it is also hopeless to expect to achieve the real objectives if monetary currents are running strongly against their realization.

What are some of the real goals? One may think of them as general well-being, today or over some longer run. But what makes up well-being? Material goods and services certainly play a part. We are better off, other things being the same, with greater rather than lesser wealth and material income. Yet the conditions under which the income is produced and consumed also affect well-being. Stability up to some point is to be preferred to instability, security to insecurity. Freedom, too, is valuable in itself. So are justice and dignity and the other elements of the good life—elements of fundamental importance extending far beyond the scope of monetary policy but nevertheless affected by it.

A real goal about which we hear much today is growth—economic progress. For good reasons we want to raise total output; even more to be sought is higher efficiency and productivity throughout the economy so that per capita incomes can go up. Many of us also emphasize specific elements of growth, such as housing or health or schools—desirable real objectives. At times a dominant real goal is to win a war.

Most of the things we seek are personal, not collective. Nevertheless, choices involving the country as a whole must be made. The economist must not assume that his rating of social goals is necessarily the best. Choice of collective goals must be the public's own responsibility. Yet this country has not arranged in precise, orderly fashion the national or social objectives that it seeks, nor indicated their relative desirability.

Any discussion of monetary policy, then, must suffer from a lack of clarity of goals. Such uncertainty—even confusion and at times inconsistency—presents the policy maker, and the economist who tries to help him, with problems of the most perplexing, most difficult nature.

MONETARY GOALS

The goals that we shall examine are essentially monetary. In appraising them, however, we shall also consider their appropriateness for helping achieve real objectives. First, however, we face a related, basic issue—"rules versus authorities."

Rules Versus Authorities

The issue is this: (1) Monetary policy and directives for action can be stated in terms that are clear, definite, and precise. (The statements would be embodied in laws passed by Congress.) Human beings in carrying out the policy would be left little (or no) room for judgment or discretion. (2) In contrast, the monetary system can be framed to give power to be used by authorities (an individual or a group) as they think best in the light of the conditions which actually develop; officials might be told to seek certain general objectives, or they might be given no explicit guidance. The first kind of policy is one of *rules,* the second one of *authorities.* Between the clear extremes lie possibilities of compromise.

Arguments in Favor of Rules.[3] The argument for fixed rules has several facets. One derives from the fact that the monetary system makes up such a vital part of the economic framework. If this part is certain, if men know as clearly and definitely as possible, then individuals and businesses can arrange their affairs more efficiently than if they are uncertain about what may develop in this important part of economic life. Expectations, it is argued, will be more certain. There is less room for surprise. Society can largely eliminate one source of risk—and risk is a cost.

A second reason is that if rules are fixed, changes in monetary policy

[3] For a classic statement see H. C. Simons, "Rules versus Authorities in Monetary Policy," *Economic Policy for a Free Society* (Chicago: University of Chicago Press, 1948), pp. 40–77. See also E. S. Shaw, "Money Supply and Stable Economic Growth," in *United States Monetary Policy* (New York: The American Assembly, Columbia University, 1958), pp. 49–71; M. Friedman, "Should There Be an Independent Monetary Authority?" in L. B. Yeager, ed., *In Search of a Monetary Constitution* (Cambridge: Harvard University Press, 1962).

will not make things worse. Adhering to a rule strictly assures protection against some human errors. Even if the rule may not be best for every situation, there is no danger of bad selection of alternative actions or bad timing as authorities try to meet changing conditions. Thus, the public avoids not only the costs of uncertainty but some of the risks of poor policy. At the worst, the argument runs, we may sacrifice little to obtain this gain because the potential superiority of flexible over fixed policy will not be large, whereas the losses from shifting to an inappropriate policy can be substantial.

Moreover, the process of selecting a fixed rule would require careful analysis and extensive public discussion. The final definition of policy would doubtless represent more carefully, and certainly more widely, considered thought than would the various decisions of an authority having extensive discretion. The rule would be selected to further the general public interest, whereas specific use of authority is subject to pressures exerted by those concerned more with special than with the general interest.

Proponents advance more arguments: Merely by being fixed so that all groups could adjust with equal opportunity, the rule would serve the general interest. If the rule were widely endorsed, it would have support which would reinforce other pressures to pursue policies to make it effective. Human weakness and incompetence would offer less of a threat because they would be countered by public opinion.

Finally, the record of discretionary management has by no means been brilliant. Evaluating the record is difficult, of course, if only because one cannot know what would have been produced by different actions. Nevertheless, the accomplishment certainly does not in itself provide a convincing testimonial to the superiority of authority over rule.

Arguments against Rules.[4] The major argument against reliance upon fixed rules is that discretion may be used wisely to meet needs as they develop. No two sets of economic conditions, after all, are identical; the future is unknown. How can men, with all their limitations as human beings, set a general rule for the future which will serve as well as the best that men can devise as conditions actually develop? Can we not get the best results if the monetary system is adaptable?

A fixed rule can hardly serve all desirable goals equally effectively, and a policy well suited to achieving one goal (such as price stability) may be poorly adapted for another (economic growth), which may increase in

[4] See G. W. Mitchell, "Statements . . ." *Federal Reserve Bulletin,* March 1964, pp. 308–16; Dr. Mitchell is a professional economist and a member of the Board of Governors of the Federal Reserve; J. M. Culbertson, *Full Employment or Stagnation?* (New York: McGraw-Hill Book Co., 1964).

relative importance. Insulation from troubles coming from other countries may require flexibility in monetary policy. Moreover, not enough is known about the ability of officials to implement a rule, almost any rule, to be confident of success. Experts point out serious difficulties in applying any proposed rule.

Conclusion. The great majority of those who have made policy, and of those who have executed it, prefer considerable discretion. They believe that monetary policy can contribute most when it is framed and administered in the light of conditions as they develop, where needs are constantly changing, always complex, and not foreseeable with certainty. The fetters of a fixed rule might restrain needlessly and impose avoidable costs.

Although the argument for "authorities" seems to have gained general adherence, two points need emphasis. (1) There is no assurance that discretion will be used competently in a world of great complexity. Mistakes may do considerable harm. (2) The lack of certainty about monetary policy itself creates problems for business. The conditions which call for action by the authorities thereby become more complex because, in a sense, the freedom which authorities welcome creates some of the problems they dread.

Congress is not likely to go the full distance in adopting a policy of fixed rules.[5] It might, however, define more clearly the goals that it wishes the monetary authorities to seek. Such clarification could mark an advance. What might be some of the possible monetary objectives?

Control of the Quantity of Money

Perhaps the clearest-cut monetary goal would be to regulate the quantity of money itself. The objective is less ambitious than others to be discussed later. And it could be achieved. The control envisaged would be more rigorous than is possible now, when private decisions also influence the expansion and contraction of bank loans—and therefore the stock of money. The quantity of money to be outstanding would be determined by rule or authority. Anyone seeking to borrow money would have to get it from the existing stock; commercial bank *creation* of deposits to lend to him would be impossible.

What method might be used? The requirement that demand deposits be backed by 100 percent reserves offers a possibility worth more

---

[5] Two more or less fixed rules—the gold standard and the balanced government budget—had considerable weight for decades. Yet they did not control in the sense of displacing other guides of policy.

attention than our space permits.[6]   The monetary authorities controlling reserves would then have one-for-one control of the quantity of money. If such a plan or, more realistically, one less rigid were adopted, what might be the guides or standards of the amount of money?

1. One possibility would be to *fix the quantity of money* once and for all.   Clearly, then, no economic disturbance could arise out of changes in the quantity of money.   A single objection, however, dooms this suggestion: In a growing economy, the price level, including wage rates, would decline as total output increased.   (The price decline would be due not to productivity growth but to expansion of total production.)   In our economy, however, price declines on the scale that would be involved would create intolerable strain.   Rigidities are too numerous and too severe.

2. A more nearly realistic possibility would be to *increase the stock of money at some steady and definite rate*.   (The rate of increase might be on a per capita basis.)   No one, then, need have any doubt about the amount of money in the economy, next month or next year.   Once the policy had been determined and necessary changes made in financial institutions to assure practical implementation, the monetary authorities would have no discretion.   Every week or month the FR would buy enough assets (government debt) in the open market to build the money stock as agreed upon, possibly with seasonal adjustment.   Or the Treasury would adjust its financing—debt refunding, new borrowing, and currency issue— to provide the expansion.   The injections of new money might be set to equal as nearly as possible the expected growth in the economy so that the price level would be essentially stable.   Or the amounts might be adjusted to move the price level upward or let it slide downward.   The heart of the proposal is the fixed, definite change in the quantity of money without regard to apparent success in reaching a given price level or other goal.

A proposal so rigid may seem unduly restrictive.   Would the gain— the removal of what has been a source of economic instability, changes in the rate of money creation and destruction—be worth the loss of freedom

[6] The debate over 100 percent reserves finds the students of money still divided on the desirability and even the feasibility of shifting from the present system of fractional reserves to one in which each dollar of demand deposit would have to be matched by a dollar of legal reserve.   A leading advocate of 100 percent reserves now proposes that member banks be paid interest on their deposits at the Federal Reserve.   This proposal would help meet one of the major objections of banks, namely, that their earning capacity would be drastically reduced if they were not allowed to operate on fractional reserves.   See Milton Friedman, *A Program for Monetary Stability* (New York: Fordham University Press, 1960).

to change the quantity of money?[7]   Few economists favor the strict rule. For one thing, it does not conform to our tradition.   More important, however, is the belief that in a world of freedom and uncertainty men should try to adapt monetary policy to the conditions which do actually arise.   And one weakness is clearer today than it was even a few years ago.   "Money" is not easily defined.   Close, and not-so-close, substitutes exist.   Changes in the totals of substitutes can upset the results expected from a policy of fixed growth of the money stock.

Nevertheless, the proposal deserves serious and sympathetic attention, even by persons inclined to favor discretionary authority over a fixed rule.

Control of the Total of Money Payments

Any policy based on strict control of the quantity of money has an inherent weakness.   It ignores velocity.   Is there, then, a policy which deliberately takes account of velocity?   One approach would seek to regulate either the total of money payments (MV), or the total of income payments (MV_y).   The goal would probably be some stated, regular increase in the aggregate.   Regulation of the total of money payments would be a more powerful instrument of economic control than one limited to the quantity of money.

Achievement, however, would be very much more difficult.   Velocity is the result of the way millions of economic units act.   Though a central authority can control M within narrow limits, it cannot control the *use* of M.   (Among the problems for which there is yet no good solution is the changing importance of "non-income" uses of money, such as the purchase and sale of securities.)   The use of money is the most decentralized, the most dispersed, of economic realities.   A proposal which includes allowances for changes in V is quite a different thing from one which involves M only.   In fact, the working out of the policy would have to rely upon those changes which the monetary authorities are actually able to make— changes in M.   These would be larger or smaller, depending upon the *expected* movements in V.

Is a goal which can be achieved only by correct forecasts of V overly ambitious?   So it would seem.   Yet the monetary policies most widely accepted today do, at least indirectly, involve this more ambitious objective.   This fact is true of the pursuit of price-level goals.

---

[7] History records many occasions on which discretionary monetary action rather than strict adherence to a rule could have served the public interest.   Nevertheless, an advocate of the strict control of the stock of money must not necessarily abandon his case when presented with such evidence.   He may argue that the trouble which seems to call for remedial action would not have developed if his plan had been in effect earlier.

Price-Level Goals

There is no question that money does affect price levels. There is no question that changes in price levels influence human welfare greatly. Perhaps, then, price-level goals are most appropriate for monetary policy, even though they are not sufficient for all public policy.

What might such a goal be? It might be stable prices, year in, year out—or some change in the level, rising or falling, at a definite rate. But what prices or price level? And there is the hard, practical problem of finding ways to use monetary policy to achieve a price-level goal.

Price-Level Stability

Price-level stability would enhance confidence and certainty. Plans would no longer need to allow for a kind of doubt that inevitably adds to costs and impairs the performance of the economy. Compared with the instability of the past, a stable price level is immensely desirable. (Not everyone, however, agrees that it is the best price-level objective.) If prices were stabilized, one force making for cumulation and the magnification of change during business fluctuations would have disappeared.

The division of labor in the broadest sense can be carried out most efficiently when the value of money is stable, when this important part of the economic framework is fixed. The greatest advantages are to be expected when the longest-range decisions are involved.

Money would be more nearly neutral in the sense that changes in its purchasing power would not influence decisions on matters of great variety and significance. Such neutrality, like that of the mile or the second, or the surgeon's scalpel or any other instrument or intermediary, helps men arrange their important affairs most effectively.

Price-level stability is a concept which the public is likely to understand, which seems essentially clear and straightforward. In fact, however, both concept and measurement prove elusive.

Declining Price Level as Productivity Rises

The argument for a falling price level (rising value of money) has one major support—a downward drift of prices will reflect one of the underlying real factors of a progressive economy, rising productivity, *output* per unit of *input*. As human and mechanical resources become more productive, there are both equity and efficiency arguments for reflecting this improvement as an increase in the purchasing power of money.

The *equity* reason is that a drop in prices will make the gains in proauctivity available to everyone in the economy; everyone uses money to buy goods and services. If the price level is stable, some members of society (the millions who have retired) will not be able to share in the benefits of rising productivity because in practice they are not able to negotiate changes in their money incomes. To some extent, however, these people probably contribute to the increase in productivity; after all, at least some of an economy's progress results from broad social developments, such as public education and tax-financed research and governmental capital formation.

Who will argue seriously that the downward drift of real costs is due solely to the efforts of those directly engaged in current production? Yet it is only they who can benefit by bargaining today. Moreover, the high interdependence of the economy reduces the possibility (1) that the sources of progress productivity can be identified accurately or (2) that they are likely to lie only where bargaining power is strong. In fairness to everyone, it is argued, policy should seek to let the entire public get some of the benefit in the form of lower prices.[8]

The *efficiency* argument, in essence, runs as follows: The process of resource allocation will operate most effectively if money costs and prices reflect changes in technological conditions. *Relative* prices should change in response to changes in relative real costs. A stable price level in an economy of falling real costs is certain to mean that relative prices will not reflect new costs accurately.

Moreover, price level stability will tend to bring "windfall" gains where individual prices do not drop as productivity rises. The windfalls will induce somewhat erroneous and wasteful decisions along the lines of any inflation. Downward pressure on prices will serve the public in another way—it will tend to force businesses to step up efforts for efficiency.

Although there is merit in these arguments for a price level to drop as productivity rises, they have won few supporters. The opposing arguments are as follows:

1. Some observers believe that as a matter of justice the gains in productivity ought to go to those actively and directly engaged in bringing them about.

2. The prospect of enjoying the fruits of cost reduction provides a powerful incentive to produce them. If the general price level is stable rather than trending downward, those producers who succeed in lowering costs have a greater chance of benefiting. The pressures of competition,

[8] If throughout the whole economy output per manhour and per other unit of input, *i.e.*, if productivity were to rise about 3.0 percent a year, a price-level decline of perhaps 1.0 percent a year would provide some benefits for the general public. Still more would remain to be shared among those in a position to bargain in the market.

of course, will operate to force individual prices down as costs fall.   Nevertheless, in a regime of general price stability the business which contributes to progress by reducing inputs per unit of output will not face the added pressure of monetary forces tending to reduce the price level.

3. Declining prices, it is argued, are bad for business psychology. Optimism may droop when prices tend to fall.   Those who hold inventory suffer losses—or run the risk of such misfortune.   Business is a little less buoyant.   Firms may hold lower inventory than needed for greatest efficiency, and they may slightly delay expansion, modernization, and the purchase of more advanced equipment if they expect the price level to be lower next year than this.

Whatever the balance of the pros and cons, an institutional force assures rejection of a falling price level as a policy goal.   Strongly organized groups do not want it, certainly not for what they sell.   Labor unions press for, and employers agree to, wage rate increases which equal or exceed improvements in productivity.   And these forces have enough power to overweigh any politically feasible monetary pressures designed to translate falling *real costs* into declining prices for output of the companies involved.

Consequently, if the general price level were to fall, the less powerfully situated sellers of labor and products would have to bear the great bulk of the effects.   There is no reason to believe that these are the groups whose productivity increase is highest.   Nor is there any presumption that the relative position of those with weak bargaining strength would become any better than it is today.   And how could the public ever reach agreement on the amount of decline to seek?

Chapter 22 examines inflation, a rising price level, and rejects it as an acceptable objective.   If we rule out a falling price level as politically out of the question, one price-level goal remains.   It is a good one.   A stable price level as an objective is eminently defensible on economic grounds and probably acceptable politically.

What Price Level?

Any policy which is directed toward a price level goal requires a clear concept of the "level" which is involved.   The general concept is familiar. At times the housewife will be correct in charging that "prices are going up."   Judging the amount of change, however, baffles even the experts. At most times, many prices are changing—some are going up while others are dropping.   Often it is not indisputably clear whether the changes combine into a net rise or fall of the general level or whether the moves roughly offset each other.   Any price level objective requires both a precise, definite *concept* and a satisfactory device for *measuring* it.

The making of index numbers of prices has progressed greatly in the last generation.   (See Appendix B.)   Statistical methods have been refined, and the collection of basic source data has improved.   Nevertheless, neither of the two major indexes—the one covering wholesale prices, the other, consumer goods and services—is satisfactory as a guide for major policy.   A third, the much broader measure used for adjusting GNP figures, is more complex; despite serious drawbacks, it probably has most promise for the long run.

Today most support would probably be found for the Consumer Price Index.   With more funds to make it better—by taking more accurate account of quality changes, new products, and services, including those of government and by covering more types of consumers and consumption items—this index could inspire confidence.

The Wholesale Price Index, however, has the merit of being more sensitive and of giving earlier indication of some changes.   Unfortunately, this index assigns more weight than is appropriate for stabilization purposes to products which are traded in international markets and which as a result are not subject to large influence from domestic monetary policy.   Moreover, the WPI accords less weight to labor and services than their role in the economy warrants.

The preparation of public opinion and the building of support for a price-level objective requires that the public see the difference between stabilizing an *index* and stabilizing *particular* prices.   Freedom for individual prices to rise and fall with changes in demand and supply is essential for economic efficiency.   The policy objective would be to stabilize the average.

If we should settle upon a truly comprehensive index; if we were to insist upon prompter collection and wider sampling of data used for computation; and if we frequently modernized the bases and methods—we would have a measure deserving of confidence.   Admittedly, honest, scientific doubt about the best procedures for making price indexes will remain.   And another problem might appear—pressures from interested groups (1) to modify the index (or fail to modify it) or (2) to control one or more key items artificially for special purposes.   Such difficulties have arisen in a few countries when heavy reliance has been placed on an index, but they are not likely to be serious if the strains are moderate.[9]

---

[9] France, for example, has used a price index in regulating wage rates, especially in government and in the many governmentally-owned utilities and other enterprises. To manipulate the index, *i.e.,* to keep it from reflecting the full extent of price increases, especially in the 1950's, selected items in the index were subjected to price controls which helped prevent at least the official price quotations from rising.   Other products and services were subsidized (bread, and fares on the subway and buses in Paris) to restrain increases in the index.

It is in times of war or postwar distress and disorder—or when internal policies are markedly inflationary—that stabilization programs using price indexes encounter great pressures to manipulate the index. One partial protection against such a danger is to use a very broad index. Then manipulation of the whole by interference with a few items is likely to seem too difficult to consider seriously.

Before examining "real" objectives, we look briefly at two others.

Preserving the International Economic Position

Monetary policy might focus on maintaining some relation to foreign economies, such as the volume of trade, the balance of payments, the price of foreign exchange, or some total holding of gold (or its equivalent). Central banking as it developed in England and spread to other countries attached very high importance to such objectives. For many years such goals were not influential in U.S. monetary policy. Since 1960, however, the considerations they involve have required attention and will continue to do so.

The ability to buy and sell, to borrow and lend, abroad with a minimum of restrictions is an "asset" of incalculable value. Yet it can be eroded by monetary disturbances. Domestic monetary developments influence the relations of one currency to those of other lands. The influence of real features of international economic relations can be "upset" by monetary change. Consequently, real advantage may come to an economy from adapting its internal monetary affairs to the requirements of conditions abroad. As we saw in Part Four, however, what any one country can accomplish will depend in part upon what others do. Sometimes policies which seem best suited to domestic needs conflict with those suited to international needs.[10]

Interest Rates

Another possible objective might be a certain level—or perhaps a pattern—of interest rates or bond prices. Such a goal has little intrinsic merit or appeal (except to one or another special group). Admittedly, interest-rate control may seem to be a helpful intermediary for achieving an objective of some significance. For example, during and after the

---

[10] For the United States the problem is more complex than that facing other countries, Great Britain excepted. Should we try to preserve the position of the dollar as a "reserve" currency? Do we gain enough from the dollar's role as a currency to which others tie to justify the costs? What are the benefits? the costs? The answers are not clear. See H. G. Grubel, "The Benefits and Costs of Being the World Banker," *The National Banking Review*, December 1964, pp. 189–212.

Great Depression, key officials here and in some other countries concluded that monetary policy should be directed toward achieving a "low" level of interest rates to favor investment.

Efforts to do so produced results which demonstrated that such a relatively narrow objective, while perhaps useful in some circumstances, can become sadly inappropriate for others. Interest rates are prices. Any success in keeping some or all of them at artificial levels over any considerable period will lead to needless economic trouble. As a policy objective, interest-rate control as such can hardly be achieved in the long run. To the extent that it is, we have no assurance that the results will be more good than bad; but we do have compelling *a priori* reasons for expecting the adverse effects to be predominant.

REAL OBJECTIVES

"Real" rather than monetary objectives receive wide support—high-level employment, reduction of cyclical fluctuations, and economic growth. All are desirable. No problem arises in justifying either their importance or the desirability of such goals as personal freedom and competition as opposed to monopoly, equity in income distribution, expanding opportunity for the individual to develop his capacities, better housing, and so on. But difficult problems do arise in trying to answer such questions as: What can monetary policy do to help or hinder the realization of these objectives? What practical limitations, conflicts, or obstacles might appear?

Each of the three most prominent goals—full employment, stability, and growth—has been the subject of a large literature. Each presents problems which differ from, and yet are related to, the others. The attainment of each involves much more than wise monetary policy, as we shall see. One requirement is a definition of the goal itself.

Measurement of Unemployment

Full employment is probably the real goal with the greatest appeal. Accumulating experience, however, proves that measuring employment, or unemployment, accurately requires better methods than we now use. During the Great Depression this measurement problem was not serious; it was clear that unemployment, by any reasonable definition, vastly exceeded the amount desirable for economic adjustment. In the 1950's, however, there was dispute about how much truly significant unemployment really existed.

Controversy increased in the 1960's. A special commission of experts concluded that the methods of estimating, while essentially reliable, need improvement.[11]   Proposals need not be described here.   The present (1964) procedure rests upon a monthly Census Bureau sampling of the population; 35,000 households in 330 areas are covered.   The questioners seek to find how many people without jobs are looking for work, including some persons who are not actively searching for jobs but who report that they might do so if they had hope of success or were not sick.   (In several countries only persons listed on employment exchanges as seeking work are counted.)   Critics of the results argue that the sampling methods give inadequate weight to areas where unemployment is exceptionally high; that many persons do not report themselves as being in the labor force because they have no hope of getting work; that to show a person working only a few hours a week as employed is misleading; that many people at work are in jobs which fail to make best use of their capacities.   Official figures fail to make explicit allowance for "short time," misemployment, and for those, such as some housewives, who would prefer to enter the labor force if jobs were available.

Unfortunately, we have no reliable data on the jobs open but unfilled.   Even when business is not booming, these jobs are probably more numerous than most of us would expect.   This fact does not, however, detract from the need to face the challenge of excessive unemployment; but we should know much more about the kind and location of jobs open.

Opinions differ as to how much frictional unemployment is desirable in our economy—the inevitable time between jobs as workers seek better opportunities, idleness during slow seasons, young entrants to the labor force who are "shopping around," and so on.   Nor do we have a good definition or measure of "structural" unemployment; undoubtedly, however, some joblessness results from inability to move to other areas, from ignorance, poor health, decline of particular industries, demand for rates of pay which exceed a person's worth, lack of qualifications for the kinds of jobs that exist, discrimination, changing technology (automation), laws and union restrictions, and so on.

For practical purposes, there is considerable feeling that employment of 96 percent of the labor force—4 percent unemployment—as now measured would be reasonably satisfactory.   It would represent substantial improvement over the recent record.   In mid-1964 as the economy prospered, the employment rate for men with families was nearly 98 percent; the high unemployment was in the younger age groups.

Measurement of "full" or "capacity" utilization of plant and equipment also stumps the experts.[12]   Businessmen themselves have differing

[11] R. A. Gordon, Chairman, and others, *Measuring Employment and Unemployment*, (*Report*) *President's Committee to Appraise Employment and Unemployment Statistics* (Washington: Government Printing Office, 1962).

[12] A. Phillips, "An Appraisal of Measures of Capacity," and C. L. Schultze, "Uses of Capacity Measures for Short-Run Economic Analysis," with discussion by S. Fabricant and M. Cohen, *American Economic Review*, May 1963, pp. 275–313.

judgments about the most desirable level of operation, on the average and at peaks. What to the outsider may seem wasteful idleness of a factory, store, bank office, railroad, or entertainment facility, may provide constructive flexibility and in fact permit operations throughout the year (meeting the needs of peak periods), or over the long run, which serve the public efficiently. Nevertheless, our economy has too often had more undesired idleness of nonhuman productive capacity than is consistent with maximizing public welfare.

QUESTIONS

1. What are some of the limitations on the goals which may be attained through monetary policy?

2. How does the old saying "You can lead a horse to water but you cannot make him drink" apply to the actions of the monetary authorities on easing credit? on tightening it?

3. What dangers of "authorities" may be eliminated or reduced by "rules"? What dangers of "rules" can be avoided by relying on "authorities"? Can both be combined effectively?

4. Make a study of proposals for requiring commercial banks to hold 100 percent reserves.

5. What do we mean by "stabilizing the price level"?

6. "On the whole, the arguments for a stable price level are more convincing than those for a declining level." Discuss.

7. Could the monetary authorities effectively control the quantity of money? Why?

8. "The Federal Reserve can no longer ignore balance-of-payments problems in determining domestic monetary policy." Discuss.

9. What is the difference between a real and a monetary objective?

10. Study the problems of defining "full employment."

11. "Business decisions are speculations on future Federal Reserve policies. . . . This involves distortion." Discuss this quotation in light of the "rules vs. authorities" distinction.

12. "As productivity advances, the change may be reflected in increased wage rates or lower prices. Although there are good arguments for favoring the latter, the structure of our economy is such that we must accept the former and be content if wage rate increases do not outstrip productivity gains." Comment.

CHAPTER 22   *INFLATION*

THE PREVENTION of inflation appears in any full list of monetary policy objectives.   Does it seem to be a rather negative goal?   No more so than the prevention of disease.   In fact, inflation is a form of economic illness —one closely related to money.

NATURE OF INFLATION

Inflation, **a fall in the purchasing power of the unit of money,** seems to be about as old as the use of money and almost as general.   Through the sweep of history, in one country after another, the monetary unit has lost buying power.   Since 1939 it has struck some countries terribly and has been a harrassing problem over most of the world.   Unfortunately, it will continue to plague mankind—as a threat if not as a fact—directly and indirectly, in more ways than we may recognize.   Fortunately, however, no inexorable fate prevents man from dealing effectively with this age-old problem.

Inflation is an increase in prices on the average (the general price level (P)).[1]   Fig. 22.1 shows the record since 1913 as measured by one price index.   Not every price may rise.   Some may even fall.   For example, from 1950 to 1964 the price of vegetable oils fell by one-third, plywood by over one-tenth.   The prices that do rise will certainly not all go up in the same proportion.   Differences in the movements of a few

---

[1] More than one definition of "inflation" appears in the writings of professional economists.   Popular usage has others; for example, one or more of the forces, such as money creation, which ordinarily leads to the price-level result, or a drop in the price of the monetary unit relative to foreign currencies.   The usage here serves best for most purposes.   For a comprehensive discussion see M. Bronfenbrenner and F. D. Holzman, "Survey of Inflation Theory," *American Economic Review,* Sept. 1963, pp. 593–661; and J. W. Conard, "The Causes and Consequences of Inflation," Commission on Money and Credit, *Inflation, Growth, and Employment* (Englewood Cliffs: Prentice-Hall, 1964), pp. 1–144; includes many charts.

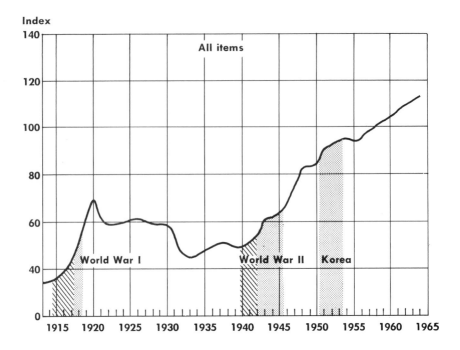

FIGURE 22.1

Consumer Price Index, 1913–64
(1957–59 = 100)

Source: *Statistical Abstract*

broad groups of prices are revealed in Fig. 22.2 for 10 years beginning well after the end of Korean hostilities. The average went up. Average of what? The best average would, of course, include everything, properly weighted. A broad and accurate index of consumer prices can serve satisfactorily, yet not perfectly.[2]

For some periods there can be no doubt that average prices have gone up even though experts will disagree on the amount. Sometimes, however, there will be doubt whether prices on the average have risen. The price index may be known to have defects, but their effects may not be clear in amount or even in direction. Suppression, concealment, improvement or deterioration of quality, introduction of new products and services, and the disguising of price changes can blur the picture.

Inflation is a matter of many degrees; the term is applied to changes

[2] As shown in Appendix B, our Consumer Price Index does not meet all of the requirements of an adequate index.

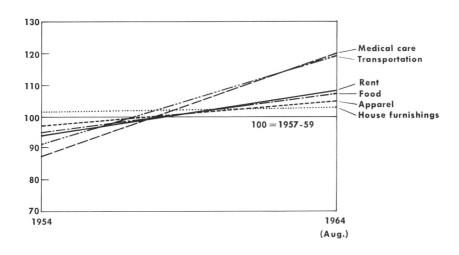

FIGURE 22.2

Consumer Prices, Changes in Selected Groups of Items, 1954–64
(1957–59 = 100)

with a range as great as that between the speed of the snail and the flight of a jet. Using the same term, "inflation," for all degrees of price-level increases can be misleading, for the differences are sometimes greater than the common features. Some inflations have been astronomical—the German inflation after World War I (average prices rose by about 400 billion times) and the Hungarian, Chinese, and Greek inflations after World War II. The currency loses all purchasing power except in tens of billions. Other inflations overwhelm society, profoundly disrupting economic life, but without making the money worthless. The Italian lira and the French franc after World War II fell to one-fiftieth or so of their 1939 value; but despite costly disorganization, economic life adjusted. Brazil and Chile have had vastly worse experiences.

Then there are inflations like those since 1940 in Britain, the United States, Canada, Scandinavia, and other areas; on the average, prices doubled, tripled, or even quadrupled. Or we may compare the 25 percent increase in this country from 1945 to 1948 with the 9 percent increase from 1955 to 1958—two inflations but hardly of the same sort. Table 22.1 shows for a score of countries how the purchasing power of the unit of money (the reciprocal of consumer prices) has changed in a decade free of major war.

TABLE 22.1

Changes in the Purchasing Power of Money, Selected Countries, 1953 to 1963 [a]

Country	Purchasing Power in 1963 (1953 = 100)	Annual Rate of Loss of Purchasing Power (compounded)
Venezuela	92	0.9
United States	88	1.3
Canada, Belgium	87	1.4
Switzerland	84	1.8
Germany	82	2.0
India, Ireland, Austria	78	2.4
United Kingdom, Netherlands	77	2.6
Italy, Norway	75	2.9
Japan	72	3.2
France	66	4.0
Mexico	59	5.0
Israel, Spain	55	5.7
Argentina	9	21.1
Brazil	6	24.4
Chile	5	26.3

[a] Based on official cost-of-living or consumer price indexes. Accuracy undoubtedly varies through a considerable range.

Source: First National City Bank.

We shall think more clearly if we do not use the same word for all these varied types of price-level change. "Hyperinflation" is a good term for the most extreme type. For less serious cases, however, there is no generally accepted vocabulary for distinguishing degrees of severity. Modifiers such as "rapid," "huge," "slow," "mild," and "creeping" must serve.

Another problem of terminology arises. Is inflation a process or a result? Usage is not clear, but we shall generally use the term for the process of change, or the rise. Before proceeding, two warnings are in order. Any discussion of the effects, bad or good, of inflation inevitably suffers from the fact that inflation is a phenomenon of widely differing degrees. Moreover, results depend upon human reactions which in turn depend upon a host of varied factors.

INFLATION'S ILL EFFECTS

In one land after another, in one generation after another, experience has taught this: *Inflation is evil*—not perhaps 1 percent in 5 years but certainly 5 percent in 1 year. Why? The record gives some clear answers. Other reasons are less obvious. The seriousness of the effects depends, of course, upon the magnitude. In this country the *big* inflations took place long ago—during the Revolution and in the South during the Civil War. World War I brought short but sharp inflation, now largely forgotten. More Americans remember the doubling of the price level during and after World War II, but this memory grows vaguer.

Human Hardship and Injustice

Inflation brings injustice to human beings, sometimes harsh injustice. People whose wealth consists of claims on money—pensions, life insurance, savings accounts, bonds—find that what they can get for their money diminishes. The dollar that was worth 5 quarts of milk when it was saved will buy only 3 or 2—or less than a cupful. Inflation expropriates wealth. It takes buying power without giving in return, and without regard to the "ability" or the need of the persons who lose. It destroys personal wealth, unequally and inequitably.

Especially pitiful are the cases of people who had saved to support themselves when they could no longer work—in retirement or when illness strikes. Human misery follows—aged widows with pensions which will buy only a fraction as much as the dollars they gave up during the lifetime of economizing. Accompanying the expropriation is a psychological factor which aggravates the sense of hurt. Some people—debtors—benefit from being able to use cheaper dollars to meet their obligations. The profits of some businesses rise not because of good service to the public but because of price changes; some workers find it possible to get wage increases which more than match the price rises; and some property values go up more than the average of prices. The observation of such good fortune adds to the bitterness of those who suffer.

Only a little less distressing than the fate of those whose savings lose much of their value are the nagging troubles of people whose incomes chronically lag behind the price rise—clergymen, some landlords, college teachers, local government employees, persons with fixed-income investments. In contrast, during and shortly after World War II, while our price level was almost doubling, the average incomes of farmers tripled; doctors did almost as well; miners and domestic servants gained by about one-and-a-half times; the earnings of bank and insurance company and Federal government employees just about kept pace with price rises.

Supply and demand in different occupations cannot adjust quickly enough to keep relative rates of pay in healthy balance. Neither justice nor economic efficiency will be served by the changes in earnings which accompany inflation. Many obstacles to mobility keep workers in jobs where pay lags; those who cannot retrain themselves are trapped. People who work as much and as well as ever suffer, not only in relation to others but even in absolute terms, as the purchasing power of their pay checks falls.

Holders of dollars lose. Most dollars are owned by businesses. Those with relatively large holdings—frequently those using a high proportion of labor—suffer the most but perhaps without realizing the fact.

Relative Price Changes and Resource Allocation

Many, though not all, prices change as the price level rises. Some prices respond more quickly, and to a greater degree, than others. Price *relationships change*. No one can be absolutely certain that the stable-price-level price relations lead to better resource allocation than when the price level rises. Yet there is powerful reason to believe that the disturbance of *price relations* due to inflation will result in less efficient allocation of productive capacity.

Inefficiency in Business

Less dramatic results are economically and socially corroding. Because each inflation has had unique features, economists have uncertain bases for generalizing about what would happen during future inflations.

Changes in the value of money make the efficient conduct of business harder. Rational calculation gets more difficult with any loss in the reliability of the unit for measuring and regulating financial relationships. Speculation is encouraged. Accountancy, our tool for systematic record keeping, and an indispensable aid to the analysis of alternatives, loses some of its usefulness if the unit on which it is based—the dollar, franc, or mark —itself changes.

Businesses encounter a new source of risk. Judgment of alternatives which involve the future must become less accurate as the measure for calculation, money, loses reliability. Because the truth is obscured or distorted by the changing value of the dollar, firms will not undertake some ventures which would benefit the community. They go ahead with others which seem wise in dollar terms but whose underlying justification does not warrant such a use of resources. Today's best judgment will often be made wrong by the changes which inflation itself produces. To escape higher costs, companies which expect inflation may build productive capacity before it is needed; such premature development leads to idleness and prevents the adoption later of improved techniques.

Some firms, gainers from the chance to sell at prices which move up more rapidly than apparent costs, overestimate their true profit. Managers overstate the chances that this profit will continue. Consequently, they overextend themselves, expand beyond the demands of the market, and make other wasteful decisions. In this way inflation adds to the opportunities people have to make mistakes.

Inflation which is associated with high demand for labor has had a tendency to induce some decline in human effort. Assured jobs and rising money income for much of the working force can lead to relaxation in the determination to work as well as possible. Careless, slovenly work will be more common when employer discipline loses the support of workers' fear of unemployment.[3] What may seem only a small decline in average human effort—say 2–4 percent—subjects the economy to a large loss.

When inflations go to extreme lengths, in amount or in duration, another loss becomes increasingly costly though often recognized. People use time and effort to overcome the consequences of inflation instead of trying to produce efficiently. Human resources are diverted from creative activity.[4] Inflation drives a wedge between private and social interest; the individual can serve himself without benefiting the public. Large inflation weakens normal market incentives for specialization and for making efficient use of time and skill.

Disruption and wasteful use of resources will also result because the individual can expect to benefit from circumventing the price increase, either by beating it (getting ahead) or by using it (holding things for a further price rise). Inflation at a rapid rate increases the effort devoted to kinds of speculation which serve no social benefit and more probably harm the economy. The individual or business, for example, finds the hoarding of goods attractive. Yet more than normal spoilage, expense, and obsolescence may result. The hoarding may deprive business pipelines of needed raw materials and thereby both slow down production and make it more expensive. Some people who get large increases in income spend wastefully.

Impairment of Capital and Discouragement of Saving

In the long run (and the period envisioned is less than even a decade), inflation is likely to reduce the country's capacity to produce by

[3] Inflation does not necessarily stimulate employment over the long run. In short periods, however, inflation and strong demand for labor are likely to go together. Inflation can bring deterioration in the quality of work through another channel, the resentment some people feel at being left behind in the race of income and prices. Government employees may sometimes react in this way. Where civil service laws make jobs highly secure, there is considerable leeway for slackening of effort.

[4] The skilled laborer, seeking some potatoes, may trudge to the country looking for a chance to do some work for a farmer or to trade a pair of shoes. The mechanism of distribution has broken down. The normal arrangements for exchanging the fruits of skilled labor for food do not then function well.

eating away the community's capital. The process of capital erosion may be indirect and, unfortunately, far from obvious. Typical business financial records will value plant and equipment at original, not today's higher replacement, cost. Consequently, in deciding on the depreciation element of expense to use in decisions on output and selling prices, businesses will use amounts which are too small to pay for replacing the productive capacity at inflated prices. In effect, then, the consuming public does not pay adequately for the capital it uses up in getting goods and services.[5] Where buildings and longlived equipment are involved, the gradual consumption of capital may be concealed for many years. Illusory inventory profits only complicate the problems.

Eventually, experience must alert businessmen and their accountants to this problem. "Once fooled, ever wise." Cannot managers learn to prevent the loss of capital by computing cost on a replacement basis? Difficulties exceed the merely difficult. Who can know future replacement costs? Differing judgments may lead to short-run competitive pressures that work against adequate allowance for inflation. When prices are regulated by governments (such as public utility rates, rents, and other prices if price control prevails), authorities may refuse to recognize costs based on replacement. Long-term contracts, such as leases, may also prevent prices from reflecting the rise in the expense of replacement. Thus even when businessmen recognize the problem, prices may not rise enough to maintain the capital needed to continue the supply over the long run.

Moreover, income tax laws generally ignore the rise in replacement cost. The costs used in computing taxable earnings rest on past rather than replacement prices; "earnings," then, are overstated. Since tax rates have become very high, tax collectors will take so much of "earnings" (including capital which, because of inflation, appears in the accounts as earnings) that businessmen may find themselves unable to finance the replacement that they know is wise.[6]

Inflation may endanger the capital supply in another way—by discouraging savings and perhaps even by stimulating families to consume their capital. Expectation of a decline in the purchasing power of money will reduce the attractiveness of new saving relative to consumption. Moreover, owners of bonds or savings accounts who expect more inflation can expect to benefit by liquidating such assets and buying goods. The

---

[5] Prices, in other words, fail to induce desirable economy in consumption. That is, they understate the scarcity of goods and services relative to the costs of maintaining the sources of supply.

[6] If inflation were large or prolonged, this distortion would become too great to be ignored. Depreciation allowances would probably be altered, as has happened in some countries, to recognize higher replacement expenses. But much damage could be done before adequate correction. Moderate inflation has rarely induced governments to allow sufficient remedy.

real value of dollars held by businesses declines. Stockholders may press for larger dividends, reducing retained earnings.

There is danger, however, in generalizing about the influence of inflation on new saving and on the preservation of property acquired in the past. Some saving will be made even though the saver cannot expect to get back as much purchasing power as he gives up. Who does not want to command some resources in the future—for example, after retirement? Some people may even try to save more if they expect prices to rise. In the short run some saving is more or less compulsory—payments into pension funds and mortgage reduction—and not closely related to changes in the value of money.

Windfalls and some unusually good profits provide funds which may be easily saved. Although inflation does strike at the attractiveness of holding claims to a fixed number of dollars—savings accounts and bonds—equities present a different prospect. The ownership of property whose value is expected to rise as much as the price level is as attractive as ever. And there will be greater incentive to acquire property which, because of inflation, seems likely to rise more than prices generally. Inflation may conceivably induce some people to save more if they can expect to get assets which may enable them to profit from inflation. But are such assets available? Real estate and common stock come to mind. But who will sell? On what terms? In general, no substantial quantity of investment assets seems likely to rise in price more than the expected increase in the price level. The kinds of assets built, and investment in general, will reflect forecasts about changes in the prospective purchasing power of money.

Discouragement of Use of Debt Contracts

Inflation adds to uncertainty, and uncertainty is a cost. It is a cost which the saver will not freely bear except for compensation of some kind. To the extent that people can acquire only assets which give a fixed claim in dollars—assets which offer no compensation for the risk of inflation—new saving will tend to be lower than under price stability, unless interest rates rise "enough." Will they? Some such adjustment will tend to occur. But what if monetary authorities are trying to restrain interest-rate increases to forestall discouragement of investment?

Markets, unfortunately, cannot work perfectly in adjusting interest rates when the amount of future price-level increases is unknown. When the amount—if any—of future inflation is not certain, borrowers are properly reluctant to contract to pay interest rates which can be justified only by a specific amount of inflation. If the long-term equilibrium interest rate were 5 percent, possible lenders expecting inflation of 2 percent a year would need to find borrowers willing to agree to pay 7 percent over a long period. Would the productivity of the project warrant such a commitment? Uncertainty about two things—the amount of inflation to actually develop and the prospects of a particular venture—will affect decisions. The result of such compounded uncertainty resulting from the prospect of inflation will reduce the supply of funds for *lending* more than it reduces the supply of saving. Interest rates, especially for the long run, will rise. Yet doubts about the future course of prices must persist. Some people may think the higher interest rate excessive and curtail borrowing and investment plans. Others will think it too low and offer fewer dollars for lending.

For the supplier of funds, inflation makes debt contracts unattractive. The savings account, bond, life insurance contract, mortgage loan, and other such fixed-dollar claims become less inviting. The saving which such contracts have facilitated will be discouraged. Men will devise various substitutes, one form or another of equity purchase, but imperfectly and incompletely. Decades might be required to devise new contract forms to match the merits of long-term debt.

Uncertainty about Relative Attractiveness of Future Jobs

The possibility of inflation on a large scale complicates an inevitably difficult task—the choice of occupation. Who can tell how much possible future changes in the price level may alter the relative attractions of different jobs? Young people face more uncertainties about the future when the price level has been changing. Experience loses some of its reliability as a guide if part of the results in the past came from price-level changes, or if there is doubt about the course of future prices.

Difficulties in International Economic Relations

An inflationary economy will get out of adjustment with other lands. If domestic prices go up more rapidly than do those abroad, the country's exports will be priced out of some foreign markets. Meanwhile, rising money incomes within the country will lead to domestic consumption of some goods that would otherwise be exported and will also raise the demand for imports. Falling exports and rising imports will create balance-of-payment problems. (See Chapters 18 and 20.) Another result is probable—the imposition of import restrictions and barriers which obstruct trade and investment and which depress real income (at home and abroad) because they reduce competition and in various ways create inefficiency in resource allocation. The losses can be costly even though largely unseen.

Restrictive Measures to Prevent Inflation as a Source of Economic Distortion

As the public experiences inflation and grows increasingly annoyed at one or another of its results, voters will probably support direct government restrictions to deal with this or that problem. Perhaps rents will be controlled, or public utility rates kept from rising, or subsidies given to one or another industry, or spending on new capital formation put under government license, or collective bargaining made subject to governmental control, or prices and wages generally restricted, or monetary ease used to try to keep interest rates from rising, or imports regulated to help prevent deterioration in the balance of payments. In the short run, no one of these policies is likely to do much good, though perhaps not much harm.

Over any substantial period, however, direct controls can seriously damage an economy. Some of the bad effects will be concealed and utterly beyond measure. The public can have no way to learn what would have developed under freer conditions. Yet the chances of wasteful distortions of production and of consumption, under direct controls, are decidedly greater than the chances of improved productivity. The allocation of resources will be poorer than if buyers and sellers were free to try to make their desires effective. The price mechanism can no longer operate with full effectiveness.

Relative prices give misleading guidance to producers and consumers. In time, seriously wasteful distortions can get encrusted or embedded in the economy. Year after year they depress real national income. One restriction breeds more. Extensive government control of life may grow out of regulations adopted piecemeal and designed to offset the forces of inflation. Few people may like many of the controls; the majority of the public may dislike the total mass of restrictions. Yet to restore freedom seems dangerously risky because of the shocks that would be involved.

The controls may in fact do little to restrain inflation. They may merely direct, and concentrate, the forces into channels different from those the public would freely prefer. As long as the underlying forces creating inflation exist, direct controls can in the long run do little to restrain it. Unfortunately, the restrictions can do much to make the economy less efficient.

Social Dissension

Small inflations and those quickly ended may do little damage to the social structure, but either large or prolonged price-level increases can work tragic distress. They create a source of discontent and dissension. Inequality in sharing the burdens and reaping the gains of inflation becomes evident; the groups suffering come to oppose the others. Demagogues find opportunity to seek power by stirring up trouble, encouraging community cleavage.

The social cohesion which we usually take for granted, and which is essential for a good (even a tolerable) society, disintegrates. Rancor, bitterness, and loss of scruple are likely. Self-pity and animosity cut the value of human life. More than a small part of the public tries to evade regulations. Respect for law drops. Corruption grows. Where inflations are large, crime increases. The reasons include not only the disintegration of traditional mores and the efforts to profit by evading regulations but also in some cases the sheer necessity of illegal action to survive.

Aftermath

Inflation is not necessarily self-perpetuating, though stopping it proves difficult, especially if it has begun to snowball. When the price rise finally stops, the effects of inflation do not end. The aftermath, too, has problems to be charged against inflation. The "correction" of maladjustments requires the shifting of resources; bankruptcy and unemployment above "normal" are inevitable. Restrictive policies may lead to serious strains, disruptions, and unemployment.[7] In addition to the essential minimum of adjustment, further disruption may develop as processes of cumulative business contraction are established.

ARGUMENTS FOR INFLATION

Good effects are sometimes claimed for inflation. The arguments have enough plausibility to help explain why inflationary policies receive support, or why in some countries the opposition is weak.

Inflation has been endorsed by some revolutionaries as a method of expropriating the property of the middle and upper income groups—a form of bloodless revolution. (This argument would perhaps have little applicability where, as in the United States today, middle and lower income groups are large owners of debt instruments, and upper income groups are owners of equities.) Beyond question, inflation can destroy

---

[7] As the Italian economy boomed for many years, forces making for price-level increases gained momentum. In 1963, after consumer prices had gone up almost 15 percent in 2 years and wage rates by nearly 15 percent in less than 15 months, the need for restraint could not be denied. The sources of easy money were restricted in the summer of 1963; in the last half of the year, bank credit rose "only" 11 percent compared with 16 percent the year before. Then tighter measures were applied. Business received a shock. Considerable unemployment resulted. See Bank for International Settlement, *Annual Report . . . 1964* (Basle: The Bank, 1964), *passim.*

important elements of a society, shifting wealth, power, and income.[8] When the Communists took over Hungary after World War II, for example, inflation seems to have been stimulated deliberately to expropriate the propertied groups.

Less extreme, but sometimes cited even in this country in justification of inflation as a tool for expropriation, is this argument: Some inflation may do good by cutting the burden of debt, such as that of government. The less each dollar is worth, the smaller the sacrifice needed to pay a specified number of dollars of interest and principal. Nice for debtors![9] The creditors, of course, suffer a loss equal to the gain of others.

In a serious emergency another argument is more defensible. Moderate inflation may help transfer productive resources in ways that are desirable. When an economy comes up against a severe strain, such as war, it needs a big shift of productive capacity, and quickly. Changes in relative prices within a given price level, which is our peacetime mechanism for shifting resources, plus such emergency direct controls as allocations of key materials and labor and rationing, may not transfer enough resources in the short run. A rise in some prices and wage rates will speed the shift of productive capacity. To attempt the same result by reducing prices and wage rates in industries producing "civilian" goods is, at best, slow. Boosting prices and wages in military industries, however, may be easy.

Moreover, even a general price increase, including consumer goods, may help the war effort; those whose incomes do not rise proportionately will be under pressure to reduce consumption and thus free resources for more urgent needs. True, inflation is not essential for cutting consumption and thereby making capacity available for military production; taxes might also do the job.

Some economists see possible advantage in more or less persistent but *mild* inflation. A small (perhaps 1 or 1½ percent) rise in the price level from year to year may stimulate business, give it useful buoyancy—useful to society. Profits, it is argued, will tend to be higher than otherwise.[10] Good profits improve the outlook of businessmen and encourage economic

---

[8] There would be no immediate change in fixed plant and equipment or in housing, and perhaps little reduction in goods in process. For a time, the productive organization in a physical sense could survive almost unscathed if raw materials and goods in the production pipeline were not depleted.

[9] Serious use of this argument has come from not a few persons concerned with the burdens of war debt. Men who would not openly endorse government repudiation of its debt have nevertheless supported inflationary policies to cut the burden of war debt.

[10] Businesses always hold some inventory. Mild inflation from year to year will tend to enable business to sell each batch of output at a price level slightly higher than the level at which it incurred the costs for those goods. Moreover, an upward price trend makes it easier to put into effect price increases which are planned for any reason, and to make them sooner. For reasons noted earlier, other forces have adverse effects on real profit, especially over the long run.

expansion. Profit growth in itself can provide a form of forced saving, *i.e.,* the rise in prices which adds to profits may force the public to consume less. If tax rates are not exorbitant, such profits make more funds available, as well as add incentive, for economic expansion.

Fig. 22.3 illustrates another aspect of the problem. As total demand in the economy approaches the full-employment level of output, more and

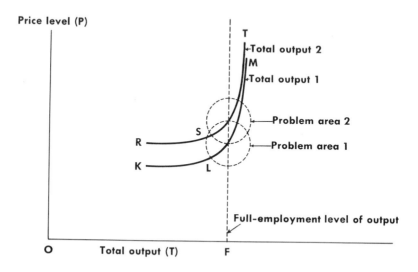

As output rises from *K* to *L*, prices rise only a little. Expansion beyond *L*, however, leads to marked increases in the average level of prices and wages even before the economy reaches full employment. Though output can exceed *OF*, the excess results from "overfull" use of productive capacity.

At the higher level of prices, more dollars are needed to buy the full-employment—or any total—output. Some of the higher prices and wages are inflexible downward. Therefore, if demand drops, the amount of output (employment) will be measured, not on KLM but on RST, the curve which reflects the higher wages and prices.

FIGURE 22.3

Relation of Total Output (Employment) to the Level of Prices

more of the increase in buying is reflected in rising prices rather than in increased employment. In such a situation, the demand which will produce full employment is a demand which tends to raise prices. Not a few economists believe that the inflation is better than the unemployment. The choice involved is one of the most difficult of modern economic policy. If the choice were required only once, most of us would "trade off" some inflation for the higher real income due to fuller employment. But the same choice may have to be made again. When the higher price level and full employment have been reached, the new equilibrium will not necessarily continue. The forces which created the original distress may still operate. Will they not shift conditions—and the curves—so that full employment can be reached only at a still higher level of prices?

Whatever the merits of the arguments that a little inflation helps business, and that some inflation is a low price to pay to get full employment, the arguments provide no "justification" for inflation if one cannot safely assume that inflation will be limited to regular, and certainly small, amounts. And there is an even more crucial requirement: *the public must not expect what is coming.* If businessmen, unions, persons with savings, and consumers know about the "little inflation" ahead, they will take the price increase into their calculation. In doing so, they will deprive the future inflation of expected stimulating effects.

Such inflation will give little or no *long-run* boost to the economy. Interest rates, prices, wage rates, and supplies of factors will adjust to allow for the price rise which seems certain. Nevertheless, because certainty is impossible, under- or over-compensation for price trends will give rise to economic wastes and distortions, as discussed earlier. And there is the probability that once the "little" proves ineffective, a bigger dosage will seem desirable.

Some economists, although not endorsing a policy of moderate inflation, still favor a slight inflationary bias. They believe that it will encourage growth. A policy seeking price stability is likely to have some restrictive elements, producing at times avoidable unemployment. Moreover, the monetary authorities trying for price stability, it is widely recognized, sometimes make errors which lead to general economic contraction, or depress the rate of growth below the reasonable potential, some loss of employment. A bias which involves a little inflation, the argument runs, will offer protection against a greater evil. May not a downturn produced by anti-inflationary action cumulate into something serious? Better, perhaps, to act always to avoid deflation, recognizing that some mistakes—on the inflationary side—are probable. At most, however, the argument will justify only a small amount of inflation over a decade. And adoption of a policy of a little inflation invites more because the rise in prices and costs makes more dollars necessary to "buy" full-employment output.

The arguments against inflation greatly outweigh those in favor. Let us be clear, however. "Inflation" means different things. A price level rise of 2 percent is a different thing from one of 20 or 200 percent. We should not react to the small rise as if it were a big one. The inflations which have caused so much misery were big inflations. But the start was always small. It is wise to set the avoidance of inflation, any inflation, as a major goal. Willing acceptance of a "little" inflation can weaken the defenses against more rapid inflation, and then something more serious.

CAUSES OF INFLATION

The following discussion of the causes of inflation, for the most part, summarizes earlier material. A review of the writings of recent years would suggest that disagreement is wide, even among professional economists. In fact, however, agreement is great and significant.

The Pull of Demand

One price, or many, can rise only when buyers are both able and willing to pay more.[11] In general, the level of prices will not increase unless the public makes larger money payments—MV.[12] Buyers may step up spending because they have more money, or because they decide to use the same quantity more energetically (rapidly). Significance lies in both the *quantity of money* and the *behavior* of the public in using it.

The problem, however, is deeper. *Why* do the quantity of money and velocity—why do consumption, investment, and government buying—change? The concern is with the whole economy, not with merely a small number of individual units. What causes the causes of inflation?

What "causes" the consuming public to have more money? Some is borrowed from banks or such other lenders as consumer finance agencies (which in turn may get the money by borrowing from banks). Typically, however, more of the increase in consumer spending power is a result of an increase in income. Most income of most people comes from employers. Where, then, can employers as a group get more money to pay more in wages? They ordinarily do so by (1) borrowing from banks or (2) selling to someone else, perhaps the government, who in turn borrows. Additional money can also come from printing presses (new currency has been highly important in some inflations) and from abroad (buoyant demand for exports has added to inflationary pressures in several lands at various times since World War II).

Why will businesses and individuals borrow to spend? The probable benefits seem greater than the costs. The better that business prospects

---

[11] A business with something to sell may raise its asking price, but we are not realistic in saying that this is "the price" unless some buyer actually pays it.

[12] If the volume of goods and services declines, the price level may rise even though money payments do not expand. If the quantity of goods and services rises, prices may remain stable despite higher spending.

seem, the greater the reason for business borrowing. One cause of a cause of inflation, therefore, is a favorable business outlook. Whatever creates a belief among businessmen that the volume of profitable transactions is going to rise, also creates a likelihood that businesses will try to borrow and spend more. Businesses also find a *need* to borrow more when prices rise. More dollars are required to conduct the same physical volume of business. Thus a price rise itself provides a cause for more borrowing.

Governments borrow or issue new currency when their spending, notably for war but for other reasons as well, exceeds revenue.[13] They borrow from banks, directly or indirectly, primarily because this method is cheaper than borrowing from other lenders. (See Chapters 24 and 25.)

Banks will be *able* to increase their lending only if they have the necessary reserves. They will be *willing* to do so only if they are able to get from borrowers such interest rates, security, and other terms as seem satisfactory.

The Keynesian approach directs attention to changes in the way that people try to use an existing income. If the public tries to save less while consuming and investing the same as before, the expansion in income may take the form of a price level increase. The forces influencing the desires to save and to invest affect buying and in this way underlie price-level changes.

What about production? Cannot output grow with spending to offset price-raising tendencies? That depends. When idle productive capacity is more than nominal, a rise in spending can lead to an increase in output, perhaps without much change in unit cost. If so, no appreciable price-level change will result. When the economy is running with essentially no idle capacity, however—or when bottlenecks choke off expansion while other capacity has obvious potentiality for greater use—the possible growth of output is small. The appearance of more purchasing power will not be matched by an increase in new goods. Consequently, whoever is getting more money and trying to spend it will add his demand to that of others for about the former volume of output—and thereby tend to raise prices.

Cost Push: Sellers' Inflation

Since World War II we have seen much blame placed on those pressures which raise costs—the *cost push,* "sellers' inflation," or perhaps "institutionalized inflation."

---

[13] The inflations of Latin America have been due to domestic developments largely unrelated to war, though in part resulting from expenditures on military forces.

As commonly stated, the arguments have little merit. They can, however, help us understand the process of inflation. Assume that a firm's profits have been about normal but that its cost of production per unit rises, perhaps because of an increase in wage rates. Then the goods or services that it offers will be supplied (on a sustained basis, *i.e.,* over the long run) only at prices which cover the new and higher costs. What is true for one firm will be true for most. If unit costs rise, so must prices over the long run. But what makes wage rates or other costs rise? Why do sellers insist upon higher prices?

For business as a whole, of course, much the largest element of cost is the payment for labor. If money wage rates (plus fringes) increase more than labor productivity, an important element of cost rises.[15] Employers have compelling reason to try to get more for their output. They will raise their asking prices, reconciling themselves to the probability of some drop in the number of units sold. If wage rates go up throughout a large part of the economy, the upward pressures on prices will exist in so many places that the general price level must be affected.

But what makes wage rates rise? One immediately thinks of unions demanding more, powerful unions which can force industries to shut down unless wage rates are increased. Who will deny that union pressure to push up wages can produce results? Yet employers must think that they can afford to pay more. If managers believed that the consuming public would not be able and willing to pay higher prices, businesses would in general put up vigorous opposition to union demands and risk strikes rather than grant increases in the major element of cost. Union attitudes will be influenced by employer resistance based on effective buyer resistance to higher prices.

Will wage rates rise only when the public has spending power to pay, when demand exists to absorb the push? To answer, we must distinguish individual cases from the whole economy. At any time some unions can get their wage rates up even if consumer buying power is dropping. Yet if many unions succeed in raising wage rates when total purchasing is stable, unemployment must result. (Workers getting more per hour may have more money to spend; but, of course, whoever pays them, has fewer dollars.) The dollars that consumers spend will buy fewer man-hours when the price of a man-hour rises. The existence of unemployment, however, will tend to reduce wage rates in the freer parts of the market, certainly to keep them from rising. (Most of the labor force is not in

---

[15] The crucial factor is the change in wage rates in relation to output per man-hour worked, labor productivity after allowing for costs of new machinery and other expenses which contribute to improved performance. To simplify, however, we shall generally refrain from referring to productivity each time such reference would be appropriate.

unions.) The total wage bill cannot increase unless there is money to pay it.

Costs are not likely to *push* up prices *in general* unless there is demand *pulling* them up as well.[16] But will cost rises themselves add to the stock of money or to velocity? They may. Authorities can control M, though they may have more difficulty doing so if particular prices are being pushed up. Suppose, for example, that construction unions and builders force up the costs of new housing.[17] Rather than permit extensive unemployment and a slowdown in building, the monetary authorities may permit an easing in the financing of construction that leads to an increase in M.

Conceivably, there will be conditions in which velocity will rise because of pressures from the cost side. Beyond question, V did rise during the postwar period when costs were rising. But the connection between costs and velocity is difficult to prove or disprove.

The possible effect of "cost push" must depend significantly upon the strength of "demand pull." If demand is strong and highly inelastic, higher costs are readily passed into price. Sometimes there is such a demand, notably that of governments for armaments, especially during war. And a national government, unlike the ordinary buyer, may have little to worry about in paying higher prices. It can resort to the banking system. When it does so, it injects new money into the economy, adding more "demand pull" and accentuating the whole process. On occasion there are other buyers whose demands are also inelastic and can be financed by an increase in M or a rise in V. When sellers (and the unions involved) know of inelastic demands, the chances of wage-price increases in the sectors of the economy affected may be substantial.

Is there a wage-price spiral?—something like this: Higher wage rates mean higher costs and cause prices to rise; the higher cost of living then leads to employee demand for higher wage rates; these are eventually granted, sending prices up again, then wages, etc. This sort of process seems to have operated for a quarter of a century—in not a few lands—

[16] The prices of imports may go up because of forces in world markets. Heavy demand from abroad may also act to raise the domestic price level. Thus inflation may be "imported" as forces outside the country raise costs, prices, and demand. The Netherlands, for whom imports are highly important, experienced a rise in prices of imports of more than 20 percent in 15 months to early 1964. This increase helped break down a policy of wage restraint. Wage rates shot upward by almost 15 percent within a few months. The United States will be affected differently by price-level developments abroad than will countries more heavily dependent on imported raw materials.

[17] One index of costs of residential construction shows a rise of about 15 percent from 1957 to 1964, a period in which unemployment was generally much above minimal and in which the index of wholesale prices of construction materials rose by less than 3 percent.

with only intermittent lapses. Some causal relation between wage and price increases is obvious.

As ordinarily expressed, however, the argument is incomplete. Someone must pay the higher wages and prices—with money. So we must ask: Do increases in wage rates, or other costs, lead to more M or higher V (or some combination)? Possibly. Higher wages, or any other cost-increasing factor (including perhaps even some taxes), may conceivably stimulate growth in the money supply. For example, the employer may borrow more from banks to meet a larger wage bill or other cost increase. Consequently, if monetary expansion is easy, cost increases may be inflationary—not really because of the obvious or surface connection between costs and prices but because of the indirect effect through growth in the money stock. The spiral will stop quickly if monetary conditions are not favorable.

Cost increases give sellers an impetus to be aggressive in taking advantage of opportunities created by growth of money demand to charge more. Some firms are not always getting the highest prices consistent with maximizing profit; a cost increase may stimulate them to push upward more energetically. Although such reactions may raise some specific prices, the effects on the whole price level are less clear. Consumers will presumably spend less on other things, the prices of which will then tend to fall.

Around three million workers are covered by escalator clauses; these provide that wage rates will go up if the cost of living, as measured by some index, rises. If inflation starts, therefore, more wage increases and price rises seem inevitable—at least if monetary expansion somehow permits. (Government willingness to "go along" in paying higher prices on its purchases will make quite a difference when, as during a period of high military spending, it is a big buyer.) [18]

Another factor sometimes cited is the widespread business practice of "mark-up" pricing; if the standard mark-up is 40 percent, an increase in the cost of an item from $1.00 to $1.10 will increase the mark-up from 40 cents to 44 cents. To assign much inflation-creating power to this practice is shortsighted. Are buyers both able and willing to pay the 4 (plus 10) cents more? How can we account for such ability and willingness if they do exist? A still more puzzling challenge is to find why the business waited for the cost increase to take advantage of the opportunity for higher profit, 4 cents a unit. The argument that mark-up prac-

---

[18] Escalator clauses may also help slow price level increases. If workers know that the purchasing power of their wages will be sustained, the union may be less aggressive in demanding wage increases to protect its position. It need not press to get ahead of the others (temporarily) to keep from getting behind over a longer period.

tices help create inflation may have some validity, but probably not much. Some prices will go up a little faster.

Farm Price Supports and Other Factors

Supports for some farm product prices are tied closely to Federal government finance and thereby with possibilities of money creation. If an inflation gets started and raises the costs of things that farmers buy, without correspondingly increasing the prices of designated farm products, the Federal government is committed to guarantee bank loans to farmers, with stored crops as collateral. The government in some cases buys and stores farm products. It restricts production. The quantity of farm output offered for sale in the market is reduced, and new money may be injected into the economy to pay the cost. The rise in agricultural prices will increase the cost of living for consumers a little; this rise will add to pressures for higher wage rates and reduce (nonfarm) saving. The forces of the inflationary spiral are strengthened a bit. Can they be sustained? They can if the money supply (or velocity) rises adequately.

Many prices are "administered" by the seller. He has more choice than the seller in a purely competitive market. Some economists believe that the power to "administer" price has been used to put prices above the levels that would otherwise prevail—and to raise them more rapidly. Steel prices in the 1950's are cited as an example. The evidence, however, is incomplete and conflicting, but the effects on the price level as a whole have probably been small.[19]

Another development deserves notice. Congress seems to have agreed implicitly to raise Social Security retirement benefits more or less in phase with increases in consumer prices—at approximately two-year intervals. Payroll taxes have also been increased. The net effect of these changes has been slight in terms of current flows of dollars.

However, the conditions just discussed can have another, indirect effect. Some groups (other than debtors) now seem to be moderately well insulated from the immediate evils of inflation. Why, then, should they cooperate in opposing it? Perhaps even more inflation would suit them. A union with an escalator clause might be acting in its own interest in opposing inflation control; measures to prevent a rise in the price level might bring its members some unemployment, while price increases seem unlikely to damage members' real income.

[19] H. W. Briefs, *Pricing Power and "Administrative" Inflation* (Washington: American Enterprise Institute, 1962); J. W. Markham, "Administered Prices and the Recent Inflation," Commission on Money and Credit, *Inflation, Growth, and Employment* (Englewood Cliffs: Prentice-Hall, 1964), pp. 145–75.

Why should those farmers protected by government policies give support to anti-inflationary measures? Some businesses, too, profit from inflation. Many more find, or hope to find, prospects better under the conditions which favor some inflation. Even the aged who are protected by rising Social Security benefits may feel little reason to press for control of inflation.

Finally, as noted earlier, an inflationary move (on a scale greater than we have experienced since the Korean fighting) may get impetus from a force it engenders. It can reduce willingness to save and to hold liquid assets. If prices are rising, the public will prefer to spend money now instead of later. The lessons that people learn increase the difficulty of getting the public to do what is needed to escape from the clutches of inflation.[20]

CREEPING INFLATION

Inflation has so generally been the result of war and its aftermath that until recently we have not thought of the normal operation of the economy as inflationary. Today things may be different. Increases in the price level may characterize our future—creeping, not dramatic, price rises. The judgments of economists, however, differ widely.

In the more highly developed lands, the reasons for fearing a gradual upward drift in the price level can be expressed as follows: (1) Powerful groups of sellers exert irresistible pressures to raise the prices that they charge, including the price of labor. Higher prices mean a drop in the quantity of output sold. (2) Rather than permit large amounts of resources to remain idle for any extended period, governments will inject new money into the economy. The first set of forces raises particular prices from the cost side, while the second works on demand in the aggregate.

Fortunately, some things also work to lower prices. Increased productivity is the chief factor—the result of improvements in technology, more capital, increasing worker skill, better management, more domestic and foreign competition. But will modern institutions permit rising productivity to be reflected in lower prices? Workers in an industry where productivity is improving will prefer higher wages to lower prices of what they produce, for they may buy little or none of the output of their firm.

---

[20] Taxes present conflicting forces. Taxes may contribute to inflation by raising prices of taxed products (some of which are in the consumer price index), by encouraging inefficiency in business spending (where the after-tax cost of deductible expenses seems low enough to justify outlays not worth their pre-tax price), and by favoring leisure over work. The net effect of such reactions, however, is unlikely to be important. Two other possibilities demand recognition. High and progressive taxes tend to reduce saving but also soak up an increasing portion of rising income.

The employer for somewhat the same reason may wisely prefer higher unit profits to lower consumer prices.[21]

The existence of strong sellers' groups—businesses sheltered from the full force of competition, unions, farmers with marketing organizations and price supports protected by government—presents an inflationary bias. Union members want more income. Increases in productivity in some firms will amply support wage rate increases. Employers may not resist wage rises of generous amounts, especially when operations are expanding so that new workers must be recruited. The industries with the highest growth in productivity may be pacesetters in wage increases. Substantial differences in wage rates for equal skills can hardly persist for long. Yet in most industries productivity increases will not equal those of the pacesetters. If anything like the same wage rate boosts are granted broadly, unit costs must rise on the average. Employment, on the other hand, will fall, or in an expanding industry rise less than otherwise.

Perhaps union and employer will combine to restrict potential competitors. Union leaders will see the limits to what the employer in a competitive world can pay. But perhaps the union can help employers—*e.g.,* construction contractors in many cities—to "cooperate" to reduce competition and to make higher prices effective so that wage rates may rise. The workers who as a result are not employed in this industry must compete for jobs elsewhere. Will wage rates in those jobs tend to fall? Resistances to wage-rate cuts are so strong throughout much of our economy (and many abroad) that the unemployed are not likely to be absorbed on any broad scale by declines in wage rates.

However, governments, here and in other lands, have pledged themselves to maintain full employment. We know how to accomplish this goal—by enough stimulating (inflationary) finance. To fulfill its commitment to minimize unemployment, a national government will provide financial stimulation by fiscal and monetary action. This stimulation can continue until full employment is achieved at the higher price and wage level.

Without the threat of serious unemployment, the argument continues, the normal restraint on wage demands and price increases is greatly weakened. Generally adequate total demand provides a climate in which high profit margins are consistent with good volume. Businesses with monopolistic powers need have less fear of overpricing their products.

Can we envision in the future, the old "corrective"—a serious "shake-out," a wiping out of some of the money supply, unemployment, price reductions, lower wage rates, lower prices? Four postwar recessions brought no drop in price levels, while each expansion has witnessed an increase.

---

[21] A falling price level brings the benefits of increasing efficiency to everyone as a consumer. If a smaller group—a portion of the working force—can get the same total gain, each of the individuals will get more.

Such predictions (of what national governments will do) are largely political. Ten years ago it seemed more likely than it does today that "modern politics has an inflationary bias." The more recent experience does suggest that Washington—under both Republican and Democratic Presidents—will be more reluctant than some of us had expected to inject new purchasing power into the economy when unemployment stays above 5 percent or even more.[22] If so, the chances of chronic, creeping inflation are smaller—and the chances of more than minor unemployment are greater—than once seemed likely.

Competition at home and from abroad may be more pervasive and more powerful than assumed in restraining wage demands and profit margins. Nevertheless, some groups are always behind others. As one group moves up to get even with some other, it perforce moves ahead of still others. A few spearheading groups will provide upward momentum, perhaps intermittent, perhaps rarely large, but always upward. The public may then look to easy money to support the higher costs (prices), and to offset the employment-reducing effect of price increases. The process has self-perpetuating features which may or may not accelerate.

Some economists, as noted earlier, believe that the worst effects of inflation at a rate of 1 or 2 percent a year are not so bad as the effects of failure of the economy to use resources as fully as could be expected with more monetary stimulation. Policies which can protect us against *any* inflation, it is argued, will lead to avoidable unemployment and will thereby slow economic growth. Is there any real prospect of getting as much domestic competition as is needed for full employment without some upward drift of prices? Answering "No," these economists believe that the practical problem is to learn to live with inflation, while pursuing full employment and economic growth as the major objectives. But other economists believe that the inflation in itself will hamper growth.

In some countries the problem takes a different form. The determination to develop the economy rapidly leads to investment programs that exceed the resources available from voluntary savings and foreign sources. Total spending rises to inflationary levels. The rate of price rise may be slow, but experience indicates a tendency for the process, once started, to gain momentum. Various restrictions on international trade and finance may insulate the economy, but the pressures from outside cannot be controlled fully.[23] Compulsion may be substituted for freedom

---

[22] One explanation is that gold outflow and a deficit in the balance of international payments would be aggravated by expansionary domestic policies.

[23] A few Latin American countries have learned that after a time a distasteful reckoning cannot be avoided. France in the postwar years succeeded in recording a high growth rate along with inflation at a higher rate than we associate with "creeping"; during this time, however, France was able to draw on outside help when balance-of-payments difficulties developed into crises.

as a source of saving. The eventual result is not yet clear beyond dispute.

Moreover, some economists believe that the problem is much exaggerated and may not even exist. Price indexes, they say, show increases when in fact there are none because of biases in the index which, for example, make inadequate allowance for quality improvements. Yet it is by no means clear that the index has such a bias or what it is that a more comprehensive index would show about prices of all consumer goods and services. We end on uncertainty.

APPENDIX TO CHAPTER 22
INFLATION CONTROLS OTHER THAN MONETARY AND FISCAL

How can inflation be prevented? The answer depends partly upon how far back in the chain of causes we wish to look. The basic elements are much the same in all industrial economies. (1) One thing would do more than all others—ending war and the threat of war, for war has been the greatest cause of inflation. (2) A rather different approach to fundamentals would be to weaken the power of special interest groups. It is these groups which can force the public to pay higher prices for specific goods and services. These groups can also force the public, as a method of preventing unemployment, to increase the money supply to "validate" a *level* of prices which is consistent with the increase in these specific prices. Antitrust policy can help, but it can meet only a small part of the problem. (3) Opening the economy freely to the world would help keep our price level from rising more than that of the world in general.

None of these proposals offers as much practical promise as we should like. But other possibilities are available. Two major possibilities are examined in the next two chapters. Four others are considered briefly in this appendix.

Price and Wage Control

Controls on specific prices and wages have been suggested. What if Uncle Sam were to say: "This is the top price you may ask or the highest wage you are allowed to offer?" Except temporarily, such controls would not do much to check a rise in the price level if the basic monetary forces were inflationary. However, if the controls help check the growth in the money supply, they help restrict an underlying source of inflation. In doing so, they work on more than symptoms.

Price controls to check inflation are pointless unless the level at which prices are set is below the price that would otherwise prevail. Why check the retail price of coffee at 80 cents a pound, if the free market price would be 70 cents? If the control price is lower, say 60 cents, enforcement becomes a problem. If people are able, and wish to pay more for a product rather than do without it, the seller might benefit by holding out for a price above the control point. Government authorities would face difficulties in preventing violations. Enforcement staffs are too small. Regulations become incomprehensible. Easily concealed violations—such as giving short weight, changing product quality, and altering the terms of sale and the services provided—are hard to prevent. Except for a relatively few items —utility rates, for example—which with their terms of sale can be defined precisely and regulated easily, price controls cannot be enforced effectively over any long period if other inflationary forces are strong.

Besides outright violation, there will be far more "adjustment." Honest buyers and firms will find ways within the law to maneuver for their own benefit. Some prices will be controlled effectively at levels below those which would prevail in the free markets. But consumers will then be left with more money than they would otherwise have to spend on things—goods and services—not tightly controlled. An obvious result will be an increase in the upward pressures on prices in the latter areas.

Enforcement depends upon many things, such as the community's general standards of law observance, the respect for the price control effort, the depths of patriotism, the structure of production and distribution (the greater the number of firms, the more difficult the policing job), the availability of uncontrolled items on which consumers can spend, the variety of goods and services, and the degree of product standardization.

A fundamental difficulty is where to set the controlled prices or wages. The obvious move at the start may be to freeze a given structure. The economy, however, is always changing. On the "freeze" date someone will have been out of line and have a good case for "relief." Others then join in demanding adjustment. Moreover, prices in world markets are beyond control. New businesses start producing. In all such situations, what *criteria* ought to be used in setting and adjusting prices? How are wage rates to be set? Powerful pressures will be exerted for higher price ceilings and wage rates. A businessman may find that the most profitable way to use his energies becomes the influencing of authorities to alter ceilings, rather than producing more efficiently. Direct controls invite corruption and manipulation (by either controllers or their outside critics) for political purposes. The labor or farm group with strategic votes, or the business group with unusual power, may show officials how to make an exception. Incompetence can cause waste; an error in setting the price of nails, for example, may discourage production of nails and hold up construction generally.

Since some wage contracts and farm parity prices are now tied to price indexes, would not control of the *index* help check an upward trend? If key prices do not rise, perhaps wage rates can be held in check; then business costs and other prices can be kept from rising. During a war this argument has merit, but the valid reasoning is less obvious than may appear. How can such a policy check growth in the stock of money or a rise in velocity? With the demands of government as a buyer highly inelastic, some businesses which supply military needs may have little incentive to keep costs under tight control. Unions, too, can benefit from seeking more. Price controls, however, may force businesses to keep charges and costs down—and unions to get along without wage rate increases—and thus restrain both the prices paid by government and its deficit. The smaller the Treasury's deficits, the less the stimulus to the monetary forces that make for inflation.

Carried further, the argument may justify government subsidies to depress key prices. To prevent the price of, say, bread from rising from 20 to 25 cents, government could pay bakers 5 cents a loaf and force sale at 20 cents. Yet since government spending may be a major source of inflationary pressure, an increase in such spending would seem undesirable. Would it not merely stimulate more inflation? There is at least a possibility that it might not. If an item of added spending prevented still greater spending by government, consumers, or business, it could actually serve to check inflation. (Subsidies can also stimulate marginal production.)

Controls on wages and salaries can help prevent inflation for at least a time. They slow down the growth not only of wage income, which is consumer buying power, but also of business costs which would otherwise lead to larger government and business spending and to the expansion of the money supply. Can wage and salary controls be enforced? For most firms, control is not really possible. However, many wage rates are set by union-management contracts which can be checked by central authorities. In such cases officials may exercise considerable control on contract terms during a great national emergency. The same may be true in an economy with extensive governmental direction. Of course, the "controllers" may not in fact do as much as they could to coerce others.

In this country, under the conditions inviting wage controls (war), there would be a "shortage" of labor at established wage rates. Employers would face difficulties getting enough manpower at prevailing rates. They would be under pressure to make concessions to get the labor needed to turn out the products demanded by government or other insistent buyers. Labor costs per unit of output would rise, even if the nominal wage structure were retained. Employers would upgrade employees—giving job titles somewhat higher than skills justify, as a means of meeting the conditions of the market. To hold workers at official wage rates, employers would have to tolerate absenteeism, tardiness, sloppy work, high waste, indifference to customers, and other sources of inefficiency and evidence of poor quality work.   Costs would rise.

To attract and hold workers, larger outlays for recruiting, training, and providing attractive conditions would be needed.   Moreover, when labor is "short" and higher wage offers cannot be provided as inducements, an employer during slack periods (a design changeover) may hold on to workers for whom he has no jobs rather than risk losing them permanently —a short-run waste.   Enforcing a system of wage controls in an economy as varied as ours is costly.   And if workers are not sympathetic, sustained enforcement requires essentially dictatorial methods.

Controls on specific prices and wages hinder economic adjustments that are very much to be desired.   (The industry with almost the longest record of government regulation—the railroads—is not the healthiest. The industry on which we spend most for government aid—farming—is not the healthiest.)   Even in periods of normal business, myriads of changes are inevitable every day.   The more easily the economy can adjust to them, the greater its efficiency in doing what people want.   Prices, including the prices of labor, are a major instrument for guiding adjustments. Price rises induce more output and greater care in consumption; wage increases attract labor to the kinds of work for which demand is growing. Price and wage reductions do just the opposite.   By many small changes at many margins, a large amount of adjustment is made throughout the economy, smoothly, constantly, impersonally, and, it seems, automatically.

More adjustment is needed at some times than at others.   The conditions that give rise to inflation, at least in the case of a major emergency, are those which call for large changes.   Price and wage controls, however, deprive society of the use of its basic device for inducing adjustments. Desirable shifts of resources become more difficult.   Clumsy and inefficient controls on output, centralized allocations of materials, compulsions imposed on labor (human beings who want to do something else), and innumerable distortions and disruptions, all these are likely when market forces are seriously curbed by controls.

Wage-Price Guidelines

The 1962 economic report of the President proposed "guidelines" for wage-rate increases and called upon businesses to exercise restraint in pricing—"to hold the line."   A few months later the President exerted so much pressure when steel companies raised prices that managements retracted.   Whether the higher steel prices would have "stuck" in view of unused capacity at the time will never be known.   What is clear is that the President's influence had results. For constructive, long-run control, however, the potentialities of such methods can hardly be promising.

In proposing wage guidelines, the Administration said, "The general guide for noninflationary wage behavior is that the rate of increase in wage rates (including fringe benefits) in each industry be equal to the trend rate of overall productivity increase. General acceptance of this guide would maintain stability of labor cost per unit of output for the economy as a whole —though not of course for individual industries." [24] There followed a series of exceptions which recognized numerous important realities of economic life. The net result was to open so many potential exceptions and special cases that the guideposts could not be "operational"—usable in practice. In any case, union leaders and business management (so far as one can judge a large group from the statements of a relative few) both refused to accept the guideposts. And the Secretary of Labor helped mediate a labor dispute with wage-rate increases outside the limits of the guidelines even with generous allowance for the flexibility of the "exceptions."

The proposal resembles somewhat the "incomes policies" of certain European countries, *e.g.,* France and the Netherlands. For several years government, union, and business leaders agreed on economic policies which restrained inflation. By 1964, however, the strains had proved too great for continued success.

Bills have been introduced in Congress to require leading industries to give advance notice of proposals to raise prices. A Federal agency would review the "propriety" of each proposed increase; the proposals, however, include little to indicate the standards of what would be approved. Given the tens of thousands of prices charged by many large companies, the variety of competitive factors, the inevitable doubts about cost allocation, the slowness with which government often acts when only a relatively few specific issues face an understaffed agency—in view of these and other conditions, the proposal is utterly unrealistic.[25] It would, at least, have the effect of discouraging price reduction if there is any prospect that an increase later will be desired.

Output Growth

An increase in the amount of goods offered for sale (more T) will tend to cause prices to fall. Yet as more goods are produced, the incomes

[24] *Economic Report of the President* . . . . *1962* (Washington: Government Printing Office, 1962), p. 189. For an evaluation see N. W. Chamberlain, "The Productivity Dogma," *Challenge,* June 1964, pp. 3–6.

[25] Controversy about price discrimination under the Robinson-Patman Act has proved long, expensive, and indecisive even when only a few prices are at issue.

of producers rise; the proceeds of sales of goods and services, in fact, make up the rise in incomes. In this respect, then, the larger output does not "soak up" excess purchasing power, since production creates its own income. Increased output will not then act as a cure for inflation. Yet we must ask where the buying power comes from—more M or higher V? To the extent that MV does not rise as much as T, there will be a decline in P.

Nevertheless, both directly and indirectly, output expansion can help check inflation. As families and businesses receive more income, their savings plus income-tax payments tend to rise more than proportionately. Consequently, there is less to be spent for the added output than the income received for its production; the new output, therefore, can absorb some of any former excess purchasing power.

Another result is probably more important. As greater production generates added income, laborers and all producers have less need to press for higher *rates* of pay. To illustrate, assume that a man has been receiving $100 for working a forty-hour week ($2.50 per hour). Then prices (or taxes) rise 10 percent, and he demands an increase to $2.75 an hour to maintain his purchasing power; if such an increase were granted, it would add force to the cost-price push. By working four hours a week more, however, he could maintain his real income without a cost-increasing rise in his wage rate. This solution leads to more output (at the sacrifice of leisure). Instead of quarreling over the sharing of a "short" supply, the community produces more to distribute. More work, of course, may not be pleasant. Yet if people do not have the quantity of goods and services that they wish, what other solution is possible?

Something will depend upon the costs of added output. A highly favorable opportunity exists when capital equipment that would otherwise be idle can be used. The community, in a sense, has little real cost in using it. As overhead cost is spread over a larger volume of output, the cost per unit declines. One unfavorable factor, however, is now built into our system; laws and many labor agreements require employers to pay from 150 to 200 percent of the normal rate for hours worked above 40 or so per week. The money labor cost of the added output is therefore likely to be above average, especially if output per man-hour falls somewhat.

Encouraging Saving

An increase in voluntary saving which reduces consumption can help prevent inflation. (If an increase in saving is matched by an increase in spending on investment goods, there will be no net effect on the price level.) How, then, can saving—and, of course, not spending money that has already been saved—be increased? Appeals to patriotism, provision of convenient ways to save, modifications in the tax system, and higher interest rates can all help.   Confidence in the future purchasing power of the dollar is also important.   However, we know too little about the determinants of voluntary saving.

Compulsion is also possible.   During a war it may prove defensible in principle and effective in practice.   In peacetime, however, the possibilities are not great, except perhaps temporarily.   Unless people are regimented far more than would be possible—to say nothing of desirable—an increase in compulsory saving, *e.g.,* in Social Security taxes, would probably lead to adjustment of private saving.   No one, of course, can be certain about the net result; but there is no firm basis for expecting much salvation on this score.

QUESTIONS

1. "No one will endorse hyperinflation, and for good reason.   The opposition to more moderate inflation, however, is less strong, and also for good reason."   Comment.

2. What are the bad effects of inflation?   For each, explain, specifically, how inflation is responsible—in whole or in part—for the unfortunate results.

3. What is "creeping inflation"?   What are its causes?

4. What are the arguments cited in favor of some inflation?   Do they seem convincing?   Why?

5. Can there be inflation without an increase in the stock of money?

6. Explain what is meant by "demand pull"? by "cost push"?   Are they entirely separable?   Why?

7. Why may the general price level rise before the economy reaches full employment?

8. "There are real dangers to any inflation—even 'creeping.'   Yet under certain conditions there may be other goals for which it would be worth tolerating 'creeping' inflation."   Discuss.

9. In what ways does inflation add to the difficulties of business management?

10. What is the relation between inflation and a country's purchases and sales abroad?

11. What, if any, part do organized groups play in creating forces of inflation?

12. In what sense are full employment and a stable price level competing objectives of policy?

CHAPTER 23   *IMPLEMENTING*

MONETARY POLICY

CHAPTER 11 described the tools of monetary policy. More than once reference to their use has crept into our analysis. A more systematic examination is now possible.[1] Unfortunately, however, gaps in knowledge remain.

THE INSTRUMENTS OF MONETARY POLICY

Three chief instruments of monetary policy are available to the officials of the Federal Reserve:[2] (1) open market operations; (2) the charge made for member bank borrowings, the (re)discount rate, and (3) changes in reserve requirements. Although each differs somewhat from the others in its workings, we can largely ignore the differences here.

The monetary authorities, in fact, do have some additional instruments for implementing policy. If we look more broadly to the public as a whole, we see that still more devices are available. Perhaps the most powerful tool of all is the possibility of building new ones. What, for

---

[1] Panic or danger of widespread financial collapse would require more sweeping action than the types discussed in this chapter. It is difficult to visualize the development of such a crisis. A serious international "run" on the dollar combined with a domestic crisis might produce strains which could not be met under provisions of existing law. The kinds of action called for would probably be fairly clear to experts. Congress and the President would presumably act unless a stalemate were to develop between a majority of one party on Capitol Hill and a President of the other in the White House, such as happened in 1931–32. See H. P. Minsky, "Can 'It' Happen Again?," in D. Carson, ed., *Banking and Monetary Studies* (Homewood: R. D. Irwin, Inc., 1963), pp. 101–11.

[2] These officials, for the sake of convenience, are often spoken of as "the monetary authorities." This term may also be used for a somewhat broader group, including key officials of the Treasury and perhaps others with regulatory or lending power.

example, can match in monetary significance one great innovation of the 1930's, the insurance of bank deposits? Our job at this point, however, is to learn what the authorities can do with their present power. Yet even they have doubts about the extent and nature of the influence they exert.

Two complicating factors will illustrate why officials will not be confident about the results of policy actions. (1) The liquidity position of the economy has changed greatly in the last 35 years. The early 1930's witnessed a drastic reduction of liquidity—currency, demand deposits, and assets with very high degrees of moneyness. The total of liquid assets fell far below the amounts needed for reasonably full operation of the economy at prices then prevailing. By 1940 much of the damage had been restored. During the war the volume of liquid assets grew tremendously. At war's end the economy was excessively liquid. Gradually, however, we "worked off" this liquidity. The volume of business rose; so did prices. By 1960 it seemed that we needed about all the liquidity that existed to finance the current volume of business. The public had become much more dependent upon current flows of money to finance buying and lending. Federal Reserve officials concluded that, as a result, the economy had become more sensitive to monetary policy. But by how much? No one knows for certain. Velocity may go up or down—and still remain beyond official control. And what is the importance of the post-1960 increase in time deposits and other assets having considerable liquidity but less than that of money? (2) Deficits in the balance of international payments cannot be ignored in making domestic policy. But how will different monetary policies affect the balance of payments in the next few months and for the longer run?

THE PROCESS OF MONETARY CHANGE

Each of the three tools operates upon the quantity of money, or the potential quantity of money. Each affects the ability of banks to make loans. Each, therefore, influences interest rates.[3] In other terminology, use of the instruments affects liquidity.

Expansion

Let us assume that by open-market purchases, or by a reduction in reserve requirements, the authorities enlarge the capacity of banks to create demand deposits for lending. What is the process by which such action affects the economy?

[3] For a description of the nature and role of interest rates and monetary policy by two Federal Reserve economists, see S. H. Axilrod and R. A. Young, "Interest Rates and Monetary Policy," *Federal Reserve Bulletin,* Sept. 1962, pp. 1110–37.

Banks earn income from the interest (1) charged on loans or (2) earned on securities. Because earning assets mean income, banks will tend to acquire such assets when they can, *i.e.,* when they have excess reserves or when they feel free to borrow at the "Fed." Making a loan, of course, is a two-party process. There must be a borrower as well as a lender. Demand as well as supply must influence the lending-borrowing process. Sometimes, there may be many bank customers more or less anxious to increase their borrowings on terms satisfactory to the bank. To the extent that this condition exists, any enlargement in the capacity of banks to lend will be followed promptly by an increase in loans.

If the new reserves are not used fully in this way, the banks will probably purchase (short-term) securities. Some banks may in fact welcome an opportunity to build up their secondary reserves, which may have been drawn down to meet earlier loan demand. Prices of the types of debt instruments involved tend to rise; yields drop. The sellers now have money instead of short-term debt. Such an increase in the holding of money will lead to some rise in spending on consumption and investment. Moreover, as prices of outstanding debt go up, securities become more easily sold, increasing public liquidity and creating some capital gains. When short-term interest rates go down, some investors seek yields higher than those obtainable on short-term securities, and prices of longer-term bonds go up. Owners of such assets feel wealthier.

Meanwhile, the process of loan expansion moves along, perhaps gradually. Some businesses and consumers (possibly even state and local governments) are on the margin—inclined to borrow if they can do so more easily. News gets around that loans are more easily obtained. Rising asset prices enhance the ability to provide collateral. Newspapers report that interest rates are lower. Some bankers seek out borrowers.

Fig. 23.1 shows what happened in 1958–59. As the "Fed" increased bank reserves early in 1958, bank lending changed little. But the purchase of securities rose markedly. Late in the year, however, loans rose, and banks sold securities to permit loan expansion.

As company treasurers, housing developers, and other borrowers meet with bank officers to arrange new financing—and to discuss the retirement or renewal of outstanding loans—more effects of easier reserve conditions appear. The loans negotiated are somewhat larger, repayment schedules are relaxed a little, and an occasional applicant who would previously have been disappointed gets a loan. Some holders of money begin to use it more freely because they recognize that if they wish they can borrow without difficulty. Here and there someone whose wealth has grown because of an increase in the price of outstanding bonds becomes more willing to spend on consumer and producer goods.

The effective liquidity of the public increases as the stock of money and the salability of assets rise. The demand for money (and close sub-

stitutes) to hold becomes more completely satisfied.   As a result spending
rises.   The growth of spending justifies optimistic expectations and in itself
adds to the demand for loans.   To accommodate borrowers, banks dispose

FIGURE 23.1

Commercial Bank Loans and Security Holdings, 1958–59

Source: Federal Reserve Bank of New York

of secondary reserves.   Who are the buyers?   Businesses, financial institutions, and state-local governments are attracted by better conditions—
yields and marketability.

Although some responses to a Federal Reserve increase in bank lending capacity appear within a few days, the complete process takes quite a
while.   The full effects cannot appear for many months.   One elaborate
study suggests that almost all of the change in interest rates will appear in
the first quarter of a year after an increase in lending capacity (open-
market operations and lowering of reserve requirements).[4]   The rise in
demand deposits will be spread almost equally by quarters over nearly two
years.   Outstanding borrowing of the public will decline slightly at first
and then rise over 18 months to a level several times the initial change.

Business expansions vary in ways which cannot be foreseen.   The
"time path" of the changes can never be known for certain in advance—
especially the amount of change at various stages (second month, seventh
month, etc.).   Much depends upon the state of the demands for (1) loans

[4] F. De Leeuw, "Financial Markets in Business Cycles: A Simulation Study,"
American Economic Review, May 1964, pp. 309–23.   The author notes that the findings are "not intended as realistic predictions"; he presents them as hypotheses about
how financial markets would operate under conditions of a particular, complicated
model constructed to take account of a vast body of knowledge.

and (2) money to hold. The loan expansion (or contraction) in itself influences the level of business and hence the desire for more borrowing. And so does the public's reaction to an increase in the stock of money. As business improves, deposit turnover picks up.

The demand for borrowed funds changes, in amount and elasticity. The spending of earlier borrowings will raise the demand for new ones as business expansion proceeds. When the profit outlook is improving; as sellers become more aggressive or have more attractive offerings for consumers and businesses; as orders from customers rise; when taxpayers vote authorization for more local bond issues; if borrowing in other countries has become more difficult; if the desire to acquire deposits for their liquidity has been met or if it actually drops—the existence of any or all of these, plus other conditions, will increase (and their opposite will decrease) the demand for loans. The amount of any such increase in demand, of course, will depend upon many factors—the cash which may have been accumulated, the ability to economize on the use of cash balances, the ability to finance from internal sources, the expectation of future need for funds and the ability to borrow, the degree of business optimism, the rise in prices, tax obligations, and so on.[5]

Neither a business nor an individual will as a rule borrow and pay interest to hold money idle. As loans are concluded, the recipients will ordinarily increase their spending, *i.e.,* they will buy more (for investment and consumption) than if they had not obtained the loan. The rise in buying is an increase in total demand, one which may be felt at points far distant from the locality where the loan was made. The effects on national income are widely diffused.

The new money will not lie idle after the original borrower's spending, especially after the general demand for liquidity has been satisfied. The added money will continue to flow through the economy. Will it circulate with the velocity which has been prevailing or at a significantly different rate? Or, using the Keynesian approach, one may ask about the multiplier effect of the new money. For example, will the rate be around 1.5, 2, or 3?

We cannot answer these queries with certainty. Yet, beyond question, the expansive effects of money creation will not disappear with the borrower's spending of the loan proceeds. The actions of monetary authorities in enabling banks to lend more will produce effects which spread widely in place and time. Some will go where demand is already high and resources are being utilized about to their capacity; prices will rise. Part of the demand increase, however, will go to sectors in which labor and

---

[5] Increases in business, consumer, and government borrowings are not confined to loans which involve an expansion in the stock of money. Growth of *credit* is not confined to growth in *money*. Some borrowers may get money which had been held idle. The rate of new saving can rise.

capital are partially idle. At least some of the increase in demand will extend into later phases of the cycle and contribute toward propelling a boom to excesses which in turn sow the seeds of later economic distress.

Responses to an expansion of reserves (and also to a contraction) may be partly speculative. If the beginning leads to a belief that the move will continue, the short-run effect will be considerably greater than if lenders and borrowers believe that the change in monetary conditions which they have just observed will not be duplicated. The possibility of speculative exaggeration magnifies the problems of the authorities.

Contraction

A restrictive policy seems to operate more rapidly than one of expansion. The path, too, differs somewhat, but for the most part is the opposite of the expansion process. Federal Reserve officials will never wish to propel the economy into recession, but at times they do impose restraint— "tighten" money. They can do so while permitting bank-lending capacity to expand but at a rate below the rate of growth of the economy's potential.

If the FR reduces the capacity of banks to lend, a process of contraction sets in. Banks can, of course, discount at the FR, but the possibilities are limited. Banks must reduce their liabilities—and assets—or at least not let them grow while the economy tries to expand. Disposal of secondary reserves does not increase the overall availability of funds but does tend to lower security prices. The lesser availability of loans; lower prices of securities; higher interest rates; greater pressure to repay loans—these combine to reduce the volume of money and of spending. Or in an economy which ought to expand from month to month, they slow the rate of growth of the money stock. The effects continue, apparently lasting for a year or more after the initiation of a policy of restraint. This lag or spillover, unfortunately, adds something to the forces of contraction after business has turned down. The long-run trend of the economy is upward. Therefore, restrictive pressures will appear if monetary action merely prevents expansion or keeps it below normal.[6]

Summary

The results of any action by the central bank depend in part upon the reactions of borrowers and of untold millions of users of money. The

[6] Since World War II actual declines in demand deposits (ignoring normal seasonal change and two or three minor drops for a month or so) occurred in the winter of 1948–49, after August 1957, and from October 1959 to June 1960, all periods of business contraction. Except to a slight degree in 1957, time deposits were not rising during these periods of monetary contraction.

amount and the *timing* of the consequences are always subject to more than a little doubt. A study of actual experience found that at 5 months after the initial action, from 20 to 54 percent of the full effects of an expansionary policy might be expected, and from 34 to 70 percent of the results of restrictive policy.[7]   Such ranges are clearly too wide for comfort.

Of course, the *direction* of the response is clear—a fact of considerable importance. If money creation is made easier—if bank lending capacity is increased—the stock of money will grow. If liquidity rises, money on hand will be used more freely. Interest rates will tend to fall and investment rise. For these related reasons, the flow of money payments gets larger. So does national income in money terms.

On the other hand, if money creation is made more difficult, the stock of money (liquidity) will grow more slowly, or perhaps actually decline. Buying will tend to fall. Rising interest rates reduce investment. Exceptions to these generalizations (with their "other things being the same" condition) will appear, but only in unusual conditions and for brief periods. Year in, year out these conclusions can be relied upon to guide policy makers, but guide only. For unknowns remain. What will be the *amount* of any response? *When* will *how much* appear? In what sectors of the economy? With what secondary effects? Will the total results do more good than harm for the public as a whole?

INTEREST RATE OR AVAILABILITY? OR BOTH?

Keynes was only one of many economists supporting the conclusion that, at least in the short run, money produces its effects on the economy chiefly through its influence on the rate of interest. After World War II, however, emphasis shifted somewhat. Perhaps the dominating factor is not so much the rate of interest—the cost of credit—as the ability to get, or make, loans.

What part, then, do ups and downs in the interest rate play in an economy's adjustment to a change in the capacity of banks to lend? Opinions vary. The tendency in recent years has been to look to the *availability* of loan accommodation and to assign the interest rate itself a less important role than was once customary. Interest rates, of course, exert influence in more than one way.

Interest rates to many borrowers are "sticky." The rate that the bank charges does not always reflect changes resulting from action by the monetary authorities, at least not fully. Big borrowers, however, know as well as do the banks themselves when the monetary authorities have

---

[7] T. Mayer, "The Inflexibility of Monetary Policy," *The Review of Economics and Statistics,* Nov. 1958, pp. 358–374. The figures are his "intermediate" estimates.

changed bank lending power. Certain key interest rates—and the related prices of government and other debt—are determined in highly competitive financial markets; anyone who looks can see what has happened. After the central bank has increased bank reserves, the treasurers of large firms will press for lower rates, perhaps play one bank against another, threaten to go to the money market, and often succeed in getting rates down. Bank-lending officers seeking to build loan volume will sometimes take the initiative in offering lower rates. Without question there are many margins where interest rates are anything but sluggish.

Nevertheless, the interest-rate effects of actions are not always clear. When the policies of the authorities in providing reserves to stimulate business begin to work and the economy picks up, the demand for borrowed funds tends to rise. Consequently FR actions giving banks greater lending power may be accompanied by only a short-lived drop in interest rates. The policies may work, however, and work significantly, by keeping interest rates from rising as much as they would otherwise. Interest rates may go up and money appear tighter in spite of the policy of ease. Such apparently paradoxical results can come from increases in demand impinging upon a supply which has grown relatively less, not from any reduction of the supply itself.

The direct significance of changes in the rate of interest on the incentives and the willingness to borrow is a matter of continuing debate. Many types of investment spending do not respond sensitively to changes in interest rates. However, both proof and measurement are exceptionally difficult. The key issue, of course, is not whether all investment is sensitive to interest costs but whether there is *enough* that does respond to make interest-rate change a useful instrument. Let us look at different parts of the market.

If businesses, consumers, or governments want to borrow for *short* periods, interest-rate *differences* are small in relation to the benefits from using loans and to the other costs of operation.[8] Consequently, interest changes as costs have little influence on the quantity of loans demanded. In other words, the elasticity of demand for short-run borrowings is low; other things being the same, the quantity of borrowing for short-run uses responds only slightly to a larger percentage change in the rate of interest. And it is short-term rates over which the monetary authorities have most influence.

For longer-lived projects, however, interest rates can be decisive. In terms of total costs, interest bulks much larger for a 30-year project than

---

[8] Consumers are frequently, but by no means always, unresponsive to finance rates charged on installment debt; the consumers who are best informed about the cost of borrowing tend to be more responsive to differences in rates. F. T. Juster and R. P. Shay, *Consumer Sensitivity to Finance Rates: An Empirical and Analytical Investigation* (New York: National Bureau of Economic Research, 1964).

for one of 3 years or 3 months. Interest as a price can have significant effect on the quantity of borrowing and of investment in long-run undertakings.

One clear connection between interest rates and investment in recent years involves housing. The volume of housing "starts" has tended to rise as interest rates drop and to fall as interest costs increase. Many other factors also influence the results, but the record confirms the testimony of builders and bankers that interest-rate changes do affect construction of new housing.

In general, it seems, utility and other business investment in plant and equipment depends upon a complex of considerations in which the interest rate as a cost has only moderate importance. A careful econometric analysis found evidence that some effects with a lag of about a year are significant. State and local government borrowing is also dominated by factors other than the interest rate. Nevertheless, at least in the short run, some connection does exist between interest cost and state-local borrowing. Higher interest rates do cause some projects to be abandoned, curtailed, or postponed.

Interest-rate changes have another effect. They influence the movement of capital from one country to another. The chain of reactions which will result can influence the domestic economy, but we need not repeat the analysis of Chapter 18.

Availability applies to the nonprice (*i.e.,* other than interest) elements which influence the amount loaned and borrowed—knowledge of market conditions, record of past borrowing, friendship, desire for diversification by the lender, concern for future dealings, compensating-balance requirements, extent of competition, line-of-credit agreements, and so on. In the short run, stickiness and imperfections in loan markets prevent the forces of supply and demand from working their effects in the "classic" manner only. But how long can a banker's desire for larger income, or a borrower's concern for lower cost, be outweighed by market imperfections? How long will nonprice rationing have a significant effect? Some economists believe that delay will be short and the size of any gap between actual and equilibrium terms will be "not large."

Another type of result also proves difficult to evaluate. When money tightens and interest rates rise, the prices of outstanding debt drop. When a bank holds such assets, it may become reluctant to sell them to get funds for lending. Incurring capital losses is unwelcome. As a result, it was suggested after World War II, banks become "locked in." But to what degree? At the most, apparently, the effect is small. (Banks can charge capital losses fully against other income in computing income tax.) If there are better uses of assets than securities at current yields, bankers are generally willing to sell to take advantage of better opportunities even if capital losses must be realized.

In judging the operation of monetary policy in ways other than through the effects of interest as a cost, increasing attention is given to the significance of changes in the prices of financial assets. How do families, businesses, and financial institutions react to changes in net worth? If someone becomes wealthier as money becomes "easier," and interest rates fall and bond prices go up, an expansion of activities will result—not always, but in some cases. Capital gains (or losses) must have some influence on consumer buying. Changes in the prices of securities which may be used as collateral for borrowing also have some effect. Rising market prices of assets held by financial institutions tend to increase the willingness to lend, at least marginally. The increase in net worth thus operates to counteract for some of the public the tendency, when interest rates drop, to reduce velocity of circulation of money. Conversely, rising interest rates and tighter money tend to produce the opposite results through the influence on capital values.

Other observers, however, and this group includes some having very close contact with the loan market, have concluded that availability can exert an independent influence more or less indefinitely. Every loan has aspects other than the amount involved and the interest rate. There is the collateral or borrower's equity in relation to the loan. There is the duration. There is the relation of the borrower's income to the amount needed to service the loan, *i.e.,* to pay interest and repay the principal. And there are other elements. Variations in each make a loan more or less attractive. Bankers consider them as well as the rate of interest. So do borrowers.

Ordinarily, a considerable number of actual or potential borrowers want more funds than they can get. An increase in bank reserves enables banks to give fuller accommodation to some customers at about the same rate of interest. Tighter money does the opposite. Such loan "rationing" operates in different ways—varying the weight given to past records and current financial position of applicants for loans, altering the requirements about maintaining balances, extending or shortening schedules for loan repayment, paring down loan requests by different amounts ". . . [The] influence of availability is subtle, manifold, and ubiquitous." [9] It is not

[9] Howard S. Ellis, "Limitations of Monetary Policy," The American Assembly, *United States Monetary Policy* (New York: Columbia University, 1958), p. 154; see also Guttentag, "Credit Availability, Interest Rates, and Monetary Policy," *The Southern Economic Journal,* Jan. 1960, pp. 219–28. In the words of the Federal Reserve: "In some cases, the stated interest rate may not change, but the rate may be effectively varied through changes in other factors. . . . In market sectors where interest rates tend to be less flexible, lenders give more emphasis to nonprice factors in allocating funds among borrowers whenever credit condition demands press actively against the supply of funds. . . . Federal Reserve anti-inflationary actions, therefore, tend to be accompanied by both rising interest rates and more emphasis by lenders on credit standards and other nonprice factors in allocating funds. Counterrecession actions taken by the System, on the other hand, tend to be associated with declining interest rates and reduced emphasis by lenders on nonprice influences." Board of Governors . . . and Treasury . . . , *The Federal Reserve and the Treasury: Answers to Questions from the Commission on Money and Credit* (Englewood Cliffs: Prentice-Hall, 1963), p. 71.

measurable. It *is* important. Generally, it operates to reinforce interest rate changes. But not always. In a period of recession, for example, even though interest rates are dropping and reserves are plentiful, bankers may become more cautious and tighten their nonprice loan conditions. During boom times they may do the opposite. Not all bankers will attach the same weight to these conditions. Not all changes, in fact, may be in the same direction.

MANAGEMENT OF MONETARY POLICY—AN ART [10]

According to highly respected bankers and economists, central banking, *i.e.,* successful central banking, is an art. It is certainly not a science. The financial system is complex. The interrelationships are beyond number; they change, as a rule gradually but sometimes rapidly. The economy never ceases to change, and each year brings some new developments of far-reaching import—in technology, for example. No less important, however, are basic stabilities. Men and women have freedom, and they use it; but they also keep to habitual practices. Consequently, there are always doubts about what will result from any action of the monetary authorities.

How, then, can a central banker discharge his responsibilities effectively? The answer will run somewhat as follows: Before he gets his appointment he will have acquired extensive knowledge, broad acquaintance with the economy, and mature judgment. He should have studied monetary theory and processes intensively. As an official he will have access to information of many types from sources everywhere in the economy and from central bankers in other parts of the world. He must seek out this information, study it, reach tentative conclusions, check them with other knowledgeable people, invite criticism, revise and modify where called for, and then act.

If he is part of a group, like the Board of Governors in this country, he will discuss the problem with his colleagues; and a majority will reach

[10] K. Brunner and A. H. Meltzer, in a study for the House Committee on Banking and Currency, conclude that officials attach undue importance to "tone," "feel," "credit," "liquidity," and other concepts which are inadequately defined and are used in different senses in different contexts. Neither the policy makers nor the staff have given adequate priority to pushing the basic monetary research that present-day analytic tools and theories make possible. Relations with the academic community have been sporadic and spotty. The System fell far behind modern developments in the use of statistical, econometric, and other analytic tools adaptable to monetary analysis. See . . . Committee on Banking and Currency . . . House . . . , *The Federal Reserve System after Fifty Years,* Vol. 2 (Washington: Government Printing Office, 1964, pp. 926–38 and 1050–66. Governor Mitchell denied the validity of some of the criticism, especially as applied to current conditions. "As of right now the System is stepping up its attention to research on basic monetary problems." *Banking,* Aug. 1964, p. 43 ff.

a decision. Intuition and feeling as well as rational judgment play a part. One or two strong personalities may dominate. Today's decision may need to be revised tomorrow as something new appears. Success involves the ability of one or a few men to predict what millions of others will do under conditions which are, inevitably, somewhat uncertain. And as these millions, and the central bankers, act, they influence each other. The responses change the conditions which were assumed when the policy was adopted. Does the policy then become a bit obsolete? Perhaps so—at least we must recognize that the monetary policy appropriate for one set of conditions may be ill suited—or even better suited—for another set.

The public has no assurance that the managers of its money have the artistry required for the kind of monetary management they attempt. Perhaps they do. Among the difficulties they face, not the least is pressure from the public. At times good central banking requires toughness and imperviousness to public criticism, including that from powerful members of Congress. Yet there have been cases—here and abroad—in which monetary authorities were wrong and some critics more nearly right than the central bankers. Officials rarely acknowledge that on this or that specific occasion they made a mistake; but several times in recent years FR leaders have said that their actions will not always be right. When things turn out well, however, they may claim credit for the accomplishment.[11]

TIMING: GRADUALNESS

The art of central banking is to a great degree the art of timing. One merit claimed for monetary policy, especially in comparison with fiscal policy discussed in the next chapter, is that the monetary authorities can act promptly as soon as action seems desirable. Moreover, changes in monetary policy can be put into effect gradually in small stages. Gradual action is ordinarily (but not always) to be preferred to large, sudden, jerky change.

Every day that the banks are open, the Federal Reserve engages in open market operations. The process is continuous in the sense that hour after hour technicians of the Federal Reserve Bank of New York, in touch

[11] Prof. Friedman, after reading all the annual reports of the Federal Reserve since 1913, points out that when things were going well, the reports say that the "favorable course of events is largely a result of the handling of this delicate instrument [monetary policy] by the monetary authority." In years of depression, on the other hand, the reports emphasize that "[the power of] monetary policy is highly limited, and that it was only the skillful handling of such limited powers as were available that averted disaster." M. Friedman . . . Committee on Banking and Currency . . . House . . . , *The Federal Reserve System after Fifty Years*, Vol. 2 (Washington: Government Printing Office, 1964), p. 1171.

with Board officials in Washington, make decisions to buy or sell. Their actions affect bank reserves. Sometimes the actions are merely "passive," or "defensive," offsetting changes which go on in the financial system so that the total of bank reserves will not be altered.[12] Sometimes the actions involve a little net change, purchases exceeding sales by a small amount or vice versa. One day's results may counterbalance those of the day before or add to them as a part of a "dynamic" policy of altering bank reserves. Always, there is open market action. Consequently, small changes in bank-lending capacity can be made easily and large changes worked out smoothly over time. The pace of change may be adapted to the apparent requirements of developing conditions.

A somewhat different aspect of gradualness exists in the fact that the FR stands ready to lend to member banks at any time. Here the banks have the initiative. Temporarily, at least, a bank feeling strain on its reserve position can get relief—at a price. Discount rates are always in effect. They can be changed at short notice. True, such changes are not made so smoothly as the day-to-day alteration in the FR holdings of government debt. Moreover, the effects of change in the rate are probably slower to appear and less easy to predict than the effects of open market operations. The rate is a tool whose value cannot be measured accurately but a tool which is at hand for use by the authorities. It supplements and can be augmented by open market operations. And to some extent System officials can relax or tighten the intangibles which influence the granting and renewal of bank requests for accommodation.

FR officials can feel their way cautiously, or act boldly. They "lean against the wind," harder at some times than at others.[13] Officials can speed up or slow down or reverse any policy. They need not try to persuade any public body. In fact, they do not ordinarily attempt to explain why they are changing policy, or failing to change, or what results they expect.

In contrast, any policy requiring Congressional action must be formulated, presumably after the evidence becomes available; there must be checking to be certain that the proposal will survive criticism. Then hearings before Congressional committees and voting will ordinarily take months. Partisan opposition is inevitable, delays are almost as certain, and compromise may be required by considerations largely unrelated to the issue. By the time a new policy can be put into effect after Congressional

---

[12] The Federal Reserve tries to smooth out disturbances which result from changes in public holdings of currency, the shifting of Treasury deposits, the movement of deposits among banks with different reserve requirements, changes in "float," shifts of deposits of foreigners, and gold flows. See R. V. Roosa, *Federal Reserve Operations in the Money and Government Securities Markets* (New York: Federal Reserve Bank of New York, 1956).

[13] Because there is a lag between monetary policy action and its effects the FR, it is said, should "lean against the winds of future months."

action, conditions will have changed from those which prompted the original recommendation. In the time gap, the monetary authorities could have initiated, adopted, and modified policy many times.

Unfortunately, the timing of monetary action and the realization of the results are not the same. At any moment the monetary authorities know that actions taken weeks and even months in the past are building up their results, perhaps is some cumulative fashion, with the total effect obscured by varied lags and myriad developments growing out of other origins. The lags are especially significant where construction is involved —the type of spending which seems to be most sensitive to interest rate changes.

Sometimes gradualness is not the best procedure. Because of a sudden development, possibly in foreign affairs, or because of delay in taking action, a move on a big scale may be needed. Taking it once and for all may well be wiser than successive steps which prolong the process. If restriction is required, the initial shock may be painful, but decisive action may be better than dragging out the unpleasantness. Moreover, if the public believes that what has been done is all that is involved, then there is no temptation to speculate on later moves by the monetary authority. Certainty is better than doubt. Yet can there really be certainty? The big, bold step may not in fact be enough. Or it may be too much.

FORECASTING

Few tools would be more useful for successful monetary control than something to reveal the economic future, a crystal ball or a carefully constructed formula or set of equations with the necessary data for their use. Men with power to act need to know what will happen if they do not change policy, and what will happen as a result of each of several courses that they may take. Tremendous efforts devoted to both the development of forecasting techniques and the collection of data and computer processing have advanced our knowledge. Nevertheless, a significant amount of uncertainty about the next year or two remains.

Part of the uncertainty concerns the margin of doubt itself. Can we judge within ± 3 percent, or may the error be ± 5 percent? Perhaps one or more of the techniques now available will give answers which are always right (except for negligible error). We do not know. The problem is inherently baffling.

Any system for predicting economic events must recognize the fundamental fact that human life always changes. Men and women are free to change their minds, to act differently from the way they did last year or last month or from the way they expected to be acting now. How many of us a year ago would have made an accurate prediction of our present earnings and buying? Forecasts of individual actions would often have been off the mark by an amount which is large in relation to any margin of doubt.

Nevertheless, there *are* great central stabilities. Most economic activity goes along about as it did last week or at the corresponding time last year. And there is another type of stability—change of a particular type will often produce about the same response in the future as in the past. Unfortunately, the problem of economic prediction is not solved by knowing what will happen to the great bulk of economic activity. What is in doubt is the marginal activity, the response where conditions are somewhat different from those of the past. Serious concern, for example, will not arise over the 1.2 million housing starts which are certain but over the hundred thousand, more or less, which builders may or may not begin.

In economic forecasting lags are important. Two types of lag must be distinguished.[14] (1) Events—such as business decisions to change investment spending—take place before the authorities can learn about them. Some gaps between the decision of, say, corporate directors and the announcement are short, but many involve weeks, and some months. At any time the facts available to makers of policy, in government and in business, lag behind both decisions and events to a widely varying extent. (2) Recognition that the economy has changed direction takes time. Not all the indexes will reveal change with equal promptness; divergent, contradictory indications often appear. Some interpreters may be unduly complacent, some unduly apprehensive. Weeks may pass before the specialists agree.

People use their economic freedom enough so that the total volume of economic activity next year is subject to doubt, rarely 8 percent of GNP but always involving many billions of dollars of output and at least hundreds of thousands in employment. Moreover, the economy is always changing. The future can never duplicate the past. Even if nothing else were to change—and much always does change—experience gained in the past would in itself insure a future at least somewhat different from anything that has gone before.

The monetary authorities in their forecasting face another problem. Their own forecasts as well as their actions will change conditions. Obviously, officials believe that what they do will have an effect. But they are the first to admit that they cannot be certain of its size. Moreover, whatever the authorities do—even if it is merely a decision to continue a course of action—will be known to the public. Some businesses, and perhaps even some households, will change their own plans as a result of

---

[14] In executing policy, additional lags complicate problems. After recognizing a change, the authorities require some time to decide on what to do. Then when they have taken action the results appear after varying time delays.

their interpretation of what the monetary authorities believe to be the general economic outlook. If the heads of several giant corporations have confidence in the judgment of FR officials, any decisive action by the monetary authorities may induce some revision of corporate policy—not only because of the monetary change itself but also because of a revision of expectations. Yet who can be confident of the size and the nature of these derivative results of official forecasts? The uncertainty that they introduce is tiny in relation to national income—but possibly important in relation to the range of doubt about fluctuations in national income.

The more prosperous the economy, the larger the margin of freedom. We find it easier to do something different when income and wealth are high or have risen. We may step up our saving or go on a buying spree. Businesses comfortably stocked with goods for processing and sale may decide to let their inventories drop; prospering firms may speed up their investment in new plant and equipment. Imports or exports may change for unexpected reasons. Federal, state, and local government finances present no end of surprises. Errors in estimates of U.S. government tax receipts and expenditures range from the inconsequential to the highly significant.[15]

Is there any wonder, then, that the monetary authorities try to "feel out" the market, probing to test the forces which operate beyond the frontier of what is known? The policy of gradualness gets support from the existence of doubt about what lies ahead. Moreover, because the economic future is uncertain the Federal Reserve feels that it must not commit itself to *specific* actions in the future, such as maintaining any set of interest rates or price levels. Officials believe that to do so would, among other things, change conditions in ways which could be undesirable and whose correction would require a different policy. Some banks and businesses would act on the basis of the commitment. Only by a miracle would the new market conditions of demand and supply then give an equilibrium at the commitment level determined earlier.

Nevertheless, the uncertainties about short-run forecasts provide some of the basis for arguments that monetary policy should be dominated by known rules. These, it is argued, would eliminate much of the danger of error arising from the use of discretion by human authorities. Under-lying forces and long-run trends can be determined with greater accuracy than the changes of the next few weeks or months.

[15] For example, we can look at the fiscal years 1947 through 1963. The estimates of revenues made in January for the twelve months beginning the next July erred on the average 10 percent—from 1 to 26 percent; 7 proved too low, 10 too high. The average error of spending estimates was 6 percent with a range from 0.1 to 15 percent; 11 were too low, 6 too high. Tax Foundation, *Federal Fiscal Issues,* 1964 ed. (New York: The Foundation, 1964), p. 49.

"BILLS-ONLY"

For a decade after the Federal Reserve-Treasury "accord" of 1951 (Chapter 25), the Federal Reserve imposed on itself a limitation in the use of its major instrument—open market operations. Pursuing a policy of "minimum intervention," it confined its purchases and sales to short-term debt, Treasury bills as a rule. The controversy which this policy aroused involves more than market techniques and, though recently dormant, may reappear.

FR officials preferred general control, such as action on bank lending capacity, over selective controls, such as particular interest rates. The chief direct objective in open market operations was felt to be to alter the total of bank reserves. What counts in altering reserves is the *amount* of securities that the FR buys and sells. The *types* of securities bought or sold make little difference in the total effect on bank reserves. However, the prices of some types of securities—some interest rates—will be directly affected more than will others when the "Fed" buys or sells one type rather than another, and especially when some of the issues have relatively thin markets.

Advocates of the "bills-only" policy believe that it concentrates change on the type of asset which is most nearly like money. This is the type with much the largest and broadest market. The very short-term securities can be bought and sold most easily and with a minimum of disturbance on the prices of other securities. And, the FR asked, is it not in the public interest to avoid direct official interference with the prices of long-term debt? These prices can vary through several percentage points. Anyone holding such debt assumes an interest-rate risk. For most holders risks may not be important. However, for the dealers in government debt who hold the inventories needed for a "broad, deep, and resilient market," the risks are large in relation to operating profit and capital. The "bills-only" policy kept the risks of holding such debt lower than when the Federal Reserve stands ready to buy or sell long-term debt and thereby to alter bond prices, without notice and without necessarily reflecting basic market conditions.

The money and capital markets are fluid. Change in any one place will be diffused broadly but not necessarily equally or quickly. The whole level and structure of interest rates will feel the effects as the forces of demand and supply react to an impulse at any point. No one, however, can know in advance what will be the relative power of these varied and complex forces. If the monetary authorities try to anticipate demand and supply in various parts of the market, errors are possible—perhaps distortions which will themselves create new difficulty. Speculation can have virtually no effect on the prices and yields of short-term securities.

Longer-term issues, however, do fluctuate. When the Federal Reserve deals in such issues for the purpose of affecting bank-lending capacity or the interest-rate structure, the argument runs, a new uncertainty exists. No one could be sure whether as a result the market would become less stable. Such instability could communicate itself to the submarkets for corporation and state-local bonds.

Critics of "bills-only" argue that the purchase and sale of longer-term government debt would generally be more effective in offsetting cyclical fluctuations. It is not enough, they believe, to change the lending capacity of the banking system. If specific interest rates and types of lending can also be altered as the parts of the economy change in relation to each other—and promptly rather than with avoidable lags—is it not foolish to fail to do so if the power exists? The influence of interest-rate changes on investment is far less at the "short" than at the "long" end of the maturity range. If monetary policy must work out through a chain from short-term to long-term interest rates, months may be required, months which might be saved by acting directly on long-term rates and in those sectors of the market where action seems most desirable.

The cleavage between the opponents of "bills-only" (advocates of selective controls) and the defenders, with their preference for reliance on general controls, was widened by doubt about the workings of monetary policy. Those who believe that monetary policy works out primarily through effects on the interest rate tend to criticize "bills-only." For it is long-term interest rates which influence investment the most. The more quickly these rates can be altered, then, the more effective is monetary policy—assuming that lenders and borrowers do not delay in expectation of additional central bank action in the particular part of the market involved. On the other hand, someone who believes that the quantity of money itself, largely independent of interest-rate change, is the significant aspect of monetary policy will be more sympathetic to "bills-only."

To some extent, in fact, the debate missed a central point—that Treasury-Federal Reserve relations are involved. One or both *must* intervene in various parts of the market. During "bills-only" most of the responsibility lay with the Treasury as it decided what types of debt to sell in the refundings. More or less of any one issue affects the part of the market in which it is traded.

No one knows whether or how long it would have required critics of "bills-only" to win out had not considerations of international finance entered. Then the desire to "twist" the rate structure added a persuasive force. A rise in short-term interest rates seemed desirable to prevent the exodus of funds to foreign financial centers. But a reduction in long-term rates was called for to help raise employment, especially in construction.

FINANCIAL INTERMEDIARIES AND THE EFFECTIVENESS OF MONETARY POLICY

One respect in which the present differs from the past is that financial intermediaries—insurance companies, savings and loan associations, savings banks, credit unions, and other institutions—have grown more rapidly than commercial banks; new ways of handling financial affairs have developed; government debt and other debt of high quality greatly exceed the pre-war proportions.[16] As a result the responsiveness of the economy to changes in monetary policy has been altered. A little or a lot? And in what respects? Economists disagree.

Two points, however, give rise to little or no disagreement.[17] (1) The operations of financial intermediaries do not directly affect the quantity of the means of payment. These institutions do not possess that distinctive characteristic of commercial banks—the ability to create or destroy the medium of exchange. (2) Yet the intermediaries unquestionably influence the amount of "work" that can be performed by any given stock of money. They act as a sort of cushion or buffer between the monetary authorities and the spending public, between those who spend for consumption and those who buy investment goods.

The intermediaries themselves increase and decrease their holdings of demand deposits. In doing so, they may alter somewhat the velocity of circulation. Intermediaries also influence liquidity. These institutions acquire assets of low liquidity (such as mortgage loans and long-term bonds) in exchange for their own liabilities, which have much greater liquidity. True, the shares of a savings and loan association, or the borrowing right of a person in his life insurance policy, are not as liquid as money. Equally true, however, is the fact that they can substitute for demand deposits in meeting some of the needs for liquidity. Consequently, as the public builds up (or reduces) its claims against financial intermediaries, the potential limits of V change. Moreover, as intermediaries buy or sell long-term debt, they affect interest rates in ways

[16] One meaning of the word "institution" is "a way of doing things." In this sense the line of credit (see Chapter 5) is an institution. Firms which have virtually complete assurance of ability to borrow may be largely insulated from monetary policy in the short run.

[17] It was once feared that wide ownership of government and other long-term debt by financial intermediaries might impede monetary policy. Restrictive action would raise interest rates and lower bond prices. Resulting capital losses might disturb business. In practice, however, the institutions have not reacted to declines in bond prices as was feared. Moreover, the widespread holding of debt has tended to make more institutions feel, and more quickly, the effects of actions by the monetary authorities.

which may accentuate or counteract influence of the monetary authorities.[18]

Officials do not yet know how the growth of financial intermediaries will affect responses to changes in monetary policy in the future, nor how much monetary policy may need to be modified as a result.

DEBATE ABOUT THE USE OF MONETARY POLICY

Both the popular press and scholarly literature raise objections to the use of monetary power, objections which constitute practical obstacles of no small size. Every use of monetary power will affect the economic position of "real, live human beings." Yet not all are affected equally. Let us restate: Actions decided upon because of their influence on the general level of the economy will not influence all parts of the public in the same proportion. Our monetary system, for example, is tied in with the granting of credit (loans). Monetary policy is to some extent credit policy, and we are not all equally concerned with credit.

Monetary actions have selective, directional, distributive effects which are more welcome, or more sharply condemned, in some parts of the economy than in others. There is discrimination (but compared with what alternatives?) between borrower and nonborrower (and lender and nonlender) and among borrowers whose demands for loans have different elasticity. Owners of some kinds of assets are affected more than others. The effectiveness of capital markets and doubtless other factors will influence the result.

Retarding Economic Growth

Most complaints arise over restrictive policies.

Monetary restraint will hurt the economic prospects of actual or potential borrowers, not only when the price of loans rises but perhaps even more when some of the credit sought is refused. Businessmen who find themselves unable to finance economic opportunities which look promising will naturally complain about a shortage of loan funds. Is it not unfair, discriminatory, and even foolish for the FR to add to the difficulties of businesses which are trying to expand? If the country needs economic growth, why put obstacles in the way of a business which is sufficiently

---

[18] Purchases and sales also affect velocity because at least some of the money used by the buyer or seller would have been idle.

optimistic to go into debt to try to enlarge its operations? If a growing community wants to borrow to build new facilities, or if a young couple wants a loan to set up a household, will not monetary restraint hurt them unfairly?

Such questions can raise strong emotions, especially if excited by political debate. When influential individuals and groups—and politicians reflecting them—press their own interests, embarrassing difficulties face monetary authorities who believe that the general public welfare requires unpopular restrictive action.

And it is the *general public welfare* which monetary policy should serve. Everyone uses money. The rate at which the stock of money expands affects everyone. Monetary expansion *can* be too rapid. As an economy approaches full use of resources, growth of the money stock to finance investment will be inflationary. The limits to economic growth under such conditions are set by *saving,* not money. Yet we can expect strong temptation to meet the demand for saving (credit) by creating money. And when the temptation is likely to be strongest, at the peak of a boom, resistance is most in the public welfare.

Nevertheless, some economists believe that monetary policy has a bias which retards economic growth, at least a little. Monetary restriction, it is argued, takes hold more on investment than on consumption, while policies of ease do relatively little to add to investment. Here, certainly, is a topic which calls for more facts and analysis.

Discrimination

One argument customarily made for using monetary policy to counteract business fluctuations is that the effects are distributed broadly throughout the whole economy. They are *not* limited to those individuals who feel the initial impact. The process is impersonal in the sense that government officials do not deal directly with this borrower or that. They alter part of the framework of the economy to meet the needs of the whole public. Within the slightly changed conditions, everyone rearranges his affairs as well as he can as he adjusts to other changes which are constantly taking place. Unfortunately, the need to adjust to monetary change inaugurated by an official agency, and the ability to do so, are not equal for everyone.

Let us first consider the effects on interest rates and on the prices of government debt and other property. The effects of FR actions on interest rates are marginal and mixed with the influences of other, more powerful, forces. The financial world knows that the Federal Reserve possesses and will use power to influence interest rates. This knowledge affects the decisions of buyers and sellers of debt. They will take account of the possibilities in their private actions. Any uncertainty will be reflected, albeit imperfectly, in market prices of securities. If there is consensus that FR action will on balance be stabilizing, the uncertainty element in price will be less than otherwise. If so, then official action *reduces* the "discriminations" which market forces would create. Short-term securities, of course, cannot vary much in price, and even since the abandonment of "bills-only" it is these which are most involved in action by the "Fed."

A second alleged discrimination is that people who borrow in periods of tight money suffer as compared with those who borrow when money is easy. Any price system—or any nonprice rationing—will affect people differently depending upon *when* they do some specific thing. The objection raised about monetary policy, however, is that official action contributes to the outcome. The defender of monetary policy replies that by preventing wider fluctuations, monetary action reduces the discriminations which the market would otherwise produce.

The availability feature of borrowing is a third aspect of discrimination. As monetary policy makes short-term loans more or less available (regardless of the interest cost), not everyone is affected equally. Some borrowers have easier access to bank accommodation than do others. (Firms which can rely on internal financing—the use of undistributed earnings and depreciation funds—will not suffer from inability to borrow from banks in times of tight money.) When banks find their lending capacity reduced, or rising less than the demand for loans, bankers do favor some customers. These may get all the credit (loans) they seek. Other customers will get less than they want, and some, conceivably, nothing. Who will tend to be favored?

The facts needed for a full answer are not available. A study of 1955–1957 experience when policy was restrictive revealed that small firms with good credit ratings got as good an accommodation from banks as large firms.[19] *Established* borrowers did have an advantage over new ones, profitable firms over unprofitable. Study of a longer period found that the impact of monetary restraint tended to be concentrated in monetary centers and least important in farm areas.[20] Arrangements for granting credit can certainly be improved. But facilitating increases in the stock of money in boom periods will not provide the best answer.

There is no assurance that the "best" uses of loanable funds, as any of us may judge, are the uses which get the money. But what system would yield such a result? When resources are limited, someone must do without. If banks were allowed to create more money to meet loan

[19] For analysis of the data see G. L. Bach, "How Discriminatory Is Tight Money?" D. Carson, ed., *Banking and Monetary Studies* (Homewood: R. D. Irwin, Inc., 1963), pp. 254–90.

[20] R. J. Laurence, "Bank Location and the Differential Effects of Monetary Policy—A Case Study," *National Banking Review,* June 1964, pp. 513–530.

demands, who would benefit and who suffer? Perhaps the increase in money demand would bring disadvantages greater than any benefits.

Effects on Income Distribution

Interest is a price. If government alters the price of anything—wheat or loans—its action affects both the recipients and those who pay. Use of monetary policy is occasionally condemned because of its effects on the distribution of income—easier money benefiting debtors at the expense of creditors, tight money the opposite. FR action which leads, or is alleged to lead, to higher interest rates will arouse criticism that banks are being favored (perhaps especially big banks which some people charge have undue influence over the System). Banks will demand higher rates from borrowers. Whatever may have been the case in the past, debtors and creditors in our economy are now so intermixed that few if any clear lines (by income, area, age, occupation, etc.) will be found. And the effects of monetary policy on the amount of interest paid and received, balancing one year with another, will rarely be more than inconsequential.

SELECTIVE CONTROLS

Recent questioning of monetary policy includes the criticism that controls which are presumably general do in fact discriminate. Some discrimination, it is argued, is against the public interest. Consumer lending, for example, seems to be affected very little by monetary ease or restraint; yet it contributes more than a little to cyclical fluctuation. Monetary tightness to restrain a boom and prevent inflation, we hear, also brings needless unemployment in some parts of the economy. Would it not be more sensible to restrain only in sectors where there is trouble? During recession would it not be wiser to ease those portions of the economy where business is weakest rather than to relax generally and perhaps spur price and cost increases in the prospering sectors?

Another and essentially different argument is that selective credit controls might direct funds to better advantage for the economy, regardless of cyclical problems. The issue here, however, involves *credit,* not money. If there is a problem, its solution must rest predominantly upon redirection of the flow of new saving, not revision of the money-creating mechanism.

Unfortunately, the discussion of selective controls tends to confuse monetary and credit problems. They are not the same. The economy's need for money is one thing. Quite another are its relative needs for different types of investment—plant and equipment, housing, depressed-area development, agriculture, etc. Changes in the money stock designed to meet a need for loanable funds (credit) produce continuing results as the flow of money through the economy remains affected. Selective controls which combine monetary and credit policies would involve a larger mixture than today of two different sets of considerations. The difficulties of making and executing policy would probably be multiplied.

Many types of selective "control" by government now exist. The differentials in our tax system, for example, operate selectively. So does governmental spending. Various credit programs—to aid housing or curb the use of credit on the stock market—are selective. During World War II and Korean hostilities, the Federal Reserve exercised special controls over installment credit, and during the Korean period over real estate credit. The FR sets the maximum rates payable by member banks on time and savings accounts. Debt management has selective aspects, and so does open market policy.

Would it be possible and desirable to use selective monetary controls to influence more effectively those sectors of the economy which seem to be the source of cyclical trouble? Uneven buying of consumer durables is now destabilizing; fluctuations in inventory contribute to cyclical movements.

Both rest in part upon the use of funds from commercial bank lending. And sometimes a temporarily depressed industry, such as housing, or one suffering from longer-run difficulties, might be aided by easier credit.

With the benefit of hindsight one can spot past situations in which a different credit policy in a specific part of the economy could have helped. But would controls designed now and drawing upon this knowledge be suitable in the future? Would they be applied wisely? Why not operate through the market to meet our needs as we, as individuals, see them rather than through government? To date, certainly, there is no consensus on the answers to such questions.

There is so much that we do not know about how the gathering forces in the economy will develop that action always involves some risk. The groups affected will naturally press their own interests, with results which may not be best, say, for monetary development. Possibilities of evasion and avoidance of regulations are bound to become more serious as time passes. It is highly doubtful that the apparent success with consumer credit control during wartime emergencies could be duplicated under peacetime conditions without vastly more rigorous policing. The financial world is flexible. Businessmen are ingenious. Not many economists have enough confidence in our ability to devise satisfactory techniques of enforcement to look with favor on controls over consumer borrowing.[21]

[21] A statistical analysis of the data for 1959–61 lends more support to the probable efficacy of selective controls than is implied in the discussion here; the availability of bank loans apparently influences borrowers so that the accessibility of alternative sources of credit will influence results to more than minor extent. If so, selective controls on bank lending can be expected to exert significant effect. J. Cohen, "What Do Bank Loans Really Finance?," in D. Carson, ed., *Banking and Monetary Studies* (Homewood: R. D. Irwin, Inc., 1963), pp. 387–407.

With present knowledge of how selective controls would function, it is difficult to have the firm confidence we should like. Certainly more study is needed.

Reliance upon monetary policy is criticized because it seems to work and because it seems not to work. Among bankers, monetary officials, and economists one will find no unanimity about the results that we can count upon obtaining from various monetary policies. Nor can we be certain about the actions which the monetary authorities will take as conditions develop. There will, however, be widespread agreement that monetary policy need not—and will not—carry the entire stabilization load. We turn next to its partner.

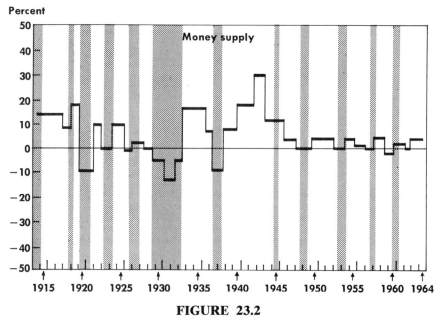

FIGURE 23.2

Rates of Change in the Stock of Money, by Periods, 1914–64

(Shaded areas represent periods of economic contraction)

Source: Federal Reserve Bank of St. Louis

QUESTIONS

1. "There are three main tools of monetary policy. Although only one of these affects the money supply directly, all three operate in one way or another on the ability to lend." Discuss.

2. "Although each tool of monetary policy has its advantages and

disadvantages in particular situations, their use cannot be isolated. Each must be used to supplement and reinforce—or at least not used to counteract—the others." Comment.

3. What is the relation between the ability of the banking system to lend and the level of economic activity? What role does the rate of interest play?

4. What is the process or path by which open market operations influence the level of business activity?

5. What problems do the difficulties of forecasting pose for monetary policy? Do they necessarily indicate that no monetary policy at all is the best solution? Why?

6. What was "bills-only"? Summarize the arguments for and against such policy.

7. What effects will the growing importance of financial institutions other than commercial banks have on the effectiveness of monetary policy?

8. What criticisms are raised against monetary policy? Do they lead to the conclusion that monetary policy is useless? too powerful?

9. Explain how monetary policy may be used to combat both inflation and depression.

10. What is meant by "availability"? How does it influence changes in the stock of money?

11. "Selective monetary controls deserve serious consideration. Yet one who believes in freedom will reject the use of selective controls in time of peace." Discuss.

12. From a study of recent annual reports of the Board of Governors of the Federal Reserve System describe the considerations which were apparently responsible for major decisions. In retrospect, what, if any, actions were unfortunate for the economy?

CHAPTER 24   *FISCAL POLICY AND ITS RELATION TO MONETARY POLICY*

MONETARY policy has a partner—fiscal policy. Although differing, the two are intimately related. The term "fiscal policy" has no universally accepted definition. We shall use it in our context to cover the things governments do in raising revenue and in spending, whether or not the actions are designed consciously to achieve national income (price level or employment) goals.[1]

Fiscal policy extends beyond the customary limits of money and banking. Yet the effectiveness of monetary policy depends so much upon government finance—and the results of fiscal policy depend so much upon monetary policy—that the analysis of money and banking requires some consideration of fiscal policy. This chapter, however, makes no pretense to full coverage of fiscal theory and practice.

AN OUTLINE OF FISCAL ACTIONS

Most interest centers on national government finances, though state and local affairs must be covered in any complete analysis.

An Essential Difference Between Monetary and Fiscal Policy

One distinction between what government can do with fiscal policy and what it can do with monetary policy stands out. By fiscal action, government can intervene *directly to change the flow of income*. By monetary action, government *can change the conditions* in which families and

---

[1] Management of government debt is not ordinarily included as an element of fiscal policy. We discuss it in the next chapter.

businesses *may* alter the flow of income.[2] In principle, then, fiscal policy would seem to be the more direct, the more predictable, and hence the more useful. In practice, however, the complexities of fiscal policy offset some of the apparent advantages of its directness.

General Principles of Revenue and Expenditure
Change to Alter National Income

This section (drawing upon Chapter 16) deals primarily with initial-stage or first-round effects, multiplier considerations being generally ignored. Government, using the power of *taxation,* takes from families and businesses some of the income that they receive (or would otherwise receive).[3] The dollars thus taken are not available to pay for consumption, nor can they be used for the private purchase of investment goods. The tax money is withdrawn from the income stream. It cannot create private demand for goods and services.

Government *spending,* on the other hand, puts money into the income stream. The spending may be for *goods and services*—military equipment, rental of office space, or the work of teachers. Or the spending may consist of *transfers,* such as grants to the needy aged or subsidies to farmers. In either case we can assume that what the government pays out is income to the recipients; it enhances their purchasing power.

If the amount which governmental units withdraw by taxation is just equal to what they pay out as spending, there is no net change in total private purchasing power. Let us assume that equal totals of taxing and expenditures have equal effects on the income stream.[4] Obviously, however, balance is not assured. (1) Taxes may exceed spending. Govern-

---

[2] Monetary policy, by changing the prices of securities, affects net worth in ways which some economists might consider changes in income.

[3] For simplicity we shall treat as taxes various non-tax revenues—charges such as those for postage, fines, etc.—but not proceeds from the sale of debt.

[4] This assumption is made to avoid complications. It would probably be rejected by most economists. A dollar increase in taxes is not likely to reduce private spending by quite a dollar, on the average. Some of the effect will be to reduce saving without an offsetting cut in investment. On the other hand, the dollar of taxes may cut private spending on consumption plus investment by more than a dollar; borrowing to buy may be less when taxes rise. The net effects of *changes* in tax collections are not clear. And the results after conditions have had time to "settle down" are even more uncertain and obscure. For a discussion of the "balanced budget multiplier" theory see W. A. Salant, "Taxes, Income Determination and the Balanced Budget Theorem," *Review of Economics and Statistics,* May 1957, pp. 153–161.

Drawing upon the work of Prof. Cunningham of Columbia University, Dr. H. Sharpe finds that a dollar of government spending on its own payroll has an expansion effect of 1.18 while the income tax has a negative multiplier of 1.55. Government purchases of privately produced goods and services have virtually the same positive multiplying power as the negative effect of income taxes. Each dollar of business investment in plant and equipment is estimated to lead to $2.27 rise in GNP. These findings are preliminary and await more extensive testing. H. Sharpe, *The Weekly Bond Buyer. . . .* December 14, 1964, p. 1.

ment finances will then tend to reduce the income flow, taking out more than is put back. (2) Or spending may put more into the income stream than taxes take out; if so, fiscal action tends to expand the flow of income. In the first case government has a budget *surplus,* in the second a *deficit.*[5]

The public has power to alter the national income by changing the relation between government spending and taxes.

By raising or lowering spending, by lowering or raising tax collections, the Federal government can, other things the same, raise or lower GNP. GNP consists of $C + I + G$ (ignoring net foreign investment). If GNP is $650 billion, it can rise to $655 billion only if one or more of the three elements rise by a total of $5 billion net. If G were to rise by $5 billion with no drop in C and I, GNP would become $655 billion. If G were to remain the same but taxes rose to reduce C by $4 billion and I by $1 billion, GNP would drop to $645 billion.

Assume that the Federal budget has been balanced. Then government spending is reduced $5 billion, or taxes are increased to cut C and I by a total of $5 billion. Moving in this way from a budget balance to a $5 billion surplus will reduce national income, other things being the same. On the other hand, moving to a $5 billion deficit would raise national income. Here, it would seem, is an easy means of controlling the level of national income. How can anything so important be so simple? Unfortunately, neither the theory nor the practice turns out to be quite so simple. Great problems arise in getting the totals of revenue and of expenditure which promise to be best. Additional problems arise in financing the result.

The way in which the surplus or deficit is financed—as well as its size—has an important influence on the total effect on national income. And it is here that monetary factors become involved in a decisive way. The national government can use the financing of a deficit or a surplus to expand or to contract the stock of money. In doing so, it can magnify or counteract the direct effect of a deficit or surplus on the income stream. The government has the opportunity, which it may use constructively or waste sadly, to make fiscal and monetary policy work together.

Note a contrast: Businesses and families with budgetary deficits (or surpluses) may also borrow from banks (or repay) and thereby influence the stock of money and the flow of income. What they do is not necessarily

---

[5] The concept and measurement of budget surplus, deficit, and balance are more complex than we can describe adequately here. For fiscal policy purposes the best measure is the generally unfamiliar "federal receipts and expenditures in the national income accounts." The "cash consolidated" concept is much the same; it is far more appropriate for fiscal policy analysis than the "administrative" budget. The latter excludes Social Security taxes and benefits, most highway revenues and spending, and some other items. The "national income accounts basis" provides a more accurate measure of timing, especially from one quarter of the year to another, than does the "cash consolidated" presentation. Federal budget and national income accounts now provide figures on all three bases.

best for the economy as a whole. The national government, however, can act in the interest of the entire public. And it can act on a big scale if big-scale action seems desirable.

The general principles can be restated. If private buying for consumption and investment—$C + I$—is greater than the value at current prices of the output available for the nongovernmental sectors of the economy, prices will tend to rise. However, if private buying is less than enough to purchase the full-employment output at current prices, the economy will not produce to its full capacity (unless prices fall "enough," a possibility that is slight in the short run). In either situation the government can use the financing of its own activities to *balance the accounts of the whole economy* at a higher or lower level of prices or output (in some combination).

Surplus Financing to Restrain the Economy— Prevent Inflation

The government can *reduce* the economy's total buying, *e.g.,* to ward off inflation, by either (1) cutting government expenditure, (a) its own

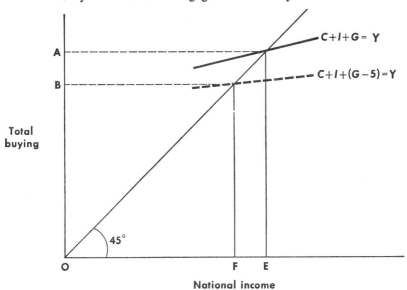

If total buying is OA, gross national income will be OE If government buying is reduced, national income will drop to OF, assuming no reduction in tax rates. The same result could be produced by tax increases which reduce $C + 1$ while G remains unchanged, but the magnitudes would differ.

FIGURE 24.1

Reduction in Government Spending Cuts
National Income: No Change in Tax Rates (Simplified Case)

demand for goods and services or (b) those transfer payments which permit others to demand goods and services without producing an equivalent, or (2) raising taxes. Either policy, or a combination, will force down total buying. Fig. 24.1 presents a simplified illustration. Tax collections will go down as national income falls. Therefore, the difference between G and T before and after will be greater than 5. In general, we shall ignore this aspect of the result to focus on the financing and its significance.

Fiscal action can thus reduce aggregate demand.

In the financing of the national government, the public has a tool for helping prevent an increase in the level of prices. However, the *amount* by which the private sectors cut their spending (consumption and investment) in response to a change in government finances will depend in part upon private willingness and ability to borrow.

Private buying may fall by less than the increase in taxes (or the drop in receipts from government spending) because some businesses and families are willing to add to debt to maintain their buying. But can they borrow? The answer depends upon the capacity and the inclination of banks to lend. The lending position of the banks can be influenced not only by monetary policy in the sense we have been using but also by the way in which the government handles its finances.

Let us now assume that the budget moves from balance to surplus.

Retiring Publicly-Held Debt. If the Treasury uses the surplus to redeem debt held by the general public, the private economy ends with no change in its holding of money. Taxpayers or beneficiaries of spending have less money, but former bondholders have more.

Our illustrations will assume that the surplus results from a rise in tax collections rather than a reduction in spending. Those who had held bonds

Treasury Uses Budget Surplus to Retire Debt Held by General Public
(Billions of dollars)

Public holding of demand deposits		Treasury	
Taxpayers	−5	Receipts from taxpayers	+5
Bondholders	+5	Payments to bondholders	−5

Changes in stock of money   0

may increase their buying for consumption or, more probably, try to put the money to work financing private investment. The net contractive effect of the surplus may then be small—especially if there is an active demand for funds to finance investment. Banks can meet loan requests which they had previously rejected. Note another possibility. A budget surplus, which reduces the public debt and which may be desired for that result, need have no depressing effect if the demand for loans is high.

Retiring Bank-Held Debt. What will be the results if the Treasury retires debt held by commercial banks?

Treasury Uses Surplus to Retire Debt Held by Commercial Banks
(Billions of dollars)

Commercial banks				Treasury		
Assets	Liabilities			Assets	Liabilities	
first step				*first step*		
	Deposits of taxpayers	−5				
No change				Funds received from taxpayers	No change	
	Deposits of Treasury	+5			+5	
second step				*second step*		
				Deposits at commercial banks	Debts due	−5
Government debt	−5	Deposits of Treasury	−5			
					−5	

Change in money stock (demand deposits) −5
Change in legal reserves 0
Excess reserves—enough for 5 of demand deposits

As the first step, checks from taxpayers build up the Treasury's accounts at commercial banks. In the second step, deposits are wiped out as the Treasury exchanges its new deposits for bank-held government debt. As a result, banks hold less government debt; and the stock of money (demand deposits) has dropped. The effect is to put downward pressure on business. Bank reserves at the Federal Reserve have not changed, but earning assets have gone down.

The reduction of deposit liabilities while reserves are unchanged puts the banks in a position to buy securities in the open market to maintain income; the sellers receive newly created deposits (money), some of which will certainly be put to use. Banks will also try to expand loans. Private borrowing will become easier. Loans leading to deposit (money) creation will tend to rise. Although the stock of money may not rebound immediately to the level before the Treasury retired its debt, an upward movement is probable. The recreating of money will be associated with a growth in private spending, as borrowers use the proceeds of loans or as sellers of securities use the dollars they receive. Consequently, the initial tendency of the budgetary surplus to depress business may soon wear off. The time lapse depends, among other things, upon the demand for loans, the willingness of banks to lend, and the inclination of sellers of securities to hold on to cash.

Retiring Debt Held by the Federal Reserve. The Treasury may repay debt held by the Federal Reserve.[6] If so, funds are transferred from the private accounts of taxpayers in commercial banks to the Treasury account at the FR.   The commercial banks lose in the first step deposit liabilities (taxpayers' accounts).   In the second step the banks lose an equal volume of assets (deposits at the FR which have gone into the Treasury's account there).   The assets which commercial banks lose are reserves which permit them, as a group, to lend on a multiple basis.   If the banks are fully "loaned up" when the Treasury retires debt, they will find themselves under pressure to reduce deposit liabilities.   Thus the initial force of contraction will be supplemented by *additional* response from the banks.

This response, however, can be offset, fully or partially, by action of banks in borrowing from the Federal Reserve.   And the monetary authorities may use any one or more of their powers to influence bank lending capacity—especially open market action.   The FR itself can neutralize, accentuate, or counteract the monetary effects of the Treasury's use of its surplus.   Within wide limits, the effectiveness of fiscal policy, therefore, depends not only upon the size of the budgetary surplus but also upon the Treasury's choice of what debt to retire and upon what the FR authorities do.

Treasury Uses Budget Surplus to Retire Debt Held by Federal Reserve
(Billions of dollars)

Federal Reserve		Commercial banks		Treasury	
Assets	*Liabilities*	*Assets*	*Liabilities*	*Assets*	*Liabilities*
		first step		*first step*	
		No change	Deposits of taxpayers −5		
			Deposits of Treasury +5	Funds received from taxpayers +5	No change
second step		*second step*		*second step*	
	Deposit of commercial bank (legal reserve) −5	Deposit at FR −5	Deposits of Treasury −5	Deposit at commercial bank −5	No change
No change	Deposit of Treasury +5			Deposit at FR +5	
third step				*third step*	
Government debt −5	Deposit of Treasury −5			Deposit at FR −5	Debt outstanding −5
		Change in stock of money	−5		
		Change in legal reserves	−5		

[6] In practice, under our system, the decisions about debt holdings by the Federal Reserve rest with the System, not the Treasury.

Accumulation of Cash Balances. The Treasury may use a budgetary surplus not to reduce debt but to build up its cash balances. (1) If the Treasury keeps the funds on deposit at commercial banks, the result is a reduction in velocity, *i.e.,* the *increase* in the Treasury's balance has a velocity of zero as long as the funds are held idle. As a result, presumably, the average velocity of all deposits will drop. (2) If the Treasury transfers deposits from commercial banks to the FR, however, the banks lose reserves just as if the Treasury had retired debt owned by the FR. The lending power of the commercial banks drops. Not only the budgetary surplus but also its use thus operate to reduce the flow of national income. Yet the FR can, if it wishes, offset—or reinforce—the monetary aspects.

Roles of Both Fiscal and Monetary Action. The importance of monetary policy in the total process leads us to ask, "Does fiscal action, the surplus, do anything which monetary action could not accomplish, and accomplish without the unpleasantness of taxes which help produce the budget surplus?" Fiscal policy most certainly does play a role of independent importance.

The original withdrawal from the income stream is a direct restrictive action. This withdrawal itself reduces the flow of income and aggregate demand. Such repressive effect of a budgetary surplus reduces the load which monetary policy might otherwise need to carry, *e.g.,* as an anti-inflationary force. The larger the surplus, the smaller the job remaining for changes in the monetary sphere if the two are to work in the same direction.[7] But a large budget surplus may be inadequate for halting inflation in the absence of restraint on the quantity of money. (If the demand for money —loans—and interest rates are high, monetary policy can perhaps do the whole job without special support from fiscal policy.) A budgetary surplus when the monetary authorities are trying to encourage business, however, will make the "money task" harder, perhaps impossible if the demand for money and loans is inelastic and interest rates are very low.

Deficit Financing to Stimulate the Economy

Monetary factors are no less vital in determining the eventual effectiveness of fiscal policy in stimulating the economy. The fiscal program which will raise national income is one by which government (1) increases the amount of money it pours into the income stream through spending (2) while holding constant or reducing the amount it takes out by taxation. The clearest way to conceive the relation is to assume that the government runs a budget deficit.

The deficit must be financed. The government can do so in different

---

[7] A budgetary surplus is a form of saving. It may conceivably be sufficiently large to meet enough of the demand for loans, to prevent inflation without a rise in interest rates. Obviously, the result will depend upon the condition of demand for loans.

ways. The choice of method will affect the amount of "boost" given the economy. The stimulating effect, if any, of a deficit can vary greatly. The considerations are roughly the opposite of those described in the financing of a surplus.

Borrowing from the General Public. The Treasury may sell new debt to the general public, including savings institutions. (1) The money will come, at least to some degree, from funds that would otherwise be used for spending on investment goods—perhaps on some new construction project. To this extent there will be no net stimulating effect, for private spending will drop, offsetting government addition to the income stream. (2) But if some of the new debt is bought with money that would otherwise be idle, spending (velocity) for the economy as a whole rises; the system gets a stimulus. There is no way, of course, for the Treasury to limit bond sales to those members of the general public who will pay with dollars which would otherwise remain unused for consumption or investment. Therefore, sales of new debt to the general public are likely to have less stimulating power than the remaining methods of financing a deficit.

Borrowing from Commercial Banks. Sales of debt to commercial banks can lead to the creation of deposits. The new money gets into circulation as the Treasury spends. In effect, a portion of government buying is financed by new money. The economy gets an expansionary boost as the added money circulates. In selling debt to commercial banks, however, the Treasury cannot be certain of the amount by which demand deposits will actually increase.

(1) The banks may lend less to business and consumers in order to lend more to government. For example, the banks may have no excess lending capacity. If so, how can they expand their total lending? They may accommodate the Treasury—but at the expense of other customers. A deficit can be financed by sale to the banking system with no creation of money, or no more than otherwise.

(2) But if banks have excess reserves, they can buy government debt—and increase their earnings by creating new deposits for the Treasury without reducing other loans and security holdings. (Why would banks buy the new debt if they had not gone into the market earlier to use excess reserves to buy government debt? The terms of the new issues may be more attractive.) Such financing will be stimulating. The possibilities, however, are ordinarily small *unless* the monetary authorities also increase legal reserves (or reduce reserve requirements) because banks do not customarily have undesired excess reserves. The FR, of course, can always add to reserves, with or without a budgetary change, but the effect will depend upon the state of demand for loans. We compare two cases: (a) If business is booming, a bit of monetary ease can lead to money creation without a budget deficit; business demand for loans will be active enough to assure that added lending capacity will lead to new money which

will be injected into the economy promptly. (b) Now we consider a period of recession, low interest rates, and excess reserves. In these conditions a monetary policy of ease will be weak relative to fiscal policy which includes a deficit financed by expansion of the stock of money; the Treasury is the "demander" of new money like businesses in the prosperity case. Treasury demand can be satisfied without requiring any other borrower to "go without."

Borrowing from the Federal Reserve. The Federal Reserve may enlarge its holdings by the amount of the new Treasury debt. In doing so, the FR increases the Treasury's checking account by an equivalent amount. As the Treasury uses these new deposits to pay its bills, the recipients will deposit the checks in their own accounts at commercial banks. These banks thereby get larger deposits at the FR. These deposits are legal reserves which support multiple expansion of commercial bank deposits. Some such expansion is virtually certain, not next week but as the months pass. In times of high prosperity, full expansion can be expected soon. During recession, multiple expansion will be slower and perhaps incomplete.

Clearly, financing a deficit by selling debt to the central bank will do much more than either of the other types of financing to raise the flow of money income over time. As always, however, the total effect will depend upon other conditions in the economy, such as the demand for loans. And the results can be accentuated or offset by open market (or other FR) action.

Currency Issue. Currency issue remains as another possibility. Instead of selling bonds, the government can print currency to use in paying its bills. Some of the new currency will continue to circulate as an addition to the hand-to-hand medium of exchange. Some, and probably most, of the new paper money will flow to the commercial banks and increase their legal reserves. Multiple expansion becomes possible. The eventual result will resemble, to a large extent, that from Treasury sale of debt to the FR.

Opposition to currency issue for deficit financing has strong emotional foundation. The printing of currency has occurred when governments are unable or unwilling to tax adequately or to borrow on satisfactory terms. Currency issue has gone with serious economic illness. It has accompanied that monstrous calamity, hyperinflation. Nevertheless, price-level increases need not be associated with currency issue—not any more so than with borrowing from banks.[8]

To the Treasury, currency has one advantage over borrowing. Paper

---

[8] Conceivably, the growth of M in the form of currency may lead to an increase in V. The public may become more distrustful of paper money than it would be of an equal amount of bank deposit expansion. V may then become somewhat higher than if currency were not expanding.

money requires no payment of interest. The Treasury gets an interest-free loan. The public, however, may not really want to make such a loan, *i.e.,* families and businesses may not want to hold more currency. Then the new paper money will flow to the banks—which must then handle larger deposits, probably at some increase in operating costs. Legal reserves, as noted above, will rise, and thus, in turn, will the ability of banks to lend and to earn income. Today, of course, direct Treasury sale of debt to the FR (or FR acquisition of Treasury debt in the open market) can yield essentially the same results as currency issue, because the Fed now refunds its marginal (incremental) income to the Treasury.

In short, the total consequences of fiscal policy depend upon more than the differences in income flows which result *directly* from tax and spending changes. The effectiveness also depends upon the monetary policy used in dealing with budgetary results and upon the responses of the economy to changes in monetary conditions. In turn, of course, fiscal policy can supplement or counteract monetary policy. The success of any monetary policy will rest to varying degrees upon the way in which the government is handling its own finances.

PROBLEMS OF DISCRETIONARY FISCAL ACTION FOR STABILIZATION

The potentialities of fiscal and monetary policy working in harmony are indeed tremendous. Moreover, one of the two can do much to offset undesired results of the other. Perhaps here is one of modern man's great accomplishments, one enabling him to manage rather well a branch of his affairs that once seemed beyond rational control. Yet the problems of using the "new" knowledge are tougher than economists once thought. The uncertainties of forecasting discussed in Chapter 23 are common to both fiscal and monetary policy. Other practical problems are more pertinent to one than to the other.

We look first at implementing what is called "discretionary" fiscal policy. By this we mean tax or expenditure action which is taken for the *specific* purpose of *altering* the *level* of *national income* (to stimulate *output* or to prevent a rise in the *price level*) in the months or the year or so ahead.

Responsibility for Decision Making

One difference between fiscal and monetary action is the *location* of responsibility for control.

Monetary policy is largely made and executed by a few administrators who have considerable freedom within a framework fixed (a) by Congress and (b) by existing financial institutions. The central decisions can be made quickly and in amounts designed (in light of the best knowledge available) to produce the result desired. Unfortunately, there is no assurance that the decisions will be good. (Moreover, as indicated in Chapter 23, the responses to changes in monetary policy can lag many months behind the action.)

Discretionary fiscal policy depends largely upon the work of Congress. *Major* changes must be the result of Congressional action.[9] Congress is not unable to act quickly. Yet the preponderance of evidence is that action will be slow. Why?

Inadequate Public Understanding

Both Congress and the Executive Branch react to, as well as try to lead, public opinion. As late as 1963 the public in general was not prepared to support tax reduction to stimulate the economy when the Federal budget deficit was substantial and when expenditures were continuing to rise rapidly—but when unemployment of men and of equipment were wastefully high.[10] At other times since the war, public understanding of the basic economic factors had also impeded discretionary fiscal policy action by government. In 1963, however, there was a contrast. The President and his whole Administration made a sustained and determined effort to explain the elementary economics of tax reduction to energize a somewhat lethargic economy. The educational results were disappointing.

The eventual tax cut came more from the influence, pressure, and support of a relative few (including most economists and some leading businessmen) than from any groundswell of public endorsement.[11]

Varied Interests Involved

Fiscal policy changes involve matters of taxation and spending which are important in and of themselves—not merely for their effects on the

[9] Debt management is more like monetary policy. The Treasury has discretionary power in what it does in refinancing the debt already outstanding.

[10] The terms "substantial" and "rapidly" reflect judgments which are the author's estimate of public attitudes. The budget which President Kennedy presented in 1963, shortly before his tax-reduction-to-stimulate-the-economy message, estimated an administrative budget deficit of $11.9 billion for the approaching fiscal year; expenditures recommended were $23.3 billion above the 1960 level and $4.5 billion over that of the year then ending.

[11] Of a sample of 321 academic economists, 84 percent favored tax reduction; the average cut endorsed was $11 billion. Chase Manhattan Bank, *Business in Brief*, Nov.-Dec., 1963, p. 4. To get the tax bill through Congress, President Kennedy, President Johnson, and leaders in both Houses of Congress pledged to cut, or at least to work to stop the growth of, Federal expenditures. From the point of view of economy and efficiency in resource use, cuts in Federal spending were perhaps highly desirable. But the macroeconomic considerations—the effects on the level of national income in the short run—of such reductions would tend to offset some of the stimulating effects of tax reduction. The need to promise such expenditure actions suggests that public opinion had by no means come to understand the economic lessons which academicians and the Administration had been trying to teach.

national income. (Implementation of monetary policy suffers less from deliberate pressures exerted by varied groups on the process of making decisions.) The choices can mean much to one or another group, enough to justify extensive effort in persuading Congress; the months taken in hearing arguments delay action. *Timing* of Congressional decision proves difficult to predict. Inescapably, however, timing of cyclical stabilization actions has crucial significance. Timing governs the *speed* with which a desirable result can be obtained. Moreover, the amount of action eventually "required" will depend upon the period during which developing forces can build up, perhaps feeding on themselves. The prompter the remedy, the less required.

Specific tax and spending policies are varied. Each has independent importance; each requires explicit attention for its stabilization effects. The "mix" of eventual actions which Congress and the President decide upon may differ appreciably from what expert judgment would prescribe— or from what even the most powerful official prefers.

The President has great power, but it is far from complete. When President Truman vetoed tax reduction in 1948 because he thought it potentially inflationary, Congress overrode the veto. In January 1963, President Kennedy began to exert the tremendous influence of his position to get a prompt tax cut to stimulate business. Yet Congress deliberated until February 1964 before passing a new tax bill. And its features departed materially from the original recommendations of the White House. A President, of course, can be wrong. Whether right or wrong, his general policy may not get enough votes in Congress unless several interest groups receive concessions.

"Fiscal policy" consideration of specific revenue and spending measures must take account of "normal" criteria of tax justice, past commitments, administrative feasibility, reversibility, and other such factors—as well as of the effects on national income. Such diverse considerations are hard to compare with each other. What if the tax reduction most likely to stimulate a "droopy" economy appears unfair to many people? What if a spending cut with the greatest possibilities of reducing inflationary pressures would slow down a highly desirable public project? What if a tax increase to check inflation seems likely to retard economic growth? Will a specific change upset Federal-state-local relations? Can a spending increase be cut back later? Such questions indicate some of the many practical problems which arise in attempts to use fiscal policy measures to supplement, or to take the place of, monetary actions to stabilize the economy.

Judging Probable Effectiveness

Other problems of making discretionary fiscal policy work raise more than minor challenges. What, for example, is the effectiveness of different kinds of tax and of spending changes for achieving national income objectives? When we think in terms of big aggregates of "taxes" and "expenditures"—the totals which are parts of the national accounts—we may be excused for assuming that each dollar has equal effect.[12] Yet in fact some may have more influence than others. Sales taxes, for example, probably do more (per dollar collected) to curb consumption than does the revenue from the upper brackets of the income tax. The latter, however, will probably cut new investment, especially some kinds of risk taking, more than does sales tax revenue (per dollar received). But our knowledge is incomplete.

Some types of government spending may give rise to larger series of private spending than will other types. Then, too, some dollars may have more effect under some conditions than under others.[13] Again, we know less than we should like about the potential effectiveness of different types of fiscal action.

Lags and Timing

The time between becoming fully aware of the desirability of a tax or expenditure change and the start of an action which embodies the change —this period tends to be long in relation to either the expansion or the contraction phase of a business cycle. The problem is more than one of forecasting and more, also, than one of getting the President and Congress to act. The additional factor involves "getting rolling," and at a desirable speed. Some tax changes can be put into operation quickly and without serious difficulty—changes in commodity taxes, for example, or even a higher or a lower rate of income-tax withholding.[14] Other tax revisions, however, may for months have little effect on actual collections—income taxes, personal and corporate, not subject to withholding.

Some changes in spending programs require a year or more before the results are significant. Such lags are especially important where construction is involved—planning and making detailed specifications, buying or condemning land, advertising for competitive bids, letting contracts, and starting work. Nevertheless, even a Federal commitment to spend can affect the economy by inducing private spending before the actual payment of money by the Treasury—"can" but not "certainly will." But try to

[12] Even this statement is not valid because the results depend upon the method of financing and the general condition of the economy.

[13] A corporation profits tax that collects funds which would otherwise remain for a time in the firm as unused dollars in the bank (V of zero) would for a time have little net deflationary effect. Under other conditions, however, the same amount of tax would reduce ownership equity of a business which would serve as the basis for substantial borrowing for expansion; if so, the tax would produce a restraining effect greater than the amount of tax itself.

[14] In 1964 changes in the rate of withholding of personal income tax went into effect 6 weeks or less after the new tax law signed by the President.

imagine the difficulties of slowing down a building project once the contract has been awarded and work has gotten under way!

Some Federal spending can change promptly. An example would be increases, and possibly even decreases, in welfare payments where administrative organizations exist. If the quick-response taxes or spending are what seem desirable for reasons such as equity and economic efficiency, fine and good. If not, however, the choice becomes tantalizing and reduces accordingly the net attractiveness of fiscal policy measures.

Tax and expenditure adjustments deliberately designed to counter "normal" business cycles call for more frequent changes than are ordinarily feasible in our system of government. A parliamentary system like that in Britain or Canada lends itself somewhat better to frequent or "delicate" changes; even reversals of policy can follow promptly upon agreement within the Cabinet that action is required.

Why not, then, modify our system to help solve the timing problems? Why not give key U.S. officials—perhaps the President and a dozen or so leaders of Congress—considerable discretion to act promptly to alter fiscal policy? (Other officials have discretion to alter monetary policy.) Congress might specify that when certain price or employment developments occur, such a group, taking account of all evident trends in the economy, could act within certain limits.

In 1962 President Kennedy proposed that the President be given authority to lower personal income tax rates by not more than 5 percentage points upon Presidential declaration that the Employment Act required such change. The tax cut would go into effect within 30 days of submission to Congress unless rejected by a joint resolution; it would remain in effect for 6 months unless revised or renewed. He also asked for a standby public works program. Under it the President would be authorized to initiate accelerated spending within 2 months after the seasonally adjusted unemployment rate had risen in at least 3 out of 4 months (or in 4 out of 6 months) and had risen to a level at least one percentage point higher than its level for 4 months (or 6 months) earlier.[15] Various other formulae have been suggested.

Such proposals have appeal. Deliberately arranged increases or decreases in the income flow might offset much of any undesired change in the private sectors of the economy. Despite the potential promise of such plans, however, Congress refuses to give up even a small amount of its control of finances. The reluctance rests in part upon doubt about the economic merit of the plan and in part upon fears of political results—Congress vis-à-vis the Executive, one party versus the other.

The practical difficulties of getting timely Congressional action, and of putting the changes into operation, are discouraging. One phase of a cycle

[15] Both the tax and spending proposals had more features and qualifications than presented here. *Economic Report of the President . . . January 1962,* p. 18-20.

can run its course before a need is recognized, leaders formulate and present a proposal, Congress acts, and the change in taxes or spending begins to influence the income stream.

In fact, there is a possibility that *well-intentioned action will do more harm than good.* Why? Because it is excessive, poorly timed, or "oversold." A policy which for a few months is genuinely helpful can work damage later. The harm done then may equal or exceed the earlier benefits. Aids to construction, for example, may exert their major effect when private demands have become stronger; the aids then raise costs and thereby reduce the quantity demanded later. Spending programs are difficult to reduce, and taxes hard to raise, even when boom conditions are adding to forces of inflation.

Another difficulty grows out of the extent—or the narrowness—of public understanding. A public which is told one year that a budget deficit will best serve the economy may not react favorably to admonitions next year for a budget surplus.

Each year's regular consideration of the budget, of course, affords some opportunity for discretionary action which takes account of the economic outlook for the coming year or so. At least a few, more or less normal, tax and spending decisions can be modified to help meet near-term stabilization needs. The number of items in today's Federal budget—and cash spending equal to nearly one-fifth of GNP—must provide basis for hope that "normal" budgetary decisions can take deliberate account of cyclical needs on a scale that is more than minor. Anticyclical considerations, however, cannot always dominate. Postwar cycles have provided little basis for hope that the President and Congress will produce the discretionary fiscal policy which will have the anticyclical effect so many economists have believed possible.

Areas of Greatest Promise

Fiscal action for stabilization offers promise in meeting two rather different needs. (1) One is to adapt the *basic structure* of public finances to meet persisting stabilization needs. (2) Major and exceptional disturbances are not inconceivable—nor beyond remedy; the actions they require are of the types already discussed—on a scale of appropriate size.

One set of structural features involves automatic stabilizers. Another group would counterbalance an undesirable tendency or trend in the economy toward inflation or unemployment.

AUTOMATIC FISCAL STABILIZERS

Rather more by accident than by design, this country and some others have acquired fiscal stabilizers which work automatically. Moves to strengthen and to extend these built-in compensatory devices do not require that the selection of tax or expenditure measures be designed for this purpose alone. Every tax or spending decision must satisfy other criteria—efficiency, service to the general public, fairness, and so on. Yet where there are choices about features of the fiscal structure, one criterion ought to be the relative effectiveness of each in offsetting business fluctuations.

Major Features of a System of Automatic Stabilizers

Let us look at 4 elements which provide automatic stabilizers.

1. One is a *revenue* system which (without changes in rates and exemptions that require Congressional action) will bring in *progressively* more revenue as the national income rises, especially as income rises toward the point where inflation will develop. The rising "tax take" will thus assure that more and more of the *increases* in income are unavailable for financing private consumption and investment.

2. When business drops, however, a more rapid rate of decline in tax collections will leave a bigger percentage of income available for private spending—GNP drops 2 percent, tax collections 4 percent. Money to finance private demand will drop less in percentage terms than national income because tax payments fall relatively more—and without the necessity of new Congressional action.

Government *spending* can move in the opposite pattern.

3. Government's role will be stabilizing if the government's own demand for goods and services—or the demand that it helps generate through transfer payments—falls as private demand rises.

4. In a recession, however, an automatic increase in Federal spending will reduce the decline in the economy. A rise in government buying, for example, can offset some of the drop in private buying.

If revenues and expenditures thus move in different directions as the level of national income rises or falls, changes in the *net budget position* will develop without deliberate planning and action by officials. Such budget shifts can exert forces in the right direction, especially if financed "correctly" and if reinforced by monetary policy. The amounts, it is true, can hardly be ideal. But to have them in the right direction helps. And today they are large.

Government Spending

First, however, we note a stabilizer that is not, strictly speaking, an "automatically offsetting" factor—the *mass* of government spending.

There is a vast bulk of outlay which does not change, at least not with any fluctuations in business activity. If private consumption and investment were to fall (or rise) by 3 or even 6 percent, major items of public spending would not respond. Congress, state legislatures, and city councils would not change the great body of spending, especially not within the 25 months or so of half of an ordinary cycle. Items of Federal-state-local spending which will remain essentially stable (as far as cyclical forces are concerned) are now relatively more important than before World War II. They equal perhaps one-fourth of the GNP. Here, then, is one vast sector of the economy in which "snowballing" will neither start nor tend to add cumulatively to cyclical change in other sectors.

Some government spending does fluctuate, however, and in the *opposite direction* from private spending. This expenditure changes automatically in ways that help stabilize total spending in the economy.

Benefits to the unemployed are the largest. These payments (with a few exceptions) are paid for by state payroll taxes. As regards stabilization, however, the financing is essentially Federal. Payments are made from Federal trust accounts whose management can be tied in with monetary policy. The money begins to reach the unemployed two weeks or so after the last pay check, as a matter of right and with little uncertainty. The payment will often be half or a bit more of the former "take-home" pay (what the worker had been getting after deductions). Most of it will be spent promptly. The V of this money, at least initially, is high. If some of the M is newly created by the banking system, the total stimulating effect in the short run can be substantial. These payments help put a floor under consumption spending. During the 1957-58 recession, for example, monthly benefits rose from $113 million in September 1957 to around $400 million a month in the spring of 1958. They dropped to about $170 million a month in the summer of 1959, then rose to over $300 million in March 1960 as business sagged. For the mass of workers, therefore, unemployment need not lead to the drastic cuts in buying that used to be inevitable. Benefits generally last from 4 to 6 months or until the person gets work. This support of buying does not last indefinitely, but because the unemployed are to large extent a shifting group, consumer buying will be sustained better than if an equal number of persons without jobs consisted of the same people month in and month out; benefits would expire for many.

Other government spending may also rise automatically. Anyone over age 65 (and women over 62) with Social Security coverage can, as a matter of right, claim benefits when work ceases. The checks come each month until income from work begins again, if it does. Each year more Americans reach the eligible age and can count upon this stabilizing element of income.

Governments also provide various types of relief or welfare assistance more or less automatically, *i.e.,* under arrangements which are largely fixed without regard to short-run business fluctuations.   The Federal government has 5 programs of grants in aid to states for the needy—for the aged, households with dependent children, the blind, the permanently disabled, for which all states qualify—and medical aid for the aged, not yet available in all states.   The money is paid on the basis of need.   States and localities, in addition, have programs for helping the poor who do not fall into one of the four Federally-aided groups.   Total payments rise somewhat as business conditions drop, and fall a little as income rises.[16]

Revenues

More important stabilizers are those in the revenue system, chiefly income taxes.   The personal income tax now reaches almost every worker; so does the Social Security payroll tax.   Most earners are subject to marginal tax rates of at least 18 percent (more in many states), nearly all of which is withheld at source.   Several million people pay still higher marginal rates by quarterly declarations.

Thus when personal income rises, an average of nearly one-fifth of the rise flows automatically to the Treasury in the form of income tax.[17] (Here, indeed, is a powerful check to any tendency toward large inflation.) On the other hand, when national income falls, *disposable* income declines by a smaller amount; for example, if earnings fall $10 a week, take-home pay goes down by around $8, as taxes make up the remainder.   The automatic stabilization effect of the personal income tax could be increased by applying withholding at the progressive rates which apply to most brackets of taxable income, rather than restricting withholding to 14 percent, the lowest bracket rate.

The corporation income tax is an even bigger stabilizer.   The rate which applies at the margin to most business profit is nearly 50 percent (higher in many states).   Profit, of course, is the most volatile element of national income.[18]   The Treasury absorbs almost half of the increases in

---

[16] The programs of aid to agriculture are complicated; there is no assurance that they will be cyclically stabilizing.

[17] The tax reduction of 1964 changed conditions so that figures based on earlier experience must be modified to a degree not measurable by late 1964.   Formerly, income up to $2000 for a single person and $4000 for a married couple was taxed at one rate, 20 percent.   Now 4 different rates apply as new brackets in this range were created.

[18] From the second quarter of 1959 to the first quarter of 1961, the annual rate of corporate profit (before tax, and seasonally adjusted) fell by 22 percent while compensation of employees rose 4 percent.   From the first quarter of 1961 to the last quarter of 1963, the profit rise was almost 40 percent while compensation of employees rose 19 percent.

net earnings when business expands, and about half the drop in profit when business declines (down to the point where losses appear). In some cases, the Treasury even shares losses. Today, a business, whether or not incorporated, which suffers a loss in one year may recompute its income tax for the three preceding years. Funds become available to the business when they are likely to be very much needed. These dollars also help prevent forced liquidation, even bankruptcy, and thereby temper the force of evils which add to the pressure of cumulative contraction.

Commodity, other excise and employer payroll tax collections also have a stabilizing effect. The revenue system exerts a substantial stabilizing effect. In the 1960–1961 recession, corporation income tax changes alone equaled more than half as much as the drop in GNP, while the personal income tax was one-sixth as large.

The total of automatic stabilizers makes up a powerful arsenal for fighting cycles. In postwar recessions the total of tax plus expenditure stabilizers has ranged around half or more of the decline in GNP; in recoveries the offset has been somewhat smaller—around 30 percent.[19]

This feature of our economic structure helps explain the mildness of postwar fluctuations.

STRUCTURAL FISCAL CHANGE FOR
PERSISTING NEEDS

What changes in the structure of the fiscal system would contribute more to stability? Viewing the total economy in proper perspective will always be difficult. Who can be certain whether a need will persist? Does an undesirable condition which seems destined to last indefinitely present a need for public action? If so, what? The judgments of specialists vary, and the past record of some who speak with assurance does not always inspire confidence in their prescience. Let us look at two possibilities.

1. Suppose that the public seems likely (a) to save too little in relation to what it wants to spend on investment goods and (b) to pay less in taxes than it orders government to spend. As a result there will be a tendency for total demand—C plus I plus G—to pull up prices. Monetary policy must then be weighted on the restrictive side. We may then expect more from it in preventing inflation than monetary policy can carry without truly undesirable consequences. Moreover, the Federal fiscal system does lead to bigger deficits during business contraction than surpluses in expan-

[19] W. Lewis, Jr., *Federal Government Fiscal Policy in the Postwar Recessions* (Washington: The Brookings Institution, 1962).

sion. The resulting growth in public debt, though by no means foreboding disaster, causes concern in some circles.

What might be done? (a) A different *overall* tax-spending balance could help offset the tendency—more taxes, less spending. The Treasury would become less of a net demander of loan funds. It might even become a net supplier over a business cycle. Over the years, then, interest rates—and also consumer demand—would tend to be lower on the average. (b) The kinds of taxes and spending might be adapted to help counteract the "shortage" of savings or the "excess" of investment plus consumption. In fact, however, even if there were agreement on the existence of the need, economists (and politicians) would find it difficult to agree on the changes which would be most effective, while also meeting other needs and wishes of the public.[20] To date, at least, voters are not obviously willing to provide budgetary surpluses for either anti-inflationary purposes or to ease the task of the managers of the monetary system.

The rising trend of national income (as distinguished from cyclical expansions) provides more revenue automatically from any given set of tax rates. The secular rise in tax collections may outpace the growth of Federal spending. The "growth power" of spending, however, exhibits vigor as existing programs expand and new ones are adopted and grow—in spite of talk about controlling the growth of Federal spending.

2. The second possibility is that conditions like those of the 1930's may reappear—not extreme but continuing stagnation. Investment, year in and year out, was then lower than needed to match the savings which would be made at high levels of national income. If such a condition seems more than temporary, modifications of tax and spending policies might help shift the balance in a better direction. They could do what monetary policy could not: (a) Deficits could be used to pump income into the economy much of the time, and (b) the tax system could be modified to give positive incentives (or reduce disincentives) to investment. Federal tax changes in 1962 were designed in part to encourage business investment, especially in machinery and equipment but with an inevitable "spilling-over" into buildings.[21]

Yet here again, the responsible prescription proves to be less easy than appears on the surface. One asks, "What will be called for in an

---

[20] Further reduction in the highest income tax rates would doubtless stimulate private saving—and probably investment as well—not only because more savings would be available (*e.g.*, the closely owned business), but also because of better incentives.

[21] Businesses received a credit offsetting tax up to 7 percent of tax, subject to numerous restrictions. Deductions for depreciation were increased for most businesses, whether or not incorporated; the total deductible remained limited to the amount originally put into the facilities. The change was an alteration in the timing of deduction so that much more was deductible in the early years, less later.

unknown future? What structural changes will produce the most appropriate totals? Which of the possible tax revisions would be preferable, those to curb saving or those to stimulate investment?" Answers are not clear.

Business recoveries in 1959–60 and 1961–62 were incomplete and laggard. One reason given by some economists who had studied the problem intensively was what is now called "fiscal drag"; the Federal revenue system siphoned off too much of the rising income too soon. Consumer and business ability to buy, therefore, did not get high enough to purchase the full employment output at prevailing prices.[22] A growing national income with sharply rising tax receipts, it was said, would be repressed repeatedly by tax collections too large in relation to aggregate demand. The economy would not reach full employment unless tax rates were reduced below the levels of the 1964 law, or expenditure programs enlarged above those of 1964. This line of argument received extensive professional support.

CONCLUSION

Fiscal policy offers no complete substitute for monetary policy. The two, if they work consistently, can accomplish much. The cooperation is of great importance. Fiscal action offers a convenient device for accentuating the effectiveness of monetary policy—and vice versa. The financing of deficits and surpluses inevitably involves monetary factors.

The total results depend upon both the fiscal and the monetary element of the combination. Fiscal policy, though potentially a great boon to mankind, is not the simple "economic engineering" once envisioned. Automatic stabilizers can be counted on for many substantial results. When we want more, however, the problems of judgment and action will be perplexing.

When the economy is booming and the need is for restraint, monetary action can generally suffice. It is likely to be easier than raising taxes or cutting government spending. Enough tightening can prevent expansion, and even force contraction, in the stock of money so that prices stop rising. Under such conditions tax reduction or increase in Federal spending would call for more stringent monetary action.

When the economy is receding or in the doldrums, monetary ease may bring only small and slow stimulus. Tax reduction or expenditure increase, if financed appropriately, can give a direct and virtually certain boost.

If the budget is in deficit when the economy is booming, monetary

[22] The argument, of course, rests upon certain assumptions about monetary conditions. If the rising tax receipts reduce the Federal deficit, will not more funds be available for business borrowing? What will be the responses? Clearly, answers to these questions will depend in part upon conditions of the time and place.

policy can offset inflationary tendencies. If for some reason (such as serious balance-of-payments deficits) "tight" money seems necessary when the economy is suffering excessive unemployment, fiscal policy can provide stimulus as the Treasury borrows where private business finds the cost too high.

QUESTIONS

1. What is fiscal policy? What do its supporters mean when they say that fiscal policy operates directly on the income stream whereas monetary policy does not?

2. "It is not the magnitude of government expenditures that counts in affecting national income but the size of expenditures in relation to the size of taxes." Discuss.

3. Explain how a budget deficit, a surplus, and balance may affect the level of economic activity. Which is most appropriate to fight a recession? Why?

4. What can a businessman learn about the economic outlook from forecasts of budget surpluses or deficits?

5. Show by means of balance sheets of the banking system how the financing of a deficit influences the effects of the deficit on the economy.

6. "One reason business should welcome a Federal budget surplus is that the Treasury retires debt and in so doing increases the capital available for financing business." Discuss.

7. What are some of the problems of discretionary fiscal policy? Which are problems for monetary policy as well and which are not? What advantages and disadvantages of fiscal policy are not shared by monetary policy?

8. What difficulties does the American political process hold for the implementation of a stabilizing fiscal policy?

9. What are "automatic stabilizers"? Describe those which are most important.

10. How can monetary action offset the effects of a Federal budget surplus? a deficit?

11. What advantages and disadvantages do built-in stabilizers possess compared with discretionary stabilizers? What are the arguments for and against relying exclusively on automatic stabilizers?

CHAPTER 25   *THE TREASURY AND MONETARY POLICY: WAR FINANCE: DEBT MANAGEMENT*

FROM the days of Alexander Hamilton, and in fact from times long preceding the establishment of the United States, government finances and the monetary system have been closely related. The relations have changed, as have the institutions for dealing with them. War has been the chief source of both change and problems. Business fluctuations, however, have also played a part. And concern for economic stability and economic growth must influence Treasury financing. Day-to-day handling of Treasury cash balances cannot be divorced from the operations of the Federal Reserve. Nor can the Fed ignore the Treasury's problems. Central banking and national government finance merge at many points.

BORROWING AND MONEY CREATION

National governments control the mechanism for creating money. Voters and public officials—in Congress, the White House, and the Treasury—sometimes like to have the national government get money without requiring the sacrifices of taxpaying. Borrowing offers one means of doing so. It has appeal. Debt, however, requires the payment of interest. The cost of borrowing in freely competitive markets may be higher than is attractive. But national governments have a tempting alternative. They can use the money-creating mechanisms to get funds "cheaply."

In the normal course of events, responsible governments do not make large use of the power to create money as a substitute for taxation. When the pressure gets heavy, however, the public may support the "easy way," and not only during war. Unfortunately, what seems easy will on occasion, but not always, prove hard in the end. In fact, when productive capacity is under-utilized, the use of taxes instead of borrowing will sacrifice an opportunity to benefit the economy. In the Treasury's access to the institutions for creating money, therefore, modern man has both problems and opportunities. Each is of not inconsiderable importance and complexity.

Although everyone prays that financing war will never again become necessary, we review the experience of World War II. A summary can present the major economic problems, illuminate postwar developments, and throw light on issues which remain very much alive.

FINANCING WORLD WAR II [1]

Despite tax increases, borrowing became necessary with the pre-Pearl Harbor rise in armament spending. Interest rates were then at depressed levels, by historical standards. Long-term rates were approximately half those of the 1920's; short-term rates were less than one-fourth of the level which had prevailed through much of our history. The banking system had large excess reserves.[2] Banks could create deposits at virtually no cost, either in operating expense or in the sacrifice of desirable lending alternatives.

Under such conditions of potential supply, low interest rates on bank loans would be expected. Moreover, extensive unemployment of men and of plant and equipment remained through 1941. Considerable armament spending could therefore be financed by creation of demand deposits without threatening significant inflation. For a time, in fact, such financing would facilitate the acquisition of military equipment by the use of resources otherwise idle and do much to keep the armament program from dragging down a depressed economy.

The Treasury naturally chose to borrow from commercial banks. It also sought to borrow from individuals and institutions other than commercial banks—and to do so at interest rates about like those of the 1930's. Private savers would freely lend for long term at low interest rates. Treasury officials welcomed the depressed rate level not only because it would help keep the interest cost down. They also believed that over the long run low interest rates would need to prevail if private borrowing to pay for modern plant, equipment, and housing was to be adequate for full employment. During 1940 and 1941 commercial banks increased their

[1] A. G. Hart and E. C. Brown, *Financing Defense* (New York: Twentieth Century Fund, 1951); H. C. Murphy, *The National Debt in War and Transition* (New York: McGraw-Hill Book Co., 1950).

[2] This abnormal condition was in part a result of the fact that gold had been sent to this country because of the political disturbances in Europe during the 1930's.

holdings of Federal debt by one-third. Demand deposits rose by about the same fraction. The average interest rate on total Federal debt fell slightly to 2.5 percent in 1941.

By early 1942, however, the economy was approaching full use of its productive capacity. And the demand for borrowing became that of a nation fighting a gigantic war—one whose end could not be foreseen. Conditions were most decidedly different from those of 1940. What should the Treasury do to finance deficits which, despite big tax increases, would inevitably be large? The alternatives fell within a range of uncertain size.

Near one limit was the possibility of leaning heavily on commercial banks. If the Federal Reserve would cooperate, the Treasury could be virtually certain of borrowing the dollars required—and at low interest rates. Equally certain, however, was the fact that the resulting increase in the stock of money would add inflationary pressures. Toward the other limit was the possibility of offering an interest rate high enough to stimulate savings and to attract them from private, noninflationary lenders. This approach would obviously raise the dollar cost of borrowing. And was it a practical alternative? (A rise in interest rates would have been of no help in curbing business investment spending; various direct controls effectively restrained investment in plant and equipment except as approved for the war effort.) Many economists believed that the amount which would be saved out of income would not rise significantly with any feasible boost in interest rates. (Even a less pronounced rise would disrupt financial markets, sending the prices of existing long-term debts below par.) The Treasury, it was generally agreed, could not in fact borrow enough without resorting to commercial banks and money creation.

In 4 calendar years, 1942–1945, Federal debt more than quadrupled, rising by over $200 billion. Today, when the economy is so much bigger, and the dollar will buy only about half as much as in the early 1940's, we can scarcely appreciate the significance of this mammoth change.

When the history was eventually revealed, the record showed that the Treasury and the Federal Reserve had decided early to continue about the *pattern* of interest rates, and the *low level,* established before Pearl Harbor. Treasury bills were to yield ⅜ of 1 percent; long-term marketable bonds were to yield 2.5 percent; issues of intermediate periods were to bring varying yields between these limits. Commercial banks would be supplied with enough expansion of reserves (by open market policy) to support the increased deposits to be created for the government.

The FR gradually absorbed most of the low-yielding Treasury bills. As time passed, more and more of the public sensed what the officials were doing and became convinced that the pattern of rates would remain effective—*i.e.,* that monetary authorities would somehow prevent the prices of outstanding Treasury obligations from falling below par. Consequently, private owners of Treasury debt tended to shift to longer-term, higher-yield, issues. Even 20-year bonds appeared almost as liquid (free from interest rate risk) as 90-day Treasury bills and certificates for one year and certainly much more rewarding. Within varying limits, a central bank can exert powerful influence on the quantity of money and the rate of interest, but it cannot overcome inherently irreconcilable results. Having determined to control the rate of interest, the FR had to create whatever money was needed.

In the years 1942–1945, commercial banks increased their holdings of government debt by $69 billion.[3] For the most part this portion of the debt was monetized. The Federal Reserve acquired $22 billion. The total supply of money grew some $66 billion. (Velocity, however, fell.) By no means all of the debt increase was sold to banks. Individuals, insurance companies, and other non-bank institutions bought more than the banks, nearly $137 billion in all. Government trust funds acquired $18 billion. The average rate of interest on Federal debt even fell to 1.9 percent in 1945. No one knows what might have been required to have gotten enough further private saving to have eliminated, say, half of the inflationary bank borrowing. Selling efforts were vigorous, especially for savings bonds, but the offer of greater rewards for saving was not really tried.[4] Virtually no use was made of compulsion to lend to the government, but heavy reliance was placed on wage and price controls and other direct regulations to slow the rise in prices. Forces of inflation were "repressed" or "suppressed." The economy became increasingly liquid.

Today, we can scarcely visualize another consideration—fear that difficulties in getting cash might hinder the war effort. Responsible officials believed that even an appearance of Treasury trouble in getting dollars might hurt America's prestige abroad. Ready access to ample cash seemed essential for morale.

DEBT MANAGEMENT FROM
WORLD WAR II TO THE "ACCORD"

Continuing problems remained for the Treasury after hostilities ceased. Revenues remained high enough so that, with the steady growth

[3] Actual operations were more complex than the text discussion can suggest. In some respects the debt operations were carried out very skillfully. Yet there were features that are hard to justify—notably the ease with which the public could borrow from banks to buy higher-yielding Treasury debt. "Playing the pattern" of pegged interest rates could sometimes bring profit, e.g., as a ⅞ percent one-year certificate approached maturity and competed with a ⅜ percent bill.

[4] After having sold a substantial volume of long-term debt yielding 2.5 percent, the Treasury became more reluctant to see interest rates rise. The price of outstanding bonds would drop. Government credit might have suffered more than warranted by any rational appraisal. Here was a risk greater than Treasury officials felt justified in taking.

of United States government trust accounts (about $2.5 billion a year), net new borrowing from the public was not required from 1946 to 1952. Refundings, however, presented a continuing problem.

At war's end, the volume of short-term debt was large, and every day the rest of the debt came closer to maturity. Moreover, much long-term debt was redeemable at the option of the bondholder. (During the war one point used in selling savings bonds had been that they could be turned in for cash to purchase consumer goods once peace returned.) The Treasury always had to be able to provide cash to those seeking to redeem bonds. In short, even though the total debt was not growing, the government continually faced the need to borrow substantial sums.

In peace as in war, the Treasury wanted to borrow at rates of interest that would keep the taxpayer's costs low. The total interest expense would inevitably be large, greater than total Federal spending in most prewar years. A difference in interest cost of one percentage point a year was $2.5 billion at war's end (and over $3 billion now). Another consideration influenced the Treasury in the late 1940's—a belief that the government should respect implied if not explicit wartime commitments to keep the price of marketable long-term bonds (with their "low" interest rates of around 2.5 percent) from falling below par.[5]

Over the years, of course, lenders would benefit from an upward shift of interest rates, but an unsophisticated public might be disturbed by a fall in the price of outstanding bonds. Again, hindsight helps us see that the fears were exaggerated. At the time, however, they carried great weight.

For the last half of the 1940's, the FR accepted what in fact was the paralysis of its real authority. The System agreed to enable banks to continue to lend to the Treasury at low rates for refundings. As part of the same related program, the FR agreed to help keep the price of long-term bonds from falling below par, *i.e.,* to peg the price to maintain yields at 2.5 percent or less. *Stable* prices for bonds, it was felt, would lead to better markets for sale of refunding issues as well as for all financing.

Moreover, strong demand for loans was well-nigh certain to induce banks to create more deposits if reserves were available. The public began to make more use (in spending) of deposits created during the war, money which on the average had had a very low V. The economy was so near full employment that little growth of output was possible. Here, then, were the makings of a rise in the price level—increases in both M and V when T could not grow with equal speed. This condition was just the kind in which monetary restraint could hold down the growth of total consumer and investment buying.

---

[5] Besides the implied promises to maintain the prices of marketable bonds, Treasury officials feared the effects of (a) a drop in bond prices on the net worth of banks and other financial institutions and (b) a rise in interest rates on business willingness to invest over the long run.

The FR, however, was seriously handicapped by its "agreement" to peg the prices of Treasury bonds and to keep the long-term rate of interest from rising. If monetary action restricted bank lending, the Treasury as a frequent borrower (for refundings) would have had to pay higher interest rates. As long-term interest rates rose, the drop in price of outstanding long-term government debt would create uncertainties and doubts about the worth of Federal bonds.

The FR refrained from using its power to force the monetary tightness which was needed to slow the rise in the price level. Congress, with one exception, refused the System's requests for special powers to restrain banks, such as higher reserve requirements or a supplementary reserve of government debt which would in effect have required banks to retain Treasury debt rather than sell it to get dollars to lend. In 1947, it is true, the rate on Treasury bills was unfrozen. It tripled. The basic problem remained, however. The FR was still unable to try to keep the amount of money payments in line with the value of full-employment output at the prevailing level of prices. The index of consumer prices rose by about 20 percent from 1946 to 1948.

For a time the interest cost of the government debt rose only slightly —one-tenth—from 1946 to 1950. Here was an apparent victory for Treasury policy. Yet it was an expensive defeat; the increase in costs of other things that the government bought was undoubtedly greater than the savings in interest.

Economists and others became more convinced that the low interest rate policy was poorly adapted to the underlying needs of the economy. Productivity of capital was distinctly higher than prevailing interest rates. Liquidity built up during war was not being "contained." Inflation continued, neither steadily nor dramatically but persistently. A business downturn in 1948 aroused some fears of depression and for a year or so weakened the force of arguments for restrictive monetary policy. The fighting in Korea, however, brought a surge of private borrowing from banks and an upward movement of prices which without question could have been restrained by tighter money. Still, the FR was shackled by the agreement that Federal bonds were not to fall below par; nor could the Treasury be allowed to fail in its borrowing efforts. Heavy increases in taxes were voted to help stem inflation, an inflation growing in part out of developments which monetary action could have forestalled. Fiscal policy was called upon to help compensate for an inappropriate monetary policy. Conflict between the Treasury and the FR could no longer be concealed. The Treasury would offer new securities at interest rates below those which would prevail in free markets. The offering could be a success only if the FR would assist.

By early 1951 the criticism of the inflationary, low-interest-rate policy became so strong that the Treasury yielded. In an "accord" of

March 1951 the FR and the Treasury agreed that the rigid support of long-term bonds to yield about 2.5 percent was to be abandoned. Pegging the price of long-term bonds was to end, and the market for government debt was to be essentially free. The FR thus regained powers over the money supply that it had lost in accommodating the Treasury. Rediscount rate and open market policies could now be used more freely; fear of their effects on the price of government debt, and on the interest cost to the Treasury, was no longer controlling. Prices of government bonds fell without the adverse effects that had been feared.

For the first time in almost 20 years, the FR was trying to operate a slightly tight money policy. The details of the transition are not important here except to note that Treasury operations and the market for Federal debt both adjusted to a sweeping change of conditions more easily than many observers had expected. The passing years, however, brought new problems about as rapidly as old ones were met.

CONTINUING PROBLEMS OF TREASURY RELATIONS TO THE MONETARY SYSTEM

Problems involving monetary policy remain for the Treasury—and will continue.[6]

Ability to Borrow to Meet Emergencies

In this uncertain world, the Treasury must be prepared for financial needs growing out of political, military, and economic crises. Who can say what amounts may have to be borrowed on short notice and under conditions of great surprise? And for as long as we can see, refunding will present nagging problems; difficulties can become acute if world emergencies arise when a huge refunding is due. If non-bank holders of debt suddenly become less willing to relend to the Treasury, a situation worse than embarrassing may develop.

---

[6] For data and interpretation see *Annual Report of the Secretary of the Treasury;* W. L. Smith, "Monetary Policy and Debt Management," in Joint Economic Committee, *Staff Report on Employment, Growth and Price Levels* (Washington: Government Printing Office, 1959), especially pp. 409–428; J. R. Schlesinger, "Insulation of the Government Securities Market: Objectives, Techniques, and Implications," and J. Tobin, "An Essay on Principles of Debt Management," Commission on Money and Credit, *Fiscal and Debt Management Policies* (Englewood Cliffs: Prentice-Hall, 1963), pp. 219–65 and 143–218, respectively; *The Federal Reserve and the Treasury. Answers to Questions from the Commission on Money and Credit* (Englewood Cliffs: Prentice-Hall, 1963) contains material on debt management and other topics covered in this chapter.

Therefore, until world conditions become more settled, the Treasury needs access to the money-creating mechanism. The FR must not impose monetary policies which will seriously restrain the Treasury during great emergencies. Congress will not always vote taxes that are adequate to meet crises. To borrow new savings made by the public will be slower— and may appear more expensive—than borrowing from banks, especially if banks are given reserves to support deposit creation.

What is easiest for the Treasury may also be most palatable to much of the public. Yet what is most tasty is not always healthiest. A danger cannot be denied: The continuous possession of power which is needed for emergencies may tempt its use when conditions are not truly emergency. If the Treasury has easy access to banks, abuse is possible. Some of the fault may lie with Congress for voting to spend more than it will raise in taxes. Or responsibility may lie with an Executive Branch which is reluctant to offer to pay interest rates adequate to attract enough loan funds from sources other than banks.

Changing Competitive Position of Federal Debt

The Treasury's borrowing problems are affected by competition.

1. Federal guarantee and insurance of FHA and VA mortgage loans, as well as of some other private debts, makes them almost as secure as Treasury debt. The volume of such loans has grown by billions every year. The interest yields are higher than on Federal debt.

2. High income tax rates create incentive for corporations, including banks and insurance companies, to seek tax-exempt state-local debt rather than Federal debt, whose yield is taxable—except as the Treasury offers sufficiently higher interest rates.

3. Net borrowing of around $5 billion a year by states and localities adds to the total demand for borrowed funds.

4. High income tax rates encourage businesses to finance growth by borrowing rather than by selling common and preferred stock; interest payments are deductible in computing taxable income, dividends are not.

5. The insurance of bank deposits and shares in savings and loans institutions makes the insured amounts in effect as safe as Federal debt for the long run and not subject to fluctuation in the short run. Frequently, such deposits are more convenient. And interest yields in many areas are higher.

6. Many persons and institutions with savings prefer to acquire equities (including real property) rather than debt. (a) The fear of inflation persists and with it some disinclination to hold long-term debt, except at interest yields which cover risk against loss in the purchasing power of money. (b) The owner of a government bond can expect to get back no more dollars than he owned originally, but the owner of a share of common stock may benefit from growth of the economy.

7. Considerations of international finance must be taken into account.

These developments can be overcome—by paying the necessary price. On a debt of $320 billion, however, even a small increase in the average rate means no small total.

Interest Cost

The gross annual interest cost of the Federal debt rose from $3.6 billion in 1945 to an estimated $11 billion in 1965. Most of the rise was due to an upward trend of interest rates—from an average of 1.9 to 3.5 percent on Federal debt—but the debt itself also rose. The total annual cost, equal to half of all state-local spending on public schools, is large even in relation to the Federal budget.

The net cost is less. The Fed's refunds to the Treasury now average nearly 9 percent of the total interest paid on all Federal debt. Most owners of debt pay income tax so that some of their interest income, and a bigger portion of any rise, returns to the Treasury. But if these holders did not own Federal debt, would they not have put their funds into other income-producing assets? If so, the Treasury would presumably get about the same tax revenue. Therefore, it seems hardly accurate to conclude that the interest cost of the Federal debt is reduced by the estimated income tax on the interest paid on such debt.[7]

The interest expense to taxpayers must cause concern. Responsible officials will try to economize on this cost in a manner consistent with the realization of other objectives of public policy. Unfortunately, it is rare to find clear agreement on the relative importance of objectives, especially since we do not know how much interest cost can be related to how much of some other result.

The Treasury can ordinarily borrow at any or several of a variety of interest rates, since long-, intermediate-, and short-term rates always differ. (Currency issue, another alternative, involves no interest.) Just as interest costs vary, so do the benefits obtained by the Treasury and the owner of the security. The nearer a security (whether a 90-day bill or a

[7] Two special cases offer possible exceptions: (a) commercial bank holdings that would have no counterparts if the Treasury had not issued the debt and (b) private ownership resulting from saving that would not have been made if the Federal borrowing had not been undertaken.

25-year bond) is to maturity or redemption at the owner's request, the higher its liquidity. To both the Treasury and various security purchasers, how much will more or less liquidity be worth in relation to more or less interest? Interest costs are easy to measure. But present knowledge does not enable us to measure the economic effects of differences in overall liquidity—the proportions of short- to longer-term debt.

At any one time there will be some, not accurately determinable, least-cost combination of borrowing. However, as the Treasury borrows —X amounts for 90 days, Y amounts for 4 years, etc.—the relations between interest rates will shift. The Treasury is such a big borrower— even when the total debt is not growing—that its own actions affect the interest rate pattern. And, of course, the maturity distribution of new issues which seems least expensive for this year will not always prove cheapest over 5 or 10 years because of changing conditions in the market for refundings.

The future of interest rates is never clear. Success in keeping interest costs down this year can prove costly later when the rate pattern has changed—and vice versa.

The men who make the decisions will never be free from an insidious temptation. At any one time the monetary authorities have some control over at least short-term interest rates. Next month's interest bill for the Treasury can certainly be pared a trifle by open-market operations or other FR actions. On the other hand, tightening money to serve the apparent needs of the whole economy will increase the cost of new Treasury borrowing. When minimizing interest costs is high among the objectives of Federal policy, the conflict with desirable monetary policy will sometimes be troublesome. One difficulty appears when the volume of short-term debt is so great that frequent refundings loom large in the money market. A problem of different character sometimes arises when the Treasury can borrow at long-term rates which seem favorable but when such borrowing conflicts with employment objectives.

Refundings and Routine Debt Management

Even when the Federal debt is not growing, borrowings are large— large, that is, in relation to the amounts which the financial markets can accommodate readily. The debt tends to grow shorter, on the average, month after month. In May 1964 the average maturity of marketable interest-bearing public debt was 5 years, 1 month. Annual refundings tend to become larger. The resulting churning in the money and capital markets creates some disturbance which can hardly help the economic system, though any harm is not easily identified.

"Routine" management of outstanding debt has monetary implications.

As the Treasury repays maturing debt, it puts money into the hands of former owners of debt. As the Treasury sells new debt to get dollars for the repayments, it draws funds from the market. It also supplies types of debt which are not necessarily the same as those being repaid. By its choice of new debt forms—and to some extent by its choice of which debt issues to repay—the Treasury affects the supply of securities offered and available in the market. In doing so, it influences at least the pattern of interest rates in the short run.

The Treasury's actions inevitably affect the monetary conditions which the FR also tries to influence. The timing of FR actions can hardly ignore the Treasury's refunding schedule. The government cannot be allowed to fail to get the dollars needed to pay its debts. At times of major refundings, therefore, the FR must stand ready to assist, not by buying the new debt (except under the most unusual of conditions) but by assuring reserves to the banking system if the banks are to be called upon, directly or indirectly. When a major Treasury financing is in prospect or under way, the FR will be reluctant to tighten money even if conditions generally require restraint.

Refundings of Treasury bills take place weekly on an auction basis. Prices fluctuate freely to clear the market. Refundings of longer-term issues are now concentrated in 4 or 5 large offerings each year rather than in many small ones. The timing is arranged to adjust as well as possible to the receipt of taxes, and other seasonal factors, and thereby to reduce interference with monetary policy. For most of the time the FR can feel more or less free from need to let Treasury problems outweigh what seem to be the requirements of the general economic situation.

Large offerings, however, do give rise to discontinuities—big amounts at infrequent intervals, $18 billion in one 30-day period in 1963 (not counting weekly bill offerings). The market may be in a poor position to absorb at a satisfactory price, and in adequate amounts, types of issues which for the longer run promise to be best. The FR then has the opportunity to help the market "digest" the offerings by either purchasing itself or aiding others to buy. The need for such help may be foreseen, or it may develop from a mistake in judgment in planning the offerings or from surprises in national or world affairs. Difficulties arise in providing such aid, however, when "appropriate" action cannot be distinguished clearly from what will be inappropriate over the longer run.

Anticyclical Management of Outstanding Debt

The way in which Federal budget surpluses and deficits are financed, we saw in Chapter 24, will have significant influence on monetary conditions and the trend of economic activity. Even if the amount of debt outstanding is not changing, its management can influence the economy. The debt must be managed. The choices about methods to be used will involve part of the "mix" of total public policy for economic stabilization. The *pattern* of the interest-rate structure, the total of liquidity, and the wealth of holders of debt—all these are subject to some "nudging," or more.

To Restrain a Boom. Assume that high prosperity shows signs of generating trouble: the creation of capital facilities beyond the reasonable prospects of profitable use in the years just ahead; efforts to increase both capital formation and consumption when bottlenecks choke off the expansion of production; price and cost maladjustments whose "correction" will create wasteful and disturbing trouble which will spread through the economy; debt-financed consumption which "steals markets from the future" and promises distress before the effects work themselves out fully; the spawning of inefficiency and of commitments which cannot be liquidated without bankruptcy and a variety of other painful distresses; threats to the balance of payments. Under such conditions monetary restraint is desirable. If the Treasury wishes to aid, it has power to do so. It can also make things worse.

The major means by which the Treasury can help check a boom, assuming no change in the total of outstanding government debt (*i.e.,* no surplus or deficit), is to rely more heavily on long-term issues while reducing those that are most like money. Any increase in Treasury demand for funds for long periods will tend to raise long-term interest rates. The Treasury soaks up some funds which would otherwise be used for financing private investment. Prices of outstanding long-term bonds (which are not yet near maturity) will drop, reducing somewhat the liquidity of holders of such debt—and perhaps their propensity to spend. As yields rise, however, bonds become more attractive relative to newly created capital goods; consequently, the demand for new investment goods will sag a little, and to some extent financial intermediaries will shift preferences to government debt from mortgages, etc., so that funds available for investment in new housing, plant, and equipment drop slightly.

With the proceeds from the sale of long-term debt, the Treasury can reduce the stock of money by retiring bank-held debt. The FR can check the capacity of the banks to make offsetting loans so that private borrowing from banks does not increase as the Treasury's declines. The Treasury may also borrow on long term in order to (1) retire debt held by the FR or (2) reduce the volume of currency outstanding. Various combinations of debt (and currency) changes are conceivable.

To Moderate Recession. During a recession the opposite emphasis is required if the Treasury is to do its best to reinforce monetary policy (without a change in the debt total). The logical action will replace long-term issues with debt sold to commercial banks or to the FR. If more debt goes to commercial banks, however, there may be little stimulus unless the FR acts to enlarge bank lending capacity. At the very least, the increase in bank loans to the Treasury must not be allowed to induce commercial banks to reduce their private lending. Reduction of the outstanding volume of long-term debt will raise bond prices (lower yields).

The liquidity of the public increases as the money stock grows and as prices of existing long-term debts rise. The rise in net worth—capital gains—of bondholders may induce an increase in consumption and investment spending. As long-term rates of interest tend to fall, existing bonds become less attractive, compared with newly created capital goods. Spending on new investment thus appears relatively more inviting. The Treasury, by paying of bonds, will add to the funds available for long-term borrowing.

Potential Effectiveness. If the Treasury wishes to help reduce cyclical fluctuations, it should not increase long-term borrowings when business is poor, however attractive such action may be for (1) reducing the interest cost of the debt and (2) stretching out the average maturity to make the job of future refundings easier. The potentialities are for marginal change—not huge and dramatic shifts. Moderation in the right direction is the practical objective. The ordinary business cycle does not call for a change of the magnitude that would move, say, a tenth of the total debt from one end of the maturity spectrum to the other. Nor does all change need to involve extremes; the alternatives are not just 90-day bills and 30-year bonds but shorter and longer issues within a large range. And obviously, the amount and type of debt change which is desirable depends upon the monetary policy pursued.

To state the general principles is decidedly easier than to develop in detail a practical program for applying them. Treasury officials recognize the principles but are reluctant to accept the responsibility for using debt management for anticyclical purposes. The net amount which could be accomplished does not appear to justify the cost in the sacrifice of other objectives, such as (1) keeping the annual interest charge as low as reasonably possible, and (2) preventing the average maturity of the debt from growing so short that noninflationary management in the future becomes unduly difficult.

The interest cost of countercyclical debt management does appear in the Treasury's expenses; the public benefits are less obvious. The Treasury also faces another obstacle—criticism if it draws upon limited supplies of savings for long-term and thereby slows down housing, business, and state-local construction during prosperity. Action to restrain a boom is not popular.

Borrowing for long periods during booms when interest rates are high will commit the Treasury to paying the high rate later when borrowing costs might be lower; any stabilization benefits may not justify the cost. On the other hand, failure to borrow on long-term when interest rates are low will appear costly later when rates rise.

A more fundamental question arises. Can debt management do more than can be accomplished by monetary policy? Now that "bills only" has been abandoned, open market operations can produce much the same influence on the pattern of interest rates.

Moreover, what is the relation between the short and the long portions of the interest rate structure? Money is fluid. Borrowers have various alternatives. Anticyclical debt management is a form of selective control. Results are never easily kept under the restraint which one or the other person may wish. Finally, the desirability of lengthening the debt is so great that even during slack times the sale of long-term issues has supporters, especially since the monetary authorities can create ease to offset restrictive pressure. Debate centers around the question of how extensively different compartments of the market for funds are separated from each other.

The Interest Rate and Debt Ceilings

Although Congress has given the Treasury great freedom in managing the debt, restrictions create problems—(1) a statutory limit on the amount of debt which may be outstanding, and (2) a ceiling of 4¼ percent which may be paid on bonds for 5 years or more.

The debt limit serves a useful purpose by forcing Congress to look at the relations between expenditures and taxes more closely than if no net borrowing were required. The limit can also get in the way of efficient Treasury financing. More than once the resort to expensive and clumsy substitutes for outright borrowing has been required. At times, too, denial of "elbow room" for the Treasury to maneuver has complicated debt management for no good result.

The interest-rate ceiling remains as a World War I legacy. For 40 years it was of no significance because (a) the Treasury was not borrowing or (b) the market rate was lower. In 1959, however, the Treasury found that it could not borrow for long term except at rates above the ceiling. All borrowing had to be for less than 5 years. Large Federal demands helped to raise short-term rates above those for the longer term for a short time. What were the arguments against reform? The most articulated reason made little sense. Defenders of the ceiling said that removal would affect new investment. Statutory interest ceilings, however, do not determine market interest rates. The forces of demand and supply make interest rates.

The ceiling prevents the Treasury from borrowing for more than 5 years when the market rate exceeds the 4¼ percent specified in World War I. If market forces do not themselves result in higher rates, and they did not for long periods in the 1930's, 1940's, and 1950's, the ceiling has no effect. When the ceiling "trap" has closed, however, the Treasury must pay for other opportunities. The ceiling remains to complicate debt management and to force the use of shorter-term issues when they are not best for the economy.

Shortening-Term Debt

Is the transformation of the Federal debt into a mass of obligations mostly due within less than 4 years a cause for concern? More accurately, how much concern?—for there is no dispute that some problems would be reduced if more of the debt were longer-term. Frequent refundings of billions unsettle the financial community. They add to the difficulties of FR monetary management.

Another problem whose significance is even harder to evaluate is the effect on the economy of the growth of highly liquid assets. As a 20-year bond approaches maturity, it becomes more liquid; when it has only a year or so to run, it is very like money. But does the owner act differently? If so, how? In some cases, certainly, the increase in liquidity will tend to reduce the inclination to hold money. The spending from any given amount of money (velocity) will rise. If the monetary authorities knew the result, they could offset it by appropriate adjustments in the quantity of money.

One fact is clear. A very large Federal debt will be with us as long as we can see. Would it not be realistic and wise, therefore, to put more of the debt into long-term form? At one time long-term debt required considerably higher interest than short-term debt. Lengthening the debt then seemed costly. More recently, however, short- and long-term interest rates have been closer together most of the time.

A "stretching out" of the average maturity of the debt is desirable, especially in the over-20-year range, not in large and sudden moves but gradually.

Possible Changes in Debt Management

Now that nearly half a generation has passed since the end of the war which created most of the debt, and the interest cost has gone much higher and the average time to maturity grown much shorter, one must ask how debt management might be improved. Economists differ, and so do bankers and the dealers who participate most actively in the market for government securities. We comment briefly on the major suggestions.

1. The statutory interest-rate ceiling on long-term bonds does harm and no apparent good. While no one can be sure about the future of interest-rate levels, there is a high prospect that Treasury borrowing for over 5 years will require interest rates above 4¼ percent—especially if the new debt issues are to be sold at times other than recession, when sale would have a somewhat depressing effect on business. If long-term interest rates move to the levels that often prevailed before the 1930's, the restriction on the Treasury will prevent sale of issues running more than 5 years.

2. The increased sale of long-term bonds might be encouraged by frequent offers, perhaps on "tap" or by auction, of modest amounts which would be within the capacity of the market to absorb. A single type of issue could be offered, with the price varying as market interest rates change; the variety of outstanding debt would not become unduly complex.

3. Auction sales of other than bills was tried twice in 1963 with at least moderate success. The objective is to get better terms for the Treasury than when traditional methods are used. Further experimentation is desirable.

4. Removal or relaxation of the debt ceiling would assist in getting more flexible and efficient management of the existing debt. The ceiling probably has some salutary effect in forcing Congress occasionally to look at Federal finances as a whole. Unhappily, the ceiling at times also adds to the difficulties of the Treasury in managing the debt.

5. "Advanced refundings" have been successful in helping the Treasury market longer-term debts. When a long-term bond comes close to maturity, it loses some of its attraction to holders who seek relatively permanent commitment of their funds. By offering to exchange a 20-year bond a year or two before maturity for new long-term issues, the Treasury reduces the essentially unconstructive churning in financial markets and keeps more debt than otherwise in permanent portfolios.

6. Banks and perhaps other financial institutions might be required to hold more debt than they would freely. Such use of compulsion could in some circumstances contribute to more effective control of the monetary system. If so, the decision should be made on such grounds alone. Otherwise, a free economy ought to eschew rather than promote policies such as the imposition of a special cost—in effect, a tax—in the form of compulsion on banks to put funds into securities which are less attractive than other uses of bank resources.

7. Closely related is a proposal to require commercial banks to hold higher reserves—say 20 instead of 12 percent—with the FR providing the reserve totals appropriate for the stock of money needed. FR holdings of Treasury debt would then be greater than otherwise; the cost of this debt to the Treasury would be negligible since the interest is returned by the "Fed." Commercial bank earnings would suffer except as banks could raise their charges to the public.

8. Some observers believe that the Treasury should make greater use of "call" features so that if market rates of interest go down, refunding would be easier. But original purchasers of bonds would insist upon a higher yield to compensate for the risk. Could the Treasury really outsmart the buyers of bonds?

9. Improvements in marketing methods are possible. The biggest problem is to stimulate the sale of long-term debt, for the short-term market seems efficient and highly competitive.

10. Finally, we need to study continually the ways in which debt management and monetary policy are related in an ever-changing economy—and how their combined results influence the economy.

RESOLVING CONFLICTS BETWEEN THE EXECUTIVE BRANCH AND THE FEDERAL RESERVE

The present system provides checks and balances. Neither the Treasury nor the Federal Reserve is fully independent of the other. Nor are other agencies, including the White House. An administration cannot count upon monetary policies which it believes desirable or essential for carrying out its programs. Sometimes officials disagree. In the majority of cases mutual understanding is reached. The economy must often benefit from the fact that each group of officials must develop the best reasoning possible to convince the other and, in turn, give serious consideration to counter-arguments. Sometimes, however, conflict of opinion remains.

Today we have no mechanism for settling such conflicts. The President does not have the authority. Congress cannot do the job as specific issues arise. Some new arrangement does seem called for. It might consist of a small group made up of one or two top men from the Federal Reserve, an equal number from the Treasury, one or more from the Council of Economic Advisers, and perhaps the President. Treasury officials recommend against restoring them to ex officio memberships on the FR Board; the responsibilities would call for greater expenditure of time than can be spared from other duties. In a showdown such a group could compel the Federal Reserve and the Treasury to pursue coordinated policies—with explanations made public. Such a change would reduce the independence of the Federal Reserve. Yet events have already cut into this independence.

QUESTIONS

1. Discuss the effects on the economy of war financing which consists of (a) increasing taxes, (b) borrowing by money creation from commercial banks, (c) borrowing from the "Fed," (d) printing money, and (e) borrowing from the public.

2. Which methods were used during World War II?

3. What is meant by the "pegging" of interest rates on government securities? What are the arguments for and against such pegging during war? during peace?

4. "The interest cost saved by the 'pegging' was by no means so important as the inflation which developed after the war. The FR should have been free to prevent postwar inflation by monetary restraint." Discuss.

5. What problems does management of the Federal debt present, assuming no change in the size of the debt? How can debt management be used as an anticyclical instrument?

6. What was the "accord"? What significance did it have for monetary policy in the 1950's? Why may Treasury-Federal Reserve policies conflict?

7. What is the debt limit? the interest rate ceiling? Does either serve a useful function? Why?

8. "The possibility that debt management can play a larger role in stabilization rests on the close tie between debt management and monetary policy." Discuss.

9. What are the reasons for trying to increase the average length of the public debt outstanding? How is monetary policy involved?

10. Describe an actual "advanced refunding." (Data are obtainable from the *Treasury Bulletin.*)

CHAPTER 26 *THE MONETARY SYSTEM AND LONG-RUN ECONOMIC GROWTH*

THIS CHAPTER, the shortest, deals with what may seem most important. Two things account for the apparent "short-changing" of space allocation. (1) At various points the material already covered has in fact, if not explicitly, dealt with economic growth—for example, moderating recessions and the waste they bring. (2) The gaps in our knowledge remain uncomfortably wide. Perhaps within a decade a reasonably complete, systematic discussion can be written. Today, however, we must be content with a summary which recognizes lack of certainty at many points.

"Economic Growth," as the term will be used here, means rising *real income per capita* over the long run. It includes not only those elements of income which appear in the national income accounts but intangibles as well. Sadly enough, measurement is less precise than it is often assumed to be.

THE SOURCES OF GROWTH

An enormous output of literature on the causes of growth has not yet resulted in general agreement on the relative importance of innumerable forces. Some of these forces help to raise real income; others impede it. Invention and expansion of knowledge in the broadest sense, capital accumulation and investment, the improved effectiveness of market processes in guiding resource allocation and in stimulating efficiency in production and distribution, the press of incentives and the vigor of enterprise—all these aid growth.

Their opposites, and such things as the wastes of urban congestion, racial discrimination, compliance with needlessly complex tax laws, forced obsolescence, preventable illness, the total weight of taxes and the specific features of tax and government expenditure programs, political stability and security, a social system which in both obvious and subtle ways encourages effort toward the new and the better—all these are among the elements which we know influence the growth of an economy. The use of resources on a massive scale for defense, private and governmental inducements to malallocation of resources, featherbedding, immobilities, ignorance of new techniques—all these retard growth. Both sets of forces differ in their fundamentals from whatever is involved in money and finance. Yet they all exist, and they all work their effects, in a money economy.

The quantity and quality of research and education are far removed from the direct influence of the monetary authorities; the Board of Governors can do little to induce children to study more diligently or researchers to be more imaginative. And so with most other elements. But not all. Changes in the value of money, which the Board does influence, and changes in interest rates, over which the Board has some influence, certainly affect investment in new productive facilities as well as the level of employment.

Perhaps monetary change has more than minor effect on the quality of human effort. Who can be sure? Bad monetary policy can certainly do immense harm to the complex of tangible and intangible forces which influence the accomplishment of an economy. If good policy does nothing more than eliminate the harmful potential of bad policies, a contribution, and a large one, will have been made. It may be unobtrusive, even unnoticed, but still wonderfully constructive compared with "what would have been."

Not long ago the Joint Economic Committee of Congress undertook a special investigation of "Employment, Growth, and Price Levels." Two dozen special studies by staff members and outside economists, together with extensive hearings at the time and since, yielded masses of data, interpretation, and opinion on the problems which are of chief concern here. Considerable divergence of views remains among professional economists. For example, the value of price-level stability is still debated. So, too, is the question of the relative influence of tax and interest-rate policy on investment. Nevertheless, the areas of agreement are extensive.

MONEY TO STIMULATE IN THE SHORT RUN

Our economy has operated at capacity for only a fraction of the time, even in the last decade when our knowledge of economics ought to have permitted better performance. Measures to bring total business activity nearer to the best level more of the time ought to speed growth. Of course, our judgment of how nearly the economy approaches capacity will depend upon how "capacity" is defined.

"Capacity operation" may reasonably be conceived as including some resource idleness at all times. Growth will certainly be easier when the expanding sector can draw upon resources not being utilized, instead of being compelled to pull them away from active use, with all the disruptions then involved. Yet our economy has fallen below the desirable level too much of the time. Filling some of the gaps would raise current real income. If a large portion of most of the gaps of a generation, or even a decade, were eliminated, the cumulative gain would be substantial. Consumers would have more, and capital accumulation would be greater, than in the world as it exists.

Society has an inviting opportunity. During much of the time it can try to spur business by monetary stimulation. For a time certainly, an injection of newly created money into the economy will lead to more output of goods and services. This possibility will not be debated.

Still, there is a debate. It ranges over the question, "What monetary (and fiscal) stimulation will do more good than harm over the years?" Assume, for argument only, that growth is the overriding objective. Then, when the economy is operating below capacity, will actions to ease money thereby stimulate output and lead to a net growth of desired output? Or will some of the injections impede the achievement of full and efficient output over the years by leading to price distortion and malallocations?

Can one justify "tightness" of money on a moderate scale—difficult as may be any definition of the concept of "tight money"—when business is less than booming? Can restraint contribute to growth over the longer run? Most economists would probably agree that some monetary restraint even in other than boom periods will contribute to certain price-cost relations, and to resource allocation, which will be better for the long run than those which might develop if money were "easier" more of the time.

Nevertheless, economists have no consensus on the degree and amount of monetary restraint desirable. Here we are at a frontier of economics. Some economists cite the desirability of stimulating growth as a reason for easier money and more money creation over a larger portion of cycles than in the 1950's and early 1960's. Others cite long-run growth considerations as the basis for monetary caution. Are there any assured grounds for settling the argument? Not completely—but continued study can probably reduce the area of doubt. How serious, really, are wage, price, and other rigidities and immobilities? How do the hard rigidities get entrenched? Does stimulating monetary action do more harm than good by encouraging and reinforcing (downward) inflexibilities?

Saving and Investment for Growth

Growth requires continuing enlargement of capital facilities—factories, schools, utility facilities, goods in process (inventory), housing, and other productive capacity. Increasing the stock of capital on any significant scale calls for extensive saving. Money creation cannot do this task. Consequently, our ability and our willingness to save will set limits to the economy's capacity to grow.

Factors Influencing Saving

Chapter 15 discussed the factors which determine the volume of saving. Two points call for comment here.

1. Inflation can, at least for a time, lead to *forced saving* in the sense that rising prices force the public to consume less. More of the economy's production than otherwise then becomes available for capital formation. Perhaps a policy of moderate inflation, one too small to produce serious disturbance, will aid capital formation. This possibility has had more than a little appeal in underdeveloped countries. The results, to the extent that they can be identified, differ; so do the evaluations. It is the author's judgment that over the long run any addition to net saving will at best be small.

2. Governments save by collecting more in revenue than they spend.[1] The amount of such saving which is possible while maintaining full employment at prevailing prices will depend in part upon monetary policy. The easier monetary conditions, the tighter fiscal policy can be, *e.g.,* the higher taxes and budget surpluses can be without tending to depress the economy. In other words, by easing monetary policy, society can raise its savings by using the taxing power, without depressing business. The principle receives wide endorsement among economists, but few venture confident predictions about relative magnitudes.[2]

---

[1] Governments ordinarily pay for large amounts of capital expenditure out of current revenues. Moreover, state-local governments use current revenue to pay off debt incurred to pay for capital projects built earlier. The total amounts spent from current revenue to finance capital formation may or may not exceed depreciation. Our data do not permit accurate estimates but some net capital formation probably occurs in the government sector even when budgets are balanced. If governments run deficits of, say, $10 billion net and borrow the whole amount from savers, a tax increase (or a cut in spending on consumption-type outlays) of $5 billion will in effect make more savings available for private investment.

[2] See J. Tobin, "Economic Growth as an Objective of Government Policy," and discussion by H. G. Johnson and H. Stein, *American Economic Review,* May 1964, pp. 1–27.

The financial system has another type of influence on decisions to save. One thing that counts is the availability of institutions to receive, to hold, and to put to use funds saved in ways that encourage both saving and productive use of the results of thrift. The United States seems well supplied with such institutions, even though numerous opportunities for improvement undoubtedly exist. This country, unlike the typical under-developed land, does not have ahead of it the job of establishing good savings institutions as a step toward growth. The amount of saving depends, of course, upon a host of factors—from the pressures of the tax system to the persuasion of business to get us to spend more on consumption—which are not within the scope of money and banking.

Investment

Many factors influencing investment were discussed earlier. One which comes within our proper concern is that emphasized by Keynes. Savings which are not, in effect, used to buy newly created capital goods represent more than the obvious wasted opportunity. Saving which is not matched by investment tends to depress national income. The dangers are widely recognized by economists. So are the inflationary effects of efforts to spend more on investment goods than the public wants to save. Economists continue to search for the monetary and fiscal policies which will reduce the possible wastes of both types of maladjustment.

A second feature of the savings-investment problem is that of *allocation*. How can savings be directed to the uses in which productivity will be greatest? Some investment alternatives are more attractive than others. The speed of economic growth will depend in part upon the success with which the economy directs savings into the most productive uses. The problem is inherently difficult because the choices involve the unknown.

One general proposition commands attention. The speed and thoroughness with which an economy can make use of the fruits of research and technical progress will depend upon the ability to finance new capital goods. Perhaps one-third of the rise in productivity, such as output per hour of work, has been the result of technological progress.[3] To take advantage of the advances in science and the arts, investment in new capital equipment is frequently essential. Such investment will generally consist of business facilities—notably machinery and equipment—as contrasted with housing. More accurately, the quality and the quantity of capital per job are directly related to output per hour; such capital, the quality element especially, embodies many of the advances of technology.

[3] E. F. Denison, *The Sources of Economic Growth in the United States and the Alternatives Before Us* (New York: Committee for Economic Development, 1962).

A distinction can be made between *extensive* investment, more of the same type of such facilities as housing or highways or stores, and *intensive* investment, meaning more of better type per job. The difference cannot be distinguished sharply, but making it helps point out the desirability of encouraging the types of investment which have potential for embodying the myriad benefits of the progress of science and the arts.

How closely do our institutions come to directing the resources available for new investment into what will prove to be the best opportunities? No one can be sure, but leaders can—and should—try to find opportunities for improving arrangements. What are the strong, and what are the weak, elements today? Can the features of strength be carried over to the places that are weak? How can the good, and the poor as well, be made better?

One approach consists of improving the rationality of investment planning within business firms. Apparently, much capital planning by business makes little or no explicit use of the best methods now available. The cruder, intuitive methods used so widely may give overall results about as good as those which would be derived from the more refined methods —but probably not. The spread of knowledge, the force of competition, and confidence in interest rates can help. But in the making of choices within the firm market forces operate imperfectly.

Moreover, the market's allocation of investment funds among business firms is criticized. Large, well-established, and profitable companies have readier access to dollars for expansion and modernization than do small and new firms and those with low profits. This to-him-who-hath-shall-be-given condition challenges the economy. Not all small or new firms are unprofitable. But often several years are needed to establish a convincing profit record. In the meantime, less capital will generally be available than economic realities would warrant.

The problem is not whether society can improve its allocation of new capital. Improvement *must* be possible. The question is "How?" In trying to meet one problem, we do not want to create others, such as directing more of limited resources into small, unprofitable, and new ventures with low productivity. Interjecting the political process into lending to small business, and providing various subsidies, not all of which are open for the public to see, may help speed growth. But they may not. They certainly do not eliminate the desirability of imaginative effort by business—including institutions with money for investment—to learn how to uncover more alternatives and to select among them more wisely.

Government investment—in schools, streets and highways, sewerage and sanitation facilities, airports, hospitals, prisons, etc.—presents difficult challenges. The decisions must be made through the political process. The choices involve estimates of social priorities. These are inevitably difficult to arrange on any scale on which people will agree, to say nothing of balancing at the margin.

How can we improve the methods for making choices about investment in the governmental sector? Some decisions have, at best, lacked brilliance—spending $800 or so an acre of taxpayers' money to develop more land for agricultural output, when hundreds of millions of taxpayers' dollars were being spent each year to take land out of cultivation. But why raise such an issue here? Although governmental investment may seem far removed from money and banking, one connection is evident. If representatives of the public are to choose wisely, they must use accurately a rate of interest which measures the worth of sacrificed alternatives.

We rely upon the financial system to balance the elements of supply and demand for loanable funds and cash balances. The better the system does so, the better it reveals a level and a pattern of interest rates that reflect human preferences—and the better the public can decide on the use of resources in public investment. Policies which "artificially" modify relative interest rates may lead to poorer allocation—or better. Good evaluation of results requires much evidence.

The allocation of savings for investment can never fully transcend the personal and the local nature of parts of the market. Elements of imperfection and monopoly will always remain. But some imperfections have been reduced, such as the broadening of markets for mortgages and for short-term loans. Each element of success will help in making our savings contribute a bit more toward growth.

FUNDS FOR POINTS OF GROWTH

The firm, industry, or region which is to grow must have financing. Dollars are necessary, of course, but they are not sufficient. Creating money will not make goods. The funds can come from two kinds of sources—from current and past savings or from the creation of new money by the banking system.

Sometimes the distinction between the sources will be clear. For example, the builder who gets funds for a new housing project from a savings and loan association, or a telephone company which finances expansion by the sale of stock to individuals and pension funds—both draw on savings. But if a business borrows from a commercial bank, the funds may be newly created.[4] Growth financing from savings may not be easily

---

[4] The commercial bank may, of course, create a deposit which merely matches another which was wiped out as a borrower repaid a loan. A commercial bank may also lend dollars which have come to it through deposits in savings accounts.

distinguishable from that from money creation. The significance, however, lies not in what is recognized but in the underlying economic reality.

One merit claimed for a decentralized and flexible banking system is that it can provide funds at the points of growth in the economy. Moreover, the amounts that become available can be related to the growth prospects. True—if the banks exist. And if the managers are imaginative, aggressive, and intelligent. In a changing economy new banking facilities must be available where shortly before no such need existed. Lethargic or merely traditional bank management where dynamism is called for will retard progress.

Will not an economy which wants to grow be wise to assure funds to the businesses, households, and governments with the best prospects of productive use? If the funds represent savings, the answer will be "Yes." Unfortunately, there is no certainty that in a decentralized system the new savings will go to the institutions whose customers have the best growth prospects.

If deposit creation is involved, the problem becomes more complex. The socially desirable limits on the expansion of the money stock are likely to be narrower than will be recognized by the particular bank or the potential borrower. The ability to provide funds readily at points of economic expansion constitutes a tool for growth—but a danger, too. Here we see in a clear form the issue between credit (loans) and money. If money expansion results, the new money will not be "confined." It will flow through the economy. The results may be generally beneficial. They may also be cyclically disturbing and tend to raise the price level more or less permanently. Rarely can we know the full consequences in advance.

MONETARY STIMULUS FOR DISTRESSED SECTORS

Years of general prosperity have revealed widely different levels of accomplishment in the various parts of the economy. Chronically depressed sectors remain—regional (from submarginal agriculture to city slums), industrial, and those where a region depends heavily upon an industry which does poorly.

Individuals and some rather large groups—even some living in relatively prosperous areas—continue to lag far behind the great majority.

These parts of the economy present a difficult problem, and a significant opportunity. In the sectors which do well, productivity improvements generally will be gradual. In contrast, the more depressed sectors offer opportunities for large percentage gains.[5] Can some deliberate use

---

[5] Humanitarian considerations reinforce the arguments for special effort to raise productivity where it is lowest, as well as to provide assistance to the aged and others who are unable to work and are in financial need.

of the monetary and financial system aid significantly in realizing the potentialities?

Credit will sometimes be productive in stagnating sectors more so than in those which are prospering. Free markets will not always value adequately all costs and benefits, including those we call "social" or "collective." Urban redevelopment, for example, presents investment opportunities which private accounting will not evaluate accurately.[6]

In general, however, directing capital into depressed sectors as a stimulant to growth for the economy as a whole seems unwise unless the prospects are good enough to overcome a presumption that "going against the market" is wasteful. For example, the anti-poverty proposals sent to Congress in 1964 included plans for additional loans for (a) farmers with very low income and (b) businesses which would employ persons long unemployed or with very low income. In both types of cases the loans would be available only if the applicants could not meet the "relaxed" terms of existing private and governmental credit programs for farmers and small businesses. Some "payoffs" might be dramatically high, but the prospects of loss would not be small—loss which would consist of the sacrifice of better opportunities to use capital.

Growth consists in part of shifting labor and other resources from uses of low to those of higher productivity. Consequently, special efforts for the submarginal, such as unusual financial aid, may actually retard growth by discouraging constructive mobility. Moreover, spot depression may reflect prices, wages, and costs which are out of line with productivity and demand; special stimulants may then buttress a price-cost relation which is untenable over the long run.

There is temptation to use special financing, selective credit aids, to meet particular problems. In the short run success may appear. Yet over a "not very long run" the outcome may well be failure, even though not evident. Growth is a long-run matter.

FRONTIERS OF RESEARCH

The interior of the atom and the extensions of outer space are subjects of extensive research. "Money," however, has received only a relative trifle of governmental and private funds for study. Fortunately, however, the Federal Reserve has stepped up research on monetary and financial problems. Private inquiry also grows.

---

[6] Unfortunately, disadvantages also exist. Long delays in getting a program under way can lead owners to postpone private projects. The social costs of relocating families can be greater when government uses the *compulsion of eminent domain* than when private owners must pay to get people to move freely.

The prospects of progress in understanding the roles of money and the financial system have never seemed more promising than in the mid-1960's.

QUESTIONS

1. How can improvements in financial markets encourage economic growth?

2. "Good monetary policy is necessary for healthy economic growth, but it is by no means sufficient." Discuss.

3. Under what circumstances, if any, will creation of money encourage the expansion of real income?

4. "An adequate money supply is necessary for economic growth—but too much money may cause inflation and actually impede growth." Comment, especially on the definition of "adequacy."

5. "The growth of the economy requires investment. A low interest rate encourages investment. Therefore, the monetary authorities should bias their policies toward low interest rates." Discuss.

6. "There is not much that *monetary* action can do to alter the rate of economic growth. *Credit* policy, however, can be devised to help, or hinder, growth." Discuss.

7. What monetary policies might increase voluntary saving?

APPENDIX A   *MONETARY DEVELOPMENT: HIGHLIGHTS IN UNITED STATES EXPERIENCE*

OUR UNDERSTANDING of money and banking today can be increased by a knowledge of the financial experiences of our great-grandfathers, perhaps even of their great-grandfathers. The "crusty old past" is still with us; the financial system that we use is an inheritance. Some of it was built long before anyone had the understanding of economic issues which only a little serious study will now provide. Space permits no more than a brief summary.

THE COLONIAL PERIOD

Currency problems nagged the colonists from the very first. Difficulties over money accounted for some of the friction with Britain and at one time or another led to economic, social, and political strain within the colonies. Banks and deposits in the modern sense were unknown. As in Europe at the time, money was thought of as coins. However, not many decades after the foundation of the first new colonies a sad history of experiment with paper money began.

As a rule newcomers to this continent brought little money. Many were poor. Those who had some wealth tended, wisely, to bring it in the form of clothing and equipment for the house and their work. Mines in what is now the United States yielded no significant amount of precious metals to provide the essentials for coining money. If settlers were to get money, therefore, they had to export more than they imported (or borrow on long term). The dominant tendency of the colonies, however, was to try to import more than they could export. Even frugal living provided only a small surplus of output over consumption. The colonists wanted much more capital equipment from abroad than they were able to pay for by exporting. The trade balance with the West Indies did yield the colonies an inflow of coins, but the specie obtained was needed at once to pay for imports from Europe.

Domestic developments, meanwhile, created a need for more money (means of payment) to facilitate an expanding trade over a growing area. Accounts were expressed in terms of British pounds and shillings, but a variety of Spanish and other foreign coins of differing weights and fineness made up much of what circulating medium there was in the colonies—never, it seemed, enough. To help compensate for the shortage of coins, colonists made extensive use of barter, usually a clumsy and inefficient substitute. They also resorted to the use of various commodities as mediums of exchange.[1] Failure always resulted, even after temporary successes, because all the commodities had defects as money. Lack of uniformity of currencies among colonies added to the difficulties of trade among them.

Massachusetts in 1652 began to mint coins, "pine tree shillings," from metal obtained by melting foreign coins. It never succeeded in providing "enough," however. Clipping (cutting off some of the metal) and counterfeiting added to the difficulties of using coins throughout the entire period.

Beginning in 1690, colonies (or banks chartered for the purpose) issued paper money (bills of credit), which they made legal tender. Bank notes appeared in 1712, when South Carolina established the first land bank. Other colonies followed the example. Paper money was issued with mortgages on land as security. Experience accumulated over half a century. Governmental bills of credit and land-bank notes had varying histories. The quantity of some issues was limited; they maintained their value and helped facilitate local exchange. More often, however, one or another pressure—need to finance military operations, dissatisfaction with shortages of capital or with means of payment—led to overissue. Then the bills became acceptable only at different and changing discounts.

Britain in 1751 began a series of moves to suppress the issue of paper money in the colonies. Success was varied—more often disappointing than satisfactory. The shortage of an acceptable circulating medium added to economic difficulty. Those of us who have always lived in a world with a monetary system which provides an ample circulating medium

---

[1] Some colonies tried to attract coins from other colonies by raising the value in shillings at which, say, the Spanish dollar would circulate locally. Prices and other aspects of commercial dealings, however, would adjust to counteract such artifices. See Arthur Nussbaum, *A History of the Dollar* (New York: Columbia University Press, 1957), Ch. 1.

have little comprehension of the problems which arise when transactions are impeded seriously by lack of means of payment.

FROM 1775 TO THE 1830's [2]

If any conclusion in political economy defies contradiction it is that military operations are expensive. British attempts to get the colonies to bear more of the costs of their own defense did much to spark the revolt of 1775. When the colonies found themselves required to finance military activities, the problems proved to be more than merely difficult.

How could the Continental Congress, with no taxing power (and conducting a war in part against taxation), finance the Revolution? It relied on paper currency. So did the individual colonies. Overissue brought substantial loss of value. The purchasing power of "continentals" fell until a unit would buy only about 2 percent as much as a unit of specie.[3] The notes were legal tender. As they depreciated, debtors were able to discharge their obligations with only a small fraction of the value originally received—to the obvious loss of creditors.

Foreign metal coins continued to circulate, but in relation to the volume of transactions at prevailing prices the quantity of coins was inadequate. The variety compounded complexity.[4]

Confusion continued during the years after fighting stopped. A decline in the price level gave rise to agitation for issue of paper money, as evidenced by Shays' Rebellion. The war and postwar disruption of life resulting from monetary disorder, the evidence of waste and hardship growing out of monetary instability, led to serious study of the problems of money. The analysis was available to the framers of the Constitution. They agreed that states should be deprived of the power to coin money, to emit bills of credit, or to make anything but gold and silver legal tender. Congress got the exclusive right to coin money. (The Constitutional Convention voted down a proposal to give Congress the power to issue bills of credit; many years later, however, the Supreme Court upheld the issue of paper money by the national government during the Civil War.) When the new government was established, the memory of inflation was still vivid —and repulsive.

---

[2] B. Hammond, *Banks and Politics in America from the Revolution to the Civil War* (Princeton, N.J.: Princeton University Press, 1957).

[3] In other words, the price level rose, not astronomically but by multiples. A large volume of business, however, was done on a barter basis.

[4] One source of coins was the British army, as it paid for supplies. Some of the French loans to the colonies came in the form of specie. It was only in 1948 that a popular referendum in New Hampshire repealed a provision of the state constitution dating from 1784 which made the shilling the monetary unit.

To meet immediate needs, the new 1789 Congress authorized the Treasury to accept certain foreign coins in payment of Federal taxes. Shortly after Hamilton in 1791 proposed a more permanent coinage system, Congress approved. This act provided for minting both silver and gold coins; the ratio between the dollar values of the two metals was fixed at 15 to 1. All specie presented would be minted, and all coins were legal tender. Congress also fixed the value of certain foreign coins in relation to the dollar and made them legal tender.

Use of the bimetallic standard was intended to help overcome difficulties arising from the scarcity of precious metals. Unfortunately, the hopes were largely frustrated. Difficulties in making a bimetallic system work had not been foreseen. They soon appeared, however. The rigid relationship between the prices of the metals fixed by law for monetary purposes was not the same as that determined by market forces, including demand and supply abroad. In relation to silver, gold proved to be underpriced as money. In other words, relative to silver it was worth more as specie and for payment abroad than in coin form. (Spain and France priced gold higher in relation to silver.) Few gold coins were issued, and fewer still circulated. Here in a sense was an illustration of Gresham's Law: "Bad money [overpriced silver] drives out good."

Although more silver was minted, a considerable part went abroad.[5] President Jefferson, therefore, ended the minting of silver dollars in 1806. Production of fractional silver coins continued, but they, too, tended to go abroad in payment for imports. The new nation was inconvenienced by lack of coins for day-to-day transactions; use of foreign coins, however, helped fill the gap.

Paper money did even more to meet the need for a medium of circulation. The first and second Banks of the United States (1791–1811 and 1816–1836), though chartered and partly financed by the United States government, were private institutions. They issued paper money in limited quantities. It circulated widely, and it did not depreciate in relation to specie.

Increasingly, however, the public relied upon paper money issued by state banks. Although the Constitution prohibited states from issuing money, banks chartered by the states were deemed to have the authority to issue their own notes. These banks certainly did so—sometimes to the point of serious abuse, issuing far more than specie and other asset holdings could justify. Printing bank notes cost little. Banks would then turn this currency over to borrowers, receiving interest-bearing IOU's. Borrowers

[5] The United States and the Spanish dollars were presumably to circulate as equals in the West Indies. But the United States dollar would yield more silver when melted down than was needed to coin a Spanish dollar. Consequently, there was profit to be made from exporting United States silver dollars as a commodity, *i.e.,* for their specie content. It is no wonder that they did leave.

used the notes to pay for goods and services—if others would accept these pieces of paper. Acceptability depended to a large degree upon confidence in the bank. This trust, in turn, depended upon belief in the bank's ability and willingness to exchange specie for its notes, upon demand.

Acceptability varied. Much of the currency did depreciate. Notes of many banks were not in fact convertible into specie, except with considerable difficulty, some of which resulted from deliberate attempts by banks to put obstacles in the way of persons seeking specie. Some notes became worthless because the issuing bank failed. Holders of notes suffered through no fault of their own, except their willingness to accept the currency. Several thousand kinds of money (plus many counterfeits) with different values per dollar (as shown on the face) circulated. Doing business was complicated by the confusing currency situation. "Bank Note Reporters and Counterfeit Detectors" indicating the current value of these notes appeared on a weekly basis. Various kinds of remedies for the mess were attempted.

State governments imposed some restrictions on issue of notes. The two Banks of the United States, and other agencies, made a point of insisting upon convertibility. For example, upon receiving notes of a bank which appeared to have overissued, the Bank of the United States would present them for redemption.

The Suffolk System, which started in Boston in 1824, was notably successful. If a bank would keep specie available to assure that its notes could be redeemed, it would not be prodded. But if it failed to do so, the banks trying to enforce higher standards would persistently send its notes for redemption in specie. Considerable success was finally achieved. After the second United States Bank lost its influence, however, the "policing" was weak in many parts of the country.[6] Americans suffered more from issue of poor currency by state banks than we are likely to realize today. Gradually the usefulness of high-quality bonds and other relatively liquid and safe assets as backing for currency came to be recognized.

Public attention focused on problems of the issue of bank notes. Deposit banking and the use of checks, however, grew steadily. The first bank was established in 1782. After 10 years 14 were operating. They made short-term loans, primarily to commercial firms. By 1809, the date of the first bank failure, there were about 75 banks. The great majority operated well. They loaned for short periods to merchants of good credit standing; in so doing these banks did not merely make loans of their capital, as was assumed, but actually created deposits. Only gradually, and incompletely, did bankers and a few others come to realize that deposit

[6] Louisiana after 1842, however, was especially strict in regulating the reserves supporting bank notes.

liabilities were essentially the same type of obligations as bank notes. During the War of 1812 banks suspended specie payment, while continuing to handle deposit accounts and transact business with bank notes.

THE 1830's TO 1861

The decade of the 1830's, like that of a century later, brought important changes. In 1834 Congress altered the silver-gold mint ratio to 16 to 1. Gold, as a result, was slightly overvalued (becoming the "bad" money of Gresham's law). In growing quantities gold came to the mint for coinage; silver coins tended to disappear.

The question of rechartering the second Bank of the United States developed into one of the most emotion-laden, controversial issues of the time. By 1830 the bank had a record of at least a decade of good, though not always popular, service to the country. New York interests wanted the bank replaced by one with headquarters in New York, not Philadelphia. President Jackson opposed renewing the bank's charter. He argued that the bank was a monopoly, unduly influenced by foreigners and Easterners. Jackson vetoed a bill to recharter the bank, and nothing was provided to take its place. Uncertainty during the years of debate disturbed business. Then when defeat was clear, the bank began a policy of contraction. This, together with such developments as a new governmental requirement that payments for public land be made in specie, helped bring on a sharp drop in business in 1837. The bank continued to operate on a limited scale under a state charter; it expanded its loans substantially in 1838, trying to support the price of cotton. Over the world, however, there was deflation. This country could not avoid the downward trend of prices while on a metallic standard and thus tied to prices abroad. The bank, and many others, failed. About one-fourth of the country's stock of money was wiped out. The depression was deep and prolonged.

The decision against rechartering the second Bank of the United States had unfortunate consequences for the whole economy. With the bank's loss of power went a much needed force for preventing deterioration of state banking standards. The first "free banking" laws were enacted in Michigan and New York. Other states followed the example, but too often without the men, assets, and experience of the East. Standards in many cases were low indeed. In a few states, however, no incorporated banks existed as late as 1852—testimony to popular opposition to favoritism and monopoly. The public was dependent upon unincorporated banks without supervision.

For a generation the country had no institution to serve the functions of a central bank. There was no national paper money. The disappearance of silver brought a shortage of "small change" which impeded the transaction of ordinary business. Foreign coins, which circulated generally, and postage stamps met only part of the need. Year after year the country suffered from the inadequacy of its money and banking facilities.

The need of the growing land for more money was met in part by accident. Gold output rose as a result of the discoveries of 1849. In 1853 Congress finally took an obviously desirable step and reduced slightly the specie content of fractional coins. No longer would there be a profit in exporting or melting coins, for the market price of the silver in a coin was now less than its money value.

Hundreds of new banks were established. Many failed. The currency issued by many others depreciated, but unevenly. In some states, unfortunately, regulation was lax.[7] Throughout this period, as earlier and later in our history, large segments of the public wanted "easy" money. The country was short of capital. Creating money seemed to be a way to meet the needs. Unhappily, it also created considerable distress—more in some areas than others—because the money proved defective. A few state governments owned and operated banks successfully. From 1837 to 1860 a dozen states enacted laws requiring cash reserves for bank notes outstanding and, in four cases, for deposits.

Some trouble arose from the working of the Independent Treasury System established in 1846. Congress wanted to protect the Federal government against losses resulting from failures of state banks. Therefore, it required not only that payments to the United States be made in specie, as had been the rule for some years. Congress also required that the money be held in the Treasury's own vaults in Washington or in subtreasuries in other leading cities. Thereafter, as money flowed into and out of the Treasury, the specie available for backing notes of state banks rose and fell. Fluctuations in revenue receipts and in government spending could move significant quantities of gold or silver from the banks and back. The certainty that specie would have to be turned over to the Treasury had one salutary effect. Banks were forced to be more cautious than some would have been otherwise.

By 1860 much experience had been gained, often at heavy cost. The best banking practices reflected great progress. They were spreading and

---

[7] Two examples will illustrate. After a long search, an agent enforcing redemption of currency found the "Bank of Morocco" in two Indiana log cabins. The bank's owner, a blacksmith, had enough gold to redeem the $1000 of notes presented to him. But he implored the agent not to disclose the location of his bank to others. In 1855 a Treasury supervisor found the subtreasury in Indiana "in a tavern adjoining the barroom with which it was connected by a door with glass lights, so that the subtreasurer might, when in the bar-room, see into his office. The entrance for the public was through a back passage under a stairway. The office was divided into two rooms by a temporary partition, lighted by a single window defended by iron gates. The silver was kept in wooden boxes, the gold in an iron safe. The subtreasurer slept in one of the rooms with his weapons." (Arthur Nussbaum, *A History of the Dollar*, New York: Columbia University Press, 1957, p. 95.)

improving.   It is hard to judge what would have developed had the nation not then been torn by a great war.

A war that is big militarily—as was the Civil War—is big economically. Such wars bring great monetary change to all belligerents.   The Confederacy suffered from substantial inflation.   It tried, at times with impressive results, to meet hard and changing financial problems; some of the experience can throw light on underlying problems of monetary processes.[9] Nevertheless, events in the North must get our attention because they had more lasting influence.   Although Congress raised taxes, borrowing and money creation financed the vast bulk of the war's cost.

Shortly after fighting began, the Treasury sold an issue of bonds for which payment in gold was required in a relatively short period.   Banks could not meet the demands and suspended redemption of bank notes in specie, a suspension which was to last 18 years.

Greenbacks during the Civil War: Inconvertible Paper Money

The government issued paper money, $450 million in 1862–63, called "greenbacks" because of their color.[10]   (About $347 million still circulate.) Printing currency seemed an easier way to get funds for armaments than equal tax increases.   The new money was not convertible into specie. (State banks had suspended specie payment by late in 1861.)   The new Federal currency was made legal tender.   As time passed, however, the notes fell substantially in terms of gold—30 percent and even more; that is, a $10 gold coin would buy more than $10 of greenbacks in the same market.   The domestic price level just about doubled in the North from 1861 to 1865.   Almost all fractional coins except the one-cent piece disappeared, for they became worth more as metal than as money.   Irritating shortages of coins created difficulties in paying for ordinary transactions; various paper expedients never satisfactorily met the needs.

---

[8] See M. Friedman and A. J. Schwartz, *A Monetary History of the United States, 1867–1960* (New York: Columbia University Press for the National Bureau of Economic Research, 1963).

[9] E. M. Lerner, "Inflation in the Confederacy, 1861–1865," in M. Friedman, ed., *Studies in the Quantity Theory of Money* (Chicago: University of Chicago Press, 1956), pp. 163–75.

[10] The national government had not issued paper money since the Revolution, except for relatively small and unusual issues during the War of 1812.   These were sold as interest-bearing notes which were easily transferable and circulated as currency.

Establishment of the National Banking System

A development with more lasting importance was the establishment of the national banking system. The founders had two chief objectives: to help sell government bonds, and to improve the quality of the country's paper money.

Congress provided for the granting of a new type of national charter to any bank which would meet designated requirements, involving capitalization, reserves, and regulation by the Comptroller of the Currency. These banks were required to buy Federal bonds, which, of course, paid interest. In addition, the bank could issue currency with the bonds as collateral; this currency could be given to borrowers in exchange for interest-bearing IOU's. The maximum issue, originally, was 90 percent of the lower of the par or market value of the bonds, not exceeding the bank's capital. A national bank, then, was able to get something like double interest on funds it used to buy Federal debt. Was there any benefit for the general public? One was clear—national bank notes were always backed by government bonds.[11] Now the country had currency which was of uniform value everywhere and which would not lose value if the issuing bank failed.

National banks were also required to keep reserves against *deposit* liabilities—25 percent in the case of banks in large cities, 15 percent in others.[12] Vault cash counted as reserves. Deposits in banks in financial centers also counted up to varying limits. The great mass of banks could keep three-fifths of their required reserves in the form of deposits in banks in large cities. Such deposits yielded interest. Consequently this portion of a bank's reserves would not be "dead weight" so far as income was concerned. The bank owing the deposit, of course, was subject to potential demands on short notice.

Congress imposed a tax of 10 percent a year on state bank notes, effectively dooming them to extinction. The total outstanding dropped from $239 million in 1863 to $4 million in 1867. Several hundred banks changed from state to Federal charters. Having lost an important source

---

[11] Other safeguards were established to assure full redeemability of this currency, which was the obligation of private institutions. The limit of notes to 90 percent of the lower of par or market value of the pledged bonds meant that a falling bond market would reduce the note-issue potential; however, any rise above par would not increase it. National bank notes, unlike greenbacks, were not "lawful money"; but this limitation had no practical significance, and the notes were accepted on a parity with other currency. The amount of new currency issued was not in fact as large as the volume of Federal debt would have permitted. Changes in the provisions governing issue were made in 1900, and the volume of notes grew.

[12] New York, Chicago, and St. Louis were designated as central reserve cities; banks in these cities had to keep 25 percent of deposit liabilities in vault cash. Banks in the 49 reserve cities could keep half their 25 percent reserves in the form of deposits in central reserve cities.

of income, they hoped to make it up by issuing national bank notes even though in some respects state laws offered greater operating freedom.

Resumption of Specie Payment

Monetary problems provided issues of popular concern in the last part of the century. This was a period with serious economic stresses, of growth but also of depression. Should the greenbacks be retired? Should all currency be redeemable in specie? What should be the relation between gold and silver? Was there enough currency? The public debated such questions with great intensity.[13]

Gold coins continued to circulate at a fluctuating premium over greenbacks. Banks carried two kinds of deposit accounts, one in gold dollars (largely for international transactions) representing the equivalent of a physical quantity of gold, and the other in greenbacks or their equivalent. The two kinds of dollars could exist side by side because they were not interchangeable at a fixed rate.[14]

What issues were involved in the arguments over making the gold and paper dollars equal? The wartime and immediate postwar view was that resumption of specie payment was the proper course of action. Those who favored "sound" money wanted Congress (1) to resume specie payment, *i.e.,* to make greenbacks convertible into gold, and (2) to retire or reduce the amount of greenbacks outstanding so that resumption would be possible. Wartime inflation had produced hardships which were associated with paper money that could not be converted into gold. Reversal of the process appealed to some. Moreover, price level reductions would aid the restoration of exports. In the East, banks had issued enough national bank notes so that business could be transacted without heavy reliance on greenbacks as circulating medium.

Opponents of the resumption of specie payment and greenback retirement argued against reducing the supply of money. Doing so would hurt debtors by depressing prices and raising the value of the dollars in which repayment had to be made. Moreover, large areas had few note-issuing banks and probably would have suffered more than minor inconvenience

---

[13] The Greenback Party elected fifteen members of Congress in 1878.

[14] The relation between the two dollars was determined primarily by the international balance of payments. Demand and supply forces for the gold dollar in world markets reflected the purchasing power of gold in the United States and other economies, notably the British. In addition, however, expectations about relative prices in the future influenced speculative holdings. Moreover, capital inflow into the United States increased the demand for dollars or the supply of gold or its equivalent.

in carrying on day-to-day transactions if other types of currency had not been available.

During hostilities the U.S. price level, in terms of gold at the prewar dollar price, had risen to about twice the world level. Making the dollar once again convertible into gold required extensive adjustment. Since prices in the rest of the world rose little, alignment of the gold dollar with other currencies required either a downward movement of prices in the United States or a cut in the gold content of the dollar. The latter, devaluation, as a possible alternative, received slight attention, the general assumption being that resumption would be on the old gold basis. Therefore, deflation of prices as quoted in currency was required to get them on the level with prices as expressed in gold. Such a process would strain the economy by altering economic price relations and by creating uncertainty.

Congress voted to reduce the volume of greenbacks somewhat, to $347 million, using budget surpluses to pay holders. But Congress postponed until 1879 the final move of making greenbacks fully convertible to gold. The total stock of money did not grow with the economy in the 1870's. Expanding production, therefore, put downward pressure on prices, averaging nearly 4 percent a year and bringing a drop to about the 1860 level. Such deflationary force helps account for depression from 1873 to 1879.[15] But this process aligned domestic prices with those abroad in terms of gold and permitted smooth resumption with little domestic or foreign demand for gold.[16] Fortunately, exports held up. Although the period after resumption was generally one of rapid economic growth, there was a downward trend of prices over much of the world.

NATIONAL BANK NOTES

One happy feature of monetary history after the Civil War was the good quality of national bank notes. All circulated at par regardless of the issuing bank; holders of notes did not suffer when a bank failed; counterfeiting was far less a problem than before. Yet all was not rosy. The quantity of notes depended on the size of the Federal debt and the amount held by national banks. Budget surpluses, however, permitted reduction in the Federal debt and with it a decline in the basis of note issue. Other

[15] In the modern world such deflationary forces would probably bring even worse unemployment and decline in real output. Prices and wage rates were then more flexible downward than they are today. Recent research indicates that real output grew more and more rapidly—an average of over 4 percent per year in the 10 years to 1879—than has been attributed to this period.

[16] Any of the greenbacks redeemed for gold had to be reissued; consequently, the Treasury's gold holdings were subject to continual drain if the public wished.

factors also reduced somewhat the attractiveness of note issue in the 1880's.[17] Publicly-held notes fell from $331 million in 1880 to $159 million in 1891.

The total of coin and currency outside the Treasury did not grow as rapidly as the economy expanded. Nor could the volume of currency increase to meet seasonal needs or the requirements of a liquidity crisis. More elasticity in currency supply was widely demanded.

Bimetallism as an Issue

A protracted dispute over bimetallism reflected tensions and involved issues like those in the debate on greenbacks. Silver had lost its monetary role, except for incidental use in fractional coins, as a result of its undervaluation at the rate of 16 to 1 in 1834. A revision of the coinage laws in 1873 omitted silver dollars from the list of coins which would be minted at the free option of the public. At the time, silver was worth more in other uses, and there was no reason to seek to have it coined. Very soon, however, the market price of silver dropped. Output from mines increased; and European governments, shifting to the gold standard, sold rather than bought silver for monetary use.

As the price of silver fell from about $1.36 an ounce to $1.12 (by 1879), silver producers sought a better market. They pressed for authority to convert silver into coins at a price of $1.29, as had been possible before 1873, i.e., at the 16 to 1 ratio. They received support from farmers seeking higher prices for their crops, from debtors hoping to be able to get dollars more easily, and from others who felt that monetary ease might help pull the country out of hard times. Opposition to the "Crime of '73" was a rallying point for protesting groups other than the silver miners.

Congress did go some distance (in 1878 and 1890) in providing for limited Treasury purchase and coinage of silver, but by no means enough to raise the price of silver to its earlier level. Silver's price in 1890 was lower than in 1880. This apparent failure was not the only disappointment. The bulky silver dollars proved unpopular. The Treasury, therefore, issued more convenient silver certificates, backed by the coins. This new paper money was interchangeable with greenbacks and national bank notes, and these were convertible into gold. Consequently, the holder of a silver certificate could in practice get gold for it. Yet the total gold available to the Treasury was only a small fraction of the claims whose payment in gold might be demanded. The monetary system was inherently

---

[17] As the Treasury purchased bonds for retirement, bond prices rose. When the price was much above par, a bank might profit little or not at all from buying bonds to support currency because the maximum amount of national bank notes permitted was related to face value.

vulnerable in that it rested upon fractional reserves when both the fraction and the actual reserves were small.

A weakening of public confidence in the ability of the Treasury to provide gold made people more anxious to convert their currency to gold while this was still possible. Gold had a world position; it could be used to buy foreign currencies at definite prices. Paper dollars were of less assured worth abroad, and silver's value as metal was below the value assigned for monetary purposes. Owners of dollars and dollar securities, especially foreigners, who had doubts about being able to get gold at any time, or who thought that the gold equivalent of paper dollars would decline, tended to convert dollars to gold. Capital inflows suffered, thus reducing the availability of foreign exchange (gold). The Treasury's stock of gold was not large in relation to the currency outstanding; moreover, the Treasury had no assured mechanism for replenishing gold holdings once they had been reduced. The silver purchase program, by its adverse effects on gold flows (and reserves for deposit creation), probably slowed the growth in the total stock of money, rather than increased it as was generally expected.

Serious difficulty arose in the early 1890's. Demands for gold threatened to exhaust the Treasury's holdings. Uncertainty about the country's ability to maintain the gold standard was itself disturbing and discouraged capital flow, while inducing foreigners to return American securities in exchange for dollars which were converted into gold. Sudden shifts of money holdings also disturbed business. In a sense, governmental policy, or doubt about the persistence of any policy, unsettled not only the financial community but also business in general. Panic developed in 1893. The public demanded currency, draining it from New York banks to the interior and from banks into private pockets. Some banks failed. Distrust spread. Gold left banks and the country. Banks then suspended or limited payments in currency. The panic ended as restriction of cash payments by banks stopped the currency drain. The gold problem continued, however, aggravated by a general decline of prices abroad which added to America's balance of payments difficulties.

The monetary system, resting on a small fractional gold base, had long been vulnerable. No complete remedy was obvious. One partial remedy, however, did seem clearly desirable. It was to end the purchase of silver. Such purchases, without in any way adding to the country's gold stock, were leading to the growth of currency which could in effect be converted to gold. President Cleveland in 1893 succeeded in getting Congress to end the requirement that the Treasury continue to purchase silver; the price went down further. And world prices kept on dropping. Gold left the country, not only because of balance of trade but also because of speculation against the dollar.

The Treasury's gold reserve dropped to $45 million in early 1895. A syndicate of private bankers headed by J. P. Morgan provided the

Treasury with gold from Europe and made funds available in London to reduce the need for gold to finance American imports and capital outflow. (The syndicate received U.S. bonds on favorable terms.)   Confidence improved.   Speculation against the dollar dropped.

In 1896 William Jennings Bryan, nominated for the presidency by the Democrats after his eloquent "Cross of Gold" speech, fought for free and unlimited coinage of silver at the rate of 16 to 1.   (The prevailing free market rate was about 33 to 1.)   He wanted an expansion in the stock of money as a means of halting and reversing what had been a protracted and large price deflation. 'The power of supporters of coinage for silver led foreigners to question America's ability to maintain the gold standard. Gold exports rose.   A syndicate of firms engaged in financing foreign trade and investment agreed to end outflows of gold and to borrow abroad for meeting demands for foreign exchange.   This action ended the crisis. Bryan lost.

The seriousness of the issue diminished after 1896.   World gold output increased with new discoveries and new refining methods.   An expansion of exports in physical volume and at higher prices helped finance the import of gold.   The banking system improved.   In 1900 Congress placed the country on an unqualified gold standard, and silver became an issue of slight public interest.

Banking Developments

Although monetary problems aroused the greatest attention, the less dramatic changes occurring in banking were more significant.   The use of checks and deposit banking became increasingly common in the growing business world.   The money supply in the modern sense expanded because demand deposits became more and more the means of payments.   Total deposits grew from around $1 billion in 1872 to over $5 billion in 1900. In the late 1860's the ratio of deposits to reserves rose by about half. Through the rest of the century there was a fluctuating but gradually rising ratio of deposits to reserves.

The number of banks increased.   State commercial banks not only survived the tax which drove their notes from circulation, but in the last two decades grew in number from 650 to 5007.   Much of the explanation is to be found in the ability of state banks to make a profit by creating deposits to lend.   National banks, too, got the bulk of their income from "deposit," rather than "currency," lending.

The growth in banking was uneven.   Much was not healthy.   It consisted of local and often small banks whose capital was inadequate for the risks assumed and whose managements were weak.   An impatient public gave considerable support to "easy" bank formation.   The country was still anxious to expand more rapidly than its savings (plus capital imports) would finance. How could a shortage of funds be made up?

Banks seemed to offer a partial solution. Many businessmen and farmers saw in local banks a source of much needed funds. Money expansion seemed to be a way to meet needs for capital. Unhappily, many of the local loans were inherently risky; others were needlessly poor; the downward drift of prices tended to reduce the value of collateral and borrowers' other assets. The typical bank had too little capital to assume any appreciable risk; moreover, there were no adequate arrangements for pooling or spreading risk over many banks or localities. All too often solvency could not survive losses that were inevitable, to say nothing of those somewhat less but always to be expected.

Moreover, the banking system as a whole was unable to meet liquidity crises—the sudden demand for a great increase in cash. The country's total stock of currency was small and inelastic. Reserve requirements, however, were rigid. Furthermore, they were set in terms of cash, *i.e.,* the city banks which in effect held the fundamental reserves for the banking system were required to keep them in currency or gold.

Cash drain from banks could not be offset by central bank action to prevent deposit contraction from growing.[18] Strains came—occasionally, even, panics as in 1873, 1884, and 1893.

During the period after 1879 velocity of circulation declined slowly. The public gradually came to hold more money per unit of business done.

1900 TO WORLD WAR I

At the turn of the century, coinage and currency problems seemed essentially settled. Yet the basis was one that could scarcely last. The quantity of currency grew somewhat as new gold entered the system and as changes in the law made the issue of national bank notes more attractive. Every year of population growth and of business expansion, of course, increased the need for coins and paper money for the conduct of daily affairs, but there was no assurance that the movements would harmonize. As noted earlier, the currency system had a more serious defect. The needs of a liquidity crisis could not be met—and the expansion of deposits which the owner had the right to demand in currency at any time created an ever-growing potential demand for currency.

Banking growth continued to meet needs for additional means (and facilities) of payment. The economy prospered. Output rose substantially, and the price level went up about 2 percent a year on the average.

---

[18] The Treasury had no way to issue fiduciary currency (except minor elements of the fractional coinage).

One dramatic episode stands out in this period—the financial panic of 1907. In the Spring business began to flatten out. Gold left the country. The stock of money declined. Late in the autumn five relatively small New York banks whose owners had speculated unsuccessfully had difficulty meeting demands for cash. Then a large trust company, suffering adverse clearing house balances, suspended payments. Other trust companies and banks suffered from runs. Stock market prices collapsed.

Country banks demanded currency in exchange for their deposits in New York. Loans were called. Banks restricted payments of currency (which then went to a premium of as high as 4 percent over deposits), largely ending the cumulation of contraction. Substitutes for currency were issued. The crisis passed, and restrictions on payment of currency by banks ended early in 1908.

This experience demonstrated that the commercial banking system had defects requiring reform. It was these apparent defects, or some of them, that the founders of the FR System sought to remedy.

Criticism was leveled against the nature of the reserve requirements of national banks. The permission of all but central reserve city banks (those in New York, Chicago, and St. Louis) to count their own deposits in reserve city and central reserve city banks as part of their legal reserve meant that the actual currency holdings were much less than total legal reserves.[19] Increasingly, banks loaned to within 2 or 3 percent of the maximum permitted by reserves so that the potential response to minor changes would be prompt and disturbing.

The inflexible nature of the reserve requirement was another defect. Once a bank got a penny below the legal requirement, it could make no new loans. Moreover, it would have incentive to try to liquidate some existing loans; if the public sensed the existence of difficulties, confidence in the bank's ability to survive would suffer, possibly starting new trouble.

The country was vulnerable to a liquidity crisis. The public had a legal right to demand several times as much currency as existed. When currency withdrawals rose, banks experienced pressure to reduce loans because legal reserves fell. Moreover, those banks which were unable to meet the claims of their depositors suspended payment or in some cases failed. If a bank suspending payment were one in which other banks held part of their legal reserve, trouble would spread. Here was a grave weakness. It resulted largely from two related conditions: At times there was not enough currency; less important, the currency existing was used inefficiently. Currency, of course, when held by banks, was, along with

[19] The shifting of currency from one bank to another could lead to magnified changes in total legal reserves. If a country bank deposited currency in a reserve city bank, which then deposited in a central reserve city bank, three banks had legal reserves resting on the same currency.

gold, "high-powered money," the legal reserves which governed the potential volume of bank deposit liabilities.

What was already, in all probability, the biggest economy in the world had no way to expand the stock of currency to meet the extra demands of crisis or even the less serious, but largely predictable, changes of the seasons.[20] Each bank was on its own, plus any help (or minus drains) from those with which it did business. The action which promised to serve best the emergency needs of the individual bank—drawing cash from financial centers—tended to weaken the banking system as a whole.

The country had no "system" in the sense of a rationally coordinated structure whose parts would work harmoniously for the benefit of all.[21] There was no effective way to prevent the development of crisis or, if one did arise, to deal with it effectively. Critics argued that expansion and contraction of money and credit were not being regulated by a competent, impartial agency charged with responsibility for the country as a whole.

Another criticism, having less merit, was that currency was not elastic to meet the changing "needs of trade." This reflection of the "real bills" doctrine was to be influential in planning the Federal Reserve.

There were other weaknesses. Means of preventing poor lending were scanty and inflexible. Controls on state banks varied widely but in general permitted bankers more freedom than proved to be in the public interest. In all too many cases, state banks had leeway under the law to make more weak loans than was safe for depositors or good for the economy. National banks, too, had considerable freedom in granting loans. And where legal restrictions did apply, such as the prohibition of real estate loans, some lending that would have been in the public interest may have been impeded; at least, national banks could not compete equally with state banks.

The central market for "discounts," the notes which borrowing businesses had given their banks, and other short-term debt that could serve as secondary reserves, were developed much less fully than European experience indicated might have been feasible. One result was that banks wanting reserves could not readily get them from banks with excess funds by exchanging assets. Check collection over long distances was slow and costly.

[20] The Aldrich-Vreeland Act of 1908 permitted banks to issue emergency currency under restricted conditions. This law was viewed as providing only a temporary solution. It was put to the test once and proved highly successful. When war broke out in 1914, banks met sudden public demands for cash by releasing $300 million of such emergency currency (previously printed). The crisis passed with no effects like those of earlier panics.

[21] The Treasury could influence the money market and bank reserves somewhat by the way it handled its deposits and debt financing. It did not have all the powers needed to operate effectively as a "central bank," but its intervention was frequent and at times salutary. For example, it would ease pressure on banks by shifting gold or currency from its own vaults to banks.

The Federal Reserve, which began operations in 1914, did promise to meet many of the needs, at least moderately well. Its objectives, as seen at the time it was established, were "to furnish an elastic currency, to afford means of rediscounting commercial paper, to establish a more effective supervision of banking . . ." and "[to accommodate] commerce and business." The present concept of much broader responsibility (including some control over the general level of employment and prices) developed slowly over a generation of momentous events. Monetary policy as we envision it today was yet to be conceived. Congress gave no explicit guides for determining actions.

WORLD WAR I TO THE GREAT DEPRESSION

Shortly before the FR System began to operate, World War I created unforeseen conditions. A heavy inflow of gold resulted from European buying in this country. The FR was unable to neutralize this large and abrupt change. The stock of money rose about 45 percent and wholesale prices 65 percent. Velocity, too, went up.

After the United States became a participant in fighting, Federal budget deficits soared. The System itself bought no appreciable amount of Federal debt, but it actively helped commercial banks to increase the supply of money. The banks did so by creating deposits for the Treasury, directly or indirectly. Commercial banks (or their borrowing customers) acquired government debt; they paid with newly created demand deposits. How did commercial banks get the lending capacity? The FR provided the reserves that the banks wished, chiefly by means of lending to member banks (they rediscounted), at rates of interest no higher than those on government debt. Velocity continued to rise. So did the price level. The FR's objective was not to control prices but to aid the war effort by preventing money shortages from imposing obstructions to production and exchange. In fact, System officials viewed the increase in the stock of money more as a result than a cause of price rises.

For more than a year after the end of the war, the FR facilitated a continued rise in bank lending. Prices also rose sharply, about 25 percent from 1918 to mid-1920. Within the FR there was dispute about the possibility of curtailing borrowing for speculative purposes without damaging "legitimate" uses of credit. By raising the rediscount rate the System could have restrained the growth in the stock of money. The Treasury, however, opposed such action because management of the public debt would have become more difficult.

The FR eventually reversed its policy and induced monetary contraction, partly in response to gold exports which had reduced legal reserves. Some months after the rediscount rate went to 6 (later to 7) percent, the stock of money dropped. The inflationary bubble burst. Prices fell drastically, and business contracted sharply. In retrospect, it is easy to see errors in FR policies, notably the failure to act as soon as would have been desirable—to restrain in 1919, not a year later—and then the failure to reverse the restrictive policy earlier than mid-1921.

Domestic currency problems were unimportant during the 1920's, but not banking problems. Although 1921–29 was a time of general prosperity and rising real income, nearly 6000 banks failed, most being in agricultural areas. The distress created by failures, though worst in the immediate localities, spread beyond them. Yet in the financial centers and in Washington remarkably little concern developed.

Commercial banking changed in many ways. Commercial loans dropped in relative importance while real estate and security loans rose. Bank loans to installment finance companies helped in the growth of new methods of consumer buying. Banks held more government debt. Through affiliates many became active in the marketing of securities. Trust activities expanded.

National banks found themselves at a serious competitive disadvantage compared with state banks—in types of lending permitted, trust activities, branching, purchase and sale of securities, and numerous other aspects of banking. The national banking system declined in relative importance as several of the largest obtained state charters or were absorbed by state banks. Legislation in 1927 gave national banks more freedom to compete with state banks. One result, unfortunately, was that standards were lowered. The dual banking system did stimulate some competition but of a type which made for poor banking, deterioration of credit standards, and in some cases speculative excesses.

The total stock of money grew steadily, but so did output of the economy; the price level was essentially stable. Business fluctuations were moderate. The FR made perhaps the first conscious attempt in monetary history to use the power of the central bank to promote internal economic stability while maintaining international balance.[22] On occasion, however, it found itself limited by pressures from abroad; it was reluctant to adopt short-run policies that would hurt friendly countries seeking to protect their gold positions and restore the international gold standard.[23] It was in this period that open market operations became important as an instrument of policy. The Federal Reserve Bank of

[22] The Board's Tenth *Annual Report* (1923) contains a pioneering analysis of problems of credit control without, however, setting out workable guides. The approach rests on the real bills doctrine, the importance of meeting the "needs of trade," the desirability of distinguishing "productive" from "speculative" use of credit.

[23] Several countries had established their currencies at levels in relation to gold which proved to be precarious. With little gold, or gold exchange, "cover," such currencies were vulnerable to relatively mild strains on the balance of payments.

New York under the presidency of Benjamin Strong gained a commanding position, but rivalry and conflict between the Board and the 12 banks simmered. The stock market boom, resting on speculation financed by credit, brought the dispute to a head in 1928. Could the use of credit to buy stocks be curbed without hurting business?

The Board, having eased money to help recovery in 1927, favored "direct action," specifically confrontation with bankers making speculative loans and even forbidding rediscounting by banks which were lending for security speculation. The FR banks, however, argued that the System had no legal right to deny rediscounting privileges, that any direct pressure should be applied in exceptional cases only, and that the way to check stock market speculation was to raise the rediscount rate.

Ten attempts by the FR Bank of New York to raise its rediscount rate in early 1929 were disapproved by the Board. In May it directed the 12 FR banks to press those member banks making large and extended use of rediscounting to curtail such borrowing. Effects were slight. Decisive action was delayed, and even today experts are not agreed on what would have been the wisest policy at different stages. The FR feared that measures to limit the availability of money for speculation would depress business by depriving it of funds. Monetary restriction and high interest rates in this country, it was also argued, would attract funds from abroad and thereby put embarrassing pressure on foreign countries. Bank reserves and the stock of money rose only a little in the late '20's but velocity (turnover of demand deposits) went up markedly. The price level was stable. This was not a decade of inflation.

The rediscount rate was eventually raised, in August at about the time that business turned down. When stock prices collapsed in October, no banking crisis followed. Banks at first rediscounted to get reserves for loans to borrowers who found other credit sources contracting. Then deposits began to decline.

To October 1930, the stock of money dropped about 2.6 percent. Evidence available today shows that in the past such a decline had been associated with severe business contractions. Velocity fell relatively more. Business got worse. Bank failures grew in number and importance. Closing of the Bank of the United States in New York in December 1930 accelerated the growth of distrust. All over the country people converted deposits to currency. Each dollar of increase in currency holding by the public could require a $14 drop in deposits as the fractional reserve system operated. Liquidity difficulties appeared. Banks sold securities, depressing bond prices and reducing the net worth of banks. Banks showed less willingness to help each other than in earlier crises, *e.g.*, 1907. Bankers pressed borrowers to repay loans and became increasingly reluctant to extend ordinary loan accommodation. Fortunately, the crisis passed.

But a new one developed in mid-1931, aggravated by a bank failure in Austria and bank closings in Germany. Distrust spread. Once again deposits were converted to currency, and the money stock fell rapidly.

What was the FR doing? Not much. The System failed to provide the assistance that might have been expected to meet the internal currency drain. Then came an external drain as foreigners withdrew gold, following Britain's abandonment of the gold standard in September. The FR raised the rediscount rate sharply and did not replenish reserves by open market operations. Financial leaders feared that action to ease domestic monetary conditions ("inflating") might lead to a dangerous loss of gold.

Member banks increased their rediscounts. However, because of the aversion to being long in debt to the FR and public sensitivity to any possible evidence of bank difficulties, banks proceeded to liquidate assets. Naturally, bond prices dropped further.

The theory of central bank operations as it had developed (with emphasis on the real-bills doctrine) offered little guidance for dealing with what was happening. The prompt rebound of business from the drastic drop in 1921 may have dulled the sense of urgency a decade later. Statistical indicators of what was happening were inadequate, nothing like those today. The System's leaders did not for over 2 years seek legislation to aid in coping with exceptional needs. The banking world showed little or no interest in reform of the banking system.

Congress in 1932 took two helpful steps. It established the Reconstruction Finance Corporation, with authority to support banks needing help. The funds were to be borrowed from the Treasury. The RFC could add to bank capital (and liquid assets) by purchasing a special issue of preferred stock for cash; or, by lending to a bank, the RFC could increase the liquid funds available.[24] It did both, but not enough to reverse the trend. By this time the commercial loan ("real bills") principle had been made obsolete by events; banks had only a relatively small quantity of such loans to rediscount. In effect, then, gold backing of currency was required. In the Glass-Steagall Act, Congress granted the FR more power; this law permitted the FR to count government debt, as well as commercial paper and gold, as part of the collateral for FR notes. Consequently, currency could be issued more freely to meet the growing demand for money to hoard. Taxes were also increased, hardly a constructive move.

Federal Reserve fear that Congress would pass inflationary legislation if something more were not done led to large open market purchases

---

[24] The RFC provided other, much needed, financial assistance to state and local governments, railroads, insurance companies, and businesses. Unfortunately, the effectiveness of the RFC aid to banks fell sharply during the last bank crisis because Congressional leaders, in opposition to President Hoover, insisted on making public the names of banks getting help. Such disclosures discouraged banks from seeking aid and gave rise to doubts about the safety of a bank that did, leading to withdrawals of deposits, adding to the currency drain, and depleting bank reserves.

until Congress adjourned—$1 billion from April to August. The added reserves offset the effects of some loss of gold and enabled the banks to reduce rediscounts and in some cases to acquire excess reserves. Interest rates fell, and bond prices rose. Business improved a little.

Then conditions got worse.[25] They developed into panic in the months between the election of 1932 and the assumption of responsibility by the new administration. Bank failures rose again. Despite President Hoover's request for cooperation from President-elect Roosevelt in the four months between election and inauguration, no such support was forthcoming even as conditions worsened. The stock of money fell sharply in early 1933. Several states declared "bank holidays," permitting banks to restrict withdrawals or in some cases forbidding them. Internal and external currency drains gained momentum; domestic hoarding of gold rose. Each dollar of gold going into domestic hoarding could require a $29 reduction in deposits.

Monetary tragedy brought immeasurable human suffering. Deflation on a massive scale crushed the country. The officials, it goes without saying, did what they believed was best for the country. They failed. Their actions were inappropriate, "too little, too late," and now difficult to explain —for example the lack of action to prevent bank failures, especially after 1930 as the FR failed to act even as many member banks were forced to close.

International factors complicated the problem for the Federal Reserve, but the weight attached to such considerations was greater than the realities warranted. Wide room for independent action by the FR existed regardless of foreign stresses. Because of the great size of this country monetary policies here affected other economies—and often adversely. For example, American deflationary policies and refusal (as in 1930–31) to let incoming gold have an expansionary effect added to balance-of-payments difficulties abroad, aggravated distress and uncertainty, and induced deflationary measures in economies losing gold.

Differences of opinion within the System,[26] especially between the Board

[25] The reasons for reversal of the slight recovery are not clear. The campaign preceding the 1932 election included exaggerated statements hardly of a kind to inspire confidence. Rumors that President-elect Roosevelt would devalue the dollar were not denied, leading to gold hoarding and export. The financial structure of banks was weak. The uncertainty pervading the economy remained powerfully oppressive.

[26] The Federal Reserve Bank of New York advocated anticontractionary policies time and again when the Board and most of the other banks wanted to do nothing or to pursue more restrictive policies. One practical difficulty of getting action was the size of the group participating in decision making—the Board and 12 bank presidents; when a committee has trouble getting agreement, the result will often be "no action." More serious, however, was the power of the 11 banks representing different regions of the country; few of the officers showed understanding of the national situation. A still deeper source of trouble was attachment through the System to the real bills doctrine, with focus on the "needs of trade" and the credit market, rather than on the stock of money.

and the Federal Reserve Bank of New York, complicated matters.   The System, torn by internal conflicts of view, failed to act as central banks exist to act in times of strain and crisis.   If the FR in the early months of 1930 had done just about what it did later in the year in lowering rediscount rates and in open market operations, the forces of cumulative contraction would not have built up so strongly.   If the open market purchases of 1932 had been made a year earlier, conditions would not have continued to deteriorate as they did.   An untold number of bank failures might have been prevented by earlier actions.   The "real" economy suffered needlessly, and on a mammoth scale, from monetary mismanagement which helped convert what might have been a "normal" recession into a prolonged and unprecedented tragic depression.

1933 TO WORLD WAR II

Every bank in the country was closed on March 6, 1933, just after President Roosevelt was inaugurated.   Emergency steps were necessary. Even if the months after the election had been used to develop carefully considered plans—and such was not the case—conditions had deteriorated so tragically that special measures were required.

Congress at once gave the President sweeping authority over banking, currency, and foreign exchange.   Banks that regulatory authorities found to be sound were allowed to open, about 12,000 out of 17,300 within three weeks; some others reopened later.   The RFC provided over $1 billion of capital to 6139 banks, made loans to many others, and provided $900 million to closed banks to speed their distributions to depositors.   Although the measurements are unsatisfactory, the first few months of 1933 witnessed a decline of one-sixth or so in the stock of money.

The President received power to direct the FR to buy government debt in the open market; he could require the Treasury to issue $3 billion of new currency to pay costs of government; he might establish bimetallism or reduce the gold content of the dollar by half and accept some silver from abroad in payment of war debts; all forms of currency were made legal tender.   Here was almost a Congressional mandate for monetary expansion.   Yet the powers granted were discretionary.   For the most part they were unutilized.

Exporting of gold was made subject to Treasury license and for a time generally suspended; the Treasury "nationalized" all privately owned gold (except that for industrial uses), paying in dollars.

The clause in contracts requiring payment in gold was repealed in June 1933.   The market price of gold rose, and beginning in September a daily official price was set—higher from day to day.   The purpose was to raise the price level as a whole.   The dollar prices of some internationally traded items did go up.   Domestic prices, however, were affected little since the new gold policy did virtually nothing to increase the number of dollars in circulation in this country. Early in 1934 Congress provided for revaluing the gold stock; most of the "profit" went into a fund to help stabilize the dollar in world markets. Currency for domestic uses was separated from gold, and private ownership of gold was drastically restricted. The President eventually set the gold price at $35 an ounce, and from that time on the dollar price of gold was stable.

Gold then entered this country on a large scale, not only because a given amount of gold would buy more dollars and American goods and services but also because of fear of more stringent controls abroad and of war, fear which induced capital export from Europe. The devaluation of the dollar in terms of gold made monetary expansion potentially easier. The change did not, however, directly provide much expansion here, except in the form of gold imports. Economies losing gold, however, found themselves under pressure to deflate, a policy which added to their troubles, then to devalue, and to institute various direct controls on foreign trade and investment.

Silver became an issue once more. Representatives of the silver interests, receiving support from advocates of monetary expansion, were unsatisfied by the President's slight use of discretionary authority to buy silver. They succeeded in 1934 in getting Congress to direct the Treasury to purchase silver at prices above those in the market.[27] In essence, a production subsidy was given silver producers in the form of monetary legislation. Purchase was to continue, gradually, until the market price equaled $1.29 an ounce or until Treasury holdings (valued at that price) were one-third the value of the gold stock. Purchase at home and abroad proceeded but never came near to the "goal" set for eventual accomplishment. Payment was made in silver certificates—$2 billion eventually. The extent to which the money stock in fact increased on balance will never be clear because we cannot be sure how Federal Reserve actions on other parts of the money supply would have differed.

Many features of the banking legislation of the 1930's remain and have been described in the text; brief reference will serve here. The composition of the FR Board was changed, with the Treasury members being removed. The Board was given more authority over the 12 Federal Reserve banks. The determination of monetary policy thus shifted clearly from the country's financial to its political center. The Board received power to alter

[27] The purchase program raised the world price of silver. Two-thirds of the purchases came from abroad, especially from the monetary stocks of China and Mexico. Their currencies, being tied to silver, appreciated relative to the currencies of other countries. Their exporting became more difficult while importing was encouraged, aggravating balance-of-payments difficulties. The draining of silver from China disrupted her financial system, led her shift to a paper standard, and contributed more than a little to her many troubles in the 1930's and later. After 1941, the Treasury purchased only domestically-mined silver. Some was drawn from stocks to use during the war. Later the Treasury sold silver for industrial use.

reserve requirements of member banks, to regulate margins required for the purchase of securities on stock exchanges, to make direct loans to industry, and to withdraw use of its facilities from any member making what it believed to be improper use of its credit facilities. The Federal Open Market Committee was established.

The FR was allowed greater scope for helping member banks in time of crisis. More generally, it was empowered to depart from the real bills, or commercial loan, theory of operations. It could now follow a procedure recognizing the use of government debt as an asset in the structure of the financial system. The flexibility of issuance of FR notes was increased. Retirement of national bank notes and minor types of currency began.

Commercial banks could no longer have investment affiliates; double liability on stock in national banks was removed; payment of interest on demand deposits was prohibited; and the interest rates paid on time deposits were made subject to FR control. The Comptroller of the Currency was given authority to decide which securities member banks might hold; rules affecting branch and group banking were altered. Most important, perhaps, was the establishment of the Federal Deposit Insurance Corporation.

The banks that had survived the crisis of the early 1930's generally sought to build their liquidity. Lending was cautious; banks acquired short-term, high quality investments in preference to business loans, especially if the potential borrower was not the very best of credit risks. Legal reserves did go up. Until monetary authorities adopted a policy of sterilizing gold (December 1936 through 1937), imports of gold added to legal reserves of member banks, enabling them to reinforce their reserve position.

But the stock of money did not grow in the multiple fashion which would have followed if commercial lending had responded "normally."

National income, starting from a very low base, rose rapidly. Yet by 1937 recovery was incomplete, and unemployment remained high. Meanwhile, wholesale prices rose one-third in about 3 years, also from a seriously depressed base but enough to cause concern.

FR policy during much of this period was essentially passive. Open market operations were directed toward maintaining the FR portfolio and influencing the interest rate structure, *not* toward altering the total of FR credit. Discounting almost disappeared. The rediscount rate was reduced to historically low levels, and System officials believed that an easy money policy was in effect. Yet the discount rate was above the free market rates then prevailing. Consequently, banks used methods of getting reserves which were less expensive than rediscounting—but which did not expand reserves and bank lending capacity. FR policy became increasingly concerned with Treasury financing of large budget deficits and the maintenance of an "orderly market" in government securities.

Interest rates on top-quality debt dropped to levels lower than ever before, but debts of less than high quality continued to command much higher returns. Lenders were reluctant to take risks. Even though banks gradually acquired large amounts of excess reserves as a result of gold imports, bank lending to business increased hardly at all. The ratio of deposits to reserves dropped by almost half. Velocity rose somewhat. The ratio of deposits to currency also went up as the public regained confidence in banks and returned currency to be able to resume the use of bank accounts.

In 1936 the FR used its new power to raise reserve requirements. Why? It did not intend to check business expansion. The objective was to regain "control" of money and credit by absorbing excess reserves which had resulted largely from gold inflows. These reserves did have an inflation potential. Eventually, it seemed, restraint would be needed. Such appeared to be the situation early in 1937. Prices had risen substantially. The business expansion had lasted nearly four years—long by historical standards—and prices were still going up. Reserve requirements were raised again in two close steps, drastically reducing the remainder of excess reserves. Unfortunately, business activity dropped sharply. The decline began in May but was not clearly recognized until autumn.

The causes of this drop and the factors accounting for its severity are still subject to debate. The balancing of the Federal government's cash budget in mid-1937 removed one force for expansion. Numerous New Deal policies were interpreted as "anti-business"; some raised costs (especially labor costs); some discouraged private investment by raising taxes, enlarging the threat of government competition, and attacking the hope of profit in other ways.

Did the monetary action contribute to the causes of the recession? The doubling of reserve requirements within a few months was an abrupt move on a large scale. It wiped out excess reserves to which banks had become accustomed and which they apparently wanted. The FR argued that removal of excess reserves did not require banks to contract deposits. Other students of money, however, believe that the forced retardation in the expansion of the stock of money must have curbed business expansion and intensified the contraction, one of the steepest on record.

The recession of 1937 converted many economists, in and out of government, to the belief that major reliance should be placed on fiscal policies to stimulate business. Confidence in monetary policy was at a low ebb. Businesses with good credit standing, it was concluded, did not need to borrow. Banks, having seen that risky loans could bring heavy loss, would not lend on any substantial scale to many of the businesses which did want to borrow. The general reluctance to invest in new plant, equipment, housing, etc., persisted; after all, there was an embarrassing amount of idle capacity. For all these reasons, it seemed, low interest rates and easy money could not give much of a positive stimulus to the economy.

Although we now see that this view contained much error, it prevailed to exert a strong influence on postwar government policy.

Gold continued to enter the country, and the policy of sterilization was relaxed. The rediscount rate was reduced after the recession had become serious in 1937, and reserve requirements were cut slightly in 1938. The stock of money rose rapidly from late 1937. National income also went up, while prices remained relatively stable until the outbreak of war in Europe.

The banking system was highly liquid when World War II began. Gold imports and several years of government deficits financed by sale of debt to banks had brought to the asset structure of the system a degree of liquidity without precedent. Interest rates were low, especially those for short periods and those on longer-term issues of borrowers with highest credit standing. War finance, as noted in the text, rested on this unusual level and pattern of interest rates. The problems that resulted plagued the economy until well into the 1950's.

APPENDIX B   *INDEX NUMBERS*

COMPARING aggregates or bundles of different things is always difficult —and often necessary.   One tool for doing so is the index number.   We are concerned with index numbers of prices.

Three problems generally arise in computing price indexes. (1) There must be a formulation of the purposes that the index is to serve. A price index for measuring the cost of living will have different characteristics from an index of the prices of internationally traded raw materials or the costs of constructing factories.   (2) What kinds of data are available?   In addition to making the best use of the figures which exist and avoiding the use of data which are known to be poor, we may be able to fill some gaps.   An index which is to appear monthly may need to be rather different from one which can utilize annual data.   (3) The selection of a base period also requires care.   If the base period itself is somewhat exceptional—a time of unusually high or low prices—comparisons with it may be at least slightly misleading.   The use of two or three years instead of one as the base can reduce the danger of the period itself being unusual.

Measurement of changes of a single price requires merely looking at the price alone.   If the price of an item rises from $1 to $2, most of us can sense readily the meaningful size of the change.   But if the change is from 90 cents to $1.08, we may find more difficulty in sensing the importance.   How, then, can we relate the two prices to compare them easily? We use a *price relative*.   Assuming that the first price, 90 cents, is the base, we assign it a figure of 100.   The new price in relation to 100, then, will be the same as $1.08 to 90 cents, or $\frac{108 \text{ cents}}{90 \text{ cents}} \times 100$, that is 1.2×100, or 120.   The 18-cent price rise was 20 percent of the original price.

A more compelling reason for using relatives arises when we are working with the prices of many different items.   The prices of some things are low per unit—milk is perhaps 25 cents a quart.   Some other prices are several times as high—shoes, $15 a pair.   Some are still higher—autos at $2500.   Suppose that these prices rise as follows:

			Price relative
Milk	$0.25 to	$0.30	120
Shoes	$15.00 to	$16.50	110
Autos	$2500.00 to	$2550.00	102
Total	$2515.25 to	$2566.80	3)332(110.7 [a]

[a] Average of the price relatives, not of the new prices themselves.

For the three items together the new price relative, computed by comparing the new prices $\left(\dfrac{\$2566.80}{\$2515.25}\right)$ with the old, is 102.25. Yet the price of milk is 20 percent higher than before, the price of shoes 10 percent. The comparatively small percentage increase in auto prices almost completely obscures the much greater percentage increases in other prices because their money amounts are small relative to the amount for the auto.

Quite another result appears, however, if we deal with the *relatives* of the individual items rather than with the absolute amounts. The unit in which the price is quoted no longer makes any difference in the result. By adding the relatives and dividing by the number, in this case 3, we obtain a significantly different figure—110.7. Even this figure, however, may not serve us well. Does it give proper attention to the comparative importance of the three items? If not, how can relative significance be measured? We need some basis for assigning the importance, *i.e., weighting* items in the way that is significant for the purposes sought. But how?

One method is to weight according to the significance in the base period. We do so by assigning importance on the basis of the amount spent, that is, the *quantity* in the base year multiplied by the *price* in that year. For example, let us assume three items as follows, substituting gasoline for the auto:

	Base year purchase			*Current year*	
				Price	Cost of base-year quantity
Milk	400 quarts at 25¢	$100		30¢	$120.00
Shoes	1 pair at $15	15		$16.50	16.50
Gasoline	100 gallons at 30¢	30		32¢	32.00
		$145			$168.50

Dividing the current year total by that of the base period $\left(\dfrac{\$168.50}{\$145.00}\right)$, we get 116.2. To obtain the quantities bought for $100 in the base year, one must now spend $116.20. The price in the base year, p_o, times the quantity in the base year, q_o, for each item is computed. All totals are added. This total becomes the denominator. For subsequent years the quantity in the base year, q_o, is multiplied by the price in the later year, p_i, for example. These are then totaled and become the numerator. Division (and multiplication by 100) gives the relative for the total with each item weighted by the quantity purchased in the base year, as follows:

$$\frac{p_i q_o + p_i' q_o' + p_i'' q_o'' + \ldots p_i^n q_o^n}{p_o q_o + p_o' q_o' + p_o'' q_o'' + \ldots p_o^n q_o^n} \times 100$$

In essence, the method illustrated is the one used by the Bureau of Labor Statistics in computing both its Consumer Price Index for Urban Wage Earners and Clerical Workers—CPI—and its Wholesale Price Index.[1] The CPI is the result of extensive effort, including major changes in 1964. Only a few highlights can be mentioned here. In 1960–61 a detailed survey of a carefully selected sample of consumers in 66 metropolitan areas and smaller cities determined how much was spent on a wide range of items. From the findings the BLS selected about 400 items to make up a typical "market basket" of what these consumers bought—all of the most significant items and a sample of those of lesser importance. The base period remains as before, the three years 1957–59. Therefore the cost of buying this assembly of goods and services in the years 1957–59 was computed and serves as 100.

To find prices in later periods, the Bureau makes regular surveys. In some cases its trained agents go into stores and price items every month, in other cases every three months. For some prices, such as those of utility services and fuel, BLS gets data by mail. The individual items are defined as carefully as possible, and great effort is made to get answers which are accurate. From time to time one product or service will be dropped and replaced by one which has become more important, with statistical "linking" of old and new. Technicians and consultants from the industry or profession involved help in the judgments required for such changes. The weighting of some of the major groups of items is shown below:

---

[1] For technical reasons the BLS uses a slightly different method which gives the same result. The amount spent on each item in the base is multiplied by the percentage of price change.

	Percent of total of all items used in computing the Consumer Price Index
Meats, poultry, and fish	5.63
Dairy products	2.80
Food away from home	4.54
Household appliances	1.36
Men's and boy's clothing and upkeep	2.86
Autos and related goods and services	12.64
Medical care	5.70
Homeownership	14.27
Rent	5.50
Reading and recreation	5.94

This type of weighting does not take account of changes from year to year in the relative importance of the items we are trying to measure. Patterns of consumption change so that some items in the market basket become more important and others less. In fact, movements of relative prices will in themselves tend to shift the pattern of purchases. A drop in the price of one item and a rise in the price of another will tend to change the quantities of each purchased. Consequently, base-period quantities are not representative of quantities bought one year or five or ten years later. To ignore shifts in quantities is to ignore change that, for our purposes, may be highly important. Yet serious practical difficulties make it impossible to revise the contents of the market basket to keep abreast of change. Moreover, weighting on the basis of current quantities will not represent base-period conditions in which we are interested for making comparisons. Here, then, is an index number problem for which no fully satisfactory solution is available.

The CPI introduced in 1964 weighted food at 22.43 compared with 28.18 in the index based on early 1950 patterns of consumption. Another illustration of the significance of differences in changes of quantities was presented with the change of another index, that computed by the Federal Reserve Board for measuring industrial production. The basis for computing the index was revised in 1959 to take account of changes in the economy and of the availability of new data. The Board found that the newer index showed manufacturing and mining in May 1959 to be 162 percent of the 1947–1949 average; the older index had shown 155. From 1947 to 1959 consumer goods output had increased 58 percent on the average. Yet production of some items, such as air conditioners, had gone up by over 400 percent; residential electricity rose 272 percent, soft drinks 84 percent; production of a few items—cooking stoves, woven floor coverings, men's suits and coats, and home radios—had actually dropped. The weighting of output on the basis of earlier conditions had failed to reflect these divergent trends.

The Consumer Price Index has been criticized by both laymen and experts. Although the BLS makes serious efforts to adjust for quality change, no known procedure can be fully satisfactory. Some quality improvements and some cases of deterioration are not reflected adequately. There is no clear indication whether, on balance, over the years the index has a bias which over- or under-states the effect of quality change.[2] New products may not appear as soon as would be appropriate. One criticism of using this index as a measure of the price level in general is that there are important parts of the economy to which it does not apply. Among consumers, for example, it does not apply well to the buying of retired persons, those who do not live in urban areas, and professional, technical, and management personnel, or proprietors.[3] It does not cover industrial raw materials, construction, and producers' goods.

How do we use an index number to adjust—"deflate" is the commonly used term for the process—for changes in the levels of prices? Assume that 1957–59 is the base period of 100. The Consumer Price Index in the summer of 1964 was 108, *i.e.*, $108 was then needed to buy the bundle of consumer goods obtainable for $100 in the base period. The purchasing power of the dollar had fallen. To find the amount, we divide the base-year figure, 100, by the current-year figure, 108—getting 92.6. The purchasing power of the dollar, we find by this process of deflation, had dropped by 7.4 percent.

The Wholesale Price Index covers about 1900 items organized in 16 major categories. Data are obtained from quotations on organized exchanges but chiefly from reports by some 2000 companies. The base period is 1957–59; weighting for the most part is based on transactions as reported in the *Census of Manufacturers*, supplemented and modernized from time to time. Iron and steel are weighted 5.5, livestock 3.5, natural

---

[2] A committee of experts reported as follows: "If a poll were taken of professional economists and statisticians, in all probability they would designate (and by a wide majority) the failure of the price indexes to take full account of quality changes as the most important defect in these indexes. And by almost as large a majority, they would believe that this failure introduces a systematic upward bias in the price indexes—that quality changes have on the average been quality improvements.

"We have very little evidence at our disposal with which to support—or deny—the belief in progressive quality improvement. Indeed we are impressed with how little empirical work has been done on so widely held a view and potentially so important a problem. Even the concept of quality change is not free of difficulty." Price Statistics Review Committee of the National Bureau of Economic Research, *The Price Statistics of the Federal Government.* . . . (New York: National Bureau of Economic Research, Inc., 1961, p. 35).

[3] The new index covers single persons in urban areas whereas before 1964 only family consumption was represented.

rubber 0.1, toys 0.5, and machine tools 0.8. Part of the index is computed daily. Weekly figures for the entire body of commodities are based on sample data.

The index is much too broad—and yet also too narrow—for most uses. Since services and sales at the consumer level are not included, the WPI omits so much of the economy that it cannot serve to represent all major price movements. Yet it covers so many industries and groups of products that none can be represented adequately by the whole index. The chief practical use, therefore, centers on the various subgroups. Business contracts often provide for price adjustments on the basis of change in an element of the index. Groups of items, of course, will fluctuate much more than the average of 1900 items. For example, from 1958 to October 1964 the total index varied by less than 2 points around 100; the subgroup of 22 basic commodities, however, rose and fell through a range of over 10 points; in the 12 months to October 1964, the WPI was essentially stable, but the key metals subgroup rose 30 points while that for foodstuffs fell 4 points.

For measuring changes in prices for the economy as a whole, increasing use is made of the "implicit price deflator" computed annually by the Department of Commerce for use in connection with national income and product accounting. The Department determines the price relative for each type of output in the Gross National Product. Each category is weighted according to its relative importance in total output. The degree of accuracy varies, *e.g.,* allowance for quality change, precision of the underlying price quotations, and weighting. With 1954 as the base year of 100, the following changes have appeared:

	Price relatives		Percentage
	1947	1963	increase
Personal consumption expenditures	84.6	113.4	34
New construction	76.6	122.9	60
Producers' durable equipment	76.8	120.9	58
Government purchases of goods and services			
Federal	80.8	130.2	60
State and local	71.5	136.4	92
Total gross national product	83.0	118.5	43

The smallest increase shown is in the consumer sector. The Consumer Price Index, therefore, does not reflect adequately the full range of changes in prices in the economy.

BIBLIOGRAPHY

THE literature on money and banking is extensive. The quality varies widely. What is good at one time may lose some or all of its usefulness as conditions change. And this is a subject area in which there is much change—in the events themselves, in the focus of interest, and in the analysis. This bibliography will suggest where the student may start looking for additional material. In general, only recent titles published in this country are cited; many of these, however, will indicate older and foreign sources. Numerous titles not included here are cited in footnotes referring to a specific topic.

BIBLIOGRAPHICAL AIDS

The student seeking material on any topic will do well to start by consulting a professionally trained librarian. And, of course, the card catalogue of the library will ordinarily provide useful guidance. General sources of bibliographical aid are the *United States Catalogue of Books,* the *Readers' Guide to Periodical Literature,* the *Industrial Arts Index,* the *Public Affairs Information Service,* and the *New York Times Index.* Unfortunately, none of these sources can be complete. They tend to be especially weak on materials in government documents, an important source for monetary matters.

Much of the most valuable material on money, banking, and related topics appears in articles in scholarly journals—*The American Economic Review, Economic Journal, Review of Economics and Statistics, Journal of Finance, Journal of Political Economy, Quarterly Journal of Economics,* and several others. The American Economic Association *Index of Economic Journals,* a series of volumes, indexes under a detailed classification system articles in around 90 different journals beginning with 1886. *The American Economic Review,* appearing quarterly, lists the articles in each issue of the major domestic and foreign journals. The monthly magazine *Banking* focuses on topics of interest to bank managements.

STATISTICAL AND OTHER SOURCE MATERIAL

The monthly *Federal Reserve Bulletin* contains a wealth of statistical information. In addition to tables which appear each month, special studies are included from time to time, and certain information is given regularly on a quarterly or less frequent basis. The *Bulletin* also includes a list of other Federal Reserve publications. Each of the twelve Federal Reserve banks publishes a monthly review; format and emphasis vary. The *National Banking Review,* published quarterly by the Comptroller of the Currency, presents data on national banks. The Bureau of the Budget *Statistical Services of the United States Government,* rev. ed., 1963, and Wasserman, P., E. Allen, A. Kruzas, and C. Georgi, *Statistics Sources* (Detroit: Gale Research Co., 1962) give helpful guidance.

The *annual reports* of the Board of Governors of the Federal Reserve System, the Federal Deposit Insurance Corporation, the Comptroller of the Currency, the Secretary of the Treasury, each of the twelve Federal Reserve banks, and some of the state departments of banking ordinarily contain both statistics and interpretation. The Federal Reserve publishes a monthly chart book. A few of the most important sets of data appear in the annual *Statistical Abstract of the United States.* The annual *Economic Report of the President* contains both statistics and analysis of monetary developments in the setting of the whole economy. The Department of Commerce's monthly *Survey of Current Business* and the Treasury Department's monthly *Treasury Bulletin* are also useful sources.

For historical information the student has the Federal Reserve's inclusive study, *All-Bank Statistics, 1896–1955,* and *Historical Statistics of the United States, Colonial Times to 1957.*

From time to time committees of Congress receive and publish data and opinions on monetary matters. The Joint Economic Committee does so each year. The Senate Committees on Banking and Currency and Finance and the House of Representatives Committees on Banking and Currency and Ways and Means deal with problems of money, banking, and finance at irregular, but frequent, intervals.

Textbooks

Barger, H., *Money, Banking, and Public Policy* (Chicago: Rand McNally, 1962).

Chandler, L. V., *The Economics of Money and Banking,* 4th ed. (New York: Harper & Row, 1964).

Haines, W. W., *Money, Prices, and Policy* (New York: McGraw-Hill Book Co., Inc., 1961).

Hart, A. G., and P. B. Kenen, *Money, Debt, and Economic Activity,* 3rd ed. (Englewood Cliffs, N.J.: Prentice-Hall, Inc., 1961).

Horvitz, P. M., *Monetary Policy and the Financial System* (Englewood Cliffs, N.J.: Prentice-Hall, Inc., 1963).

Klise, E. S., *Money and Banking,* 3rd ed. (Cincinnati: South-Western Publishing Co., 1964).

Robertson, D. H., *Money* (Chicago: University of Chicago Press, 1959).

Trescott, P. B., *Money, Banking, and Economic Welfare* (New York: McGraw-Hill Book Co., Inc., 1960).

Whittlesey, C. R., A. M. Freedman, and E. S. Herman, *Money and Banking: Analysis and Policy* (New York: Macmillan, 1963).

More Specialized Studies

Ahearn, D. S., *Federal Reserve Policy Reappraised, 1914–1959* (New York: Columbia University Press, 1963).

Alhadeff, D. A., *Monopoly and Competition in Banking* (Berkeley and Los Angeles: University of California Press, 1954).

Ascheim, J., *Techniques of Monetary Control* (Baltimore: The Johns Hopkins Press, 1961).

Anfricht, H., *Central Banking Legislation* . . . (Washington: International Monetary Fund, 1961).

Bailey, M. J., *National Income and the Price Level* (New York: McGraw-Hill Book Co., Inc., 1962).

Barger, H., *The Management of Money—A Survey of American Experience* (Chicago: Rand McNally, 1964).

Beckhart, B. H., ed., *Banking Systems* (New York: Columbia University Press, 1954).

Burgess, W. R., *The Reserve Banks and the Money Market,* rev. ed. (New York: Harper and Bros., 1946).

Burns, A. F., *Prosperity Without Inflation* (New York: Fordham University Press, 1957).

Burstein, M. L., *Money* (Cambridge, Mass.: Schenkman, 1963).

Chandler, L. V., *Benjamin Strong, Central Banker* (Washington: Brookings Institution, 1958).

Chase, S. B., *Asset Prices in Economic Analysis* (Berkeley: University of California Press, 1963).

Commission on Money and Credit. Volumes on Financial Institutions: *The Commercial Banking Industry; The Consumer Finance Industry; Life Insurance Companies as Financial Institutions; Management Investment Companies; Mortgage Companies; Mutual Savings Banks; Property and Casualty Insurance Companies; The Savings and Loan Business; The Federal Reserve and the Treasury.*

Volumes on Monetary and Fiscal Policy: *Federal Credit Agencies; Federal Credit Programs; Fiscal and Debt Management Policies; Impacts of Monetary Policy; Inflation, Growth, and Employment; Monetary Management; Private Capital Markets; Private Financial Institutions; Stabilization Policies.* (Englewood Cliffs, N.J.: Prentice-Hall, Inc., various dates, generally 1963).

Copeland, M. A., *A Study of Moneyflows in the United States* (New York: National Bureau of Economic Research, 1952).

Culbertson, J. M., *Full Employment or Stagnation?* (New York: McGraw-Hill Book Co., Inc., 1964).

Dewey, D. R., *Financial History of the United States,* 11th ed. (New York: Longmans, Green and Co., 1931).

Domestic Finance, Subcommittee on, House [of Representatives] Committee on Banking and Currency. A series of studies on various aspects of banking and monetary policy appeared in 1963 and 1964. Available from Government Printing Office, Washington.

First Boston Corporation, *Securities of the United States Government,* 21st. ed. (New York, 1964).

Fischer, G. C., *Bank Holding Companies* (New York: Columbia University Press, 1961).

Friedman, M., ed., *Studies in the Quantity Theory of Money* (Chicago: University of Chicago Press, 1956).

Friedman, M., *A Program for Monetary Stability* (New York: Fordham University Press, 1960).

Friedman, M., and A. J. Schwartz, *A Monetary History of the United States, 1867–1960* (New York: Columbia University Press for National Bureau of Economic Research, 1963).

Gaines, T. C., *Techniques of Federal Debt Management* (New York: Free Press of Glencoe, 1962).

Garvey, G., *Debits and Clearings Statistics and Their Use,* 2nd ed. (Washington: Federal Reserve System, 1959).

Goldenweiser, E. A., *Monetary Management* (New York: McGraw-Hill Book Co., Inc., 1951).

Goldsmith, R. W., *Financial Intermediaries in the United States Since 1900* (New York: National Bureau of Economic Research, 1958).

Gurley, J. G., and E. S. Shaw, *Money in a Theory of Finance* (Washington: Brookings Institution, 1960).

Haberler, G., *Prosperity and Depression,* 3rd ed. (Lake Success, N.Y.: United Nations, 1946).

Hall, G. R., and C. F. Phillips, Jr., *Bank Mergers and the Regulatory Agencies—Application of the Bank Merger Act of 1960* (Washington: Federal Reserve System, 1964).

Hammond, B., *Banks and Politics in America from the Revolution to the Civil War* (Princeton: Princeton University Press, 1957).

Hansen, A. H., *Monetary Theory and Fiscal Policy* (New York: McGraw-Hill Book Co., Inc., 1949).

Hansen, A. H., *A Guide to Keynes* (New York: McGraw-Hill Book Co., Inc., 1953).

Hodgman, D. R., *Commercial Bank Loan and Investment Policy* (Champaign, Ill.: University of Illinois, 1963).

Homer, S., *A History of Interest Rates* (New Brunswick, N.J.: Rutgers University Press, 1963).

Horwich, G., *Money, Capital, and Prices* (Homewood, Ill.: R. D. Irwin, Inc., 1964).

Johnson, H. G., *Alternative Guiding Principles for the Use of Monetary Policy* (Princeton, N.J.: Department of Economics, Princeton University, 1963).

Johnson, R. W., *Financial Management,* rev. ed. (Boston: Allyn and Bacon, 1962).

Kessel, R. A., *The Cyclical Behavior of the Term Structure of Interest Rates* (New York: Columbia University Press, 1965).

Lewis, W., Jr., *Federal Fiscal Policy in Postwar Recessions* (Washington: The Brookings Institution, 1963).

Ludtke, J. B., *The American Financial System* (Boston: Allyn and Bacon, 1961).

Lutz, F. A., and L. W. Mints, eds., *Readings in Monetary Theory,* sponsored by the American Economic Association (Homewood, Ill.: R. D. Irwin, Inc., 1951).

Madden, C. H., *The Money Side of the Street* (New York: Federal Reserve Bank of New York, 1959).

Meek, P., *Open Market Operations* (New York: Federal Reserve Bank of New York, 1962).

Meigs, A. J., *Free Reserves and the Money Supply* (Chicago: University of Chicago Press, 1962).

Meiselman, D., *The Term Structure of Interest Rates* (Englewood Cliffs, N.J.: Prentice-Hall, Inc., 1962).

Mints, L. W., *Monetary Policy for a Competitive Society* (New York: McGraw-Hill Book Co., Inc., 1950).

Money, Trade and Economic Growth, Essays in honor of J. H. Williams (New York: The Macmillan Co., 1951).

Nadler, M., S. Heller, and S. Shipman, *The Money Market and Its Institutions* (New York: Ronald Press Co., 1955).

Nussbaum, A., *A History of the Dollar* (New York: Columbia University Press, 1957).

Patinkin, D., *Money, Interest, and Prices* (New York: Harper & Row, 1956).

Phelps, C. W., *Factoring and Accounts Receivable Financing as a Method of Business Finance* (Baltimore: Commercial Credit Co., 1957).

Prochnow, H. V., ed., *The Federal Reserve System* (New York: Harper and Bros., 1960).

(Radcliffe) Committee on the Working of the Monetary System, *Report,* Cmnd. 827 (London: H. M. Stationery Office, 1959).

Reed, E. W., *Commercial Bank Management* (New York: Harper & Row, 1963).

Robinson, R. I., *The Management of Bank Funds,* 2nd ed. (New York: McGraw-Hill Book Co., Inc., 1962).

Robinson, R. I., *Money and Capital Markets* (New York: McGraw-Hill Book Co., Inc., 1964).

Robinson, R. I., ed., E. W. Boehmler, F. H. Gane, and L. C. Farwell, *Financial Institutions,* 3rd ed. (Homewood, Ill.: R. D. Irwin, Inc., 1960).

Roosa, R. V., *Federal Reserve Operations in the Money and Government Securities Markets* (New York: Federal Reserve Bank of New York, 1956).

Saulnier, R. J., *The Strategy of Economic Policy* (New York: Fordham University Press, 1963).

Saulnier, R. J., H. G. Halcrow, and N. H. Jacoby, *Federal Lending and Loan Insurance* (Princeton: Princeton University Press for the National Bureau of Economic Research, 1958).

Sayers, R. S., *Modern Banking,* 6th ed. (Oxford: Clarendon Press, 1964).

Selden, R. T., *Trends and Cycles in the Commercial Paper Market* (New York: National Bureau of Economic Research, 1963).

Viner, J., *Problems of Monetary Control* (Princeton, N.J.: Department of Economics, Princeton University, 1964).

Welfling, W., *Bank Investments* (New York: American Institute of Banking, 1963).

Woodworth, G. W., *The Money Market and Monetary Management* (New York: Harper & Row, 1965).

INDEX

Debt (*Cont.*)
  public, *see* Government debt
  repayment and saving, 261, 263
  retirement, 265, 324, 325
  structure, 259
Debtor, 472, 529, 535
Decentralized banking, 524; *see also* Unit banking
Declining price level, 380, 409, 411, 412, 532, 537, 548
Default risk, 118ff.
Defense costs, *see* War
Defensive action, Federal Reserve, 189, 462
Deferred availability cash items, 157, 178
Deferred payments, standard of, 11, 14; *see also* Inflation
Deficit financing, *see* Deficits, budgetary
Deficits, balance of payments, 387ff., 415
Deficits, budgetary, 483ff., 520
Deflation, *see* Declining price level
Demand:
  aggregate, *see* Aggregate demand
  for borrowed funds, 67, 259ff.; *see also* Interest
  for cash balances, 315
  for currency, 158
  effective, 287
  for loanable funds, 93, 130, 259ff.; *see also* Interest
  for money, 238, 241ff., 403, 453; *see also* Velocity
  pull, inflation, 434
Demand deposits, 3, 9, 15, 16, 34, 43, 228, 455; *see also* Deposit creation; Money

Denison, E. F., 521
Deposit banking, development, 531
Deposit creation, 9, 25ff., 188, 278, 451, 485
Deposit destruction, *see* Contraction of money
Deposit insurance, *see* Insurance, bank deposit
Deposit service charges, 76
Deposits:
  as assets, 25
  bank, *see* Balance sheet; Monetary policy
  competition for, 56
  defined, 26ff.
  derivative, 32, 465
  at Federal Reserve, 27, 42; *see* Reserves
  government, 43, 175
  as liabilities, 25
  safety of, 134ff.
  savings and loan association, 203
  time and savings, *see* Time deposits
Depreciation, 244, 263, 276, 296, 300, 302, 327, 426, 471, 496
Depressed areas, 524
Depression, 231, 250, 327, 331, 341, 547
Devaluation, currency, 376, 380, 384, 391, 537, 549
Development plans, 386
Dewey, D. R., 564
Direct investment, 356
Direct loans to business, Federal Reserve, 194
Direct placement, 205
Directors, bank, 52, 82
Disaster relief, 209
Discount, nature of, 41, 91, 112ff.

Discount rate and discounting at Federal Reserve, 160, 182ff., 209, 462, 543, 546, 551
Discount window, 185
Discounts, 178, 186, 207, 297
Discretionary: fiscal policy, 486
  management of money, 407
Discrimination, and monetary policy, 469ff.
Discriminatory controls, foreign exchange, 381
Disposable personal income, 285, 289, 397, 494
Disruption, international, 378ff.
Dissaving, 292
Distortion, 429
Distress loans, 90
Distressed sectors, 524
Diversification, loan, 47, 49, 82, 140, 213
Dividends, 202, 204, 218, 285
Dividends, stock, bank, 51
Divisibility, and coinage, 18
Division of labor, 5, 6, 12, 411
Documentary bill, 345
Dollar:
  and gold, *see* Gold and gold standard
  international role of, 389, 391, 415
  unit of account, 5, 6, 10, 12, 13, 14, 15, 528
Dollar:
  shortage, 385
  surplus, 385
Domestic developments and foreign exchange, 381ff.
Double liability, 48

International financial relations (*Cont.*)
costs of production, 390; *see also* Inflation
currencies, relations, 360, 366, 385
devaluation, *see* Devaluation
dollar shortage and surplus, 385, 389, 391
exchange rates, 360, 366, 370ff.
and Federal Reserve, 153, 154, 157, 173, 415, 467, 545
forward markets, 352
goal of policy, 415
and gold, 161, 174, 360ff, 536
income change, 363, 384
inflation, 370, 381, 386, 428, 442
and interest rates, 365, 394, 457, 458
investment, 357, 365, 458, 507
letters of credit, 347
liquidity, world, 393
market for foreign exchange, New York, 348
payment mechanism, 342
price changes, 360
purchasing power parity, 367
United States, position of, 385, 389ff.
International Monetary Fund, 356, 378ff., 394
Intuition in central banking, 461
Invention, 517
Inventory buying, 239, 294, 307, 321, 326ff., 413, 431, 473
Investment, financial, 25, 108, 197, 262, 551;

see also Financial intermediaries; Liquidity; Portfolio policy
Investment, real, 293ff.
accelerator, *see* Accelerator
business, 260, 280, 287, 324, 458, 501; *see also* Fluctuations, business
and costs, 298, 322, 327; *see also* Construction costs
definition, 293
deflation and, 413
determinants, 263, 280, 294ff., 321, 325, 333, 511, 521
and economic growth, 521
and fluctuations, *see* Fluctuations, business
governmental, 301, 458, 506, 520, 522
and inflation, 425ff.
and interest, 314, 317, 403, 511; *see also* Interest
international, 356, 365, 390
inventory, *see* Inventory
multiplier, *see* Multiplier
replacement, *see* Depreciation
and saving, 300, 426, 448, 520
taxation and, 426, 489, 496
Investment banking, 25, 42, 71, 116ff., 212
Investment, dealers, 84
Investment funds (trusts), 213
Investment tax credit, 496
Ireland, 422
Issue, currency, 3, 22, 158

Israel, 386, 422
Italy, 13, 421, 422, 430

Jackson, A., 532
Jacoby, N. H., 566
Japan, 392, 422
Jefferson, T., 530, 532
Jobs, *see* Employment
Johnson, D. G., 209
Johnson, H. G., 383, 401, 520, 565
Johnson, L. B., 487
Johnson, N. O., 393
Johnson, R. W., 92, 565
Joint Economic Committee, 518, 562
Journal of Finance, 561
Journal of Political Economy, 561
Juglar cycle, 319
Juster, F. T., 457
Justice, Department of, 47

Kenen, P. B., 355, 565
Kennedy, J. F., 171, 487, 488, 490
Keynes, J. M., 242, 269, 280, 283, 456, 521
Kitchen cycle, 319
Klise, E. S., 563
Knowledge, expansion of, 517
Kondratieff cycle, 319
Korean hostilities, 193, 194, 382, 420, 473, 504
Kruzas, A., 562

Labor, Secretary of, 447
Labor unions, 436, 441, 445
Lags:
fiscal policy, 481, 489
forecasting, 463ff.
monetary policy, 405, 453, 455, 467
Land bank notes, 528
Land prices and federal aids, 208
Latin America, 435, 442
Laurence, R. J., 471
Leased wires, 157

Massachusetts, 200, 202, 528
Maturity of debt, 120, 508, 511
Maximum interest on time deposits, 43, 473
Mayer, T., 238
McKie, J. W., 214
Measured income, 254
Measurement, money for, 6
Mechanization, bank 54ff.
Mediation, financial, *see* Financial intermediaries
Medium of exchange, 5, 8, 35, 203, 226, 340, 528
Meek, P., 565
Meigs, A. J., 191, 566
Meiselman, D., 566
Meltzer, A. H., 460
Member banks, 163ff., 172, 178, 450; *see also* Federal Reserve Banks
Membership, advantages of Federal Reserve, 151
Mergers, bank, 47, 144
Metals as money, 15, 18
Mexico, 422
Michigan, 532
Military expenditures, 208, 356, 388, 396, 528; *see also* War and war finance
Minimum balance, 81, 82
Minimum intervention, *see* "Bills only"
Mining, 254
Minnesota, 48
Minsky, H. P., 329, 450
Mint and minting, 13, 158, 528ff.
Mint ratio, *see* Bimetallism
Mints, L. W., 565, 566
Mitchell, G. W., 407, 460

Mitchell, W. C., 319
Mobility, resource, 332, 423, 446, 525
Modigliani, F., 283
Monetary authorities, 450
Monetary policy; *see also* Fluctuations, business; Monetary theory
an art, 401, 460ff.
availability, 456
"bills only," *see* "Bills only"
broad nature of, 402, 470
conflicts, 469, 515
contraction, 455
currency and, 168
discrimination and, 470
"easy" money, 191, 499
expansion, 451, 485
and financial intermediaries, 468
and fiscal policy, 476, 483ff., 499
forecasting, 463
history, 526ff.
implementing, 4, 152, 226, 450
importance of, 4, 225
instruments, 403, 408
interest rates, 274, 456
lags, *see* Lags
limitations, 401ff.
liquidity, 453
liquidity, 453; *see also* Liquidity
necessity, 4
objections to use of, 402, 469ff.
objectives, 401ff., 515
open market operations, *see* Open market operation
path (process) of monetary change, 451
reserves, 167, 170; *see also* Reserves, bank; Rules vs. authorities

Monetary policy (*Cont.*)
rules vs. authorities, 406
selective controls, 472
"tight" money, *see* "Tight" money
timing, 461
Monetary standards, 16ff., 529ff.; *see also* Gold
Monetary system, 3ff.
Monetary theory; *see also* Monetary policy
cash balances approach, 235ff.
equation of exchange, 227ff.
inadequacies, 232
income version, 233, 237
interest, *see* Interest
money, demand for, 238; *see also* Demand for money
national income approach, 311ff.,
quantity approaches, 225ff.
scope of, 225
transactions version, 227, 236
and velocity, *see* Velocity
Monetizing debt, 26, 33
Money, *see also* Monetary theory
acceptability, *see* Acceptability
asset, 21
and bank failures, 243
and banks, *see* Bank and banks
changes in stock, 239, 252, 278, 311
circulation, velocity of, *see* Velocity
coins, *see* Coins
commodity standards, 17, 226; *see also* Bimetalism
controls, 16

Money (*Cont.*)

creation, 9, 25ff., 188, 208, 252, 277ff., 451, 499, 523

and credit, 276; *see also* Credit

currency, *see* Currency

and cycles, business, 325, 329ff.

debt, 9, 21

definition, 3, 8, 14, 410

demand deposits, *see* Demand deposits

demand for, 238, 241ff., 403, 453

evolution, 16, 527ff.

flows, 10, 235, 285, 401, 403, 451, 476

as framework, 4, 193, 486

functions of, 6ff., 411

and gold, *see* Gold

holding, motives for, 10, 236, 241ff.

illusion, 238

and inflation, *see* Inflation

interest and, 217ff., 312

and intermediaries, financial, *see* Financial intermediaries

legal tender, 9, 158

liquidity, 9; *see also* Liquidity

management of, 3, 16, 401ff., 450ff.; *see also* Reserves

market, 108, 112, 132, 543

medium of exchange, 5, 8, 35, 203, 226, 340, 528

metal, 15, 18; *see also* Bimetallism

ownership of, 242

paper, *see* Paper money

payments, control of, 410

Money (*Cont.*)

precautionary motive, 245

price of, 9

primitive, 18

qualities of good, 12

quantity, significance of, 225ff., 434, 452ff.; *see also* Equation of exchange; Inflation

speculative motive, 246, 536

standard of deferred payment, 11

standards, 23

stock of, 3, 16, 25, 35, 242, 268, 452ff.

store of value, 10

substitutes, 15, 104, 105, 121, 244, 246, 292, 410; *see also* Liquidity; Time deposits

transaction motive, 242, 313, 324

value of, *see* Price level

Money market, 104, 175; *see also* Open market

Moneyness, 15, 248

Monopoly, 48, 148

Moore, G. S., 342

Moore, T. G., 47

Moral risk loans, 75, 86

Moral suasion, 185, 193, 546

Morgan, J. P., 539

Morris, Robert, Associates, 89

Morris Plan, 218

Mortgage debt, 76, 84, 132, 201, 204, 205, 209, 258, 259, 265, 327, 523

Motivations, 233, 237, 253; *see also* Expectations

Multiple unit banking, 48

Multiplier, 303ff., 322, 324, 339, 454

Municipal debt, *see* State-local borrowing and debt

Murphy, H. C., 500

Murphy, J. L., 327

Mutual funds, 213

Mutual savings banks, 25, 150, 152, 200, 202

Nadler, P. S., 67

National accounts, balancing, 479

National Bank Acts, 46, 76, 166, 535

National Bank notes, 535, 537, 551

National Banking Review, 562

National Banking System, 46, 535

National income approach, monetary theory, 283ff.

National income concept, 283, 284

National product, 229, 284

Nationalization of gold, 549

NATO, 386

Natural rate of interest, 280

Near money, 292; *see also* Money, substitutes

"Needs of trade," 64, 182, 543, 545

Negotiability, 26, 99, 100, 347

Net national product, 18, 284

Net worth, 88

Netherlands, 422, 437, 447

Neutral money, 411

New banks, 46, 56

New Deal, 552

New Hampshire, 529

New nations, 371

New products, 558; *see also* Innovations

Present worth, 297

President, U.S., 147, 487ff., 515

Pressure groups, 436, 441, 443, 445, 488, 522; see also Public opinion

Price control, anti-inflation device, 443

Price effect, 364, 384

Price index, 229, 419ff., 443, 445

Price level, 5, 7, 226, 229, 413, 534
and borrowing, 261
changes in, and expectations, 291
goals, 410, 518
and gold flows, 364
and natural rate of interest, 280
and relations among prices, 426

Price regulation, 426

Price relative, index number, 554, 557

Price supports, farm, 78, 439, 494

Prices, relative, 7, 426, 525

Prices of capital goods and investment, 298, 299, 322

Prices vs. jobs. 315, 440, 441, 446

Primary deposit, 32

Primary reserves, 122

Prime rate, 93, 258

Priorities, asset policy, 122

Private debts, 17, 26, 33, 259

Pro forma balance sheet, 88

Process of monetary change, 451ff.

Prochnow, H. V., 566

Producer's durable equipment, price change, 559

Productivity, 260, 276, 381, 411, 435, 436, 440, 446, 504, 521

Profit, 178, 494
bank, 49, 50, 51, 167
and cycle, 323, 324, 325
inflation and, 424, 431

Progress, technical, 300

Progression, tax, 492, 494

Promissory notes, 39, 99, 101

Propensity to consume (save), 289ff.

Property taxes, 244

Prosperity, phase of cycle, 324, 333

Protective investments, 123, 126

"Prudent man" rule, 211

Psychology, *see* Expectations

Public Affairs Information Service, 561

Public housing, 208

Public opinion, 193, 462, 487

Public responsibility, 5

Public utilities, 254, 426

Purchasing power, money as store of, 8, 10, 14, 237; *see also* Inflation

Purchasing power parity, 367

Qualities of money, 12ff.

Quality, loan, 90, 145, 183

Quality and price index, 443, 558

Quantity of money, 4, 17; *see also* Money control of, 403, 408

Quantity theory of money, 227ff.

Quarterly Journal of Economics, 561

Quota, 391

Radcliffe Committee, 566

Railroads, 214, 446

Rationality, 424, 522

Rationing, loan, 459; *see also* Availability

Ratios, 88

Readers Guide to Periodical Literature, 561

Real balance effect, 235, 238, 313, 338

Real bills doctrine, 62, 65, 543, 545, 547, 548

Real costs, 4, 19, 412

Real estate, 84, 230, 232, 235, 263, 427, 506

Real estate loans, 78, 79; *see also* Mortgage debt

Real forces:
capital productivity, 280
interest, 257

Real objectives, 4, 6, 416

Realized investment (saving), 301

Receivership, 212

Recession, 323, 326, 334, 441, 485, 493, 510, 552

Recognition lag, 464

Reconstruction Finance Corporation, 547, 549

Redeemability, currency, 22, 166, 535

Redeemable debt, 503

Redeposited reserves, 535, 542

Redevelopment loans, 85

Rediscounting, *see* Discount rate and discounting

Reed, E. W., 566

Reform, monetary, 4, 170

Refundings, 61, 71, 261, 508, 509

Regionalism, Federal Reserve, 149

Registration, new securities, 212

Regulation, bank, 51, 82, 117, 128, 201, 220,

533, 543; *see also* Examination, bank
Reinvestment of earnings, 44, 202
Relationships, price, 7, 266ff., 285, 424
Relatives, price, 554, 557
Relief, *see* Welfare aid
Rent control, 426
Rental income, 284, 285, 287
Repayment, loan, 69ff., 77, 204, 261
Replacement cost and inflation, 426
Replacement investment, 300
Reports, bank, 52, 151, 152
Representative full bodied money, 17
Repressed inflation, 502
Repurchase agreements, 105ff., 189
Required reserves, *see* Reserves
Research, 154, 157, 518, 521, 525
Reserve cities, 165, 170
Reserve currency, international, 391, 415
Reserves:
  advances, *see* Advances
  cities, 165, 166
  computation, 169
  correspondent banks, 57
  cost to bank, 125, 169
  creation of, for banking system, 169, 173ff.
  creation of, for individual bank, 156, 171ff.
  currency, 159
  deficiency, 169
  discount, *see* Discount rate and discounting
  equation, 177
  excess, *see* Excess reserves
  Federal reserve control,

163ff., 450, 457, 460, 466, 480ff., 500, 515
  fractional, 20, 27, 49, 167, 539
  free, 191
  function of, 27, 167, 170
  and gold, *see* Gold
  graduated, 171
  as idle assets, 125, 169
  and inflation control, 435, 455, 465, 469
  legal, 28, 33, 34, 40; *see also* Reserves, required
  loss, 50
  management, bank, 191
  member bank classification, 164
  National Bank Acts, 535
  net free, 191
  open market operations, *see* Open market operations
  origin of, 169
  primary, 122
  purposes of, 17, 27, 167
  reform, 170
  required, 33, 163ff., 450
  response to change, 452
  revision of requirements, 27, 164, 180, 450, 484, 515
  secondary, *see* Secondary reserves
  state banks, 57
  time deposits, 164
  vault cash, *see* Vault cash
Reserves, valuation, 41
Resource allocation, 199, 333, 424, 429, 521, 522, 523
Responses to monetary change, 452ff.
Restrictions and inflations, 429

Restrictive policy, 386, 455, 469
Resumption specie payment, 536
Retirement income, 292, 427
Revenue system, *see* Tax and taxation
Review of Economics and Statistics, 561
Revival, cyclical, 321
Revolution, American, 529, 534
Revolving credit, 75
Rigidities, 311, 315, 332, 380, 409, 429, 441, 519
Risk:
  assets, 51
  bank, 49
  as cost, 406, 424
  credit, 118ff., 459
  default, 118
  interest rate, 119, 258, 265, 312, 466
  international, 352, 371
  and investment, 489
  of lending, 76, 77, 85, 86, 132, 216, 271, 274, 427
Robert Morris Associates, 89
Robertson, D. H., 235, 563
Robertson, R. M., 148
Robinson, R. I., 121, 122, 566
Robinson-Patman Act, 447
Roosa, R. V., 462, 566
Roosevelt, F. D., 134, 548, 549
Routing symbols, 156
Rules vs. authorities, 406
Run, international, 450
Runs, bank, 136, 175, 383, 542
Rural electrification, 207
Russia, 392
Rutgers University, 56

Sacrifice, and interest, 281